Stefan Buczacki's
PLANT DICTIONARY

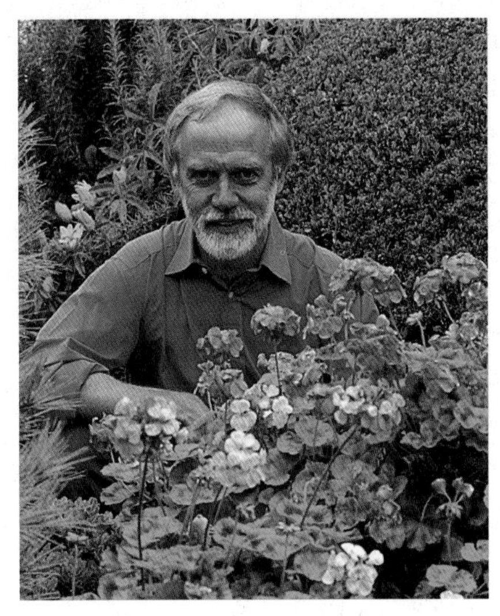

STEFAN BUCZACKI'S

PLANT DICTIONARY

HAMLYN

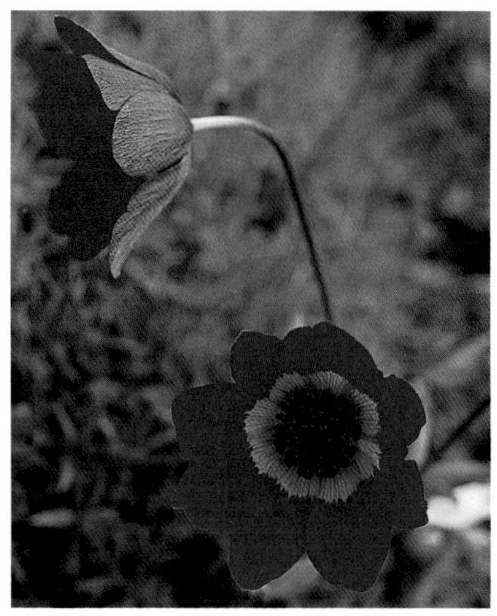

Publishing Director *Laura Bamford*
Creative Director *Keith Martin*
Executive Editor *Julian Brown*
Editor *Karen O'Grady*
Design Manager *Bryan Dunn*
Designer *Ginny Zeal*
Picture Researcher *Mel Watson*
Production Controllers *Julie Hadingham, Clare Smedley*
Researcher *Casey Horton*
Illustrator *Vanessa Luff*

First published in Great Britain in 1998
by Hamlyn
an imprint of Reed Consumer Books Limited
Michelin House, 81 Fulham Road, London SW3 6RB
and Auckland, Melbourne, Singapore and Toronto

ISBN 0 600 59378 9

A catalogue record for this book is available from the British Library

Printed in Europe

CONTENTS

INTRODUCTION

There are currently around 75,000 species and varieties of hardy garden plants available to gardeners. Some are very familiar, very common and on sale at countless nurseries and garden centres. At the other extreme are many that are rare, obscure and obtainable only occasionally from specialist suppliers. Neither I nor anyone else has seen them all or grown more than a small fraction of the total. Nonetheless, the choice of plants for my own garden has long been a process of try and then retain or reject. Also I have been more fortunate than most in the number of other gardens and nurseries that I have been able to visit and the number of expert growers whom I have been privileged to meet. I have, over the years, therefore seen a very large number of cultivated plants.

It's on this experience that I have prepared the selection of around 6,000 plants in this book. I have attempted to sift out the best from the more commonly available plants that you will find at your local centre. And whilst I have included relatively few that are truly difficult to obtain I have described a considerable number that I feel should be much better known and that will repay a little effort in the search. It is, however, a personal selection because attractiveness or satisfactory yield or performance is very much in the perception of the beholder. Nonetheless, whilst there is no definitive yardstick of plant quality, the closest that we have is the Award of Garden Merit (AGM) of the Royal Horticultural Society, a distinction granted only after careful assessment by a panel of experts. You will find a considerable number, although by no means all, of the plants in this book have been granted this accolade.

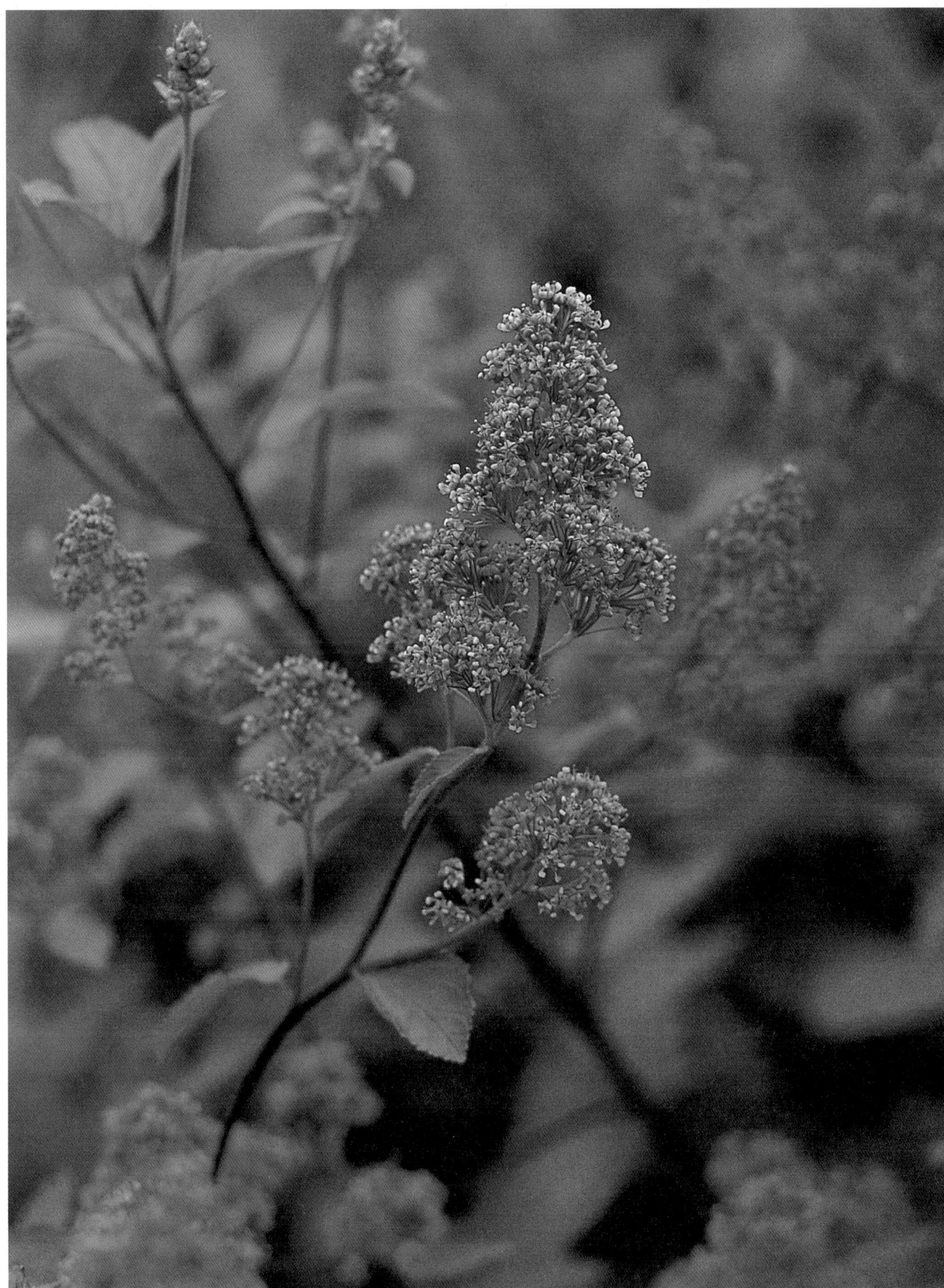

How to use the book

The text is arranged alphabetically by Latin genus name, and within each genus, mainly by alphabetical arrangement of species and the varieties derived from them. If you don't know the Latin name for a plant that interests you, you should first refer to the English-Latin name listing on page 306. For each plant genus, I have given the family to which the genus belongs. I have long felt that gardeners derive more interest and enjoyment from their gardening when they are aware of the relationships between garden plants. And it has a practical dimension too in that within many families will be found types of plant requiring similar growing conditions. A full list of every plant family represented in the book, with their salient features, is given on pages 312-320.

Under each genus entry, I have indicated the overall scope of the group (annuals, trees, climbers and so forth), although not all types within each genus may be represented in my selection here. This is especially so with warm climate groups; we may for instance only be able to grow a few small half-hardy annuals from a particular sub-tropical genus during the summer whereas the genus as a whole includes types that in their native habitat are shrubs and trees. I have given this information, however, because, once again, I believe it is of interest and adds to the satisfaction of gardening. I have also given an indication of relative hardiness (in terms of the minimum winter temperature that the plant can tolerate (see table opposite). Also, for ornamentals, I have described them as small, medium or large (as an approximation of height although this is generally an indication of overall size too). The ranges obviously differ from annuals and alpines at one end of the spectrum to trees at the other (a very small tree would be a very big annual) and this will be evident from the detailed sizes given in the list of my recommended varieties.

In each entry, I have usually also outlined the types of flowers to be found in the group and sometimes foliage too, followed by a brief summary of the preferred growing conditions, methods of propagation, pruning and other important aspects of cultivation. Finally, the measurements given are the maximum height and maximum width that the plant can be expected to attain under average growing conditions. So 60cm/45cm equates to height/width.

Although this book stands readily on its own as a reference work, it will be found even more valuable if used in conjunction with its companion, *Stefan Buczacki's Gardening Dictionary*. There I have described the way that these many different types of garden plant can be grown, cared for and used as parts of an overall garden design.

HARDINESS CHART

Category	Minimum winter temperature	
Very Hardy	-20°C *or below*	(-4°F *or below*)
Hardy	-15°C *to* -20°C	(5°F *to* -4°F)
Moderately Hardy	-10°C *to* -15°C	(14°F *to* -4°F)
Fairly Hardy	-5°C *to* -10°C	(23°F *to* 14°F)
Barely hardy	0°C *to* -5°C	(32°F *to* 23°F)

Abelia Caprifoliaceae

Large semi-evergreen/deciduous flowering shrub. Moderately hardy to hardy. Elliptical to rounded leaves; funnel-shaped flowers, 0.5-5cm (¼-2in) long, summer to autumn. Thin out old wood of evergreen species after flowering and of deciduous species in late winter. Take softwood cuttings in early summer, semi-ripe cuttings late summer. ❀ 'Edward Goucher', semi-evergreen, 2cm (¾in) long mauve-pink flowers, 1.5m/2m(5ft/6½ft). *A.* x *grandiflora*, evergreen or semi-evergreen, 2cm (¾in) long pink flowers tinged white, 2m/3m (6½ft/10ft); *A.* x *g.* 'Francis Mason', yellow leaves marked dark green.

Abies *Silver Fir* Pinaceae

Evergreen trees. Hardy. Short, usually soft needles, sometimes streaked silver beneath. Conspicuous, erect, blue female cones; pendent male cones green at first, later purple to brown. Cones ripen and disperse seeds and scales in one season. No routine pruning. Sow ripe seed in autumn or late winter. Most species are too large for gardens but a few slow growing or dwarf forms make fine plants. ❀ *A. concolor* (White Fir) 'Compacta' (syn. 'Glauca Compacta'), dwarf, grey-blue foliage, green or pale blue cones 50cm/75cm (1¾ft/2½ft); *A. koreana* (Korean Fir), needles dark green above, silver beneath, a beautiful plant, slow growing but not dwarf, violet-blue cones at a younger age than any other conifer I know, 10m/4m (33ft/13ft); *A. nordmanniana* (Caucasian Fir), foliage bright green, white beneath, 40m/6m (130ft/20ft); *A. n.* 'Golden Spreader', dwarf, prostrate, golden yellow needles, pale yellow undersides, 1m/1.5m (3ft/5ft); *A. procera*, bright blue-grey to grey-green foliage, green cones, 25-45m/6-9m (73-146ft/20-30ft).

above Although fairly reliably hardy, I find *Abelia* x *grandiflora* a better plant in milder areas where it retains its leaves for much of the winter.

above right *Abutilon megapotamicum* is quite the most striking member of the genus that is hardy enough for British gardens, although it will benefit from shelter.

Abutilon Malvaceae

Deciduous or evergreen flowering shrubs/small trees, annuals and perennials. Tender to barely hardy. The shrubs are the best known but are suitable for growing outdoors only in the mildest areas,

particularly near the sea; in less mild but frost-free areas they require a sheltered west- or south-facing wall. Prune frost-damaged shoots in spring, cutting back at least 15cm (6in) into healthy wood. Take semi-ripe cuttings in early autumn. ❀ A. 'Canary Bird', evergreen, bell-shaped pendent lemon yellow flowers, spring to autumn, 3m/3m (10ft/10ft); *A.* x *hybridum* 'Kentish Belle', evergreen/semi-evergreen, pendent, funnel-shaped yellow and red flowers with purple stamens from summer to autumn, 1.5m/1.5m (5ft/5ft); *A. megapotamicum*, evergreen/semi-evergreen, trailing or climbing, lance-shaped to elliptical leaves, a charming plant with red and yellow flowers with purple stamens from summer to autumn, a variegated form is inferior, 2.5m/2.5m (8ft/8ft); *A.* x *suntense*, deciduous, mallow-like, violet-purple flowers, some white, late spring to early summer, 2.5m/2.5m (8ft/8ft). *A.* x *s.* 'Jermyns', my favourite, a beautiful variety, grey-green toothed leaves, dark mauve flowers, 5m/3m (16ft/10ft); *A. vitifolium*, lavender-blue flowers, 9cm (3½in) in diameter, 5m/2.5m (16ft/8ft).

Acacia Mimosaceae

Large evergreen/deciduous flowering shrubs and small trees. Tender to barely hardy. Can only be grown successfully outdoors in frost-free or mild areas in a sheltered position. Fern-like foliage of lance-shaped to elliptical leaves. In some species the 'leaves' are modified leaf stalks (phyllodes). Clusters of tiny, petal-less, bright yellow flowers with numerous long stamens give a very appealing feathery appearance. No routine pruning. Take semi-ripe cuttings in summer or sow seed in warmth in spring. ❀ *A. baileyana*, large evergreen shrub or small tree, bright yellow inflorescences from winter to spring, 5-8m/3-6m (16-25ft/10-20ft); *A. dealbata*, evergreen tree, much the hardiest and most reliable species, small rounded clusters of delightful fragrant, feathery flowers in spring, 15-30m/6-10m (50-100ft/20-33ft).

Acaena *New Zealand Burr, Bidi-Bidi* Rosaceae

Small evergreen perennials/alpines. Very hardy. Most provide rather vigorous ground cover with wiry stems, pretty rounded spiky inflorescences and tiny leaves, red in autumn. Usually raised from seed but multiplication by removal of rooted runners from established plants is easier. Be warned that most are too invasive to plant in confined spaces; I've made the mistake. Trim straggly growths in early spring. ❀ *A buchananii*, greenish flowers, 2.5m/75cm (8ft/2½ft); *A. saccaticupula* 'Blue Haze', steel-blue flowers, 15cm/1m (6in/3ft).

Acantholimon Plumbaginaceae

Small evergreen alpine. Hardy. Mound-forming species for rock gardens or walls with rosettes of sharply pointed dark green leaves, dense clusters of funnel-shaped flowers from early to mid spring. Increase in spring by layering, sowing seed in containers in open frames or taking softwood cuttings. ❀ *A. glumaceum*, more tolerant of wet conditions than other species, cushions of stiff, lance-shaped leaves, sprays of rose-pink flowers in summer, 5-8cm/20-30cm (2-3¼in/8in-1ft).

Acanthus *Bear's Breeches* Acanthaceae

Medium/large semi-evergreen perennial for the back of the border. Hardy. Glossy, prickly leaves and very striking tall spikes of white, pink or mauve flowers. Cut back dead flower spikes after flowering. Best propagated by root cuttings in winter, alternatively in spring by division or by sowing seed in a cold-frame. ❀ *A. mollis*, mauve and white flower spikes in midsummer, 1.5m/90cm (5ft/3ft); *A. spinosus*, pure white and purple flowers from late spring to midsummer, 1.2m/60cm (4ft/2ft).

Acer *Maple* Aceraceae

Small/medium trees. Most are at least moderately hardy. Among the most appealing deciduous garden trees, although their flowers are predominantly greenish and individually rather uninteresting. The most attractive feature of many is their autumn leaf colour, invariably best when warm days contrast with cold nights in early autumn. Among over one hundred species however are some large or otherwise unsuitable garden types such as sycamore and field maple. They are tolerant of most soils but usually best in slightly acidic conditions. Most, especially the Oriental types, are unsuccessful in windy or very wet sites, although the smaller forms are very good in containers. Maples should not be pruned as they are very prone to coral spot disease which will infect through pruning cuts. They are difficult to strike from cuttings and named forms do not come true from seed. ❀ *A. griseum* (Paper-bark Maple), chestnut brown, peeling bark, deep red autumn colour, demand always exceeds supply, 4m/8m (13ft/25ft); the Japanese maples *A. japonicum*, *A.*

far left *Acaena microphylla*. All of the New Zealand members of the genus *Acaena* are attractive, both in foliage and flower, but they aren't plants for restricted space.

left I believe *Acer grosseri hersii* is the prettiest of all the snake-barked maples; the bark positively glows in a low winter sun.

right *Achillea filipendulina*. *Achillea* is a big genus and includes some uninteresting weeds but the varieties of *A. filipendulina* are among the very best of border perennials.

shirasawanum and *A. palmatum* have given rise to a huge range of varieties with many different leaf shapes and varying intensity of autumn colour. The named forms are grafted and usually expensive: *A. shirasawanum* 'Aureum', pale green in spring, yellow in summer, red-orange in autumn, 2m/3m (6½ft/10ft); *A. palmatum*, palm-shaped green leaves, red in autumn; *A. p. atropurpureum* and *A. p.* 'Bloodgood', palm-shaped deep purple leaves, red and scarlet in autumn; *A. p.* 'Osakazuki', seven-lobed olive green leaves, vivid red autumn colour, 3m/5m (10ft/16ft); *A. p. dissectum*, finely divided, fern-like green leaves, red-orange in autumn; *A. p. d.* Dissectum Atropurpureum Group and 'Garnet', similar but with deep purple leaves, changing to red-orange in autumn, 'sells on sight' as nurserymen say, 1.2m/1.5m (4ft/5ft); *A. maximowiczianum* (syn. *A. nikoense*), yellow flowers, leaves pale beneath, red in autumn, 3m/15m (10ft/50ft); *A. negundo* (box elder), distinct foliage, not three-lobed but rather like an ash, the best form is 'Flamingo', with pale pink leaf variegation although it may produce shoots bearing green leaves which must be cut out, 5m/8m (16ft/25ft); *A. platanoides* (Norway Maple), 'Crimson King', deep red-purple leaves, little change in autumn, the most attractive large maple for gardens, 8m/25m (25ft/80ft); *A. p.* 'Drummondii' is little over two-thirds the size with lovely pale green, yellow-edged leaves; Snake bark maples: *A. davidii*, green-purple bark with paler stripes, no autumn colour, 8m/15m (25ft/50ft); *A. grosseri hersii*, superb grey-olive green lined bark, orange and red autumn colour, always an eye-catcher in my own garden, 8m/14m (25ft/47ft); *A. capillipes*, red-purple bark with pale lines, orange and scarlet autumn colour, 7m/15m (23ft/50ft).

Achillea *Milfoil, Yarrow* Asteraceae

Herbaceous hardy perennial for the border and rock garden. Some species are semi-evergreen. Both tall and dwarf types have flattened heads composed of tiny flowers that are borne in tightly-packed or loose clusters held well above the foliage. Most have grey-green, fern-like leaves, with a characteristically spicy scent. Tall species make good cut and dried flowers. Best in well-drained soil in a sunny position. Cut back tall-growing species to soil level at the beginning of winter. Divide in early spring or sow seed in growing positions; some varieties self-seed rather freely. ❀ *A. ageratum*, broad white inflorescence, 60cm (2ft); *A.* 'Coronation Gold', golden yellow flowers, 1.5m (5ft); *A.* 'Fanal' (syn. 'The Beacon'), mat-forming, slightly rounded inflorescences of tiny red flowers with yellow centres, broad bi-pinnate leaves, green to grey-green, 75cm/60cm (2½ft/2ft); *A. filipendulina* 'Cloth of Gold', light green leaves and deep lemon-yellow inflorescence, 1.5m (5ft); *A. f.* 'Gold Plate', bright yellow inflorescence, slightly recurved, 1.5m (5ft); *A. grandifolia*, white inflorescences, 90cm/60cm (3ft/ 2ft); *A.* 'Huteri', pure white; *A.* x *lewisii* 'King Edward', hummock-forming, semi-evergreen with pale yellow inflorescence, suitable for rock gardens, 8-12cm/23cm (3¾-5in/9in); varieties of *A. millefolium* (Common Yarrow), include 'Cerise Queen', cherry-red flowers with white centres, 60cm/60cm (2ft/2ft); *A.* 'Moonshine', bright yellow flowers, 60cm/50cm (2ft/1¾ft); *A. ptarmica* (Sneezewort), has narrow, lance-shaped toothed leaves, mid-green, and white, daisy-like flowers, 30-90cm/ 60cm (1ft-3ft/2ft); *A. sibirica* Summer Pastels Group, flowers in a wide range of colours, including white, cream, various shades of pink, purple, crimson and yellow.

Aconitum *Monk's-hood* Ranunculaceae

Small/large hardy herbaceous perennial suitable for the more shaded border or woodland garden. Rich green leaves variously kidney-shaped to elliptical; hooded flowers in shades of dark purple, blue and white borne on flower spikes held well above the leaves. All parts are highly toxic and leaves may cause skin irritation when handled. Tall forms must be staked. Dead-head once flowering is finished. Divide in spring; some varieties can be grown from seed sown in spring in a cold-frame. ❀ A. 'Bressingham Spire', deep violet flowers from midsummer to autumn, 90-100cm/30cm (3ft-3ft/ 1ft); *A.* x *cammarum* 'Bicolor', blue and white flowers mid- to late summer, 1.2m (4ft); *A. carmichaelii*, purple-blue flowers in early autumn, 1.5-1.8m/30-40cm (5ft-5½ft/12-1½ft); *A. c.* 'Arendsii', rich blue flowers in autumn, 1.2m/30cm (4ft/1ft); *A. hemsleyanum*, deep purple-blue flowers midsummer to early autumn, 2-3m/1m (6½ft-10ft/3ft); *A.* 'Ivorine', ivory-white flowers late spring to early summer, 90cm/45cm (3ft/1½ft); *A. napellus*, violet-pink flowers midsummer to late summer, 1.5m/30cm (5ft/1ft).

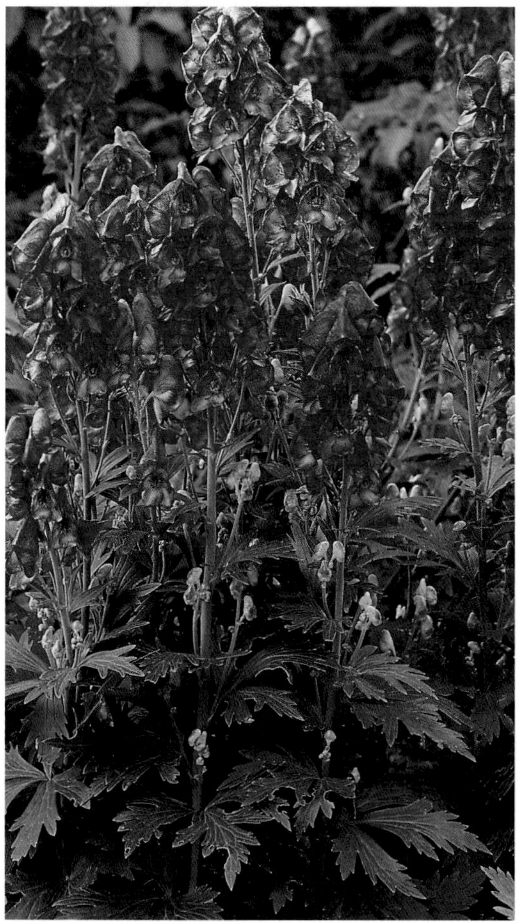

left *Aconitum carmichaelii* 'Arendsii'. The Monk's Hoods take their name from the cowl-shaped flowers but whilst very beautiful, they are also toxic and not plants for gardens with young children.

Acorus *Sweet Flag* Araceae

Small/medium water marginal perennial. Barely hardy to hardy. Linear or strap-shaped leaves smell of orange when crushed, insignificant green inflorescences 5-7cm (2in-2¾in) long in midsummer. Requires a position in full sun or light shade at depths of 10-30cm (4-1ft). Cut back dead foliage in autumn. Propagate by division every three to four years in spring. *A. calamus*, deciduous, insignificant brown-green flowers, followed in warm areas by red fruit, 1.5m/60cm (5ft/2ft); *A. c.* 'Variegatus', leaves striped cream and white, 60-90cm/60cm (2ft-3ft/2ft).

Actaea *Baneberry* Ranunculaceae

Medium herbaceous hardy perennial. Clump-forming species with light green dissected leaves and spikes of fluffy white flowers in spring followed by the main attraction, clusters of pea-sized white, black or red (and toxic) fruits. Cut back after fruiting is finished. Divide in spring or sow ripe seed in a cold-frame in autumn. ❀ *A. alba* (syn. *A. pachypoda*), light green leaves, white fruits with a black spot carried on bright red stalks, 90cm/45-60cm (3ft/18-2ft); *A. rubra*, spherical red fruits on slender green stalks, 45cm/30cm (1½ft/1ft); *A. spicata*, glossy black fruits on green stalks, 45cm/45cm (1½ft/1½ft).

Actinidia Actinidiaceae

Large deciduous climber. Moderately hardy to very hardy. Woody, twining stems with ovate, oblong or heart-shaped toothed leaves, clusters of white, sometimes fragrant flowers usually followed by fruit. Some species require both male and female plants to produce fruit. Suitable for growing in trees or on pergolas and walls, where it will need additional support. Thrives best in moist, fairly rich soil in full sun. No pruning of ornamentals but *A. deliciosa* pruned as grapevine. Sow seed in a cold-frame in autumn or spring, take semi-ripe cuttings of current year's growth in late summer or layer low-growing branches.

❀ The best ornamental species is *A. kolomikta*, pale green heart-shaped leaves tipped with white at first, as if dipped in paint, later deep rose pink, fragrant white flowers in early summer, sometimes followed on female plants by small green-yellow fruit, 6-7m (20-23ft). The main species with sweet, edible fruit is *A. deliciosa* (syn. *A. chinensis*) (Chinese gooseberry or Kiwi fruit), self-fertile or separate male and female plants, large heart-shaped leaves with bristly margins, flowers cream-white at first, later yellow, followed by hairy brown edible fruit, prune as grapevines, 30m (100ft); *A. d.* 'Blake', self-fertile, early-flowering female, *A. d.* 'Hayward', late-flowering female; *A. d.* 'Jenny', self-fertile female, *A. d.* 'Tomuri', male counterpart of 'Hayward'.

below Gardeners sometimes become frustrated with the climber *Actinidia kolomikta* because it often takes a few years before the striking foliage colours become really intense.

right *Adonis amurensis* 'Fukujukai'. This Eastern Asian species is popular with Japanese gardeners and this is one of several varieties that originated in Japanese nurseries.

Adenophora
Gland Bellflower Campanulaceae

Small/large herbaceous hardy perennial. Oval to lance-shaped, sometimes downy green leaves. Tall inflorescences of violet or blue, mainly bell-shaped flowers. Propagate by seeds in spring or basal shoot cuttings in late spring. ❀ *A. bulleyana*, clusters of narrow-petalled blue flowers in late summer, 1.2m/45cm(4ft-1½ft); *A. liliifolia*, fragrant blue or white-blue flowers in late summer, 45cm/30cm (11/2ft-1ft); *A. potaninii*, bell-shaped, pale blue-violet flowers from mid- to late summer, 60-90cm/30cm (2ft-3ft/1ft); *A. tashiroi*, pendent violet flowers on slender stems from mid- to late summer, 10-50cm/15cm (4in-1¾ft/6in).

Adiantum *Maidenhair Fern* Adiantaceae

Deciduous, semi-evergreen and evergreen ferns. Some are barely hardy, others vary from tender to very hardy. Hardier species are suitable for the alpine garden, fernery or in woodland. Thin, black to dark purple-red wiry stems; delicate fronds of tiny, more or less rounded leaves. Cut down dead foliage in spring. Divide in early spring. ❀ *A. pedatum*, hardy, deciduous, erect lime-green fronds on dark brown or black stalks, 30-40cm/30-40cm (1-1½ft/1-1½ft); *A. venustum*, very hardy, usually evergreen but deciduous in areas where winter temperatures fall below about -10°C (14°F), green fronds with black stalks, newly emerging fronds brown-pink, 15cm/15cm (6in/6in) or more.

below *Adiantum pedatum*. So many of the lovely Maidenhair ferns aren't truly hardy but my experience has been that this North American and Asian species is one of the most reliable.

Adonis Ranunculaceae

Small annuals and hardy herbaceous perennials, of which the perennials are best known. Fern-like foliage, bowl-shaped flowers are one of my garden's greatest delights in late winter and early spring; like a rather grand aconite. Divide in spring after flowers have faded, replanting immediately, or sow seed in a cold-frame. ❀ *A. amurensis*, clump-forming, finely cut leaves, single golden yellow flowers appear before the foliage, 30-40cm/30cm (12-1½ft/1ft). *A. a.* 'Flore Pleno', double yellow flowers with a green tinge.

Aegopodium *Ground Elder* Apiaceae

Small but invasive hardy herbaceous perennials. Only one species is recommended for cultivation and is commonly used for ground cover where conditions are poor. Propagate by division in spring or autumn. ❀ *A. podagraria* 'Variegatum', said not to be as invasive as the green form, but don't believe it, mid-green leaves with white margins, umbels of cream-white flowers in early summer, 30-60cm (12-2ft)/indefinite.

Aeonium Crassulaceae

Medium evergreen perennial/ biennial. Tender succulent used in summer as bedding, in containers or temporarily in a rock garden. Leaves form a rosette. Tiny star-shaped flowers 8-15mm (¼-½in) in diameter from spring to summer. Sow seed in warmth in spring or take leaf cuttings in early summer. ❀ *A. arboreum*, narrow, shiny, bright green leaves, yellow inflorescences from spring to early summer, 60cm/1m (2ft/3ft); *A. a.* 'Atropurpureum', extremely dark red and maroon leaves.

Aesculus
Horse Chestnut Hippocastanaceae

Large deciduous trees/medium-large shrubs, only for very big gardens. Moderately hardy. Most have coarse, flaking bark, sticky leaf buds and large palmate, toothed leaves. Large flowers in beautiful cone-shaped inflorescences, 15-40cm (6-1½ft) long, in late spring, followed by fruit ('conkers') in autumn. Sow seed in a seed bed in autumn or buy named plants. ❀ *A.* x *carnea* 'Briotii', leaves golden yellow in autumn, rose-pink inflorescences up to 20cm (8in) long, knobbly round fruit, 20m/15m (60ft/50ft); *A. flava* (syn. *A. octandra*) medium/large tree with good autumn colour, yellow flowers late spring to early summer, 15-20m/10-15m (50-60ft/33-50ft); *A. indica*, colourful leaves, bronze in spring, glossy mid- to dark green in summer, yellow or orange in autumn, white inflorescences sometimes flushed pink, black knobbly fruit, 15m/15m (50ft/50ft); *A. parviflora*, medium/large, suckering shrub, leaves bronze in spring, later mid-green, sometimes yellow in autumn, white flowers with red anthers on upright inflorescences, smooth, pear-shaped fruit, 3m/5m (10ft/16ft); *A. pavia* (syn. *A. splendens*) medium/large shrub or small tree, shiny green leaves turn red in autumn, bright red inflorescences from early to midsummer, smooth, oval fruit, 5m/5m (16ft/16ft).

Aethionema *Stone Cress* Brassicaceae

Small evergreen/semi-evergreen perennials, sub-shrubs and annuals. Moderately hardy. Narrow, usually grey-green or blue-green leaves form thick, sometimes spreading mats. Masses of tiny flowers held well above the leaves. Suitable for rock gardens or stone walls; lime-tolerant. Sow seed in a cold-frame in spring, divide in spring or autumn or take semi-ripe cuttings in midsummer. ❀ *A. grandiflorum* (syn. *A. pulchellum*), sub-shrub, large pale pink inflorescences from early to midsummer, 20-30cm/20-30cm (8-1ft/8-1ft); *A.* 'Warley Rose', sub-shrub, deep rose-pink flowers from late spring to midsummer, 15-20cm/15-20cm (6-8in/6-8in).

Agapanthus Alliaceae

Medium hardy and half-hardy perennials, some evergreen. Long, arching strap-shaped leaves in clumps, round or pendent umbels of trumpet- or bell-shaped flowers on tall, smooth bare stems, followed by seed-heads. Good for cutting (flowers) and drying (seed-heads). Suitable for borders and containers but always best close to the sea. Mulch in winter. Divide established clumps in spring.

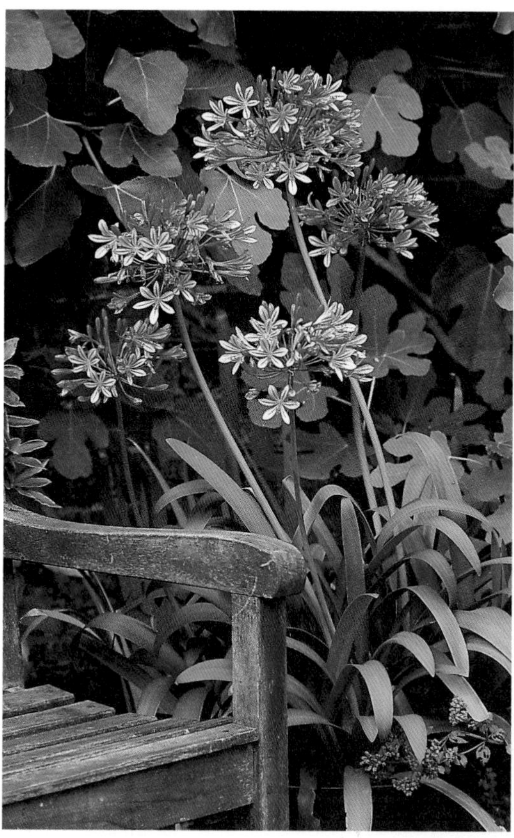

left *Agapanthus* 'Headbourne Hybrids'. *Agapanthus* are among the largest and most striking of summer flowering bulbs but unless you live in a mild area or at the coast, this variety is always the one to choose.

❀ *A. campanulatus*, deciduous, slightly flattened umbels of blue, sometimes white, bell-shaped flowers from mid- to late summer. 60-120cm/45cm (2-3½ft/1½ft); *A.* 'Headbourne Hybrids' (syn. 'Palmer's Hybrids'), evergreen, much the best for general use, variable shades of dark and light blue flowers from mid- to late summer, 1m (3ft); *A.* 'Lilliput', dwarf, compact variety, slightly flattened umbels of dark blue flowers, 40cm/40cm (1½ft/1½ft).

Agastache *Giant Hyssop* Lamiaceae

Medium/large short-lived, half-hardy perennial. Bushy, erect plants with pointed, toothed, ovate to lance-shaped leaves, most smelling strongly of aniseed, spikes of mainly red or purple flowers lasting from midsummer to autumn. Needs winter protection in cold areas and a mulch in autumn in mild places. Cut to soil level in spring. Take semi-ripe cuttings in late summer, divide in spring or sow seed in early summer.

❀ *A.* 'Firebird', orange flowers, 60cm/30cm (2ft/1ft); *A. foeniculum*, violet-blue flowers, 90-150cm/30cm (3-5ft/1ft); *A. mexicana*, best grown as an annual, crimson flowers, 60cm/30cm (2ft/1ft); *A. rugosa*, mint-scented leaves, white and hairy beneath, purple flowers, 90-120cm/60cm (3-4ft/2ft).

Agave *Century Plant* Agavaceae

Large evergreen perennial. Tender to barely hardy. Rosettes of succulent, prominently toothed leaves, strap-like, with vicious spines at the tip. Inflorescences of funnel-shaped flowers, arising from the centre, may take 8–20 years to appear and are usually followed by fruit. The leaves of most species die after flowering; the offsets remain to continue growing. Suitable for growing outside only in mild areas. Remove offsets in spring or autumn or sow seed in warmth in spring. ❀ *A. americana*, broad inflorescences of bell-shaped, cream-white or yellow-green flowers in summer, 2m/3m (6½ft/10ft); *A. a.* 'Variegata', yellow leaf margins, less hardy.

right The very hardy Chinese tree *Ailanthus altissima* has been in British gardens since 1751. Perhaps the fact that it is still not widely known is due to it really being a plant for big gardens.

Ageratum Asteraceae

Small half-hardy annuals. Suitable for the edges of borders. Compact foliage of small, ovate, mid-green leaves, fluffy mounds of soft blue flowers in summer. Thrives best in full sun in a sheltered position in any but dry conditions. Sow seed in warmth in spring. ❀ Several modern, compact varieties are named after seas; among the best is *A.* 'Adriatic', mid-blue flowers in early summer, 15-20cm/15-20cm (6-8in/6-8in); *A.* 'Blue Mink', an older, taller type, powder-blue flowers, 20-25cm/15-30cm (8-10in/6in-1ft).

Agrostemma *Corn-cockle* Caryophyllaceae

Medium hardy bedding annuals. Narrow lanceolate, mid-green leaves, trumpet-shaped flowers in summer with five notched petals, long, pointed sepals held well above flowers. Rather weak stems need support. Sow seed in flowering positions in early spring or autumn. Self-seeds freely once established. ❀ *A. githago*, hairy sepals, purple-red flowers, often with a white centre, or white flowers, 60-90cm/30cm (2ft-3ft/1ft).

Agrostis *Bent Grass* Poaceae

Annual and perennial grasses. Moderately hardy. Perennials are particularly suitable for wildflower meadows or borders. Most thrive in well-drained soil in full sun. Propagate by division from mid-spring to early summer. ❀ *A. canina*, 'Silver Needles', evergreen mat-forming perennial for sun or partial shade, erect stems, mid-green leaves, red-brown inflorescences early to late summer, 6cm/30cm (2¼in/1ft).

Ailanthus *Tree of Heaven* Simaroubaceae

Large deciduous trees and shrubs. Hardy. Tolerant of urban pollution and therefore used as a street tree but also makes a fine specimen in large gardens. Large, pinnate, ash-like leaves, winged fruit in autumn. May be cut back hard in spring if shrubby growth is desired but I much prefer to see it grown as a specimen tree with no routine pruning. Propagate by sowing seed in autumn in a cold-frame, by suckers or by root cuttings in winter. ❀ *A. altissima*, leaves 60-100cm (2ft-3ft) long, red at first, later green, terminal clusters of green flowers in summer, male and female flowers on separate plants, followed on female trees by red-winged fruit in autumn, 25m/15m (80ft/50ft).

Ajuga *Bugle* Lamiaceae

Small hardy bedding annuals and evergreen/semi-evergreen rhizomatous ornamentals. Suitable for ground cover although in my experience, their value is seriously limited by their susceptibility to mildew. Those that I describe here are evergreen or semi-evergreen. Oblong to ovate or narrow needle-like leaves, spikes of tubular two-lipped flowers in spring or summer. Mulch in spring and autumn.

right *Ajuga reptans* 'Catlin's Giant'. If only the ajugas didn't suffer from mildew, I'm sure they would be even more popular. This is the biggest and boldest of them.

Divide established plants in spring or autumn. ❀ *A. reptans*, evergreen, spoon-shaped, glossy dark green leaves, blue flowers late spring to early summer, 15cm/60-90cm (6in/2-3ft); *A. r.* 'Alba', white flowers; *A. r.* 'Atropurpurea', glossy, dark purple leaves, blue flowers; *A. r.* 'Braunherz', glossy dark brown-purple leaves; *A. r.* 'Burgundy Glow', silver-green leaves with bronze or pink margins; *A. r.* 'Catlin's Giant', brown-purple leaves, inflorescences 20cm (8in) long, vigorous; *A. r.* 'Multicolor', bronze leaves with yellow, gold or red markings; *A. r.* 'Variegata', green leaves, with cream margins.

Akebia *Chocolate Vine* Lardizabalaceae

Large deciduous/semi-evergreen climber. Moderately hardy. Mid-green palmate leaves, often tinted bronze when young. In mild areas male and female flowers are produced in spring. In long hot summers the flowers are followed in autumn by curious purple fruit. No regular pruning needed but plants may be pruned after flowering to limit size. Support young plants and give winter protection in early years. Layer or take semi-ripe cuttings in autumn, or sow seeds in spring. ❀ *A. quinata*, semi-evergreen, small deep-purple flowers with vanilla (or supposedly chocolate) scent, 6m/6m (20ft/20ft).

Albizia Mimosaceae

Deciduous shrub/small tree. Tender to barely hardy. Finely divided foliage, small, fluffy inflorescences from early to midsummer. In cold areas, thrives best in poor to moderately fertile well-drained soil in full sun. Can also be grown as a climber against a wall. Cut out frost damaged shoots in spring. Sow seed in spring, take semi-ripe cuttings in summer or root cuttings in winter. ❀ *A. julibrissin* 'Rosea', fern-like leaves, white to pink flowers, 6m/6m (20ft/20ft).

Alcea *Hollyhock* Malvaceae

Large hardy perennials and biennials but I find them all much better when grown as an annual or biennial as this helps avoid rust, to which it is very prone. One of the best-loved plants of cottage gardens with rather rough, slightly lobed leaves and tall, slender inflorescences of single or double shallow, funnel-shaped flowers. Cut down and destroy stems after flowering. Sow seed in midsummer and plant out transplants in early autumn. ❀ *A. rosea*, biennial, light green, rather hairy, rounded, lobed leaves, single flowers in white and shades of purple, pink and yellow from early to midsummer, 1.5-2.5m/60cm (5-8ft/2ft); *A. r.* 'Chater's Double Group', biennial, double flowers in bright or pale shades of red, blue, yellow, pink; *A. r.* 'Nigra', single, flowers very dark purple-red, verging on black, 2m (6½ft); *A. rugosa*, biennial, fairly rust-resistant, deeply lobed leaves, pale yellow flowers up to 12cm (5in) in diameter, 3m/60cm (10ft/2ft).

left *Alchemilla alpina.* This neat, compact species is the one to choose if you love the genus but find *Alchemilla vulgaris* to be too big and invasive.

Alchemilla *Lady's Mantle* Rosaceae

Small herbaceous deciduous/semi-evergreen perennials and alpines. Barely hardy to very hardy. Low-growing clumps of leaves, feathery inflorescences of tiny green-yellow flowers in summer. The flowers of some are good for cutting and drying. Tolerant of most types of soil except very dry or heavy, wet conditions, but thrives best in deep, rich loam in sun or partial shade. Remove flowers when they fade and become untidy and cut foliage to soil level in late autumn. Divide in spring or autumn, sow seed in spring or remove self-sown seedlings. ❀ *A. alpina*, moderately hardy, dark green round or kidney-shaped leaves with serrated lobes, smooth surface, hairy beneath, flower clusters held erect, usefully smaller and neater than the more familiar *A. mollis*, 8-12cm/50cm (3¼-5in/1¾ft); *A. conjuncta*, blue-green leaves, deeply lobed, smooth above with silver hairs beneath, green flowers from early summer to late autumn, 40cm/30cm (1½ft/1ft); *A. erythropoda*, round, sharply toothed, hairy blue-green leaves, flowers from late spring to early summer, 20-30cm/20cm (8-1ft/8in); *A. mollis*, very hardy and drought-tolerant, self-seeds freely, hairy, shallow-lobed light green leaves with toothed edges, frothy green-yellow inflorescences in summer, I think this is probably the loveliest deciduous ground cover perennial, 50cm/60cm (1¾ft/2ft).

below The hollyhock, *Alcea rosea,* in all its forms, is a classic cottage garden plant; but rust disease must be kept under control.

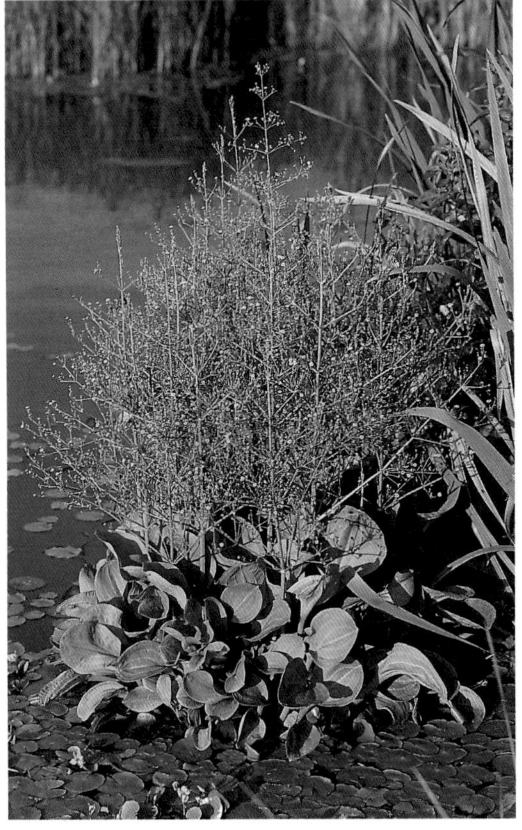

right You really need space to grow *Alisma plantago-aquatica*; even then, it makes sense to remove flower heads before the seed is set and the seedlings dispersed far and wide.

Alisma *Water plantain* Alismataceae

Water marginal. Deciduous, moderately hardy perennial up to 75cm (2½ft) tall. Basal rosette of green-grey, elliptical to lance-shaped leaves 25cm (10in) long held above the water. Suitable for shallow parts of large pools. Best in full sun at depths of 0-20cm (0-8in) but survives in depths of up to 30cm (1ft). Cut back dead flower spikes in the autumn. Divide clumps in spring every three to four years. Buy established plants or grow from seed. ❀ *A. plantago-aquatica*, self-seeding and invasive, white gypsophila-like flowers 10mm (½in) in diameter on branching sprays from mid- to late summer, 50-75cm/50cm (20-2½ft/1¾ft).

Allium *Onions* Alliaceae

Bulbous or occasionally rhizomatous ornamental and edible perennials and biennials. Very hardy to hardy. Edible species (see below) are onions, garlic, shallots, chives and leeks. Ornamental alliums are useful for growing in clumps in borders; smaller species are attractive among alpines in the rock garden. All produce delightful terminal umbels of brightly coloured flowers, mainly in pinks, mauves, and blues, some yellow or white. Umbels are spherical or shaped like a shuttle-cock and are suitable for drying for winter decoration.

Ornamental alliums thrive best in well-drained soil in an open, sunny position. Sow seed in growing positions between October and April, plant bulbs in October at three to four times their own depth. Divide established clumps of spring-flowering species once flowers have died down, summer-flowering forms in the autumn. ❀ *A. caeruleum*, linear mid-green leaves clasping the stems are followed by large spherical umbels of blue flowers in summer, 60cm/2.5cm (2ft/1in); *A. carinatum* ssp. *pulchellum*, elongated umbels, 3cm (1¼in) in diameter, of deep purple, cup-shaped pendent flowers in midsummer, linear, semi-erect leaves, 30-60cm/8-10cm (12-2ft/3¼-4in); *A. cernuum*, clump-forming, summer flowering with pink bell-shaped flowers held in loose, pendent umbels, strap-like, narrow, semi-erect basal leaves, 30-70cm/8-12cm (1-2¼ft/3¼-5in); *A. cristophii*, grey-green basal, strap-shaped leaves edged with hairs, ribbed stems, loose, semi-spherical umbels, 20cm (8in) in diameter, of light purple, star-shaped flowers in summer, 30-60cm/15-20cm (1-2ft/6-8in); *A. cyathophorum* var. *farreri*, narrow strap-shaped, mid-green basal leaves held erect, small, loose umbels of violet-blue, cup-shaped flowers with pointed petals in summer, 15-30cm/5-10cm (6in-1ft/2-4in); *A. flavum*, umbels of yellow bell-shaped flowers in summer on thin arching stalks, linear, grey-green semi-erect leaves clasp lower stems, 10-35cm/5cm (4-1ft/2in); *A. giganteum*, a massive plant with a huge bulb, very tall with broad, strap-shaped basal leaves, light green, large globe of star-shaped rose-lilac flowers in summer, 1.5-2m/15cm (5ft-6½ft/6in); *A. karataviense*, small, spring-flowering, broad, decorative grey-purple to grey-green basal leaves with distinctive red margins, star-shaped pale pink flowers in spherical umbels, 15cm (6in) in diameter, 20cm/25-30cm (8in/10in-1ft); *A. moly*, bright yellow star-shaped flowers in dense umbels, 5cm (2in) in diameter, summer, semi-erect grey-green,

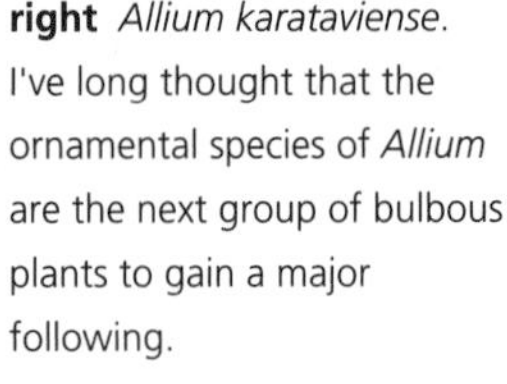

right *Allium karataviense*. I've long thought that the ornamental species of *Allium* are the next group of bulbous plants to gain a major following.

lance-shaped, clump-forming basal leaves, striking but rather invasive, 15-25cm/5cm (6-10in/2in); *A. oreophilum*, dwarf with loose umbels of rose pink, bell-shaped flowers in early summer, linear semi-erect basal leaves, mid-green, 5-20cm/3cm (2-8in/1¼in); *A. sphaerocephalon*, dense elliptical umbels of pink-purple to dark red, bell-shaped flowers in summer, sometimes with bulbils, linear, semi-erect basal leaves, 50-90cm/8cm (1¾ft-3ft/3¼in).

Onions

Bulbous vegetable. Most onions are biennials grown as annuals. The majority are sown in spring as seed or sets and are ready for harvesting from late summer onwards. Some varieties will reliably survive over winter following an autumn sowing. Onions require full sun; most give best results in a light, well-drained and well manured loam. They are vulnerable to a number of pests and diseases: onion fly, stem and bulb eelworms, downy mildew, onion smut, soft rot and storage rots, white rot (which is especially problematic as it persists for many years in the soil) and virus.

Bulb onions (*A. cepa*) are generally divided into four main types: main bulb crop; overwintering bulb crop; spring, salad or bunching onions; and pickling onions, although immature bulb varieties can be used as spring onions. Maincrops are harvested in late summer from early spring or late winter sowing or planting. ❀ 'Ailsa Craig', large, pale, globe-shaped, a traditional exhibition variety best sown in warmth in January; 'Balstora', globe-shaped with golden brown skin, keeps well; 'Bedfordshire Champion' a large old English variety, keeps well; 'Hygro' F1, heavy cropping mid-season onion, slightly flattened globe, keeps well; 'Senshyu Semi-Globe Yellow', Japanese variety for autumn sowing, very hardy; 'Stuttgart Giant', long-lasting, semi-flat globe; 'The Kelsae', a good globe-shaped exhibition onion with mild flavour, doesn't keep well; 'Brunswick', red-skinned with mild flavour; 'Purplette', tiny with purple-red skin, mild flavour, good for cooking or pickling, can be pulled young and used as a spring onion; 'Southport Red Globe', an old exhibition variety, keeps well, sow in autumn or early spring. Spring onions: 'Ishikura', a spring onion for overwintering, does not form bulbs; 'White Lisbon' the best spring onion for sowing early spring; 'White Lisbon Winter Hardy', the best spring onion for overwintering, harvest early spring. Pickling onions thrive in a light, but poor soil: 'Barletta', traditional Italian white pickling onion; 'Paris Silver Skin', spring or pickling onion, fast grower.

Shallots (*A. c.* Aggregatum Group) form clumps of small bulbs. Cultivate as bulb onions, planting bulbs in late winter or early spring although a few varieties can now be grown from seed. The young leaves can be harvested and eaten as spring onions. ❀ 'Atlantic', early, heavy cropper, stores well; 'Golden Gourmet', yellow skin, my most reliable variety, stores well; 'Hative de Niort', flask-shaped bulbs, deep brown skin, an excellent exhibition shallot; 'Sante', equally good for exhibition or eating, red-brown skin, very good flavour and keeps well, don't plant before April or it will run to seed.

The Egyptian or tree onion (*A. c.* Proliferum Group) is a perennial onion with bulbils at the top of the stems instead of flowers, to be used like shallots. An attractive and interesting plant.

The Welsh onion (*A. fistulosum*) is a tuft or clump-forming non-bulbous onion with many stems, so resembling a spring onion. The narrow shoots can be used as spring onions and the leaves eaten like chives.

Leeks (*A. porrum*) require a long growing season and thrive best when transplanted and grown in an open position at temperatures no higher than 24°C. The soil should be fertile and moisture-retentive. ❀ 'King Richard', early, harvest summer to early winter; 'Mammoth Pot', thick-stemmed, for use in winter; 'Musselburgh', the traditional and most reliable winter leek.

left *Allium cepa* Proliferum Group. The tree onion is a fascinating plant; and a useful one too for its bulbils can be used for cooking all year round.

above Red skinned onions are extremely valuable for their mild flavour and resistance to neck rot. *Allium cepa* 'North Holland Blood Red Redmate' is equally good as a bulb or salad onion.

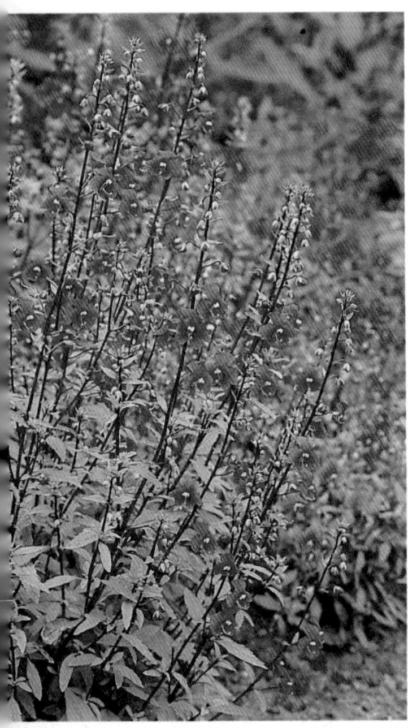

above *Alonsoa warscewiczii. Alonsoa* is one of the forgotten garden genera. The gardeners of the nineteenth century loved them and displays like this suggest that a return to serious favour is over-due.

Garlic (*A. sativum*) requires an open site with well drained, light soil. To obtain the best results in all but very cold areas, plant cloves in autumn, otherwise delay until early spring. Buy edible cloves from shop and split for planting.

Chives (*A. schoenoprasum*) These hardy perennial herbs, thrive in sun or partial shade, in a medium loamy, well-drained soil. Sow seed in early spring and transplant to their permanent position in late spring. Divide established clumps in autumn.

Chinese chives (*A. tuberosum*) are clump-forming perennials with flat leaves; sow seed or divide in spring.

Alnus *Alder* — Betulaceae

Small/large, fast-growing deciduous trees and shrubs for large gardens with water. Hardy. Simple, toothed leaves, male and female flowers produced separately on pendent catkins, usually followed by fruit. Most are suitable for all soils except chalk but thrive best in damp conditions. No routine pruning. Take hardwood cuttings in winter or sow seed when ripe.

❀ *A. cordata*, glossy, oval leaves, dark green, yellow catkins in groups of three to six in late winter, oval fruit in summer, tolerant of more alkaline, drier soil, 25m/6m (80ft/20ft); *A. glutinosa*, bushy, irregular-shaped dark green leaves, lighter on undersides, yellow-brown catkins in late winter, early spring, oval fruit in summer, 20m/10m (60ft/33ft); *A. g.* 'Imperialis', about half the size of the species, lighter green, finely cut leaves; *A. incana*, graceful tree requiring drier soil than most others, dark-green leaves, hairy and grey-white beneath, yellow-brown catkins late winter, early spring, oval fruit in summer, 20m/10m (60ft/33ft).

Aloe — Aloeaceae

Small/large tender evergreen perennials, shrubs and trees. Small plants used as summer bedding in cold areas. Thick, succulent, spiky leaves form a rosette from which panicles of bell-shaped or funnel-shaped flowers emerge. Sow seed in spring or divide in spring or summer.

❀ *A. vera* (syn. *A. barbadensis*), used as the basis of a number of skin creams (but be aware that the sap of some species is astringent), lance-shaped, toothed grey-green leaves with red spots when young, 45cm (1½ft) long, yellow funnel-shaped flowers in summer, 60-90cm (2ft-3ft)/indefinite.

Alonsoa — Scrophulariaceae

Small/medium evergreen perennials. Barely hardy and generally grown as annuals for summer bedding and borders. Asymmetrical, spurred flowers in shades of orange and red, sometimes white. Take semi-ripe cuttings in late summer or sow seed in spring in warmth. ❀ *A. meridionalis*, pointed ovate to lance-shaped, toothed mid-green leaves, red or orange flowers in summer, 30-90cm/30cm (1-3ft/1ft); *A. m.* 'Pink Beauty', pink flowers; *A. warscewiczii*, lance-shaped, toothed, dark green leaves on red stems, loose inflorescences of spurred scarlet or white flowers from summer to autumn, 30-90cm/30cm (1-3ft/1ft); *A. w.* 'Peachy-keen', soft apricot flowers.

Alopecurus *Foxtail grass* — Poaceae

Small/medium annual and perennial grasses. Moderately hardy. Some perennial species are suitable for rock gardens or mixed borders. ❀ *A. pratensis* 'Aureovariegatus', perennial for the front of the border, loose clumps of bright yellow and green striped leaves, 45cm/50cm (1½/1¾ft).

right If you are choosing a variegated grass, try to select one such as *Alopecurus pratensis* 'Aureovariegatus' that also offers appealing inflorescences.

Aloysia Verbenaceae

Medium deciduous/evergreen shrub. Barely hardy. In cold areas best grown in a warm sheltered position, preferably against a south- or west-facing wall. Prune frost-damaged plants to soil level in spring. Take softwood cuttings in summer. ❀ *A. triphylla* (syn. *A. citriodora*) (Lemon-scented Verbena), bushy deciduous shrub with coarse, lance-shaped green leaves with lemon fragrance, used as flavouring or for pot pourri, slender sprays of tiny white or pale purple flowers in summer, 3m/3m (10ft/10ft).

Alstroemeria
Peruvian Lily Alstroemeriaceae

Medium hardy herbaceous perennial growing from a tuber, spreading to form clumps 1m (3ft) or more in diameter. Erect habit with linear to lance-shaped, usually mid-green, leaves on twisted leaf stalks. Showy, funnel-shaped flowers in summer in open umbels at the ends of stems. Many species and varieties make long-lasting cut flowers. Thrives in light, rich, fairly free-draining soil in full sun, with some shelter from cold winds. Intolerant of thin dry soils. Cut back leaves to soil level as they fade. Mulch young plants and those in cold areas in winter. Divide in autumn or very early spring, handling tubers carefully and replanting immediately, or sow seed in a cold-frame in spring. Young shoots may be eaten by slugs and snails. ❀ *A. aurea* (syn. *A. aurantiaca*), umbels of orange or yellow flowers with dark red blotches, summer, 1m/45cm (3ft/1½ft); *A. a.* 'Orange King', red-orange flowers; *A.* Ligtu Hybrids, the best overall garden varieties, wide range of soft pinks, scarlets, and yellows with contrasting flecks and streaks, early summer, 1.2m/45cm (4ft/1½ft); *A. psittacina* (syn. *A. pulchella*), green flowers marked deep red on purple-spotted stems, summer, 1m/45cm (3ft/1½ft).

Althaea Malvaceae

Large perennials and annuals. Very hardy. Clump-forming, with round, lobed, velvety and toothed light green leaves and sturdy stems. From summer to autumn pink or blue-purple flowers are produced at the leaf axils. Flowers are similar to those of the hollyhock (*Alcea*), although smaller. *A. officinalis* has medicinal and culinary uses. Thrives in most soils if fairly moist, in full sun. On windy sites, tall species need staking. Mulch in spring and autumn, cut down to soil level in autumn. Sow seed in growing position in spring or divide in spring or autumn. ❀ *A. officinalis* (Marsh Mallow), velvety, round to ovate, soft hairy leaves on downy stems, soft violet-pink flowers with prominent purple-red centres, singly or in groups, 1.5-2cm (½-¾in) in diameter, 2m/50cm (6½ft/1¾ft).

above *Alstroemeria* Ligtu Hybrids. Probably better known as cut flowers than garden plants, alstroemerias are nonetheless easy to grow. This range of hybrids between two Chilean species is by far the best.

Alyssum Brassicaceae

Small annuals, hardy herbaceous perennials and evergreen sub-shrubs. Simple green, grey or silver-grey leaves, small yellow or white flowers in early summer. Trim lightly after flowering to maintain the shape. Take softwood cuttings in early summer or sow seed in autumn or spring in a cold-frame. ❀ *A. montanum*, small grey leaves, tiny yellow scented flowers in spring, 15cm (6in); *A. m.* 'Berggold', bright yellow scented flowers in early summer, 10-15cm (4-6in); *A. spinosum* (syn. *Ptilotrichum spinosum*) 'Roseum', pale pink to deep rose-pink flowers, 30-50cm/30-50cm (1-1¾ft/1-1¾ft). For white garden alyssum, see *Lobularia*.

Amaranthus *Amaranth* Amaranthaceae

Medium/large half-hardy bedding annual. Suitable for containers or borders. Most have decorative, pendent flower tassels useful for cutting and drying. Taller varieties and those on exposed sites require support. Sow seed in warmth in mid-spring. *A. caudatus* can be sown in growing positions in mid-spring. ❀ *A. caudatus* (Love-lies-bleeding), pale green leaves, brilliant red tassels from mid- to late summer, 1-1.5m/45-75cm

(3-5ft/18-21/2ft); *A. c.* 'Viridis', bright green tassels fading to off-white; *A. hypochondriacus*, purple-tinted leaves, erect flower spikes of deep red flowers midsummer to mid autumn, 90-120cm/30-45cm (3ft-4ft/1-1½ft); *A. h.* 'Green Thumb', green flowers, 60cm/40cm (2ft/1½ft); *A. h.* 'Pygmy Torch', purple foliage, crimson flowers, 60cm/40cm (2ft/1½ft).

Amaryllis
Jersey Lily, Belladonna Lily Amaryllidaceae

Bulbous ornamental. Barely hardy. A genus with a single species, grown for its showy flowers. Mulch in autumn. In cold areas requires protection from frost and cold winds. Sow seed in warmth as soon as ripe or lift older plants in spring and remove large offsets. ❀ *A. belladonna*, dark green, strap-shaped, leaves on tall purple to purple-green stems, pink or white fragrant, trumpet-shaped flowers in autumn, 60cm/10cm (2ft/4in); *A. b.* 'Johannesburg', light pink flowers.

above *Amelanchier lamarckii* was the first ornamental tree that I planted in my own garden; I do believe it remains the loveliest.

Amelanchier
Snowy Mespilus, June Berry Rosaceae

Small deciduous tree/large shrub. Very hardy. My favourite small garden tree. All species are spring-flowering and most offer attractive autumn colour. Small ovate to oblong leaves, usually bronze or bronze-tinted when young, masses of white star-shaped flowers followed by small attractive fruit. Maintain tree-like shape of suckering species and varieties by removing suckers once a year; otherwise no routine pruning. Rooted suckers can be used for propagation, or take softwood or semi-ripe cuttings in summer. ❀ *A. canadensis*, suckering shrub, leaves downy, white when young, mid-green summer, yellow-orange and red in autumn, white flowers followed by blue-black fruit, 6m/3m (20ft/10ft); *A.* x *grandiflora* 'Ballerina', shiny mid-green leaves in summer, red and purple in autumn, white flowers followed by red fruit deepening to dark purple, 6m/8m (20ft/25ft); *A. lamarckii*, much the best form, erect shrub or small tree, bronze leaves in spring, later dark green, orange and red in autumn, white flowers followed by dark purple fruit, 10m/12m (33ft/40ft).

Amicia
Papilionaceae

Large perennial or sub-shrub. Fairly hardy. Erect hollow stems bear mid-green leaves with conspicuous midribs. In cold areas requires a sheltered, warm sunny position, preferably near a wall, with protection from wind. Sow seed in warmth in spring, take root cuttings in late spring or semi-ripe cuttings in summer. ❀ *A. zygomeris*, leaves composed of two heart-shaped leaflets, clusters of yellow pea-like flowers, sometimes flushed purple, summer to autumn, followed by flattened narrow seed pods, 2.2m/1.2m (6¾ft/4ft).

Ammi
Apiaceae

Small/medium-sized hardy bedding annuals and biennials with finely divided leaves and striking fluffy clusters of white flowers in the summer. Plants require staking to prevent wind damage. Sow seed in spring. ❀ *A. majus*, fast-growing annual, fern-like mid-green to blue-green leaves, round, laced umbels of tiny white to cream-white flowers on branching stems from midsummer to autumn, 1.2m/40cm (4ft/1½ft).

Ampelopsis
Vitaceae

Large deciduous climbers. Fairly hardy to moderately hardy. Suitable for growing on fences, walls, tree stumps and pergolas. Oval, lobed or divided leaves often vividly red and yellow in autumn. The rather insignificant inflorescences may be followed by fruits, but for me, the autumn colours of the foliage offer the real glory. Climb by tendrils but mature specimens may need additional support. Mulch late autumn and spring. Prune in late winter or early spring to limit size and encourage new growth. Take semi-ripe cuttings or layer in sum-

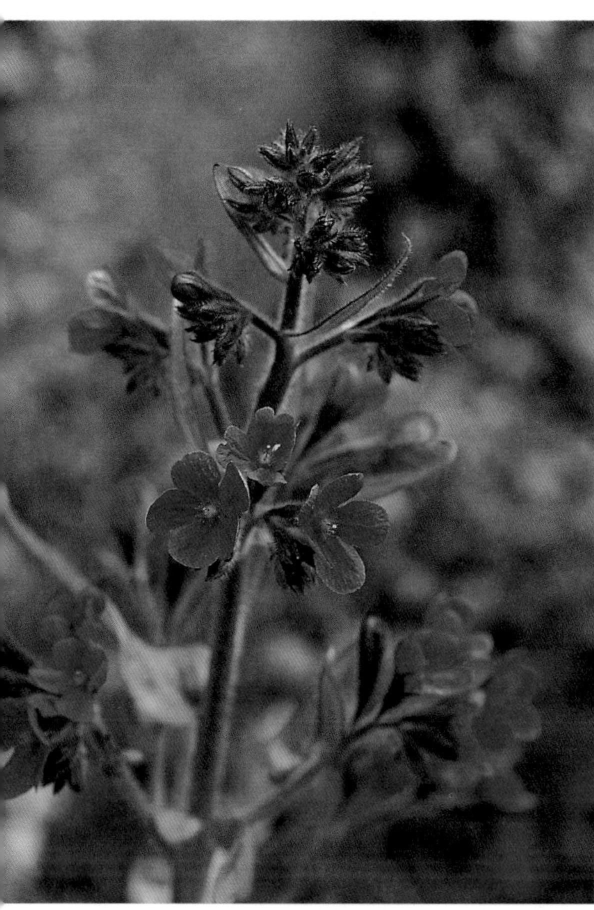

left *Anchusa azurea* 'Loddon Royalist' is one of the few herbaceous perennials that offers intense rich blue flowers.

mer, or sow fresh seed in winter. ❀ *A. glandulosa* var. *brevipedunculata* (syn. *A. brevipedunculata*), clusters of tiny green flowers in late summer, followed in warm summers by fruits 6cm (2¼in) in diameter, pink-purple at first, later blue, 8m (25ft); *A. megalophylla*, large leaves up to 60cm (2ft) long, ovate, lobed, mid-green, pale beneath, clusters of tiny green flowers in late summer, sometimes followed by purple-black fruits, 10m (33ft).

Anagallis *Pimpernel* Primulaceae

Small half-hardy bedding annuals, biennials and evergreen perennials. Fairly hardy to moderately hardy. Very short stalkless leaves, bell-shaped to flattened flowers that characteristically close when cool. Sow seed in a cold-frame in spring, take softwood cuttings or divide in spring. ❀ *A. monellii*, beautiful short-lived evergreen, best grown as an annual, glossy green leaves, narrow and pointed, abundant bright blue, sometimes red or pink flowers from mid- to late summer, 10-20cm/40cm (4-8in/1½ft); *A. tenella* 'Studland', fairly hardy evergreen perennial, requires damp soil, pale green round to oval leaves, erect, bell-shaped, fragrant deep pink flowers from spring to summer, 5-10cm/40cm (2-4in/1½ft).

Anaphalis *Pearly Everlasting* Asteraceae

Small/medium hardy herbaceous perennial. Grey-green woolly leaves and white 'everlasting' inflorescences, always popular with flower arrangers. Cut flowering stems back to soil level in spring or autumn. Propagate by division in early spring, by basal or stem tip cuttings in spring or early summer, or sow seed in a cold-frame in spring. ❀ *A. margaritacea*, lance-shaped leaves, downy white beneath, pearl-white flowers from midsummer to autumn, 60cm/60cm (2ft/2ft); *A. m.* 'Neuschnee', more compressed, with longer leaves, 45cm/45cm (1½ft/1½ft); *A.m.* var. *yedoensis* (syn. *A. yedoensis*), larger, with larger inflorescences, 75cm/60cm (2½ft/2ft).

Anchusa Boraginaceae

Medium/large hardy bedding annuals, biennials and herbaceous perennials. Lance-shaped to elliptical leaves, sometimes coarsely hairy or bristly, large clusters of tubular flowers in summer. Cut back stems of perennials in autumn. Take basal cuttings in spring, root cuttings in winter. Sow annuals in warmth in early spring, biennials in late winter and perennials in a cold-frame in spring. ❀ *A. azurea* 'Dropmore', tall spikes with abundant deep blue, purple flushed flowers from late spring to early summer, 1.8m/60cm (5½ft/2ft); *A. a.* 'Loddon Royalist', much the best form, a lovely plant, royal blue flowers, 1m/60cm (3ft/2ft).

Andromeda *Bog Rosemary* Ericaceae

Dwarf evergreen shrub. Very hardy. Lance-shaped leaves, umbels of small pitcher-shaped flowers on the ends of slender wiry stems in spring and early summer. Suitable for rock gardens (provided you select one of the less vigorous forms and damp borders and I think one of the unjustifiably neglected plants of the acidic soil garden. Mulch annually in spring and trim to shape after flowering. Take softwood cuttings from early to midsummer or sow seed in early autumn.

❀ *A. polifolia* (syn. *A. rosmarinifolia*), erect or low-growing twiggy shrub, narrow, leathery, blue-green leaves, white beneath, clusters of soft pink flowers in late spring or early summer, 40cm/60cm (1½ft/ 2ft); *A. p.* 'Alba', (syn. 'Compacta Alba'), pure white flowers, 15cm/20cm (6in/8in); *A. p.* 'Compacta', broad leaves, coral pink flowers flushed white, 30cm/20cm (1ft/8in); *A. p.* 'Macrophylla', very low-growing, broad dark-green leaves, pink and white flowers, 5-15cm/25cm (2-6in/10in).

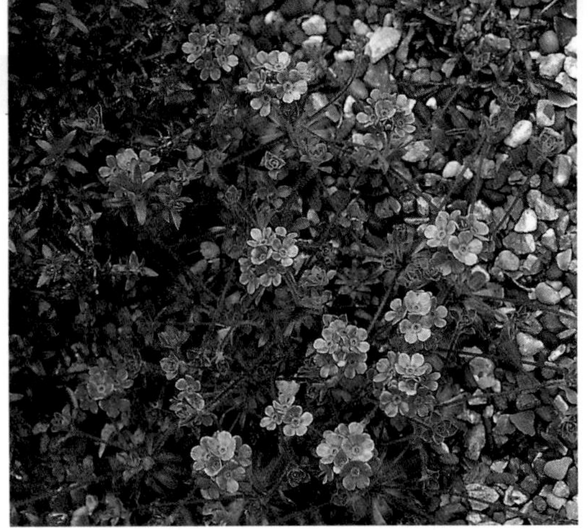

right *Androsace sempervivoides* is one of a group of these arrestingly individual members of the family Primulaceae that was first introduced to our gardens around 100 years ago.

Androsace *Rock Jasmine* Primulaceae

Small annuals, evergreen perennials and alpines. Moderately hardy. Those I describe here are all evergreen alpines and most form compact cushions of foliage, often composed of soft hairy leaves held in rosettes. Abundant flowers from spring to autumn. Like so many other of the best alpines, require protection from winter wet. Sow seed in autumn or take tip cuttings in summer. ❀ *A. carnea*, neat rosettes of bright green, narrow, pointed leaves with hairy margins, clusters of pink flowers on 6cm (2¼in) stalks carried above the foliage, 5cm/8-15cm (2in/3¼-6in); *A. lanuginosa*, trailing, silky-haired stems, grey-green, oval, soft hairy leaves, clusters of lilac-pink or light pink flowers from mid- to late summer, 5-10cm/10cm (2-4in/4in); *A. sarmentosa*, mat-forming, spreads by runners, narrow, elliptical, silver-haired leaves, deep pink flowers from summer to autumn, 5-10cm/30cm (2-4in/1ft); *A. s.* 'Sherriff's', pale pink flowers; *A. sempervivoides*, mat-forming, spreads by runners, rosettes of leathery, deep green leaves, fragrant bright pink flowers in spring, 2.5-5cm/15-20cm (1-2in/6-8in).

Anemone Ranunculaceae

Small/large rhizomatous, tuberous, or fibrous-rooted ornamentals. Barely hardy to very hardy. I have little hesitation in listing *Anemone* among the most important genera of garden ornamentals. Most have deeply divided, toothed, basal and stem leaves. Cup- to saucer-shaped flowers, singly or in clusters, with prominent centre, often on multi-branched stems, produced in early spring, summer or autumn. Cultivation depends on the species and variety (see below). Divide rhizomatous species in spring or after the leaves have died down; divide tuberous species in summer when dormant. Fibrous-rooted species resent disturbance and are best raised from ripe seed in a cold-frame in autumn or early winter. Alternatively divide in spring and replant immediately or take root cuttings in spring.

❀ *A. blanda*, tuberous, clump-forming, dark green leaves, solitary and beautiful deep blue, white or pink rather flat flowers in spring, thrives in well-drained, humus-rich soil in sun or partial shade, or light sandy soil in full sun, protect with mulch in winter, 15cm/15cm (6in/6in); *A. b.* blue, various shades of blue; *A. b.* 'Radar', deep red, white-centred flowers; *A. b.* 'White Splendour', pure white flowers, pink undersides; *A. coronaria* De Caen Group, tuberous but I'm convinced, much better grown as an annual; they just don't have the ability to persist, single or semi-double blue, red and white flowers in spring, lovely as cut flowers but you will need to grow plenty, thrives in light sandy soil in full sun, protect with winter mulch, 30-45cm/15cm (1-1½ft/6in); *A. c.* St. Brigid Group, double flowers in various shades of pink,

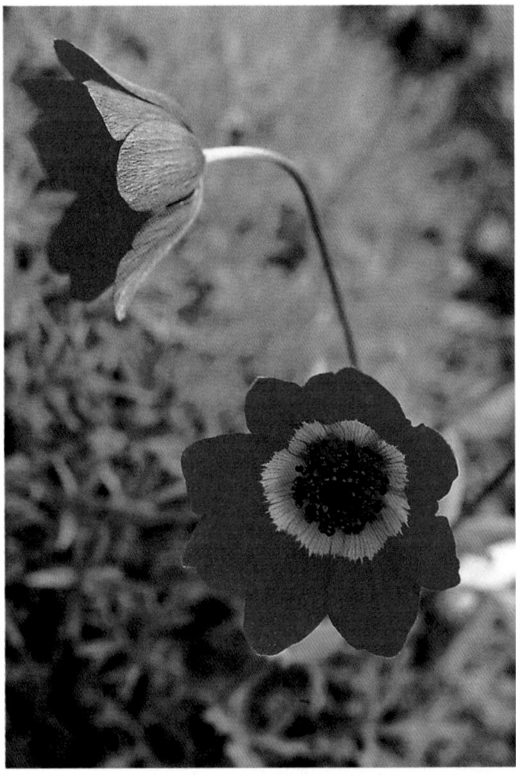

far right *Anemone coronaria* De Caen Group has striking flowers in the first year but don't expect it to be reliably perennial.

blue and white in spring; *A. hupehensis* 'Bowles' Pink', medium, fibrous-rooted perennial, dark-green leaves, hairy beneath, clusters of deep purple-pink flowers mid- to late summer, thrives best in moist, fertile soil enriched with humus in sun or partial shade, mulch spring and autumn, 60-90cm/40cm (2ft-3ft/1½ft); *A. h.* 'Hadspen Abundance', pink-red flowers; *A. h.* var. *japonica* 'Prinz Heinrich', vivid pink flowers; *A. h.* var. *j.* 'September Charm', rose-pink flowers late summer to early autumn; *A.* x *hybrida*, border perennials for late summer, can be invasive but plant where they have room to spread as they are glorious, 75cm/50-60cm (2½ft/1¾-2ft); *A.* x *h.* 'Honorine Jobert', single pure white flowers flushed pink on undersides, much the best variety; *A.* x *h.* 'Königin Charlotte', large semi-double light pink flowers frilled at the edges, flushed pink beneath; *A.* x *h.* 'Richard Ahrends', rose-pink flowers; *A.* x *lesseri*, fibrous-rooted, clump-forming, hairy mid-green leaves, red-pink flowers singly or in clusters in summer, best in well-drained soil enriched with humus in sun or partial shade, 40cm/30cm (1½ft/1ft); *A. multifida*, rhizomatous, mid-green leaves, cream-yellow flowers in summer, well-drained soil enriched with humus, sun or partial shade, 30cm/15cm (1ft/6in); *A. nemorosa*, rhizomatous, low-growing with creeping stems, deeply-cut mid-green leaves, abundant white solitary flowers from spring to early summer, thrives in moist, well-drained soil enriched with humus, in partial shade and a lovely plant when growing naturally in woodland, 8-15cm/30cm (3¼-6in/1ft); *A. n.* 'Alba Plena', white flowers, pale yellow centres; *A. n.* 'Allenii', lavender flowers, paler beneath, yellow centres; *A. n.* 'Robinsoniana', lavender-blue flowers with grey undersides; *A. n.* 'Vestal', double white flowers; *A. ranunculoides*, rhizomatous, mat-forming, mid-green leaves, single deep yellow flowers in spring, thrives in moist, well-drained soil enriched with humus in partial shade, 5-10cm/45cm (2-4in/1½ft); *A. rivularis*, fibrous-rooted, hairy dark green leaves, clusters of white flowers, sometimes blue on undersides, from late spring to early summer, best in well-drained soil enriched with humus in sun or partial shade, 60-90cm/30cm (2ft-3ft/1ft); *A. tomentosa*, fibrous-rooted, mid-green leaves, pale pink flowers from late summer to mid autumn, thrives in moist soil enriched with humus, in sun or partial shade, 1-1.5m/60cm(3-5ft/2ft).

above I still think *Anemone* x *hybrida* 'Honorine Jobert' is the best variety of these rather invasive perennials although pinks are available too.

Anethum *Dill* — Apiaceae

Medium annual or biennial herb. Fairly hardy but best grown as a half-hardy annual. It has both culinary and medicinal uses. Intolerant of cold and wet. Sow seed in the growing position at monthly intervals from mid-spring to summer, protecting early sowings with cloches. Prone to run to seed but this isn't a big problem as the seeds can be used in the kitchen too. ❀ *A. graveolens*, characteristic feathery grey-green leaves, with fragrance strongly reminiscent of parsley and caraway, produced on solitary, hollow ribbed stem, yellow-green flowers on flattened umbels in summer, followed by aromatic seeds, 60-30cm (2-1ft).

Angelica — Apiaceae

Large herbaceous perennials and biennials. Very hardy. Pinnate leaves 30-90cm (1ft-3ft) long. Large umbels of small, usually green-white or green-yellow flowers produced in the second year, followed by brown fruit. Cut down to soil level in autumn and mulch in spring and autumn. Sow seed in growing positions in spring.

❀ *A. archangelica* (syn. *A. officinalis*), the culinary and medicinal perennial herb, best grown as a biennial, extremely light green leaves 60cm (2ft) long on tall, hollow ribbed stems, both stems and leaves are aromatic, green-white flowers early and midsummer, self-seeds freely, 2m/1.2m (6½ft/4ft); *A. gigas*, biennial or short-lived perennial, toothed, mid-green leaves 30-40cm (1-1½ft) long, umbels of dark purple flowers on dark red stems from late summer to early autumn, 1-2m/1.2m (3ft-6½ft/4ft).

left *Anemone nemorosa* 'Allenii' is one of a range of attractively coloured forms of the beautiful native white wood anemone.

far right *Anthemis sanctijohannis*. Unexpectedly introduced to gardens from Bulgaria only 50 years ago and sadly, a plant that always takes second place to its taller relative *A. tinctoria*.

Antennaria *Everlasting* Asteraceae

Small evergreen/semi-evergreen perennials. Hardy. Low-growing, carpet-forming plants for use among paving, for edging and ground cover but can be invasive in rock gardens. Woolly, sometimes hairy, spoon-shaped, silver-green aromatic leaves, clusters of fluffy, daisy-like flowers on short leafless stems, good for drying. Divide in spring or sow seed in spring or autumn. ❀ *A. dioica*, grey-green leaves with hairy undersides, small white or pale pink inflorescences, 5cm/45cm (2in/1½ft); *A. microphylla* (syn. *A. rosea*), rose-pink inflorescences, 5cm/45cm (2in/1½ft); *A. parvifolia*, brown inflorescences with pink or white tips, 8cm/30cm (3¼in/1ft).

right *Antennaria dioica* is a pretty but rather 'rough and ready' native alpine; good where you need to cover a large area of stony ground.

Anthemis Asteraceae

Small/medium annuals and evergreen perennials. Fairly hardy to hardy. Most are mat- or cushion-forming, suitable for ground cover. Feathery, finely dissected leaves, aromatic in some species. Daisy-like flowers, yellow or white with yellow centres. Require a free draining, light sandy soil in full sun or partial shade and intolerant of damp, cold situations. Trim lightly in spring, cut back in autumn. Sow seed in a cold-frame in spring, take basal cuttings in summer or divide established plants in the spring. ❀ *A. punctata* ssp. *cupaniana*, low-growing evergreen perennial, leaves silver-grey in spring and summer, later grey-green, single white flowers with yellow centres on short leafless stems in early summer, some later, 30cm/90cm (1ft/3ft); *A. sancti-johannis*, evergreen perennial, hairy grey-green leaves, yellow-orange flowers with yellow centres, summer, 60-90cm/60cm (2-3ft/2ft); *A. tinctoria* (Dyers' Camomile), fern-like leaves, green above, grey, downy beneath, cream-yellow to golden-yellow, summer to autumn, 1m/1m (3ft/3ft); *A. t.* 'E. C. Buxton', pale yellow flowers; *A. t.* 'Sauce Hollandaise', pale yellow flowers fading to cream; *A. t.* 'Wargrave', cream-yellow flowers, 90cm/90cm (3ft/3ft).

Anthericum Anthericaceae

Medium hardy rhizomatous herbaceous perennials. Clumps of narrow, grass-like leaves; clusters of star-shaped flowers reminiscent of lilies are produced in spring and summer, followed by seed capsules suitable for cutting and drying for arrangement. Sow seed in a cold-frame in spring or autumn or divide established plants in spring. ❀ *A. liliago* (St. Bernard's Lily), white flowers with prominent yellow centres from late spring to early summer, 60-90cm/30cm (2-3ft/1ft); *A. ramosum*, smaller white flowers in summer, 90cm/30-60cm (3ft/1-2ft).

Anthoxanthum *Vernal Grass* Poaceae

Small perennial grass. Hardy. Tufted, aromatic leaves. ❀ *A. odoratum*, broad, evergreen leaves, good for drying, when, like many grasses, they become more strongly aromatic, cream-white flower spikes from late spring to early summer; 18-50cm/12-30cm (7in-1¾ft/5-1ft).

Anthriscus Apiaceae

A genus of small/medium annuals, biennials and perennials that includes the commonest wild member of the family, cow parsley. Hardy. Finely dissected, fern-like leaves, umbels of tiny flowers. Sow seeds in a cold-frame in spring or autumn or divide mature plants. Sow seeds of *A. cerefolium* in growing positions; established plants will self-seed.

❀ *A. cerefolium* (Chervil), bright green leaves with flavour reminiscent of aniseed, white flowers in midsummer, 50cm/24cm (1¾ft/9½in); *A. sylvestris*, 'Ravenswing', biennial or short-lived perennial, laced, dark brown-purple leaves, white flowers with pink bracts from late spring to early summer, 1m/30cm (3ft/1ft).

Anthyllis Papilionaceae

Small hardy bedding annuals, hardy herbaceous perennials and shrubs for the border or rock garden. Finely divided palmate or pinnate leaves, cream, yellow or red flowers in clusters or singly. Sow seed in autumn or take semi-ripe cuttings in summer. ❀ *A. vulneraria* (Kidney Vetch), annual or short-lived perennial, rounded inflorescences of flowers are either yellow or cream, usually tipped red or purple, or various shades of red, purple, orange or white, 20-60cm/80cm (8-2ft/2½ft), *A. v. coccinea*, red flowers.

Antirrhinum
Snapdragon Scrophulariaceae

Small/medium annuals, perennials, alpines and sub-shrubs. Barely hardy to hardy. Ovate to lanceolate leaves, spikes of tubular flowers from early summer to autumn. Among the best loved of old garden flowers but out of favour for many years because of rust disease although some modern forms have fairly good resistance. Thrives best in fertile, well-drained, alkaline or neutral soil enriched with humus, in sun or partial shade. Shrubby species require a sheltered site in very well-drained soil. Sow seed of *A. majus* in warmth in early autumn or spring. Take semi-ripe cuttings of shrubby species in summer or sow seed in a cold-frame in autumn or spring.
❀ *A. majus*, short-lived perennial best grown as an annual, dark green leaves, spikes of scented flowers from summer to autumn in single colours of orange, yellow, pink, red and white and various shades and combinations of these, 25cm-1.2m/15-60cm (10in-4ft/6in-2ft). The following are good dwarf varieties: 'Floral Carpet Series', bushy, 15-30cm (6-8in); 'Kim Series', 15cm (6in); 'Magic Carpet', trailing habit, 15cm (6in); 'Royal Carpet Series', bushy, rust-resistant, 20cm (8in); 'Tahiti', bushy, rust-resistant, 20cm (8in); 'Tom Thumb', 15cm (6in). Medium-sized varieties: 'Coronette Series', bushy, rust resistant, 45cm (1½ft); 'Monarch Series', rust resistant, single or mixed colours, 40-45cm (1½ft); *A. m.* ssp. *majus* 'Taff's White', white variegation on leaves, 40cm (1½ft). Tall varieties: 'Giant Foreman', branching habit, 1m (3ft); 'Madam Butterfly', double flowers, 60-80cm (2-2½ft).

Apium *Celery, Celeriac* Apiaceae

Leafy salad and bulbous vegetables. Moderately hardy. Divided pale green leaves on thick, ribbed stems, umbels of tiny green-white flowers followed by seeds. Thrives in rich, damp soil enriched with humus in a sheltered position in sun or partial shade; never forget that celery is naturally a bog plant and must have plenty of water. Sow seed in warmth in late winter or early spring for transplanting. ❀ *A. graveolens dulce* (Celery), available in two forms, traditional or trenched and self-blanching: 'Celebrity', early, self-blanching, resistant to bolting, less stringy than most; 'Giant Red', red stems, late maturing, long standing and hardy, (the more red pigment, the hardier the variety); 'Giant White', white, early; 'Golden Self-Blanching', dwarf, not frost hardy, best harvested late summer, yellow leaves; 'Lathom Self-blanching', resistant to

above *Anthriscus sylvestris* 'Ravenswing'. Although that invaluable kitchen herb chervil is the best known member of this genus, here's a very attractive herbaceous ornamental that deserves wider recognition.

left *Antirrhinum majus* Monarch Series. Resistance to rust disease is essential in snapdragons and this is one of the more reliable varieties.

above Celery 'Lathom Self-Blanching'. Although I really believe that blanched celery has the best flavour, I know that many gardeners find self-blanching varieties like this one to be much less trouble.

right *Aquilegia* McKana Hybrids. These very popular if rather spidery flowers offer a wider range of colour than you will find anywhere in the genus.

bolting; *A. g. rapaceum* (Celeriac), hardy biennial grown as an annual, the edible swollen base is a corm, best harvested from late autumn onwards; *A. g. r.* 'Balder', stores well; 'Monarch', cream flesh.

Aponogeton Aponogetonaceae

Small submerged perennial plants. Tender to barely hardy. Leaves, varying from linear, elliptical to lanceolate, float on the surface of the water or are sometimes submerged. Tiny flowers are borne in clusters in summer. Sow seed when ripe, water in warmth or divide crowns in spring. ❀ *A. distachyos* (Water Hawthorn), evergreen in mild areas, grey-green, mat-forming foliage, spikes of white flowers with dark anthers, with scent reminiscent of hawthorn, held above the water surface from spring to autumn, followed by fruit, 60cm/1.2m (2ft/4ft).

Aquilegia *Columbine* Ranunculaceae

Small/medium hardy herbaceous perennials and alpines. Smaller species are suitable for the rock garden or alpine house and I feel that this is an under-valued genus, more diverse than is generally appreciated. Relatively large, many-lobed leaves, light green to grey-green. Funnel-shaped flowers, most with prominent spurs arising from each of the five petals. All parts are toxic. Fairly short-lived but self-seed and hybridise freely. Thrive in most well-drained soils in full sun or partial shade but intolerant of heavy soils. Alpines require gritty soil in full sun. Cut back border plants to soil level after flowering; dead-head alpine species. Mulch in autumn and spring. Sow seed in a cold-frame in spring or sow ripe seed in summer; divide established plants between autumn and spring.

❀ *A. alpina*, bright blue flowers, slightly curved spurs, late spring to early summer, 45cm/30cm (1½ft/1ft); *A. bertolonii*, dwarf species, small violet-blue flowers, incurved spurs, from early to midsummer, 30cm/10cm (1ft/4in); *A. canadensis*, striking masses of small red-and-yellow flowers on branching stems from late spring to midsummer, 60-90cm/30cm (2-3ft/1ft); *A. chrysantha*, yellow flowers strongly flushed pink, 90cm/60cm (3ft/2ft); *A. discolor*, pale blue and white flowers 10cm/15cm (4in/6in); *A. flabellata*, blue or lavender flowers with white or cream tips, short hooked spurs, from mid-spring to early summer, 10-30cm/10-15cm (4in-1ft/4-6in); *A. f.* 'Ministar', alpine, bright blue and white flowers; *A. f. pumila*, larger, 10-20cm (4-8in) tall; *A. f. pumila alba*, compact, white flowers 10cm/10cm (4in/4in); *A. formosa*, thrives in moist, partially shaded position, flowers usually red and yellow, sometimes entirely red, 60-90cm/45cm (2-3ft/1½ft); *A. fragrans*, requires rich soil, will tolerate partial shade, fragrant flowers, pale yellow or cream with pale lilac or white, from early to midsummer, 14-40cm/45cm (5½in-1½ft/1½ft); *A. longissima*, very large curved spurs, yellow flowers frequently with paler sepals, in summer, 60-90cm/45cm (2ft-3ft/1½ft); *A.* McKana Group, hybrids with abundant large flowers in bright, often assertive, shades of blue, yellow and red, with very long spurs flared at the top, from late spring to midsummer; could not be described as a subtle variety 75cm/60cm (2½ft/2ft); *A. saximontana*, alpine, tolerates partial shade, deep violet-blue flowers with yellow-white petals, short hooked spurs, 10-15cm/15cm (4-6in/6in); *A. vulgaris*, (Granny's Bonnet), the much loved old cottage garden plant, deep red, blue, purple, and red-purple flowers, occasionally pink or white, in early summer, 90cm/45cm (3ft/1½ft); *A. v.* 'Adelaide Addison', old variety with double blue and white flowers; *A. v. flore pleno*, another old variety with double, deep purple flowers; *A. v.* 'Nivea' (syn. 'Munstead White'), pure white flowers; *A. v.* 'Nora Barlow', a striking plant pink with green petals, looks old but isn't; *A. v.* 'Ruby Port', double flowers, dark maroon-red; *A. v. stellata*, white or shades of blue or pink with spreading sepals, lacks spurs, 90cm (3ft).

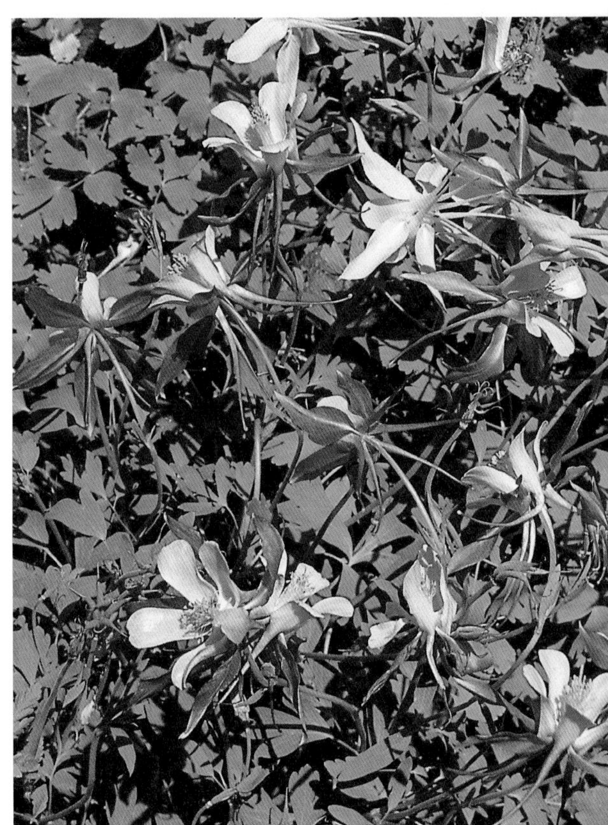

Arabis *Rock Cress* Brassicaceae

Small evergreen perennials and alpines. Mat- or cushion-forming with tiny leaves, abundant four-petalled flowers on spikes held above the foliage. Most are intolerant of winter wet. Trim after flowering to promote new growth. Take softwood cuttings in summer, sow seed of species in spring or autumn or divide established plants after flowering. ❀ *A. alpina* 'Flore Pleno', rosettes of green leaves, double white flowers in spring, 15-20cm/45cm (6-8in/1½ft); *A. blepharophylla* 'Frühlinszauber' (syn. 'Spring Charm'), toothed dark green leaves, fragrant purple-pink flowers late spring early summer, 10cm/20cm (4in/8in); *A. alpina* 'Variegata', green leaves with broad yellow margins, fragrant white flowers, 15cm/50cm (6in/1¾ft); *A. ferdinandi-coburgi* 'Old Gold', shiny green leaves variegated gold, white flowers in late spring, 5-8cm/30-40cm (2-3¼in/1-1½ft); *A. procurrens* 'Variegata' (syn. *A. f. c.* 'Variegata'), glossy mid-green leaves with cream-white margins, may be flushed pink, white flowers late spring, 5-8cm/30-40cm (2-3¼in/1-1½ft).

Aralia Araliaceae

Large deciduous shrubs or small trees. Very hardy although it doesn't look it. Large paired leaves, yellow, orange or purple in autumn. Clusters of tiny white or green-white flowers sometimes followed by black fruit. Give shelter from strong winds and mulch in spring and autumn. No routine pruning. Sow seed in a cold-frame in winter or use suckers. ❀ *A. elata* (Angelica Tree), suckering shrub, pinnate grey-green leaves on spiny stems, white flowers in broad clusters late summer to early autumn, 10m/10m (33ft/33ft); *A. e.* 'Aureovariegata', green leaves with yellow margins, 5m/5m (16ft/16ft); *A. e.* 'Variegata' (syn. 'Albomarginata'), leaf margins are cream-white.

Araucaria Araucariaceae

Medium/large evergreen trees. Tender to hardy. A very striking plant but usually grown in quite the wrong place. Given plenty of room and planted in groups, it can be arresting. Stiff, overlapping scale-like, dark green leaves, triangular or needle-like. Male and female cones usually produced on separate plants. No routine pruning. Sow seed in autumn; cuttings difficult without special facilities. ❀ *A. araucana* (syn. *A. imbricata*) (Monkey Puzzle Tree), leaves are arranged in a spiral on tiered branches, dark brown ridged bark, 15-25m/7-10m (50-80ft/23-33ft).

above *Arbutus unedo.* Not least of the attractions of this lovely small tree are that, just as with oranges, the flowers and fruits are present at the same time; although sadly they are less palatable than either oranges or strawberries.

Arbutus *Strawberry Tree* Ericaceae

Small/medium evergreen trees or shrubs. Fairly hardy to moderately hardy. Glossy green leaves, pitcher-shaped flowers are usually followed by spherical strawberry-like fruit. Some species have attractive flaking bark. No routine pruning. Sow seed in spring or take cuttings of *A. unedo* in midsummer. ❀ *A.* x *andrachnoides* (syn. *A.* x *hybrida*), small tree, reddish branches, white flowers sometimes flushed pink in late autumn, early winter, rarely followed by fruit, 8m/8m (25ft/25ft); *A. unedo*, large shrub/small tree, tolerates alkaline soils, rough, dark brown flaking bark, white flowers produced at the same time as red, but barely edible strawberry-like fruit, 8m/8m (25ft/25ft).

Arctostaphylos *Bearberry* Ericaceae

Deciduous and evergreen shrubs and small trees. The one I describe here is a moderately hardy, creeping shrub that makes good ground cover on acidic soils. The tiny pitcher-shaped flowers are followed by spherical fruit. Cut back in spring if necessary to control growth. Layer in spring or take heel cuttings of lateral shoots during summer. ❀ *A. uvaursi*, evergreen, slow-growing prostrate shrub, small white or pink flowers mid to late spring, red fruits, 20cm/1.5m (8in/5ft).

Arctotis *African Daisy* Asteraceae

Small half-hardy bedding annuals and half-hardy perennials. Woolly leaves and stems; solitary daisy-like flowers on long stems from midsummer to autumn. Sow seed in warmth in early spring or autumn, or in flowering positions in late spring. ❀ *A.* x *hybrida*, 'Apricot', silver-green leaves, dark-centred apricot-yellow flowers, 45-50cm/30cm (1½-1¾ft/1ft); *A.* x *h.* 'Flame', bright orange-red; *A.* x *h.* 'Wine', deep red.

above *Argyranthemum frutescens* 'Jamaica Primrose'. Once called chrysanthemums and still popularly known as marguerites, these charming daisies are usually and mistakenly imagined to be only white.

Arenaria *Sandwort* Caryophyllaceae

Small half-hardy to hardy annuals and shrubby evergreen perennials for the rock garden. Mat- or cushion-forming foliage of tiny leaves, above which masses of flowers are produced in spring and summer. Sow seed in a cold-frame in autumn or early spring; divide *A. balearica* and *A. montana* after flowering, *A purpurascens* in spring. ❀ *A. balearica*, white star-like flowers from spring to summer, 1cm/30cm (½in/1ft); *A. montana*, saucer-shaped white flowers, 2-5cm/30cm (¾-2in/1ft); *A purpurascens*, star-shaped purple flowers, 2-5cm/20cm (¾-2in/8in).

Argemone *Prickly Poppy* Papaveraceae

Medium/large hardy bedding annuals and perennials. Prickly, thistle-like leaves, delicate flowers resembling poppies; an interesting mix. Sow seeds in warmth in spring. ❀ *A. mexicana*, sea-green leaves with silver veins, slightly fragrant pale to deep yellow flowers in summer, treat as half-hardy annual, 1m/30-40cm (3ft/1-1½ft).

Argyranthemum *Marguerite* Asteraceae

Small evergreen sub-shrubs. Barely hardy. Finely dissected green, blue-grey or occasionally silver-grey leaves, daisy-like single or double flowers in various shades of pink, yellow and white from late spring to early autumn. Suitable for borders or containers; some make lovely and popular standard plants in containers. Most are good in seaside gardens and in cold areas it's sensible to take plants under cover in winter. Pinch out growing tips to encourage dense growth and cut back flowering shoots of previous year's growth in early to mid-spring. Take softwood cuttings in spring or semi-ripe cuttings in summer. ❀ *A. foeniculaceum*, white flowers with yellow centres, 80cm/80cm (3ft/3ft); *A. frutescens*, abundant flowers, white with yellow centres, 70cm/70cm (2¼ft/2¼ft); *A. gracile* 'Chelsea Girl', white flowers with yellow centres, 60cm/60cm (2ft/2ft); *A.* 'Jamaica Primrose', primrose-yellow flowers with darker centres, 1.1m/1m (3½ft/3ft); *A. maderense* (syn. *A. ochroleucum*), yellow flowers, 50cm/1m (1¾ft/3ft); 'Petite Pink' (syn. 'Pink Delight'), abundant small, light pink flowers with yellow centres, 30cm/30cm (1ft/1ft); 'Powder Puff', pale pink double flowers, 50cm/1m (1¾ft/3ft); 'Vancouver', double pink flowers, rose-pink centres, flowers fade to buff-pink, 90cm/90cm (3ft/3ft).

Arisarum Araceae

Small tuberous and rhizomatous ornamentals. Moderately hardy. Suitable for rock gardens and make good and interesting subjects for woodland gardens in mild areas. Arrow-shaped, clump-forming prostrate leaves, tubular spathes. Sow seeds in a cold-frame in spring or divide established plants between late summer and autumn. ❀ *A.proboscideum*, glossy mat-forming foliage, in late spring, early summer, maroon and white spathe, drawn out and elongated into a peculiar tail-like appendage at the top, like the rear view of a mouse disappearing down its hole, 15cm/25cm (6in/10in).

Aristolochia Aristolochiaceae

Shrubs, perennials, evergreen and deciduous climbers. Tender to moderately hardy. The leaves are heart- or kidney-shaped. Produce curious

left *Arisarum proboscideum* is quite one of the oddest but most appealing little plants that you will see. It belongs to a family that never fails to surprise and astonish.

curved or S-shaped petal-less, white, purple-brown or maroon flowers with inflated bases, darker markings, often described as resembling a Dutchman's pipe. Climbers need strong supports. Cut back untidy shoots after flowering. Sow seed in spring or take semi-ripe cuttings in summer. ❀ *A. clematitis* (Birthwort), moderately hardy perennial with narrow, tubular, light yellow, brown or yellow-brown flowers with pointed, curved upper lips from spring to midsummer, 90cm/60cm (3ft/2ft); *A. macrophylla* (syns. *A. durior*, *A. sipho*) (Dutchman's Pipe), very hardy twining, deciduous climber, solitary, rounded, yellow-green and brown flowers with purple markings in summer, well hidden among foliage, 8-10m (25-33ft).

Armeria *Thrift, Sea Pink* Plumbaginaceae

Small hardy alpine. Rosettes of linear to strap-like green to grey-green leaves form mounds of foliage. Round inflorescences of small cup- or saucer-shaped flowers on leafless stems. Intolerant of clay soils but will tolerate very alkaline conditions. Trim shoot tips and flower stems after flowering. Divide established plants in early spring, take basal cuttings in late summer or sow seed in a cold-frame in autumn or spring. ❀ *A. alliacea* Formosa Hybrids, spherical flower heads in various shades of rose, pink and white in summer, good for cutting, 45-60cm/30cm (18-2ft/1ft); *A. juniperifolia*, purple-pink to white flowers in late spring, 5-8cm/15cm (2-3¼in/6in); *A. j.* 'Bevan's Variety', very small, tight hummocks, deep rose-pink, almost stemless flowers, 5cm/15cm (2in/6in); *A. maritima*, one of the most familiar and best loved plants of the sea cliff, abundant white, purple or pink flowers from late spring through to the summer, 20cm/30cm (8in/1ft); *A. m.* 'Alba', large white flowers.

Armoracia *Horseradish* Brassicaceae

Evergreen perennials. Hardy. Can be invasive and should be confined. Contact with the sap may cause skin irritation. Sow seed or take root cuttings in spring. ❀ *A. rusticana*, herb with pungent root, elliptical, toothed, coarse leaves, clusters of small white flowers on branching stems from late spring to late summer, 60-90cm (2ft-3ft); *A. r.* 'Variegata', leaves irregularly splashed with white but just as invasive.

Arnica Asteraceae

Small/medium rhizomatous perennial. Moderately hardy. For borders or large rock gardens. Neat clump of mainly basal leaves, yellow daisy-like flowers on long stems in summer. All parts of the plant are toxic. Sow seed in a cold-frame in autumn or divide established plants in spring. ❀ *A. chamissonis*, lance-shaped leaves, clusters of flowers from mid- to late summer, 90cm/45cm (3ft/1½ft); *A. montana*, broad oval to lance-shaped leaves, solitary yellow or yellow-orange flowers, sometimes in bunches of two to three, 50cm/30cm (1¾ft/1ft).

left *Armeria maritima* 'Alba' is a plant very familiar to older generations of British gardeners because of its appearance on the much lamented pre-decimal three pence piece, a coin supposed to encourage thriftiness.

right *Artemisia arborescens* 'Faith Raven'. There are few garden plants with more silvery foliage than the artemisias which most appealingly combine a striking colour with a finely feathery appearance.

Artemisia

Wormwood, Mugwort Asteraceae

Small/large hardy and half-hardy herbaceous perennials, herbs, alpines and evergreen or semi-evergreen shrubs and sub-shrubs. The perennials are important plants for mixed borders or herb gardens; some of the smaller species make good ground cover and are valuable in rock gardens. Most have silver or pale grey feathery leaves, sometimes with a pungent fragrance reminiscent of aniseed. Tiny round yellow or white flowers, solitary or in clusters at the ends of stems, are produced in summer and autumn. Shrubby species grow best in any well-drained soil in a sunny position; most hardy perennials thrive in light soil, although *A. lactiflora* is best in moisture-retentive soil. Protect dwarf, woolly-leaved species from winter wet; in cold areas the less hardy shrubs and sub-shrubs require the protection of a warm sunny wall. Taller perennials may require staking. Trim shrubs to maintain shape and cut back *A. absinthium* and, if desired, other woody types in spring to within 15cm (6in) above soil level. Divide in autumn or take semi-ripe cuttings from shrub species in summer.

❀ *A. abrotanum* (Southernwood), hardy, bushy semi-evergreen sub-shrub with aromatic, downy, grey-green leaves, dull yellow flowers in late summer, 90cm/60cm (3ft/2ft); *A. absinthium* (Lad's Love, Old Man, Absinthe), evergreen sub-shrub, not reliably hardy, deeply dissected silver-grey leaves with silky hairs, grey-yellow flowers in late summer, 90cm/60cm (3ft/2ft); *A. a.* 'Lambrook Silver', silver foliage, tiny yellow mimosa-like flowers in summer, 75cm/60cm (2½ft/2ft); *A. alba* 'Canescens' (syns. *A. canescens*, *A. splendens*), semi-evergreen, silver leaves, yellow-brown flowers in late summer, 45cm/30cm (1½ft/1ft); *A. arborescens*, evergreen sub-shrub, not reliably hardy, aromatic silver-white leaves, yellow flowers from summer to autumn, 1m/1.5m (3ft/5ft); *A. a* 'Faith Raven', is similar but hardier and much better; *A. caucasica* (syns. *A. assoana*, *A. pedemontana*, *A. lanata*), small shrub with spreading habit, deeply-cut, fern-like, silver-green leaves, 30cm/15cm (1ft/6in); *A. dracunculus* (French Tarragon), not reliably hardy, dark green lance-shaped leaves have an anise-mint flavour, small green-yellow flowers in late summer, 1m/45cm (3ft/1½ft); *A. d. dracunculoides* (Russian Tarragon), hardier but with a more bitter flavour, not as refined as French tarragon, paler leaves, 1.2m/45cm (4ft/1½ft); *A. lactiflora* (White Mugwort), irregularly cut dark green leaves, plumes of cream-white flowers from late summer to autumn, 1.5m/60cm (5ft/2ft); *A. ludoviciana* (syns. *A. palmeri*, *A. purshiana*, *A. gnaphalodes*) (Western Mugwort, Cudweed), hardy perennial, aromatic lance-shaped woolly leaves, silver-white on young plants, greener when mature; white-grey flowers from midsummer to autumn, 1.2m/60cm (4ft/2ft); *A. l.* 'Silver Queen', silver leaves, plumes of tiny yellow-grey flowers, 75cm/60cm (2½ft/2ft); *A. l.* 'Valerie Finnis', silver-grey leaves, white when young, 60cm/60cm (2ft/2ft); *A. pontica* (Roman Mugwort), low-growing, aromatic, rhizomatous sub-shrub, downy grey-green leaves, yellow-grey flowers in early summer, 40cm/80cm (1½ft/2½ft); *A.* 'Powis Castle' (syn. *A. arborescens* 'Brass Band'), woody-based semi-evergreen perennial, feathery silver-grey foliage, plumes of silver flowers flushed yellow in late summer, 60m/90cm (2ft/3ft); *A. schmidtiana*, low-growing semi-evergreen perennial, downy silver leaves, plumes of small yellow flowers in summer, 30cm/45cm (1ft/1½ft); *A. s.* 'Nana', silver-grey silky leaves, 8cm/30cm (3¼in/1ft); *A. vulgaris* (Mugwort) 'Variegata', aromatic perennial, dark green leaves flecked with white, 1.7m/1m (5½ft/3ft).

Arum Araceae

Small to medium tuberous ornamentals. Barely hardy to moderately hardy. The glossy green leaves are shaped like arrowheads and die down after flowering, usually reappearing in late autumn or early winter. Tiny petal-less flowers are produced at the base of the spadix, which is partly enclosed by a leaf-like spathe, and followed by dense clusters of striking orange or red fruits on an erect stalk. They are plants of arresting appearance although some species have an unpleasant odour. All parts of the plant are toxic and may cause skin irritation. Suitable for mixed borders and planting in moist places under trees. Divide established plants or remove offsets after flowering. ❀ *A. creticum*, barely hardy, sweetly scented, cream or yellow spathe, yellow or purple spadix in spring, 30-50cm/15cm (1-1¾ft/6in); *A. italicum*, dark green leaves with white veins, yellow-green spathe, yellow spadix in early summer; *A. i.* ssp. *italicum* 'Marmoratum' (syn. *A. i.* 'Pictum'), prominent pale green to white marbled leaves, 30cm/15cm (1ft/6in); *A. maculatum*, leaves sometimes marked with black, green-white spathe in spring, sometimes with purple margin, purple or yellow spadix, 20-30cm/15cm (8-1ft/6in); *A. pictum*, the least hardy species, best grown in an alpine house, white-veined leaves, dark purple spathe in autumn, 15-25cm/15cm (6-10in/6in).

left *Arum italicum* ssp. *italicum* 'Marmoratum'. Anyone who admires the native wild arum will love this richly variegated relative.

Aruncus *Goat's Beard* Rosaceae

Small/large hardy herbaceous perennial. Pinnate, toothed green leaves with many leaflets, sometimes yellow or red in autumn. Feathery plumes of tiny white or cream flowers in midsummer, followed on female plants by green seed pods. Suitable for waterside or woodland plantings. Self-seeds freely; remove dead flowers if seedlings are not required. Divide established plants or sow seed in a cold-frame in mid autumn or early spring. ❀ *A. aethusifolius*, leaves tinted pink or red in autumn, terminal panicles of cream-white flowers on wiry stems from early to midsummer, 25-40cm/25-40cm (10in-1½ft/10in-1½ft); *A. dioicus*(syn. *Spiraea aruncus*), separate male and female plants, fern-like leaves turn pink or red in autumn, pyramidal flower plumes of cream-white flowers on male plants, green-white on females, 2m/1.2m (6½ft/4ft); *A. d.* 'Glasnevin', 1.2m/60cm (4ft/2ft); *A. d.* 'Kneifii', lacy leaves, cream-white flowers.

Asarina
Climbing Snapdragon Scrophulariaceae

Small trailing evergreen perennial. Barely hardy. Suitable for growing on a wall, in a rock garden, as ground cover or in raised beds and troughs. Protect with cloches in winter. In cold areas grow in containers and move inside in autumn. Propagate by sowing seeds in warmth in early spring or taking tip cuttings during late spring or early summer. ❀ *A. procumbens*, sticky grey-green, kidney-shaped leaves covered in soft hairs, pale yellow flowers resembling snapdragons, with deep yellow throats and purple veins, are just hidden among the foliage from early summer to early autumn, 5cm/60cm (2in/2ft).

Asarum
Wild Ginger, Asarabacca Aristolochiaceae

Small rhizomatous ornamental, the rhizomes smelling of ginger. Moderately hardy. The species I describe here are all evergreen, but the leaves may be damaged in cold winters. Kidney-shaped or heart-shaped leaves and urn-shaped flowers hidden among foliage, followed by oval fruit. Make very good ground cover in shady positions. Divide in early spring, sow seed in warmth or in a cold-frame in autumn. Self-seeds readily.

❀ *A. caudatum*, hairy purple-red flowers in spring, 15cm/ 40cm (6in/1½ft); *A. europaeum*, satin smooth green leaves sometimes marked silver, green-purple flowers in early spring, 8cm/30cm (3¼in/1ft).

right *Asplenium scolopendrium* Crispum Group. The variety that exists within many fern species is considerable; with this familiar native, it is quite bewildering.

Asclepias *Milkweed* Asclepiadaceae

Medium/large annuals, perennials, shrubs and sub-shrubs. Tender to moderately hardy. Oval, elliptical or lance-shaped leaves, orange, pink or red flowers resembling crowns from late summer to autumn are followed by tufted seed heads which split to reveal seeds with silky hairs. Milky sap may cause skin irritation. Sow seed of tender species in warmth in late winter, or divide in late spring; sow seed of perennials in a cold-frame or take basal cuttings in spring. ❀ *A. curassavica* (Bloodflower, Indian Root), evergreen sub-shrub often grown as an annual, clusters of red-and-orange flowers, sometimes white or yellow when propagated from seed, 1m/60cm (3ft/2ft); *A. incarnata* (Swamp Milkweed), hardy perennial, tubular pink-purple or white flowers, 1.2m/60cm (4ft/2ft); *A. tuberosa* (Indian Paintbrush, Butterfly Weed), hardy herbaceous perennial, orange-and-red flowers or orange-and-yellow flowers from midsummer to early autumn, 90cm/30cm (3ft/1ft).

above Few varieties match *Asparagus* 'Connover's Colossal' for flavour but as with all varieties, the secret of success is not to over-crop.

Asparagus *Asparagus* Asparagaceae

Ornamental and edible evergreen and deciduous perennials, climbers and sub-shrubs. Tender to moderately hardy. Fern-like, arching and/or spreading, leafy stems, small white flowers sometimes followed by red, purple or black fruits. The ornamental species are all tender. Hardy edible varieties thrive in very well-drained, rich sandy soil. Sow seed in warmth in early spring or outside in a seed bed. Alternatively, and I think better, buy two-year old frame-raised crowns in early spring. Mulch with straw in early spring. ❀ Edible asparagus are forms of the hardy *A. officinalis*, perennial vegetable, of which there are both male and female forms, the females producing orange-red fruits but the male varieties are best for cropping. 'Connover's Colossal', early crops of thick spears; 'Franklim' F1, thick spears; and 'Lucullus' F1, long thin spears.

Asperula *Woodruff* Rubiaceae

Small annuals, deciduous or evergreen perennials, alpines and dwarf shrubs. Moderately hardy. Foliage usually in pretty whorls, clusters of slender, tubular, star-shaped flowers from spring to

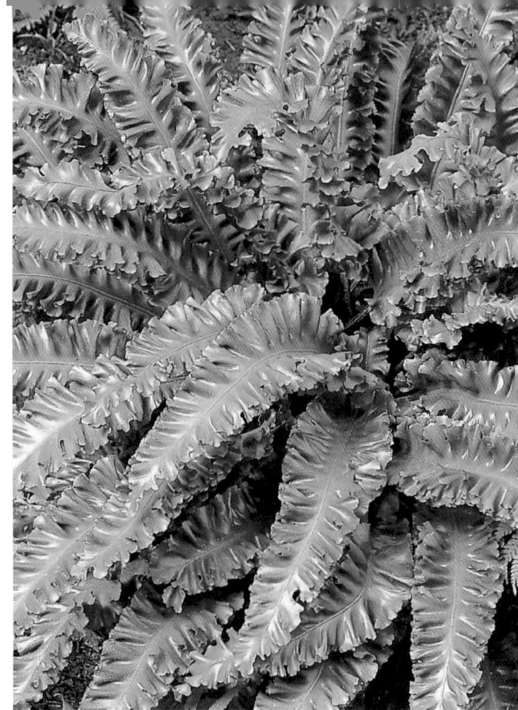

early summer. Sow seed in a cold-frame in spring or divide established plants in late summer or autumn. ❀ *A. gussoni*, evergreen, red-pink, late spring, 5cm/15cm (2in/6in); *A. sintenisii*, pink flowers, early summer, 10cm/20cm (4in/8in).

Asphodeline *Jacob's Rod* Asphodelaceae

Medium/large biennials and hardy herbaceous perennials with rhizomatous roots. Clump-forming, grass-like leaves and spikes of star-like flowers from early spring to summer. Sow seed in a cold-frame in spring or divide established plants in late summer or early autumn. ❀ *A. liburnica*, perennial, grey-green leaves, light yellow flowers, 1m/30cm (3ft/1ft); *A. lutea* 'Yellow Asphodel', perennial, grey to dark green foliage, fragrant yellow flowers, late spring followed by green seeds, 1.5m/30cm (5ft/1ft).

Asphodelus Asphodelaceae

Small to medium bedding annuals and perennials. Moderately hardy. Long, narrow, clump-forming basal leaves and clusters of star-shaped flowers with prominent stamens encircled with brown or white bracts on leafless stems. Those I include here are true perennials. Sow seeds in a cold-frame in spring or divide mature plants in early spring. ❀ *A. albus*, perennial best grown as an annual, star-shaped white flowers with pink veining, prominent stamens, in mid- to late spring, 90cm/30cm (3ft/1ft); *A. fistulosus*, short-lived perennial with pink-white flowers with soft brown central vein on each petal, surrounded by white bracts in early to midsummer, 45cm/20cm (1½ft/8in).

Asplenium *Spleenwort* Aspleniaceae

Small/large evergreen and semi-evergreen perennial ferns. Tender to very hardy. Most have clumps of rippled, ribbon-like green leaves. Hardy species are excellent for woodland gardens or borders, some for rock gardens and dry walls. Divide established plants in the spring. ❀ *A. scolopendrium* (Hart's Tongue Fern), very hardy, broad undulating leaves, 45-70cm/60cm (1-2¼ft/2ft); *A. s.* Crispum Group, crimped leaves, frilled margins, 30cm/60cm (1ft/2ft); *A. s.* Cristatum Group, leaves divide twice, forming tassels at the tips, 60-80cm (2-2½ft); *A. s.* 'Kaye's Lacerated', torn or frayed leaf margins; *A. s.* Undulatum Group, wavy leaf margins; *A. trichomanes* (Maidenhair Spleenwort), evergreen or semi-evergreen, long, slender leaves with small rounded leaflets on glossy dark midribs, 15cm/20cm (6in/8in).

Aster *Michaelmas Daisies* Asteraceae

Small to medium annuals, biennials, hardy herbaceous perennials and sub-shrubs. Tender to hardy. Those I describe here are hardy perennials. Lance-shaped leaves, sometimes with soft hairs, daisy-like inflorescences in a variety of colours, produced singly or in clusters from summer to autumn. Flowers are good for cutting. Smaller species are suitable for the rock garden, larger ones for borders. Thrive in most soils if not waterlogged, in full sun, light or partial shade. Mulch in autumn and cut down after flowering. Taller plants need support. Sow seed in a cold-frame or divide mature plants in spring or autumn. Alternatively, take basal cuttings in spring. Many species and varieties (especially older forms) are devastated by mildew and the resistant varieties of *A. amellus* are much the best of the traditional border Michaelmas daisy type for the modern garden.

❀ *A. alpinus*, single purple or purple-blue flowers with a yellow centre from early to midsummer, 25cm/45cm (10in/1½ft); *A. amellus* 'Brilliant', pink flowers with yellow centres, late summer to autumn, 75cm/45cm (2½ft/1½ft); *A. a.* 'King George', blue-violet flowers with yellow centres, 45cm (1½ft); *A. a.* 'Rosa Erfüllung', pink flowers, 60cm (2ft); *A. a.* 'Veilchenkönigin', (syn. 'Violet Queen') violet flowers, 30cm/45cm (1ft/1½ft); 'Combe Fishacre', white flowers tinged with pink, brown-yellow centres, midsummer to mid autumn; 90cm/30cm (3ft/1ft); *A. divaricatus*, sprays of tiny white flowers with brown-yellow centres from midsummer to mid autumn, 60cm/60cm (2ft/2ft); *A. ericoides* 'Blue Star', some mildew resistance, clusters of pale blue flowers from late summer to late autumn, 1m/30cm (3ft/1ft); *A. e.* 'Golden Spray', white flowers with golden centres; *A. e.* 'Pink Cloud', pink-mauve flowers; *A.* x *frikartii*, blue flowers with orange centres in late summer and

above *Aster novi-belgii* 'Marie Ballard'. There's no denying that the best colour range occurs in some of the older, 'traditional' Michaelmas daisies but few have the mildew resistance of the newer introductions.

left *Aster* x *frikartii*. One of the main attractions of this classic Michaelmas daisy is that it has a high resistance to mildew.

autumn, 70cm/45cm (2¼ft/1½ft); *A.* x *f*. 'Mönch', mildew resistant, lavender-blue flowers from summer to autumn; *A. lateriflorus*, white to violet flowers with pink centres from midsummer to mid autumn, 1.2m/30cm (4ft/1ft); *A. l.* 'Horizontalis', lilac flowers with rose-pink centres in autumn, leaves copper-pink in autumn, 60cm (2ft); *A. l.* 'Prince', similar to 'Horizontalis' but with leaves and stems stained purple; 'Little Carlow', some resistance to mildew, blue-violet flowers with yellow centres, 90cm/45cm (3ft/1½ft); *A. novae-angliae*, violet flowers with yellow centres, early autumn, 1.5m/60cm (5ft/2ft); *A. n.* 'Andenken an Alma Pötschke', bright pink semi-double flowers, early autumn, 1.2m (4ft); *A. n.* 'Harrington's Pink', pink flowers with yellow centres, autumn; *A. n.* 'Herbstschnee', white flowers with yellow centres in late summer, early autumn, 1.2m (4ft); *A. novi-belgii* 'Ada Ballard', lavender-blue flowers from midsummer to mid autumn, 90cm/90cm (3ft/3ft); *A. n.* 'Audrey', lavender-blue flowers, 35cm (1ft); *A. n.* 'Fellowship', deep pink double flowers, 90cm (3ft); *A. n.*'Jenny', double purple-red flowers, 30cm/45cm (1ft/1½ft); *A. n.* 'Lady in Blue', semi-double lavender-blue flowers; *A. n.* 'Marie Ballard', double lavender-blue flowers, 90cm (3ft); *A. n.* 'Winston S. Churchill', double red flowers, 90cm (3ft); *A. pringlei* 'Monte Cassino', white flowers with yellow centres, 1m/30cm (3ft/1ft); *A. sedifolius*, mildew resistant, lavender-blue flowers, late summer to early autumn, 1.2m/60cm (4ft/2ft); *A. thomsonii* 'Nanus', mildew resistant, light lilac flowers, summer to autumn, 45cm/25cm (1½ft/10in).

right *Astilbe* 'Deutschland'. White astilbes look lovely in dappled shade; some of the colours however are just too luminous for their own good.

Astilbe — Saxifragaceae

Small/large hardy herbaceous perennials. Suitable for damp borders and bog gardens. Fern-like leaves with toothed lobes, mid- to deep green; immature leaves are copper-coloured. Plumes of tiny flowers, white or shades of sometimes shocking red, pink or purple, are produced in summer and followed by seedheads. Blending pink astilbes with other flowers is one of life's challenges. Thrive in moist, rich soil in light shade. Mulch in autumn and spring. Divide established plants in autumn or spring, otherwise leave undisturbed. Sow seed in warmth in spring.

❀ 'Aphrodite', glossy bronze leaves, red flowers, midsummer, 40-60cm/60cm (1½-2ft/2ft); *A.* x *arendsii*, 'Brautschleier', bright green leaves, flowers white at first, later cream-yellow in early summer, 75cm/75cm (2½ft/2½ft); *A.* x *a.* 'Fanal', bronze to copper foliage, deep red flowers, early summer, 60cm/45cm (2ft/1½ft); *A.* x *a.* 'Snow-drift', white flowers, 60cm/45cm (2ft/1½ft); 'Bronce Elegans' (syn. 'Bronze Elegance'), dwarf, green bronze-tinted foliage, arching sprays of cream-and-pink flowers, summer, 30cm/25cm (1ft/10in); *A. chinensis pumila*, dwarf, mid-green leaves, rose- purple flowers, summer to autumn, 25cm/20cm (10in /8in); *A. chinensis taquetii* 'Superba', rose-mauve flowers 1.2m (4ft); *A.* x *crispa* 'Perkeo', very finely divided dark green leaves, bronze when immature, rose-pink flowers, summer, 20cm/20cm (8in/8in); 'Deutschland', white flowers, late spring, 50cm /30cm (1¾ft/1ft); 'Inshriach Pink', dwarf, pink flowers, 36cm (1¼ft); *A.* x *rosea* 'Peach Blossom', peach flowers, midsummer, 60cm/45cm (2ft /1½ft); 'Sprite', pale pink flowers, late summer followed by rusty red seedheads, 50cm/1m (1¾ft/3ft).

Astilboides — Saxifragaceae

Large hardy perennial. One species grown mainly for its attractive foliage. Divide in spring.

❀ *A. tabularis* (syn. *Rodgersia tabularis*), very large, slightly hairy light green leaves 1m (3ft) in diameter with scalloped margins, produced on stout stems. Feathery plumes of tiny cream-white flowers from early to midsummer, 1.5m/1.2m (5ft/4ft).

Astrantia *Masterwort* Apiaceae

Medium hardy herbaceous perennial. Clump-forming foliage of lobed leaves above which umbels of small flowers encircled with a collar of papery bracts are produced in summer. Equally lovely in a shady border and as a cut flower. Sow seed in a cold-frame or divide in spring. ❀ *A. carniolica rubra*, finely divided leaves and purple-red star-like flowers and bracts, 30cm/30cm (1ft/1ft); *A. major* 'Hadspen Blood', small green or pink flowers, sometimes purple-red, with green bracts, sometimes flushed pink from early to mid-summer, 30-90cm/45cm (1-3ft/1½ft); *A. m.* ssp. *involucrata* 'Shaggy' (syn. 'Margery Fish'), green-white flowers with large pale green bracts, 60cm/45cm (2ft/1½ft); *A. m. rosea*, deep pink; *A.m. rubra*, dark purple-red; *A. m.* 'Sunningdale Variegated', leaves have irregular cream-yellow margins, pale pink-white flowers; *A. maxima*, pink flowers.

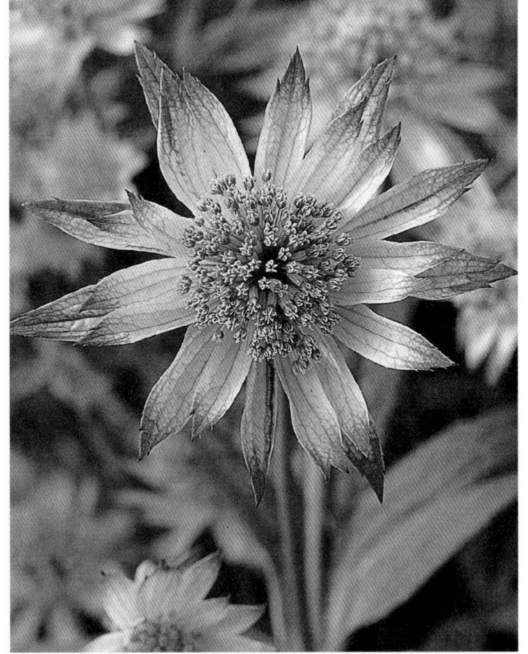

left *Astrantia* 'Shaggy' is quite the loveliest of the paler coloured *Astrantia* varieties; however, it is a shame that its original name, which commemorated the great gardener Margery Fish has been replaced.

Athyrium Athyriaceae

Medium/large deciduous fern. Barely to moderately hardy. Simple or bi-pinnate leaves. A moist, slightly shaded position is essential. Divide in spring. ❀ *A. filix-femina* (Lady Fern), pale green laced fronds on red stalks becoming arched when mature, 1.2m/60-90cm (4ft/2-3ft); *A. f.* 'Frizelliae', extremely pretty with rounded lobes grouped along either side of the midrib, 20cm/30cm (8in/1ft); *A. niponicum* var. *pictum* (syn. 'Pictum') (Japanese Painted Fern), very pale green leaves, sometimes appearing silver-grey, on maroon-tinted midrib are held almost horizontal to the ground, 30cm/30cm (1ft/1ft).

Atriplex *Orache, Salt Bush* Chenopodiaceae

Large half-hardy annuals, perennials and small semi-evergreen/evergreen shrubs. Moderately hardy. The genus includes the leafy vegetable orache. Shrubs are suitable for borders and hedging, particularly in coastal areas as they are resistant to the effects of salt spray. No routine pruning. Take softwood cuttings of *A. halimus* in summer; sow seeds of *A. hortensis* in the early spring. ❀ *A. halimus*, dense oval or fairly angular grey-green leaves with a silvery surface, insignificant yellow flowers, spring, 1-2m/50cm-1m (3-6½ft/1¾-3ft). *A. hortensis rubra* (Red Orache), edible red-purple spinach-like leaves, green or red inflorescences, 1.2m/30cm (4ft/1ft).

Aubrieta *Aubretia* Brassicaceae

Small evergreen perennials or alpines. Hardy. Suitable for rock gardens, dry walls and rocky banks. Small, ovate to oblong green leaves, sometimes toothed and hairy. Clusters of blue, red or mauve flowers in spring. Trim back hard after flowering. Sow seed in a cold-frame in autumn or spring or take basal cuttings in summer. The species I describe here are all about 15cm/60cm (6in/2ft). ❀ *A.* 'Alix Brett', double red-pink flowers; 'Aureovariegata', single pale lavender flowers, gold-green leaves; 'Doctor Mules', rich violet flowers; 'Green-court Purple', semi-double, deep purple flowers; 'Purple Cascade', single, deep purple flowers; 'Red Carpet', single flowers, deep red.

Aucuba *Spotted Laurel* Aucubaceae

Large evergreen shrub. Very hardy. For containers, hedging, and one of the best shrubs for shady sites, dry soils and polluted areas. Oval, slightly toothed, bold green leaves, some heavily marked with yellow or gold. Insignificant flowers are followed by red, sometimes white or yellow fruit if both male and female species or varieties are planted together. No routine pruning. Take softwood cuttings in early summer or hardwood cuttings in late autumn or winter. ❀ *A. japonica* 'Crotonifolia', female, glossy, leathery, pale green leaves blotched with gold, 3m/3m (10ft/10ft); 'Golden King', male, is similar with larger splashes of gold; *A. j. longifolia*, female, narrow pale green and glossy lance-shaped leaves; 'Picturata', male, leaves with

above *Aucuba* varieties are generally distinguished by the presence or absence of fruits and by the pattern of leaf variegation but *Aucuba japonica longifolia* unusually has narrow, elongated leaves.

irregular yellow central mark and yellow spots within the leaf margins; 'Rozannie', bisexual, green leaves; 'Salicifolia', female, unexpectedly and distinctively green, narrow, willow-like leaves, bright red fruits in autumn; 'Variegata' (syn. *A. j. maculata*), both male and female plants available, leaves densely gold speckled.

Aurinia *Brassicaceae*

Small biennials, evergreen perennials and subshrubs. Hardy. For borders, rock gardens, banks. Those I describe here are all evergreen perennials. Hummocks of hairy, lance-shaped leaves, clusters of four-petalled white or yellow flowers. Sow seed in a cold-frame in autumn or take softwood cuttings in early summer. ❀ *A. saxatilis* (syn. *Alyssum saxatile*), evergreen, toothed, hairy grey-green leaves, bright yellow flowers from late spring to early summer, 20cm/30cm (8in/1ft); *A. s.* 'Citrina', sprawling, grey-green foliage, sprays of tiny pale lemon yellow flowers, spring; *A. s.* 'Compacta', dwarf, gold-yellow flowers, 10cm/30cm (4in/1ft).

Azara *Flacourtiaceae*

Large evergreen shrubs and small trees. Barely hardy to moderately hardy. Shrubs are suitable for training against a wall. Glossy green elliptical to ovate leaves, clusters of fragrant petal-less flowers with prominent stamens, sometimes followed by pale purple or white fruits. Needs shelter in cold areas. Remove damaged shoots after flowering. Take semi-ripe cuttings in summer. ❀ *A. dentata*, shrub or small tree, fragrant yellow flowers from late spring to early summer, 3m/3m (10ft/10ft); *A. microphylla*, small tree, the hardiest species, very dark green leaves, vanilla-scented, green-yellow flowers, late winter or early spring, 10m/4m (33ft/13ft); *A. m.* 'Variegata', leaves have pale yellow edges; *A. serrata*, shrub, fragrant dark yellow flowers, midsummer, 4m/3m (13ft/10ft).

Azolla *Fairy Moss, Water Fern* Azollaceae

Small floating fern. Barely hardy, but may survive in dormant state in cold areas. Suitable for medium-sized pools. Tiny deciduous, bright green knobbly fronds turn red in autumn. Can be invasive. Propagate by transferring fronds. ❀ *A. filiculoides*, lacy, light green fronds, 1.5cm (½in)/indefinite.

Azorella Apiaceae

Small evergreen perennial. Moderately hardy. Rosettes of leathery leaves, small flowers in umbels in late spring or summer. Sow seed in autumn or take semi-ripe cuttings in late summer. ❀ *A. trifurcata* (syn. *Bolax glebaria*), glossy green leaves, umbels of tiny cream-white flowers, summer, 10cm/20cm (4in/8in); *A. t.* 'Nana', similar but more compact, 10cm/15cm (4in/6in).

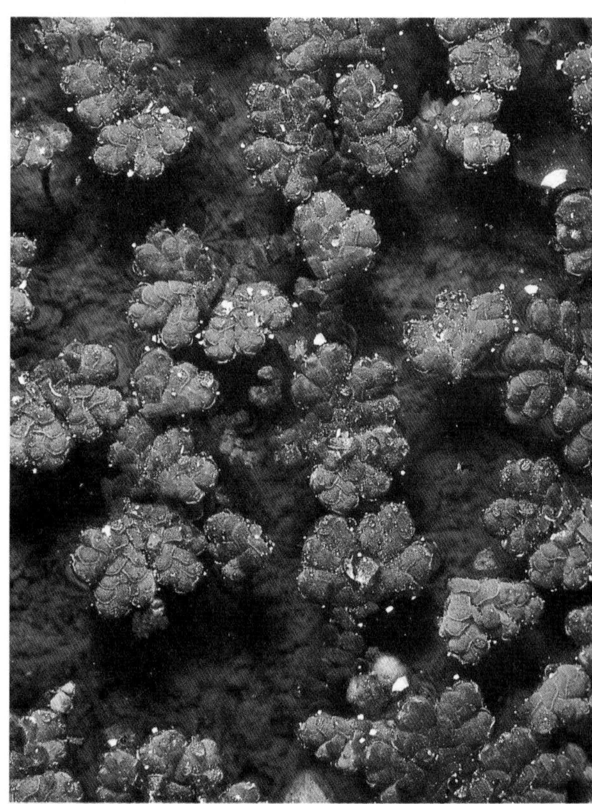

right *Azolla filiculoides*. Uniquely special, this minute floating fern turns the most glorious autumn red; but is wickedly invasive.

Ballota Lamiaceae

Small/medium herbaceous perennials and deciduous/evergreen sub-shrubs. Barely hardy to moderately hardy. Toothed or scalloped downy, sometimes velvety leaves, tubular two-lipped flowers, summer. Some give off a pungent aroma. Sow seed in warmth, divide established plants in spring or take semi-ripe cuttings of sub-shrubs in early summer. ❀ *B. acetabulosa*, evergreen sub-shrub, grey-green, slightly scalloped leaves downy white beneath, white or pink flowers flushed purple from mid- to late summer, 60cm/75cm (2ft/2½ft); *B.* 'All Hallows Green', shrubby perennial, lime-green leaves, pale green flowers from mid- to late summer, 60cm/75cm (2ft/2½ft); *B. nigra*, herbaceous perennial, hairy, coarse toothed leaves, abundant purple or pink flowers, 60cm/75cm (2ft/2½ft); *B. n.* 'Archer's Variegated', green-and-white spotted leaves, pink flowers, 1m/60cm (3ft/2ft); *B. pseudodictamnus*, dwarf sub-shrub, grey-white downy leaves, white flowers flecked purple in summer, 45cm/60cm (1½ft/2ft).

Barbarea Brassicaceae

Small hardy biennials and perennials. *B. verna*, (American Land Cress), rosettes of dark green basal leaves with a strong flavour that last well through the winter. Sow seed in growing positions in spring and during summer. ❀ *B. vulgaris* 'Variegata' (Variegated Yellow Rocket, Variegated Land Cress), ornamental biennial or short-lived perennial, glossy green toothed leaves with cream markings, small rather insignificant silver-yellow flowers, early summer, 25-45cm/20cm (10-1½ft/8in).

Begonia Begoniaceae

Small/large evergreen and deciduous perennials. Tender to barely hardy. In cold areas only a few species (although with many varieties) are suitable for use outside as summer bedding or container plants. Male flowers have two to four ovate or oblong petals, two of which are shorter than the others; female flowers, on the same plant, have four to six petals of similar size. Most species and varieties are best in a neutral soil or compost in light shade. Sow seed of species, *B.* x *tuberhybrida*. Non-Stop varieties and *B. semperflorens* hybrids in warmth in early spring. Take stem, tip or leaf cuttings of all types in spring or summer, and basal cuttings from tuberous begonias in spring.

❀ I have only described the most popular types here and because of the numerous individual varieties, have instead recommended varietal Series. Fibrous rooted types: *B. carrierei* (syn. *B. semperflorens* still widely used), invaluable summer bedding, compact, bushy plants with round, shiny dark green or bronze leaves, abundant pink, red or white bicoloured flowers from early summer to autumn frosts, 20-30cm/30cm (8in-1ft/1ft); *B. c.* Cocktail Series F1, deep bronze leaves; Excel Series, bronze

above *Begonia x tuberhybrida* Non-Stop Series F1. There's no denying that if you want assertive colours, these seed-raised begonias, with all the advantages of tuberous varieties, are the ones to supply them.

and green leaves; Olympia Series F1, green and bronze leaves; Organdy Mixed F1, the full colour range on small, compact plants with bronze or green leaves; Tuberous types: *B. grandis* ssp. *evansiana*, suitable for growing outside in mild areas, pendent sprays of pink or white flowers on fleshy stems from late summer to mid autumn, 50cm /30cm (1¾ft/1ft); 'Alba', white flowers; *B. sutherlandii*, light green trailing leaves, sometimes with red veins, orange flowers, summer, 30cm/45cm (1ft/1½ft); *B.* x *tuberhybrida* Multiflora Group, bushy, good if strident summer bedding plants, erect succulent stems, vivid red, pink, orange or white flowers, single, semi-double or double, 30cm/30cm (1ft/1ft); *B.* x *t.* Non-Stop Series F1, tuberous, raised from seed as annuals, heart-shaped mid-green leaves, single or double flowers, yellow, apricot, orange, red, pink or white, 30cm /30cm (1ft/1ft); *B.*x *t.* Illumination Series, pendent, oval mid- to dark green leaves, double pale pink or orange flowers, 60cm/30cm (2ft/1ft); *B.* x *t.* Prima Donna Series, double flowers 45cm/30cm (1½ft/1ft); Pendula Group, longer thinner stems than Multiflora Group, trailing habit, double flowers 45cm/30cm (1½ft /1ft); *B.* x *t.* Cascade Series, pendent, double flowers, red, pink, orange, or yellow 45cm/30cm (1½ft /1ft); *B.* x *t.* Sensation Series, mixed colour 30cm/30cm (1ft/1ft).

above *Bellis perennis* 'Prolifera'. It still seems remarkable to me that gardeners will grow the named varieties of the lawn daisy in one part of the garden whilst spending money to eradicate them in another.

Bellis *Daisy* Asteraceae

Small hardy perennials often grown as biennials. Suitable for summer bedding, containers and edging. Rosettes of oval, slightly hairy leaves, solitary single or double daisy flowers, white or shades of pink and red derived from the lawn daisy *Bellis perennis*. Sow seed in a seedbed in summer or divide established plants (essential with double varieties) in early spring or after flowering.

❀ Varieties range from 5-15cm/5-15cm (2-6in/2-6in). *B.* 'Alba Plena', double white flowers; *B.* 'Aucubifolia', gold-mottled leaves, single white flowers; *B.* 'Dresden China', tiny, double, pink pompon flowers; *B.* 'Monstrosa', large red flowers; *B.* Parkinson's Double White', *B.* 'Pink Buttons', pompon flowers in various shades of pink; *B.* 'Prolifera', double white flowers speckled pink and with tiny 'daughter' flowers hanging from the 'mother' bloom; *B.* 'Rob Roy', large double crimson button-like flowers *B.* 'Shrewly Gold', single flowers, golden foliage; *B.* 'Staffordshire Pink', pink flowers, tall.

Berberis Berberidaceae

Small/large deciduous and evergreen shrubs. Barely hardy to very hardy. Among the most valuable garden shrubs. Dwarf species and varieties are suitable for rock gardens, larger ones for hedging or specimen plants. Linear, elliptic to oblong or rounded leaves, sometimes spiny toothed. Stems have sharp spines. Clusters of light yellow or orange cup-shaped flowers on evergreens in spring are followed by blue or blue-black fruits; deciduous species usually produce white flowers flushed red or pink, followed by red fruits. Thrive in most well-drained soils in full sun or partial shade. Evergreens may need protection from cold winds. No routine pruning. Trim hedges lightly after flowering. Take semi-ripe cuttings in early summer.

❀ *B. darwinii*, stunningly lovely evergreen, small olive-green leaves with silver undersides, stems very spiny, brilliant orange flowers, mid-spring, 3m/3m (10ft/10ft); *B. dictyophylla*, deciduous, pale to mid-green leaves, red in autumn, light yellow flowers in late spring followed by red fruits, 2m/1.5m (6½ft/5ft); *B.* x *frikartii* 'Amstelveen', evergreen, glossy green leaves, pale yellow flowers, early summer, 1m/1.5m (3ft/5ft); *B. gagnepainii* var. *lanceifolia*, evergreen suckering shrub suitable for hedging, spiny dark green leaves, golden yellow flowers from late spring to early summer, 1.5m/2m (5ft/6½ft); *B. julianae*, evergreen, good for hedging, dark green, spiny toothed leaves with some red autumn colour, vicious long spines, slightly fragrant yellow flowers, 3m/3m (10ft/10ft); *B. linearifolia* 'Orange King', evergreen, mid-green leaves with silver undersides, large double orange

right *Berberis darwinii.* I always think it fitting that a plant commemorating someone as distinguished as Darwin should be so very, very good. He first saw this spectacular shrub growing wild in South America.

far left There are several forms of *Berberis* with a markedly upright habit but *Berberis thunbergii* 'Helmond Pillar' must be the best. It is an ideal plant for limited space.

flowers, 2.5m/2.5m (8ft/8ft); *B.* x *lologensis* 'Apricot Queen', evergreen, glossy dark green leaves similar to those of *B. darwinii* but a less impressive plant, pale orange flowers, late spring and periodically later, 4m/3m (13ft/10ft); *B.* x *media* 'Parkjuweel', semi-evergreen, glossy light green leaves, orange in autumn, sometimes until spring, yellow flowers, late spring, 2m/2.5m (6½ft/8ft); *B.* x *m.* 'Red Jewel', semi-evergreen, similar to 'Parkjuweel', leaves red-bronze at first, later mid to dark green, purple in autumn, yellow flowers, late spring, 2m/2.5m (6½ft/8ft); *B.* x *ottawensis* 'Superba', deciduous, dark purple-red leaves, rich red in autumn, yellow flowers with red markings in spring, 2.5m/2.5m (8ft/8ft); *B.* x *stenophylla*, evergreen, suitable for hedging, narrow, needle-like olive-green leaves, white beneath, fragrant gold-yellow flowers, spring, 3m/5m (10ft/16ft); *B. thunbergii*, deciduous, excellent for hedging, pale to mid-green leaves, brilliant red-orange in autumn, pale yellow flowers with red markings from mid- to late spring, red fruits, 1m/2.5m (3ft/8ft), numerous excellent varieties: *B. t. atropurpurea*, purple-red leaves, red-orange in autumn; dwarf varieties include *B. t.* 'Atropurpurea Nana', almost spineless, 60cm/75cm (2ft/21/2ft); *B. t.* 'Bagatelle', mound-forming, deep red leaves, 30cm/40cm (1ft/1½ft); *B. t.* 'Dart's Red Lady', splendid, very dark purple leaves, red-orange in autumn 1.5m/1.5m (5ft/5ft); *B. t.* 'Golden Ring', purple leaves when young, yellow-gold later, intense red in autumn 1.5m/1.5m (5ft/5ft); *B. t.* 'Helmond Pillar', upright, good in confined space, purple-red leaves, red-orange in autumn, 1.5m/60cm (5ft/2ft); *B. t.* 'Red Chief', red stems, purple in winter, purple-red leaves, orange-red in autumn, 1.5m/2m (5ft/6½ft); *B. t.* 'Rose Glow', purple leaves with pink and silver marbling, pale orange-red in autumn, 1.5m/1.2m (5ft/4ft); *B. verruculosa*, compact evergreen, olive-green leaves with spiny tips, silver undersides, semi-double yellow flowers, late spring followed by purple fruit, 1.5m/1.5m (5ft/5ft); *B. wilsoniae*, deciduous, thorny stems, blue-green leaves, white undersides, yellow flowers, early summer followed by orange-red fruit in autumn, 1m/2m (3ft/6½ft).

Bergenia *Elephant's Ears* Saxifragaceae

Small/medium evergreen/semi-evergreen perennials. Hardy. Suitable for ground cover in borders or shaded shrubberies. Rosettes of leathery, glossy green leaves, sometimes flushed red in autumn, clusters of bell-shaped flowers, white or shades of pink, red or violet, in spring. Divide in spring or autumn. ❀ *B.* 'Baby Doll', smooth, rounded green leaves tinted bronze, light pink flowers from mid- to late spring, 30cm/45cm (1ft/ 1½ft); Ballawley

left: *Bergenia cordifolia* 'Purpurea'. Bergenias do make excellent ground cover in shady places but I find they are always best in a slightly heavy soil.

Hybrids, glossy green leaves, bronze-red in winter, large pink flowers on red stalks in spring, a few in autumn, 60cm/45-60cm (2ft/ 18in-2ft); *B.* 'Bressingham White', green leaves, white flowers, 60cm/75cm (2ft/ 2½ft); *B. cordifolia*, drooping purple-pink flowers, late winter to early spring, 60cm/75cm (2ft/2½ft); *B.* c. 'Purpurea', a fine, striking plant, green leaves turn purple in winter, deep purple flowers, spring, often repeated in summer; *B. purpurascens*, glossy green leaves, vibrant dark red above in autumn, mahogany below, purple-red to pink flowers, 45cm/30cm (1½ft/1ft); *B.* 'Silberlicht', large panicles of pure white flowers turning pink in spring, 30-45cm/45-60cm (1-1½ft/18-2ft); *B.* 'Wintermärchen', small, narrow, glossy leaves, green on surface, red on underside, sometimes scarlet, tinged red in winter, deep rose flowers, early to mid-spring, 30-45cm/45-60cm (1-1½ft/1½-2ft).

above Beetroot 'Burpee's Golden' (at the bottom) is one of a number of beetroot varieties that make a refreshing change for those used to imagining them as always red.

Beta
Beet, Beetroot, Chard Chenopodiaceae

Biennials and perennials that include the root vegetable beetroot and the leafy vegetable spinach beet or chard. Moderately hardy. All species have glossy green or red-purple leaves on red stems. The roots are usually red but may be pink, yellow or white. Both beetroot and spinach beet are grown as annual vegetables. They thrive best in light, fertile, moist soil in full sun or partial shade. Sow seed (each is a cluster of individual seeds) in growing positions in early spring or summer and thin out seedlings.

❀ *B. vulgaris*, beetroot, has globe-shaped or cylindrical roots. The following varieties are those I have found particularly successful: 'Barbietola di Chioggia', an entertaining old globe variety, red and white rings when sliced; although the colour does fade on cooking 'Boltardy', bolt resistant medium-sized globe; 'Burpee's Golden', golden yellow globe with flavour similar to that of red varieties, stores well; 'Cheltenham Green Top', old variety with cylindrical root, stores well; 'Cylindra', long, cylindrical dark red roots; 'Detroit', old variety with large roots for maincrop use; 'Monopoly', dark purple-red root sometimes with paler rings, each seed producing a single seedling; 'Red Ace' F1, round to oval roots, tender, resistant to bolting, good dark red colour. *B. v. cicla*, various varieties known as spinach beet, Swiss chard and seakale beet, have crinkled or smooth edible leaves. My recommendations are 'Fordhook Giant', seakale beet, broad green leaves; 'Lucullus', seakale beet, broad green leaves with wide midrib; 'Rhubarb Chard', a Swiss chard, dark green crinkled leaves with scarlet midribs; 'Perpetual Spinach', tasty variety with green crinkled leaves, much the best substitute for real spinach on light soils where spinach runs to seed.

right It takes considerable expertise to be able to identify the various species of Himalayan white-barked birch but *Betula ermanii* is certainly one of the most attractive.

Betula *Birch* Betulaceae

Small deciduous shrubs and medium/large trees. Hardy. Good for exposed sites. Most have attractive bark and toothed, usually ovate, mid- to dark green leaves, often yellow in autumn. Some bear male and female catkins in spring. No routine

pruning, although small shoots arising on the trunk are best removed. Sow seed in a seedbed in autumn; softwood cuttings taken in summer may be difficult to strike.

❀ *B. albosinensis*, var. *septentrionalis*, medium to large tree, green leaves, yellow in autumn, orange-brown peeling bark, male catkins, 25m/10m (80ft/33ft); *B. ermanii*, may be damaged by spring frosts, green leaves, yellow in autumn, lovely cream bark peels to reveal pink to brown-pink trunk, male catkins, 20m/12m (60ft/40ft); *B. nana*, small spreading shrub, small, round, toothed leaves, glossy mid-green, yellow or red in autumn, male catkins in spring, 60cm/1.2m (2ft/4ft); *B. nigra*, fairly fast-growing tree, suitable for wetter sites, pink-orange bark at first, later brown, ridged, light green leaves, blue bloom beneath, male catkins in early spring, 18m/12m (56ft/40ft); *B. papyrifera*, shiny white bark, peels in strips when mature exposing orange-brown bark beneath, dark green leaves yellow-orange in autumn, male catkins, 20m/10m (60ft/33ft); *B. pendula*, thrives on drier soils, silver-white peeling bark, sharply toothed mid-green leaves, yellow in autumn, on pendent branches, male catkins followed by winged fruits, 25m/19m (80ft/58ft); *B. p.* 'Laciniata' (syn. 'Dalecarlica'), deeply cut leaves, very drooping branches; *B. p.* 'Tristis', symmetrical, bark remains white at base; *B. p.* 'Youngii', small tree, weeping branches; *B. utilis*, variable, like most white-barked Himalayan species, bark copper-brown, pink-brown or orange-brown, peeling, dark green leaves, yellow in autumn, 18m/10m (56ft/33ft); *B. u. jacquemontii*, arguably the loveliest of all the white-barked birches, white bark sometimes tinted pink or ochre, serrated mid-green leaves, yellow in autumn, 18m/10m (56ft/33ft).

Bidens — Asteraceae

Small annuals, perennials, and deciduous shrubs. Tender to hardy. Annuals are excellent for hanging baskets and other containers, gravel gardens and borders and have become very popular recently. Trailing or spreading, simple or pinnate leaves, sometimes fern-like, starry flowers. Sow seed in warmth in spring, or take cuttings from overwintered plants in spring. ❀ *B. aurea* 'Sunshine', feathery leaves, yellow flowers from early summer to autumn, 50cm/40cm (1¾ft/1½ft); *B. ferulifolia*, feathery foliage, golden daisy-like flowers from early summer to autumn, 30cm (1ft)/indefinite.

left *Bidens aurea* 'Sunshine' is an endearing little daisy that has become a hanging basket favourite in recent years, although a surprising number of gardeners still don't know its name.

Billardiera — Pittosporaceae

Medium evergreen perennial climber. Barely hardy. In mild areas suitable for hanging baskets, among shrubs or up tree trunks, walls and pergolas. Small, entire, often lance-shaped leaves on twining branches, bell-shaped flowers, single or in clusters, followed by fruit. No routine pruning. Sow seed in warmth when ripe in autumn or in early spring, layer in autumn or spring, or take semi-ripe cuttings in late summer. ❀ *B. longiflora*, narrow, linear to lance-shaped deep green leaves, solitary light yellow-green flowers in late summer followed by purple-blue, sometimes purple, red, pink or white fruits in early autumn, 2.1m/1m (6½ft/3ft).

Blechnum *Hard fern* — Blechnaceae

Small/large evergreen fern. Fairly hardy to very hardy. Suitable for sparse ground cover in shade. Rosettes of pinnate, leathery typically ladder-like fronds. Divide in spring. ❀ *B. penna-marina*,

below *Blechnum penna-marina* is a delightful little Southern Hemisphere fern that I have at the edge of my fernery where it grows most appealingly over damp logs.

delightful, very hardy evergreen, creeping (almost invasive), carpeting, small ladder-shaped fronds, 10-20cm (4-8in)/indefinite; *B. spicant*, very hardy, two types of frond, one evergreen and spreading, the other upright, deciduous and spore-producing, 20-50cm/60cm (8in-1¾ft/2ft); *B. tabulare*, fairly hardy, creeping, deciduous, bronze-green fronds, 1m/60-120cm (3ft/2ft-4ft).

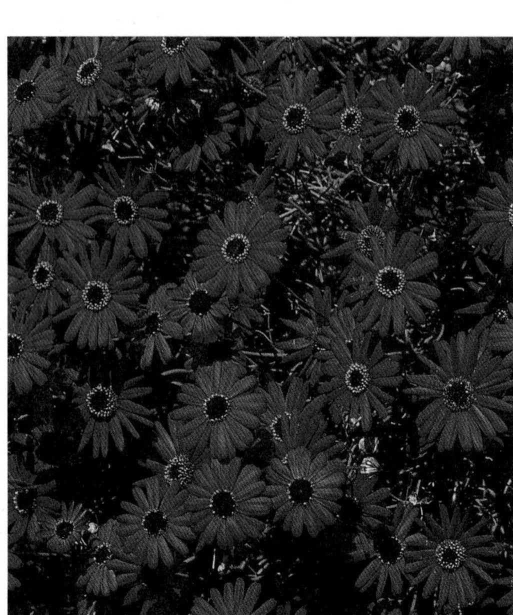

right *Brachycome iberidifolia* 'Purple Splendour'. I have been recommending these sweetly fragrant little Australian plants as container subjects for years so I'm especially pleased that they are now more widely available.

Boltonia *False Camomile* Asteraceae

Large herbaceous hardy perennial. Suitable for a position in light shade in a border. Lance-shaped, blue-green leaves, sometimes finely toothed, clusters of white, pink-purple or lilac daisy-like flowers with yellow centres. Sow seed in spring or in a cold-frame in autumn, divide in autumn or early spring or take basal cuttings in late spring. ❀ *B. asteroides*, glossy grey- to blue-green, narrow, pointed leaves, flowers white, sometimes purple, from late summer to autumn, 2m/1m (6½ft/3ft); *B. a.* var. *latisquama*, larger flowers, lilac, 1.8m/1m (5½ft/3ft).

Brachyglottis Asteraceae

Small/medium evergreen trees and shrubs, herbaceous perennials and climbers. Barely hardy to moderately hardy. Suitable for borders, smaller varieties for rock gardens; thrives in seaside locations and is tolerant of strong (but not cold) winds and dry conditions. Leaves are usually olive-green above, downy and white beneath. Clusters of daisy-like yellow flowers, summer or autumn. Propagated by semi-ripe cuttings in summer or hardwood cuttings from mid to late autumn. ❀ *B.* Dunedin Group 'Sunshine', one of the best-loved summer garden shrubs still usually referred to by its old and always incorrect name of *Senecio greyi*, low mound of grey-green or silver scalloped leaves, large clusters of yellow flowers from mid- to late summer, 75cm/1.5m (2½ft/5ft); *B. monroi*, scalloped, wavy, oblong leathery leaves, large clusters of yellow flowers, summer, 1m/2m (3ft/6½ft).

Brachycome
Swan River Daisy Asteraceae

Small half-hardy bedding annuals and deciduous/evergreen perennials. Annuals are quite excellent for hanging baskets and other containers, edging and borders. Sow seed in warmth in spring. ❀ *B. iberidifolia*, has come to be immensely significant in recent years, bushy, fairly drought-tolerant, deeply cut light green leaves, abundant blue, sometimes violet or white ('Blue Splendour', 'Purple Splendour', 'White Splendour'), fragrant daisy-like flowers with yellow centres throughout the summer, 45cm/35cm (1½ft/1ft).

Brassica Brassicaceae

Annuals, evergreen biennials and perennials, including a large range of edible vegetables. Most are moderately hardy to hardy. They thrive best in fertile, well-drained alkaline soil in full sun. Sow seed in growing positions or in a seed bed from

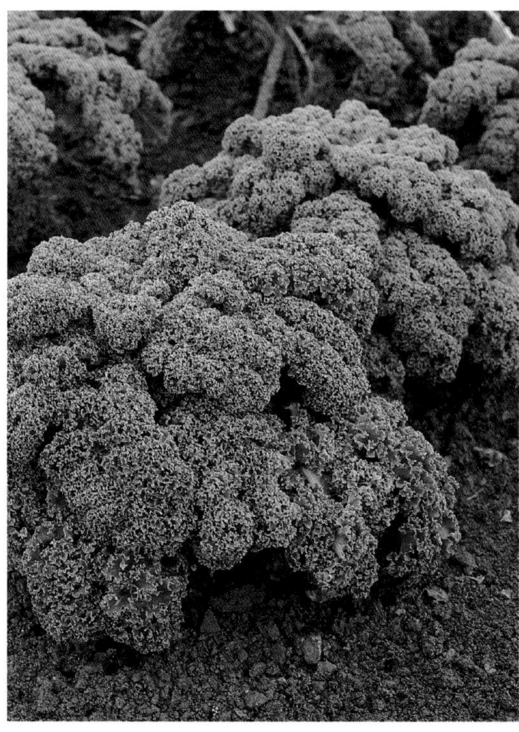

far right Kale 'Pentland Brig'. The kales are large, non-hearting cabbage-like vegetables, far too often dismissed as simply cattle fodder. In truth, they are delicious and succulent if cooked carefully.

which they are transplanted from spring to summer, depending on variety; some can be sown in warmth in early spring. Young plants of some types are available from nurseries. The brassicas are susceptible to a wide range of pests and diseases but none of these prevent them from being in every kitchen garden.

Mustard Swede Rape

The annual species *B. juncea* has given rise to a group that includes the mustard greens, brown and oriental mustards. Thrive in warm, moist, rich soil. ❀ 'Amsoi', a tender green with a mustard bite, harvested in autumn; 'Gai Choy' (syn. 'Green-in-the-Snow'), an exceptionally hardy variety with jagged, lobed or finely cut leaves, peppery flavour; 'Red Mustard'.

Rape (*B. napus*), used as substitute for mustard in salads and for mustard and cress, also for sprouting seeds, needs warm, moist soil. ❀ 'Salad Rape', milder than cress, grows more quickly.

Swede (*B. n.* Napobrassica Group), hardy biennial, larger, hardier than turnip with a milder flavour. Thrives best in light, rich soil in an open position. ❀ 'Acme'; 'Best of All'; 'Marian', spherical root with light purple skin and yellow flesh, some resistance to clubroot and powdery mildew.

Black mustard varieties (*B. nigra*), grown for its seeds, leaves, flowers and oil, include 'Burgonde', used to make French mustard, also and quite coincidentally, suitable for green manure. (For white mustard, see *Sinapsis alba.*)

Cabbages and cabbage-like vegetables

These are varieties of species *B. oleracea*, a biennial grown as an annual. They include kale, kohl-rabi, Brussels sprouts, cauliflowers and broccoli.

Kale (*B. o.* Acephala Group), generally divided into curly leafed and plain leafed types, does not form a heart. Moderately hardy, leaves and young shoots harvested in winter and early spring. Will tolerate poorer soil than cabbages. ❀ 'Dwarf Green Curled', very hardy, densely curled leaves; 'Pentland Brig', broccoli-like spears; 'Thousand Head', very hardy.

Ornamental kales/Ornamental cabbages. Hardy annuals grown for decorative purposes. Suitable for autumn bedding or containers. Usually raised from seed sown in warmth. Thrives best in poorer soil than vegetable types. Temperatures below 10°C (50°F) intensify the colour. Round to ovate, plain or frilled pink, red or white leaves. ❀ Northern Lights Series, frilled leaf margins, 25cm/50cm (10in/1¾ft).

above Cabbage 'Ruby Ball' is much the most widely available red cabbage, a vegetable that always seems to be accorded more culinary respect than its green-leaved counterpart.

Cabbages have edible leaves and a large terminal bud, the heart. They are divided into three groups according to the time of harvest: spring cabbages (and non-hearting spring greens), sown in summer for harvesting in spring to early summer; summer cabbage, sown late winter to early spring for summer to autumn harvest; winter cabbage, sown in spring for harvesting winter to spring. Most have fairly smooth leaves and either a round or pointed heart. They thrive best in well-drained, very fertile soil in full sun. ❀ Spring: 'April', dwarf, compact, pointed head, early; 'Pixie', small, hard, pointed head. Summer: 'Golden Acre', my all-time recommendation, excellent, firm, small to medium-sized; 'Greyhound', dwarf, compact, early spring; 'Hispi' F1, good for small gardens, bolt resistant; 'Minicole' F1, small, compact, late summer to early autumn, very long-standing. Winter: 'Christmas Drumhead', small for a winter variety, dwarf, compact; 'Holland Late Winter' Dutch white cabbage for storing; Red cabbages: 'Red Drumhead 2', autumn; 'Ruby Ball', summer. Savoy cabbages have crinkled leaves, often tinged blue, and are sown in early summer for harvesting from autumn to spring. 'Best of All', drumhead, solid heart, late autumn to early winter; 'Celtic', rather smooth leaves for a Savoy, late winter, 'January King Hardy Late Stock 3', medium-sized, very hardy and long-standing, mid-late winter, still, I think, by far the best Savoy.

right To my mind Cauliflower 'All the Year Round' is the best summer cauliflower; although I think that whoever first named it allowed their enthusiasm to run away with them.

Chinese broccoli (*B. o.* Alboglabra Group), a slender leafy vegetable with a small head of white or sometimes yellow flowers and a fleshy stem, rather like a small kale or leafy calabrese. ❀ 'Green Lance' F1, a quick-growing variety suitable for warm conditions.

Cauliflowers (*B. o.* Botrytis Group) have edible flower buds (curds) on thick fleshy stalks, the buds usually white but sometimes purple, orange or green. They are grouped as summer/autumn varieties and so-called winter varieties (although strictly, winter 'cauliflowers' are types of broccoli), that are harvested from early spring onwards. They require a moisture-retentive soil with a fairly high pH. ❀ Summer/autumn varieties: 'All the Year Round', misnamed old variety for summer; 'Barrier Reef', autumn; 'Dok Elgon', quick growing and, I find, probably the easiest to grow, popular with exhibitors, early to late autumn. Winter varieties: 'Walcheren Winter 1 Armado April', very large curds, the best, I have found, of the confusingly large 'Walcheren' range.

Brussels Sprouts (*B. o.* Gemmifera Group) have a single stem, and are grown for the edible lateral buds that resemble small cabbages. Best in fairly heavy, firm soil. Tall varieties require staking. ❀ 'Cambridge No 5', tall erect variety, late, my selection among open-pollinated types; 'Citadel' F1, medium-sized, late winter, reliably hardy; 'Peer Gynt' F1, small, compact, the best hybrid sprout for modern gardens, mid-autumn; 'Rubine', red sprout (turns dirty green on cooking); 'Sheriff' F1, mid to late season, claimed to have mildew resistance.

Kohl-rabi (*B. o.* Gongylodes Groups) is grown for the edible white flesh inside the swollen stem. ❀ 'Purple Vienna', purple skin, white flesh; 'Superschmelz', white skin, white flesh, very large; 'White Vienna', white skin, white flesh.

Broccoli includes those vegetables known as sprouting broccoli, Italian broccoli or calabrese and Cape broccoli or purple cauliflower. Italian broccoli/calabrese (*B. o.* Italica Group) is an annual similar in appearance to cauliflower until it produces dark green, or purple flower buds. ❀ 'Corvette F1, large central head followed by smaller shoots; 'Romanesco' (strictly, a late green cauliflower), suitable for larger gardens, late autumn to early winter, pointed lime-green heads, excellent for freezing. Sprouting broccoli, purple or white flower buds at the ends of side shoots produced either early or late, far too neglected in gardens since the introduction of calabrese: 'Green

far right Kohl-rabi 'Purple Vienna'. It's entirely appropriate that one of the best varieties should have a central European name because this is a vegetable that mystifyingly has always been more popular in Continental Europe than in Britain.

Sprouting' and 'Purple Sprouting Early', traditionally harvested in spring; 'White Sprouting Early', the equivalent of purple sprouting but with white tips. Cape broccoli/purple cauliflower, hardy, useful for overwintering: 'Purple Cape'. The vegetable known as perennial broccoli which lasts for several years if all heads are picked in spring is, strictly, a form of cauliflower; 'Nine Star Perennial' is the old, traditional variety.

B. o. Tronchuda Group, includes the tree or walking-stick cabbage, 'Jersey Walking Stick', and the Portuguese cabbage 'Couve Tronchuda', loose-centred, forms a large 2m (6½ft) or more tall leafy mid-green plant with prominent white midribs for harvesting in autumn.

Oriental greens and Turnip

Miscellaneous varieties of *B. rapa* (syn. *B. campestris*) that includes pakchoi, Mizuna and Mibuna greens. These plants originated in China and Japan where they are widely used in cooking. Most are hardy, fast-growing and easy.

❀ 'Mizuna', clumps of very finely dissected leaves, long-standing; 'Green Spray' and 'Bouquet F1', varieties of Mibuna greens, long smooth leaves, not dissected, with edible stalks and flowers. *B. r.* Chinensis Group includes the celery mustards and pak-choi: 'White Celery Mustard'; 'Joi Choi' F1, variety of the Chinese pak choi, rosettes of erect, smooth rounded leaves, pure white leaf stalks. *B. r.* Pekinensis Group, the Chinese cabbages and Chinese leaves resemble cos lettuce in shape, with stronger flavour: 'Green Rocket' F1 and 'Ruffles' F1, cream-white leaves, less prone to the bolting that used to plague some older varieties in our summers.

Turnips (*B. r.* Rapifera Group) fast maturing, fleshy roots, leaves also edible when young. ❀ 'Golden Ball', round deep yellow, stores well; 'Purple Top Milan', flattish white roots with purple markings, overwinters well; 'Snowball', early variety, sweet flavour; 'Tokyo Cross' F1, small, perfect globes.

Briza *Quaking Grass* Poaceae

Annual and perennial grasses. Hardy. Suitable for larger rock gardens and borders; a valuable grass to dry for indoor arrangements. Linear leaves, flowers are purple-brown spikelets resembling small lockets, hanging from slender, thread-like stalks in summer. Sow seed in growing positions in spring or autumn, or divide established perennials in spring. ❀ *B. media*, evergreen perennial, flat light green leaves on slow, creeping erect stems, purple-brown flower spikelets in summer, 60-90cm/30cm (2-3ft/1ft).

above The popular name of *Briza media*, quaking grass, comes from the delicate, trembling flower heads which are so prized by flower arrangers.

Browallia *Bush Violet* Solanaceae

Small half-hardy annuals, tender perennials and sub-shrubs of which one species has become very popular for hanging baskets and window boxes in summer. Slender ovate to elliptic, pointed leaves, rather sticky. Trumpet-shaped or star-shaped violet, purple, blue or white flowers from early summer to early autumn. Sow seed in warmth in early spring, or in late summer for winter and spring flowers in the greenhouse. ❀ *B. speciosa* 'Blue Troll', bushy perennial usually grown as an annual, rounded or pointed matt, sticky leaves, clear blue flowers, 25cm (10in); *B. s.* 'White Troll', white flowers.

Bruckenthalia Ericaceae

Small evergreen shrub and one of the neglected members of its family. Hardy. Suitable for the heather garden, rock garden and containers but requires lime-free soil. Linear, needle-like dark green leaves on stiff erect stems. Clusters of bell-shaped rose-pink, sometimes white, flowers from late spring to midsummer. No routine pruning. Take semi-ripe heeled cuttings in midsummer or sow seed in a cold-frame in spring. ❀ *B. spiculifolia*, dark green leaves, short spikes of pink flowers from early to midsummer, 25cm/20cm (10in/8in).

Brugmansia (syn. Datura)

Angel's Trumpet Solanaceae

Large evergreen shrubs or small trees. Tender to barely hardy. All parts of the plant are toxic if eaten. Suitable only for mild, frost-free areas but good in containers to put outside in summer. Simple, coarse, usually toothed leaves, sometimes downy. Dramatic, large solitary pendent funnel- or trumpet-shaped flowers, often scented, from late spring to autumn. Cut back hard before taking under cover in winter. Sow seed in warmth in spring or take semi-ripe cuttings in summer. ❀ *B.* x *candida* 'Grand Marnier', large shrub or small tree, matt green oblong to elliptic leaves with wavy margins, apricot-coloured flowers, lightly scented, from summer through to autumn, 3-5m/1.5-2.5m (10-16ft/5-8ft); *B.* x *c.* 'Knightii', white double flowers.

Brunnera Boraginaceae

Small hardy herbaceous perennials. Very hardy. Suitable for ground cover, woodland plantings and borders. Most need protection from cold winds. Heart-shaped or oval basal leaves, mid-green, often rough, hairy, and lance-shaped stem leaves. Small, blue or white star-shaped flowers in terminal inflorescences from mid to late spring. Divide established plants in spring or autumn, sow seeds in a cold-frame in spring or early summer or take root cuttings in winter or early spring. ❀ *B. macrophylla* (syn. *Anchusa myositidiflora*), heart-shaped, pointed leaves, tiny blue flowers on wiry stems in spring, 45cm/60cm (1½ft/2ft); *B. m.* 'Dawson's White', leaves variegated white and green, some almost entirely white, bright blue flowers; *B. m.* 'Hadspen Cream', light green leaves with cream-white margins, blue flowers; *B. m.* 'Langtrees', large, rough dark green leaves spotted silver, blue flowers.

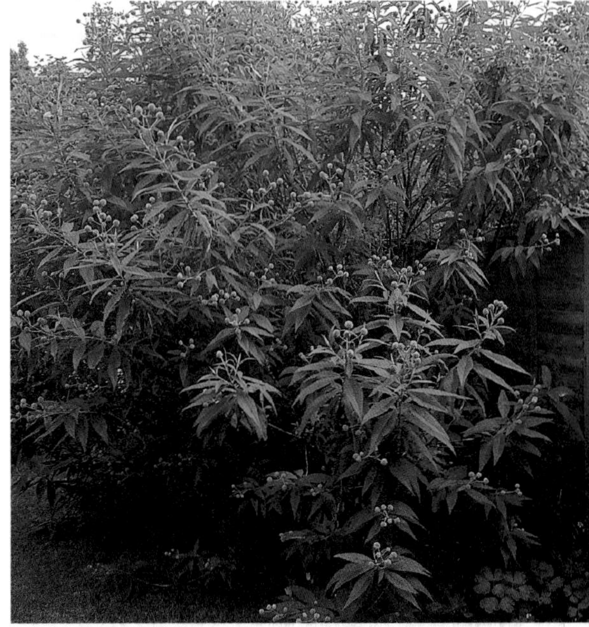

right *Brunnera macrophylla* 'Langtrees'. I think of brunneras as rather coarse versions of their relatives, the forget-me-nots and they provide robust ground cover for wilder parts of the garden.

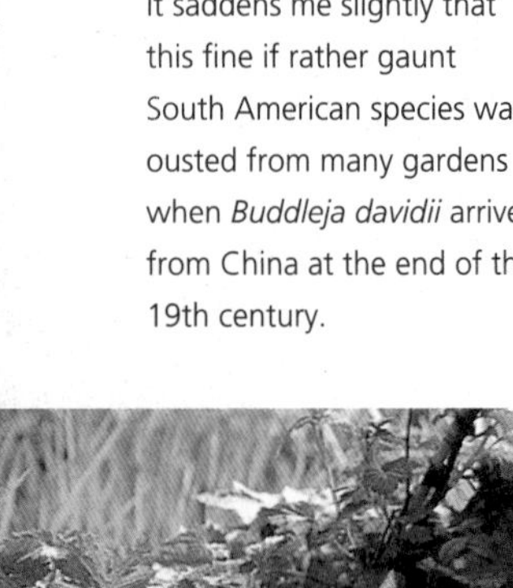

below *Buddleja globosa*. It saddens me slightly that this fine if rather gaunt South American species was ousted from many gardens when *Buddleja davidii* arrived from China at the end of the 19th century.

Buddleja Buddlejaceae

Evergreen, semi-evergreen and deciduous shrubs, trees, climbers and herbaceous perennials although those for temperate gardens are all shrubs. Tender to hardy. Suitable for mixed or shrub borders. Lance-shaped to ovate pointed leaves, usually dark green or silver-grey. Small tight panicles of tiny tubular flowers, sometimes fragrant, which in some species are extremely attractive to insects, particularly butterflies. Thrive in any fertile, well-drained soil in full sun. Pruning varies significantly with species. Propagate by semi-ripe cuttings in late summer, hardwood cuttings of *B. davidii* in autumn or winter.

❀ *B. alternifolia*, deciduous, willow-like leaves on arching branches, lilac flowers scented of honey in early summer, cut back flowering shoots as flowers fade, 4m/4m (13ft/13ft); *B. colvilei*, semi-evergreen or deciduous, dark green elliptic to lance-shaped leaves, drooping panicles of dark pink or red flowers, early summer, prune as *B. alternifolia*, 6m/6m (20ft/20ft); *B. crispa*, fairly tender, deciduous, prune hard in spring, toothed, grey-green leaves, hairy, silvery when young, fragrant lilac flowers from mid to late summer, 3m/3m (10ft/10ft); *B. davidii*, arching, deciduous, long panicles of pale purple, fragrant flowers, late summer, prune very hard in spring, the optimum time varies with region and climate and is best done about ten weeks before the last danger of any frost 3m/5m (10ft/16ft); *B. d.* 'Black Knight', deep violet flowers, *B. d.* 'Dartmoor', magenta flowers on drooping branches, *B. d.* 'Empire Blue', violet-blue with orange centres; *B. d.* 'Harlequin', cream-white variegated leaves, deep red-purple flowers; *B. d.* 'Nanho Blue', pale blue flowers, 1.5m (5ft); *B. d.* 'Royal Red', narrow panicles of red-purple flowers, *B. d.* 'White Profusion', pure white flowers with yellow centres; *B. fallowiana* var. *alba*, grey leaves, deciduous, woolly, silvery beneath, fragrant cream-white flowers from mid- to late summer, prune hard in spring, 2m/3m (61/2ft/10ft); *B. globosa*, evergreen or semi-evergreen shrub, dark green leaves brown beneath, fragrant, bright orange globular flower clusters in early summer, prune as *B. alternifolia*, 5m/5m (16ft/16ft); *B.* 'Lochinch', deciduous, green leaves, white, hairy beneath, fragrant violet-blue flowers with orange centres from mid- to late summer, 2.5m/3m (8ft/10ft); *B.* 'Pink Delight', deciduous shrub, long bright pink panicles; *B.* x *weyeriana*, orange-yellow globular inflorescences from mid- to late summer, prune hard in spring, 4m/3m (13ft/10ft); *B.* x *w.* 'Sungold', deep orange flowers in dense inflorescences.

Bulbocodium Colchicaceae

Small corm-forming ornamental. Moderately hardy. Suitable for rock gardens and naturalising in grass, also alpine houses or cool greenhouses. Linear or lance-shaped leaves appear after or with starry, funnel-shaped, almost stemless flowers in spring, sometimes late winter. Leaves die back in midsummer. Propagate by removing offsets in summer or sow seed in a cold-frame in autumn or spring. ❀ *B. vernum*, perennial, glossy dark green leaves, pink-purple flowers, 4-8cm/5cm (1½-3¼in/2in).

Buphthalmum Asteraceae

Medium hardy herbaceous perennial. Suitable for borders or wild flower gardens. Clump-forming, dark green leaves, marigold-yellow daisy-like flowers in summer, good for cutting. Propagate by division or seed sown in a cold-frame in spring or autumn. ❀ *B. salicifolium*, narrow, lance-shaped leaves, sometimes slightly hairy, 60cm/40cm (2ft/1½ft).

Butomus *Flowering Rush* Butomaceae

Large water marginal. Very hardy. Suitable for medium to large pools. Deciduous, long twisted leaves, fragrant flowers. Propagated by sowing seed in summer, division in spring during dormancy or removing root bulbils. ❀ *B. umbellatus*, rush-like leaves, mid-green, later purple-bronze, then dark green. Loose umbels of fragrant pink flowers, late summer sometimes followed by red fruit, 1.5m/45cm (5ft/1½ft).

Buxus *Box* Buxaceae

Small/large evergreen shrub or small tree. Very hardy. A superb plant for hedging, containers and second only to yew for topiary. Small round to elongated glossy leaves, dark green insignificant flowers. Shaped plants should be clipped twice a year. Take semi-ripe cuttings in summer or hardwood cuttings in autumn. ❀ *B. microphylla*, compact, rounded, elliptic to oblong leaves turn bronze in winter, 75cm/1.5m (2½ft/5ft); *B. sempervirens*, bushy, rounded shrub or small tree, glossy dark green leaves, 5m/5m (16ft/16ft); *B. s.* 'Aureovariegata', leaves splashed and mottled with cream-yellow, 2.5m/3m (8ft/10ft); *B. s.* 'Elegantissima', narrow, white margined green leaves, 1.5m/1.5m (5ft/5ft); *B. s.* 'Suffruticosa', very slow growing, matchless for dwarf formal hedging, for example in knot gardens, bright glossy green leaves, 1m/1.5m (3ft/5ft).

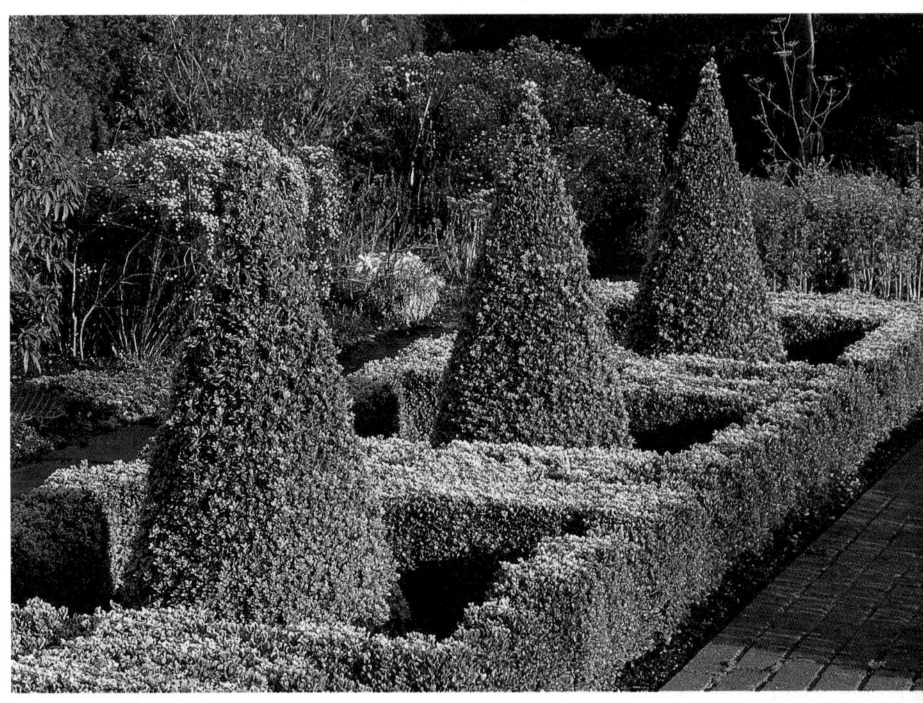

above *Buxus sempervirens* 'Suffruticosa'. This very slow growing form of box is seen here in its characteristic use, as low hedging in a formal garden, for which it is quite matchless.

Calamagrostis *Reed Grass* Poaceae

Perennial grasses. Moderately hardy. Linear leaves, branching inflorescences. Divide established plants in spring. ❀ *C.* x *acutiflora* 'Karl Foerster', clump-forming, slightly glossy, mid-green leaves, erect bronze-pink plumes, fading to straw-colour, in late summer, remaining throughout winter, 1.8m/60cm (51/2ft/2ft); *C.* x *c.*'Overdam', leaves edged and striped soft yellow-white, later fading to white, purple plumes turn grey-pink later, 1.2m/60cm (4ft/2ft).

Calamintha *Calamint* Lamiaceae

Small perennials. Moderately hardy. Suitable for rock gardens, borders and containers, preferably in full sun. Aromatic green, ovate to oblong, often toothed leaves, tubular flowers in summer. Divide established plants in spring. ❀ *C. grandiflora*, peppermint-scented pale green, toothed leaves, bright pink flowers, 45cm/45cm (1½ft/1½ft); *B. g.* 'Variegata', cream leaves speckled green; *C. nepeta*, bushy, oval, grey-green leaves, white, blue or mauve flowers, 45cm/50-75cm (1½ft/1¾-2½ft); *C. n.* ssp. *glandulosa* 'White Cloud', white flowers.

Calandrinia Portulacaceae

Small/medium evergreen perennials. Tender to barely hardy. Suitable in mild areas for rock and scree gardens and borders but in colder gardens best treated as half-hardy annuals. Usually compact with narrow, fleshy leaves and red, purple-red or white cup-shaped flowers, solitary or in clusters. Sow seeds in warmth in spring or autumn, or take stem cuttings in spring. ❀ *C. caespitosa*, linear, sprawling or cushion-forming, grey-green, hairy leaves, shiny magenta flowers with yellow centres, sometimes orange-gold or pale pink, 7cm/10cm (2¾in/4in); *C. grandiflora*, clump-forming succulent, bright green elliptic, pointed leaves, clusters of pale purple-red magenta flowers in summer, 1m/45cm (3ft/1½ft); *C. umbellata*, variable, semi-erect stems, linear to lance-shaped hairy blue or grey-green leaves, loose clusters of red flowers, 15-20cm/15-20cm (6-8in/6-8in).

Calceolaria *Slipper Flower* Scrophulariaceae

Annuals, biennials, perennials and sub-shrubs. Tender to moderately hardy, the hardy species and varieties are suitable for rock gardens, raised beds or troughs; the less hardy for summer bedding and containers. Vividly coloured pouched flowers singly or in clusters; they remind me of a frog on a stick. Sow seeds in a cold-frame in autumn or early spring, or take semi-ripe cuttings in autumn. *C. integrifolia* is propagated by softwood cuttings in late spring or summer, or by sowing seed in warmth in winter; the Herbeohybrida Group by sowing seed in warmth in spring or late summer; 'Anytime Series' at any time of the year flowering about four months after sowing. ❀ *C. biflora* (syn. *C plantaginea*), hardy evergreen perennial, basal rosettes of lance-shaped to oval leaves, dark green, loose clusters of bright yellow pouched flowers from summer to late autumn, 15-25cm/20cm (6-10in/8in); *C. falklandica*, hardy evergreen, mid-green, oblong, hairy leaves, pale yellow flowers with purple flecks at the throat, 25cm/20cm (10in/8in); Herbeohybrida Group, bushy tender biennials, oval, mid-green hairy leaves, white, red, orange or yellow flowers with darker markings in spring and summer, 30cm/25cm (1ft/10in); H. G. 'Jewel Cluster', mixed colours, spotted, 30cm/20cm (1ft/8in); H. G. 'Sunshine' F1, gold-yellow flowers, a very good hanging basket plant, 30cm/25cm (1ft/10in); *C. integrifolia*, half-hardy evergreen sub-shrub, usually grown as an annual, grey-green lance-shaped leaves, round, bright yellow flowers in late summer, 1.2m/20-30cm (4ft/8in-1ft); *C. i.* 'Kentish Hero', similar to Herbeohybrida Group but with smaller orange-bronze flowers.

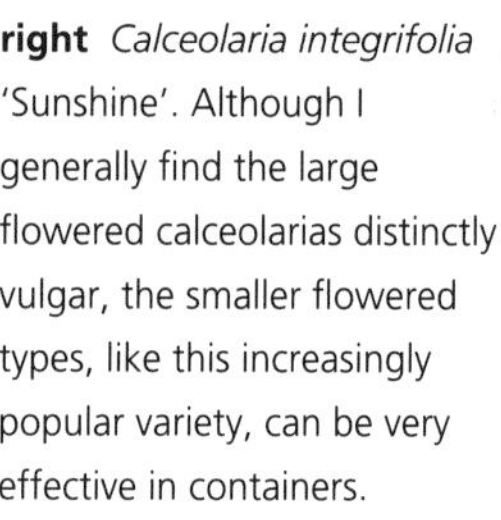

right *Calceolaria integrifolia* 'Sunshine'. Although I generally find the large flowered calceolarias distinctly vulgar, the smaller flowered types, like this increasingly popular variety, can be very effective in containers.

Callicarpa Verbenaceae

Small/large deciduous and evergreen shrubs and small trees. Tender to very hardy. Hardy species and varieties are suitable for mixed plantings. Simple opposite leaves, red, white, or pink inflorescences in summer are followed by rather amazing brightly coloured little round fruit. No routine pruning. Sow seeds in a cold-frame in autumn or spring, softwood cuttings in spring or semi-ripe cuttings in summer. ❀ *C. bodinieri* var. *giraldii*, very hardy, bushy, deciduous shrub, elliptic green leaves, red or yellow in autumn, star-shaped mauve or purple flowers from mid- to late summer, followed by clusters of fruit, 3m/2.5m (10ft/8ft); *C. b. g.* 'Profusion', leaves purple-bronze when young, pale pink flowers, almost unbelievable violet fruit.

left *Calendula officinalis* 'Fiesta Gitana'. The range of flower size and colour is very much greater in modern pot marigolds but gardeners often forget the 'pot' part of their name; they are edible kitchen herbs.

Calendula *Pot Marigold* Asteraceae

Small hardy bedding annuals, evergreen perennials and sub-shrubs. Those that I describe here are varieties of the annual herbaceous pot marigold *C. officinalis*, a long-popular culinary herb. Suitable for herb gardens and informal borders. Aromatic, lanceolate leaves on slightly branching stems. Edible vivid yellow to orange flowers from summer until autumn. Sow seeds in warmth in early spring or mid spring in flowering positions, also in late spring or early summer to provide a succession of flowers. ❀ *C. officinalis* 'Art Shades', semi-double flowers, apricot, orange and cream, 60cm/60cm (2ft/2ft); *C. o.* 'Fiesta Gitana', dwarf, double flowers, pastel oranges and yellows, some bicoloured, 30cm/30-45cm (1ft/1-1½ft); *C. o.* 'Orange King', double, a beautiful deep orange, 45cm/30-45cm (1½ft/1-1½ft); *C. o.* 'Pacific Beauty', double flowers in shades of orange, primrose or cream with red-brown centres, 60cm/60cm (2ft/2ft); *C. o.* 'Prolific', single orange flowers, main flowers producing smaller ones from their base, 40-50cm/40-50cm (1½-1¾ft/1½-1¾ft); *C. o.* 'Radio', double orange flowers with rolled petals, similar to some dahlias, 45cm (1½ft).

Calla *Water Arum, Bog Arum* Araceae

A small deciduous or semi-evergreen water marginal. Very hardy. Suitable for medium-sized to large pools. Spreads by creeping rhizomes. Glossy dark green leaves, double spathes followed by red fruits. Skin contact may cause irritation. Divide rhizomes in spring. ❀ *C. palustris*, tiny flowers in spring on green and white spadix half enclosed by white papery spathe, followed by round, bright red fruit, 25cm/60cm (10in/2ft).

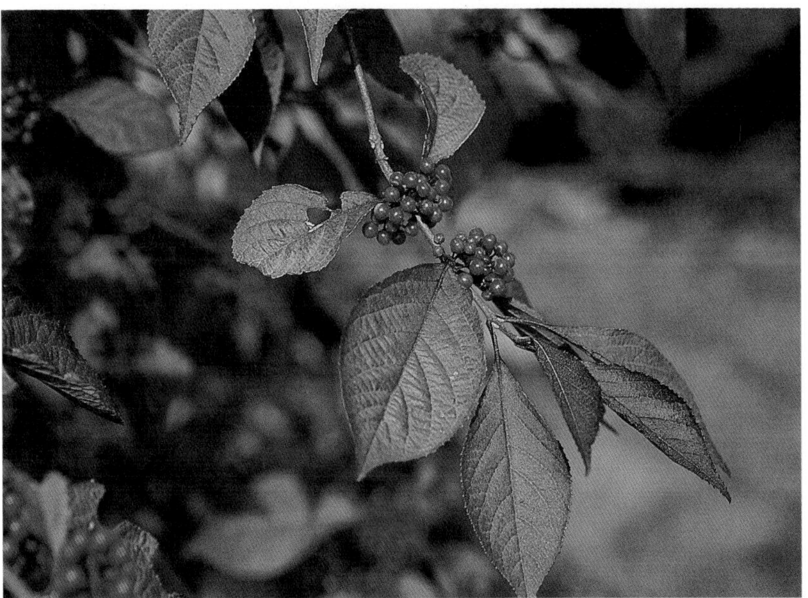

above Callicarpas, like *C. bodinieri giraldii* 'Profusion', offer some of the most unexpected and arresting of all autumn fruits.

Callistemon *Bottle Brush* Myrtaceae

Small/large evergreen trees and shrubs. Tender to moderately hardy. Suitable for shrub borders in mild areas or against a sheltered wall in colder places. Cylindrical to lance-shaped leaves, spikes of tiny flowers with long stamens, red, purple, pink, yellow, green or white. No routine pruning. Sow seeds in warmth in spring or take semi-ripe cuttings in late summer. ❀ *C. citrinus*, fairly hardy and the only really reliable species in much of Britain, variable, dark green, lemon-scented, lance-shaped leaves, bright crimson-red 'bottle-brush' flowers in summer, 1.5m-8m/1.5m-8m (5-25ft/5-25ft); *C. c.* 'Splendens', barely hardy, broad leaves, pink-red when young, crimson flowers, 2-8m/1.5-6m (6½ft-25ft/5-20ft).

above *Callistephus chinensis* Duchess Series. An old range but still one of the very best for cutting.

right The range of plant size is one of the most remarkable features of heather varieties; *Calluna vulgaris* 'Robert Chapman' is one of the taller forms and has probably the most intense winter colour.

Callistephus *China Aster* Asteraceae

Small/large half-hardy bedding annual. A genus of only one species but many cultivated forms. Erect, bushy, coarsely toothed, ovate leaves, single, semi-double or double daisy-like flowers from summer to autumn, excellent for cutting. Thrives best in fertile, moist, neutral to alkaline soil in a sheltered position in full sun. Taller varieties need staking. Sow seeds in warmth in early spring or in flowering positions in late spring. Prone to serious wilt disease when grown repeatedly on the same site.
❀ *C. chinensis* 'Chrysanthemum Flowered', compact, double flowers in white, cream, shades of blue, purple, lavender, pink, and red, 25-30cm (10in-1ft); *C. c.* Duchess Series, the best overall range for garden use and cutting, with double flowers, incurved florets, yellow, purple, red, 70cm/30cm (2¼ft/1ft); *C. c.* 'Lilliput', dwarf, pompon flowers in same mixed colours as Duchess Series, 30cm/40cm (1ft/1½ft); *C. c.* 'Milady', round, double flowers, shades of red, red-pink, blue, white, 30cm/25cm (1ft/10in); *C. c.* 'Ostrich Plume', mainly pink, crimson flowers with long feathery florets, reflexed, from late summer to autumn, 60cm/30cm (2ft/1ft); *C. c.* Princess Series, fairly wilt-resistant, incurved, semi-double flowers, quilled florets, wide range of colours, 60cm (2ft).

Calluna *Heather* Ericaceae

Small evergreen shrub. Hardy. A single species with over 500 cultivated varieties. Linear, slightly fleshy overlapping leaves, racemes of tiny bell-shaped flowers in reds, pinks, purples or white; less conspicuous than those of *Erica* because the petals are partly concealed by the sepals. Requires acidic soil, well-drained with added humus, in full sun. Cut back flowering stems to within 1.5-2.5cm (½-1in) of previous year's growth in spring. ❀ The following varieties flower from summer to early autumn (unless otherwise stated): *C. vulgaris*, 'Anthony Davis', grey-green leaves, long racemes of single white flowers, 45cm/75cm (1½ft/2½ft); 'Beoley Gold', yellow leaves, white flowers, 35cm/75cm (1ft/2½ft); 'County Wicklow', dwarf, semi-prostrate, mid-green leaves, double shell pink flowers, 25cm/35cm (10in/1ft); 'Darkness', dense, bright green leaves, dark purple-pink flowers, 25cm/35cm (10in/1ft); 'Firefly', red-brown leaves, deep orange-red in winter, deep lilac flowers, 45cm (1½ft); 'Gold Haze', bright gold leaves, white flowers, 50-60cm (1¾-2ft); 'H. E. Beale', double rose-pink flowers, summer to late autumn, 60cm (2ft); 'J. H. Hamilton', dwarf, deep pink flowers midsummer to late summer, 10cm/25cm (4in/10in); 'Kinlochruel', bright green leaves, bronze in winter, double white flowers, 25cm/40cm (10in/1½ft); 'Robert Chapman', a superb variety, leaves gold in spring, later orange, red in winter, light purple flowers, 25cm/60cm (10in/2ft); 'Silver Queen', silver-grey leaves, pale mauve flowers, 40cm/55cm (1½ft/2ft); 'Spring Cream', dark green leaves, tipped with cream in spring, white flowers, 35cm/45cm (1ft/1½ft); 'Wickwar Flame', bright

orange and red leaves in summer, copper and gold in autumn/winter, pink-mauve flowers, 50cm/60cm (1¾ft/2ft).

Caltha
Marsh Marigold, Kingcup Ranunculaceae

Small/medium water marginal. Very hardy. Suitable for medium-sized/large pools at depths of 0-15cm (0-6in). Deciduous heart- or kidney-shaped leaves, cup-shaped, gold-yellow or white flowers in spring. Propagate by division in spring or sow seed in autumn. ❀ *C. palustris*, toothed, dark green leaves, waxy yellow flowers, 10-40cm/45cm (4in-1½ft/1½ft); *C. p.* var. *alba*, (syn. *C. p.* 'Alba'), compact, solitary white flowers in spring before leaves develop, 22cm/30cm (8½in/1ft); *C. p. radicans* 'Flore Pleno', double yellow flowers, 25cm (10in).

Calystegia *Bindweed* Convolvulaceae

Large climbers. Moderately hardy. Vigorous herbaceous plants (including some vicious weeds) suitable for scrambling over fences, tree stumps and against walls. Usually oval or heart-shaped leaves, funnel-shaped flowers. Propagate by division in spring. ❀ *C. hederacea* 'Flore Pleno' (syn. *C. japonica* 'Flore Pleno'), not invasive, hairy green leaves, pink flowers from mid- to late summer, 5m/1m (16ft/3ft).

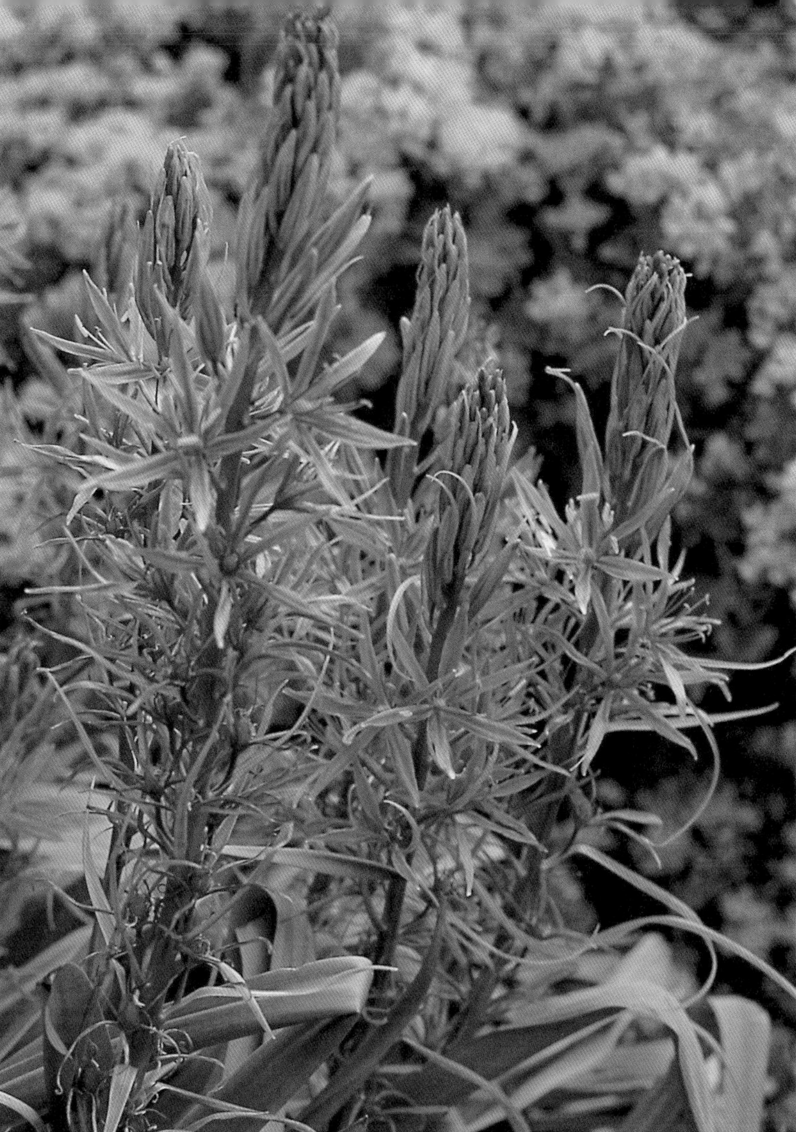

above *Camassia cusickii.* I grow this delightful feathery flowered bulb in a container where it is shown off particularly well.

Camassia
Camash, Quamash Hyacinthaceae

Small/medium bulbous ornamentals. Barely hardy to moderately hardy. Narrow linear, bright green basal leaves, inflorescences of star- or cup-shaped flowers, white, purple or blue, from late spring to summer, good for cutting if you grow sufficient. Propagate by removing offsets in late summer or early autumn. ❀ *C. cusickii*, linear leaves with wavy margins, grey-green, light or dark blue flowers in late spring, 60-80cm/10cm (2-2½ft/4in); *C. leichtlinii* ssp. *leichtlinii*, white flowers, often flushed pale green, in summer, 60-130cm/10cm (2-4½ft/4in); *C. quamash* (syn. *C. esculenta*), eaten by native American peoples, blue to violet-blue flowers in late spring, 20-80cm/5cm (8in-2½ft/2in).

Camellia Theaceae

Small evergreen trees and small/large shrubs, including *C. sinensis*, the tea plant but the many cultivated ornamental forms suitable for borders and containers are derived from very few species. Barely hardy to moderately hardy. Green ovate to elliptic or lance-shaped usually glossy leaves; glorious cup- or bowl-shaped single, semi-double or double flowers in late winter or spring; pink, red, white but not a true yellow. Requires a moist, rich, well-drained acidic soil in partial or light shade. Shelter from morning sun and cold, drying winds. No routine pruning. Propagated from leaf bud cuttings in summer or hardwood cuttings mid-autumn to early spring. The size differs with variety and growing conditions but most of my recommendations will attain about 4m/2m (13ft/6½ft), those that I have indicated as large may be 5m/3m (16ft/10ft) or more.

❀ *C.* 'Inspiration', large erect shrub or small tree, moderately hardy, oval leaves, semi-double, deep pink flowers, mid-winter to late spring; *C. japonica* 'Adolphe Audusson', spreading shrub or small tree, moderately hardy, elliptic, dark green leaves, semi-double red flowers, early spring to mid spring; *C. j* 'Elegans' (syn. *C. j.*'Chandleri Elegans'), double rose-pink flowers, mid to late spring; *C.* 'Leonard Messel', moderately hardy, large, thick, leathery

below *Camellia japonica* 'Adolphe Audusson'. The varieties of *C. japonica* tend to be less hardy than the hybrids but this is nonetheless a very good and reliable variety.

right *Camellia* x *williamsii* 'Donation' is one of the easiest, best known and most loved of all garden camellias.

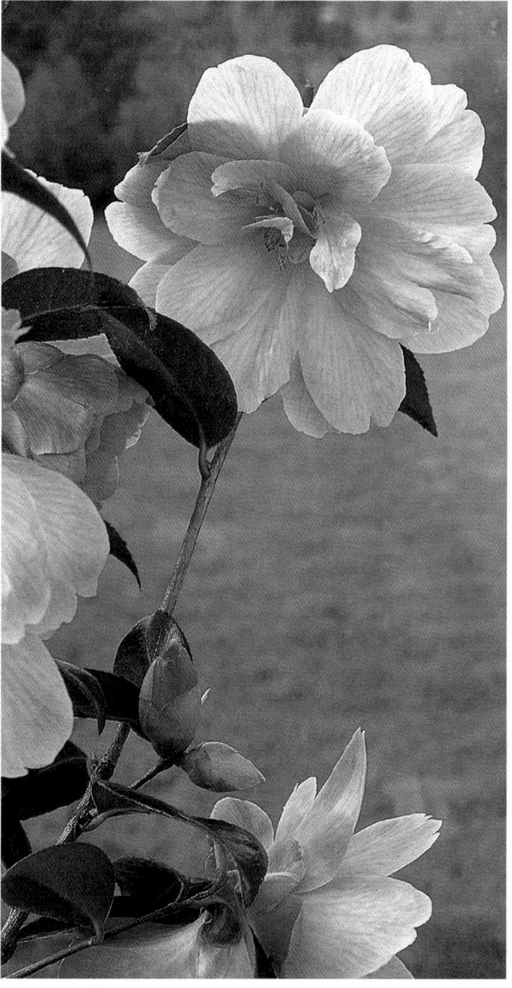

leaves, semi-double carmine flowers, mid to late spring; *C.* x *williamsii* 'Anticipation', moderately hardy, elliptic, glossy bright green leaves, double crimson flowers, late winter to early spring; *C.* x *w.* 'Brigadoon', semi-double rose-pink flowers, silver-tinged, late winter to late spring; *C.* x *w.* 'Debbie', deep clear pink flowers, semi-double to double, late winter to late spring; *C.* x *w.* 'Donation', far and away the best and easiest overall, moderately hardy, large, semi-double pink flowers, late winter to late spring; *C.* x *w.* 'Elsie Jury', deep pink double flowers shading to pale pink, late spring; *C.* x *w.* 'J. C. Williams', single pale pink flowers with dark shading, late winter to late spring; *C.* x *w.* 'Saint Ewe', single, trumpet-shaped, rose-pink flowers, early to mid spring.

Campanula *Bell flower* Campanulaceae

Small/large annuals, biennials, herbaceous perennials and sub-shrubs. Barely hardy to moderately hardy. Suitable for borders, edging and rock gardens; some are excellent for hanging baskets and other containers. Alternate, entire or toothed leaves; star-shaped or bell-shaped flowers from late spring to late summer. Cultivation requirements vary: most require moist, well-drained neutral to alkaline soil in full sun or partial shade; those damaged by frost should be grown in warmth in bright light out of direct sun, while those species that will not tolerate winter wet are best grown in a scree bed or trough. Tall perennials must be staked early. Sow seeds in cold-frame or greenhouse in spring; alpines in an open frame in autumn. Perennials are divided after flowering in autumn or increased by taking non-flowering basal shoot cuttings in spring or early summer. Those species and varieties that I describe here are all moderately hardy unless stated otherwise.

Perennial Border varieties: *C. alliariifolia*, hairy, heart-shaped leaves, erect spikes of pendent cream-white, bell-shaped flowers along one side of the stem in summer, 30-60cm/45cm (1-2ft/1½ft); *C.* 'Burghaltii', mound-forming, ovate, mid-green leaves, spikes of grey-mauve, pendent bell-shaped flowers in midsummer, 60cm/30cm (2ft/1ft); *C. carpatica*, clump-forming, solitary, upright, cup-shaped flowers in white or shades of blue and purple-blue in summer, 45cm/30-60cm (1½ft/1-2ft); *C. c.* 'Blaue Clips' (syn. *C. c.* 'Blue Clips'), sky blue flowers, 20cm (8in) mound; *C. c.* 'Weisse Clips', (syn, *C. c.* 'White Clips'), pure white flowers, 20cm (8in) mound; *C. glomerata*, lovely spreading plant but can be invasive, ovate to lance-shaped toothed dark green leaves, tubular bell-shaped white, lavender or purple flowers in summer, 10-45cm (4in-1½ft)/indefinite; *C. g.* 'Superba', deep purple flowers, 75cm (2½ft); *C. lactiflora* 'Loddon Anna', erect perennial, open bell-shaped flowers, lilac-pink, early summer to early autumn, self-seeds freely, 1.2-1.5m/60cm

far right: The alpine campanulas are an utterly charming group and *Campanula cochleariifolia* is one that I have found reliable even in partial shade.

(4-5ft/2ft); *C. l.* 'Prichard's Variety', dwarf, mound-forming, deep purple flowers, 75cm (2½ft); *C. latifolia*, clump-forming, long erect spikes of tubular white or purple-blue flowers in midsummer, 1.2m/60cm (4ft/2ft); *C. persicifolia*, evergreen, rosettes of mid-green, narrow, leathery leaves, cup-shaped flowers, white and shades of blue, purple, from early to midsummer, 90cm/30cm (3ft/1ft); *C. p. alba*, white; *C. p.* 'Boule de Neige', large, double white flowers; *C. punctata*, elongated bell-shaped pink and cream flowers, speckled crimson inside, 30cm/40cm (1ft/1½ft); *C. trachelium*, erect, with nettle-like leaves, white, lilac or mid-blue bell-shaped flowers in midsummer, 40-90cm/30cm (1½-3ft/1ft); *C. t.* 'Bernice', double, blue-lilac flowers, 40-60cm/30cm (1½-2ft/1ft).

Alpine varieties: *C.* 'Birch Hybrid', heart-shaped, toothed, slightly hairy bright green leaves, pale mauve bell-shaped flowers for a long period in summer, 10cm/20cm (4in/8in); *C. cochleariifolia*, mat-forming, bright glossy leaves, pendent bell-shaped light blue or lavender flowers from early to midsummer, 10cm/30cm (4in/1ft); *C. c.* var. *alba*, white flowers; *C. c.* 'Elizabeth Oliver', double pale blue flowers; *C.* 'E. K. Toogood', compact, heart-shaped leaves, pale blue star-shaped flowers in summer, 50cm/70cm (1¾ft/2¼ft); *C. garganica*, creeping, heart- or kidney-shaped mid-green leaves, clusters of star-shaped, bright blue-purple flowers in summer, 5cm/30cm (2in/1ft); *C.* x *haylodgensis* 'Plena', small, spreading, bowl-shaped lavender-blue flowers from early to midsummer, 15cm/20cm (6in/8in); *C. isophylla*, barely hardy trailing plant, superb for hanging baskets, saucer-shaped or star-shaped pale blue or white flowers in midsummer, 15-20cm/30cm (6-8in/1ft); *C. i.* 'Alba', pure white flowers; *C. i.* 'Kristal Blue', 'Kristal White', compact long-flowering varieties raised from seed, flowering the same year, blue or white flowers respectively, 15cm/30cm (6in/1ft); *C. portenschlagiana*, mat-forming, can be invasive although less so than the next species, clusters of tubular or funnel-shaped deep lavender flowers, mid- to late summer, 20cm/50cm (8in/1¾ft) or more; *C. poscharskyana*, spreading, often very invasive, star-shaped blue-violet flowers from summer to early autumn, 25cm/60cm (10in/2ft); *C. pulla*, low-growing, spreading perennial, solitary tubular, bell-shaped, deep violet or blue-purple flowers from late spring to early summer, 10cm/30cm (4in/1ft); *C. rotundifolia*, good for naturalising but can be invasive, pendent blue or white bell-shaped flowers from summer to early autumn, 12-30cm/12-30cm (5in-1ft/5-1ft).

above Like some other campanulas, *Campanula glomerata* can be invasive but it is worth finding a space large enough for it as it is a rich and individual plant.

Campsis *Trumpet Flower* Bignoniaceae

Large deciduous climber. Hardy. Climbs by aerial roots and suitable for training against a wall or fence or up a tree but in cold areas requires a sheltered position. Dark green pinnate leaves of oval, toothed leaflets; trumpet-shaped flowers, red, yellow and orange. Prune side-shoots to within 5cm (2in) of permanent framework in spring. Propagate by layering in autumn or winter, taking leaf-bud cuttings in early spring or softwood cuttings in early summer. ❀ *C. radicans*, terminal clusters of orange to red flowers from late summer to autumn, sometimes followed in hot summers by brown seed pods, 10m (33ft); *C. r.* f. *flava* (syn. 'Yellow Trumpet'), yellow flowers; *C.* x *tagliabuana* 'Madame Galen', glorious large clusters of flowers with yellow to orange tubes, scarlet lobes, from late summer to autumn, 10m (33ft).

Canna *Canna lily* Cannaceae

Medium/large rhizomatous perennial. Tender and best used as a tall focal point among bedding. Broad, deciduous, paddle-shaped bright green to bronze-purple leaves, lily- or iris-like cream, yellow-orange, orange-red or deep crimson flowers. Keep in containers in greenhouse over winter and divide established plants in spring. ❀ *C. indica*, dark green leaves, often flushed with bronze, iris-like red-orange flowers, sometimes marked or edged pink or yellow, from midsummer to mid autumn, 1.5m-2.2m/50cm (5ft-6¾ft/1¾ft); *C.* 'Lucifer', green leaves, red iris-like flowers, yellow margins from midsummer to early autumn,

right All forms of this extremely hardy little tree are pretty but the fine feathery leaves of *Caragana arborescens* 'Lorbergii' are especially attractive.

60cm/50cm (2ft/1¾ft); 'Golden Lucifer' is similar with gold-yellow flowers. *C.* 'Wyoming', bronze leaves, gladiolus-like orange flowers with purple veining and blotching from midsummer to early autumn, 1.8m/50cm (5½ft/1¾ft).

Capsicum *Pepper* Solanaceae

Tender annual and perennial vegetables, including chilli, bell and cayenne peppers. Those I describe here are all annuals and in cool temperate regions are only reliable in a greenhouse. Green leaves, yellow, white or pink bell-shaped or tubular flowers, solitary or in clusters, are followed by shiny fruit, usually green at first, later yellow, bright red, deep purple, brown or orange. Sow seeds in warmth in late winter. ❀ *C. annuum* Grossum Group, bell or sweet peppers, pimento, irregular bell-shaped lobed, slightly ovoid fruit. 'Ace', F1 green; 'Gypsy' F1 red; 'Salad Festival', very attractive mix of green, red, orange, yellow and deep purple fruits, but until you grow them, there's no way of knowing which colour each plant will produce; *C. a.* Longum Group includes the hot chilli peppers and cayenne pepper. Some like 'Apache' F1, have distinct names, others are vaguely called 'Cayenne' or 'Chilli' but check whether the strain you buy is mild, hot or very hot; and even then, don't entirely trust the description.

below *Capsicum* 'Salad Festival'. The problem with pepper varieties of mixed colours is that, as here, you can't guarantee to have chosen plants with the full range.

Caragana *Pea tree* Papilionaceae

Small/large deciduous shrub or small tree. Very hardy. Suitable for shrubberies or as isolated specimens and valuable in dry soil, cold, exposed or polluted areas. Among the great under-valued garden plants. Pinnate, sometimes feathery leaves, yellow, white or pink pea-like flowers, solitary or produced in clusters, in early summer, followed by seed-pods. No routine pruning. Take semi-ripe cuttings in late summer. ❀ *C. arborescens*, upright, slightly thorny shrub or small tree, elliptic or ovate green leaves, soft yellow flowers, 6m/4m (20ft/13ft); *C. a.* 'Walker', prostrate, weeping shrub, feathery leaves, usually grafted to make a lovely weeping standard.

Cardamine Brassicaceae

Annuals and hardy herbaceous perennials including some important weeds such as hairy bitter cress. Hardy. Those I describe here are all non-invasive herbaceous perennials. Simple pinnate or palmate leaves, clusters of single, four-petalled or double flowers in white and shades of pink, yellow and purple. Propagate by division after flowering, or in spring or autumn, or sow seed from early to midsummer, or autumn or spring in a cold-frame. ❀ *C. pentaphyllos*, toothed mid-green leaves, pale purple, pink or white inflorescences on nodding stems from late spring to early summer, 30-50cm/30cm (1-1¾ft/1ft); *C. pratensis* 'Flore Pleno', (Cuckoo Flower, Ladies' Smock), creeping, rosettes of deeply-cut dark green leaves, double pink or lilac flowers in late spring, 15cm/30cm (6in/1ft).

Cardiocrinum Liliaceae

Bulbous ornamental. Barely hardy to moderately hardy and ideal for large woodland gardens. Rosettes of dark green, heart-shaped basal leaves, large slender trumpet-shaped, fragrant flowers borne in clusters on long stems, followed by seed capsules. Bulbs die once the plant has flowered. Propagate by removing bulbils or sowing ripe seed in autumn in a cold-frame. ❀ *C. giganteum*, spectacular, like a huge lily, cream to white flowers streaked crimson-brown or purple inside, from mid- to late summer, 1.5-4m/45cm (5-13ft/1½ft).

Carex *Sedges* Cyperaceae

Small/large deciduous, semi-evergreen and evergreen grass-like perennials for borders, edges of waterways and pools; some species are also suitable for growing in containers. Rather coarse linear keeled leaves in tufts. Flowers are small catkin-like spikes; in some species both male and female flowers are produced on the same plant. Propagate by division from mid spring to early summer or from seed in early spring. ❀ *C. berggrenii*, evergreen, short blue-green to red-brown leaves, brown flower spikes in midsummer, 10cm/5cm (4in/2in); *C. elata* 'Aurea', (syn. *C. stricta* 'Bowles' Golden') bright gold-yellow leaves with green margins, erect black-brown flowers, male and female, in pointed clusters in summer, 60cm (2ft); *C. hachijoensis* 'Evergold', evergreen, dark green leaves striped cream-yellow in the centre, 30cm/35cm (1ft/1ft); *C. morrowii* 'Fisher's Form', evergreen, arching green leaves with cream margins, green-brown flower spikes, 40cm (11/2ft); *C. m.* 'Variegata', rough leaves with cream margins and stripes, rarely flowers, 35cm/25cm (1ft/10in); *C. ornithopoda* 'Variegata', small, compact tufts of low arching green leaves with yellow margins, 15cm/20cm (6in/8in); *C. pendula*, spreading, arching leaves, drooping red-brown 'fox-tail' flower spikes from late spring to midsummer, 1.4m/1.5m (4¾ft/5ft); *C. riparia* 'Variegata', vigorous, evergreen erect arching white-and-green leaves, dark brown flower spikes in spring, 60cm/30cm (2ft/1ft); *C. siderosticha* 'Variegata', deciduous, clump-forming, light green leaves streaked white, dark brown, insignificant flower spikes from late spring to summer, 30cm/40cm (1ft/1½ft); *C. testacea*, evergreen, fine, bright to olive green leaves, brown flowers spikes, 1.5m/60cm (5ft/2ft).

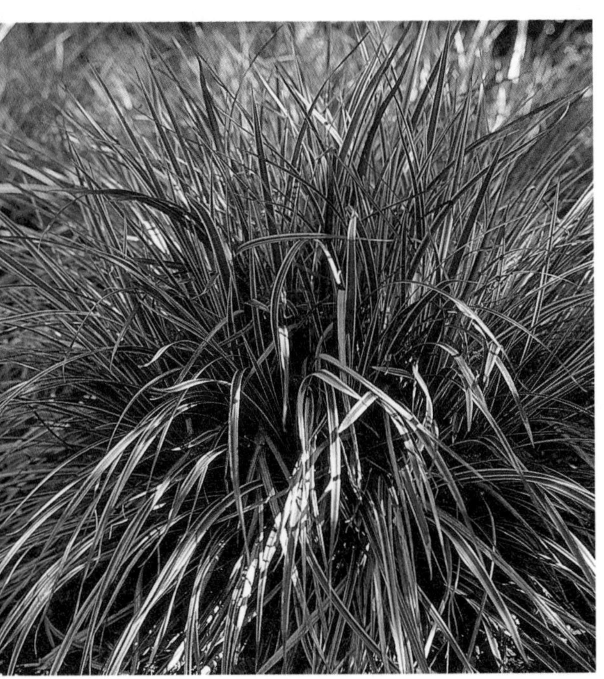

left *Carex morrowii* 'Fisher's Form'. Sedges are often confused with grasses but their leaves lend to be more coarse and tough, nonetheless pretty.

Carlina *Carline thistle* Asteraceae

Small annuals and perennials. Hardy. Those I describe here are perennials with rosettes of spiny, thistle-like leaves; spherical inflorescences surrounded by coloured bracts followed by seedheads, good for drying. Sow seeds in flowering positions or in a cold-frame in spring. ❀ *C. acaulis*, herbaceous, grey-green leaves, downy white beneath, stemless or short-stemmed purple-brown inflorescences, papery pink bracts, from midsummer to autumn, 10cm/25cm (4in/10in); *C. a.* ssp. *simplex*, dark green prickly leaves, pale inflorescences with silver bracts 8-12cm (3¼-5in) in diameter.

Carpenteria Hydrangeaceae

Medium evergreen shrub. Fairly hardy. Thrives best in a sunny sheltered position in a border or against a wall. Cut back old flowered shoots and some old growth after flowering. Take semi-ripe cuttings in summer or layer in winter. ❀ *C. californica*, erect growth, glossy lance-shaped leaves, very beautiful white, scented flowers, singly or in clusters, with golden yellow centres, from early to midsummer, 2m/2m (6½ft/6½ft).

Carpinus *Hornbeam* Corylaceae

Medium/large deciduous trees. Hardy. Suitable as a specimen tree in large gardens or for hedging. Toothed or entire veined, oval to ovate leaves give good autumn colour and then hang over winter, although less effectively than those of beech. Tiny green flowers form catkins in spring, followed (from female catkins) by tassels of winged seeds in autumn: male and female catkins are produced on

right *Caryopteris x clandonensis* 'Heavenly Blue'. It's a curious feature of several blue flowered shrubs that they are tolerant of alkaline soils and this lovely hybrid between two Oriental species is a fine example.

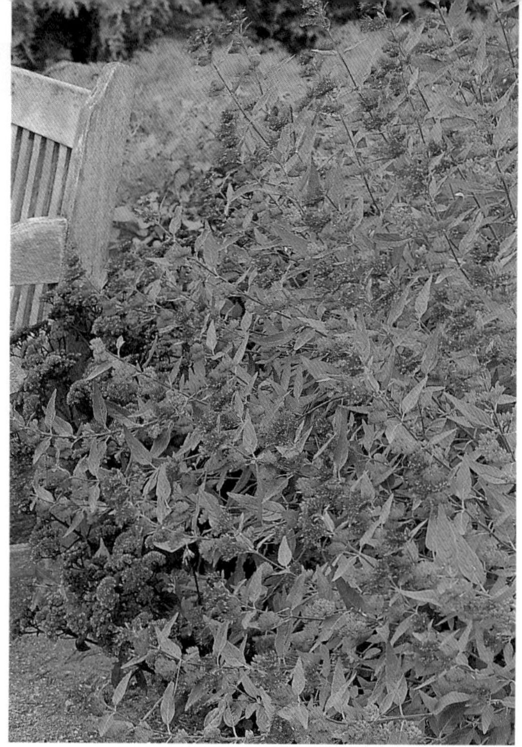

the same plant. No routine pruning, clip hedges in early summer and again in early autumn. Take hardwood cuttings in late autumn. ❀ *C. betulus*, finely serrated, ribbed, dark green leaves, yellow or red-brown in autumn, green female catkins 12cm (5in) long, yellow male catkins 3cm (1¼in) long, from late spring, 25m/20m (80ft/60ft); *C. b.* 'Fastigiata', bright, glossy green leaves turn gold and orange in autumn, 15m/12m (50ft/40ft).

Caryopteris Verbenaceae

Small deciduous shrubs. Barely hardy to hardy and will tolerate alkaline soil. Aromatic oval, pointed toothed dull grey-green leaves, clusters of small, fragrant, tubular, usually blue flowers from late summer to autumn. Prune hard in spring. Take softwood cuttings in spring or semi-ripe cuttings in early to mid-summer. ❀ *C.* x *clandonensis*, mound-forming, grey-green ovate to lance-shaped leaves, slightly toothed, hairy beneath, blue-purple flowers from late summer to early autumn, 1m/1.5m (3ft/5ft); *C.* x *c.* 'Heavenly Blue', grey leaves, dark blue flowers; *C.* x *c.* 'Worcester Gold', yellow leaves, pale lavender-blue flowers.

Cassiope Ericaceae

Small evergreen shrub. Hardy. Leaves tiny and superficially like *Calluna* but with large bell-shaped pink or, in the better forms, white flowers in spring and early summer that are closer in form to *Erica*. Requires acidic soil, well-drained with added humus, sheltered from full sun. Cut back flowering stems to within 1.5-2.5cm (½-1in) of previous year's growth in spring. Take semi-ripe cuttings in summer or remove layers. ❀ *C. lycopodioides*, a dense mat of foliage with white or cream flowers. 10cm/30cm (4in/1ft); *C.* 'Muirhead', abundant white flowers on pink stalks, 15cm/30cm (6in/1ft); *C.* 'Randle Cooke', white flowers, 15cm/30cm (6in/1ft).

Castanea *Sweet Chestnut* Fagaceae

Large deciduous trees and shrubs. Hardy. Best as a specimen tree in large gardens or in woodland. Ridged bark, toothed, veined leaves, tiny fragrant flowers on catkins followed (sometimes) by edible fruit (nuts). No routine pruning. Sow ripe seed in autumn. ❀ *C. sativa*, tough, glossy, oval dark green leaves, green-white catkins in midsummer, 30m/15m (100ft/50ft); *C. s.* 'Albomarginata', cream-white margins on leaves.

Catalpa *Indian Bean Tree* Bignoniaceae

Medium deciduous tree. Hardy. Beautiful as isolated specimens. Very large green leaves usually appear first in early summer. clusters of bell-shaped white flowers on mature trees, followed by long bean-like seed pods. No routine pruning. Sow seed in autumn or take softwood cuttings in late

far right *Catalpa bignonioides* 'Aurea'. Not the least of the appealing features of these lovely large-leaved trees is that they are remarkably drought-tolerant.

spring or early summer. ❀ *C. bignonioides*, heart-shaped deep green, aromatic leaves 30cm/20cm (1ft/8in), erect racemes of white frilly flowers with yellow and purple markings, similar to fox-gloves, from mid- to late summer, 15m/15m (50ft/50ft); *C. b.* 'Aurea', leaves bronze at first, later yellow.

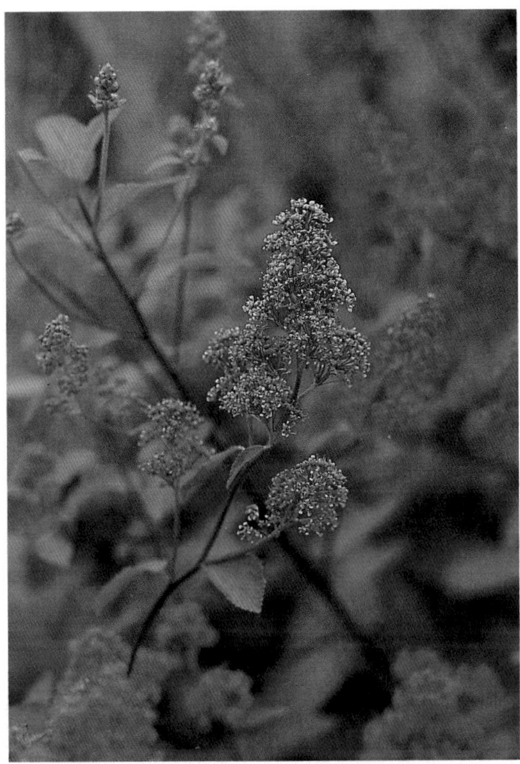

Ceanothus *Californian Lilac* Rhamnaceae

Small/large evergreen and deciduous shrubs and small trees. Fairly hardy to moderately hardy. Toothed leaves, tiny star-shaped flowers, white, pink or shades of blue, in umbels or dense panicles from spring to late summer. Thrives in fertile, well-drained soil in full sun. In cold areas the evergreen, spring-flowering species require the protection of a warm wall. Prune deciduous varieties hard in spring, early flowering evergreens against walls hard after flowering, free-standing evergreens lightly after flowering. Sow seeds in a seedbed or open frame in autumn, take semi-ripe cuttings from mid- to late summer.

Evergreen varieties: *C. arboreus* 'Trewithen Blue', oval to rounded, toothed dark green leaves, fragrant mid-blue pyramidal panicles, spring to early summer, 6m/8m (20ft/25ft); *C.* 'Autumnal Blue', branching habit, ovate, glossy green leaves, small, soft blue flowers, summer to autumn, 3m/3m (10ft/10ft); *C.* 'Blue Mound', toothed, glossy dark green leaves, large clusters of dark blue flowers, late spring, 1.5m/2m (5ft/6ft); *C.* 'Cascade', arching branches, glossy oblong finely toothed dark green leaves, light blue flowers, spring to early summer, 4m/4m (13ft/13ft); *C.* 'Concha', compact , narrow green leaves, abundant indigo flowers, late spring, 8m/1.5m (25ft/5ft); *C. impressus*, small crinkled leaves, deep lavender-blue flowers, mid-spring, 1.5m/1.5m (5ft/5ft); *C.* 'Italian Skies', small mid-green leaves, dark blue flowers, late spring, 1.5m/2.4m (5ft/6¾ft); *C. prostratus*, 'Puget Blue', low-growing, leathery, holly-like leaves, bright blue flowers, early summer, 2.1m/2.1m (6½ft/6½ft); *C. thyrsiflorus* var. *repens*, low, spreading, glossy toothed mid-green leaves, large clusters of pale to dark blue flowers, spring, 6m/6m (20ft/20ft).

Deciduous varieties: *C.* x *delileanus* 'Gloire de Versailles', erect, mid-green leaves, downy beneath, light blue flowers, midsummer to early autumn, 1.5m/1m (5ft/3ft); *C.* x *pallidus* 'Marie Simon', pale pink flowers, midsummer to early autumn, 1.5m/1.5m (5ft/5ft).

Cedrus *Cedar* Pinaceae

Large evergreen trees. Hardy. Beautiful specimen trees but only appropriate for large gardens. Dark green, yellow or silver-blue needles arranged in dense spirals. Male flowers, similar to catkins, and female flowers produced on the same tree. Female flowers are followed by barrel-shaped cones, green-purple at first, later brown. No routine pruning. Sow seeds in late autumn. ❀ *C. deodara* (Deodar), spreading branches, shoots droop at tips, leaves blue-green at first later mid-green, 40m/10m (130ft/33ft); *C. d.* 'Aurea', gold-yellow foliage in spring, green-yellow later; *C. libani* ssp. *atlantica* (Atlas Cedar), shoots turn up at tips, silver-grey bark, dark green or blue-green leaves, 40m/10m (130ft/33ft); *C. l.* ssp. *a.* Glauca Group, blue-grey foliage; *C. l.* ssp. *a.* 'Glauca Pendula', weeping branches to soil level, 4m/6m (13ft/20ft); *C. l.* ssp. *libani* (Cedar of Lebanon), spreading branches, horizontal shoots, green foliage, 40m/10m (130ft/33ft).

Celastrus *Bittersweet* Celastraceae

Deciduous and evergreen shrubs and climbers. Hardy. Simple leaves, usually toothed, small male and female flowers, often on the same plant, in summer, followed by fruit in autumn. No routine pruning but big plants may be cut hard back in spring. Sow seeds when ripe, or in an open frame in spring, take semi-ripe cuttings in summer or

left Californian lilacs exist confusingly as both deciduous and evergreen species. *Ceanothus x delilieanus* 'Gloire de Versailles' is one of the best hybrids, a cross between an evergreen and a deciduous species. Some forms of it are evergreen but this excellent variety tends to be more deciduous.

root cuttings in winter. ❀ *C. orbiculatus*, deciduous climber, round to elliptic leaves, toothed or scalloped, mid-green in summer, yellow in autumn, small, star-shaped green flowers in summer on separate plants are followed by yellow pods that split to reveal red to pink seeds, 14m (42ft); *C.* Hermaphrodite Group are self-fertile.

Celosia Amaranthaceae

Annuals, perennials and shrubs. Tender to barely hardy. Only the half-hardy bedding annuals are described here. Oval to lance-shaped leaves, tiny bright flowers in plume-shaped or bizarre and scarcely pretty cockscomb-like inflorescences in summer. Sow seeds in warmth from early to late spring. ❀ *C. argentea* var. *cristata* (Cockscomb), 'Jewel Box', dwarf, pointed, narrow leaves, velvety cockscomb-like inflorescences in mixed colours, including red, gold, yellow and pink, 23cm (9in); *C. a.* var. *c.* 'Kimono', dwarf, large inflorescences in mixed, bright colours including salmon-pink, yellow, rose-red and cream-white, 20cm (8in); *C. a.* var. *c.* 'New Look', dark red leaves, deep red plumes, 40cm (1½ft); *C. a.* var. *c.* 'Pink Flamingo'; *C. spicata* ('Prince of Wales' Feathers), 'Flamingo Feather', lance-shaped mid-green leaves, pink-tipped plumes, silver at base, 18cm/15cm (7in/6in).

Centaurea Asteraceae

Small/large annuals and herbaceous perennials. Barely hardy to moderately hardy. Simple, lobed leaves, flowers with thistle-like centres surrounded by thin petals. Sow seeds of annuals in growing positions in spring, perennials in a cold-frame in spring or divide established plants during the autumn months.

Perennial varieties: *C. bella*, feathery pale green leaves, white, hairy beneath, pale pink to purple-pink flowers, late spring to midsummer, 20-30cm/45cm (8-1ft/1½ft); *C. dealbata*, deeply cut, grey-green leaves, silver beneath, rose-pink flowers, early summer to autumn, 90cm/60cm (3ft/2ft); *C. d.* 'Steenbergii', deep pink flowers; *C. hypoleuca* 'John Coutts', spreading, elliptic to lance-shaped, light green leaves with wavy margins, grey-white beneath, fragrant pink flowers, summer, 60cm/45cm (2ft/1½ft); *C. macrocephala*, erect, rough, oblong, light green leaves, yellow flowers, mid- to late summer, glossy brown bracts, 1.5m/60cm (5ft/2ft); *C. montana*, lax, mid- to deep green, oblong to lanceolate leaves with white hairs, purple to violet-blue flowers, late spring to midsummer, 45cm/60cm (1½ft/2ft); *C. m. alba*, white flowers; *C. simplicicaulis*, mound-forming, deep green oblong to lyre-shaped leaves, grey, hairy beneath, abundant rose-pink flowers, late spring to midsummer, 25cm/60cm (10in/2ft).

Hardy Annual varieties: *C. cyanus* (Corn-flower), 'Black Ball', light chocolate-coloured flowers from early summer to early autumn, very good for cutting, 80cm/30cm (2½ft/1ft); *C. c.* 'Frosty', blue, red and pink shades tipped with white; *C. c.* 'Jubilee Gem', blue flowers, 30cm (1ft); *C. c.* 'Midget', mixed colours 15-20cm (6-8in); *C. c.* 'Polka Dot', blue, pink, carmine, white flowers, 35-45cm (1-1½ft).

right *Centaurea cyanus* 'Polka Dot'. Despite having a wider colour range than the wild species, I think these mixed varieties of cornflower really do conjure up a vision of an old meadow.

Centranthus *Valerian* Valerianaceae

Small bedding annuals and medium, hardy herbaceous perennials. Simple or pinnate leaves, red or white funnel-shaped flowers. Sow seed in a cold-frame in spring or divide established plants in early spring. ❀ *C. rubra*, perennial, lance-shaped to oval leaves, deep to mid-green, fragrant, small flowers, white, pale pink or dark red, from late spring to late summer, 1m/1m (3ft/3ft); *C. r. albus*, white flowers.

Cerastium *Chickweed* Caryophyllaceae

Small hardy annuals and perennials, including many weeds. Moderately hardy. Simple, grey or silver, usually hairy leaves, clusters of tiny star-shaped white flowers. Sow seeds in an open frame in autumn, divide in spring or take stem-tip cuttings in early summer. ❀ *C. tomentosum*, hardy evergreen perennial, can be very invasive, narrow, grey leaves, downy, white flowers throughout summer, 5-8cm (2-3¼in)/indefinite; *C. t.* var. *columnae,* more compact; *C. t.* 'Silberteppich', foliage silver grey.

Ceratostigma
Shrubby Plumbago Plumbaginaceae

Small deciduous, semi-evergreen or evergreen sub-shrubs and herbaceous perennials. Tender to hardy. In cold areas the hardier species require a sheltered position outside. Small green oval to ovate leaves, gloriously red or bronze in autumn, clusters of tubular, vivid blue flowers opening out from late summer to autumn. Prune to soil level in mid-spring. Propagate by softwood cuttings in spring, semi-ripe cuttings in summer, layering or remove suckers in autumn.
❀ *C. plumbaginoides* (syn. *Plumbago larpentiae*), low-growing hardy sub-shrub, ovate to lanceolate mid-green leaves on red stems, red in autumn, small clusters of bright blue flowers in summer, 4.5cm/30cm (1¾in/1ft); *C. willmottianum*, hardy deciduous shrub with bristly stems and leaves, pointed, diamond-shaped leaves, dark green with purple margins, red in autumn, small rich blue flowers in terminal clusters from late summer to autumn, 1m/1.5m (3ft/5ft).

Cercidiphyllum
Katsura Cercidiphyllaceae

Medium/large deciduous tree. Hardy/very hardy. A superb specimen tree, given space. More or less heart-shaped leaves change colour attractively from bronze in spring through blue-green to yellows, pinks and purple in autumn, accompanied by a curious sweet fragrance. Insignificant red male and female flowers on separate trees, clusters of seed pods sometimes form on female plants. No routine pruning. Propagate by hardwood cuttings in late autumn. ❀ *C. japonicum*, is the only species, 20m/ 5m (60ft/16ft); var. *magnificum* has a more golden autumn leaf colour and is worth searching for.

Cercis *Judas tree* Caesalpiniaceae

Small/medium deciduous trees. Moderately hardy. Striking plants because few hardy specimen trees have flowers of this colour. Broad, paper-thin, rounded, heart-shaped, bright green leaves, often yellow in autumn. Small groups of purple-pink flowers appear in spring on bare branches, followed by green seed pods. No routine pruning. Sow seeds in warmth in early spring, or take semi-ripe cuttings in summer. ❀ *C. canadensis*, in some areas may be slow to flower, heart-shaped pointed leaves, bronze at first, later green, then yellow in autumn, flowers white, deep red, purple or pink, 10m/10m (33ft/33ft); *C. c.* 'Forest Pansy', dark red-purple leaves all season, an improvement on the species; *C. siliquastrum*, rounded, blue-green leaves, bronze at first, yellow in autumn, magenta to pink flowers, sometimes white flowers, appear before and with the foliage, 10m/10m (33ft/33ft).

above Not all deep purple leaved trees are very pretty. *Cercis canadensis* 'Forest Pansy' is one of the better and less sombre ones.

Cestrum Solanaceae

Small/medium evergreen and deciduous shrubs and small trees. Tender to barely hardy. Only a few species hardy enough to be grown outside in mild areas in a warm sheltered position. All parts of the plant are toxic if eaten. Slender to narrow leaves, usually ovate to lance-shaped, clusters of tubular or funnel-shaped flowers, fragrant in some species, are followed by fruits. Cut back frost damaged shoots in spring. Sow seeds in a cold-frame in autumn or taking softwood cuttings in summer.
❀ *C.* 'Newellii', barely hardy arching evergreen shrub, ovate, dull green leaves, pitcher-shaped crimson flowers from summer to autumn, red-purple fruits, 3m/3m (10ft/10ft); *C. parqui*, barely hardy deciduous shrub, bright green willow-like leaves, tubular, night-scented green-yellow flowers, purple-brown and black fruits, 2m/2m (6½ft/6½ft).

below *Ceratostigma willmottianum*. What this stunning blue flowered shrub lacks in size, it makes up for in intensity of colour.

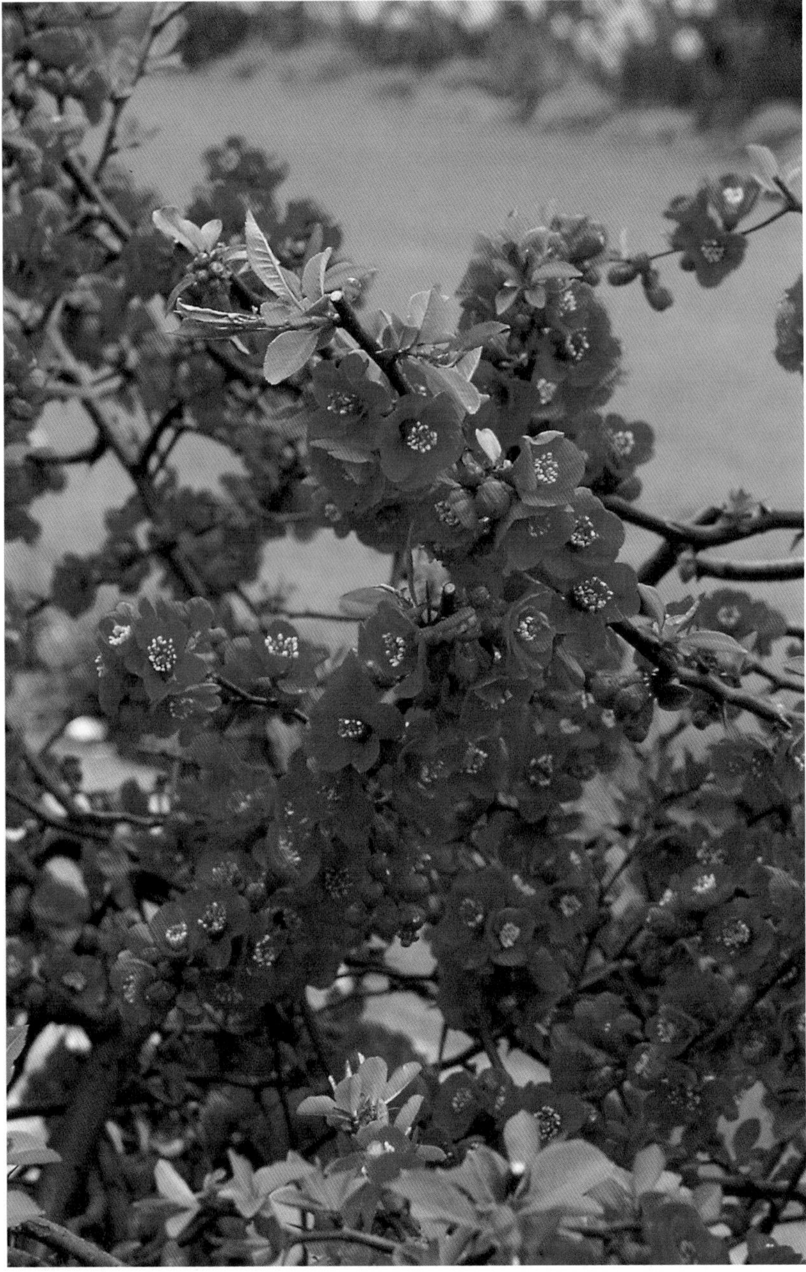

above Some of the ornamental quince varieties, like *Chaenomeles x superba* 'Knap Hill Scarlet', offer the first really bright red flowers of the season in most gardens.

right *Chamaecyparis lawsoniana* 'Ellwoodii'. As there are more varieties of this species than of any other garden tree, it's small wonder that you will be spoiled for choice.

Chaenomeles
Ornamental Quince, Japanese Quince Rosaceae

Medium/large deciduous shrubs. Hardy. Traditionally grown against a wall but I think very effective free-standing. Toothed simple leaves, double or single cup-shaped flowers, white or shades of red or pink followed by more or less edible aromatic purple, green or yellow fruit in autumn. Thrives in fertile, well-drained soil in sun or partial shade. No routine pruning on free-standing plants; on wall trained plants, cut back previous season's growth hard in spring. Sow seeds in a seedbed or layer in autumn, or take semi-ripe cuttings summer. ❀ *C. speciosa* thorny medium-sized shrub, 2.5m/5m (8ft/16ft); *C. s.* 'Geisha Girl', double apricot-peach flowers; *C. s.* 'Moerloosei' (syn. 'Apple Blossom'), large white flowers tinged pink; *C. s.* 'Nivalis'. pure white flowers; *C. s.* 'Simonii', double, dark red flowers; *C.* x *superba* 'Crimson and Gold', compact medium-sized, deep crimson with yellow centres, 1m/2m (3ft/6½ft); *C.* x *s.* 'Knap Hill Scarlet', bright red flowers; *C.* x *s* 'Pink Lady', dark pink flowers, earlier than most; *C.* x *s.* 'Rowallane', scarlet flowers.

Chaenorrhinum
Dwarf Snapdragon Scrophulariaceae

Small annuals and perennials. Fairly hardy. Simple entire leaves, two-lipped snapdragon-like flowers in shades of blue, purple and yellow. Sow seeds in a cold-frame in autumn or winter. ❀ *C. origanifolium* (syn. *Linaria origanifolium*), perennial, long oval leaves, dramatic lilac-blue flowers with dark stripes, and white or light yellow on the lip, from late spring throughout the summer months, 10-20cm/25-30cm (4-8in/10-1ft); *C. o.* 'Blue Dream', clear blue flowers.

Chaerophyllum Apiaceae

Small/medium annuals, biennials and perennials, including the bulbous vegetable, turnip-rooted chervil, not the herb chervil which is *Anthriscus* (see page 26). Moderately hardy. Fern-like leaves, umbels of small pink, white or yellow flowers. Sow seeds in a cold-frame when ripe or in early spring,

or divide established plants in spring or autumn. *C. hirsutum* 'Roseum', perennial, feathery, hairy dark green leaves, umbels of tiny lilac-mauve flowers on branched stems in early summer, 60cm/30cm (2ft/1ft). *C. bulbosum* (Turnip rooted chervil) is a tuberous rooted biennial vegetable, sow in growing positions in rich soil in spring for harvest late summer. 2m/75cm (6½ft/2½ft).

Chamaecyparis
False Cypress Cupressaceae

Small/large evergreen trees. Hardy to very hardy. Extremely varied in shape, size and colour; *C. lawsoniana* alone has given rise to more varieties than any other cultivated tree and is one of the most widely grown and useful garden plants. Immature

leaves are flat, awl-shaped and frond-like, later small, scale-like, carried in sprays. Female cones are globular and appear in autumn; spherical male cones appear in spring. Flowers are insignificant and colours in varieties' descriptions below refer to foliage. Most thrive best in sun or partial shade in good, more or less neutral well-drained soil but tolerate more acidic conditions; those with gold foliage usually require full sun to retain their colour. No pruning but all forms respond well to clipping. Propagation isn't easy but take softwood cuttings in spring.

❀ *C. lawsoniana* (Lawson Cypress) 'Aurea Densa', dwarf, slow-growing, rounded-conical, golden, 2m (6½ft); *C. l.* 'Chilworth Silver', dwarf, slow-growing, upright, blue-green when young, 1.5m (5ft); *C. l.* 'Columnaris', narrowly columnar, blue-grey, 10m/1m (33ft/3ft); *C. l.* 'Ellwoodii', slow-growing, broadly columnar, grey-green, steel blue in winter, 3m (10ft); *C. l.* 'Ellwood's Gold', compact, slow-growing, yellow-green, gold tipped, 5m (16ft); *C. l.* 'Fletcheri'. grey-green feathery, bronzed in winter, 6m (20ft); *C. l.* 'Gimbornii', dwarf, blue-green tipped with mauve in winter, 2m/1.8m (6½ft/5½ft); *C. l.* 'Green Hedger', rich green, good for hedges and screens, 25m/4m (80ft/13ft); *C. l.* 'Minima Aurea', dwarf, slow-growing, soft bright yellow showing gold on the tips, 80cm (21/2ft); *C. l.* 'Minima Glauca', dwarf, slow-growing, sea green, 2m (6½ft); *C. l.* 'Pembury Blue', narrow, silver-blue, 15m (50ft); *C. l.*'Pygmaea Argentea', dark, blue-green tipped silver-white, 2m/75cm (6½ft/2½ft); *C. l.* 'Wisselii', narrow, fast-growing tree, fern-like blue-green, masses of tiny red male cones in spring, 10m/2m (33ft/6½ft); *C. nootkatensis* 'Pendula', pendulous, dark green, 30m/8m (100ft/25ft); *C. obtusa* (Hinoki Cypress), 'Crippsii', slow-growing, rich gold, 15m/8m (50ft/25ft); *C. o.*'Nana', dwarf, slow-growing, very dark green, 75cm/100cm (2½ft/3ft); *C. o.* 'Nana Gracilis', dark, glossy green, 2m (6½ft); *C. pisifera* (Sawara Cypress), 'Boulevard', conical, soft steel blue with white stripes on undersides, tinged purple in winter, best in light shade, attractive when young but becomes misshapen with age, 10m (33ft); *C. p.* 'Filifera Aurea', gold-yellow, needs protection from full sun, 2.4m/4.5m (6¾ft/14½ft); *C. p.* 'Nana Aureovariegata', dwarf, slow-growing, dark green with golden tinges, 60cm/1.2m (2ft/4ft); *C. thyoides* (White Cypress), 'Ericoides', dwarf, soft grey-green, bronze or purple in winter, 1.5m/80cm (5ft/2½ft).

Chamaemelum *Camomile* Asteraceae

Small annuals and perennial herbs. Moderately hardy. Aromatic, feathery leaves, small daisy-like white flowers with yellow centres. Sow seeds in growing positions in spring or divide. ❀ *C. nobile* (syn. *Anthemis nobilis*), mat-forming finely-cut bright green, apple-scented leaves, abundant single flowers in summer, 30cm/45cm (1ft/1½ft); *C. n.* 'Flore Pleno', shaggy, cream-white, button-like double flowers, 15cm/45cm (6in/1½ft); *C. n.* 'Treneague', mossy, non-flowering variety with strongly-scented foliage, the species suitable for camomile lawns, must be raised from cuttings, 10cm/45cm (4in/1½ft).

above *Chamaemelum nobile* 'Treneague'. If you hanker for a camomile lawn, this non-flowering variety raised from cuttings is the plant you need.

left *Chamaecyparis pisifera* 'Filifera Aurea'. The varieties of *Chamaecyparis* with narrowly pendent shoots are among the best and this golden form is particularly good away from fierce sun.

right *Chimonanthus praecox.* The name *praecox* means early, an appropriate choice for this delightful winter-flowering shrub.

Chelidonium
Greater Celandine Papaveraceae

Small/medium short-lived perennials. Moderately hardy. Excellent for wild-flower gardens. Pinnately lobed grey-green leaves, yellow summer flowers. Brittle stems snap easily and contact with the orange sap may cause skin irritation. Sow seeds in growing positions in spring. ❀ *C. majus*, umbels of four-petalled, poppy-like flowers, self-seeds freely, but it is rarely invasive enough to be a problem 60cm/20cm (2ft/8in); *C. m.* 'Flore Pleno', double yellow flowers.

Chelone *Shellflower* Scrophulariaceae

Small/medium hardy herbaceous perennials. Simple toothed leaves, clusters of curious tubular, two-lipped flowers on erect stems from late summer to mid-autumn. Sow seeds in a cold-frame in early spring, take soft-wood cuttings in summer or divide established plants in spring. ❀ *C. glabra* (syn. *C. obliqua* var. *alba*) lance-shaped, mid-green leaves, virtually stalkless, white flowers, sometimes flushed pink, with white beards, 60-100cm/45cm (2ft-3ft/1½ft); *C. obliqua*, lance-shaped dark green veined leaves, deep rose or purple flowers, yellow beard, followed by seedheads, 40-60cm/30cm (1½-2ft/1ft).

Chenopodium Chenopodiaceae

Small/large annual and perennial herbs and sub-shrubs. Very hardy. Thrive in full sun or light shade in rich, well-drained soil. Sow seed in growing positions in spring. ❀ Only important cultivated species is the salad herb *C. bonus-henricus* (Good King Henry, Fat Hen), a large perennial often grown as an annual, triangular, dark green, spinach-like leaves, tiny flowers in leafless spikes but these are best removed when the leaves are pulled for kitchen use; 75cm/30cm (2½ft/1ft).

Chiastophyllum Crassulaceae

Small evergreen alpine. Moderately hardy. Succulent leaves, tiny yellow flowers in pendent inflorescences. Sow seeds in a cold-frame in autumn, divide established plants after flowering or take side-shoot cuttings in early summer. ❀ *C. oppositifolium* (syn. *C. simplicifolium*), ovate scalloped pale green leaves, bell-shaped deep yellow flowers in late spring; *C. o.* 'Jim's Pride', leaves splashed with cream, brighter yellow flowers, 15-20cm/15cm (6-8in/6in).

Chimonanthus
Wintersweet Calycanthaceae

Medium to large deciduous or evergreen shrubs. Barely hardy and really best grown against a sunny wall but one of the lovelier winter-flowering shrubs. No routine pruning. Sow seeds in warmth in winter or layer in mid-summer. ❀ *C. praecox*, deciduous, glossy, rough mid-green lance-shaped leaves, smooth beneath, fragrant, pendent, waxy bell-shaped yellow flowers, brown or purple inside, appear in mid-winter, 4m/3m (13ft/10ft).

Chionanthus Oleaceae

Small/large deciduous trees and shrubs. Tender to moderately hardy. Leaves often downy when immature, yellow in autumn. Four-petalled flowers, strap-shaped, in terminal clusters in midsummer, followed, especially after warm summers, by blue-purple or blue-black plum-like fruit when both male and female flowers are present. Sow seed in a cold-frame in autumn or layer. ❀ *C. virginicus*, deciduous shrub or small tree, glossy, dark green elliptic leaves, fragrant white flowers followed by small blue-black fruit, 4m/3m (13ft/10ft).

Chionodoxa

Glory of the Snow Hyacinthaceae

Small bulbous ornamental. Barely hardy to moderately hardy. One of spring's most under-appreciated delights; good for rock gardens and for naturalising among gravel and under trees but self-seeds freely and can be invasive in small areas. Linear, mid-green basal leaves, clusters of star-shaped flowers in early spring. Divide clumps after flowering, sow ripe seed in a cold-frame. ❀ *C. luciliae*, dwarf, two grass-like leaves, light blue flowers with white centres, 15cm/15cm (6in/6in); *C. l.* Gigantea Group, (syn. *C. gigantea*), rather larger overall, blue to blue-violet flowers.

Chionohebe

Scrophulariaceae

Small evergreen alpine. Moderately hardy. Tiny mat- or cushion-forming green leaves, small white or purple flowers in spring. Divide established plants after flowering or in spring. ❀ *C. pulvinaris* (syn. *Pygmaea pulvinaris*), grey-green hairy leaves, white flowers from mid-to late spring, 4cm/15cm (1½in/6in).

Choisya

Mexican Orange Rutaceae

Medium evergreen shrubs. Barely hardy to moderately hardy and best in a slightly sheltered border or against a wall. Palmate, glossy, aromatic green or yellow leaves, fragrant, white, star-shaped flowers, solitary or in clusters. No routine pruning. Take semi-ripe or soft-wood cuttings in summer. ❀ *C.* 'Aztec Pearl', small, leaves of slender, light green leaflets, white, pink-flushed flowers, almond-scented, in late spring, repeat flowers in late summer and autumn, 2.5m/2.5m (8ft/8ft); *C. ternata*, glossy, dark green leaves, clusters of white, scented flowers from late spring to summer, again in autumn, 2.5m/2.5m (8ft/8ft); *C. t.* 'Sundance', bright yellow to yellow-green leaves, flowers rarely but has unfortunately begun to supplant the green form in modern gardening.

Chrysanthemum

Chrysanthemum Asteraceae

Small/medium half-hardy bedding annuals and medium/large barely hardy perennials. For several years, perennial chrsyanthemums were placed in the genus *Dendranthema*, the genus *Chrysanthemum* itself being limited to annuals but they have now been re-unified. Annuals have a bushy habit, clusters of single, white or yellow flowers in spring and summer, or from summer to autumn. Sow seeds in a cold-frame in early spring or in flowering positions in spring and early summer. In very mild areas they may also be sown in autumn for an early display in spring. ❀ *C. carinatum* 'Court Jester', fast-growing, bright green finely divided leaves, bright yellow, orange-red or white flowers with red or orange rings, in summer, 60cm/30cm (2ft/1ft); *C. c.*'Polar Star', white flowers with brown centres ringed with yellow; *C. coronarium* 'Primrose Gem', pale green fern-like leaves, daisy-like, single, semi-double and double

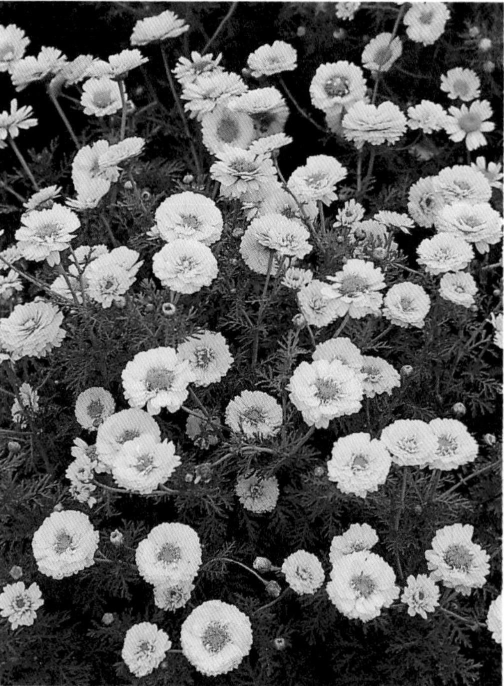

above *Chrysanthemum* 'Shirley Glorious'. The naming of chrysanthemum varieties is complex: this variety is an Early Flowering Outdoor Intermediate Medium Flowered.

far left *Chionodoxa luciliae*. This very pretty little early spring bulb self-seeds freely in my gravel garden but it is so endearing that I really can't bear to weed out the seedlings.

left *Chrysanthemum coronarium* 'Primrose Gem'. I always pinch out the centre of the young plants of this lovely annual to help encourage a bushy and more floriferous habit.

right *Chrysanthemum* 'Purple Princess'. The beautifully incurved petals are a feature of many of the very finest chrysanthemums.

primrose-yellow flowers with golden centres, in my experience, the prettiest and best, 30-45cm/40cm (1-1½ft/1½ft); *C. segetum*, fast-growing, good for wild-flower gardens, oblong to ovate grey-green leaves, solitary, single daisy-like flowers in summer, 30cm (1ft).

Perennial varieties: The perennials are bushy, semi-evergreens derived from *C.* x *morifolium* with indented, strongly spice-scented leaves and with stems that soon become woody towards the base. The flowers are double, or, in a few cases, single, but vary widely in size and form (see below) and are quite invaluable for cutting for indoor display. All require full sun and a rich, well-drained, more or less neutral soil or compost and are most simply propagated by taking basal softwood cuttings in spring. They fall naturally into two main groups. The outdoor varieties are planted outside in the spring but are generally lifted in autumn, the top growth cut down and the rootstocks (or stools) taken into a cold-frame or other protection to be kept dormant over winter. The greenhouse varieties may be grown permanently under protection in containers or soil borders but are more usually grown in containers which are kept outside during the summer and then taken into a greenhouse in early autumn for flowering. Outdoor varieties may be integrated with other plants in borders but I find the inevitable disturbance when they are lifted means they are better kept apart. All chrysanthemums will flower better if they are stopped (the central shoot pinched out) and/or disbudded. This is done in the cause of producing either a larger number of flowers (and a 'spray' habit) or, conversely, and especially for exhibition purposes, few but larger flowers. Outdoor varieties for normal display are conveniently stopped once to give a bushier plant but exhibitors develop carefully tried regimes of repeated stopping and disbudding of indoor varieties to achieve their perfect blooms.

Hybrids: Probably more varieties of chrysanthemum have been raised over the years than of any other garden plant. There are huge numbers available at any one time, each generally from only one or two nurseries, and they are also often sold for very short periods and are replaced by others within one or two seasons. Lists of individual varieties are of little value and I have restricted the descriptions here to the features of the main flower groups, most of which are available for both Outdoor and Indoor types: Incurved, a more or less spherical, large flower head with florets tightly overlapping towards the top; Reflexed, a more or less spherical flower head with the florets overlapping downwards towards the stem; Intermediate, more or less spherical flower head with the florets loosely turned upwards, not as tight as an incurved head; Anemone Flowered: a daisy-like head with a distinct division into a large central disc of tubular florets and petal-like outer ray florets; Single: a daisy-like head with a small central disc of tubular florets and outer ray florets; Pompon: small, tightly spherical head with florets closely overlapping downwards towards the stem; Charm: large numbers of small, daisy-like single lowers, rather in the manner of a Michaelmas daisy.

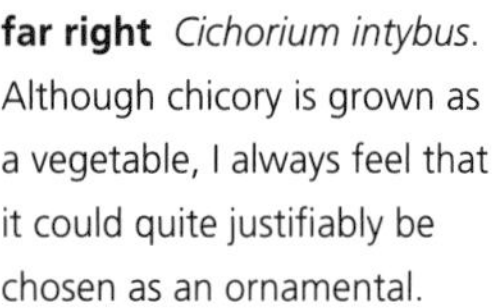

far right *Cichorium intybus*. Although chicory is grown as a vegetable, I always feel that it could quite justifiably be chosen as an ornamental.

above *Cimicifuga racemosa* is an attractive plant provided it is placed in the centre of the border where its unpleasant smell isn't apparent.

Chrysogonum *Golden Knee* Asteraceae

Small rhizomatous perennial. Moderately hardy. Low-growing and spreading, stays evergreen in mild areas, good for ground cover in damp, shaded places. May need winter protection in very cold areas. Sow ripe seed in a cold-frame or divide established plants in spring or summer. ❀ *C. virginianum*, oval, hairy, bright green leaves, single, gold-yellow, five-'petalled' flowers with yellow centres from late spring to early autumn, 24cm/60cm (9½in/2ft).

Chrysolepis *Golden Chestnut* Fagaceae

Small evergreen trees and shrubs. Barely hardy to moderately hardy and good for coastal areas. In cold places, requires some shelter. Shiny deep green leaves with yellow hairs beneath, cream-white catkins with male and female flowers in summer, sometimes followed by spiky fruit. No routine pruning. Sow ripe seed in a cold-frame in late autumn or in warmth in late winter. ❀ *C. chrysophylla*, oval, tapered, dark green leaves, fragrant catkins in summer, followed in following year by green chestnut-like fruit containing edible nuts, 12m/12-30m (40ft/40-100ft).

Chusquea Poaceae

Large evergreen bamboo. Moderately hardy. Slow-growing and clump-forming. Round, glossy smooth canes, oval or linear mid-green to dark green leaves, culm sheaths shiny white when young. Sow seeds in warmth or transplant sections of the rhizome in spring. ❀ *C. culeou*, erect, yellow-green to olive-green canes, linear, mid-green leaves, 6m/2.5m (20ft/8ft).

Cicerbita *Sow Thistle* Asteraceae

Large hardy herbaceous perennials. Best in informal plantings and woodland gardens. Rosettes of mid-green, finely divided basal leaves, smaller stem leaves. Thistle- or dandelion-like blue, violet or yellow inflorescences on tall stems in midsummer. All forms can self-seed rather aggressively but the impact of this can be lessened if the seed heads are removed before seed dispersal. Sow seeds in a cold-frame in spring or divide. ❀ *C. alpina* (syn. *Lactuca alpina*), erect, branching, mid-green lobed leaves, thistle-like pale blue inflorescences, 2.5m/60cm (8ft/2ft); *C. plumieri*, (syn. *Lactuca plumieri*), clump-forming, mid-green leaves, blue inflorescences from midsummer to early autumn, 1.3m/45cm (4½ft/1½ft).

Cichorium *Chicory, Endive* Asteraceae

Annuals and perennials. Moderately hardy. Large toothed mid-green leaves, very pretty, thistle-like or dandelion-like blue, sometimes white or pink flowers that close by mid-day. ❀ *C. intybus* (Chicory), tall perennial grown as an annual, toothed, inversely lance-shaped basal leaves, clusters of sky-blue, sometimes white, loosely dandelion-like flowers in summer; to grow as a vegetable, sow seeds in spring and harvest roots in autumn, store them in sand in dark and warmth; up to three to four weeks later the shoots or 'chicons' are ready for use, 1.2m/60cm (4ft/2ft); *C. i. album*, candelabra-like clusters of semi-double white flowers from early to midsummer, 60-120cm (2-4ft); *C. i. roseum*, small pink dandelion-like flowers in midsummer, 90cm (3ft). *C. endivia* (Endive), very similar in flower to *C. intybus* but annual; to grow as a salad crop, treat as late summer/autumn lettuce; two main groups of varieties: Broad-leaved, hardier, 'No. 5' (syn. 'Batavian Broad Leaved'); Curled, more flavour, 'Ione'.

Cimicifuga *Bugbane* Ranunculaceae

Large herbaceous perennials. Moderately hardy to very hardy. Best in a damp border or woodland. Light green, finely divided leaves, sometimes changing colour in autumn. Long spikes of star-shaped white or cream flowers. Both leaves and flowers are good for cutting. Sow ripe seed in autumn or divide established plants between autumn and spring. ❀ *C. racemosa*, clump-forming, ovate leaves divided into deeply toothed leaflets, white flowers in autumn are unpleasantly scented (like bugs), 1.2m-2.2m/60cm (4-6¾ft/2ft); *C. simplex* 'White Pearl', pale green leaves, flower buds pale green, opening to white flowers on arching stems, followed by lime-green seed-heads, 60-90cm (2-3ft); *C. s.* var. *simplex*, purple foliage.

right *Clarkia grandiflora* 'Azalea Flowered'. Clarkias are valuable cut flowers for the summer; although many gardeners will be more familiar with types like this under their old name *Godetia*.

below *Cistus* x *dansereaui* 'Decumbens'. Cistus always conjure up visions of hot Mediterranean hillsides; some such as 'Decumbens' are low-growing and especially valuable in smaller gardens.

Cirsium *Plume Thistle* Asteraceae

Large biennials and herbaceous perennials. Moderately hardy. The genus includes some pernicious weeds such as *C. arvense*, Creeping Thistle, but those I recommend are not invasive. Deeply lobed hairy leaves with bristly margins. Pincushion-like red, yellow, purple or white inflorescences in summer. Divide established plants in autumn or spring or sow seed in warmth in spring. ❀ *C. japonicum* 'Rose Beauty', short-lived, glossy dark green leaves, deep carmine inflorescences appear singly or in clusters from early to mid-summer, 1-2m/60cm (3ft-6½ft/2ft); *C. rivulare* 'Atropurpureum', spreading, glossy, dark green prickly leaves, deep crimson inflorescences, 1.2m/60cm (4ft/2ft).

Cistus *Rock Rose* Cistaceae

Small/large evergreen shrubs. Barely to moderately hardy. Suitable for dry sunny banks, containers, path edging and borders and especially good in coastal areas. Among the most characteristic shrubs of the Mediterranean. Often short-lived. Leaves oval to lance-shape. Simple rose-like flowers, each lasting one day, are produced throughout the summer. Thrives in poor, well-drained soil in full sun, sheltered from east and north winds. No routine pruning. Sow seeds in spring or take softwood cuttings in summer. ❀ *C.* x *aguilarii* 'Maculatus', sticky, bright green leaves, clusters of white flowers with crimson blotches at base of petals, yellow centres, 1.2m/1.2m (4ft/4ft); *C.* x *cyprius*, sticky, oblong-lance-shaped,olive-green leaves, white flowers, crimson-maroon blotches, 2m/2m (6½ft/6½ft); *C.* x *dansereaui*, small, dark green oblong-lance-shaped leaves, clusters of white flowers, pale yellow and crimson blotches, 1m/1m (3ft/3ft); *C.* x *d.* 'Decumbens', low, spreading, 60cm (2ft); *C.* 'Elma', glossy, deep green leaves, clusters of pure white flowers with yellow centres, 2m/2m (6½ft/6½ft); *C.* 'Grayswood Pink', low-growing, small grey-green leaves, pale pink flowers, 60cm/60cm (2ft/ 2ft); *C.* x *hybridus* (syn. *C.* x *corbariensis*), small, coarse, wrinkled leaves, dark green, paler beneath, white flowers, yellow blotches and centres, singly or in clusters, buds flushed red, 1m/1.5m (3ft/5ft); *C. ladanifer*, dull green leathery leaves, ovate-lance-shaped, clusters of white flowers with maroon blotches, yellow centres, 2m/1.5m (6½ft/5ft); *C.* 'Peggy Sammons', oval, grey-green leaves, abundant clusters of pale purple-pink flowers, 1m/1m (3ft/3ft); *C.* x *pulverulentus* 'Sunset' (syn. *C. crispus* 'Sunset'), oblong, grey-green leaves, abundant clusters of rose-pink flowers with yellow centres, 60cm/90cm (2ft/3ft); *C.* x *purpureus*, oblong-lance-shaped dark green leaves, clusters of dark pink flowers with crinkled petals, maroon blotches, 1m/1m (3ft/3ft); *C.* x *skanbergii*, oblong-lance-shaped grey-green leaves, clusters of pale pink flowers, 75cm/90cm (2½ft/3ft).

Clarkia *Clarkia, Godetia* Onagraceae

Small/medium hardy bedding annuals. Slender, erect bushy plants with branched stems. Some species and varieties were formerly listed as species of *Godetia*. Grey to green lance-shaped to elliptic leaves, sometimes toothed, clusters of paper-thin, smooth-textured azalea-like flowers, usually funnel-shaped, in pastel shades from mid-summer to early autumn. Excellent summer annuals and unexpectedly good for cutting. Thrive in fairly fertile, moist but well-drained soil in sun

or partial shade. Sow seeds in growing positions in early spring or autumn or in warmth in spring.
❀ *C. bottae*, long, narrow leaves, spikes of cup-shaped lavender-blue flowers with a white base, 25cm/40cm (10in/1½ft); *C. b.* 'Pink Joy', pink flowers; *C. concinna* 'Pink Ribbons', feathery, deep rose flowers, 30cm (1ft); *C. grandiflora* (syns. *C. amoena, Godetia grandiflora*),'Bornita', cup-shaped flowers in shades of red, orange or white, 25cm (10in); *C. g.* 'Cattleya', orchid pink, 30-36cm (1-1¼ft); *C. g.* 'Duchess of Albany', satin white, slightly frilled petals, 30cm (1ft); *C. g.* 'Satin Pink' F1, dwarf, bushy, single pink flowers, 20cm (8in); *C. g.* 'Azalea Flowers', white or pink semi-double flowers, 40-50cm (16-13/4ft); *C. pulchella*, narrow, pointed leaves, spikes of four-petalled, cup-shaped lilac flowers, 40cm/20cm (1½ft/8in); *C. p.* 'Lace', semi-double flowers in pink, purple and white; *C. p.* 'Snowflake', double white flowers; *C. rubicunda*, prostrate habit, cerise pink or mauve with a red base, 30-50cm (1-1¾ft); *C. unguiculata* (syn. *C. elegans*) 'Apple Blossom', lance-shaped, elliptic to ovate leaves, pink flowers, 30-100cm (1-3ft); *C. u.* 'Asterix', dwarf, pink, mauve or red flowers, 30cm/25cm (1ft/10in); *C. u.* 'Rhapsody'; *C. u.* 'Royal Bouquet', frilly, double flowers resembling small hollyhocks, pink, mauve or red, 90cm/30cm (3ft/1ft).

Clematis — Ranunculaceae

Small/large deciduous and evergreen climbers and herbaceous perennials; for me and countless other gardeners, the finest of all groups of climbing ornamentals. Barely hardy to very hardy. Climbing species and varieties are suitable for growing up and over pergolas, buildings, archways, large shrubs and trees; some are suitable for training against a trellised wall. Most have simple, hairy or hairless, palmate or pinnate leaves and scramble or twine by means of their leaf tendrils. Flowers vary from small bells to large saucer-shaped blooms, some scented, and are borne singly or in clusters. They are available, depending on type, in a wide range of colours, including white, cream, yellow, blue, violet, purple, red, pink and mauve. Clematis thrive best in rich, fairly light, slightly alkaline soil, usually with their heads in full sun and the roots shaded. For the purposes of pruning and other aspects of cultivation the species and varieties are divided into three groups. according to their flowering season: Group 1 are those that flower early in the year on wood produced the previous season, and are pruned lightly immediately after flowering; Group 2, those that flower in summer on the previous season's wood and are pruned fairly lightly in early spring prior to the appearance of new growth; and Group 3, those that flower in late summer on the current year's growth and are also pruned in early spring, but more severely than those in Group 2. Take semi-ripe cuttings in late summer, layer or sow ripe seed. Most forms strike readily from cuttings although some of the large-flowered hybrids are frustratingly tricky.(of species and near species) in a cold-frame.
❀ The clematis that I describe below are grouped together under the headings: early-flowering species; early-flowering hybrids; later-flowering hybrids; late-flowering species; evergreen species and herbaceous perennials.

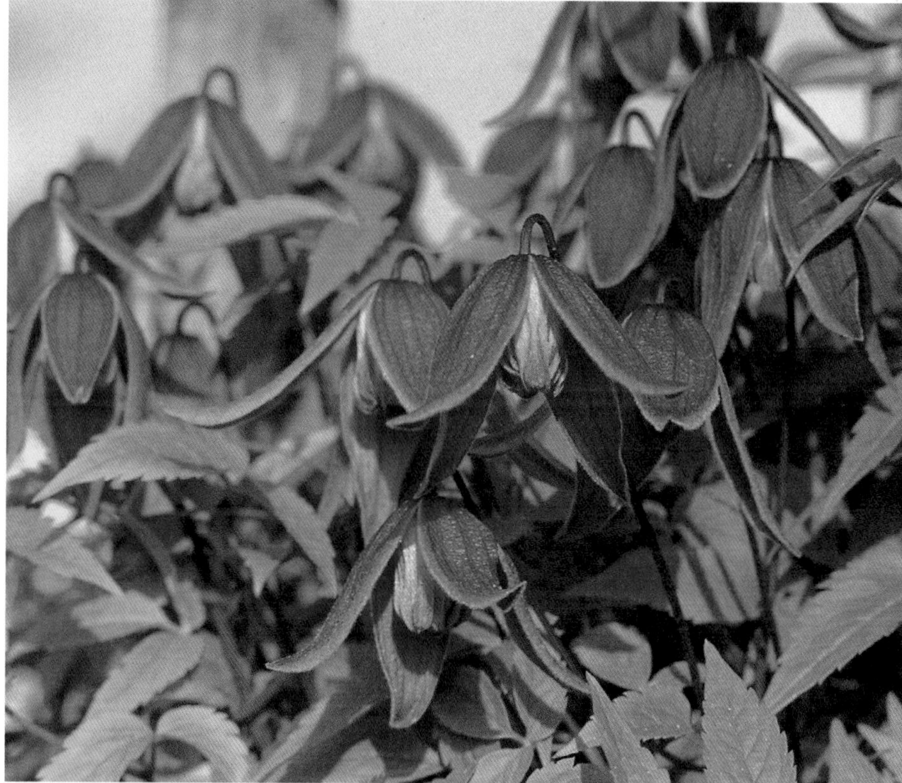

above *Clematis alpina* 'Helsingborg'. I find the bell-flowered varieties of *C. alpina* among the best of all the early flowering clematis, especially in limited space.

Early-flowering species

Clematis alpina (Group 1), hardy with open, bell-shaped white-centred blue flowers, from spring to early summer, followed by fluffy seedheads, 2-3m/1.5m (6½-10ft/5ft). *C. a.* 'Columbine', pale lavender, white stamens; *C. a.* 'Frances Rivis', large flowers, mid-blue, slightly twisted; *C. a.* 'Helsingborg', large flowers, dark blue, light brown-purple stamens; *C. a.* 'Pamela Jackman', blue, black and cream anthers; *C. a* . 'Rosy Pagoda, pale pink; *C. a.* 'Ruby', purple-pink, cream stamens tinged red; *C. a.* ssp. *sibirica* 'White Moth', white; *C. a.* 'Willy', pale pink, deeper pink undersides, cream anthers.

above *Clematis armandii.* Hardy evergreen clematis are few; this fragrant species is undoubtedly the most reliable.

C. macropetala (Group 1). Very hardy, bell-shaped blue or blue-violet semi-double flowers from spring to early summer followed by silver seedheads, 2-3m/1.5m (6½-10ft/5ft). *C. m.* 'Jan Lindmark', pale purple, blue and cream stamens; *C. m.* 'Maidwell Hall' (syn. 'Blue Lagoon'), deep mauve; *C. m.* 'Markham's Pink', sugar-pink. Early-flowering hybrids of *C. alpina* or *C. macropetala* include: 'Blue Bird', semi-double flowers, purple-blue; 'Rosie O'Grady', semi-pendent pink-mauve and white; 'White Swan', large white flowers.

C. montana (Group 1). Very hardy, single white, cream-yellow anthers, from late spring to early summer, 5-14m/2-3m (16-42½ft/6½-10ft). *C. m.* 'Elizabeth', strongly scented pale pink flowers, the best scented variety of *C. montana*, yellow anthers; *C. m.* 'Freda', cherry-pink flowers, copper foliage; *C. m.* f. *grandiflora*, white flowers with yellow stamens; *C. m.* 'Marjorie', semi-double, cream-pink, salmon-pink stamens; *C. m.* 'Pink Perfection', scented, pale pink, cream stamens; *C. m.* var. *rubens*, scented, violet-pink, yellow stamens, bronze-purple leaves; *C. m.* var. *sericea*, white; *C. m.* 'Tetrarose', deep satin-pink, straw-coloured stamens, spicy scent; *C. m.* var. *wilsonii*, white, yellow stamens, chocolate scent. Similar species: *C. chrysocoma*, less vigorous, white and pink varieties; *C.* x *vedrariensis*, pale rose-pink.

Early-flowering hybrids

The following varieties were developed from three Chinese species: *C. florida*, *C. patens*, and *C. lanuginosa*. *C. florida* types (Group 2), deciduous or semi-evergreen, double or semi-double flowers from late spring to early summer, some repeat flowers later, usually single blooms, 4m/1m (13ft/3ft): *C.* 'Belle of Woking', double silver-mauve flowers, cream anthers; *C.* 'Daniel Deronda', double mid-blue, cream stamens; *C.* 'Hakuôkan', large semi-double violet with white stamens, later single flowers; *C.* 'Proteus', peony-like, rose-lilac flowers, yellow stamens, cream anthers; *C.* 'Vyvyan Pennell', double lilac flowers, central lavender-blue rosettes, yellow anthers, later flowers blue-mauve; *C.* 'Walter Pennell', semi-double deep mauve pink, later single flowers. *C. patens* types (Group 2), very hardy, blue-and-white flowers from late spring to early summer, sometimes again in autumn, 2-3m (6½-10ft): *C.* 'Barbara Jackson', purple with broad crimson stripe, cream stamens; *C.* 'Bee's Jubilee', single flowers, deep pink, dark central bands, brown anthers; *C.* 'Doctor Ruppel', single, deep rose-pink, darker central bands, light chocolate anthers; *C.* 'Gillian Blades', single, white, cream anthers; *C.* 'Lasurstern', single, rich mauve-blue, white stamens; *C.* 'Lincoln Star', pink, broad pink central stripe, later flowers paler; *C.* 'Lord Nevill', single, deep blue, scalloped, purple-red anthers; *C.* 'Miss Bateman', single, white, red anthers; *C.* 'Nelly Moser', the most famous of all clematis, pink-mauve, darker central band, red anthers; *C.* 'Richard Pennell', rich blue, pure yellow anthers; *C.* 'The President', rich purple, silver beneath, red anthers; *C.* 'Wada's Primrose', cream-white, yellow anthers. *C. lanuginosa* types (Group 2), very hardy, usually single flowers with white, gold, brown or purple stamens, from late spring to early summer, then periodically throughout the summer, 2-3m (6½-10ft): *C.* 'Carnaby', mid to dark pink, dark central band, red anthers; *C.* 'Edith', white with red anthers; C. 'Elsa Späth', mauve-blue, red anthers; C. 'Lady Northcliffe', deep blue-purple, white stamens; C. 'Lawsoniana', lavender-blue tinted rose, beige stamens; C. 'Marie Boisellot', white, cream anthers; C. 'Mrs Cholmondley', pale blue, brown stamens; C. 'Silver Moon', silver-mauve; C. 'W E Gladstone', light blue, red-brown anthers; C. 'Will Goodwin', pale blue, yellow anthers; C. 'William Kennett', lavender-blue, dark red anthers, dark central stripe.

Later-flowering hybrids

Jackmanii Group (Group 3), very hardy, particularly suitable for informal plantings over pergolas or similar structures, usually single flowers, white and shades of red, blue, purple, from midsummer until early autumn, 2-3m (6½-10ft): C. 'Comtesse de Bouchaud', bright mauve-pink, pale yellow anthers; C. 'Ernest Markham', vivid magenta, light chocolate anthers; C. 'Gipsy Queen', velvet violet-purple, deep red anthers; C. 'Hagley Hybrid', pink-mauve, red anthers; C. x 'Jackmanii', deep violet-purple; C. 'Jackmanii Superba', velvet deep purple, green stamens; C. 'Jan Pawel II', white flowers flushed pink brown stamens, central pink band; C. 'Kardynal Wyszynski', crimson flowers, dark black-red anthers; C. 'Lady Betty Balfour', rich purple, yellow anthers'; C. Madame Edouard André', dark red, silver beneath, yellow anthers; C. 'Madame Grangé', dusky purple, silver beneath, dark brown anthers; C. 'Niobe', deep wine red, yellow anthers; C. 'Perle d'Azur', the most popular of all clematis, deep mauve, pale green stamens; C. 'Prince Charles', light violet, green stamens; C. 'Rouge Cardinal', velvet crimson, red-brown anthers; C. 'Star of India', deep purple-blue, carmine red central bands, light brown anthers;

C. *viticella* varieties and hybrids (Group 3). C. *viticella*, usually small slightly nodding flowers, bell-shaped, blue-purple or rose-red, pale yellow anthers from midsummer to autumn, 2-4m/1.5m (6½-13ft/5ft): C. *v.* 'Purpurea Plena Elegans', abundant double, purple-mauve flowers, no anthers; C. 'Abundance', wine red, cream anthers; C. 'Alba Luxurians', grey-green foliage, green tipped white flowers, black anthers; C. 'Etoile Violette', nodding violet-purple saucer-shaped flowers, yellow anthers; C. 'Huldine', cup-shaped white flowers, cream anthers; C. 'Kermesina', deep wine red, red-brown stamens; C. 'Minuet', white edged with pink-red; C. 'Madame Julia Correvon', the best of the group, wine red, golden stamens; C. 'Polish Spirit', rich purple-blue, rosy-purple stamens; C. 'Royal Velours', red-purple, red stamens; C. 'Venosa Violacea', white, veined and edged purple; C. 'Ville de Lyon', carmine, darker edged, cream stamens.

Late-flowering species

C. *tangutica* (Group 3), very hardy, abundant, solitary bell-shaped flowers, pale yellow to rich orange, 5-6m (16-20ft): C. *t.* 'Gravetye' Variety', yellow; C. *t.* 'Lambton Park', large yellow flowers; C. *tibetana* ssp. *vernayi*, and its variants C. *t.* ssp. *v.* 'Orange Peel', and C. *t.* ssp. *v.* 'LS & E 13342', nodding, thick spongy petals, yellow to green-yellow or purple-flushed; C. 'Aureolin' and C. 'Burford Variety', yellow; C. 'Corry', large lemon-yellow flowers; C. 'Bill MacKenzie', very large, open bell-shaped flowers often appear with seedheads. Similar species: C. *rehderiana*, vigorous, yellow bells.

Varieties of C. *texensis* (Group 3), moderately hardy, 2-3m (6½-10ft): C. 'Duchess of Albany', deep pink, slightly darker central band; C. 'Etoile Rose', nodding, deep rose-pink, recurved tips; C. 'Gravetye Beauty', rich crimson, paler bands outside; C. 'Princess Diana', deep pink. Similar species: C. *viorna*, pitcher-shaped, orange-brown to red-purple with cream tips; C. *crispa*, nodding bell-like, blue-purple, white-edged.

above *Clematis* 'Ernest Markham'. This lovely plant is one of a small group of later summer flowering hybrids related to Jackmanii varieties.

left *Clematis macropetala* 'Markham's Pink'. Of the two related early flowering species, *C. macropetala* varieties tend to have more red than those of *C. alpina*.

right *Clematis* 'Bill MacKenzie'. the late flowering yellow clematis are a confusing group but this is consistently thought among the finest.

C. flammula (Group 3), semi-evergreen or deciduous, star-shaped, very fragrant white flowers; *C. campaniflora* (Group 3), lilac-blue, nodding bell-like flowers.

Evergreen species (Group 1)
C. armandii, fairly hardy, saucer-shaped, richly scented white flowers, cream anthers in spring: *C. a.* 'Apple Blossom', pink flowers flushed white. *C. cirrhosa* (Group 1), barely hardy, flowers late autumn to spring, 4-5m (13-16ft): *C. cirrhosa* var. *balearica*, fragrant, pale cream, speckled red-brown, *C. c.* 'Freckles', cream-pink spotted red inside; *C. c.* 'Wisley Cream', cream with faint red markings. *C. napaulensis* (Group 1), tender, cream-yellow bell flowers, purple stamens.

Herbaceous species
The following are all medium/large very hardy herbaceous perennials. *C. heracleifolia* var. *davidiana* 'Wyevale', spreading, toothed, deeply lobed light green leaves, scented, tubular, indigo-blue flowers in summer, 75cm/1m (2½ft/3ft); *C. integrifolia*, simple inverted lance-shaped to elliptic leaves, nodding bell-like flowers, mid-blue with cream anthers, in summer, followed by attractive seedheads, 60cm/60cm (2ft/2ft); *C. i.* 'Rosea', scented deep pink flowers; *C.* x *jouiniana* 'Praecox', pale green leaves, scented, white flowers with violet margins, 3m (10ft); *C. recta*, clump-forming, grey-green leaves, clusters of star-shaped heavily scented pure white flowers from midsummer until autumn, followed by seedheads, 1-2m/75cm (3ft-2½ft).

Cleome *Spider Flower* — Capparaceae

Large half-hardy annuals and evergreen shrubs. Only the annuals are commonly cultivated. They have strong, bushy growth and can be grown in warmth for summer cut flowers. Palmate leaves, terminal clusters of single flowers with long, prominent thread-like (spidery) stamens. Sow seeds in warmth in spring. ❀ *C. hassleriana* 'Cherry Queen' (syn. *C. spinosa* 'Cherry Queen'), spines at base of leaf stalks, clusters of white, purple or violet scented flowers with prominent stamens and styles from early summer to early autumn, 1.5m/45cm (5ft/1½ft); *C. h.* 'Colour Fountain', scented, pink, violet-pink, rose-red or white, 1.2m/45cm (4ft/1½ft); *C. h.* 'Helen Campbell', white flowers; *C. h.* 'Violet Queen', violet flowers.

Clerodendrum — Verbenaceae

Deciduous and evergreen shrubs, trees and climbers. Tender to moderately hardy but most benefit from some shelter and resent disturbance. Mid-green toothed leaves, terminal or axillary, often fragrant dense clusters of flowers with cylindrical tubes and prominent stamens. No routine

far right *Clerodendrum trichotomum* is an extraordinary plant in its combination of a heady, spicy flower fragrance and the most vivid red and blue fruits.

left *Cobaea scandens* 'Alba'. The various colour forms of this Mexican climber are best grown from seed as half-hardy annuals.

pruning. Sow seeds in warmth in spring or remove suckers in autumn. ❀ *C. bungei*, fairly hardy, ovate leaves, tipped purple when young, have an unpleasant odour, very fragrant, star-shaped rose-pink flowers from summer to autumn, 2m/2m (6½ft/6½ft); *C. trichotomum*, moderately hardy, bushy shrub or small tree (in mild areas), slow-growing, ovate mid-green leaves with a strange, rather unpleasant odour when crushed, scented white flowers with red sepals from late summer to mid autumn, followed by quite remarkable turquoise-blue fruits surrounded by dark red calyces; *C. t. fargesii*, smooth leaves, bronze when young, flowers white with green sepals, abundant, lighter blue fruits, 5-6m/5-6m (16-20ft/16-20ft).

Clethra — Clethraceae

Medium/large deciduous and evergreen shrubs and small trees. Tender to very hardy. The evergreen species are usually tender: the deciduous species hardy. Requires an acidic soil. Mid-green to dark green, leathery, toothed, ovate to oblong leaves, rarely, lance-shaped, white or pink-flushed inflorescences, sometimes fragrant, from midsummer to mid autumn. No routine pruning. Take semi-ripe cuttings in summer or sow seed in warmth in spring or autumn. ❀ *C. alnifolia* (Sweet Pepper Bush), very hardy, bushy deciduous shrub, mid-green leaves with serrated margins, terminal clusters of fragrant, bell-shaped cream-white flowers from late summer to early autumn, 2.5m/2.5m (8ft/8ft); *C. barbinervis*, hardy deciduous shrub, peeling bark when mature, deep green leaves, red and yellow in autumn, arching, terminal clusters of white bell-shaped flowers from late summer to autumn, 3m/3m (10ft/10ft).

Clianthus — Papilionaceae

Medium evergreen climber or sub-shrubs. Barely hardy to fairly hardy. Only one species, *C. puniceus*, is suitable for growing outside in cold areas and then must be sheltered from cold winds. Pinnate, mid-to dark green leaves, flowers resembling lobster's claws. No routine pruning. Sow seeds in warmth in summer. ❀ *C. puniceus* (Lobster Claw, Glory Pea), spreading climber, needing support, mid-green leaves, pendent clusters of crimson-scarlet flowers from late spring to midsummer, 4m/3m (13ft/10ft). *C. p.* 'Albus', white flowers.

Clinopodium — Lamiaceae

Short/medium half-hardy bedding annuals and hardy perennials for rock gardens or the edge of borders. Small, mid-green, aromatic leaves, clusters of two-lipped flowers in summer. Sow seeds in autumn or early spring in a cold-frame or divide after flowering. ❀ *C. vulgare* (Wild Basil), perennial, hairy, oval, pointed, slightly toothed leaves, pink-purple flowers from summer to early autumn, 50cm/30cm (1¾ft/1ft).

Clintonia — Convallariaceae

Small rhizomatous ornamentals. Fairly hardy. Require acidic soil. Broad, ovate to elliptic, glossy pale to mid-green leaves, star-shaped flowers, singly or in clusters, followed by round fruits. Sow seeds in a cold-frame in autumn or divide established plants in early spring. ❀ *C. andrewsiana*, rosettes of oval or tongue-shaped leaves, clusters of bell-shaped, deep red flowers on thin hairy stalks, 60cm/25cm (2ft/10in).

Cobaea — Cobaeaceae

Medium/large evergreen and herbaceous climbers. Tender but can be grown outside in summer as half-hardy annuals for growing over pergolas, arches, walls and up trees. Pinnate leaves, large tubular flowers. Sow seeds in warmth in summer for planting in following spring. ❀ *C. scandens* (Cup and Saucer Vine), rapid-grower, grey-green leaves of three oval leaflets, a fourth leaflet in the form of a tendril, fragrant flowers green-cream at first later violet and purple, 10-20m (33-60ft).

right *Colletia hystrix* must be one of the most prickly of all hardy shrubs and in consequence, one that makes a very effective boundary.

Codonopsis

Bonnet Bellflower Campanulaceae

Small/medium herbaceous perennials with erect, sprawling or twining habit. Fairly hardy to moderately hardy. Suitable for growing in borders and woodland; smaller species in a rock garden. Ovate or oblong to lance-shaped leaves, often with an unpleasant odour when crushed. Solitary, nodding, star-, bell- or saucer-shaped flowers, sometimes marked inside. Sow seeds in a cold-frame in spring or autumn. ❀ *C. clematidea*, twining climber, bell-shaped white flowers tinged blue-green, yellow, blue, black markings inside, in late summer, 1.5m (5ft); *C. convolvulacea*, twining herbaceous climber, smooth, light green ovate leaves, lavender-blue star-shaped flowers, sometimes white, in summer, 2m (6½ft); *C. ovata*, low, spreading, hairy ovate light green leaves, pale blue flared bell-shaped flowers, orange and purple markings inside, from mid-to late summer, 30cm/30cm (1ft/1ft); *C. tangshen*, climber, deep grey-green rounded leaves, pendent yellow-green bell-shaped flowers, purple and orange markings inside, from midsummer to early autumn, 2m (6½ft).

below *Colchicum autumnale*. The 'Naked Ladies' common name of this graceful bulb alludes to the stems, bare of leaves. Sadly, this also means the flowers are easily damaged by wind and rain.

Colchicum

Autumn Crocus, Naked Ladies Colchicaceae

Small/large corm-forming ornamentals. Some are suitable for naturalising in grass although are less effective than many other bulbous plants because the naked flower stems require support and are readily damaged by wind and rain, larger species in herbaceous borders. Fairly hardy to moderately hardy. Semi-prostrate basal leaves, broadly ovate to lance-shaped, appear with or after the flowers. Goblet-shaped flowers, sometimes scented, in late autumn, winter or spring. The species I describe here thrive best in fertile, well-drained soil in an open position in full sun, and do not tolerate dry conditions. Separate dormant corms in summer. ❀ *C. agrippinum*, slightly wavy, pointed leaves, red-purple flowers on long, pale tubes, 8-10cm/8cm (3¼-4in/3¼in); *C. autumnale* (syn. *C. autumnale* var. *minor*), small lilac flowers in early autumn before leaves appear, 10-15cm/8cm (4-6in/3¼in); *C. a.* 'Alboplenum', double white flowers; *C. a.* 'Album', large white flowers; *C.* 'Lilac Wonder', deep lilac-pink flowers with a faint white stripe, in autumn, 15cm/6cm (6in/2¼in); *C.* 'Rosy Dawn', fragrant violet-pink flowers in autumn, 15cm/10cm (6in/4in); *C. speciosum*, pale to deep purple-pink flowers sometimes with a white throat, yellow anthers, in autumn, 18cm/10cm (7in/4in); *C. s.* 'Album', pure white flowers; *C.* 'The Giant', purple-violet flowers in autumn, 20cm/10cm (8in/4in); *C.* 'Waterlily', double lilac-pink flowers; 12cm/10cm (5in/4in).

Colletia

Rhamnaceae

Medium/large deciduous shrub. Fairly hardy. Suitable for a sunny sheltered border or for growing against a warm wall. In mild areas, it will produce a totally impenetrable boundary. Leaves few and inconspicuous. Succulent stems divided into many upright branches with thick, extraordinarily vicious pointed spines. Abundant small flowers, bell-shaped, sometimes fragrant, are produced on or below the spines in late summer. No routine pruning. Take semi-ripe heeled cuttings in summer. ❀ *C. hystrix* (syn. *C. armata*), spreading, sharply pointed grey-green spines, fragrant white tubular flowers on the spines, from late summer to autumn, 3m/3m (10ft/10ft); *C. h.* 'Rosea', pink buds open to white flowers.

Collinsia Scrophulariaceae

Medium, hardy bedding annuals. Particularly good for containers. Lance-shaped or ovate leaves, often hairy, two-lipped pink, white, blue or bicoloured flowers from spring to summer. Sow seeds in warmth in early spring or in growing positions in autumn or spring. ❀ *C. heterophylla*, (syn. *C. bicolour*), toothed mid-to purple-green leaves, white and lilac-pink bicoloured flowers, 60cm/30cm (2ft/1ft); *C. h.* 'Blushing Rose', white and pale pink bicoloured flowers.

Colobanthus Caryophyllaceae

Small evergreen alpines. Moderately hardy. Mat- or cushion-forming tiny leaves, fairly insignificant flowers. Sow seeds in a cold-frame when ripe or in spring, or take short leafy cuttings in spring or late summer. ❀ *C. canaliculatus*, pointed leaves, 4mm (⅛in) long, small green-white flowers in early summer, 3cm/15cm (1¼in/6in).

Colutea Papilionaceae

Medium/large deciduous shrubs or small trees. Barely hardy to moderately hardy. Suitable for coastal gardens and also areas with high levels of pollution. Pinnate leaves, clusters of pea-like flowers, yellow to red-brown, followed by inflated, bladder-like seed-pods. No routine pruning. Sow seeds in a cold-frame in spring or autumn or take semi-ripe cuttings in early summer. ❀ *C. arborescens*, tolerates dry, poor soil in sun, pale green leaves, clusters of yellow flowers in summer followed by seed-pods, green at first, later translucent, 3m/3m (10ft/10ft).

Commelina
Widow's Tears, Day-Flower Commelinaceae

Small half-hardy perennials often grown as annuals. In mild areas makes good ground cover. Mat- or clump-forming, tuberous or fibrous-rooted, leaves ovate, linear or lance-shaped, small, three-petalled saucer-shaped flowers opening and dying in one day, are produced throughout the summer. Sow seed in warmth in spring or divide established plants in spring. ❀ *C. dianthifolia*, narrow, grass-like leaves, blue flowers, much the prettiest species, 30cm/25cm (1ft/10in); *C. tuberosa*, mat-forming tuberous ornamental, narrow, lance-shaped leaves sometimes hairy, clusters of green flowers striped dark blue-purple in summer, 20cm (8in)/indefinite; *C. t.* 'Alba', white flowers.

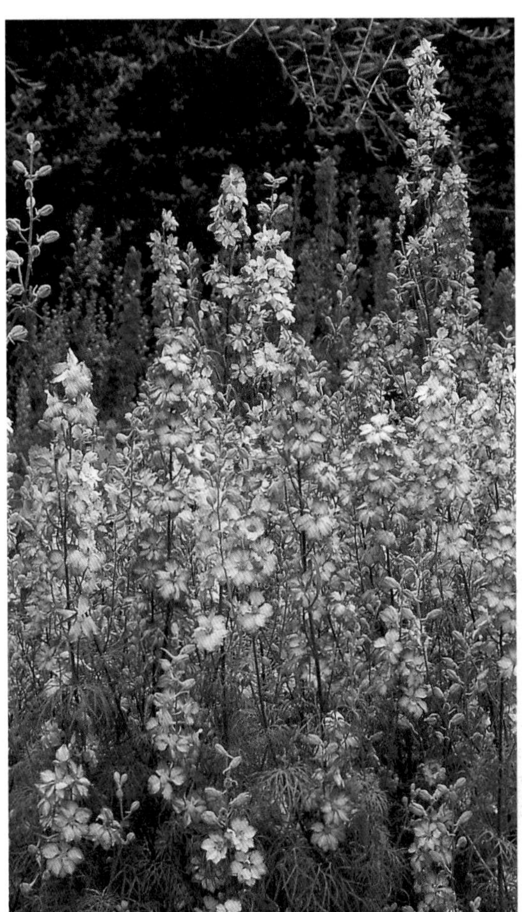

left *Consolida* 'Frosted Skies'. No garden should be without its larkspurs; and no home without them as dried flowers too.

Consolida *Larkspur* Ranunculaceae

Hardy bedding annuals. Excellent for cutting and drying for indoor display. Rounded palmate or finely divided leaves, feathery, spurred, delphinium-like flowers on long flower spikes throughout the summer. Sow seeds in growing positions in early spring. ❀ *C. ajacis* (syn. *C. ambigua*, *Delphinium consolida*), finely divided leaves, erect single or branched flower spikes, single or double flowers in white and shades of pink, violet-blue, 30-120cm/25-30cm (1-4ft/10in-1ft); *C.* 'Dwarf Hyacinth Flowered', double flowers; *C.* 'Frosted Skies' (syn. 'Frosted Sky'), semi-double white flowers flushed violet-blue, 30-45cm (1-1½ft); *C. a.* 'Imperial White King', double, pure white flowers.

right *Convallaria majalis.* The Lily of the Valley is a much loved and very fragrant plant; but it is also invasive so be sure you really know where you want to plant it.

Convallaria
Lily of the Valley Convallariaceae

Small rhizomatous perennial. Hardy. Very good for wild-flower gardens or large plantings under deciduous trees where it can be allowed free rein; it is invasive. Elliptic, green leaves, in pairs, bell-shaped fragrant nodding flowers. Thrives in moist, humus-rich soil in partial shade and always looks pathetic in dry conditions. Divide established clumps in winter. ❀ *C. majalis*, stalked basal leaves, arching clusters of very fragrant waxy white flowers 5-10mm (¼-½in) in diameter, in late spring, 23cm/30cm (9in/1ft); *C. m.* 'Albostriata', leaves striped cream-white; *C.* 'Fortin's Giant', the best form, broad leaves, large flowers 8-15mm (⅓-¾in) in diameter, 30cm (1ft); *C. m.* var. *rosea*, pale pink flowers; *C. m.* 'Variegata, green and gold striped leaves.

Convolvulus *Bindweed* Convolvulaceae

below *Convolvulus cneorum.* The name *Convolulus* for many gardeners means bindweed but this shrubby relative is not only harmless, it is also extremely attractive.

Climbing or scrambling annuals and perennials and evergreen shrubs and sub-shrubs, including some pernicious weeds. Tender to moderately hardy. Oval, heart-shaped, elliptic or lance-shaped leaves, funnel-shaped flowers throughout summer. Sow seeds of annuals in growing positions, perennials in a cold-frame in late winter or early spring. Take soft-wood cuttings of evergreen shrubs and sub-shrubs in late spring, semi-ripe cuttings in summer or divide established plants in spring. ❀ *C. althaeoides*, clump-forming perennial, can be invasive and best grown in a container, hairy, oval to heart-shaped leaves, pink flowers on climbing or trailing stems in summer, 15cm (6in)/indefinite; *C. a.* ssp. *tenuissimus* (syn. *C. elegantissimus*), more finely dissected leaves, soft hairs; *C. cneorum*, a beautiful bushy, barely hardy, evergreen shrub, silver-grey, oval to lance-shaped leaves, pink-flushed buds open to white flowers from late spring to summer, 60cm/60cm (2ft/2ft); *C. sabatius* (syn. *C. mauritanicus*), evergreen perennial, small, oval, deep-green leaves on trailing or climbing slender stems, pale blue to deep blue-purple flowers in summer, 15cm/50cm (6in/1¾ft); *C. tricolor*, annual or short-lived perennial, ovate to lance-shaped dark-green leaves, solitary royal blue flowers, flushed white, yellow centres, in summer, 30-40cm/23-30cm (1-1½ft/9in-1ft); *C. t.* 'Flagship' mixed colours including red; *C. t.* 'Royal Ensign', trailing, deep blue flowers with yellow and white centres; *C. t.* 'Red Ensign', red flowers; *C. t.* 'Rainbow Flash', blues, pinks and mauve flowers.

Coprosma
Rubiaceae

Small/large evergreen shrubs and small trees. Barely hardy to moderately hardy and in cold areas the less hardy species require overwintering in a greenhouse. Linear, rounded, oval or oblong leaves, clusters of insignificant flowers usually followed by fruits when male and female flowers are grown close by. No routine pruning. Sow seeds in a cold-frame in spring or take semi-ripe cuttings in late summer. ❀ *C.* 'Beatson's Gold', barely hardy,

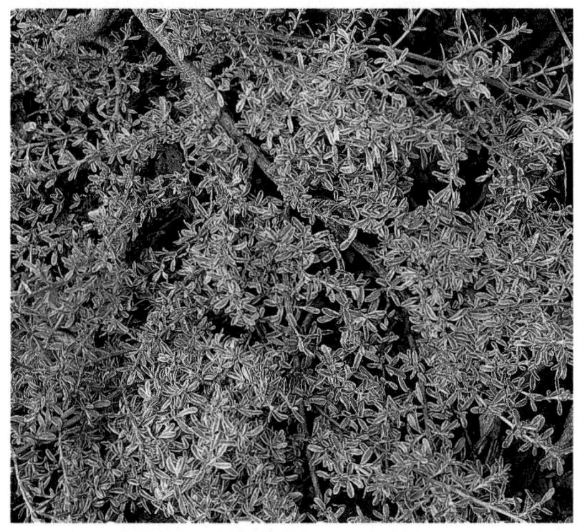

compact female shrub, bright green leaves, splashed yellow in the centre, bright red fruits in autumn, 1.5m/1.5m (5ft/5ft); *C.* x *kirkii* 'Kirkii Variegata', low, spreading shrub, deep green leaves with white margins, does not produce fruits, 60cm/100cm (2ft/3ft); *C. repens* 'Pink Splendour', tender, male, glossy leathery leaves, edged cream and pink, 2m/2m (6ft/6ft).

Cordyline *Cabbage Tree* Agavaceae

Medium evergreen shrubs and small trees. Tender to barely hardy. Large species are palm-like and rather lovely, despite the unflattering name. Suitable for growing outside in winter only in mild areas but many are good in containers and may be taken under cover in winter. Tufts or rosettes of leathery, linear to lance-shaped leaves, clusters of fragrant, cup-shaped flowers followed by fruits. ❀ *C. australis*, green, stiff, sword-like leaves borne in dense arching clusters at the top of each branch, fragrant, cream-white flowers in plume-like panicles in summer, followed by blue or white fruits, 3-10m/1-4m (10-33ft/3-13ft); *C. a.* Purpurea Group, purple or bronze leaves; *C. a.* 'Red Star', deep purple leaves; *C. a.* 'Sundance', sunset-red on leaf base, pink mid-rib; *C. a.* 'Torbay Dazzler', green leaves have bold cream stripes and margins; *C. a.* 'Torbay Red', plum-red leaves.

Coreopsis *Tickseed* Asteraceae

Medium/large hardy annuals and hardy herbaceous perennials; some of the perennials are grown as annuals. Good for cutting and especially attractive to bees. Pinnate or palmate leaves, bright yellow or yellow-orange, very fresh looking daisy-like single or double flowers throughout the summer. Sow seeds of annuals in flowering positions from early spring to early summer; perennials in a seedbed in mid-spring to flower the same year. Divide established perennials in early spring. ❀ *C. auriculata* 'Schnittgold', low, bushy perennial, oval or narrow pointed leaves, light green, often lobed, single vivid golden flowers with ragged edges from early summer to mid-summer, 80cm/60cm (2½ft/2ft); *C. grandiflora* 'Early Sunrise', clump-forming perennial usually grown as an annual, lance-shaped or palmate, lobed, leaves, semi-double deep yellow flowers flushed orange-yellow near the centre, from late spring to late summer, 45-90cm/45cm (1½ft-3ft/1½ft); *C. g.* 'Mayfield Giant', large orange-yellow flowers, needs support, 90cm (3ft); *C. rosea* 'American Dream', compact, single, rose-pink, star-shaped flowers, 30-60cm/30-45cm (1-2ft/1-1½ft); *C.* 'Sunray', spreading clump-forming perennial, grown as an annual, lance-shaped toothed leaves, double bright yellow flowers in summer, 45cm /30-45cm (1½ft/1-1½ft); *C. verticillata*, bushy perennial, fern-like mid-green leaves, clusters of single yellow flowers, 60-80cm/45cm (2-2½ft/ 1½ft); *C. v.* 'Grandiflora' (syn. *C. v.* 'Golden Showers'), dark yellow flowers; *C. v.* 'Moonbeam', lemon-yellow, 50cm (1¾ft); *C. v.* 'Zagreb', drought-tolerant, golden yellow flowers, 25-30cm/30cm (10in-1ft/1ft).

left *Coprosma x kirkii* 'Kirkii Variegata'. Plants with very small variegated leaves have a special quality and for slightly milder gardens, this is one of the best.

below *Coreopsis grandiflora* 'Early Sunrise' is probably one of the less widely grown of yellow flowered daisies but it is an easy and hardy plant that deserves to be better known.

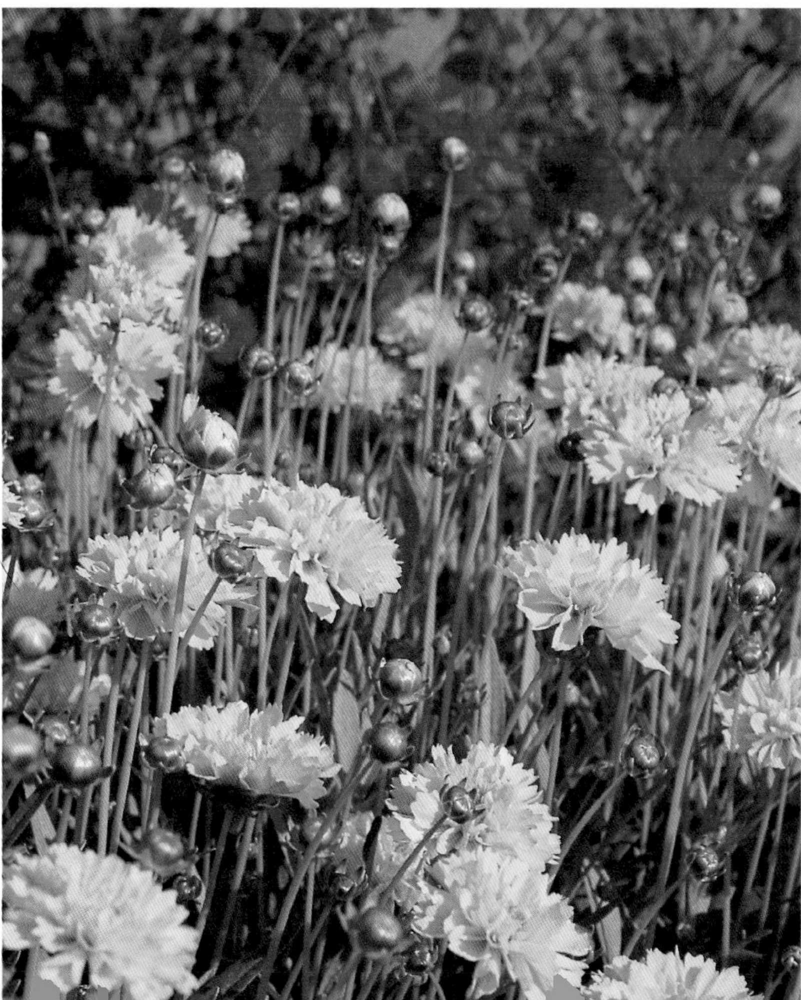

right *Cornus sanguinea*. Coloured stems are an outstanding feature of some of the best and easiest ornamental dogwoods.

Coriandrum Apiaceae

Hardy annual herbs. Basal leaves, oval or finely divided, upper leaves pinnate. Umbels of small, cup-shaped flowers, white or white flushed purple, followed by round seeds. Sow seeds in growing positions in spring; may self-seed. ❀ *C. sativum* (Coriander), pungent, aromatic edible leaves, white to mauve flowers in summer followed by small, round, sweet, spicy seeds, 15-70cm/10-30cm (6in-2¼ft/4in-1ft). The variety known as Cilantro or Chinese parsley is best for leaf production; the Moroccan variety for seed production.

Cornus *Dogwood* Cornaceae

Deciduous shrubs, small trees and perennials. Barely hardy to hardy. A wonderfully valuable genus of plants with a wide range of garden roles; some species are grown for their colourful winter stems, others for their foliage or flowers. They are suitable for a wide variety of situations, including woodland gardens and shrub borders and most thrive best in fertile, well-drained, neutral to acidic soil in full sun or light shade; *C. canadensis* thrives in more acidic soil; *C. florida*, *C. kousa* and *C. nuttallii* do not tolerate shallow, alkaline soil. Species and varieties grown for winter colour are best in full sun; summer-flowering species require shelter from spring frosts. For most species, routine pruning is necessary but plants may be shaped in late winter or early spring to maintain an attractive appearance. *C. alba*, *C. sanguinea* and *C. stolonifera* are best pruned annually in spring by cutting back almost to ground level to encourage new coloured shoots. Take soft-wood cuttings in summer (*C. alba*, *C. stolonifera* 'Flaviramea', *C. capitata*, *C. florida*, *C. kousa*) or hardwood cuttings in autumn (*C. alba*, *C. stolonifera* 'Flaviramea'). *C. canadensis* may be divided in spring or autumn and the suckers of suckering types can be replanted in early winter. ❀ *C. alba* 'Aurea', erect deciduous shrub with vivid red shoots, ovate to elliptic yellow leaves turn red or orange in autumn, clusters of white flowers from late spring to early summer, white fruit tinged blue, 3m/3m (10ft/10ft); *C. a.* 'Elegantissima', grey-green leaves with white margins; *C. a.* 'Kessel- ringii', grey-green leaves, red and purple in autumn, very dark, almost black shoots; *C. a.* 'Sibirica', red autumn leaves, bright red in autumn; *C. a.* 'Sibirica Variegata', green and cream-white leaves on deep red stems; *C. a.* 'Spaethii', oval leaves, golden yellow margins, deep red stems in winter, black fruits in autumn; *C. alternifolia*, 'Argentea', hardy shrub or small tree, branches arranged in horizontal tiers, small bright green ovate to elliptic leaves with white margins, red and purple in autumn, small white flowers in early autumn followed by red fruit, 3m/2.5m (10ft/8ft); *C. canadensis* (syn. *Chaemaepericlymenum cana-dense*), creeping herbaceous perennial, carpet- forming, glossy, mid-green leaves, red in autumn, tiny green-red flowers in clusters, surrounded by large white bracts, sometimes pink flushed, followed by round fleshy red fruit, 15cm (6in)/indefinite; *C. capitata* (syn. *Dendrobentham-iacapitata*), evergreen, button-like inflorescences surrounded by sulphur-yellow bracts from early to midsummer, followed by large raspberry-like fruit in autumn, 12m/12m (5in/5in);

above *Cornus nuttallii*. The lovely white flowers of many ornamental *Cornus* species are in reality groups of white bracts, but they are certainly none the worse for that.

C. controversa, a glorious deciduous tree, spreading branches tiered, glossy dark green elliptic leaves, grey-blue beneath, turn purple and red in autumn, white flowers in early summer followed by round, blue-black fruit, 15m/15m (50ft/50ft); *C. c.* 'Variegata', cream-white margins, 8m (25ft); *C.* 'Eddie's White Wonder', large deciduous shrub or small tree, compact, erect, leaves slightly glossy, green above, grey beneath, red and orange in autumn, abundant purple-green flowers surrounded by overlapping white bracts, 6m/5m (20ft/16ft); *C. florida* 'Cherokee Chief', deciduous tree or shrub, oval to ovate mid-green leaves, red and purple in autumn, green flowers tipped yellow, ruby-pink bracts, 6m/8m (20ft/25ft); *C. f.* 'Rainbow', compact erect, yellow margined leaves, red-purple with scarlet margins in autumn, white bracts, 3m/2.5m (10ft/8ft); *C. kousa*, deciduous tree, especially beautiful, with flaking bark, dark green leaves with white margins, crimson-purple in autumn, green inflorescences surrounded by white bracts, followed by fleshy, strawberry-like fruit 7m/5m (23ft/16ft); *C. k.* var. *chinensis*, cream-yellow bracts, leaves tinted red in autumn, red fruit; *C. k.* var. *c.* 'China Girl', very free-flowering; *C. k.* 'Satomi', deep pink bracts, leaves purple and red in autumn; *C. mas*, large hardy shrub or small tree, spreading, thrives on alkaline soil and much undervalued, clusters of tiny yellow flowers from late winter to early spring before the leaves appear, small oval dark green glossy leaves, bright red edible fruit in late summer, 5m/5m (16ft/16ft); *C. m.* 'Variegata', grey-green leaves with white margins; *C.* 'Norman Hadden', small semi-evergreen tree, mid-green leaves, yellow or pink in autumn, clusters of small green flowers surrounded by four white bracts, later flushed pink, pendent, red strawberry-like fruit in autumn, 8m/8m (25ft/25ft); *C. nuttallii*, deciduous tree, oval to ovate leaves, mid-green, sometimes red in autumn, purple and green flowers surrounded by four, six or eight white or pink-flushed bracts in late spring, followed by orange-red round fruit, 12m/8m (40ft/25ft); *C. officinalis*, large deciduous shrub or small tree, peeling bark, clusters of yellow flowers on bare twigs in large winter, similar to *C. mas* but better, rich red autumn leaves, edible red fruit, 5m/5m (16ft/16ft); *C. sanguinea*, erect deciduous shrub, ovate, mid-green leaves red in autumn, clusters of white flowers in summer followed by round, matt blue-black fruit, 3m/25m (10ft/80ft); *C. s.* 'Midwinter Fire', suckering deciduous shrub with striking yellow and red young shoots, looking from a distance like flickering flames; *C. stolonifera* 'Flaviramea', suckering deciduous shrub, ovate to lance-shaped dark green leaves, red or orange in autumn, vivid yellow-green shoots, clusters of white flowers, sometimes flushed pink, followed by white fruit, sometimes flushed blue, 2m/4m (6½ft/13ft); *C. s.* 'Kelsey's Compact', yellow-green winter shoots tipped red, 75cm/75cm (2½ft/2½ft).

Corokia — Escalloniaceae

Small/large evergreen shrubs or small trees. Barely hardy. In cold areas they thrive best outside in a sheltered border or against a warm wall. Ovate to linear leaves, small star-shaped yellow flowers in late spring, in mild areas often followed by red or orange fruit. No routine pruning. Take semi-ripe cuttings in summer. ❀ *C. cotoneaster*, small/ medium, hardier than other species, tangled wiry stems given a uniquely intriguing appearance of wire netting, tiny spoon-shaped leaves, green to dark purple, tiny yellow flowers in late spring, orange fruit, 25cm/25cm (10in/10in); *C.* x *virgata*, clusters of small, yellow, fragrant flowers in late spring, orange or yellow fruit, 3m/3m (10ft/10ft); *C.* x *v.* 'Red Wonder', abundant deep red fruits.

Coronilla *Crown Vetch* — Papilionaceae

Annuals, perennials, deciduous and evergreen shrubs. Barely hardy to moderately hardy. Pinnate, grey leaves, circular clusters of yellow flowers in spring or summer, followed by bead-like seed pods. In cold areas the species I describe here is best given the protection of a warm wall. Take softwood cuttings in summer or sow seeds in warmth in early spring. ❀ *C. valentina* ssp. *glauca*, blue-green leaves, abundant rich yellow flowers with a scent of peaches, in early summer and often again in late summer, 80cm/80cm (2½ft/2½ft); *C. v.* ssp. *g.* 'Citrina', pale yellow flowers; *C. v.* ssp. 'Variegata', cream-white leaf margins.

below *Coronilla valentina* ssp. *glauca* is not one of the best known members of its shrub family but typical in its masses of yellow flowers.

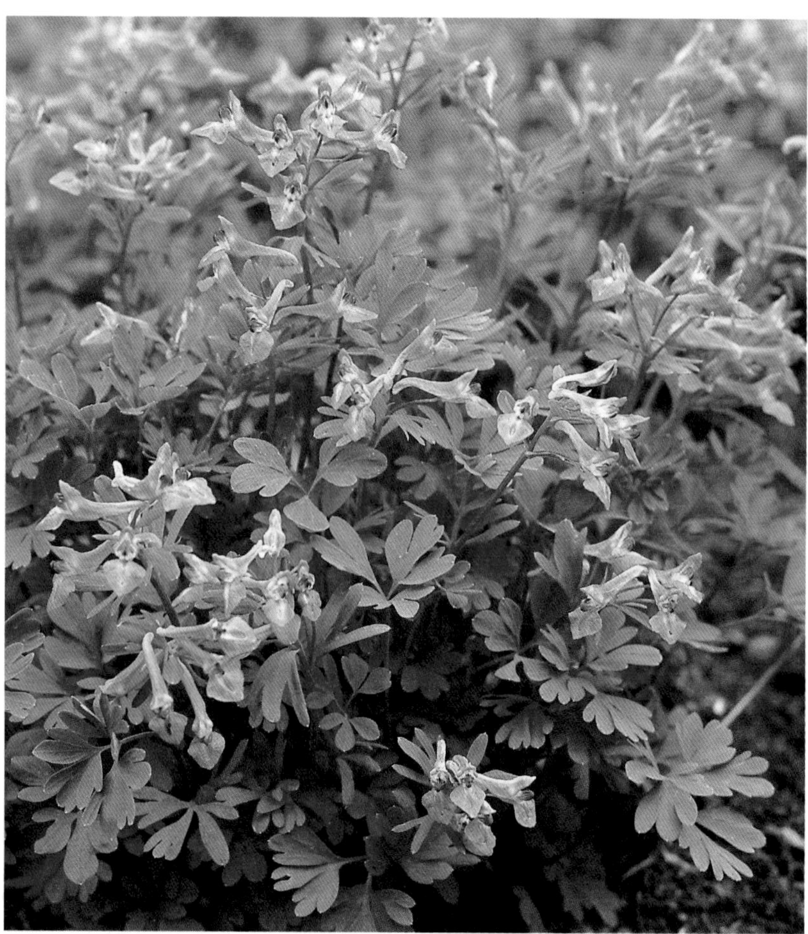

above *Corydalis flexuosa*. For a relatively recent introduction to European gardens, this Oriental species has rapidly become extraordinarily popular.

Cortaderia *Pampas Grass* Poaceae

Large evergreen or semi-evergreen perennial grasses. The biggest and most dramatic hardy grasses that can be grown in European gardens and far more reliable than bamboos. Barely hardy to moderately hardy. Tussocks of narrow, linear, stiff leaves, often blue-green. Plume-like flower panicles, silver, gold, or pale pink. Male and female flowers usually borne on separate plants. Pull out old flower shoots and foliage at the end of winter. Divide established plants in spring; seed raised plants are usually of inferior quality. ❀ *C. richardii*, olive-green arching leaves with prominent mid-ribs, arching plume in late summer, cream-white at first, later pale brown, 2.5m/1.8m (8ft/5½ft); *C. selloana* (syns. *C. argentea*, *Gynerium argentea*), slender, arching, rough-edged, blue-green leaves, silver plumes, often tinged purple or pink, from late summer to autumn, 2.5-3m/1.5m (8-10ft/5ft); *C. s.* 'Aureolineata' (syn. 'Golden Band'), rich yellow-orange leaves, fading to dark golden yellow; *C. s.* 'Pumila', compact, abundant silver-yellow plumes, mid-green leaves, 1.5m (5ft); *C. s.* 'Sunningdale Silver', silver-white plumes, 3m/2.5m (10ft/8ft).

Cortusa Primulaceae

Small herbaceous perennial. Moderately hardy. Rosettes of round or kidney-shaped, shallowly lobed leaves, bell-shaped flowers borne characteristically on one side of the flower stem. Sow seed in a cold-frame when ripe or divide established plants in spring. ❀ *C. matthioli*, crinkled, deep green leaves with red-brown hairs, pendent magenta or purple flowers on hairy stems from late spring to early summer, 20-30cm/15cm (8in-1ft/6in).

Corydalis Papaveraceae

Fibrous- or fleshy-rooted annuals and biennials, tuberous and rhizomatous perennials, most herbaceous, some evergreen. Barely hardy to moderately hardy. Fern-like leaves, tubular spurred flowers. Sow seeds in a cold-frame when ripe; divide spring-flowering species in autumn and summer-flowering species in spring. ❀ *C. cashmeriana*, barely hardy, tuberous ornamental, blue-green leaves, brilliant clear blue flowers with curved spurs in summer, 10-25cm/8-15cm (4-10in/3¼-6in); *C. cheilanthifolia*, fibrous-rooted evergreen perennial, light to mid-green leaves, spike-like clusters of spurred yellow flowers from spring to summer, self-seeds freely, 30cm/25cm (1ft/10in); *C. flexuosa*, rhizomatous, deep green slightly bronze leaves, blue-purple to deep blue flowers from late spring to midsummer, 30cm/30cm (1ft/1ft); *C. f.* 'China Blue', blue-green leaves, ice-blue flowers from spring to summer; *C. f.* 'Père David', grey-green leaves, sky-blue flowers in early spring, 15-20cm (6-8in); *C. f.* 'Purple Leaf', finely-cut purple-brown leaves, tiny blue flowers flushed red, 20cm (8in); *C. lutea* (syn. *Pseudofumaria lutea*), rhizomatous, leaves soft green above, blue-green beneath, spurred yellow flowers in oblong clusters, from late spring to autumn, 20cm/50cm (8in/1¾ft); *C. ochroleuca*, clump-forming, fibrous-rooted evergreen perennial, light green leaves, clusters of cream-white flowers, with a yellow throat, downward-curving spurs, from late spring to summer, 30cm/30cm (1ft/1ft); *C. solida* f. *transsylvanica* 'George Baker', tuberous, grey-green leaves, erect spike-like clusters of mauve-pink or red-purple flowers, downward-curving spurs, 25cm/25cm (10in/10in).

Corylopsis
Winter Hazel Hamamelidaceae

Medium/large deciduous shrubs and small trees for acidic soils. Moderately hardy but need protection from cold winds and early frosts. Oval, toothed leaves with bristly margins, heart-shaped bases. Delightful, pendent clusters of bell-shaped flowers appear in early spring before the leaves. No routine pruning. Take semi-ripe cuttings in summer, layer in mid autumn or sow seeds in a cold-frame in mid autumn. ❀ *C. pauciflora*, bushy, spreading, bright green leaves, pale yellow flowers, 5m/5m (16ft/16ft); *C. sinensis* var. *sinensis*, spreading shrub, green leaves, blue-green beneath, slightly fragrant bright yellow flowers in mid spring, 4m/1m (13ft/3ft); *C. s.* var. *s.* 'Spring Purple', purple-green leaves; *C. spicata*, dark green leaves, softly downy beneath, marrow racemes of pale green-yellow flowers with purple anthers, slightly scented, 2m/3m (6½ft/10ft).

Corylus *Hazel* — Corylaceae

Large hardy deciduous shrubs and small trees. Valuable plants, either for their edible fruits (nuts) or as ornamentals. Broad, oval toothed leaves, heart-shaped at the base, pendent yellow male catkins, tiny female flowers with red tassels occur on the same plants in late winter and early spring. Thrives well in alkaline soil but tolerates most other fertile soils in sun or partial shade. Remove suckers from suckering species and cut back the oldest one third of the shoots to soil level in spring. Layer named varieties in autumn or sow seed of species in a cold-frame in autumn. ❀ *C. avellana* (Hazelnut, Cobnut) multi-stemmed, mid-green leaves, clusters of male catkins late winter to early spring, 5m/5m (16ft/16ft); *C. a.* 'Aurea' leaves bright yellow at first, yellow-green later; *C. a.* 'Contorta', elaborately twisted shoots, wonderful for flower arranging; *C. a.* 'Cosford Cob', attractive edible nuts in autumn; *C. colurna* (Turkish Hazel), glossy dark green leaves, yellow in autumn, clusters of edible autumn nuts enclosed in fringed bracts, pendent yellow catkins in late winter, 20m/7m (60ft/23ft); *C. maxima* (Filbert), erect shrub, best grown as a multi-stemmed tree, heart-shaped mid-green leaves, edible nuts in tubular bracts in autumn, 5m/5m (16ft/16ft); *C. m.* 'Kentish Cob', abundant crops of nuts; *C. m.* 'Purpurea', purple leaves, catkins and fruit bracts, one of the best ornamental forms.

Cosmos — Asteraceae

Half-hardy bedding annuals and perennials. Simple lobed or pinnate leaves, saucer-, bowl- or cup-shaped summer flowers in red, white or pink. Taller than most half-hardy annuals and best among perennials in borders although they also look effective in large beds. Sow seeds in warmth in mid spring, in flowering positions in late spring or take basal cuttings of *C. atrosanguineus* in early spring. ❀ *C. atrosanguineus* (syn. *Bidens atrosanguineus*) perennial, spoon-shaped pinnate dark green leaves, solitary saucer-shaped, velvety brown-maroon, chocolate-scented flowers with darker centres, from midsummer to autumn, 75cm/45cm (2½ft/1½ft); *C. bipinnatus* 'Day Dream', semi-dwarf annual, good for cutting, ferny foliage of light green leaves, saucer-shaped cream flowers with orange zone, darker centre, 90cm (3ft); *C. b.* 'Gloria', large flowers, pink with rose zone, 90-120cm (3ft-4ft); *C.* 'Pied Piper Red', velvety, fluted florets on crimson-red flowers, 30cm (1ft); *C. b.* 'Purity', pure white flowers, 90-120cm (3ft-4ft); *C. b.* 'Sea Shells', fluted petals on carmine-red, pink or white flowers, 90cm (3ft); *C. b.* 'Sonata', white flowers, 60cm (2ft); *C. sulphureus* 'Ladybird', erect, bushy annual, mid-green leaves, bowl-shaped, semi-double flowers, yellow, orange or scarlet, 30-40cm (1-1½ft); *C. s.* Sunny Series, dwarf, dense, bushy, semi-double lemon yellow flowers, golden yellow and orange-red flowers, 35-45cm (1¼-1½ft).

above *Corylus maxima* 'Kentish Cob'. Confusingly, this plant is not a genuine cobnut but is the best variety of filbert.

below *Cosmos bipinnatus* 'Gloria'. Among the most reliable among taller annual daisies, *Cosmos* varieties offer a very wide range of flower colours.

above The autumn foliage colours on *Cotinus coggygria* 'Flame' are probably the most intense in the species and the 'smoke-like' inflorescences also have a pink tinge to add to the appeal.

Cotinus *Smoke Bush* Anacardiaceae

Large deciduous shrubs and small trees. Moderately hardy. Good for borders or as specimen plants. Elliptic to round green or purple leaves with attractive autumn colours. Plumes of tiny green-white flowers (smoke-like) in summer, and always best in full sun, followed by plume-like panicles of small round fruit. No routine pruning. Layer, take soft-wood cuttings in summer or sow seeds in cold-frame in autumn. ❀ *C. coggygria* (syn. *Rhus cotinus*), bushy tree or shrub, oval mid-green leaves, red, orange to yellow in autumn, fruit clusters green at first, later smoke-grey, 5m/5m (16ft/16ft); *C. c.* 'Royal Purple', still I think, the best form, dark plum-purple leaves, light red in autumn; *C.* 'Flame', dark green leaves, brilliant red and orange in autumn, flower plumes tinged pink, purple-pink fruit panicles, 6m/5m (20ft/16ft); *C.* 'Grace', oval, purple leaves, brilliant red in late autumn, purple-pink fruit panicles, 6m/5m (20ft/16ft); *C. obovatus*, excellent for autumn colour, ovate leaves, pink-brown at first, later red, purple and orange, flower plumes pale green, pink-grey fruit panicles in summer, 10m/8m (33ft/25ft).

Cotoneaster Rosaceae

Small/large deciduous, semi-evergreen and evergreen shrubs and small trees. Hardy. One of the most valuable and easy to grow of all shrub genera. Suitable for shrub borders, specimen plants, ground cover, walls and hedging. Leaves usually oval and small, flowers five-petalled, usually white and cup-shaped, followed by bright red, yellow or, rarely, white fruits in autumn, sometimes remaining throughout winter. Thrive in most fertile, well-drained soils but intolerant of water-logged conditions. Deciduous species and varieties require full sun; evergreen species will tolerate sun or partial shade. Prune deciduous species as necessary in late winter or early spring to maintain shape and healthy growth, evergreen species annually after flowering, removing dead or damaged growth in mid spring. Take semi-ripe cuttings of semi-evergreen and evergreen species in late summer, or of deciduous species in early summer. Sow ripe seeds in a cold-frame.

Deciduous species and varieties: *C. adpressus*, prostrate, dull green leaves, red in autumn, white flowers tinged red, singly or in pairs, round red fruit, 30cm/2m (1ft/6½ft); *C. atropurpureus* 'Variegatus' (syn. *C. horizontalis* 'Variegatus'), prostrate or upright, glossy mid-green leaves with white margins on arching branches, pink and red in autumn, 45cm/90cm (1½ft/3ft); *C. bullatus*, glossy, corrugated dark green leaves, red in autumn, white flowers followed by clusters of oval to spherical red fruits, 1.5m/1.2m (5ft/4ft); *C. frigidus* 'Cornubia', deciduous or semi-evergreen large shrub or small tree, peeling bark, dull green leaves, clusters of white flowers in summer, pendent clusters of almost spherical red fruits, 10m/10m (33ft/33ft); *C. horizontalis*, branches

right *Cotoneaster salicifolius* 'Rothschildianus'. One of the best among yellow-berried cotoneasters although I prefer to see it trained as a standard.

arranged in herringbone pattern, glossy green leaves, red in autumn, white flowers tinged pink in spring, very attractive to insects, abundant clusters of spherical red fruits, 1m/1.5m (3ft/5ft); *C. simonsii*, deciduous or semi-evergreen shrub, good for hedging, glossy dark green leaves, white flowers with pink stamens, scarlet fruits, 1.5m/1m (5ft/3ft).

Evergreen/semi-evergreen species: *C. cochleatus*, prostrate, mound-forming shrub, broad, shiny, oval green leaves, notched at tip, pink buds opening to white flowers in summer, red fruits, 30cm/2m (1ft/6½ft); *C. congestus*, creeping, dull pale green leaves, solitary white flowers in summer, 70cm/90cm (2¼ft/3ft); *C. c.* 'Nanus', dwarf, good in a rock garden, 50cm/50cm (1¾ft/1¾ft); *C. conspicuous* 'Decorus', mound-forming, narrow, elliptic, shiny dark green leaves, white flowers in clusters, sometimes solitary, in summer, shiny red fruit, 1.5m/2-2.5m (5ft/6½-8ft); *C. dammeri*, prostrate, ovate to elliptic mid-to dark green leaves, white flowers, solitary or in clusters, in early summer, slightly spherical red fruit, 20cm/2m (8in/6½ft); *C. floccosus*, lance-shaped to elliptic dark green leaves on arching branches, clusters of white flowers in summer, shiny bright red fruits, 5m/5m (16ft/16ft); *C. franchetii*, semi-evergreen, good for hedging, sage-green leaves, pink-white flowers in midsummer, oval orange-red fruits, 3m/3m (10ft/10ft); *C. lacteus*, useful for hedging, elliptic to ovate leaves on arching branches, dark olive to grey-green above, grey, hairy beneath, white flowers in summer, red fruit in autumn lasting into winter, 4m/4m (13ft/13ft); *C. microphyllus*, dwarf, hummock-forming, tiny leaves 15mm (¾in) long, tiny white flowers, red-pink fruits, 30cm/1m (1ft/3ft); *C. salicifolius* 'Exburyensis', arching shrub, lance-shaped bright green leaves, pale yellow fruits, sometimes tinged pink, 1.2m/1.2m (4ft/4ft); *C. s.* 'Gnom', mound-forming, purple arching shoots, lance-shaped leaves, flushed bronze in winter, 10cm/85cm (4in/2¾ft); *C. s.* 'Pendulus', suitable as ground cover but is often grafted to be grown as a standard, glossy ovate leaves, 60cm/180cm (2ft/5½ft); *C. s.* 'Rothschildianus', semi-evergreen, light green willow-like leaves, clusters of cream-yellow fruit in autumn, remaining into winter, 1.5m/1.2m (5ft/4ft); *C. serotinus*, shrub or small tree, elliptic leaves dark green above, pale green beneath, clusters of white flowers in mid-and late summer, bright red fruit, 10m/3-4m (33ft/10-13ft); *C.* x *suecicus* ' Coral Beauty', glossy dark green leaves on arching branches, bright coral-red fruits, 60cm/1.2m (2ft/4ft).

Cotula *Brass Buttons* Asteraceae

Carpeting annuals and perennials. Barely hardy. The perennial species I describe here is good for rock gardens. Finely divided pinnate or lobed, sometimes rosette-forming leaves, silver or bright green. Aster-like inflorescences from late spring to early summer. Sow seeds in warmth in late winter or early spring, or divide in autumn. ❀ *C. hispida*, hairy, silver-grey, segmented leaves, small button-like bright yellow inflorescences, sometimes becoming red with age, 7.5cm/30cm (2¾in/1ft).

above *Cotoneaster dammeri*. Probably the finest ground covering evergreen form of cotoneaster.

Crambe Brassicaceae

Medium/large hardy perennials especially suitable for coastal areas: tolerant of poor soils. Large, simple to pinnate basal leaves, sometimes a few stem leaves. Tiny fragrant flowers on large loose panicles or racemes which it is tempting to cut for indoor decoration but unfortunately, they smell strongly of cabbage. Sow seeds in a cold-frame in spring or autumn, divide in early spring or take root cuttings in winter. ❀ *C. cordifolia*, clump-forming herbaceous perennial for large gardens, large kidney-shaped to ovate deep green crinkled leaves, branching panicles 1.5m (5ft) in diameter with tiny strong-smelling flowers from late spring to mid-summer, 2.5 m-1.5m (8-5ft); *C. maritima* (Sea Kale), spreading ornamental or vegetable, notched or lobed edible fleshy, blue-green leaves, white flowers in dense racemes in early summer, 75cm/60cm (2½ft/2ft).

Crataegus *Thorn, Hawthorn* Rosaceae

Large deciduous, sometimes semi-evergreen, shrubs and small trees. Hardy. Still, I think, under-appreciated. Especially valuable for exposed areas and town gardens. Thorny branches, toothed, oval, usually small leaves, sometimes lobed, in some species with very good if brief autumn colour. Clusters of fragrant cream, red or pink saucer-shaped flowers in late spring or early summer are followed by small round fruits (haws). Thrives in most soils in full sun, although will tolerate partial shade. Difficult to strike from cuttings; sow ripe seed in a cold-frame (many types come true). ❀ *C. crusgalli* (Cockspur Thorn), small tree with very pronounced thorns, glossy, dark green ovate leaves, scarlet in autumn, clusters of white flowers with pink anthers in early summer, followed by round red fruits, 8m/10m (25ft/33ft); *C. laciniata* (syn. *C. orientalis*), compact small tree, sparsely thorny, triangular to diamond-shaped deeply cut, downy dark green leaves, grey beneath, clusters of white flowers with red anthers from late spring to early summer, orange-red or coral red fruits, 6m/6m (20ft/20ft); *C. laevigata* (syn. *C. oxyacantha*) (English Hawthorn, May) 'Crimson Cloud' rounded, shallowly lobed, glossy mid-green leaves, clusters of sweetly scented large purple-red flowers, sometimes flushed pink, in late spring, crimson fruits, 8m/8m (25ft/25ft); *C. l.* 'Paul's Scarlet' (syn. 'Coccinea Plena'), double deep pink flowers; *C. l.* 'Plena', double flowers, white at first, later pink; *C.* 'Rosea Flore Pleno', double pink flowers, still, I think, the best form; *C.* x *l.* 'Carrièrei', long glossy dark green leaves, red in autumn, often not shedding until midwinter, white flowers with pink anthers, fruits orange-red, lasting until winter, 7m/10m (23ft/33ft); *C. monogyna* (English Hawthorn), numerous thorns, ovate to diamond-shaped lobed mid-green leaves, usually orange-red in autumn, sweetly scented white flowers in late spring, ovoid crimson fruits, 10m/8m (33ft/25ft); *C. persimilis* 'Prunifolia', glossy, deep green leaves, orange or scarlet in autumn, clusters of white flowers in early summer, abundant orange-red fruits, 8m/10m (25ft/33ft).

above *Crataegus laevigata* 'Rosea Flore Pleno'. The hawthorns are greatly under-valued as blossom trees but this is one of many that prove their merits; and they are much less disease-prone than many rivals.

Crepis *Hawk's Beard* Asteraceae

Small hardy annuals, biennials and herbaceous perennials. Basal rosettes of pinnate or entire leaves, simple or compound dandelion-like inflorescences, singly or in clusters, in summer. Sow seeds when ripe in a cold-frame or take root cuttings in winter. Self-seeds freely and can become invasive. ❀ *C. incana*, rosettes of inversely lance-shaped toothed grey-green hairy leaves, pink or purple-pink flowers in midsummer, 30cm/30cm (1ft/1ft).

Crinodendron
Lantern Tree Elaeocarpaceae

Large evergreen shrubs and small trees for rich acidic soil. Impressive plants when grown well. Fairly hardy to moderately hardy, depending on the situation. Dark green, shiny leaves, narrow elliptic to oblong or ovate, beautiful bell-, urn- or lantern-shaped red or white flowers. Take semi-ripe cuttings in late summer. ❀ *C. hookerianum* (syn. *Tricuspidaria lanceolata*), small bushy tree or large shrub, moderately hardy in cold areas if given a sheltered position, toothed, leathery leaves on downy stalks, flowers in bud from autumn, opening to pendent lantern-shaped flowers the following year in late spring or early summer,

6m/5m (20ft/16ft); *C. patagua* (syn. *Tricuspidaria dependent*), shrub with broad, finely toothed leaves similar to those of the above, buds in autumn open to bell-shaped, scented white flowers from mid-to late summer, 8m/5m (25ft/16ft).

Crinum Amaryllidaceae

Small/large deciduous or evergreen bulbous ornamentals. Tender to moderately hardy. In cold areas a few species will survive in a warm, sheltered position outside. Strap-shaped basal leaves, light to mid-green, trumpet or funnel-shaped flowers in late summer. Divide clumps in spring. ❀ *C.* x *powellii*, bright green leaves, funnel-shaped pink flowers from late summer to early autumn, 1.5m/30cm (5ft/1ft). *C* x *p.* 'Album', pure white flowers.

Crocosmia *Montbretia* Iridaceae

Medium corm-forming ornamentals. Fairly hardy to moderately hardy. Suitable for herbaceous and shrub borders although some can be invasive; good for cutting. Erect, sword-shaped mid-green leaves, funnel-shaped or tubular flowers carried on either side of slender arching stems. Thrives best in sandy, moist soil enriched with humus, in sun or partial shade. Sow ripe seed in a cold-frame or divide in spring. ❀ *C.* x *crocosmiiflora*, pale green leaves, spikes of orange or yellow flowers in late summer, 60cm/8cm (2ft/3¾in); *C.* x *c.* 'Carmin Brilliant', small pink-red flowers; *C.* x *c.* 'Jackanapes', mid-green leaves, many-branched stems of orange and red flowers in late summer, 40-60cm/8cm (1½-2ft/3¼in); *C.* x *c.* 'James Coey', small, deep orange-red flowers; *C.* x *c.* 'Lady Hamilton', small yellow flowers, yellow ring on the inside; *C.* 'Emberglow', mid-green leaves, nodding, small dark red flowers on red-brown stems, in midsummer, 60-75cm/8cm (2-2½ft/3¼in); *C.* 'Lucifer', the best overall in my experience, stiff, pleated blade-like leaves, large flame-red flowers on arching spikes in summer, 1- 1.2m/8cm (3-4ft/3¼in); *C. masoniorum*, pleated mid-green leaves, orange-red flowers on arching, usually unbranched stems, in midsummer, 1.2m/8cm (4ft/3¼in); *C.* 'Severn Sunset', orange-pink flowers.

far left *Crinodendron hookerianum* is a rich and glorious South American evergreen for moist, milder gardens with acidic soil.

left *Crocosmia x crocosmiiflora* 'Sulphurea'. The modern named forms of *Crocosmia* such as this one are much less invasive than the species and older types.

Crocus Iridaceae

Small corm-forming ornamentals; the most valuable and versatile of all small 'bulbous' ornamentals. Fairly hardy to hardy. Suitable for herbaceous and mixed borders, or (large flowered 'Dutch' varieties) for naturalising in grass. Smaller species are best grown in rock gardens or troughs. Narrow, grass-like leaves, with a central stripe of silver-grey or white. Goblet- or funnel-shaped, six-petalled flowers, some scented of honey, in a variety of colours including pale and bright yellow, purple, blue, mauve, lilac, cream and white, mainly

above *Crocus ancyrensis.* I have grown this delightful crocus for many years and it is consistently the best golden variety for winter.

in late winter, early spring, or autumn. Most thrive in well-drained soil in full sun; flowers open in sunlight, close on dull days. Best planted in clumps. Divide clumps after flowering and sow ripe seed in a cold-frame. Corms may be eaten by mice and voles, and birds may pick at the flowers. ❀ *C. ancyrensis*, golden-yellow flowers in late winter, 7cm (2¾in); *C. angustifolius* (syn. *C. susianus*), deep yellow, bronze markings on outer petals in late winter and early spring, 7cm (2¾in); *C. banaticus*, lilac to purple flowers with pale inner petals in early autumn, dark green leaves appear after the flowers have faded 10cm (4in); *C. cartwrightianus* 'Albus', goblet-shaped, fragrant pure white flowers appear with the leaves in autumn or early winter, best grown in a frame or alpine house, 5cm/5cm (2in/2in); *C. chrysanthus* 'Blue Pearl', white flowers with grey-blue outer petals in late winter or early spring, 10cm (4in); *C. c.* 'Cream Beauty', rich cream rounded petals; *C. c.* 'Ladykiller', pure white flowers with deep purple markings on the outer petals; *C. c.* 'Snow Bunting', white flowers with light brown markings at the base of the petals; *C. c.* 'Zwanenburg Bronze', golden yellow flowers with purple-bronze marks on the outer petals in autumn and early winter; *C. goulimyi*, pale lilac flowers on tall tubes in mid autumn, suitable for the alpine house or outside in full sun, 18cm (7in); *C. laevigatus* 'Fontenayi', a superb and reliable winter crocus, small, fragrant lilac flowers with purple stripes on outer petals in early winter, good for naturalising or a rock garden, 75cm (2½ft); *C. medius*, deep purple flowers with rounded petals in autumn, scarlet stigmas, leaves appear as flowers fade, 10cm (4in); *C. ochroleucus*, cream-white flowers with yellow throats, leaves appear just after the flowers, 5-8cm (2-3¼in); *C. sativus* (Autumn Crocus), large flowers, 3cm (1¼in) tall, rich purple with darker veins and scarlet stigmas in mid-autumn, dull green leaves appear with or just after the flowering period, 10cm (4in); *C. speciosus*, violet-blue flowers with deeper blue veins, orange centres, in autumn, 5cm (2in); *C. tommasinianus*, pale silver-lilac to red-purple outer petals often flushed silver, in late winter to early spring, 8-10cm/25cm (3¼-4in/10in); *C. t.* 'Whitewell Purple', red-purple flowers, silver mauve inside; *C. tournefortii*, pale lilac, white anthers, scarlet centres, occasionally with light purple veins, in late autumn after the leaves have appeared, best grown in an alpine house; *C. vernus* (Dutch Crocus), 'Jeanne d'Arc', white flowers with deep purple bases, faint purple feathering, from spring to early summer, 10-12cm/5cm (4-5in/2in); *C. v.* 'King of the Blues', rich purple-blue flowers; *C. v.* 'Purpureus Grandiflorus', violet flowers with purple bases; *C. v.* 'Queen of the Blues', lilac-blue flowers; *C. v.* 'Striped Beauty', striped mauve and paler mauve with deep purple base.

right: *Crocus chrysanthus* Blue Pearl'. This is the species for early spring displays before the large flowered Dutch crocus take centre stage.

Cryptomeria

Japanese Cedar Taxodiaceae

Small/large evergreen trees. Moderately hardy. Thick, red-brown bark, narrow, wedge-shaped dark green needles giving a pronounced feathery appearance. Small male and female flowers on the same plant, followed by spherical female cones, ovoid male cones. No routine pruning although trees may be clipped lightly to improve shape. Take semi-ripe cuttings in late summer or early autumn. ❀ *C. japonica*, red-brown shedding bark, downward sweeping branches, pointed leaves, bright green, sometimes grey-green, often bronzed in winter, green female flowers, yellow-brown male flowers are followed by brown cones, 25m/6m (80ft/20ft); *C. j.* 'Elegans', leaves blue-green at first, red-brown in winter, 6-10m (20-33ft); *C. j.* 'Sekkan-sugi', cream-yellow leaves, almost white in winter; *C. j.* 'Vilmoriniana', dwarf, light green leaves tinged red-brown in winter, 80cm (2½ft).

Cucumis

Cucumber, Melon Cucurbitaceae

Small/medium vegetable fruit. Tender. Trailing or climbing annuals comprising melons, cucumbers and gherkins. In cold areas most are best grown in a greenhouse although some varieties are hardy enough to crop in a cold-frame, under cloches or in the open. Plants produce both male and female flowers: female flowers are distinguished by a swelling or pouch underneath the flower. Greenhouse varieties thrive in humus-rich loam-based soil or compost in full sun. High humidity is usually essential. The male flowers on greenhouse (but not outdoor) cucumbers should be removed before fertilisation takes place in order to produce fruit free from bitterness although some varieties, called All Female types, produce almost entirely female flowers and so render this task unnecessary. Sow seed in warmth from midwinter to late spring. ❀ *C. melo* (Melon): 'Blenheim Orange', red-orange flesh, yellow skin; 'Ogen', pale green flesh, very aromatic, medium-sized melon, in cold areas suitable for cold-frame or cloche culture; 'Sweetheart' F1, pale green skin, orange-pink flowers, very sweet, easily the best variety for colder areas where it is suitable for cold-frame or cloche culture. *C. metullifer* is an African 'horned' cucumber with rough hairy stems, oblong fruit with thick spines. *C. sativa* (Cucumber, Gherkin) Greenhouse varieties: 'Birkit' F1, All Female; 'Brunex' F1; 'Conqueror'; 'Pepinex 69' F1, All Female; 'Petita' F1, All Female small-fruited; 'Telegraph', popular exhibition variety with elongated traditional cucumber shape; Ridge cucumber varieties for growing outside: 'Burpee's Tasty Green' F1; 'Crystal Apple' (syn. 'Lemon Cucumber'), round, like a melon, white skinned at first, yellow when ripe; 'Perfection'; 'Yamato'. 'Venlo Pickling', is a gherkin best harvested when young.

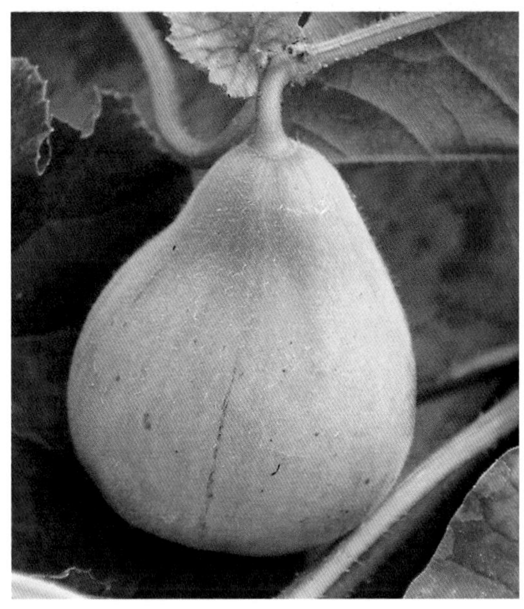

left Without doubt, Melon 'Sweetheart' is the melon for cold frames and other garden use without artificial heat.

Cucurbita *Pumpkins, Marrows, Squashes, Courgettes, Zucchini* Cucurbitaceae

Small/large vegetable fruit. Tender. Bushy or trailing annuals, the most important for garden condition are varieties of *C. pepo* for harvesting in late summer or autumn. Usually lobed, pale to mid-green, hairy, heart-shaped leaves. Wide, bell-shaped, orange-yellow edible flowers, oval or cylindrical fruit, green, cream-white or bicoloured striped skins and succulent flesh. They require fertile, well-drained humus-rich soil in full sun. Sow seeds in warmth in mid-spring or in growing positions in late spring. ❀ **Pumpkin**: 'Atlantic Giant', extremely large, orange-skin, yellow flesh; 'Mammoth', large, orange skin, yellow flesh. Winter squash: 'Butternut' F1, trailing, cylindrical, bright orange flesh; 'Autumn Queen'. **Marrows and Courgettes** (Courgettes are simply marrows cut when young): 'Custard White', a patty pan type, flattened round fruit with scalloped edges; 'Gold Rush' F1, bush type, the most reliable courgette in my experience, attractive deep yellow, slightly curved; 'Long Green Trailing', traditional variety of trailing marrow, dark green skin marked pale green and deep yellow; 'Minipak', bush type, green striped marrow to 30cm (1ft); 'Tiger Cross' F1, bush type, use as courgette when young, later

right *Courgette* 'Gold Rush'. The golden varieties of courgette and of full-sized marrow make bright and attractive contrasts to the dark green types.

as marrow; 'Vegetable Spaghetti', spaghetti-like flesh when cooked; 'Zucchini' F1, bush type, deep green cylindrical fruit.

Cuphea — Lythraceae

Annuals, perennials and sub-shrubs. Tender to barely hardy. Those I describe here are short-lived evergreen perennials suitable for growing outdoors in containers in summer. Oval to lance-shaped, slightly toothed, mid-to dark green leaves. Star-shaped or tubular flowers, singly or in clusters. Sow seed in warmth in late winter or early spring or in growing positions in late spring; take soft-wood cuttings or divide in late spring. ❀ *C. hyssopifolia* (False Heather), bushy sub-shrub, small, narrow, glossy dark green leaves, small, star-shaped white, pink or pale purple flowers from summer to autumn, 30-60cm/20-80cm (1-2ft/8in-3ft); *C. ignea* (syn. *C. platycentra*) (Cigar Flower), shrub or sub-shrub, lance-shaped to ovate glossy, dark green leaves, scarlet tubular flowers with black tip rimmed with white, 30-75cm/30-90cm (1-2½ft/1ft-3ft).

X Cupressocyparis *Leyland Cypress* — Cupressaceae

Large evergreen tree. Hardy. A hybrid between *Chamaecyparis nootkatensis* and *Cupressus macrocarpa*. Exceptionally fast growing and although a valuable screening plant for large hedges, it should be planted with caution, especially in urban gardens where it will very soon become a nuisance. Dark green, flattened sprays of scale-like leaves. Contact with leaves may irritate the skin or cause an allergy. Very small insignificant flowers from late spring to early summer, sometimes followed by small, oval yellow male cones and rounded female cones. Clip hedges at least twice each year as they will otherwise soon become unmanageable. Take semi-ripe cuttings in late summer. ❀ x *C. leylandii*, large columnar tree, dark green leaves, tinged grey on slightly drooping stems, dark brown female cones, 25m (80ft); x *C. l.* 'Castlewellan' (syn. 'Galway Gold'), plume-like sprays of golden foliage; x *C. l.* 'Robinson's Gold', leaves bronze-yellow in spring, later golden yellow and lime-green.

Cupressus *Cypress* — Cupressaceae

Small/large evergreen trees. Barely hardy to moderately hardy. Usually narrow and columnar. Tiny, overlapping, aromatic scale-like leaves. Clusters of insignificant green flowers from winter to early spring. Small round female cones, smaller oval male cones, green at first, later brown and woody, often remaining on the tree for several years. Thrives best in well-drained soil in full sun sheltered from cold, drying winds. Varieties with yellow foliage need an open position. No routine pruning but plants grown as hedging should be clipped twice each year. Take semi-ripe cuttings in spring. ❀ *C. arizonica* var. *glabra* 'Aurea' (syn. *C. glabra*), slender tree, blue-grey leaves flecked white beneath, flushed yellow in summer, 10-15m/4-5m (33-50ft/13-16ft); *C. a.* var. *g* 'Blue Ice', silver-blue foliage; *C. macrocarpa* 'Donard Gold', deep yellow foliage, in upright, spreading sprays, 15m (50ft); *C. m.* 'Gold Crest', smaller variety with feathery foliage when young, rich golden yellow leaves, 5m/2.5m (16ft/8ft); *C. m.* 'Golden Pillar', small, narrow, golden yellow foliage; *C. sempervirens* 'Stricta', very slender small tree, horizontal, flattened branches, sprays of dark green or grey-green leaves, female cones are prickly, 5m/60cm (16ft/2ft); *C. s.* 'Swane's Gold', upright, pale yellow or green-yellow leaves, 6m/1m (20ft/3ft); *C. torulosa* 'Cashmeriana' (syn. *C. cashmeriana*),

far right *Cuphea ignea*. Although too tender to be grown as a year-round garden shrub, this very pretty Central American species is excellent in summer containers.

an extremely beautiful tree but tender and suitable for growing outside only in mild areas, blue-grey leaves on long flattened pendent sprays, prickly green-brown female cones, 30m/10m (100ft/33ft).

Cyananthus

Trailing Bellflower Campanulaceae

Small herbaceous perennials. Moderately hardy. Linear to broadly rounded leaves, sometimes toothed and hairy, on prostrate stems. Funnel-shaped flowers, blue, violet or yellow, sometimes white. Sow seeds in a cold-frame when ripe or in spring, or take soft-wood cuttings in late spring or early summer. ❀ *C. lobatus*, deeply lobed, fleshy dull green leaves, bright blue flowers, hairy dark calyces, from late summer to early autumn, 5cm/30cm (2in/1ft); *C. microphyllus*, mat-forming, thick red stems, violet-blue flowers from late summer to early autumn, 2.5cm/25cm (1in/10in).

Cyathodes

Epacridaceae

Small evergreen shrubs and small trees. Fairly hardy. Heath-like, suitable for rock gardens with acidic soil. Small, overlapping linear to lance-shaped leaves, small tubular flowers singly or in clusters, followed by fleshy fruit. ❀ *C. colensoi*, narrow leaves with hairy margins, pink tips on new leaves, mature leaves blue-green, small white male and female flowers on separate plants, followed, occasionally, by white, deep pink or red fruits, 30cm/30cm (1ft/1ft).

Cyclamen

Primulaceae

Small tuberous ornamentals. tender to moderately hardy. Round or heart-shaped leaves, sometimes lobed or serrated. In some species there is silver or white marbling on the leaf surface with red beneath, making the plants almost as valuable for their foliage as for their flowers. Flowers sometimes fragrant, are nodding, with twisted reflexed petals, in various shades of pink, crimson, mauve or white. Flowering time depends on the species, but one or more type can be found in bloom at most times of the year. Hardy species thrive in most well-drained, moist soils enriched with humus, in partial shade. Barely hardy species are suitable for growing outside in mild areas although in colder gardens, they are very successful in cold-frames. Transplant 'daughter' tubers in the dormant season or sow ripe seeds in a cold-frame. ❀ *C. africanum*, tender, heart-shaped bright green leaves with paler markings, pink flowers with deep maroon mouths, appear in autumn before the leaves, 12-15cm/23cm (5-6in/9in); *C. balearicum*, barely hardy, mid-green to grey-green, heart-shaped leaves with scalloped margins and silver markings, maroon beneath, white or pale pink fragrant flowers with fine veining, appear with the leaves in spring, 5cm/5-8cm (2in/2-3¼in); *C. cilicium*, barely hardy, oval leaves, heart-shaped at the base, deep green with grey or cream-white markings, pale to mid-pink flowers from late summer to autumn, 5cm/8cm (2in/3¼in); *C. c.* f. *album*, pure white; *C. coum*, moderately hardy,

left *Cupressus macrocarpa* 'Gold Crest'. Although the Monterey cypress has been grown for many years and to some extent has fallen from favour, this is one of the best golden conifers of any type.

above *Cyclamen coum*. This is the hardy cyclamen for late winter flowering and here it is confusingly seen with the foliage of the autumn flowering *Cyclamen hederifolium*.

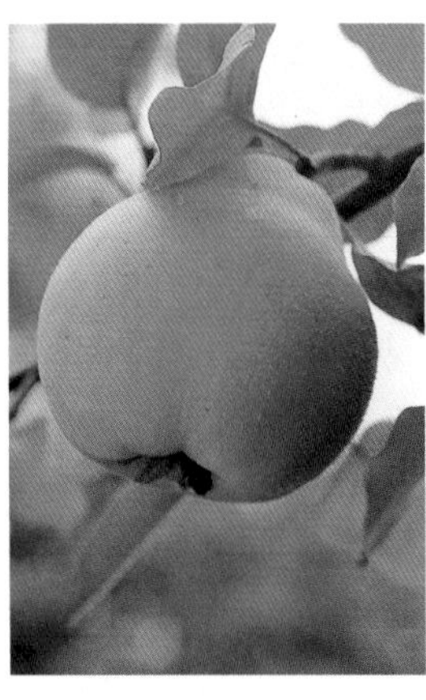

above Quince 'Vranja'. For a fruit with such a long history of cultivation, quinces are still unfortunately not common trees.

below There are relatively few good wall plants for the native plant garden but *Cymbalaria muralis* is one of the prettiest.

shiny deep green, sometimes deep green with silver markings, white, carmine or pink flowers, white rimmed mouths, appear with leaves in winter or early spring, 5-8cm/10cm (2-3¼in/4in); *C. c. album*, white flowers; *C. c.* Pewter Group, silver-grey leaves, sometimes with green margins or midribs pink or magenta flowers; *C. cyprium*, barely hardy, toothed, heart-shaped light grey patterned leaves, fragrant white flowers, carmine at the mouth, appear with the leaves in autumn, 5-8cm/15cm (2-3¼in/6in); *C. hederifolium* (syn. *C. neapolitanum*), hardy, deep grey-green, usually heart-shaped leaves with grey, cream or silver markings, pale to deep pink flowers in autumn, 15cm/23cm (6in/9in); *C. h.* f. *album*, pure white; *C. intaminatum*, barely hardy, plain green rounded leaves, marked silver-white, tiny white or pale pink flowers with pale grey veins, 6cm/9cm (2¼in/3½in); *C. libanoticum*, barely hardy, dark green, lobed, heart-shaped leaves, light green markings, in winter, pale pink flowers with a white base, red markings at the mouth, appear with leaves in winter or early spring, 10cm/15cm (4in/6in); *C. mirabile*, barely hardy, rounded leaves with scalloped margins, pale pink flowers with toothed petals, 8cm/8-10cm (3¼in/3¼-4in); *C. pseudoibericum*, barely hardy, best in alkaline soil, heart-shaped, deep green leaves with scalloped margins, grey-green or silver markings, fragrant carmine flowers from mid-summer to early autumn, 8-10cm/10cm (3¼-4in/4in); *C. repandum*, heart-shaped, deep green leaves, grey-green markings or specks, fragrant carmine flowers appear with the leaves from mid to late spring, 10-15cm/10-13cm (4-6in/4-5¼in).

Cydonia *Quince* — Rosaceae

Deciduous tree or shrub. Moderately hardy but in cold areas, best trained against a wall. Elliptic to oval leaves, yellow in autumn, flowers followed by edible fruit. No routine pruning. Always buy named varieties. ❀ *C. oblonga* 'Meech's Prolific', dark green leaves, downy beneath, solitary pale pink to white flowers in late spring followed by aromatic light yellow fruit, ripening in mid autumn, 5m/5m (16ft/16ft); *C. o.* 'Vranja', the best and most reliable variety for our climate, very aromatic fruit, pale green at first, later golden yellow.

Cymbalaria — Scrophulariaceae

Small hardy herbaceous and evergreen alpines. Small round, sometimes lobed leaves on creeping stems. Very pretty tiny flowers on slender stems and I think this is one of the easiest and most unappreciated alpines. Sow seed in winter in warmth or replant rooted stems. ❀ *C. muralis* (syn. *Linaria cymbalaria*), (Ivy-leaved Toadflax), tiny, ivy-like leaves, lilac or blue viola-like flowers with spot on lower lip and darker markings, from spring to autumn, 2cm/60cm (¾in/2ft); *C. m.* 'Nana Alba', compact, abundant white flowers; *C. m.* 'Pallidior', white flowers with yellow throat.

Cynara — Asteraceae

Large herbaceous ornamental perennials and vegetables. Barely hardy to moderately hardy. Thrive best in well-drained fertile soil in full sun protected from strong winds. Replant offsets or take root cuttings of selected strains in winter, generally less successful from seed. ❀ *C.* Scolymus Group (Globe Artichoke), very large, long arching lobed silver-grey leaves, purple thistle-like flowers from late summer to mid-autumn, suitable for cutting and drying. The edible parts are the leaf bracts and heart of the flowerheads. *C. cardunculus* (Cardoon), spiny silver-grey leaves, purple inflorescences from early summer to early autumn, grey woolly stems, The fleshy leaf bases and midribs are blanched and eaten raw or cooked. 1.5m/1.2m (5ft/4ft).

Cynoglossum *Hound's Tongue* — Boraginaceae

Hardy annuals, biennials and perennials. Narrow, rough, lance-shaped or ovate leaves, clusters of blue, sometimes pink, white or purple flowers held on one side of the curved flower stem, from spring to autumn. Sow seed in a cold-frame or divide in spring, or take root cuttings in winter. ❀ *C. nervosum*, clump-forming perennial, narrow, hairy, mid-green leaves, sprays of bright blue flowers early to late summer, 60cm/60cm (2ft/2ft).

Cyrtanthus *Fire Lily* Amaryllidaceae

Small deciduous/semi-evergreen bulbous ornamentals. Tender to barely hardy. Suitable for growing outside in mild areas only. Clump-forming, usually mid-green, strap-shaped leaves. Umbels of tubular or flared bell- shaped flowers from spring to autumn. Sow seed in warmth when ripe or remove offsets. ❀ *C. elatus* (syn. *C specious*, *C. purpureus*), deciduous, erect strap-shaped leaves, slightly fragrant, funnel-shaped bright scarlet flowers from midsummer to early autumn, 30-60cm/10cm (1-2ft/4in).

Cyrtomium Aspidiaceae

Small deciduous or evergreen fern. Barely hardy to hardy. Leathery, pinnate, leaves, leaflets sharply pointed. Sow spores in warmth in late summer, divide in spring or sectioning rhizomes in winter. ❀ *C. falcatum* (syn. *Phanerophlebia falcatum*) (Japanese Holly Fern), moderately hardy evergreen and much more tough than is usually claimed, glossy, dark green, holly-like leaflets, 60cm/1.1m (2ft/3½ft); *C. fortunei* (syn. *Phanerophlebia fortunei*), moderately hardy, dull pale green fronds, sickle-shaped leaflets, 60cm/40cm (2ft/1½ft).

Cytisus Papilionaceae

Small/large deciduous or evergreen shrubs and among the best for reliable spring flowers. Barely hardy to moderately hardy and with a tendency to be short-lived, especially on poor soil. All the species I describe here are deciduous and moderately hardy unless stated otherwise. Simple or palmate leaves, mid-green, plants sometimes leafless when older. Pea-like fragrant flowers, singly or in clusters, followed by mid-green hairy or downy seed-pods. Thrive best in fertile, light, well-drained soil in full sun. No routine pruning. Take semi-hardwood cuttings in summer or hardwood cuttings in winter. ❀ *C. battandieri*, barely hardy, best grown against a sunny wall in mild areas, large silver-green palmate leaves, a most beautiful plant with golden yellow pineapple scented flowers from late spring to midsummer, 5m/5m (16ft /16ft); *C.* x *beanii*, dwarf, linear, simple hairy leaves, 60cm/1m (2ft/3ft). *C.* 'Burkwoodii', medium-sized, erect, best in a neutral soil, intolerant of extremes, lance-shaped silver-grey leaves, clusters of red flowers with crimson wings edged with yellow, from late spring to early summer, 1.5m/1.5m (5ft/5ft); *C.* 'Hollandia', palmate leaves, abundant small, pale cream and red flowers with darker red wings, from late spring to early summer, 1.2m/1.5m (4ft/5ft); *C.* x *kewensis*, low-growing, mid-green palmate leaves on downy arching branches, almost covered with clusters of cream flowers in late spring, 30cm/1.5m (1ft/5ft); *C.* 'Killiney Red', compact, palmate leaves on arching branches, abundant red flowers with darker wings, from late spring to early summer, 1.2m/1.5m (4ft/5ft); *C.* 'Lena', compact, arching branches with simple leaves, clusters of white flowers from mid to late spring, 1.2m/1.5m (4ft/ 5ft); *C.* x *praecox* 'Allgold', dark yellow flowers; *C.* x *p.* 'Warminster', yellow flowers; *C. scoparius*, erect, tiny mid-green palmate leaves on green branches, rich yellow flowers, singly or in pairs, 1.5m/1.5m (5ft/5ft); *C. s.* f. *andreanus*, yellow flowers splashed with red; *C.* 'Windelsham Ruby', bushy, palmate leaves, large ruby-red flowers singly or in pairs, from late spring to early summer, 1.5m/1.5m (5ft/5ft); *C.* 'Zeelandia', bushy, three-palmate leaves, clusters of cream-white and lilac-pink flowers, from late spring to early summer, 1.5m/1.5m (5ft/5ft).

above *Cytisus battandieri.* There is quite simply no finer plant in this very valuable genus; the size of its flowers, the colour of its leaves and even that fresh pineapple fragrance all mark it out as a quite stunning plant.

Daboecia *St Dabeoc's Heath* Ericaceae

Small evergreen shrubs. Fairly hardy. Suitable for ground cover among other acidic -loving species such as *Calluna*. Small lance-shaped or elliptic, dark green leaves, relatively large (for a Heath) urn-shaped flowers from early summer to autumn. Take semi-ripe heeled cuttings in midsummer. ❀ *D. cantabrica* f. *alba*, lance-shaped leaves, glossy, dark green above, white beneath, spikes of white flowers from early summer to mid autumn, 25-40cm/65cm (10-1½ft/2¼ft); *D. c.* 'Atropurpurea', dark purple flowers; *D. c.* 'Bicolour', mid-green leaves, sometimes deciduous, white, red and pink flowers, sometimes striped; *D. c.* 'Hookstone Purple', large amethyst flowers in late autumn; *D. c.* 'Prolifera', grey-green leaves, pale mauve flowers; *D. c.* 'Praegerae', sometimes deciduous in cold weather, mid-green leaves, deep red flowers; *D.* x *scotica* 'Jack Drake', barely hardy, elliptic to oval leaves, dark green, clusters of ruby red flowers from late spring to mid autumn, 25cm/40cm (10in/1½ft); *D. c.* 'Waley's Red', deep magenta flowers, 50cm/65cm (1¾ft/2¼ft).

above *Daboecia cantabrica* 'Praegerae'. I have often called *Daboecia* the forgotten heather and this impressive form, named after a great Irish botanist is a typical sample.

Dactylorhiza Orchidaceae

Small to medium tuberous, deciduous terrestrial orchid. Moderately hardy. Spear-shaped leaves, fleshy, mid-green spikes of purple, red-purple, red, pink or white hooded flowers spotted or streaked, with green to purple bracts. Divide in early spring or autumn after the leaves have died down. ❀ *D. foliosa*, deep green leaves, sometimes brown, spotted pink or purple flowers from late spring to early summer, 60cm/15cm (2ft/6in); *D. fuchsii*, clumps of mid-green leaves with dark purple spots, pale pink, white or mauve flowers with red or purple marks, from late spring to early summer, often self-seeds, 20-60cm/10cm (8in-2ft/4in); *D. maculata*, bright green plain or sometimes brown or purple spotted leaves, pink, red, mauve or white flowers from mid-spring to late summer, small single tooth on wavy-edged lip, 15-60cm/15cm (6in-2ft/6in).

Dahlia Asteraceae

Small/medium tender tuberous ornamentals and half-hardy annuals. Dahlias are much misunderstood and in the right place, and of the right variety, they can enhance almost any garden. They are generally divided into two main groups: low-growing bedding dahlias, most of which are grown from seed, and taller border dahlias, named varieties, most 1.1-1.3m/60cm (3½-4½ft/2ft), that must be propagated vegetatively. All have pinnate leaves with toothed oval leaflets, mid- to dark green, occasionally, and very attractively, bronze or dark purple. The flowers vary enormously in form and size, with single, semi-double or double inflorescences, the latter including types with names such as waterlily, pompon, cactus and orchid-flowered. Those varieties that are widely used for exhibition are grouped according to the size of the flower: Giant, over 25cm (10in) in diameter; Large, 20-25cm (8-10in); Medium, 15-20cm (6-8in); Small, 10-15cm (4-6in); Miniature, less than 10cm (4in). Colours range from white through oranges and yellows to red and purples. Dahlias require rich, well-drained soil in full sun and the taller types must be staked. In all but the mildest areas the tubers must be lifted in autumn, cleaned free of soil and stored in a frost-free place. Most bedding dahlias are raised from seed sown in warmth in early spring: border varieties by taking stem cuttings or dividing the tubers.

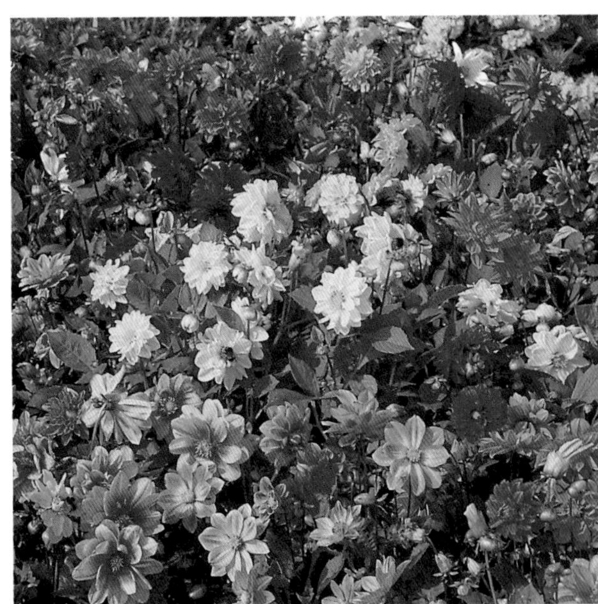

right *Dahlia* 'Rigoletto'. Bedding Dahlias like this mixture are extremely easy to raise from seed, make good cut flowers and entail none of the problems of storing tubers over-winter.

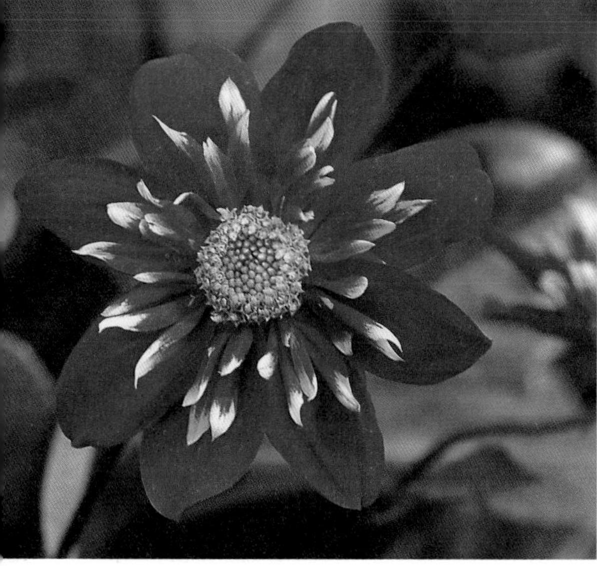

far left *Dahlia* 'Chimborazo'. The Collarette dahlias are among the less well known groups but I find them simply fascinating.

Bedding dahlias raised from seed
Grown as half-hardy annuals: 'Burnished Bronze', double and semi-double flowers in a wide range of colours and attractive bronze-green foliage; 'Coltness Hybrids' single flowers in a wide range of colours, 45-60cm (18-2ft); 'Diablo', semi-double and double, bronze-green leaves, orange, yellow, lavender, lilac and white flowers, 37cm (14¾in); 'Figaro', double, semi-double, white, yellow, red and pink flowers, 40cm (1½ft); 'Redskin', semi-double, double, bronze leaves, wide range of flower colours including scarlet, pink-mauve, orange, 45-60cm (18-2ft); 'Rigoletto', compact, double flowers, 38cm (1½ft).

Single dwarf bedding dahlias
Half-hardy annuals grown from seed: 'Preston Park', very dark green leaves, scarlet flowers with purple centres, prominent yellow anthers, 45cm (1½ft); 'Yellow Hammer', yellow flowers with bronze or dark purple leaves, 45cm/60cm (1½ft/2ft).

Lilliput varieties
Dwarf varieties not exceeding 45cm (1½ft) in height, producing abundant miniature flowers some 3cm (1¼in) in diameter: 'Harvest Inflammation', orange; 'Omo', white.

Anemone-flowered
Small, closely-grouped tubular florets surrounded by one or two rows of larger ray florets, flowers 10-15cm (4-6in) in diameter. 'Comet', dark red centre and ray florets.

Collarette
Central disk surrounded first by densely-packed small florets and on the outer rim by a row of flat, larger florets, sometimes overlapping, often bicoloured flowers 10-15cm (4-6in) in diameter. 'Chimborazo', dark red, yellow central disk and collar; 'Easter Sunday' cream-white.

Waterlily-flowered
Rather flattened, fully double flowers, from giant to miniature. Medium, 'Hugh Mather', orange to orange-brown ; Small, 'Christopher Taylor', red, silver undersides, 'Gerrie Hoek, pale pink outer florets, dark pink inner florets, 'Glorie van Heemsteede', yellow.

Decorative
Flowers flattened, usually with blunt-ended florets. Giant, 'Hamari Girl', pink, 'Hamari Gold', gold-bronze, 'Kidd's Climax', pink, flushed gold, 'Wanda's Capella', orange-yellow; Medium, 'Charlie Two', yellow, 'Lilac Time' lavender, 'Majuba', 'Suffolk Punch' blood red, bronze foliage; Small, 'Arabian Night', dark red-purple, 'Edinburgh', purple tipped with white, 'Lady Linda' clear yellow, 'Moonlight' yellow, 'Senzoe Ursula', violet, white floret base, 'White Linda', white flushed pale lavender-blue; Miniature, 'David Howard', orange yellow, 'Jeanette Carter', pale yellow, often flushed pink at the centre, 'Karenglen', orange-scarlet.

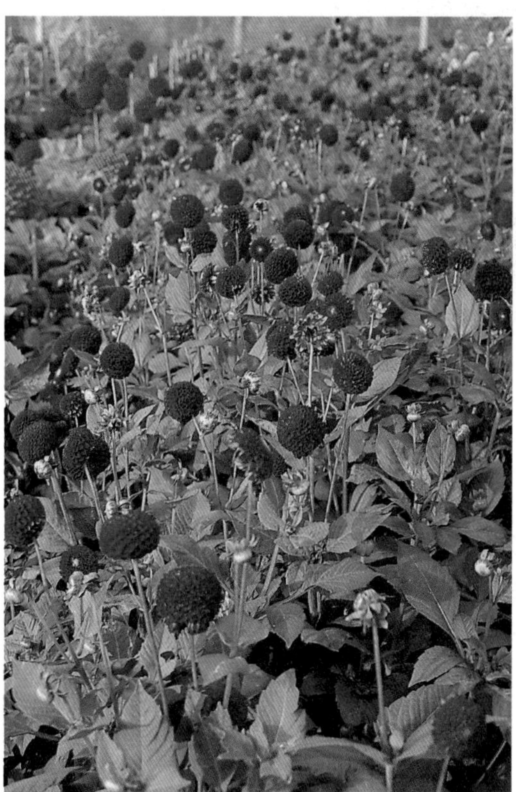

left *Dahlia* 'Moor Place'. The Pompon varieties have a neat, almost sculptural appeal and always find a place in flower arrangements.

Ball-flowered
Fully double flowers, ball-shaped, sometimes slightly flattened at the top, florets spirally arranged, blunt or rounded tips. Small, 'Fiona Stewart', 'Ruskin Tangerine', 'Vaguely Noble'; Miniature, 'Candy Cupid', lavender-pink, 'Hamari Rose'; 'Wootton Cupid, sugar pink.

above *Dahlia* 'Daleko Jupiter'. The cactus dahlias are highly individual and owe their 'spiky' appearance to an ancestry in the Mexican *Dahlia juarezii*.

right *Daphne tangutica* is one of the very best of the evergreen daphnes that I grow, offering particularly pretty flowers, attractive fruits and a reliable evergreen habit.

Pompon
More spherical than ball-flowered varieties, smaller, with incurved florets, most 5cm (2in) in diameter. 'Mi Wong', white, flushed pink, 'Minley Linda', orange-red, 'Moor Place', wine-red, 'Small World', pure white.

Cactus
Fully double flowers, florets rolled back (quilled) for more than half their length, pointed tips. Medium, 'Garden Party', 'Hillcrest Royal', rich purple; small 'Doris Day, red', 'Kiwi Gloria', white, flushed lavender-pink.

Semi-cactus
Similar to cactus but broader florets, quilled half or less than half their length. Giant, 'Daleko Jupiter', rose-red blending to pink-yellow; 'Hamari Accord', pale orange-yellow; Medium, 'Grenidor Pastelle', salmon-pink, cream bases, 'Hamari Bride', white, 'Pink Sensation'; Small, 'Dana Iris', red, 'Hillcrest Albino', white, 'Lemon Elegans', 'Radfo', 'Wittemans Superba', Miniature, 'So Dainty', gold-bronze, flushed apricot.

Miscellaneous
'Bishop of Llandaff', a truly lovely and striking plant, peony-flowered, bright red, black-red foliage, yellow anthers

Dwarf bedding
'Bednall Beauty', double, dark red, bronze-purple foliage, 60cm (2ft); 'Ellen Houston', double, scarlet, purple foliage, 40cm (11/2ft).

Species
D. coccinea, branching, red flowers with yellow centres, 1.2m/60cm (4ft/2ft); *D. merckii*, branching, pinnate mid-green leaves, saucer-shaped single pink to purple or white, purple or yellow anthers, singly or in clusters.

Danae *Alexandrian Laurel* Ruscaeae

Small evergreen shrub best treated as an herbaceous perennial. Fairly hardy. Suitable for shaded areas and use as hedging as a substitute for box. Lacks true leaves; flattened, leaf-like glossy green stems, on arching shoots, small green-yellow spherical hermaphrodite flowers on short panicles in early summer, sometimes followed in mild areas or hot summers by red fruits. Sow seed in a cold-frame in autumn or divide from autumn to early spring. ❀ *D. racemosa*, arching sprays of slender dark green shoots, small green-yellow flowers in early summer followed by red or orange fruits, 1m/1m (3ft/3ft).

Daphne Thymelaeaceae

Small/large semi-evergreen and evergreen shrubs. Barely hardy to moderately hardy. Suitable for rock gardens or shrub borders although in cold areas the least hardy varieties require some protection. All parts of the plant are very toxic when ingested; the sap may irritate the skin. Linear to ovate leaves; tubular, often fragrant flowers, singly or in clusters, in red, white, pink, lavender, lilac or yellow, in winter or from spring to summer. Some of the most

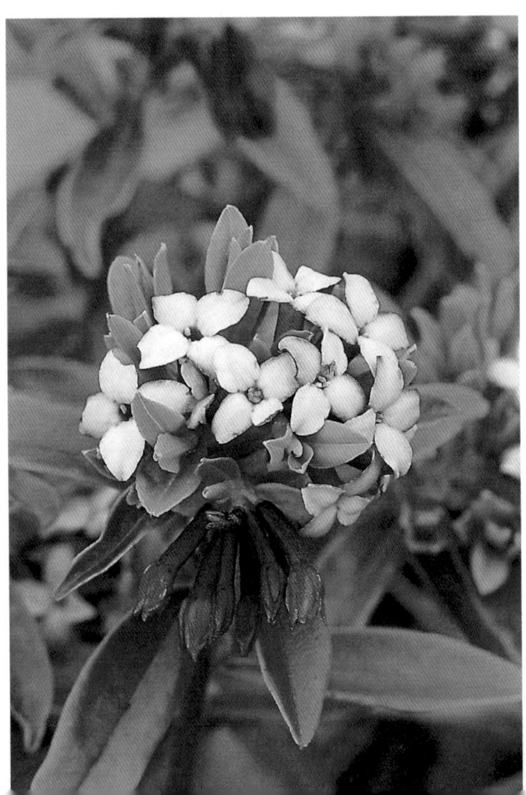

fragrant of all winter flowering shrubs belong here. Flowers are followed by oval fruits. Thrives in fairly fertile soil enriched with humus, in full sun or partial shade. Most prefer a soil bordering on neutral. No routine pruning. Take soft-wood cuttings in early to midsummer, semi-ripe cuttings in mid-to late summer, layer or sow ripe seed in a cold-frame. ❀ *D. bholua*, erect, semi-evergreen, barely hardy, leathery dark green leaves, clusters of fragrant, white pink-tinged flowers in late winter, purple-black fruits, 24m/1.5m (73ft/5ft); *D. blagayana*, mat-forming semi-evergreen or evergreen, oval, dull grey leaves at stem tips only, fragrant cream-white flowers from early to mid spring, round, pink or white fruits, 40cm/1m (1½ft/3ft); *D.* x *burkwoodii*, erect semi-evergreen, linear to inverted lance-shaped leaves, mid-green, clusters of fragrant white flowers tinged pink to pale purple, in late spring, sometimes also in autumn, 1-1.5m/1-1.5m (3-5ft/3-5ft); *D.* x *b.* 'Astrid', leaves edged with cream-white; *D.* x *b.* 'Somerset', pale green leaves, pale pink to white flowers; *D. cneorum*, low-growing, trailing evergreen, dark green leaves, grey-green beneath, profuse clusters of fragrant pale pink to deep rose-pink flowers, sometimes white, from mid spring to early summer, 15cm/2m (6in/6½ft); *D. c.* 'Eximia', deep crimson buds, deep rose-pink flowers, 20cm/2m (8in/6½ft); *D. c.* 'Variegata', pale to mid-pink flowers, leaves edged with yellow; *D. laureola*, erect evergreen, glossy green more or less lance-shaped leaves, very fragrant pale green to yellow-green flowers in late winter to spring, black fruits, 1m/1.5m (3ft/5ft); *D. mezereum*, deciduous, erect, pale green more or less lance-shaped leaves, very fragrant, pink or red-purple flowers in late winter before leaves appear, round red fruits, 1m/1.5m (3ft/5ft); *D. m.* f. *alba*, white flowers, yellow fruits; *D. odora*, evergreen, ovate to inversely lance-shaped leathery, glossy dark green leaves, clusters of fragrant purple-pink or white flowers from midwinter to early spring, 1.5m/1.5m (5ft/5ft); *D. o.* 'Aureomarginata' (syn. *D. o.* 'Marginata'), narrow leaves with irregular yellow margins, red-purple flowers, white inside; *D. pontica*, evergreen, ovate, glossy dark green pointed leaves, fragrant clusters of yellow-green flowers from mid to late spring, oval black fruits, 1m/1.5m (3ft/5ft); *D. tangutica*, erect, evergreen, elliptic, leathery leaves, pale pink flowers from late spring to early summer, sometimes in early autumn, 80cm/45cm (2½ft/1½ft); *D. t.* Retusa Group (syn. *D. retusa*), good for rock gardens, leathery, glossy, deep green leaves, rose-red buds opening to rose-purple flowers from late winter, mid-to late spring, occasionally autumn, shiny red fruits, 60cm/30cm (2ft/1ft).

Darmera — Saxifragaceae

Large hardy herbaceous perennial. Very large, dark green, veined, toothed, deeply lobed umbrella-like leaves on leaf stalks up to 2m (6½ft) in height. Astilbe-like clusters of white or pale pink star-shaped flowers appear on stems 2m (6½ft) in length in early spring before the leaves. Divide in autumn or spring or sow seed in a cold-frame in autumn or spring. ❀ *D. peltata* (syn. *Peltiphyllum peltatum*), flowers with conspicuous deep pink stamens, leaves, erect at first, later spreading, appear as flowers fade, 2m/1m (6½ft/3ft).

above *Darmera peltata*. Few herbaceous perennials provide better or more effective ground cover for large areas than this North American river-side plant.

Daucus *Carrot* — Apiaceae

Small/medium root vegetable. Hardy. A biennial grown as an annual; if left in the ground over winter, carrots will flower in the following spring. The roots of cultivated carrots are usually orange but may also be white or yellow. Thrive best in full sun or light shade in well-cultivated, well-drained deep soil that hasn't been treated with fresh manure within the previous twelve months. Sow seed in growing positions under cloches (early varieties) from winter to mid-spring, or in the open from mid-spring to late spring (maincrop). Space seed carefully to minimise thinning; foliage disturbance attracts carrot fly. Harvest from early summer onwards; store roots

right *Davidia involucrata vilmoriniana*. The plant collector Ernest Wilson described the flowers as being like white doves; so it's unfortunate that this glorious plant is often encumbered with the name of handkerchief tree.

in the ground (with straw protection in colder areas) or lift and store in boxes of sand. Apart from time of maturity, carrots fall into three main groups: short rooted, intermediate and long; they may also be tapering, stump-rooted or spherical. ❀ Early varieties (which may also be sown for a quick crop late in the season): 'Amsterdam Forcing 3'.very early, short, stump rooted; 'Chantenay Red Cored 2', can also be grown as also mid-season or maincrop, intermediate, stump-rooted; 'Early French Frame', very early, short, spherical, suitable for heavier or shallower soils; 'Fly Away' F1, which I grow also as mid-season and maincrop, intermediate, stump rooted, very good resistance to carrot fly; 'Nantes', intermediate, cylindrical rooted; 'Parmex', short, spherical, good for shallower soils; 'Sytan' F1, intermediate, cylindrical rooted, some resistance to carrot fly. Maincrop varieties: 'Autumn King 2', intermediate-long, stump rooted; 'Autumn King 2 Vita Longa', intermediate-long, tapering; stores well; 'Berlicum 2 Berjo', intermediate stump rooted; 'New Red Intermediate' and 'St Valery', very long tapering roots, ideal for exhibition but less practical for garden use.

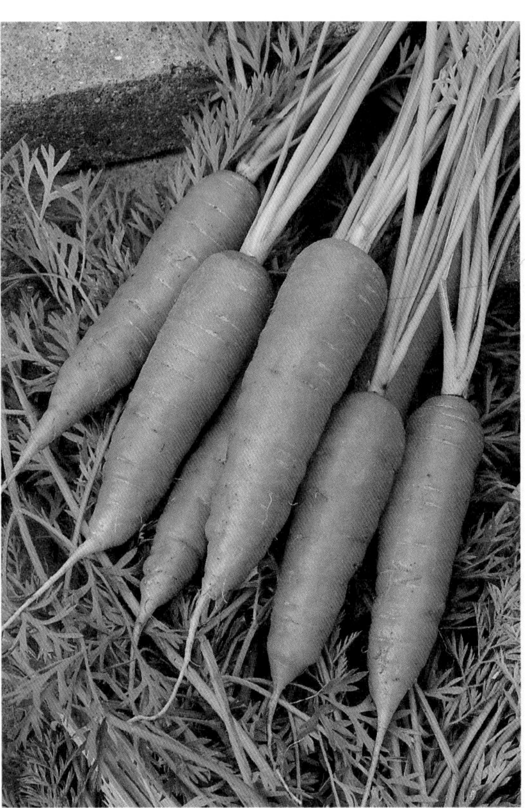

above Carrot 'Fly Away'. Very few new varieties revolutionise vegetable growing in the way that this first really effective carrot-fly resistant variety has done.

Davidia *Dove Tree* Davidiaceae

Medium deciduous tree. Moderately hardy. Rich green, simple, broadly ovate leaves, clusters of green-brown flowers under quite exquisite large white bracts, frequently described as being like fluttering white doves, appear on mature trees and are followed by oval fruit. No routine pruning necessary. Take soft-wood cuttings from mid-to late summer, layer or sow very fresh seed in a cold-frame. ❀ *D. involucrata*, toothed, deep green ovate leaves, hairy beneath, on red stems, flowers, with cream bracts, in late spring, green fruit, egg-shaped, tinged purple. during the autumn, months 15m/10m (50ft/33ft). *D. i.* var. *vilmoriniana*, grey-green or yellow-green leaves, darker beneath.

Decaisnea Lardizabalaceae

Large deciduous shrubs. Moderately hardy. Pinnate green leaves, orange-yellow in autumn, bell-shaped, petal-less flowers carried in spikes followed by seed-pods similar to those of the bean. No routine pruning. Sow fresh seed in a cold-frame in autumn or spring. ❀ *D. fargesii*, large, dark green pinnate leaves. mid-green below, tinged blue when immature, green or yellow-green pendent flowers in early summer, deep blue seed-pods in autumn, 3m/3m (10ft/10ft).

Delphinium Ranunculaceae

Small/large annuals, biennials and herbaceous perennials. Tall varieties are ideal for the back of borders, smaller types for rock gardens; most make good cut flowers. Toothed and lobed basal leaves, inflorescences of cup-shaped, spurred single or double flowers in cream, white and shades of blue, purple, yellow, pink and red. Thrive in well-drained, fertile, slightly alkaline soil in full sun, protected from strong winds. Take basal cuttings in early spring from named hybrid varieties, sow seed of species in warmth in mid-winter or in flowering positions in early spring, or take root cuttings in spring and early summer.

Species

D. grandiflorum (syn. *D. chinense*), perennial, usually grown as an annual, deep green leaves, narrowly lobed, single blue, violet or white flowers in early summer, 20-25cm (8-10in); *D. g.* 'Blue Butterfly', bright blue flowers; *D. nudicaule*, perennial often grown as an annual, lobed leaves on long stalks, single, funnel-shaped flowers, red, orange-red or yellow, red or yellow throats, unbranched stems, in midsummer, 20cm/60cm (8in/2ft); *D.* x *ruysii* 'Pink Sensation', erect, short-lived perennial, small, glossy, finely divided leaves, nodding yellow-pink buds opening to dusky-pink flowers, from summer to autumn, 1m/60cm (3ft/2ft); *D. tatsienense*, short-lived but nonetheless very lovely perennial, deeply cut, palmate leaves, mid-green, loose panicles of long-spurred, purple-blue flowers, funnel shaped, in midsummer, 20-26cm/30cm (8-10½in/1ft).

Garden hybrids

D. Astolat Group, divided leaves, flowers in shades of lilac or pink with black eyes, from early to midsummer, 1.5m/60cm (5ft/2ft); *D.* Belladonna Group, erect, branching, palmate lobed leaves, single blue, sometimes white or purple flowers with long spurs from early to late summer, 1-1.2m/45cm (3-4ft/1½ft); *D.* B G 'Casa Blanca', white; *D.* B G 'Clivedon Beauty', sky-blue; *D.* Black Knight Group, deep violet-purple, black eyes, 1.5m/60cm (5ft/2ft); *D.* Blue Bird Group, clear blue, white eye, deep blue 1.5m/60cm (5ft/2ft); *D.* B G 'Blue Jay', deep blue; *D.* Cameliard Group, lavender-blue, lavender-pink, white eyes, 1.5m/60cm (5ft/2ft); *D.* 'Connecticut Yankees Group, white or shades of blue and mauve, 75cm (2½ft); *D.* 'Emily Hawkins', semi-double or double, large light violet flowers, 1.7m/60-90cm (5ft 7in/ 2-3ft); *D.* 'Faust', semi-double, deep cornflower blue flushed purple, indigo eye, 2m/60-90cm (6½ft/2ft-3ft); *D.* Galahad Group, pure white, 1.5m/60cm (5ft/2ft); *D.* Guinevere Group, rose-lavender, white eye, 1.5m/60cm (5ft/2ft); *D.* King Arthur Group, shades of violet, white eye, 1.5m/60cm (5ft/2ft); *D.* 'Mighty Atom', semi-double violet, brown streaked eyes; *D.* Pacific Hybrids, annuals or biennials, semi-double white, pink, purple, or blue, 1.7m/75cm (5ft 7in/2½ft).

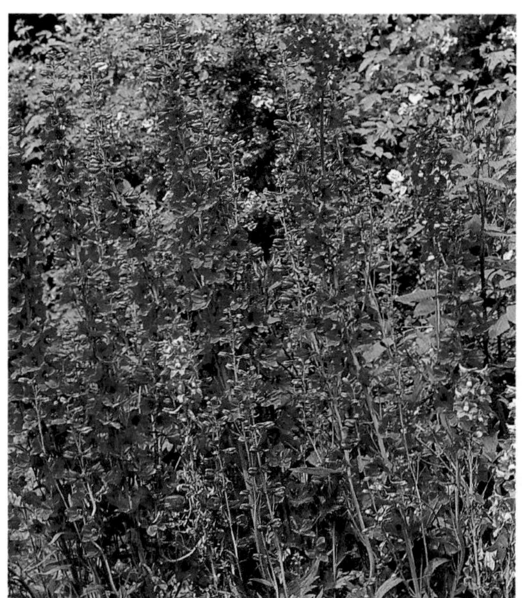

left Delightful species such as *Delphinium tatsienense* astonish gardeners who know delphiniums only as giant border perennials.

Deschampsia *Hair Grass* Poaceae

Small/large perennial evergreen or herbaceous grasses. Hardy. Tussocks of linear, thread-like or oblong leaves, shimmering panicles of small flowers. One of the better grasses for shaded places. Sow seed in growing positions in spring or autumn, or divide established plants in mid spring or early summer. ❀ *D. cespitosa*, evergreen, dark to mid-green leaves, silver-green panicles from early to late summer, remaining during winter, 2m/1.2-1.5m (6½ft/4-5ft); *D. c.* 'Bronzeschleier' (syn. 'Bronze Veil'), inflorescences silver at first, later light bronze on green stems, 1.2m/1.2m (4ft/4ft); *D. c.* 'Goldschleier', (syn. 'Golden Veil'), narrow arching green leaves, panicles silver-green at first, later yellow, on yellow stems, 1.2m/1.2m (4ft/4ft); *D. c.* var. *vivipara*, summer flowers develop into small plantlets, arching stems to the ground, 1.2m/1.2m (4ft/4ft); *D. flexuosa*, evergreen, thread-like blue-green leaves, silver-brown panicles, early to midsummer, 60cm/30cm (2ft/1ft); *D. f.* 'Tatra Gold', bright yellow-green, fine needle-thin leaves, red-brown panicles late spring to mid-summer, 50cm (1¾ft).

far left *Delphinium* Pacific Hybrids. Although much work has been put into the development of red flowered border delphiniums, blue really remains their true colour.

right *Desfontainea spinosa*. This lovely South American tree may look rather like a holly when out of flower, but in bloom, it is unmistakably special.

Desfontainea — Loganiaceae

Small evergreen shrubs for moist, acidic soils. Fairly hardy. Glossy, dark green holly-like leaves, tubular, pendent, very striking waxy scarlet flowers, yellow near the tips, from mid-to late summer. No routine pruning. Take semi-ripe cuttings in mid-summer. ❀ *D. spinosa* (syn. *D. spinosa hookeri*), needs protection from frost, small, oval, spiny-edged dark green leaves, abundant narrow, tubular flowers from midsummer to late autumn, 2m/2m (6½ft/6½ft).

Deutzia — Hydrangeaceae

Small to medium deciduous shrub. Moderately hardy to very hardy. Very free-flowering shrubs, many species with attractive arching branches. Narrow lance-shaped to ovate leaves, mid-green or grey, usually toothed, turn yellow or purple in autumn. Spherical clusters of purple, pink or white star- or cup-shaped flowers, sometimes fragrant, from late spring to early summer. Thrives best in well-drained, fairly rich soil in full sun or partial shade. The more tender varieties require some shelter from frosts. Tolerant of alkaline soils but intolerant of drought. No routine pruning. Take semi-ripe cuttings from early to midsummer or hardwood cuttings in autumn or winter. ❀ *D. compacta* 'Lavender Time', lance-shaped leaves, dark green, grey-green undersides, fragrant cup-shaped flowers in midsummer, lilac at first, later pale lavender, 2m/2.5m (6½ft/8ft); *D. crenata* var. *nakaiana* 'Nikko', dwarf, compact, narrow, pointed, rich green leaves, red-purple in autumn, white inflorescences in summer, 60cm/1.2m (2ft/4ft); *D.* x *elegantissima* 'Rosealind', erect, bushy, lance-shaped matt green leaves, pink-flushed white or pink inflorescences from late spring to early summer, 1.2m/1.5m (4ft/5ft); *D. gracilis*, pointed, toothed, lance-shaped bright green leaves, erect inflorescences of pure white, star-shaped flowers from spring to early summer, 1m/1m (3ft/3ft); *D.* 'Magicien', erect, bushy, lance-shaped, pale to mid-green leaves, yellow in autumn, clusters of star-shaped flowers edged with white, purple beneath, yellow anthers, 1.5m/1.5m (5ft/5ft); *D.* x *kalmiiflora*, narrow oval leaves, mid-to deep green, clusters of deep rose flowers, white inside, in early summer, 1.5m/1.5m (5ft/5ft); *D. pulchra*, moderately hardy, leathery dark green leaves, remaining until winter, orange-brown peeling bark, pendent sprays of white, pink-flushed flowers from late spring to early summer, 2.5m/2.5m (8ft/8ft); *D.* x *rosea*, compact, bushy, dark green oval leaves, clusters of rose-pink flowers, white inside, in early summer, 1.2m/1.2m (4ft/4ft); *D.* x *r.* 'Carminea', rose-carmine flowers tinged paler pink; *D. scabra* 'Plena', (syn. *D. crenata* 'Flore Pleno'), rough, ovate dark green leaves, double white flowers, rose-purple on the outside, 3m/2m (10ft/6½ft); *D. setchuenensis*, moderately hardy, requires shelter from cold winds, finely toothed, dull grey-green leaves, softly hairy beneath, clusters of white star-like flowers in summer, 2m/1.5m (6½ft/5ft).

below *Deutzia x rosea* 'Carminea'. These very floriferous shrubs are unexpectedly related to hydrangeas; and always appear to me, quite erroneously, as if they require acidic soils.

Dianthus

Carnation, Pink Caryophyllaceae

Annuals, biennials, perennials and sub-shrubs, many are low-growing and evergreen and most thrive best in slightly alkaline soil. Tender to moderately hardy although many of the perennial forms deteriorate rather quickly after a few years due to diseases and stock should be renewed frequently. The genus includes some of the best loved of garden flowers in Sweet Williams, pinks and carnations. The pinks and carnations are a complex group, subdivided in several rather distinct types and the sub-groups that I have used here aren't the only categories that you may find in catalogues. Most groups contain very many varieties and so I have listed here only a few representatives in each category with which I am especially familiar. Very

left *Dianthus barbatus* 'Monarch'. Sweet Williams are among my real cottage garden favourites and I'm sure that the only reason they have fallen from favour is because of their biennial habit; they take a long time to do anything.

characteristic, linear to lance-shaped pointed leaves, blue-green or grey-green. Clove-scented flowers, singly or in clusters, with tubular bases, petals sometimes fringed or bearded. Sow seed of annual species in warmth in spring, biennials in a seed bed in early summer for transplanting to growing positions in autumn. Take cuttings ('pipings') from perennial species in summer and from perpetual flowering species and Malmaison Carnations in late winter. Border carnations may be layered after flowering.

Species

Hardy perennials, ideal for rock gardens and the fronts of borders. Single flowers. Alpine species thrive in humus-rich, very well drained gritty compost, in troughs and raised beds. Other hardy species thrive best in well-drained, neutral to alkaline soil in full sun. *D. alpinus* (Alpine Pink), mat-forming, glossy dark green leaves, crimson to rose-pink flowers marked with small white spots, with bearded, toothed petals, from early to mid-summer, 8cm/10cm (3¼in/4in); *D. a.* 'Joan's Blood', rich crimson flowers; *D. anatolicus*, hummock-forming, narrow pointed deep green leaves, white flowers in midsummer, 30cm/20cm (1ft/8in); *D. arenarius*, grass-like, bright green leaves, sprays of solitary, fringed, bearded white flowers, sometimes with purple bases, in summer, 30cm/30cm (1ft/1ft); *D.* x *arvernensis*, mat-forming, linear, grey-green leaves, deep pink flowers in summer, 15cm/30cm (6in/1ft); *D. barbatus* (Wild Sweet William), Nigrescens Group, short-lived perennial best grown as a biennial, matt green leaves, flat clusters of sweetly scented deep crimson maroon flowers; *D. caryophyllus* (Wild Carnation), flattened, grey-green leaves, fragrant, toothed, single purple-pink flowers in midsummer, 80cm/15-23cm (2½ft/6-9in); *D. deltoides* (Maiden Pink), mat-forming, best for rock gardens, deep green leaves, usually solitary, sometimes in clusters, toothed, bearded cerise pink flowers in summer, 15cm/30cm (6in/1ft); *D. d.* 'Albus', white flowers; *D. d.* 'Leuchtfunk' (syn. 'Flashing Light'), vibrant cerise pink flowers; *D. erinaceus*, cushion-forming, mid-green leaves, solitary, sometimes paired, toothed and bearded pink flowers, in summer, 5cm/50cm (2in/13/4ft); *D. gratianopolitanus* (syn. *D. caesius*) (Cheddar Pink), mat-forming, grey-green leaves, highly scented, single deep pink, toothed, sparsely bearded flowers in summer, 15cm/40cm (6in/11/2ft); *D. knappii*, tufted, narrow, lance-shaped, pale grey-green leaves, sulphur yellow flowers, 30-40cm/10-20cm (12-11/2ft/4-8in); *D. pavonius* (syn. *D. neglectus*), mat-forming and excellent when grown between paving, grey-green leaves, single pale to deep pink flowers, buff undersides, in summer, 8cm/20cm (3¼in/8in); *D. plumarius* (Wild Pink), hummock- or mat-forming perennial suitable for rock gardens, narrow, pointed, grey-green leaves, extremely fragrant solitary white to pink flowers, 10-15cm/15-25cm (4-6in/6-10in); *D. superbus*, tufted, mid-green leaves, single purple-pink flowers, fringed petals, singly or in pairs, in summer, 20cm/20cm (8in/8in).

Border Carnations

Hardy evergreen though quickly deteriorating perennials. Fragrant double flowers, usually three or four to each stem, from mid- to late summer, blue-grey or grey-green leaves, smooth-edged petals, 45-60cm/40cm (1½-2ft/1½ft). Colour may be 'self', with a single colour, 'fancy', marked with

right There are some very striking colour forms among the annual carnations that are raised from seed; *Dianthus* 'Black and White Minstrels' is one of the more sober.

contrasting stripes or flecks, or 'picotee', petals margined with a contrasting colour. Thrive in well-drained soil enriched with organic matter but not easy plants to grow attractively as they flop to form an unruly tangle if not staked carefully and discretely. *D.* 'Candy Clove', fancy, white with rose red markings; *D.* 'Eva Humphries', picotee, double white flowers with purple edges; *D.* 'Mendip Hills'.

Perpetual Flowering Carnations
Half-hardy evergreen perennials for growing in warmth for cut flowers and exhibition blooms. Double flowers, sometimes scented, are selfs, fancies or picotees, 90-130cm/30cm (3ft-4½ft/1ft). Given suitable conditions they flower all year round about although hugely important commercially, they aren't easy to grow in a home greenhouse. Perpetual flowering carnations are best grown in containers of loam-based compost in bright but diffuse light, in a well-ventilated position. *D.* 'Anne Franklin', pale yellow flowers, edged and flecked with pale maroon; *D.* 'Clara', fancy, scented yellow flowers, striped salmon-pink; *D.* 'Fragrant Ann', self, clove-scented, white; *D.* 'Jacqueline Ann', fancy, fragrant white flowers, flecked rose-pink.

above *Dianthus* 'Gran's Favourite'. The pinks, whether old or modern varieties, have a charm and appeal that the large flowered carnations seem to have lost.

Malmaison Carnations
Half-hardy evergreen perennials, extremely fragrant, for growing in warmth, in a greenhouse or conservatory. Double flowers, all selfs, produced intermittently throughout the year. Leaves broad, curly, 50-70cm/40cm (20-2¼ft/1½ft). Require loam-based compost in bright but diffuse light, well-ventilated position. Very popular in

Victorian greenhouses and beginning to make a comeback with devoted growers. *D.* 'Duchess of Westminster', salmon-pink; *D.* 'Princess of Wales', large salmon-pink flowers; *D.* 'Souvenir de la Malmaison' (syn. 'Old Blush'), large blue-pink flowers.

Pinks
Pinks are excellent garden plants, much the easiest members of the genus to cultivate. They are usually divided into three groups: Old-fashioned or Garden Pinks, derived from *Dianthus plumarius*, Modern (mainly 'Allwoodii' Pinks derived from crosses between Old Pinks and Perpetual Flowering Carnations from which they derive a long flowering season) and Alpine Pinks. The first two are suitable for borders and cutting, the latter for raised beds, troughs, rock gardens and alpine houses. Old-fashioned: fully hardy evergreen perennials, clove-scented single, semi-double or double selfs, bicolours, with a contrasting centre, or laced, with petal margins and centre in a contrasting colour, 25-45cm/30cm (10in-1½ft/1ft). Require well-drained, neutral to alkaline soil enriched with organic matter, in full sun. *D.* 'Allspice', single magenta flowers mottled pale pink or white; *D.* 'Brympton Red', laced pink, single bright red with deeper crimson contrast; *D.* 'Dad's Favourite', laced, semi-double, white with purple centre, ruby-red margins, one of the more reliable laced varieties; *D.* 'Earl of Essex', bicolour, double rose-pink with darker centre; *D.* 'Inchmery', self, double pale pink; *D.* 'Monica Wyatt', bicolour, double, lavender-pink with magenta' centre; *D.* 'Mrs Sinkins', self, double fringed white, justifiably one of the most popular of all varieties of pink; *D.* 'Musgrave's Pink' (syn. 'Charles Musgrave'), bicolour, scented, single white with green eye; *D.* 'Sam Barlow', bicolour, double, scented, white with deep purple centre; *D.* 'Sops-in-'Wine', white with deep crimson-purple markings. Modern pinks: fully hardy evergreen perennials for borders and cutting, selfs, bicolours, fancies or laced,

sometimes clove-scented, mostly double flowers, 25-45cm/40cm (10in-1½ft/1½ft). Thrive best in soil enriched with organic matter, well-drained, neutral to alkaline soil, in full sun. *D.* 'Bovey Belle', self, clove-scented double, bright pink; *D.* 'Cranmere Pool', bicolour, cream-white with magenta centre; *D.* 'Devon Glow', self, double, magenta; *D.* 'Diane', deep salmon-red; *D.* 'Doris', bicolour, scented, double pale pink with darker pink centre; *D.* 'Gran's Favourite', laced, double white with cerise-pink centre and edges; *D.* 'Haytor White', self, double white; *D.* 'Joy', self, semi-double, carmine-red; *D.* 'Laced Monarch', laced, double, pink with deep red centre and margins; *D.* 'Laced Romeo', laced, cream-white, chestnut-red centre and edges; *D.* 'London Lovely,

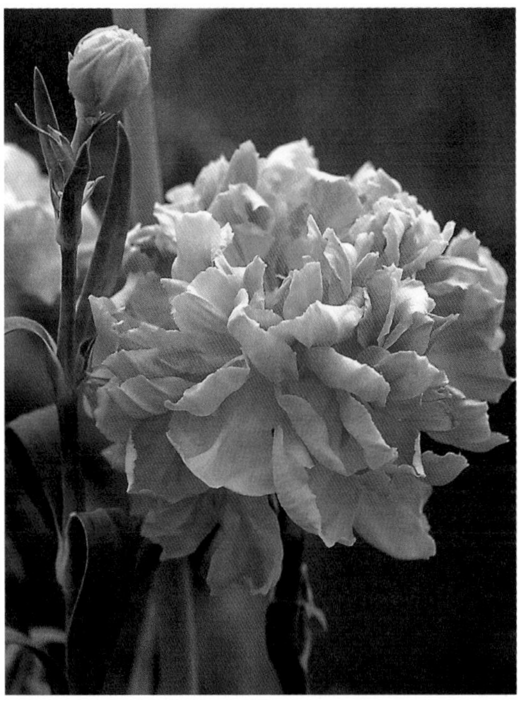

white, mauve-centre and margins'; *D.* 'Valda Wyatt', bicolour, scented, double, lavender-pink with deeper centre.

Alpine pinks, fully hardy evergreen perennials, tufts or bushy clumps of narrow grey or grey-green leaves, single, semi-double or double flowers, most fragrant, with fringed or serrated petals, in summer, 8-10cm/20cm (3¼-4in/8in). Thrive in humus-rich, gritty compost, in troughs and raised beds with good drainage. *D.* 'Allwoodii Alpinus' Group is a range of free-flowering hybrids between *Dianthus alpinus* and the modern 'Allwoodii' pinks; *D.* 'Betty Norton', single, rose with maroon centre, *D.* 'Dewdrop', single white with yellow-green edges; *D.* 'Fusilier', single rose-red; *D.* 'Inshriach Dazzler', single, deep carmine-red, fringed petals; *D.* 'La Bourboule', single, pink; *D.* 'Little Jock', single, rose-pink with crimson centre; *D.* 'Mars', semi-double, bright crimson; *D.* 'Nyewood's Cream', single, cream or ivory-white, petals smooth-edged; *D.* 'Pike's Pink', double, pale pink with dark red eye; *D.* 'Pink Jewel', semi-double, light purple; *D.* 'Prince Charming', single, pink with paler centre; *D.* 'Waithman Beauty', single, ruby-red splashed pink; *D.* 'Whatfield Gem', double, pink, laced maroon; *D.* 'Whatfield Magenta', single, magenta.

Annual Carnations

Annual carnations are varieties of the bushy, short-lived perennial or biennial species *D. chinensis* (which is more or less synonymous with a plant often called *D.* x *heddewigii*) and *D. caryophyllus* that are grown as annuals for bedding. I find they achieve their greatest impact when grown in small containers, interspersed among pots of other types of summer flowering annuals although the *D. caryophyllus* varieties seem to be rather late in flowering. Pale mid-green leaves, loose clusters of fringed summer flowers, sometimes elaborately patterned, sometimes in very assertive colours, 70cm/16-23cm (2¼ft/6½-9in). For cultivation requirements see Species, above. Varieties of *D. chinensis*: *D.* 'Baby Doll', large single white flowers, marbled crimson, 15-20cm (6-8in); *D.* 'Black and White Minstrels', very dark maroon and white, scented; *D.* 'Colour Magician', compact, small single flowers, clear white at first, later rose-pink, 25cm (10in); *D.* 'Fire Carpet', single, scarlet self, 20cm (8in); *D.* 'Frosty', double, frilly flowers reminiscent of old perennial laced pinks in a range of bicolours and tricolours, 20cm (8in); *D.* 'Raspberry Parfait' F1, dark green leaves, deep pink with dark crimson centre; *D.* 'Snowfire White', white with scarlet centre; *D.* 'Strawberry Parfait' F1, dark green leaves, light rose-pink with scarlet centre. Varieties of *D. caryophyllus*: *D* 'Lillipot' F1, dwarf, bushy, double flowers, pink, purple, yellow, scarlet and orange, some bicolours, 20-25cm (8-10in); *D.* 'Peach Delight', hardy double, peach flowers, 60-90cm (2ft-3ft); *D.* 'Red Riding Hood', small, double, fragrant cherry-red flowers, 20-30cm/38cm (8in-1ft/1½ft).

D. barbatus (Sweet William)

D. b. 'Auricula-eyed', bicolour, various colours including crimson-red, rose- and salmon-pink, with pale centres; *D. b.* 'Dunnet's Dark Crimson', bronze-green leaves, blood-red flowers; *D. b.* 'Excelsior', very fragrant, rich varied colours; *D. b.* 'Indian Carpet', crimson, purple or pink flowers, many bicoloured, 15-22cm (6-8½in); *D. b.* 'Monarch',

above *Dianthus alpinus*. The range in form among *Dianthus* types really is remarkable; however, few would deny that the tiny alpines are among the most delightful.

left *Dianthus* 'Souvenir de la Malmaison' Although these carnations must be grown in warmth, I have no hesitation in including them here as they really do have a very special charm.

white, pink, red, and purple with contrasting centres, 60cm (2ft). Sweet Williams grown as annuals: *D. b.* 'New Era', variously coloured singles and bicolours.

above The abundance of flowers and strong if slightly assertive colour have made *Diascia barberae* 'Ruby Field' a great favourite for hanging baskets in recent years.

Diascia Scrophulariaceae

Small annuals and semi-evergreen or evergreen perennials. Fairly hardy. Those I describe here are all perennials although many are grown as half-hardy annuals, especially for containers. As young plants are more free-flowering it is best to replace specimens frequently. Heart-shaped, ovate to elliptic or linear, toothed leaves, usually mid-green. Clusters of tubular, nemesia-like flowers, mainly in spring or early summer. Sow seed in warmth in late winter, take basal shoot cuttings in autumn or spring, or semi-ripe cuttings in summer or early autumn. ❀ *D. barberae* 'Blackthorn Apricot', hardy, spreading or trailing, mat-forming, glossy ovate dark green leaves, loose clusters of rich orange-cream flowers over a long period, 25cm/60cm (10in/2ft); *D. b.* 'Ruby Field', compact mat of tiny, pale green, heart-shaped leaves, dark pink tubular flowers, wide-lipped, throughout summer, a particularly good hanging basket plant, 25cm/60cm (10in/2ft); *D.* 'Coral Belle', low-growing, large deep salmon-pink flowers in summer; *D. cordata*, hardy, low-growing, almost prostrate, heart-shaped, pale to deep green, small rounded leaves, clusters of bright pink flowers, 15cm/50cm (6in/1¾ft); *D. fetcaniensis*, erect, spreading, bushy, ovate to heart-shaped deep green hairy leaves, rose-pink flowers from late spring to summer, 25cm/50cm (10in/1¾ft); *D. integerrima*, creeping, narrow, grey, lance-shaped leaves. spikes of rose-pink flowers, 30cm/50cm (1ft/1¾ft); *D.* 'Joyce's Choice', trailing, yellow-pink flowers, 30cm (1ft); *D.* 'Lilac Belle', compact, abundant purple-pink flowers throughout summer, 22cm (8½in); *D.* 'Lilac Mist', airy clusters of small light purple-pink or lilac flowers with darker flushes, 40cm (1½ft); *D. rigescens*, trailing evergreen but best treated as an annual, deeply toothed leaves, pale green at first, red-brown later, crimson-pink flowers from late spring to early autumn, 30cm/50cm (1ft/1¾ft); *D.* 'Rupert Lambert', trailing, mat-forming, elliptic to ovate grey leaves, deep pink flowers, 25-45cm (10-1½ft); *D.* 'Salmon Supreme' (syn. *D.* 'Hector Harrison'), mat-forming, heart-shaped leaves, salmon-pink flowers throughout summer, 15cm/50cm (6in/ 1¾ft); *D.* 'Twinkle', loose spikes of purple-pink flowers tinged with violet, in late spring, 30cm (1ft); *D. vigilis*, spreading, deciduous, rounded, toothed leaves, soft clear pink flowers from early summer until autumn, 30cm/60cm (1ft/2ft); *D. v.* 'Jack Elliot', leaves rounder, slightly larger flowers, shell-pink.

Dicentra *Bleeding Heart* Papaveraceae

Small/medium annuals and rhizomatous or tuberous ornamental perennials. Very hardy. Suitable for woodland plantings, rock gardens or borders. Can cause stomach upsets if ingested; leaves may aggravate skin allergies. Fern-like, finely divided leaves, mainly green, occasionally silver-grey. Pendent, red, pink or white heart-shaped flowers, often on arching stems. Thrive in well-drained, moist soil in light shade. Divide rhizomatous species in late winter or early spring, take root cuttings in winter, or sow seed in warmth in late winter. ❀ *D.* 'Bacchanal', rhizomatous perennial, ferny grey-green leaves, small clusters of dark red flowers from mid to late spring, 45cm/60cm (1½ft/2ft); *D.* 'Bountiful',

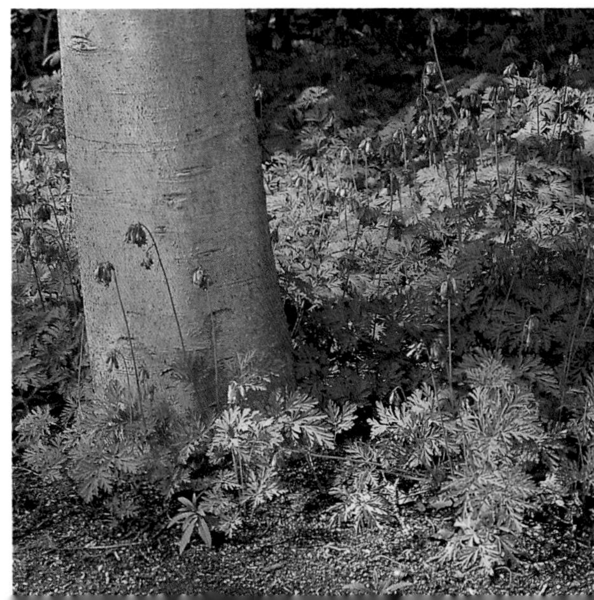

right *Dicentra formosa*. The dicentras always appear too delicate and fragile to survive in woodland gardens but they are extremely hardy and woodlands are their natural home.

clump-forming, rhizomatous perennial, pinnate, feathery mid-green leaves, clusters of nodding purple-pink flowers on red stems in late spring, sometimes to early autumn, 30cm/45cm (1ft/1½ft); *D. cucullaria*, tuberous perennial, deeply divided blue-green leaves, clusters of white flowers, sometimes tinged pink and/or yellow-tipped, in early spring, 20cm/25cm (8in/10in); *D. formosa*, rhizomatous perennial, hummocks of fern-like, deeply divided leaves on pink-tinged stems, mauve-pink flowers from spring to early summer, 45cm/60-90cm (1½ft/2ft-3ft); *D. f.* 'Alba', paler green leaves on glossy green stems, white flowers from spring to early summer; *D.* 'Langtrees', rhizomatous perennial, coarsely divided silver-grey leaves, clusters of cream-pink flowers from mid spring to early or midsummer, 30cm/45cm (1ft/1½ft); *D.* 'Pearl Drops', lobed blue-green leaves, cream-white flowers tinged pink from mid spring to early or midsummer, 30cm/45cm (1ft/1½ft); *D. scandens*, clambering perennial, deeply lobed, ovate to lance-shaped mid-green leaves, white or yellow flowers, occasionally tipped purple or pink, from late summer to early autumn, 1m/1m (3ft/3ft); *D. spectabilis*, clump-forming perennial, pale green leaves, ovate or lobed leaflets, pendent stems with rose-pink flowers in early summer, the most familiar and popular species but soon becomes lax and untidy, 1.2m/45cm (4ft/1½ft); *D. s.* 'Alba', fern-like, light green leaves, pure white flowers from late spring to early summer; *D.* 'Stuart Boothman', spreading, rhizomatous perennial, grey-green fern-like leaves, deep red-pink flowers in summer, 30cm/45cm (1ft/1½ft).

Dicksonia — Dicksoniaceae

Large evergreen or semi-evergreen tree ferns. Tender to barely hardy. Spreading pinnate leathery fronds on an upright, trunk-like rhizome. Makes a very striking specimen plant in mild areas or very sheltered woodland gardens. Be sure to obtain already rooted specimens. ❀ *D. antarctica*, tree-like evergreen, erect rhizome covered by dense brown fibrous bases of old fronds and roots, fronds pale green at first, later darker, 6m/4m (20ft/13ft).

Dictamnus
Dittany, Burning Bush — Rutaceae

Small/medium herbaceous perennial. Very hardy. Flowers and seed capsules contain a volatile oil that can momentarily ignite spontaneously. The oil may cause skin irritation when the skin is exposed to sunlight. Strongly aromatic, of lemon. Leaves pinnate, with divided, ovate leaflets. Clusters of asymmetrical star-shaped flowers with prominent stamens. Divide in autumn or sow seed in warmth in early spring. ❀ *D. albus*, clump-forming, bushy, dark green leaves, leathery, star-shaped white flowers sometimes marked with purple, in early summer, 40-90cm/60cm (1½-3ft/2ft); *D. a.* var. *purpureus*, pink-mauve flowers striped dark pink or purple, aromatic leaves.

above *Dierama pulcherrimum*. The Wand Flower is aptly named as its tall, fragile looking stems arch gracefully and wave in the wind.

Dierama *Wand Flower* — Iridaceae

Medium/large evergreen corm-forming perennial. Tender to fairly hardy. Dwarf species are suitable for the rock garden. Erect or semi-erect, narrow, grass-like mid-green to grey-green leaves, spikes of pendent bell- or funnel-shaped flowers on arching stems. Divide in spring or sow ripe seed in a cold-frame.

❀ *D. dracomontanum* (syn. *D. pendulum* var. *pumilum*). fairly hardy, slender mid-green leaves, red, rose-pink, purple-pink or mauve flowers from mid-to late summer, 60cm/30cm (2ft/1ft); *D. pendulum* (syn *D. ensifolium*), clump-forming, narrow, strap-like leaves, bell-shaped pink-purple flowers, in summer, 1-2m/60cm (3-6½ft/2ft); *D. pulcherrimum*, evergreen, erect, broad grass-like leaves, pale to deep magenta flowers, sometimes purple or silver-pink, rarely white, pendent, on clustered spikes in summer, 1-1.5m/60cm (3-5ft/2ft).

right *Diervilla* x *splendens*. Although the true shrubby honeysuckles are mostly rather tender, this related genus provides a very adequate substitute.

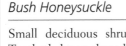

Diervilla
Bush Honeysuckle Caprifoliaceae

Small deciduous shrub, Hardy to very hardy. Toothed, lance-shaped to oblong or ovate green leaves with pointed tips, red-purple in autumn. Yellow two-lipped tubular flowers. No routine pruning. Transplant suckers or take semi-ripe cuttings in summer. ❀ *D. sessilifolia*, very hardy, narrow, elliptic mid-green leaves, flushed purple at first, small flowers from early to late summer on arching branches, 1-1.5m/1.5m (3-5ft/5ft); *D.* x *splendens*, elongated mid-green leaves, superior autumn tints, strong yellow flowers.

Digitalis *Foxglove* Scrophulariaceae

Small/large biennials and perennials. Fairly hardy to very hardy and excellent for woodland plantings or slightly shaded borders. All parts are toxic if ingested; contact may cause skin irritation. Basal rosettes of glossy or softly hairy, lance-shaped, usually mid-green leaves, tubular or bell-shaped two-lipped flowers, frequently spotted inside, usually carried on one side of the flower stem, in summer. Copes in most soils but thrives in moist, humus rich soil in light, preferably dappled shade. Sow seed in a cold-frame in early summer or in flowering positions in late spring (many species will self-seed freely) take offsets or basal cuttings in spring, or divide in early spring. ❀ *D. ferruginea*, short-lived perennial or biennial, broad, downy leaves, trumpet-shaped brown-red flowers, 1.2m/45cm (4ft/1½ft); *D. grandiflora* (syn. *D. ambigua*), very hardy evergreen perennial, best treated as a biennial, smooth, oval green leaves, pale yellow tubular flowers, 1m/45cm (3ft/1½ft); *D. g.* 'Carillon', dwarf perennial, tolerant of heavy rains, primrose yellow flowers, 45cm (1½ft); *D.* 'John Innes Tetra', perennial, grey-green leaves, bronze flowers on stiff stems, in summer, 45cm (1½ft); *D. laevigata*, moderately hardy perennial, oblong-lance-shaped dark green leaves, brown-purple to orange-brown flowers with net-like brown markings, 1m/45cm (3ft/1½ft); *D. lanata*, short-lived perennial best treated as a biennial, narrow grey-green leaves, softy hairy, cream-yellow, purple or white flowers with lighter lip and brown-purple spotting, 60cm/30cm (2ft/1ft); *D. lutea*, perennial, smooth dark green glossy leaves, pendent, pale lemon flowers, from spring to summer, 60cm/30cm (2ft/1ft); *D.* x *mertonensis*, short-lived perennial best treated as a biennial, hairy grey-green leaves, clusters of pink-buff flowers, from mid-to late summer, 90cm/30cm (3ft/1ft); *D. obscura*, fairly hardy clump-forming perennial, oblong to lance-shaped, sometimes toothed evergreen leaves, orange-yellow to red-brown flowers, marked red, from mid-to late summer, 30-120cm/45cm (1-4ft/1½ft); *D. parviflora*, perennial, narrow dark green leaves, slightly toothed, densely packed cylindrical inflorescences, orange-brown with purple-brown lip, in summer, 60cm/30cm (2ft/1ft); *D. purpurea*, very hardy biennial or short-lived perennial, oval to lance-shaped grey-green leaves, pink, purple or white flowers, 1.2m/60cm (4ft/2ft); *D. p.* f. *albiflora*, cream-white flowers (but those with purple pigmented stems tend to produce purple flowers and all purple flowered plants in the vicinity must be removed to maintain the purity of self-seeding populations), 1.2m (4ft); *D. p.* 'Sutton's Apricot', short-lived perennial best grown as a biennial, large

far right The perennial foxgloves are a real revelation after the familiar short-lived native species and *Digitalis laevigata* is my favourite.

apricot flowers, 90-150cm/60cm (3-5ft/2ft); *D. viridiflora*, perennial, lance-shaped green leaves, green-yellow tubular flowers with prominent green veins, 60cm (2ft).

Dimorphotheca Asteraceae

Small half-hardy annuals. Suitable for containers, rock gardens, temporary ground cover and sunny borders. Deeply toothed leaves with wavy margins. Daisy-like flowers from summer to autumn, close on sunless days. Sow seed in warmth in early spring or sow in flowering positions in mid spring. ❀ *D. pluvialis* (syn. *D. annua*) 'Glistening White', erect, aromatic dark green leaves, scented white flowers, tinged violet, with dark brown-purple centres, from midsummer to early autumn, 40cm/15-30cm (1½ft/6in-1ft); *D. sinuata* 'Tetra Pole Star', smaller, flowers have dark gold-brown central disk, 30cm/30cm (1ft/1ft).

Dionysia Primulaceae

Small evergreen alpine. Moderately hardy. Rosettes of oblong to spoon-shaped leaves, sometimes woolly beneath, five-petalled flowers, singly or in clusters, from spring to early summer. Sow seed in a cold-frame when ripe or in winter. ❀ *D. aretioides*, hummock-forming, hairy, toothed, oblong grey-green leaves, with inrolled margins, solitary yellow flowers, 7cm/30cm (2¾in/1ft); *D. a.* 'Phyllis Carter', flowers with narrower petals.

Diospyros Ebenaceae

Large deciduous shrubs and trees. Tender to moderately hardy. Genus contains the tree ebony (*D. ebenum*) valued for its fine wood. The two species I describe here are deciduous; *D. kaki* is barely hardy and in cold areas is best grown in a large greenhouse or conservatory. Thrives best on a warm sunny wall. Glossy, lance-shaped to broadly ovate leaves. Bell- or urn-shaped flowers; male flowers, in clusters, and female flowers, singly, borne on separate plants. Flowers on female plants may be followed by fruit if male and female plants are grown. Sow ripe seed in a cold-frame, *D. kaki* by grafting in winter. ❀ *D. kaki*, Persimmon, dark green leaves, purple, orange and red in autumn, pale yellow bell-shaped flowers in summer, male flowers, in clusters, female flowers, singly, followed by edible oval or rounded fruit, 10m/7m (33ft/23ft); *D. lotus*, Date Plum, dark green leaves, bell-shaped green flowers tinged red, from mid-to late summer, on female plants followed by inedible oval to round fruit, 10m/6m (33ft/20ft).

Dipelta Caprifoliaceae

Medium/large deciduous shrubs, similar to the much more familiar *Weigela*. Moderately hardy to very hardy. Characteristic upright, multi-stemmed, arching habit, short, simple oval leaves and clusters of *Weigela*-like tubular flowers in spring and early summer, followed by small fruits with papery wing-like projections. Tolerant of alkaline soils; excellent and unjustifiably neglected plants for mixed plantings. No routine pruning. Take semi-ripe heeled cuttings in summer or hardwood cuttings in late autumn. ❀ *D. floribunda*, fragrant pink-white flowers with orange-yellow throat, pale cream-buff peeling bark, particularly attractive in winter, 5m/2m (16ft/6½ft). *D. ventricosa*, pale pink flowers with orange throat, slightly less hardy than *D. floribunda*, 2m/1m (6½ft/3ft).

above *Dipelta floribunda*. All of the common species that arrived in our gardens from China around 100 years ago but have never received quite the recognition that I think they deserve.

Diphylleia Berberidaceae

Large rhizomatous ornamental. Moderately hardy. Extremely large dark green leaves on tall stems, attached to the centre of the leaf. cluster of bow-shaped white flowers. Sow ripe seed in a cold-frame or divide in spring. ❀ *D. cymosa*, lobed, toothed leaves with conspicuous veining, 40cm (1½ft) in diameter, rounded umbels of star-shaped white flowers from late spring to early summer, followed by round blue fruits, 1m/30cm (3ft/1ft).

Diplarrhena Iridaceae

Small/medium rhizomatous ornamental. Fairly hardy, in cold areas requires a sheltered position in the border or the protection of a wall, or growing in a greenhouse or conservatory. Fans of usually strap-shaped leaves, clusters of iris-like fragrant flowers. Sow seed in a cold-frame in autumn or spring or divide in spring. ❀ *D. moraea*, evergreen sword-shaped to linear dark green leaves, six-petalled flowers, three large outer ones, three smaller inner ones flushed yellow and purple, from late spring to early summer, 60cm/23cm (2ft/9in).

Dipsacus Dipsacaceae

Large biennials and perennials. Moderately hardy. Narrow, pointed leaves, often pairs on the stem and united to form a cup at the stem. Tiny papery flowers on a conical spiny head, in summer. Sow seed in flowering positions in autumn or spring; self-seeds freely. ❀ *D. fullonum*, biennial, prickly leaves and stems, basal leaves oblong to lance-shaped with spiny pimples, paired flower stem leaves, joined at the stem, purple-pink or white inflorescences, curved prickly bracts at base, from mid-to late summer, 1.5-2m/30-80cm (5-6½ft/1-2½ft).

Dipteronia Aceraceae

Small deciduous shrubs or small trees. Moderately hardy. Pinnate leaves, erect clusters of small green-white flowers in summer, followed by fruit. Sow seed in a seedbed in autumn, take soft-wood cuttings in summer or layer in late spring or early summer. ❀ *D. sinensis*, leaves have ovate or lance-shaped toothed leaflets, insignificant flowers in summer, followed on older plants in early autumn by clusters of red, winged fruit, 10m/10m (33ft/33ft).

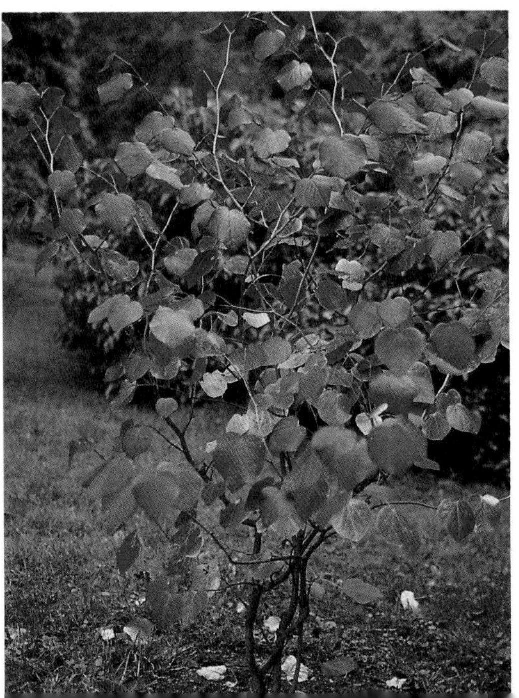

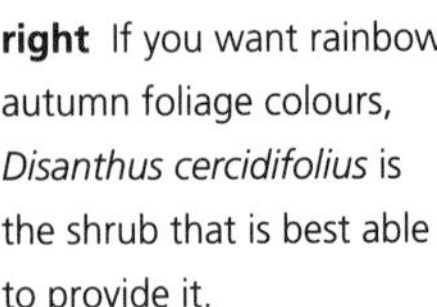

right If you want rainbow autumn foliage colours, *Disanthus cercidifolius* is the shrub that is best able to provide it.

Disanthus Hamamelidaceae

Genus of only one species, a medium-sized deciduous shrub. Fairly hardy. Ovate to rounded green leaves, orange, gold, red-purple in autumn, all colours occurring together. Sow seed in a seedbed in autumn, layer in winter. ❀ *D. cercidifolius*, blue-green leaves, heart-shaped at base, star-like purple flowers, 2.5m/3m (8ft/10ft).

Disporum Convallariaceae

Small/medium rhizomatous ornamental. Tender to moderately hardy. Ovate to lance-shaped, mid-to dark green leaves, bell-shaped or tubular trumpet- or cup-shaped flowers, sometimes pendent, white, grey-yellow, red-purple or brown-red, often in umbels, followed by black, orange or red fruits. Sow seed in autumn or divide established clumps in early summer. The species described here are all moderately hardy. ❀ *D. sessile* 'Variegatum', almost stalkless leaves with broad cream-white stripes, pendent tubular flowers, white with green tips or pale cream, from late spring to early summer, blue-black fruits in early autumn, 90cm/60cm (3ft/2ft); *D. smithii*, ovate, mid-green leaves, sometimes with wavy margins, clusters of cream-white flowers in spring, followed by bright orange oval fruits in autumn, 30-60cm/30cm (1-2ft/1ft).

Dodecatheon Primulaceae

Small herbaceous perennials. Moderately hardy. Suitable for mixed borders, beside ponds, in bog, woodland and rock gardens. Rosettes of ovate to inversely lance-shaped, spoon-shaped or oblong leaves, umbels of cyclamen-like, pendent flowers on arching stems. thrives in well-drained, moist soil enriched with humus. Sow ripe seed in a cold-frame or divide established plants in spring. ❀ *D. dentatum*, oblong to lance-shaped, toothed, pale to mid-green leaves, umbels of white flowers in spring, sometimes purple-spotted at base, conspicuous purple anthers, 20cm/20cm (8in/8in); *D. hendersonii*, ovate to spoon-shaped leaves, slightly toothed, clusters of maroon-lavender or white flowers, maroon and yellow stamens, 40cm/25cm (1½ft/10in); *D. jeffreyi*, oval pale green to mid-green sticky leaves, lavender to magenta, rarely white, flowers in clusters, maroon and yellow stamens, 60cm/30cm (2ft/1ft); *D. meadia* (syn. *D. pauciflorum*), ovate to spoon-shaped leaves, sometimes toothed, clusters of rose, rose-purple, pink-mauve flowers with yellow stamens striped maroon, from mid-spring to mid-summer, 40cm/20cm (1½ft/8in); *D. m.* f. *album*, cream-

left *Dodecatheon pulchellum pulchellum* 'Red Wings'. There is something about the swept-back flowers of these classic woodland plants that is particularly graceful.

white flowers, yellow anthers; *D. pulchellum* (syn. *D. amethystinum*), ovate to spoon-shaped, toothed pale green leaves, sometimes sticky, cerise-pink, purple and magenta flowers from late spring to summer, 35cm/15cm (1ft/6in); *D. p.* ssp. *pulchellum* 'Red Wings', deep magenta-pink flowers from late spring to early summer, 35cm/20cm (1ft/8in).

Dodonaea
Sapindaceae

Large evergreen shrubs and small trees. Barely hardy. Suitable for growing outside only in mild areas; tolerant of coastal conditions. Needle-like or oblong to more or less oval leathery leaves, sometimes pinnate, insignificant flowers, male and female on separate plants, followed by winged fruit. Sow seed in warmth in spring or take semi-ripe cuttings in summer. ❀ *D. viscosa* 'Purpurea', leathery oblong purple-red leaves, tiny green, or red flowers in spring, followed by yellow, red-brown or purple-red winged seeds in summer, 1-5m/1-3m (3-16ft/3-10ft).

Doronicum
Asteraceae

Medium/large hardy herbaceous perennials. Bright green, hairy, heart-shaped basal leaves, gold-yellow daisy-like flowers in spring. Sow seed in a cold-frame in spring or division of established plants during the autumn months. *D. excelsum* 'Harpur Crewe' (syn. *D. plantagineum* 'Excelsum'), lightly toothed leaves, heart-shaped at base, single gold-yellow flowers with darker centres, 60cm/60cm (2ft/2ft); *D.* 'Frhlindspracht', double gold-yellow flowers, 40cm (1½ft); *D.* 'Miss Mason' (syn. *D. columnae* 'Miss Mason'), bright yellow flowers, mid to late spring, 45cm /60cm (1½ft/2ft); *D. orientale* (syn. *D. caucasicum*), spreading, ovate to elliptic scalloped leaves, solitary single flowers, gold-yellow, from mid to late spring, 60cm/90cm (2ft/3ft); *D. o.* 'Magnificum', large yellow flowers, 50cm (1¾ft).

Dorotheanthus
Livinin gstone Daisy — Aizoaceae

Small half-hardy annuals. Low-growing succulent stems and leaves, leaves narrow, linear to spoon-shaped, glistening like sugar. Daisy-like flowers, white and shades of yellow, orange, red and pink, close on dull days. These are plants that have suddenly become very popular with the introduction of new colour forms. Sow seed in warmth in early spring or in flowering positions in mid spring. ❀ *D. bellidiformis* (syn. *Mesembryanthemum criniflorum*), mat-forming fleshy stems, prostrate, light green leaves, orange, pink, red, or crimson flowers, some with paler petal bases, darker central disk, 10-15cm/30cm (4-6in/1ft); *D. gramineus*, tufted, erect red stems, bright green leaves, flowers crimson, rose-pink or white, with a darker central disk, 10cm/30cm (4in/1ft); *D. bellidiformis* 'Lunette' (syn. 'Yellow Ice'), mat-forming, soft yellow flowers, brown-red disk, less inclined to close on dull days, 10cm/30cm (4in/1ft).

Draba
Brassicaceae

Small annuals and semi-evergreen/evergreen alpines. Moderately hardy. The species I describe here are alpines. Cushion- hummock- or mat-forming rosettes of linear to ovate, oblong or spoon-shaped leaves, small cross-shaped yellow flowers in clusters, from spring to early summer. Sow seed in a cold-frame in autumn, or replant rosettes of established plants during late spring. ❀ *D. aizoides*, tufted, mat- or cushion-forming semi-evergreen, narrow, green leaves, bristled at tips, vibrant yellow flowers, 10cm/25cm (4in/10in); *D. longisiliqua*, cushion-forming evergreen, tiny, downy grey leaves, rounded dense clusters of yellow flowers in spring, 9cm/25cm (3½in/10in); *D. mollissima*, hummock-forming evergreen, hairy grey-green leaves, bright yellow flowers in late spring, best grown in warmth, 8cm/20cm (3¼in/ 8in); *D. rigida* var. *bryoides* (syn. *D. bryoides*), hummock-forming evergreen, rosettes of dark green leaves with inrolled, hairy margins, bright yellow flowers, 3cm/15cm (1¼in/6in).

above Doronicums have rather fallen out from favour because of their susceptibility to mildew but if you want one, *Doronicum excelsum* 'Harpur Crewe' is probably the best.

right *Drimys winteri* derives its name from Capt. William Winter who went around the world on Drake's expedition and brought back some bark which he had used to treat scurvy in the ship's crew. A specimen of the plant wasn't collected until Cook's second voyage, 200 years later.

below *Dryas octopetala* is a greatly under-valued native plant for the alpine bed although prone to becoming rather woody and straggly with age.

right *Dryopteris wallichiana*. One of several lovely plants named after Nathaniel Wallich who studied the botany of India, although this species is from north-east Asia.

Drimys Winteraceae

Medium/large evergreen shrubs and small trees. Moderately hardy but in colder areas best grown in a sheltered position. Elliptic to more or less lance-shaped aromatic leaves, clusters of small star-shaped flowers. No routine pruning. Sow seed in a cold-frame in autumn or take semi-ripe cuttings in summer. ❀ *D. lanceolata*, erect shrub, leathery, glossy dark green leaves, light green beneath, purple-red shoots, abundant small cream-white flowers mid- to late spring, female and male flowers on separate plants, 4m/2.5m (13ft/8ft); *D. winteri*, (Winter's Bark Tree), a beautiful and much under-valued species, large shrub or small tree, large leathery leaves, blue-white beneath, umbels of fragrant ivory-white flowers in late spring, early summer, 15m/10m (50ft/33ft).

Dryas *Mountain Avens* Rosaceae

Evergreen, spreading, dwarf alpine sub-shrub. Hardy to very hardy; ideal plants for the alpine garden in well-drained, gritty soil with added organic matter, or similar compost in troughs or other containers. Dark green, rather bristly leaves and solitary, long-stalked, bell-like summer flowers with a delicacy that contrasts with the roughness of the foliage. No routine pruning. Remove rooted stems, take semi-ripe cuttings in late summer or sow fresh seed in a cold-frame. ❀ *D. octopetala*, leaves shaped like those of an oak, in dense spreading mats, erect, white flowers, 20cm/50cm (8in/1¾ft) or more; *D. o.* 'Minor', compact form with smaller flowers, 8cm/20cm (3¼in/8in); *D.* x *suendermannii*, nodding white flowers, spreading to 75cm (2½ft) or more.

Dryopteris Aspidiaceae

Medium/large deciduous, semi-evergreen and evergreen ferns. Tender to moderately hardy. The species and varieties I describe here are all moderately hardy and are among the most useful of all larger ferns. Usually, bi-pinnate or tri-pinnate lance-shaped fronds, arranged in a vase form, rather like the feathers of a shuttlecock. Divide mature plants in spring or autumn. ❀ *D. affinis* (Golden Shield Fern), semi-evergreen, or evergreen in mild areas, lance-shaped bi-pinnate fronds, gold-green at first, later rich green, gold-brown midrib, 90cm/90cm (3ft/3ft); *D. a.* 'Crispa Congesta', dwarf, evergreen, 30cm/30cm (1ft/1ft); *D. a.* 'Cristata Angustata', arching fronds with crested tips; *D. a.* 'Cristata The King', similar to 'Cristata Angustata' but broader fronds; *D. cycadina* (syns. *D. atrata, D. hirtipes*), deciduous, lance-shape pinnate bright green fronds, green midribs, 60cm/45cm (2ft/1½ft); *D. dilatata* (syn. *D austriaca*) (Broad Buckler Fern), dark green arching, triangular lance-shaped fronds, bright green midribs, stalks and midribs covered with prominent brown scales, 90cm/1.2m (3ft/4ft); *D. d.* 'Crispa Whiteside', crisped fronds; *D. d.* 'Lepidota Cristata', more finely divided fronds than 'Crispa

Whiteside', crested, paler brown scales, 90cm/45cm (3ft/1½ft); *D. erythrosora* (Japanese Shield Fern), evergreen, glossy, rose-brown fronds when young, later green, bi-pinnate or tri-pinnate, triangular, 60cm/38cm (2ft/1½ft); *D. filixmas* (Male Fern), 'Crispa Cristata', deciduous, fronds lance-shaped bi-pinnate or deeply divided, crested, mid-green fronds, green midribs, 60cm/1.2m (2ft/4ft); *D. wallichiana*, a magnificent plant, deciduous, fronds lance-shaped bi-pinnate to deeply divided, yellow-green at first, later dark green, 90-180cm/75cm (3-5¾ft/2½ft).

Eccremocarpus
Glory Flower Bignoniaceae

Medium/large evergreen or deciduous perennial herbaceous climbers best grown as half-hardy annuals. Pinnate leaves with clinging tendrils at the ends of each leaf stem. Brightly coloured tubular flowers in clusters during summer. Sow seed in warmth in late winter or spring, or take root cuttings in spring or summer. ❀ *E. scaber* f. *aureus*, light green pinnate, sometimes toothed leaves with conspicuous veining, tubular golden yellow flowers spring to autumn, 3-5m (10-16ft); *E. s.* f. *carmineus*, carmine red flowers; *E.* 'Fireworks', a seed-raised mixture with a wide colour range; *E. s.* f. *roseus*, bright pink to light red flowers; *E. s.* Tresco hybrids, flowers range from orange-scarlet and carmine-rose to golden yellow.

Echinacea *Cone Flower* Asteraceae

Large hardy herbaceous perennials. Excellent for the middle to back of sunny borders. Linear to lance-shaped dark green leaves, sometimes toothed, on hairy stems. Daisy-like flowers, purple, pink or red, sometimes white, with very distinctive and prominent cone-shaped disk, yellow-brown or orange, early summer to autumn. Thrives in any fertile, well-drained soil in full sun. Sow seed in warmth in spring, take root cuttings in late winter or divide established plants between autumn and spring. ❀ *E. purpurea* (syn. *Rudbeckia purpurea*) lance-shaped, rough, mid-green, slightly toothed leaves, rich mauve-crimson flowers, orange-brown centres, late summer to autumn, 1.5m/45cm (5ft/1½ft); *E. p.* 'Magnus', much the best variety, deep purple petals, deep orange centres; *E. p.* 'White Swan', pale green-white, with golden yellow centres, 75cm/45cm (2½ft/1½ft).

Echinops *Globe Thistle* Asteraceae

Medium/large hardy herbaceous biennials and perennials. These I describe here are all perennials. Spiky, thistle-like, deep green to grey-green leaves. Globular inflorescences of tiny flowers, usually blue or white, and very good for drying, summer to early autumn. A big, coarse plant but usefully tolerant of poor soils. Sow seed in a seedbed in mid-spring, divide from autumn to spring or take root cuttings in winter. ❀ *E. bannaticus* 'Blue Globe', clump-forming, spiny, rough, oval to elliptic dark green leaves, downy beneath, dark blue flowers mid- to late summer, 50-120cm/60cm (1¾-4ft/2ft); *E. b.* 'Taplow Blue', powder-blue flowers, 1.5m/60m (5ft/198ft); *E. ritro*, compact, clump-forming, stiff, spiny, oblong to elliptic leaves, dark green above, downy beneath, flowers metallic blue at first, later bright blue, 60cm/45cm (2ft/1½ft).

Echium Boraginaceae

Annuals, evergreen biennials, perennials and shrubs. Tender to moderately hardy. Good for mixed borders and attractive to bees and butterflies. Oblong or lance-shaped coarsely hairy leaves, which may cause skin irritation. Panicles or spikes, sometimes characteristically one-sided, of bell- or funnel-shaped summer flowers, in blue, red, purple or yellow, sometimes white. Best in fertile well-drained soil but tolerant of hot, dry places. Sow seeds of annuals and perennials in warmth in late winter, annuals also in flowering positions in spring, or take softwood cuttings in summer. ❀ *E. pininana* (syn. *E. pinnifolium*), half-hardy, short-lived perennial that dies after flowering, rosettes of lance-shaped, deep green, roughly hairy leaves, densely packed tubular mauve or purple flowers usually appear on sideshoots in the third year, mid- to late summer, 4m/90cm (13ft/3ft); *E. vulgare* (Viper's Bugloss), hardy biennial usually grown as an annual, lance-shaped, toothed dark green leaves, abundant, dense spikes of flowers, purple in bud, opening to violet, with conspicuous green calyxes, in summer, 40-60cm/ 30cm (1½-2ft/1ft).

Eichhornia
Water Hyacinth Pontederiaceae

Small floating plant. Barely hardy. In cold areas overwinter indoors in moist compost; in mild areas can be very invasive and, in some countries, its planting may be legally restricted. Submerged leaves linear to strap-shaped, surface leaves rounded or heart-shaped, in rosettes, on inflated stalks. Blue-violet, remarkably hyacinth-like flowers held above water in summer. Propagated by

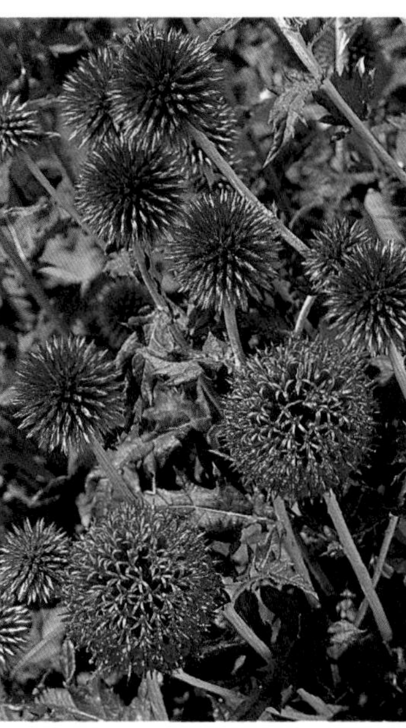

above *Echinops ritro.* I find this big, bold plant is valuable for filing large gaps at the back of the border.

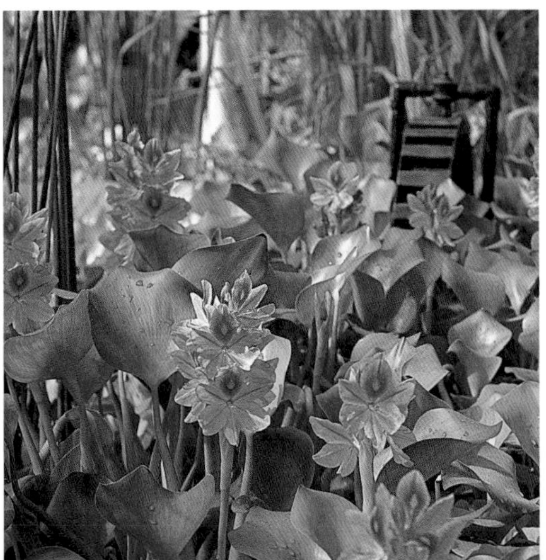

left It's not easy to find the right conditions for *Eichhornia crassipes*, a lovely South American species. Many gardens are too cold for it but in warm climates it becomes an aquatic weed.

above *Enkianthus campanulatus* is one of the lesser known Japanese members of the family Ericaceae but a good shrub for colder gardens with acidic soil.

right There are few genera with as many good variegated shrubs as *Elaeagnus* and *Elaeagnus* x *ebbingei* 'Limelight' has become one of the most popular forms in recent years.

removing off-shoots at any time. ❀ *E. crassipes*, rosettes of rounded oval leaves on inflated shiny green fleshy stalks, spikes of pale blue to violet flowers with yellow markings, 45cm/45cm (1½ft/1½ft).

Elaeagnus Elaeagnaceae

Large deciduous or evergreen shrubs or small trees. Very hardy and among the easiest and most satisfying of garden shrubs. Oblong to oval or lance-shaped leaves, white or cream-white bell-shaped or tubular flowers, usually fragrant, followed by fruits. Thrives in well-drained, fertile soil in full sun but rather intolerant of shallow soil over chalk. No routine pruning but cut out all-green shoots from variegated forms. Sow seed in a cold-frame in autumn, take semi-ripe cuttings from deciduous species in mid-summer, and evergreen species in summer. ❀ *E. commutata*, deciduous shrub, broad elliptic silver leaves, fragrant yellow-white flowers in late spring, followed by small, oval, silver fruit, 4m/2m (13ft/6½ft); *E.* x *ebbingei*, evergreen shrub, particularly good in coastal gardens, glossy dark green leaves, silver beneath, fragrant silver-scaled flowers in autumn followed by orange fruit speckled silver, in spring, 4m/4m (13ft/13ft); *E.* x *e.* 'Gilt Edge', gold-edged leaves, dark green centres, fragrant bright yellow flowers; *E.* x *e.* 'Limelight', leaves silver at first, later gold-yellow in centre, an understandably very popular plant, 3m/3m (10ft/10ft); *E. pungens* 'Frederici', evergreen shrub, shiny, small, narrow cream-yellow leaves, pendent silver-white flowers in autumn, red fruit, 4m/5m (13ft/16ft); *E. p.* 'Goldrim', narrow, dark green leaves, bright yellow margins; *E. p.* 'Maculata' (syn. 'Aureovariegata'), bold, yellow markings in centre of leaf that intensify in winter, still I think one of the best winter evergreens; *E. p.* 'Variegata' (syn. 'Argenteovariegata') narrow, cream-yellow margins; *E.* 'Quicksilver', deciduous small tree or large shrub, silver, narrow leaves, silver buds opening to yellow flowers, 4m/4m (13ft/13ft).

Elymus *Wild Rye* Poaceae

Small/large perennial grasses. Hardy. Linear, flat leaves, sometimes rolled, broad or narrow, bristled inflorescences with stalkless spikelets along the flower stalk. Sow seed in growing positions in autumn or spring, or divide established plants from mid-spring to early summer. ❀ *E. hispidus*, tufted, upright or arching linear, inrolled silver-blue leaves, insignificant narrow silver-blue flowers on erect stems, early summer to mid-summer, 75cm/ 40cm (2½ft/1½ft); *E. magellanicus*, neat, clump-forming, erect, linear, folded or flat, vivid blue leaves, narrow green and white inflorescences, 19cm (7½in) long, in summer, 15cm/30cm (6in/1ft).

Embothrium Proteaceae

Large semi-evergreen/evergreen shrubs or small trees. Fairly hardy but only really successful in mild areas, when they can be incredibly striking. Requires acidic soil. Leathery, narrow, lance-shaped to oblong leaves, clusters of waxy, brilliant red tubular flowers in summer. No routine pruning. Sow seed in warmth in spring, replant suckers in late winter or take semi-ripe cuttings in early summer. ❀ *E. coccineum*, erect shrub or small tree, fairly hardy to moderately hardy if grown in a sheltered position, dark green, oblong or paddle-shaped leaves, very narrow scarlet flowers in late spring, 10m/5m (33ft/16ft); *E. c.* Lanceolatum Group, slightly hardier, linear to lance-shaped leaves; *E.* 'Norquinco', semi-evergreen, abundant orange-scarlet flowers.

Enkianthus Ericaceae

Medium/large shrubs and small trees for acidic sites. Hardy. Most species, and those I describe here, are deciduous. Long oval to elliptic or lance-shaped toothed leaves, orange-red in autumn,

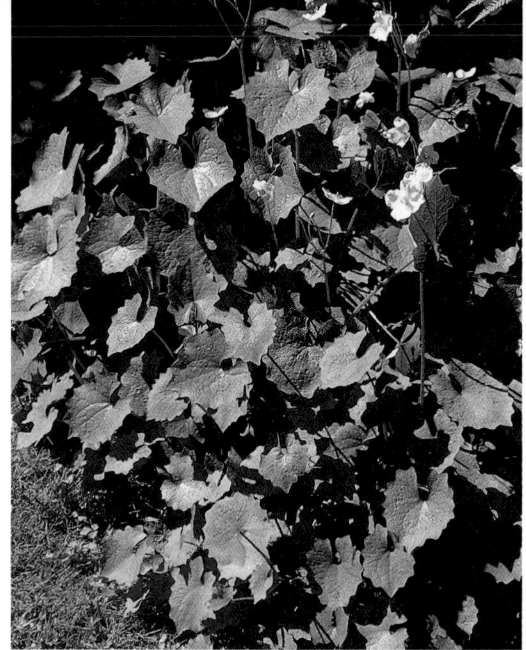

(syn. *E. angustifolium* var. *leucanthum*) (Rosebay Willow-Herb), spreading perennial, the white form is less invasive than the species, willow-like, mid-green linear to lance-shaped leaves, tapering spikes of open saucer-shaped flowers, white with green sepals, mid-summer to early autumn, 1.5m/1m (5ft/3ft); *E. dodonaei*, erect, hardy herbaceous perennial, linear toothed, hairy mid-green leaves, spikes of cup-shaped flowers, purple-pink, late summer to early autumn, 40-90cm/20cm (1½-3ft/8in); *E. glabellum*, mat- or clump-forming semi-evergreen alpine, elliptic to oval toothed leaves, glossy, deep green, tinged bronze, small funnel-shaped, cream-white single flowers in summer, 20cm/20cm (8in/8in).

left Give *Eomecon chionantha* the space, and it will reward you amply; but confine it and it can be a nuisance.

umbels of small bell-shaped flowers, mid-spring to early summer, good for cutting. No routine pruning. Sow seed in warmth in late winter or early spring, layering in autumn, or semi-ripe cuttings in summer. ❀ *E. campanulatus*, one of the hardiest species, elliptic to more or less oval leaves, dark yellow or orange-red in autumn, pale yellow-bronze flowers in summer, 4-5m/4-5m (13-16ft/13-16ft); *E. c.* f. *albiflorus*, cream-white or green-white flowers; *E. c.* 'Red Bells', compact, erect shrub, red flowers; *E. cernuus* f. *rubens*, oval grey-green leaves, dark red to purple in autumn, clusters of fringed flowers, 2.5m/2.5m (8ft/8ft).

Eomecon *Snow Poppy* Papaveraceae

Small hardy rhizomatous ornamental that is far too little known, although it can be invasive. Slightly fleshy, leathery, heart-shaped to oval or kidney-shaped, usually blue-grey or grey-green leaves, yellow or white poppy-like flowers, spring to summer. Sow seed in a cold-frame in spring, divide established plants, or replant runners. ❀ *E. chionantha*, spreading, dull grey-green, heart-shaped, kidney- or arrow-shaped leaves, clusters of glistening white flowers, late spring to mid-summer, 40cm (1½ft)/indefinite.

Epilobium *Willow-Herb* Onagraceae

Annuals, biennials, herbaceous perennials and alpines; includes many weeds but also some rather pretty ornamentals. Moderately hardy to hardy. Linear to oval leaves, four-petalled pink or white flowers, singly or in racemes, summer to autumn, followed by seedpods with fluffy seeds. Sow seed in a cold-frame when ripe or in spring, divide established plants in spring or autumn or take softwood cuttings in spring. ❀ *E. angustifolium album*

above *Epimedium perralderianum*. A plant with a mystifying name, for *Epimedium* means 'on top of the middle' but it has a far from mystifying role, being splendid ground cover for damp and shady places.

Epimedium Berberidaceae

Small deciduous, semi-evergreen and evergreen rhizomatous ornamentals. Moderately hardy and I find quite excellent for woodland gardens, rock gardens and borders; larger species for ground cover. Leathery leaves with pointed tips, bright green at first, later darker, sometimes tinged brown, copper, red or pink in spring, bronze or yellow in autumn but tend to turn brown in cold weather. Small spoon-, cup- or saucer-shaped flowers, sometimes spurred, spring to early summer. Thrives in fertile, moist, well-drained soil enriched with humus, in dappled shade. Sow ripe seed, divide established plants in autumn or take cuttings from rhizomes in winter. ❀ *E.* x *cantabrigiense*, clump-forming evergreen, oval to heart-shaped leaves, pointed leaflets, bronze tipped in spring, red or yellow flowers, mid to late spring, 30-60cm/30cm (1-2ft/1ft); *E. grandiflorum*, deciduous, oval to heart-shaped leaves, light green flushed bronze at first, pendent, spurred, yellow, white or carmine-pink or purple flowers, mid to late spring, 20-30cm/30cm (8in-1ft/1ft); *E. g.* 'Lilafee', narrow, oval leaves, bronzed at first, dark purple buds opening to light purple flowers, white-tipped spurs, 20-25cm (8-10in); *E. g.* 'Rose Queen', dark bronze-purple leaves, spurred, deep rose-pink flowers with white tips; *E.* x *perralchicum*, evergreen, tufted, round to oval leaflets, red or bronze at first, later green, pendent yellow flowers with short brown spurs, 40cm/60cm (1½ft/2ft); *E* x *p.* 'Frohnleiten', neat clumps of marbled leaves, at first red and brown, then again in autumn, gold-yellow flowers; *E. perralderianum*, spreading, clump-forming evergreen, leaves bronze when young, glossy dark green later, bright yellow flowers, short brown spurs, mid to late spring, 30cm/60cm (1ft/2ft); *E. pinnatum* ssp. *colchicum* (syn. *E. pinnatum elegans*), carpet-forming, oval to round, downy leaves, red at first, again in autumn, bright yellow, short-spurred flowers on arching stems, mid to late spring, 30-40cm/20cm (1-1½ft/8in); *E.* x *rubrum*, deciduous, but old leaves remain until spring, dying back when new leaves emerge, flushed red at first, red-brown in autumn, crimson and pale yellow flowers with short spurs, mid to late spring, 30cm/30cm (1ft/1ft); *E.* x *versicolor* 'Sulphureum', evergreen, mid-green leaflets, bronze at first, hairy, grey beneath, yellow flowers with long spurs, on wiry stems, mid to late spring, 30cm/30cm (1ft/1ft); *E.* x *warleyense*, semi-evergreen, heart-shaped, red-purple leaves in spring and autumn, pale orange flowers, 30cm/40cm (1ft/1½ft); *E.* x *youngianum* 'Niveum', semi-evergreen, neat clump of soft, pale brown leaves in spring, white starry flowers on wiry stems, 20-30cm/30cm (8in-1ft/1ft); *E.* x *y.* 'Roseum' (syn. 'Lilacinum'), mauve-purple flowers, 30cm (1ft).

right *Eremurus robustus.* I prefer to grow Foxtail Lilies with some supporting vegetation around them rather than as the isolated individuals shown here because the thin stems are prone to damage.

below *Eranthis hyemalis* Tubergenii Group 'Guinea Gold'. This is arguably the best of a very fine bunch of spring flowers whose foliage is almost as attractive as the flowers.

Eranthis
Winter Aconite Ranunculaceae

Small moderately hardy tuberous ornamental that is one of the most welcome late winter flowers. Tolerates most soils. Fairly finely dissected pinnate or palmate-lobed leaves, small gold-yellow buttercup-like flowers, mid-winter to early spring. Sow ripe seed in a cold-frame in summer or divide established plants immediately after flowering in spring. Self-seeds freely. ❀ *E. hyemalis*, bright or pale green leaves, bright lemon-yellow flowers, 5-8cm/5cm (2-3¼in/2in); *E. h.* Cilicica Group, leaves narrower, slightly bronze, pink stems, 5-8cm/5cm (2-3¼in/2in); *E. h.* Tubergenii Group 'Guinea Gold', sterile variety, bronze-green leaves, deep yellow, scented flowers, appear slightly earlier than others, 8-10cm/5cm (3in-4in/2in).

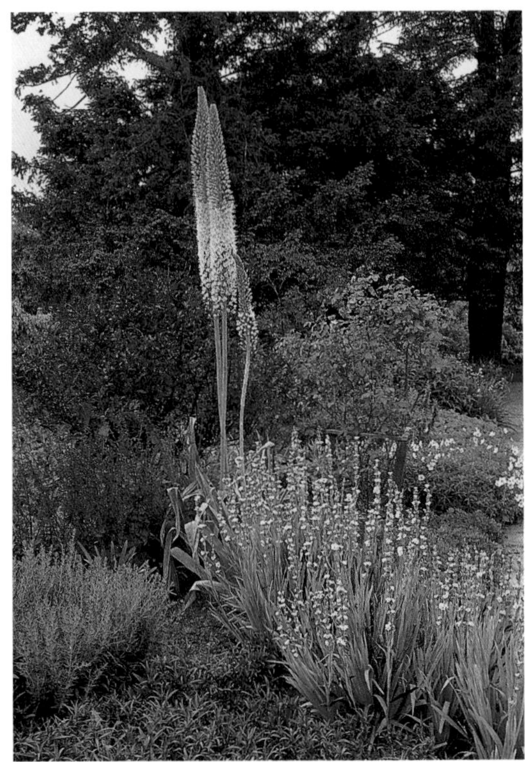

Eremurus *Foxtail Lily* Asphodelaceae

Large hardy herbaceous perennials. Best grown among other plants in the border as leaves die back after flowering. Rosettes of folded, linear to lance-shaped or strap-shaped leaves, erect clusters of star-shaped flowers, most white, pink or yellow, with prominent stamens. Divide after flowering but take care with the thin, brittle tuberous roots. ❀ *E. himalaicus*, strap-shaped leaves, white flowers with orange stamens, late spring to early summer, 1.2-2m/60cm (4-6½ft/2ft); *E.* x *isabellinus* Ruiter Hybrids, lance-shaped green leaves, small, rust-red, orange to yellow and pink flowers, late spring to early summer, 1.5m/90cm (5ft/3ft); *E.* x *i.* Shelford Hybrids, the most reliable overall, flowers ivory-white to shades of pink, yellow and orange, late spring to early summer; *E. robustus*, strap-shaped blue-green leaves, pale pink flowers with brown markings, yellow stamens, early summer to mid-summer, 75-120cm (2½ft-4ft).

Erica *Heather, Heath* Ericaceae

Small/large evergreen shrubs and sub-shrubs. Tender to moderately hardy; generally, the taller the species, the less hardy it is. Suitable as ground cover, specimen plants or hedging; few shrubs are easier to grow or care for although some do become unavoidably straggly after a few years and should be replaced. Needle-like, sometimes oval or linear leaves, usually mid-green to dark green, carried in whorls around the stems. Bell-shaped flowers, white, or shades of purple, pink and red, sometimes bicoloured and much larger than those of *Calluna*. All thrive in well-drained, acidic soil in full sun but the winter-flowering *E. carnea*, *E.* x *darleyensis* and, to some degree, *E. erigena* are alkalinity tolerant. Use shears to trim back dead flower heads in spring. Take semi-ripe heeled cuttings in mid-summer. ❀ *E. arborea* (Tree Heath), 'Albert's Gold', large, hardy, upright shrub, gold leaves, a few ash-white flowers, early to late spring, 2m/80cm (6½ft/2½ft); *E. a.* var. *alpina*, fresh green leaves, clusters of white flowers, 2m/85cm (6½ft/2¾ft); *E. carnea* (Winter Heath, Winter-flowering Heather), 'Adrienne Duncan', prostrate, spreading, bronze leaves, purple-pink urn-shaped flowers on one-sided racemes, late winter to early spring, 20-25cm/30cm (8-10in/1ft); *E. c.* 'Ann Sparkes', gold leaves with bronze tips in spring, flowers rose-pink at first, later mauve-pink, winter to mid-spring, 15cm/25cm (6in/10in); *E. c.* 'December Red', mid- to dark green leaves, flowers pink at first, later purple-pink, 15cm/45cm (6in/1½ft); *E. c.* 'Foxhollow', yellow leaves with bronze tips, leaves turn orange-red in very cold weather, 15cm/40cm (6in/1½ft); *E. c.* 'King George', pink flowers in early winter, 15cm/25cm (6in/10in); *E. c.* 'Loughrigg', flowers pink at first, later rose-pink, then mauve-pink, 15cm/45cm (6in/1½ft); *E. c.* 'Myretoun Ruby', flowers pink, later crimson, a superb variety; *E. c.* 'Pink Spangles', trailing, shell-pink flowers, later deep pink, 15cm/45cm (6in/1½ft); *E. c.* 'Springwood Pink', trailing, pink flowers, later deep pink, 15cm/40cm (6in/1½ft); *E. c.* 'Springwood White', trailing, bright green leaves, white flowers, much the best white winter heather, 15cm/45cm (6in/1½ft); *E. c.* 'Vivellii' (syn. 'Urville'), bronze-tinged leaves, purple-pink flower, later magenta, 15cm/45cm (6in/1½ft); *E. c.* 'Westwood Yellow', yellow leaves, pink flowers, 15cm/30cm (6in/1ft); *E. ciliaris* (Dorset Heath), 'Corfe Castle', upright shrub, mid-green oval leaves, tinged bronze in winter, pink flowers on long spikes, 22cm/35cm (8½in/1¼ft); *E. c.* 'David McClintock', grey-green leaves, pink and white flowers 40cm/45cm (1½ft/1½ft); *E. c.* 'Stoborough', white flowers; *E. cinerea* (Bell Heather), 'Alba Minor', compact, mid-green linear leaves, abundant white flowers, early summer to late autumn, 30cm/55cm (1ft/1¾ft); *E. c.* 'C D Eason', bright magenta flowers, 25cm/50cm (10in/1¾ft); *E. c.* 'Eden Valley', mid-green leaves, lavender and white flowers, 20cm/50cm (8in/1¾ft); *E. c.* 'Fiddler's Gold', gold-yellow leaves, red in winter, lilac-pink flowers, 25cm/45cm (10in/1½ft); *E. c.* 'Golden Hue', pale yellow leaves, tipped orange in winter, amethyst flowers, 35cm/70cm (1¼ft/2¼ft); *E. c.* 'Hookstone White', mid-green leaves, white flowers on long stalks, 35cm/65cm (1¼ft/2¼ft); *E. c.* 'Pink Ice', dark green leaves, bronze in autumn, rose-pink flowers, 20cm/35cm (8in/1¼ft); *E. c.* 'Purple Beauty', dwarf, bright purple-pink flowers, 30cm/35cm (1ft/1¼ft); *E. c.* 'Stephen Davis', upright, dwarf, abundant magenta flowers; *E. c.* 'Velvet Night', deep purple flowers; *E. c.* 'Windlebrooke', gold-yellow leaves, orange-red in winter, a few mauve flowers. *E.* x *darleyensis* species and varieties I describe here are bushy, hardy, tolerant of all soils; *E.* x *d.*'Arthur Johnson', mid-green needle-like leaves lightly tipped white and cream in spring, slightly scented pink flowers, 30cm/60cm (1ft/2ft); *E.* x *d.* 'Furzey', mid-green leaves tipped cream in spring, flowers lilac-pink at first, later mauve-pink, 30cm/60cm (1ft/2ft); *E.* x *d.* 'Ghost Hills', light green leaves tipped cream in spring, 30cm/80cm (1ft/2½ft); *E.* x *d.* 'Jack H Brummage', orange-yellow leaves, purple-pink flowers, 30cm/60cm (1ft/2ft); *E.* x *d.* 'Jenny Porter',

above *Erica carnea* 'Springwood White' is certainly the best white, winter-flowering heather and may well be the best of all white heathers.

above: *Erica vagans* 'Birch Glow'. It is when plants like this are compared with their similarly coloured counterparts in the genus *Calluna* that the flowers of *Erica* are revealed as really so very much better.

mid-green leaves tipped cream in spring, pink-white flowers, 30cm/ 60cm (1ft/2ft); *E.* x *d.* 'Kramer's Rote', bronze-green leaves, magenta flowers, 30cm/ 60cm (1ft/2ft); *E.* x *d.* 'Silber-schmelze' (syn. 'Molten Silver'), mid-green leaves, faintly tipped cream in spring, later dark green, red in winter, 35cm/80cm (1¼ft/2½ft); *E.* x *d.* 'White Perfection', bright green leaves, white flowers, 40cm/70cm (1½ft/2½ft); *E. erigena* (syn. *E. hibernica, E. mediterranea*) (Irish Heath), 'Brightness', erect shrub, linear, purple-green leaves in winter, blue-green in summer, honey-scented lilac-pink flowers in spring, 50cm/ 50cm (1¾ft/1¾ft); *E. e.* 'Golden Lady', bright gold-yellow leaves, a few white flowers, 30cm/40cm (1ft/1½ft); *E. e.* 'Irish Dusk', dark green leaves, rose-pink flowers, late autumn to late spring, 60cm/45cm (2ft/1½ft); *E. e.* 'Superba', very fragrant, shell-pink flowers, mid to late spring, 1.8m/ 50cm (5¾ft/1¾ft); *E. e.* 'W T Rackliff', compact, rich green foliage, abundant white flowers in spring, 75cm/55cm (2½ft/2¾ft); *E. lusitanica* (Portuguese Heath), upright, linear mid-green leaves, pink buds opening to cup-shaped or tubular white flowers, early winter to late spring, 3m/1m (10ft/3ft); *E.* x *stuartii* (syn. *E.* x *praegeri*) 'Irish Lemon', grey-green leaves, bright lemon growth in spring, mauve flowers, late spring to summer, 25cm/50cm (10in/1¾ft); *E. terminalis* (syn. *E. terminalis stricta*), upright, lime tolerant, linear, dark green glossy leaves, lilac-pink flowers, summer to early autumn, russet in winter, 1m/1m (3ft/3ft); *E. tetralix* (Cross-Leaved Heath), 'Alba Mollis', narrow silver-grey leaves, white flowers, early summer to mid-autumn, 20cm/30cm (8in/1ft); *E. t.* 'Con Underwood', magenta flowers, 25cm (10in); *E. t.* 'Pink Star', pink flowers, 20cm/35cm (8in/1¼ft); *E. vagans* (Cornish Heath), *E. v.*'Birch Glow', spreading, linear, dark green leaves, rose-pink flowers, mid-summer to mid-autumn, 40-80cm/80cm (1-2½ft/2/½ft); *E. v.* 'Cornish Cream', bright green leaves, off-white flowers, 35cm/65cm (1¼ft/2¼ft); *E. v.* 'Lyonesse', bright green leaves, white flowers, 25cm/50cm (10in/ 1¾ft); *E. v.* 'Mrs D F Maxwell', rose-pink flowers, a magnificent variety, 30cm/ 45cm (1ft/1½ft); *E. v.* 'Saint Keverne', pink flowers, 45cm/45cm (1½ft/ 1½ft); *E. v.* 'Valerie Proudley', bright yellow leaves, a few white flowers, 1.7m/30cm (5½ft/1ft); *E.* x *watsonii* 'Dawn', grey-green leaves, new leaves red, later gold, pink flowers, mid-summer to mid-autumn, 20cm/ 85cm (8in/2¾ft).

Erigeron *Fleabane* Asteraceae

Small/medium annuals, biennials and herbaceous or semi-evergreen/evergreen perennials. Moderately hardy. Those I describe here are all perennials and among the prettiest of daisies. Oblong, lance-shaped or spoon-shaped leaves, single or semi-double daisy-like flowers, purple, yellow, pink or orange, singly or in clusters, in summer. Sow seed in a cold-frame in mid or late spring, take basal cuttings or divide established plants in spring. ❀ *E.* 'Azurfee' (syn. 'Azure Fairy'), clump-forming perennial, more or less lance-shaped leaves, semi-double lavender flowers in summer, 45cm/45cm (1½ft/1½ft); *E.* 'Dimity', clump-forming evergreen, lance-shaped leaves, semi-double pink flowers with orange centres, 25cm/30cm (10in/1ft); *E.* 'Dunkelste Aller' (syn. 'Darkest of All'), clump-forming, lance-shaped grey-green leaves, clusters of semi-double dark purple flowers, 60cm/45cm (2ft/1½ft); *E. karvinskianus* (syn. *E. mucronatus*), spreading, elliptic to lance-shaped grey-green leaves, hairy, flowers white at first, later rose, yellow centres, self-seeds freely and a trifle invasive but a most wonderful little hardy Mexican

right *Erigeron karvinskianus.* There are few more endearing and durable little daisies. Although it can be invasive, it is never troublesome.

daisy and one of the most admired plants in my garden, 15-30cm/1m (6in-1ft/3ft); *E.* 'Quakeress', lilac-pink flowers, clump-forming, lance-shaped grey-green, single pink flowers with yellow centres, early to mid-summer, 60cm/45cm (2ft/1½ft); *E.* 'Rosa Juwel' (syn. 'Pink Jewel'), clump-forming, lance-shaped leaves, clusters of semi-double pink flowers with yellow centres, early to mid-summer, 60cm/45cm (2ft/1½ft); *E.* 'Schneewitchen', white flowers, 60cm (2ft).

Erinus Scrophulariaceae

Small hardy semi-evergreen or evergreen alpine perennials. Rosettes of wedge-shaped or lance-shaped toothed leaves, tubular flowers in spring and summer. Sow seed in warmth in autumn or early spring. ❀ *E. alpinus* (Alpine Balsam), more or less lance-shaped to wedge-shaped sticky, mid-green, deeply toothed leaves, bright pink star-like flowers, can be invasive through self-seeding, 8cm/ 10cm (3¼in/4in); *E. a.* var. *albus*, white flowers.

Eriogonum *Wild Buckwheat* Polygonaceae

Small/large annuals, alpine perennials, evergreen shrubs and sub-shrubs. Tender to moderately hardy. Linear, oval or rounded leaves, often white, woolly, flowers usually white or yellow, in summer. Sow ripe seed in early spring or autumn in a cold-frame, seed of tender species in warmth, or take semi-ripe cuttings mid- to late summer. ❀ *E. ovalifolium*, mat-forming perennial, spoon-shaped hairy silver leaves, cream or yellow flowers in summer, sometimes purple-pink later, 5cm/20cm (2in/8in); *E. umbellatum* (Sulphur Flower), deep green leaves, white, hairy beneath, umbels of cream or bright yellow flowers, mid- to late summer, later tinged red-brown, sometimes followed by copper fruit, 30cm/1m (1ft/3ft).

Eriophorum *Cotton Grass* Cyperaceae

Medium perennial sedge. Very hardy. Suitable for large bog gardens, wildlife pond edges, semi-wild situations. Slender, tough leaves, umbels of beautiful nodding, cottony white flower heads in summer but needs to be massed over a large area for real effect. You really need to mimic the wonderful natural drifts of this plant around mountain pools. Sow seed in spring or divide. ❀ *E. angustifolium*, linear grooved basal leaves, sharply pointed tips, spikes of downy white flowers in summer, 75cm (2½ft)/indefinite.

above *Erodium pelargoniiflorum. Erodiums* are too often forgotten in favour of their relatives in *Geranium* but they have a valuable charm of their own.

Erodium *Stork's Bill* Geraniaceae

Small annuals, semi-evergreen/evergreen perennials, evergreen/deciduous sub-shrubs. Barely hardy to moderately hardy. Smaller compact species are suitable for rock gardens, others for herbaceous borders but are much less appreciated than their close relatives, geraniums. Those I describe here are all moderately hardy perennials. Lobed or pinnate leaves, usually cup- or saucer- shaped flowers, in shades of pink, purple, some white and yellow, followed by seedheads with long pointed beaks. Sow ripe seed in an cold-frame, divide established plants in spring or take stem cuttings in late spring or early summer. ❀ *E. chrysanthum*, tufts of deeply divided, fern-like silver leaves, sulphur-yellow saucer-shaped flowers, summer to early autumn, 15cm/40cm (6in/1½ft); *E. glandulosum* (syns. *E. macradenum, E. petraeum* ssp. *glandulosum*), mid-green, deeply divided fern-like leaves, sprays of saucer-shaped lilac flowers, dark violet blotches on upper two of five petals, early summer to late summer, 10-20cm/20cm (4-8in/8in); *E.* x *kolbianum* 'Natasha', fern-like, silver-grey, finely divided leaves, pale pink flowers in small clusters in summer, 15cm/15cm (6in/6in); *E. manescaui*, mound-forming, fern-like, divided blue-green leaves, pink-purple flowers with dark blotches on upper two petals, late spring to early autumn, 40cm/60cm (1½ft/2ft); *E. pelargoniiflorum*, more or less rounded to heart-shaped leaves, branched, woody stems, white flowers with dark purple blotches on upper two petals, summer, 30cm/20cm (1ft/8in); *E. reichardii* (syn. *E.*

below *Eriophorum angustifolium*. The glorious sight of a drift of these delicate flower heads dancing in the breeze can add great appeal to a water garden.

chaemaedryoides), dark green heart-shaped leaves, finely toothed edges, short-stemmed white summer flowers with shell-pink to red veins, 5-7cm/15cm (2-2¾in/6in); *E.* x *variabile* 'Album', cushion-forming, mid-green leaves, scalloped or lobed edges, heart-shaped bases, single or double white flowers, veined maroon, 12cm/30cm (5in/1ft); *E.* x *v.* 'Bishop's Form', bright pink flowers; *E.* x *v.* 'Flore Pleno', double pink flowers with crimson veins.

Eruca *Salad Rocket* Brassicaceae

Annuals and perennials. Fairly hardy. The only important species is the popular annual leaf salad, rocket. Sow seeds in the growing position in spring or, in mild areas, in early autumn. Regular repeat sowings will be needed in summer as it soon runs to seed. ❀ *E. vesicaria* ssp. *sativa*, erect, lobed asymmetrical leaves, cream flowers, veined purple, late winter to autumn, strong flavoured, pleasantly sharp-tasting leaves harvested when young, 60-100cm/15-20cm (2-3ft/6-8in).

Eryngium *Sea Holly* Apiaceae

Annuals, biennials, herbaceous/evergreen perennials. Barely hardy to moderately hardy. Those I describe here are all herbaceous or evergreen perennials. Immediately recognisable, spiny oval to heart-shaped or sword-shaped leaves, cylindrical umbels or cones of teasel-like flowers, surrounded by narrow, sometimes spine-toothed, bracts. Splendid perennials for hot, dry gardens but intolerant of waterlogged conditions. Sow ripe seed in a cold-frame, take root cuttings in late winter, or divide established plants in spring. Some species self-seed freely. ❀ *E. agavifolium* (syn. *E. bromeliifolium*), rosettes of strap-shaped toothed leaves, light green, green-white umbels surrounded by spiny-toothed bracts, on branching stems, in late summer, 1.5m/60cm (5ft/2ft); *E. alpinum*, oval to heart-shaped, spiny-toothed, mid-green leaves, steel-blue or white flowers surrounded by soft metallic-blue bracts, mid-summer to early autumn, 10cm/45cm (4in/11/2ft); *E. bourgatii*, clump-forming, deeply divided basal leaves, prickly margins, silver veining, umbels of blue-green flowers, silver bracts flushed blue, 15-45cm/30cm (6in-1½ft/1ft); *E. giganteum* (Miss Willmott's Ghost), short-lived, rosettes of heart-shaped, mid-green leaves, spiny, toothed stem leaves, umbels pale green at first, later metallic silver-blue, surrounded by oval, toothed, silver-grey bracts, 90cm/30cm (3ft/1ft); *E.* x *olivieranum*, clump-forming oval mid-green basal leaves, toothed edges, lavender-blue umbels surrounded by spiny bracts, 1m/60cm (3ft/2ft); *E. planum*, clump-forming evergreen, oblong to oval, toothed, dark green toothed basal leaves, abundant umbels on branching stems of small light blue flowers, spiky blue-green bracts, in late summer, 90cm/45cm (3ft/1½ft); *E.* x *tripartitum*, semi-evergreen, rosettes of deep grey-green, coarsely toothed basal leaves, small violet-blue umbels surrounded by spine-tipped, narrow, grey-blue bracts, mid-summer to early autumn, 60-90cm/50cm (2-3ft/1¾ft); *E. variifolium,* rosettes of rich green, oval, toothed leaves, marbled white, umbels of small metallic-blue spiny flowers, mid-summer to late summer, there are few more striking variegated herbaceous perennials, 30-40cm/25cm (1-1½ft/10in).

below *Eryngium giganteum*. Popularly called 'Miss Willmott's Ghost' after the great gardener Ellen Willmott; possibly because she spread it far and wide and it keeps appearing as a reminder of her.

Erysimum *Wallflower* Brassicaceae

Small/medium annuals, biennials and evergreen perennials and sub-shrubs. Barely hardy to moderately hardy. Those species and varieties I describe here are all moderately hardy and are excellent for sunny borders, the small evergreen species make fine rock garden plants, and the biennials, which include the familiar and much-loved bedding wallflower, offer spring colour in beds and containers. Some species are toxic and can cause skin

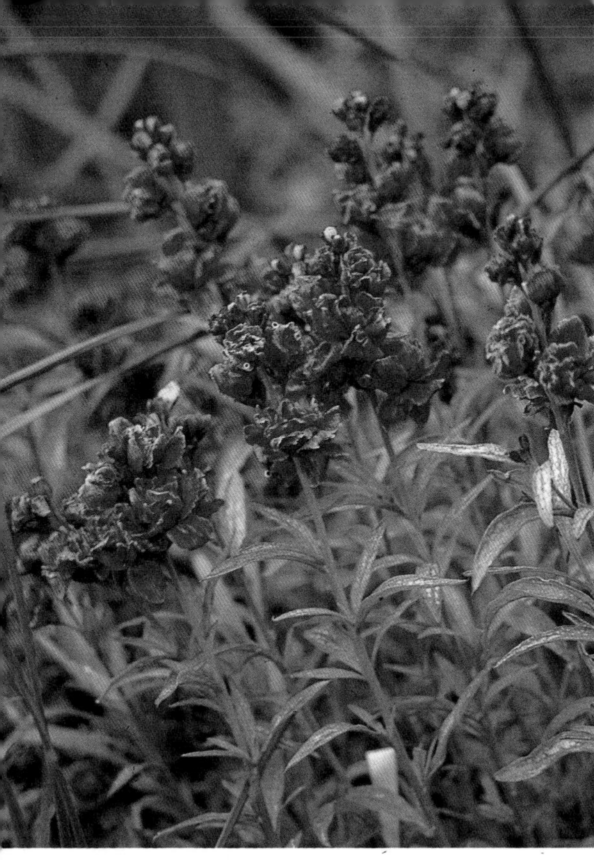

irritation. Most have more or less lance-shaped, toothed, hairy leaves and dense clusters of four-petalled, sometimes fragrant, often yellow, flowers. Sow seed (biennials) in a seedbed in late spring or early summer for transplanting in autumn; take semi-ripe cuttings of perennials in early summer. ❀ *E.* 'Bowles' Mauve', erect, evergreen perennial sub-shrub, grey-green leaves, mauve flowers, late winter to summer, 75cm/60cm (1ft/2ft); *E.* 'Bredon', mound-forming, evergreen perennial, blue-green leaves, red buds open to rich yellow flowers, mid-spring to early summer, 30cm/45cm (1ft/1½ft); *E. cheiri* (syn. *Cheiranthus cheiri*) (Wallflower), short-lived evergreen perennial usually grown as a biennial, dark green lance-shaped to more or less oval leaves, spice-scented spring flowers, red, orange, yellow, cream and bronze shades, 25-80cm/30-40cm (10in-3ft/1-1½ft); far fewer varieties exist today than in the recent past but among the best are *E. c.* 'Baden-Powell', double, yellow; *E. c.* 'Bloody Warrior', dwarf, double, ox-red, 30cm/30cm (1ft/1ft); *E. c.* 'Harpur Crewe', dwarf, double, yellow, late spring to mid-summer, 30cm/60cm (1ft/2ft); *E.* 'Constant Cheer', bushy, erect evergreen perennial, lance-shaped dark green leaves, dusky orange-red, later purple or violet-mauve flowers flushed amber, mid-spring to early summer, 30cm/60cm (1ft/2ft); *E. linifolium* 'Variegatum' (syn. *E.* 'Sissinghurst Variegated'), tufted evergreen perennial, narrow, linear to lance-shaped, wavy-edge, grey-green leaves, mauve, spring, 45cm/45cm (1½ft/1½ft); *E.* 'Moonlight', mat-forming evergreen perennial, oval, narrow, mid-green leaves, pale yellow, 25cm/45cm (10in/1½ft); *E.* 'Wenlock Beauty', evergreen perennial, elliptic to lance-shaped deep green leaves, mauve and yellow flowers flushed bronze, early to late spring, 45cm/45cm (1½ft/1½ft).

far left *Erysimum cheiri* 'Bloody Warrior'. So many of the lovely old wallflower varieties have gone that we must cherish those such as this one that still remain.

Erythronium

Dog's Tooth Violet Liliaceae

Small/medium bulbous ornamental. Moderately hardy to hardy. Oval to lance-shaped leaves, sometimes glossy, in pairs, pendent nodding, pink, white, yellow or purple flowers, petals reflexed, conspicuous stamens, late winter to early spring. A lovely bulb for the early spring woodland garden; must have rich, moist soil – intolerant of dryness. Sow seed in warmth in spring; divide established clumps when dormant. ❀ *E. californicum*, elliptic to lance-shaped mid-green leaves, mottled white, flowers pink-brown in bud, opening to cream-white, yellow centre, on purple stems, in spring, 15-35cm/10cm (6in-1¼ft/4in); *E. c.* 'White Beauty', strong-growing, dark green leaves heavily mottled brown, cream-white, lily-like flowers with red ring around base, crimson stamens; *E. dens-canis*, cultivated dog's tooth violet, mid-green oval leaves, mottled purple-brown, white, lilac or pink solitary flowers purple or blue anthers, 10-15cm/10cm (4-6in/4in); *E. d.* 'Rose Queen', deep pink flowers; *E. d.* 'Snowflake', off-white flowers, tinged mauve; *E.* 'Pagoda', elliptic, glossy dark green leaves, mottled bronze, very pale yellow flowers, brown rings at centre, in mid-spring, 15-35cm/10cm (6in-1¼ft/4in); *E. revolutum*, green leaves mottled brown, spikes of pink flowers, spring to early summer, 20-30cm/10cm (8-1ft/4in); *E. tuolumnense*, pale to mid-green leaves, often with wavy margins, spikes of bright yellow, green-veined flowers, 20-35cm/8cm (8-1¼ft/3¼in).

left *Erythronium tuolumnense*. Plant erythroniums where they will be seen prominently in a shady bed; they are too valuable to tuck out of sight.

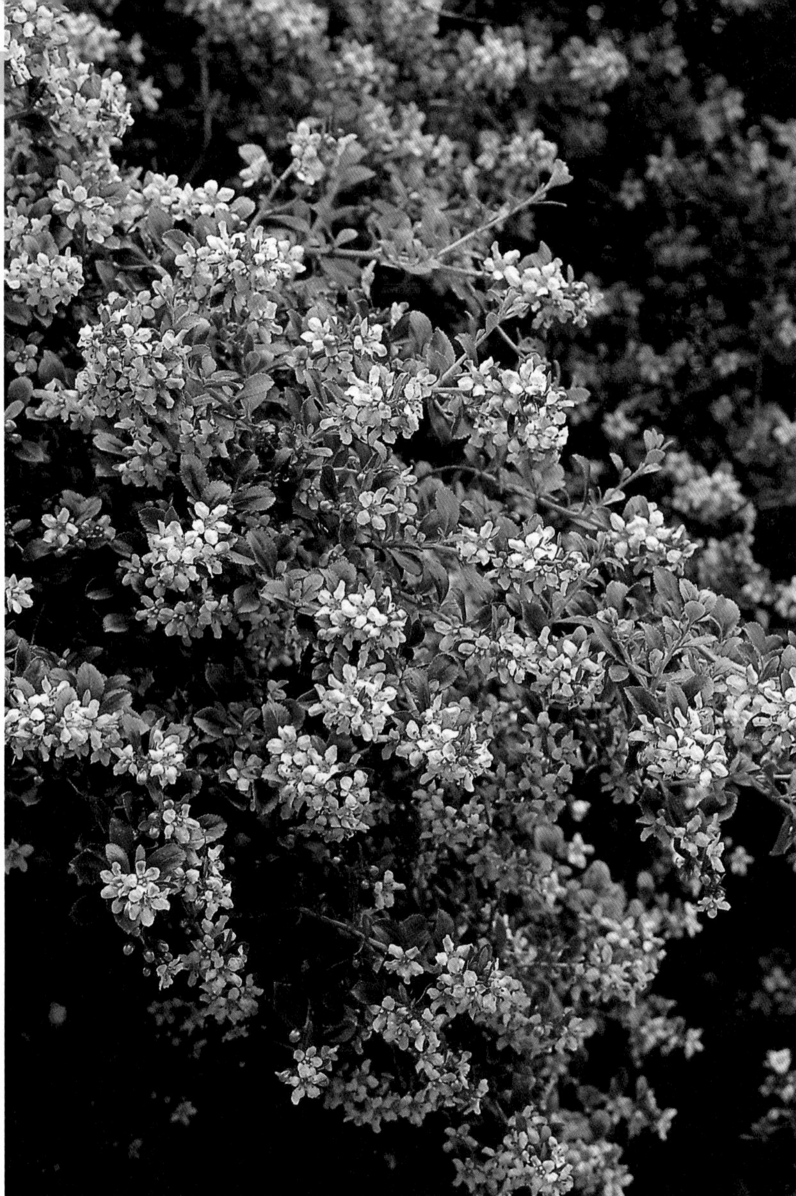

above *Escallonia* 'Apple Blossom'. Although most reliable in coastal gardens, some escallonias are hardy inland too; and this is probably the best.

right *Eschscholzia caespitosa* 'Mission bells'. Few summer annuals can match the Californian poppies for delicate flowers in pastel shades.

Escallonia — Escalloniaceae

Medium/large shrubs and small trees, many evergreen, including all those I recommend here. Fairly hardy to moderately hardy. Suitable for hedging, particularly in mild and coastal areas as they are prone to die-back in cold winters and, although they will regenerate, they are unsightly for long periods. Plants that die back in cold areas usually regenerate from old wood. Leaves glossy, narrow or broad, oval, clusters of bell-shaped, tubular, saucer-shaped flowers, white, pink or red, late spring to autumn. Thrives in fertile, well-drained soil in full sun or light shade, the less hardy species with the protection of a sunny wall. Tolerant of alkaline soil. No routine pruning when grown informally; hedges should be clipped lightly after flowering. Take softwood cuttings in mid-summer or semi-ripe cuttings from late summer to early autumn. ❀ *E.* 'Apple Blossom', compact, moderately hardy and I think much the best all-round variety, elliptic, glossy dark green leaves, pink and white flowers with incurved petals, 2.5m/2.5m (8ft/8ft); *E.* 'C F Ball', glossy, aromatic, dark green, oval to more or less oval, deeply toothed leaves, tubular crimson flowers in summer, 2.5m/2.5m (8ft/8ft); *E.* 'Donard Radiance', compact, glossy, deep green, more or less oval toothed leaves, clusters of chalice-shaped rose-red flowers, 2.5m/2.5m (8ft/8ft); *E.* 'Donard Seedling', arching, moderately hardy, more or less oval, glossy dark green leaves, pink buds open to white flowers, early to mid-summer, 2.5m/2.5m (8ft/8ft); *E.* 'Iveyi', erect, glossy, aromatic round leaves, often flushed bronze in cold weather, clusters of white flowers in mid-summer, 3m/3m (10ft/10ft); *E.* 'Peach Blossom', spreading, elliptic glossy dark green leaves, clear peach-pink, chalice-shaped flowers, summer to early autumn, 2.5m/2.5m (8ft/8ft); *E.* 'Red Elf', spreading, glossy, dark green, oval to more or less oval leaves, tubular crimson flowers, early to mid-summer, 2.5m/4m (8ft/13ft); *E. rubra* 'Crimson Spire', barely hardy, upright, glistening dark green oval, toothed leaves, bright crimson tubular flowers in summer, 5m/5m (16ft/16ft); *E. r.* var. *macrantha*, excellent for coastal hedging, glossy aromatic leaves, tubular rose-crimson flowers, 3m/3m (10ft/10ft).

Eschscholzia
California Poppy — Papaveraceae

Small hardy annuals and perennials. Those I describe here are all annuals for borders and rock gardens; good cut flowers. Light to blue-green, finely divided, fern-like leaves, solitary, cup-shaped, four-petalled, silky poppy-like flowers in shades of red, yellow and orange, sometimes white, spring to summer. Few summer annuals offer such vivid yellows and oranges in combination with such delicacy of form. Thrives in fairly poor, well-

drained soil in full sun. Sow seed in flowering positions in mid-spring or early autumn; autumn-sown seedlings require winter protection in cold areas. ❀ *E. caespitosa*, dwarf, tufted, very finely divided leaves, numerous scented yellow flowers in summer, 15cm/15cm (6in/6in); *E. c.* 'Sundew', lemon-yellow, fragrant flowers, 5cm (2in); *E. californica*, mat-forming, sometimes hairy, blue-green, finely-cut lance-shaped leaves, most orange, some red, white or yellow, long curved blue-green seedpods, 30cm/15cm (1ft/6in); *E. c.* 'Ballerina', fluted, semi-double or double, red, pink, yellow, or orange flowers; *E. c.* 'Dali', scarlet flowers, some with yellow centres, 25cm (10in); *E. c.* 'Mission Bells', large double flowers, shades of cream, pink and orange; *E. c.* 'Thai Silk', a lovely selection, single or semi-double fluted, silky wavy-edged flowers, red, pink or orange, tinged bronze, 20-25cm (8-10in); *E. c.* 'Monarch', pale green feathery leaves, semi-double or single cerise, red, orange, carmine and yellow flowers.

Eucalyptus *Gum Tree* Myrtaceae

Large evergreen shrubs and trees. Tender to hardy. There are rather few reliably hardy species and all tend to make large, dominant trees. I feel they are all better when pollarded annually in spring to produce the distinctive and attractive juvenile foliage which is usually stalkless, rounded and very aromatic; the mature leaves are usually sickle-shaped. Peeling old bark reveals colourful new colours beneath. Umbels of petal-less buds in early summer opening 12months later to tufts of white or cream filaments, followed in mild areas by seed capsules. Thrives in well-drained, moderately fertile soil in full sun, most are intolerant of chalk. Needs protection from cold winds. Sow seed in warmth in spring or summer. ❀ *E. coccifera* (Tasmanian Snow Gum), large hardy tree, wind-resistant, suitable for hedging when pruned and grown as a shrub, immature leaves elliptic, green or blue-green, later lance-shaped, grey-green, peppermint scented, bark smooth, mottled pale grey or white, white flowers in spring and early summer, 18m/7m (56ft/23ft); *E. dalrympleana* (Mountain Gum), hardy species, tolerant of chalk, grey-green leaves, bronze when young, 20m/8m (60ft/25ft); *E. globulus* (Blue Gum), suitable only for very mild areas, leaves silver on immature plants, later blue-green, smooth shedding bark, 15-50m/10-25m (50-165ft/33-80ft); *E. gunnii* (Cider Gum), erect, spreading, hardy, silver-blue immature leaves, later sickle-shaped, shedding bark, showing yellow or pink to orange new bark, 10-25m/6-15m (33-80ft/20-50ft); *E. parvifolia* (Kybean Gum), barely hardy, tolerant of chalk, narrow blue-green mature leaves, 15m/10cm (50ft/4in; *E. pauciflora* (Snow Gum), hardy, immature leaves grey-green, oval to elliptic, later lance-shaped, pendent, glossy dark red to orange-yellow twigs, 8-20m/6-15m (25-60ft/20-50ft); *E. p.* ssp *niphophila*, small tree, leathery grey-green leaves, 6m (20ft).

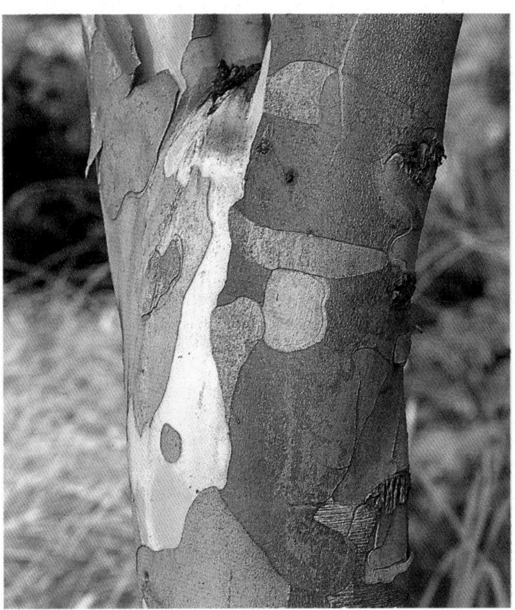

left *Eucalyptus parvifolia*. Although there's much to be said for keeping eucalyptus pruned small, where space and climate do permit them to reach tree size, the bark is often an added attraction.

Eucryphia Eucryphiaceae

Medium/large deciduous, semi-evergreen or evergreen shrubs and trees. Barely hardy to moderately hardy. Less hardy species require a sheltered position in cold areas and all are best in rich, moist, slightly acidic soil. A well-grown tree in flower is a glorious sight. Leathery, simple or pinnate green leaves, white, sometimes cup- to saucer-shaped fragrant flowers with prominent stamens, late summer to autumn. No routine pruning. Take semi-ripe cuttings in early summer or layer. ❀ *E. glutinosa*, medium-sized deciduous tree or large shrub, glossy dark grey-green leaves, orange-red in autumn, white flowers, mid- to late summer, 10m/6m (33ft/20ft); *E.* x *intermedia* 'Rostrevor', small evergreen tree, barely hardy, oblong, simple or trifoliate leaves, slightly toothed, dark green above, paler beneath, small white cup-shaped flowers in mid-summer, 6m/1.5m (20ft/5ft); *E.* x *nymansensis*, evergreen tree, alkaline-tolerant, glossy, leathery, dark green leaves, clusters of large white flowers, late summer to early autumn, 12m/1.8m (40ft/53/4ft); *E.* x *n.* 'Nymansay', much the most reliable all-round variety, simple to trifoliate, elliptic to oblong, serrated, dark green leaves, large purple-white flowers in late summer, 15m/5m (50ft/16ft).

above Our native shrubs are often passed by in the search for something exotic. *Euonymus europaeus* 'Red Cascade' demonstrates the beauty that lies close to home.

right *Eupatorium purpureum maculatum* 'Atropurpureum'. Reliably hardy, fragrant and an excellent plant to give purple to the herbaceous border.

Euonymus Celastraceae

Evergreen, deciduous and semi-evergreen climbers, shrubs and trees. Barely hardy to moderately hardy. An exceedingly important genus of shrubs for foliage and fruiting appeal; often maligned for being too common and easy to grow. Variable leaf shape, many oval, toothed or scalloped, deciduous species with scarlet or yellow autumn leaf colour; in evergreen species leaves usually marked with yellow or white, sometimes pink, insignificant flowers in spring or summer, followed by winged or lobed fruit, often splitting very attractively to reveal orange seeds in winter. All parts are toxic when eaten. Thrives in well-drained soil in full sun or partial shade but evergreen species require shelter from cold winds. No routine pruning but all-green shoots on variegated forms should be cut out promptly. Sow ripe seed in a cold-frame, take semi-ripe cuttings in summer. ❀ *E. alatus*, deciduous shrub, oval to elliptic, toothed dark green leaves, brilliant crimson-pink in autumn, red-purple fruit splitting to reveal orange seeds, 2m/3m (6½ft/10ft); *E. a.* 'Compactus' (syn. *E.* 'Ciliodentatus'), smaller, compact, good for low hedging, 1m (3ft); *E. europaeus*, deciduous shrub or small tree, narrow oval mid-green leaves, green-white flowers in spring, abundant rose-red seed capsules, opening to reveal orange seeds, 2m/1.2m (6½ft/4ft); *E. e.* 'Red Cascade', bright red or purple leaves in autumn, profuse clusters of red-pink fruit, splitting to reveal white and orange seeds, 2m/1.2m (6½ft/4ft); *E. fortunei*, very hardy, prostrate, creeping or climbing evergreen shrub, glossy dark green leaves, oval, toothed, pink capsules enclosing orange seeds, 3m/2m (10ft/6½ft); *E. f.* 'Emerald Gaiety', narrow bright green leaves, cream-white leaf margins, tinged pink-bronze in winter, 1m/1.5m (3ft/5ft); *E. f.* 'Emerald 'n' Gold', bright green leaves, broad, bright yellow margins, tinged pink in winter, 1m/1.5m (3ft/5ft); *E. f.* 'Silver Queen', dark green leaves with broad white margins, tinged rose in winter, can be grown as a climber, 1.5m/1.5m (5ft/5ft), to 6m (20ft) as a climber; *E. f.* 'Sunspot' (syn. 'Gold Spot'), compact, deep green leaves, central gold blotch, tinged red beneath in winter, a magnificent plant, doubly so when it produces fruits; *E. japonicus*, evergreen shrub or small tree, toothed, leathery, oval to elongated oval leaves, glossy dark green, fruit spherical, pink with white flush, 4m/2m (13ft/6½ft); *E. j.* 'Aureus' (syn. 'Aureopictus'), dark green leaves with gold centres; *E. j.* 'Microphyllus Albovariegatus' (syn. 'Microphyllus Variegatus'), white margins on leaves; *E. j.* 'Ovatus Aureus' (syns. 'Aureovariegatus', 'Marieke'), dense, compact, yellow leaves tinged green, green leaves tinged yellow, 2m/1.5m (6½ft/5ft).

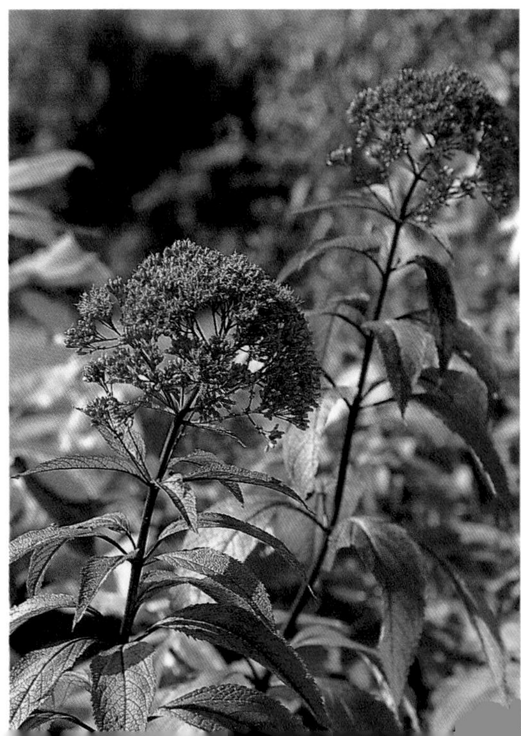

Eupatorium Asteraceae

Herbaceous perennials and evergreen shrubs. Tender to very hardy; all those I describe here are hardy. Leaves usually toothed, dissected, sometimes entire. Tubular flowers on erect stems, sometimes in fluffy clusters, sometimes singly. Sow seed in warmth in spring or in a cold-frame in autumn, divide established perennials in spring or autumn, or take stem cuttings of shrubs in summer. ❀ *E. cannabinum* (Hemp Agrimony), aromatic green, divided, toothed leaves, dense clusters of white, pink or purple flowers, late summer to early autumn, very attractive to butterflies, 1.5m/1.2m (5ft/4ft); *E. purpureum*, coarse, oval leaves, scented of vanilla when crushed, clusters of pink-purple flowers, late summer to autumn, purple stems, 2.2m/1m (6¾ft/3ft); *E. p.* ssp. *maculatum* 'Atropurpureum', deep purple-red flowers on mottled stems.

Euphorbia Euphorbiaceae

Annuals, biennials, semi-evergreen and evergreen or herbaceous perennials, and deciduous and evergreen sub-shrubs, shrubs and trees although all of those grown in British gardens are treated as herbaceous perennials. Tender to moderately hardy. Unusual flowers, known as cyathia, are petal-less, with small green petal-like bracts. Each cyathium has reduced male and female flowers contained in a cup formed by two bracts, usually yellow-green, and a ring of small glands, sometimes colourful, that secrete nectar. Few genera have enjoyed so much increased interest in recent years, and few other plants offer so much variety from such unappealing sounding attributes. All parts of the plant are toxic and may cause skin and eye irritation and are also dangerous if eaten. Thrives in a well-drained soil in full sun, some usefully in shade. May be cut back to soil level after flowering. Sow seed in spring in a cold-frame, divide established plants in spring or autumn or take softwood cuttings in late spring or early summer. ❀ *E. amygdaloides* 'Purpurea', narrow elongated oval leaves, purple, sometimes fading to mid-green, yellow flowers, 75-80cm/30cm (2½-2½ft/ 1ft); *E. a.* var. *robbiae* (syn. *E. robbiae*), leathery, shiny, dark green leaves, paler beneath, flowers on long spikes, valuable as ground cover in shade but invasive; *E. characias*, linear to elongated oval, grey-green leaves, *E. c.* ssp. *wulfenii*, tolerant of dry conditions, magnificent large clumps of blue-green leaves, huge inflorescences of lime-green flowers, early to late summer; *E. c.* ssp. *w.* 'Lambrook Gold', bright gold-green flowers; *E. cyparissias*, linear leathery blue-green leaves, yellow in autumn, yellow-green flowers, sometimes orange, invasive, 20-40cm (8in-1½ft)/indefinite; *E. c.* 'Fens Ruby', young shoots flushed red-purple; *E. c.* 'Orange Man', flowers flushed orange, leaves orange-tinted in autumn; *E. dulcis*, oblong to more- or-less lance-shaped leaves, dark green or bronze-green, red, gold, orange in autumn, green-yellow flowers in early summer, 30cm/30cm (1ft/1ft); *E. d.* 'Chameleon', purple leaves, yellow-green flowers tinted purple; *E. griffithii* 'Dixter', upright, linear-oblong to lance-shaped leaves, very dark green, tinted copper, red midribs, red and

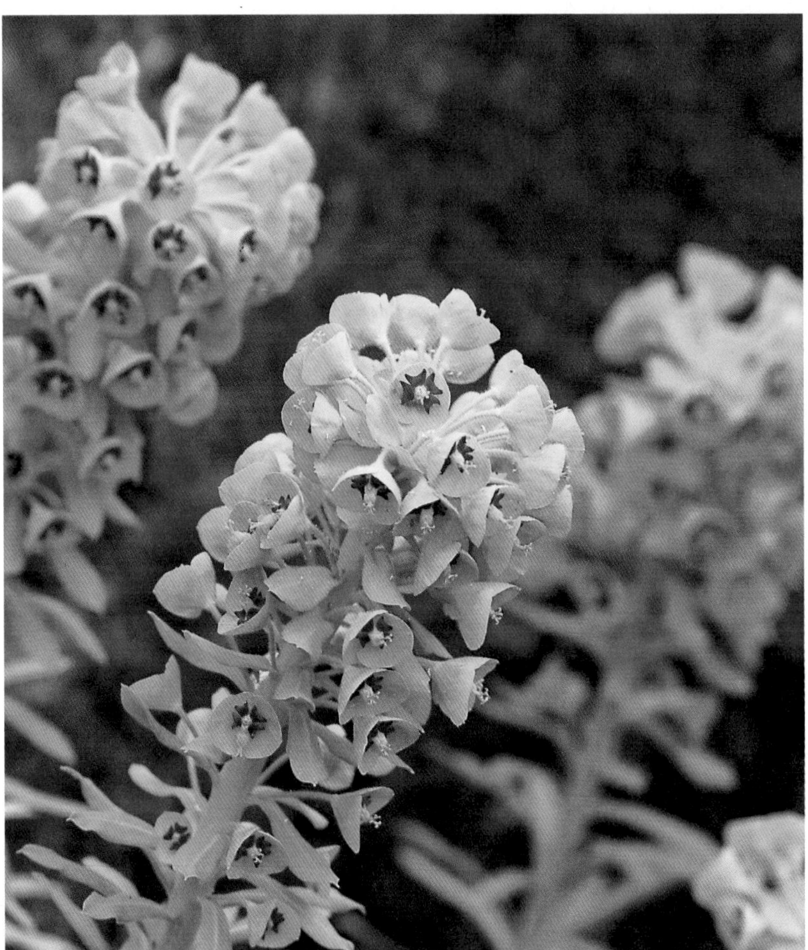

above *Euphorbia characias wulfenii*. One of the best of the big border euphorbias, but variable, so see it in flower before you buy.

yellow in autumn, yellow and orange flowers in early summer, 1m/75cm (3ft/1ft); *E. g.* 'Fireglow', yellow and orange-red flowers; *E.* x *martinii*, narrow grey-green leaves on red stems, sometimes tinged purple at first, clusters of yellow-green flowers with dark glands, spring to mid-summer, 1m/1m (3ft/3ft); *E. mellifera*, (syn. *E. longifolia*), barely hardy, light green leaves, pink margins, yellow central veins, honey-scented flowers, yellow-green bracts, gold to red glands, mid-spring, pea-like, waxy fruit, late summer to

above *Euphorbia griffithii* 'Fireglow'. Some of the more recent euphorbia introductions have revealed a stunning display of original colours; this is by far one of the finest.

autumn, 2m/2.5m (6½ft/8ft); *E. myrsinites*, oval to round succulent leaves, blue-green, umbels of green-yellow flowers, in spring, 10cm/30cm (4in/1ft); *E. palustris*, bright green oblong to lance-shaped leaves, orange in autumn, deep yellow flowers in late spring, 90cm/90cm (3ft/3ft); *E. polychroma* (syn. *E. epithymoides*), elongated oval to elliptic leaves, dark green, yellow and bright green flowers, mid-spring to mid-summer, 40cm/60cm (1½ft/2ft); *E. p.* 'Candy' (syn. 'Purpurea'), dark purple-green leaves, pale yellow flowers; *E. sikkimensis*, young shoots bright pink, lance-shaped to linear-oblong, dark green leaves marked red, later soft green, red margins, red veins, yellow and green-yellow flowers, mid-summer to late summer, 1.2m/45cm (4ft/1½ft).

Euryops Asteraceae

Annuals, herbaceous perennials, evergreen shrubs and sub-shrubs. Barely hardy to moderately hardy. A lovely but still far too seldom grown group of 'daisy bushes' with silvery foliage. Linear or lance-shaped to oval leaves, daisy-like flowers. No routine pruning. Sow seeds in warmth in spring, take semi-ripe cuttings in summer or softwood cuttings in spring. ❀ *E. acraeus* (syn. *E. evansii*), dwarf evergreen shrub, moderately hardy, flattened, leathery, narrow silver-grey leaves, a profusion of canary yellow flowers, late spring to early summer, 30cm/30cm (1ft/1ft); *E. pectinatus*, moderately hardy, small evergreen shrub, grey, downy shoots, deeply lobed leaves, rich yellow flowers, late spring to early summer, 1m/1m (3ft/3ft).

Exochorda *Pearlbush* Rosaceae

Medium/large deciduous shrub. Moderately hardy. Elongated oval or oblong leaves, sometimes toothed, cup- or saucer-shaped white flowers in spring or summer. No routine pruning. Sow seeds in a seedbed in autumn, or take softwood cuttings in summer. ❀ *E. giraldii* var. *wilsonii*, large shrub, elongated oval leaves, pink-green at first, later, pale green, red-veined, white flowers to 25cm (10in) in diameter, in late spring, 3m/3m (10ft/10ft); *E.* x *macrantha* 'The Bride', an outstanding spring-flowering shrub, once seen in bloom, not lightly forgotten, mound-forming, arching shrub, light green elongated oval leaves, clusters of white flowers, 3cm (1¼in) in diameter, late spring to early summer, 2m/3m (6½ft/10ft).

Fagus *Beech* Fagaceae

Large deciduous trees. Very hardy. Suitable for hedging, specimen trees or woodland plantings and arguably the loveliest native forest tree; but only the more or less fastigiate forms are suitable for any other than large gardens. Smooth, ribbed, pointed leaves, oval to elliptic, green or coppery-purple, russet in autumn. Leaves remain throughout the winter on immature trees, young shoots and hedges. Insignificant green flowers, male and female on same plant, in late spring, on mature trees followed by brown fruits (mast) with prickly coverings. Thrives in most rich, free-draining soils, in full sun or partial shade. Intolerant of heavy clay. No routine pruning as a specimen plant; clip hedges in early summer and early

right *Exochorda macrantha* 'The Bride'. Several plants are called 'The Bride'. They invariably have white flowers but I am convinced this is the best among a fine collection.

autumn. Sow ripe seeds in a seedbed or in pots in a cold-frame. ❀ *F. sylvatica*, best for hedging, erect, rounded, smooth bark, silvery-grey on older trees, green leaves, 25m/15m (80ft/50ft); *F. s.* 'Dawyck Gold', more or less fastigiate, gold leaves, pale yellow-green in summer, 18m/7m (56ft/23ft); *F. s.* 'Dawyck Purple', more or less fastigiate, purple leaves, 20m/5m (60ft/16ft); *F. s.* var. *heterophylla* 'Aspleniifolia', deeply lobed pale green leaves; *F. s.* 'Pendula', weeping; *F. s.* 'Riversii', dark purple leaves.

left *Fagus sylvatica* 'Dawyck Gold'. Beeches really aren't trees for small gardens but this beautiful fastigiate form will occupy less room than most.

Fallopia — Polygonaceae

Large hardy herbaceous climber. Suitable for growing up large walls, over pergolas, into big, old trees, but needs support at first. Very fast growing and vigorous; can be very invasive but does nonetheless have its uses, particularly in big, wilder gardens. Triangular or oval green leaves, panicles of green-white, white or pink flowers in late summer, sometimes followed by small fruit. Prune as hard as necessary in spring to contain growth. Sow seed in a cold-frame when ripe or in spring, take semi-ripe heeled cuttings or layer in summer. ❀ *F. baldschuanica* (Russian Vine, Mile-a-Minute Vine), vigorous, heart-shaped leaves, sprays of pink-flushed white flowers, 12m (40ft).

Fargesia — Poaceae

Large evergreen bamboos. Barely hardy to moderately hardy. Smaller species are suitable for growing in containers but need protection from wind. Canes are useful for cutting. Linear to lance-shaped leaves, bright to mid-green. Flowers in attractive panicles. Propagate by detaching and replanting rooted canes, or take cuttings of cane sections of young plants in spring. ❀ *F. murieliae*, clump-forming, canes erect, yellow-green, leafless in first year, later arching with narrow pointed, bright green leaves, 4m/1.5m (13ft/5ft); *F. nitida*, spreading, clump-forming, arching canes flushed dark purple, dark green leaves, 5m/1.5m (16ft/5ft).

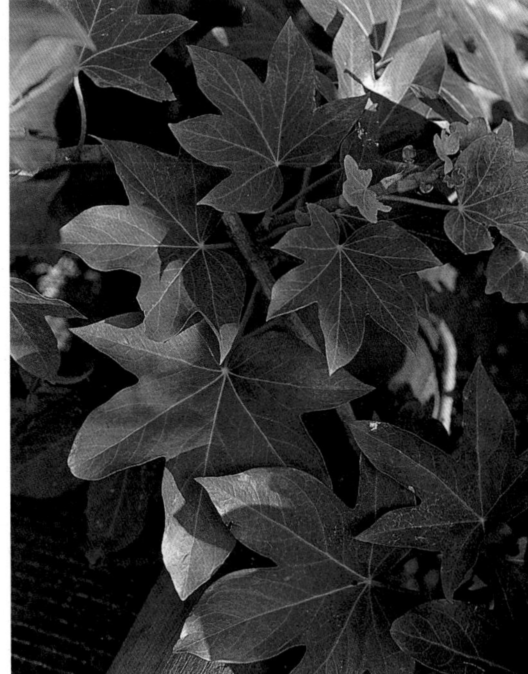

above *x Fatshedera lizei*. One of the few inter-generic hybrids in gardening; an unmistakable cross between *Fatsia* and *Hedera* (ivy).

x Fatshedera — Araliaceae

Small to medium evergreen shrub (*Fatsia* x *Hedera*). Moderately hardy; much hardier, I always think, than it looks. Tolerant of air pollution, coastal sites and shade. Large palmate, lobed, glossy dark green leaves, umbels of small, inconspicuous green-white flowers in autumn. No routine pruning. Take semi-ripe cuttings or softwood cuttings in early summer. ❀ x *F. lizei*, spreading, large leathery leaves, sterile green-white flowers in autumn, 1.2-2m/3m (4-6½ft/10ft); x *F. l.* 'Annemieke', less vigorous and less hardy, leaves variegated yellow with central bright yellow-green mark, 1.5m/1.5m (5ft/5ft); x *F. l.* 'Variegata', grey-green leaves with narrow cream-white edges, yellow veining, 1.5m/1.5m (5ft/5ft).

Fatsia — Araliaceae

Large evergreen shrub or small tree. Moderately hardy. Especially suitable for coastal sites, containers, courtyard gardens and herbaceous borders. In cold areas requires shelter and protection in winter. Divided, leathery, glossy, palmate leaves, umbels of white flowers in late summer, followed by black grape-like fruit. No routine pruning. Sow seed in warmth from early to mid-spring or take softwood cuttings in early summer. ❀ *F. japonica*, similar to x *Fatshedera* but with larger leaves, lobed, mid- to dark green, cream-white globular flowers, 1.5-4m/1.5-4m (5-13ft/5-13ft).

Felicia *Kingfisher Daisy* Asteraceae

Small annuals, perennials and evergreen sub-shrubs. Tender to barely hardy. Oval or elongated oval leaves, absolutely arresting daisy-like blue flowers with yellow centres, in summer; small blue daisies are always something special. Sow seed in warmth in spring, take stem-tip cuttings in late summer or divide established plants in early spring. ❀ *F. amelloides*, barely hardy evergreen sub-shrub, often grown as an annual, stalkless green leaves, light blue flowers, with yellow centres, 30-60cm/30-60cm (1-2ft/1-2ft); *F. a.* 'Santa Anita', larger, hardier rich blue flowers; *F. a.* 'Variegated', leaves variegated white; *F. amoena*, bushy annual or short-lived perennial best raised in warmth and put outside in summer, elliptic to linear grey-green downy leaves, blue flowers with yellow centres, 30-50cm/30-50cm (1-1¾ft/1-1¾ft); *F. bergeriana*, dwarf, mat-forming, half-hardy annual, grey-green, hairy, lance-shaped leaves, clear blue flowers with yellow centres, mid-summer to mid-autumn, 25cm/25cm (10in/10in).

below *Felicia amelloides* 'Santa Anita'. Probably the best clear blue flowered daisy that I have grown.

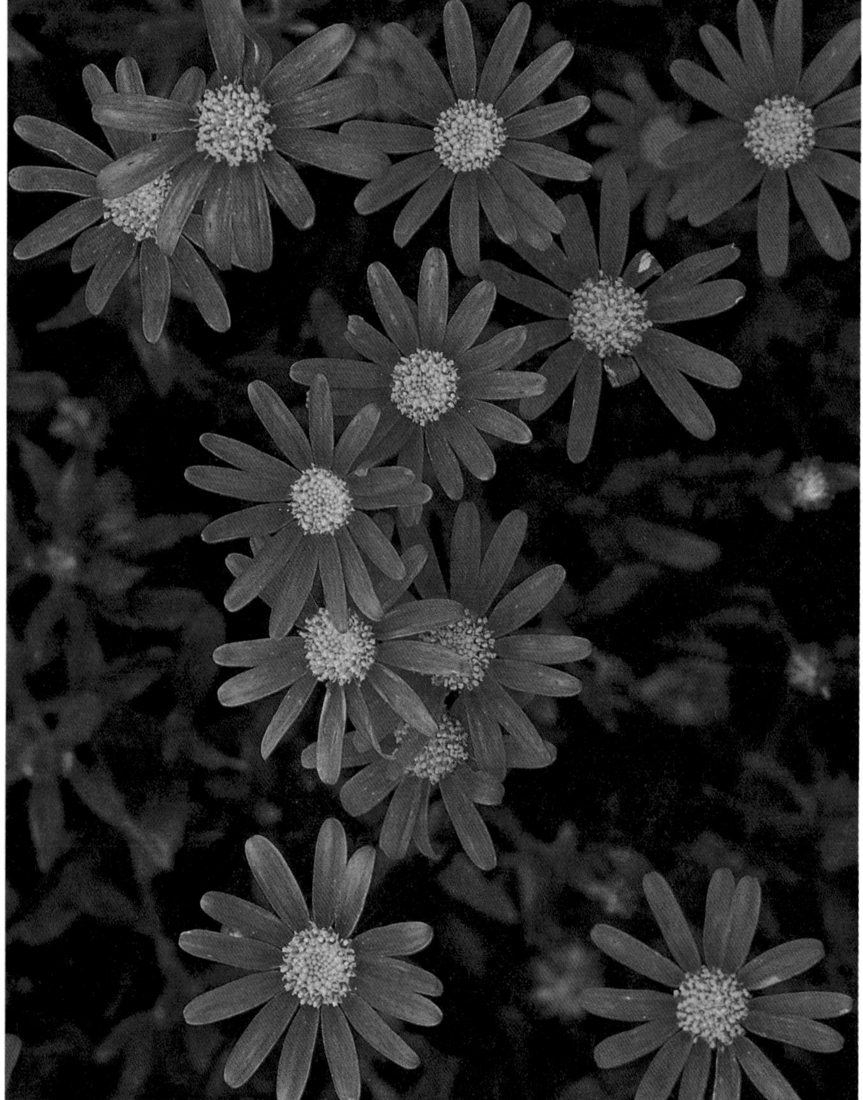

Festuca *Fescue* Poaceae

Small to medium deciduous or evergreen perennial grasses. Hardy. Suitable for the border or rock garden, smaller species or varieties for edging. Leaves rolled, flat or folded, lance-shaped, spikes of brown-green, sometimes glaucous flowers, spring to summer. If you want a reliable blue-foliaged grass, this is the place to find it. Sow ripe seed in autumn or spring or divide established plants in spring. ❀ *F. amethystina*, erect, clump-forming evergreen, narrow linear leaves, spikes of green to violet flowers on violet stems in early summer, 45cm/25cm (1½ft/10in); *F. glauca*, erect or arching evergreen, inrolled, intense steel-blue, fine leaves, bright blue-green flowers flushed violet late spring to summer, 30cm/25cm (1ft/10in); *F. g.* 'Blaufuchs', brighter blue flowers; *F. g.* 'Golden Toupee', yellow-green, tightly rolled leaves, bright yellow in spring; *F. valesiaca* var. *glaucantha* 'Silbersee' (syn. 'Silver Sea'), compact, clump-forming, sometimes semi-evergreen, very fine blue leaves, powder blue, pale green-white or purple flowers, mid- to late summer, 20cm/15cm (8in/6in).

Ficus *Fig* Moraceae

Large deciduous shrubs, small trees or evergreen perennials. Tender to moderately hardy. Best grown against a wall for reliable fruiting. Erect or trailing large, coarse, mid-green divided leaves with round lobes, toxic if eaten. Large, teardrop-shaped edible fruit containing the insignificant flowers ripen in the second year in cool temperate climates. Thrives on poor soil, preferably in dry conditions, fan-trained against a south- or south-east facing wall. Prune in spring, taking care to leave a proportion of the small embryo fruits which form at the tips of the shoots. Take semi-ripe cuttings in summer. ❀ *F. carica* 'Brown Turkey', large deciduous shrub or small tree, palmate, lobed leaves, pear-shaped green-brown, purple-tinged fruit with red flesh, 3m/4m (10ft/13ft); *F. c.* 'Brunswick', large brown-tinged fruit, skin should be removed before eating; *F. pumila*, evergreen trailing or climbing perennial for very sheltered walls, barely hardy, bright green, heart-shaped leaves, later oval, green hairy fruit, tinged purple, ripening in late summer, 3-5m (10-16ft).

Filipendula *Meadowsweet* Rosaceae

Small/medium rhizomatous ornamental. Moderately hardy. Suitable for borders, watersides and other damp places, good for cutting. One of the loveliest native plants of wet pastures and stream-sides. Pinnate leaves with lobed leaflets, plumes of flowers, pink, white or red, late spring to early summer. Sow seed in warmth in spring or in a cold-frame in autumn, take root cuttings in late winter or early spring or divide established plants in spring or autumn. ❀ *F.* 'Kahome', dark green, deeply cut leaves, deep rose-pink inflorescences in mid-summer, 60cm/45cm (2ft/1½ft); *F. purpurea*, clump-forming, toothed, pinnate leaves, crimson-purple stems, carmine-red flowers, fading with age, 1.2m/60cm (4ft/2ft); *F. rubra* 'Venusta' (syn. *F. r.* 'Venusta Magnifica'), spreading, clump-forming, pinnate, vine-like leaves, large flat heads of fragrant, deep rose-pink flowers in mid-summer, 1.8-2.5m/1.2m (5¾-8ft/4ft); *F. ulmaria* (syn. *Spiraea ulmaria*) (Meadowsweet), clump-forming, pinnate, more or less lance-shaped leaves, veined, downy beneath, very fragrant, tiny cream-white flowers in spring, 60-90cm/90cm (2-3ft/3ft); *F. u.* 'Aurea', gold leaves in spring, later pale green; *F. u.* 'Flore Pleno', double flowers; *F. u.* 'Variegata', leaves striped and marked yellow; *F. vulgaris*, rosettes of fern-like leaves, bronze buds opening to pendent panicles of double, cream flowers, in mid-summer, 60cm/45cm (2ft/1½ft); *F. v.* 'Multiplex' (syn. *F. v.* 'Plena'), double flowers.

Foeniculum *Fennel* Apiaceae

Large herb and vegetable. Very hardy. All parts are aromatic, with an anise-like scent, and are used for culinary and medicinal purposes; also makes an extremely attractive foliage perennial. Very finely cut, feathery leaves, flat umbels of tiny yellow flowers followed by seeds. Thrives in moist, fertile, well-drained, light sandy soil in full sun or light shade. To avoid self-seeding remove flowers; cut down in late autumn. Sow seed in growing position in spring; *F. vulgare* 'Purpureum' is best propagated by dividing young established plants. ❀ *F. vulgare* (Fennel, Herb Fennel)), bright green, glossy leaves with hair-like leaflets, tiny yellow flowers, mid- to late summer followed by grey-brown seeds, can be invasive, 1.8m/45cm (5¾ft/1½ft); *F. v.* 'Purpureum' (syn. *F.* 'Bronze') (Bronze Fennel), leaves bronze-purple at first, later glaucous, produces both green and bronze seedlings; *F. v.* var. *dulce* (Florence Fennel, Finocchio), usually grown as a biennial, bulbous stalk forms in the first year and is eaten as a vegetable, raw or cooked, harvested from late summer to winter, flowers the second year, 60cm/45cm (2ft/1½ft); *F. v.* var. *dulce* 'Cantino', bolt-resistant, bulbs ready for harvesting from late summer; *F. v.* var. *dulce* 'Herald', bolt-resistant.

Forsythia Oleaceae

Small/large deciduous shrubs, sometimes semi-evergreen. Moderately hardy. Suitable as specimen plants, informal hedging and for training against a wall. Very familiar but none the less valuable early spring-flowering shrubs. Toothed or entire leaves, simple or palmate, narrowly tube-shaped, flared, four-petalled flowers, usually on bare branches, from early to mid-spring. Thrives in moderately fertile, moist, well-drained soil in full sun or partial shade. Cut out the oldest one-third of the shoots annually after flowering. Take semi-ripe cuttings in late summer. ❀ *F.* 'Beatrix Farrand', bushy, deciduous, oval, toothed mid-green leaves, rich yellow flowers with orange markings, in spring, 2m/2m (6½ft/6½ft); *F.* 'Fiesta', rich green leaves, gold and cream markings, gold-yellow flowers, early to mid-spring, 1.5m/1.5m (5ft/5ft); *F.* x *intermedia* 'Lynwood', compact, dark green lance-

left Never be put off by the fact that *Foeniculum vulgare* 'Purpureum' self-seeds freely; it is readily kept in check and looks wonderful with old roses.

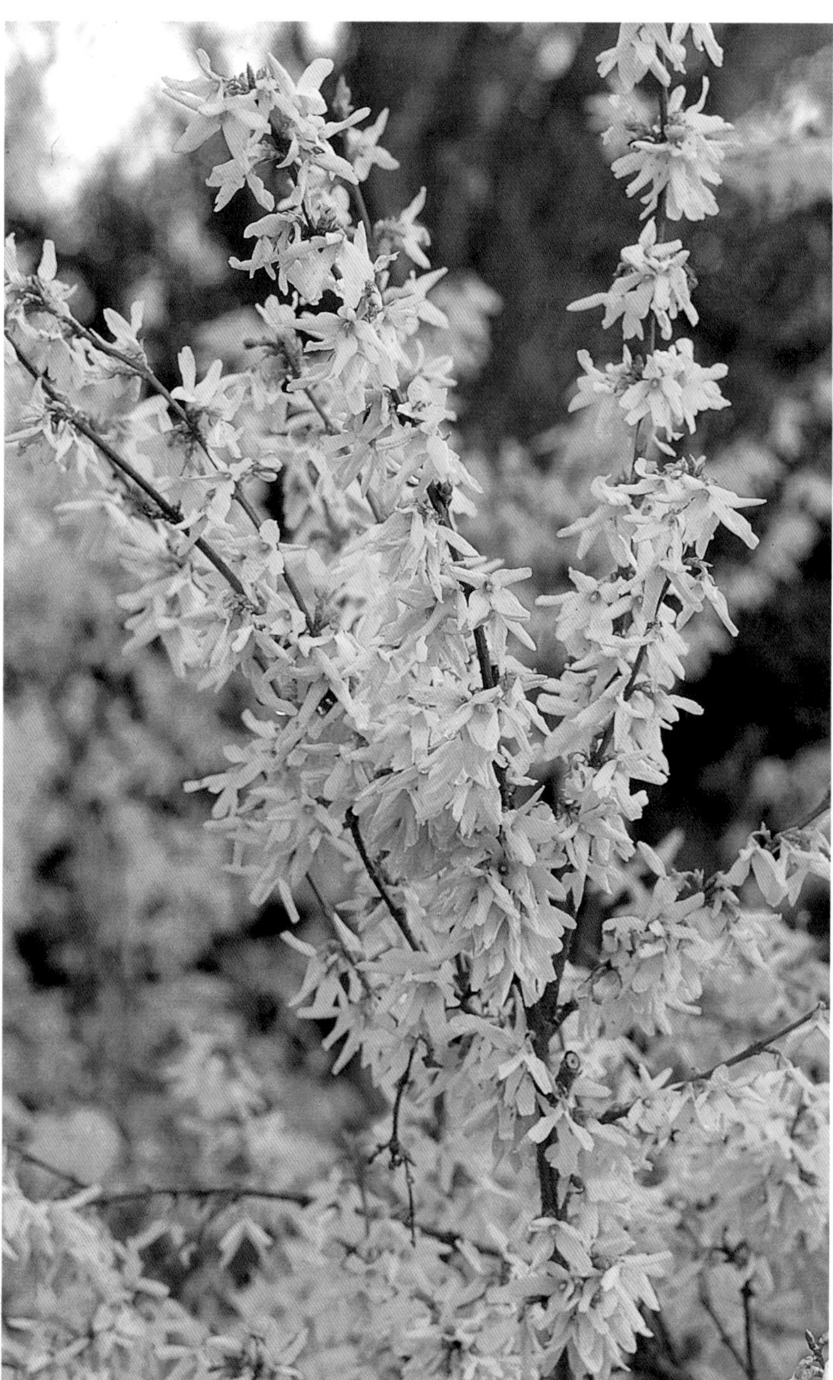

above *Forsythia* x *intermedia* 'Spectabilis'. Although many other varieties have appeared since, I still think this form (from c. 1906) is the best.

shaped, toothed leaves, abundant large yellow flowers with broad petals, in spring, 3m/3m (10ft/10ft); *F.* x *i.* 'Minigold', oblong, mid-green leaves, small, deep yellow flowers, early to mid-spring, 1.8m (5¾ft); *F.* x *i.* 'Spectabilis', mass of deep yellow flowers, an old variety but still, I think, the best both in the quantity and quality of its very rich flowers, 2m/3m (6½ft/10ft); *F. suspensa*, rambling, erect or arching, good when trained against a north- or east-facing wall, oval mid- to dark green leaves, clusters of yellow flowers, early to mid-spring, 3m/3m (10ft/10ft).

Fothergilla Hamamelidaceae

Small to medium deciduous shrubs. Moderately hardy. Dark green, broad oval leaves with toothed tips, pale and hairy beneath, red, orange or yellow in autumn and one of the best shrubs for autumn colour. Spikes of petal-less, 'bottle-brush' flowers of close-set cream stamens. Thrives in moist, well-drained acidic soil enriched with humus, in full sun or partial shade. Sow seeds in a cold-frame or seedbed in autumn or layer. ❀ *F. gardenii*, bushy, dark green oval to elongated oval leaves, toothed, bright red, yellow and orange in autumn, spikes of fragrant small white flowers in spring before the leaves appear, 1m/1m (3ft/3ft); *F. g.* 'Blue Mist', blue-green leaves; *F. major*, erect, rounded shrub, glossy toothed, dark green leaves, red, orange and yellow in autumn, fragrant white, sometimes pink-flushed flowers, late spring to early summer, before the leaves appear, 2.5m/2m (8ft/6½ft).

Fragaria *Strawberry* Rosaceae

Hardy herbaceous perennials. Palmate leaves with toothed-edged leaflets, white flowers, sometimes pink, usually five-petalled, followed by strawberry fruit. Requires moist, fertile, well-drained, neutral to acidic soil in dappled shade or full sun. For reliable fruiting, strawberries should be grown on short-rotation, rather like vegetables, and the stock replaced with new, virus-free plants every two or three years. Strawberries can be divided into two groups: the large- and small-fruited culinary strawberries; and the ornamental strawberries.

Large fruited, summer cropping strawberries

'Cambridge Vigour', early, heavy cropping, replace after two years; 'Elvira', early, heavy cropping; 'Redgauntlet', early to mid-season, heavy cropping, will produce a second crop in good summers; 'Royal Sovereign', early to mid-season, the variety by which others are judged, low cropping, disease-prone, crop for one year only; 'Cambridge Favourite', mid-season, the standard British commercial variety, heavy cropping, long cropping period, resistant to mildew but prone to red spider mite which can troublesome in dry areas and hot summers; 'Elsanta', mid-season, heavy cropping, prone to disease; 'Hapil', mid-season, good on light soils and in dry summers; 'Honeoye', mid-season, heavy cropping; 'Bogota', late, heavy cropping, replace after two years; 'Pegasus', late, heavy cropping, good disease resistance; 'Pandora', late, heavy cropping, good disease resistance, not self-fertile so must be grown with another variety.

left Strawberry 'Aromel'. Without peer as a late-fruiting strawberry; and there's much to be said for having the bulk of your crop late in the season; there are just too many strawberries in early summer.

Remontant ('Perennial') strawberries
'Aromel', moderate cropping, crops twice but to obtain the best benefit from the autumn crop, remove the first flowers in late spring; 'Rapella', fairly heavy cropping, low disease resistance and best in warmer areas.

Small-fruited (alpine) culinary varieties
'Baron Solemacher', very tiny fruit with good, sweet flavour, fairly heavy cropper; *F. vesca*, wild European strawberry; *F. v.* 'Alexandra', sweet flavour, larger than 'Baron Solemacher' but fewer fruit.

Ornamental strawberries
F. x *ananassa* 'Variegata', rather striking cream and green leaf variegation; *F.* 'Pink Panda', oval, toothed leaflets on red-green stems, bright pink flowers, late spring to mid-autumn, rarely fruits, 10-15cm (4-6in)/indefinite; *F. vesca*, bright green oval toothed leaves, white flowers followed by red fruit, 30cm (1ft)/indefinite; *F. v.* 'Multiplex (syn. 'Plymouth Strawberry'), few small flowers, small red fruit, few stolons; *F. v.* 'Variegata', variegated grey-green and cream leaves.

Fraxinus *Ash* — Oleaceae

Medium/large deciduous and evergreen trees. Fairly hardy to moderately hardy. All those I describe here are moderately hardy. Suitable for exposed sites and polluted areas, and medium to large gardens, but bear in mind that ash is seldom a beautiful tree. Light to dark green pinnate leaves, some with panicles of insignificant petal-less flowers, others with ornamental flowers or winged seeds. No routine pruning. Requires moist, well-drained fertile neutral to alkaline soil in full sun. Sow seed in an open-frame in autumn or spring. ❀ *F. angustifolia* 'Raywood' (syn. *F. oxycarpa*), erect, glossy, dark green leaves, plum-purple in autumn, 20m/12m (60ft/40ft); *F. excelsior*, spreading, pinnate dark green leaves, yellow in autumn, black buds in winter, 30m/20m (100ft/60ft); *F. e.* 'Jaspidea', yellow leaves in spring and autumn, yellow shoots in winter; *F. e.* 'Pendula', mound of weeping branches beneath which nothing will grow, 15m/8-10m (50ft/25-33ft); *F. ornus*, pinnate, dark green leaves, purple-red in autumn, clusters of fragrant cream-white flowers, late spring to early summer, 15m (50ft).

Freesia — Iridaceae

Small corm-forming ornamentals. Barely hardy. Usually grown as a greenhouse plant; some specially prepared corms are suitable for growing outside in summer but are best treated as annuals with fresh stock obtained each year. Narrow, sword-shaped to linear-lance-shaped leaves, funnel-shaped, usually highly fragrant, flowers in bright colours, winter to late spring. Requires pots

below If you really do want an ash tree for your garden, *Fraxinus excelsior* 'Pendula' is one of the very few suitable as a garden tree.

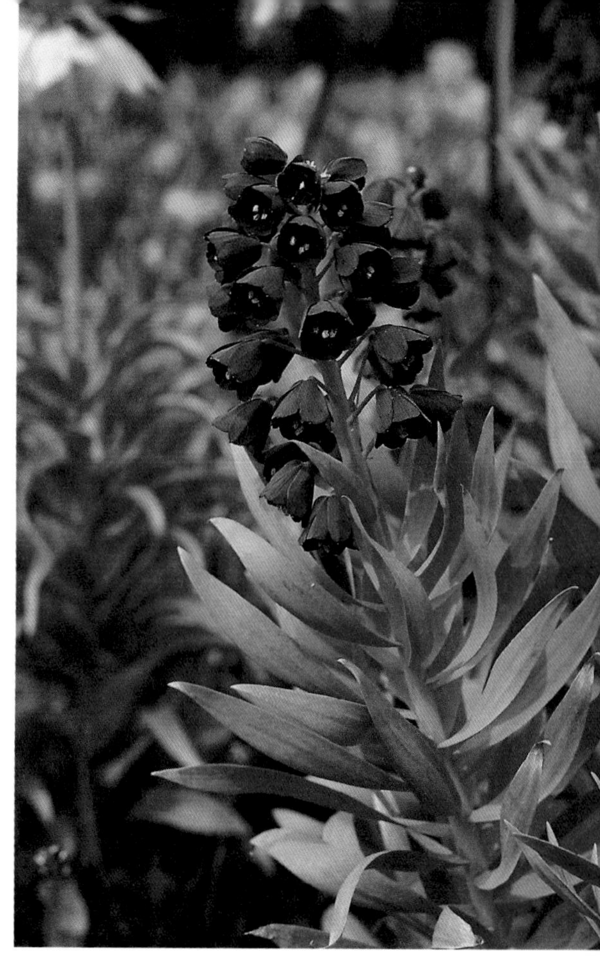

right *Fritillaria persica*. One of the most glorious of all fritillaries but a very variable plant so do buy your bulbs from a reputable source.

of loam-based compost with added grit in a cold-frame with good ventilation, moved when mature into full sun. Outdoors, plant in well-drained, fertile, moist soil in full sun. Sow seed in warmth in summer or winter or remove small offsets in autumn. Species and varieties in single colours are difficult to obtain and freesias are almost invariably only available as scented flowers in mixed colours of mauve, white, yellow, pink, red, orange, and lilac blue.

Fremontodendron Sterculiaceae

Large evergreen or deciduous shrubs or small trees, tending to be rather short-lived and to die suddenly without warning or evident reason. Fairly hardy but in cold areas best grown against a warm, sunny wall where it may for brief periods tolerate temperatures down to -15°C (5°F). Rounded, lobed, hairy dark green leaves, stunning large waxy yellow petal-less flowers, spring or summer to autumn. Hairs from leaves and stems may irritate eyes and skin. Sow seed in warmth in spring, take semi-ripe cuttings in late summer. ❀ *F.* 'California Glory', semi-evergreen, hardier than others, erect at first, later spreading, dark green leaves, tufted hairs above, brown densely hairy beneath, angled buds, lantern-like, open to saucer-shaped deep yellow flowers, late spring to mid-autumn, 6m/4m (20ft/13ft); *F. californicum*, evergreen or semi-evergreen, dull dark green leaves, hairy, pale brown beneath, hairy above, yellow flowers, summer to autumn, 6m/4m (20ft/13ft).

Fritillaria *Fritillary* Liliaceae

Small/large bulbous ornamentals. Barely hardy to moderately hardy. Most are suitable for sunny borders and rock gardens, some for damp woodland or meadows. The genus includes some of the most striking and least known of medium-sized bulbs. Lance-shaped or linear leaves. Flowers bell-shaped, tubular or shallow saucer-shaped, pendent, with conspicuous nectaries, followed by seed capsules. Most thrive best in areas with dry winters and summers and damp springs. Woodland species require moisture-retentive soil enriched with leaf mould or humus, full sun to light shade. Species suitable for rock gardens thrive in moderately fertile, sharply drained soil, in full sun. Sow seed in autumn in a cold-frame, remove and replant bulbils or divide offsets in early spring; leave established plants undisturbed for as long as possible. ❀ *F. acmopetala*, narrow, lance-shaped, grey-green leaves, bell-shaped flowers with three pale green outer petals, three inner purple-brown petals, singly or sometimes in clusters, in spring, 40cm/5-8cm (1½ft/2-3in); *F. camschatcensis*, glossy lance-shaped light green leaves, clusters of large cup-shaped flowers, very dark purple, almost black, sometimes yellow-green, in early summer, 45cm/8-10cm (1½ft/3-4in); *F. imperialis* (Crown Imperial), much the best known species, glossy, pale green leaves, lance-shaped, ring of bell-shaped orange, yellow or red flowers, crowned with erect leaf-like bracts, in early summer, 1.5m/25-30cm (5ft/10in-1ft); *F. i.* 'Aurora', bright red-orange flowers; *F. i.* 'Maxima Lutea', large lemon-yellow flowers; *F. i.* 'Rubra', deep orange-red; *F. i.* 'Rubra Maxima', taller than 'Rubra' 1.5-2m (5-6½ft); *F. meleagris* (Snake's Head Fritillary), linear, grey-green leaves, solitary or paired flowers, white or pink-purple or purple flowers with conspicuous purple-pink markings in a chequered pattern, in spring, a beautiful plant but difficult to establish in gardens; it needs undisturbed water meadows, 30cm/5-8cm (1ft/2-3in); *F. m. alba*, white flowers; *F. michailovskyi*, glaucous, narrow leaves, clusters of red-brown flowers with darker markings and green on edges of petals, in early summer, 10-20cm/15cm (4-8in/6in); *F. pallidiflora*, lance-shaped, glaucous leaves, cream angular bell-shaped flowers with faint red-brown markings, unpleasantly scented, in early summer, 40cm/5-8cm (1½ft/2-3in); *F. persica*, grey-green, lance-shaped leaves, glaucous, clusters of narrow, bell-shaped green-brown to deep-purple flowers in spring, 1m/10cm (3ft/4in); *F. pontica*, lance-shaped glaucous leaves, some in groups of three around the flowers, sometimes edged red-brown, in spring, 15-20cm/5cm (6-8in/2in); *F. uvavulpis* (syn. *F. assyriaca*), narrow bell-shaped flowers with recurved yellow tips, chocolate brown, yellow inside, 20cm/5cm (8in/2in).

Fuchsia Onagraceae

Deciduous and evergreen shrubs and trees. Tender to hardy. In all except the mildest areas, most fuchsias are treated as half-hardy perennials and overwintered in a greenhouse. Only a relatively few species are widely cultivated; more popular are the 800 or more, usually tender varieties grown in containers for summer displays. The numbers are so enormous, and so many really are very similar, that my modest selection here is limited to those that I have grown personally. Despite the vast numbers, however, all have certain common features: the leaves are mid-green, oval to lance-shaped and the pendent flowers comprise a tube with four overlapping petals and four spreading sepals at the mouth, the sepals and petals often in contrasting colours. Hardy species are best in fertile, well-drained soil, in full sun or partial shade. Container-grown species or varieties may be in either soil-less or loam-based compost. It is important to distinguish growth habits; trailing varieties for instance will be needed for hanging baskets, upright types for specimens among other plants. Apart from plants trained as standards, tender fuchsias stored overwinter under protection should be cut back by two-thirds in spring. Small bush varieties hardy enough to be left outdoors over winter may be cut back to soil level in spring or simply have old and dead growth thinned out. Hedges should be clipped lightly after flowering. Sow fresh seed of species in warmth, take softwood cuttings in spring or semi-ripe cuttings in late summer. All varieties are tender unless stated otherwise. ❀ *F.* 'Alice Hoffman', upright, single, tube and sepals carmine, corolla white, pink-veined; *F.* 'Annabel', upright, double, tube and sepals rich pink, corolla lavender; *F.* 'Beacon', upright, single, tube and sepals scarlet, corolla mauve-pink; *F.* 'Billy Green', upright, elongated tubes (Triphylla type), olive-green leaves, tube, sepals and corolla pink-salmon; *F.* 'Brutus', upright, single, tube and sepals cerise-crimson, corolla deep purple; *F.* 'Cascade', trailing, single, tube and sepals white with red flush, corolla rich rose; *F.* 'Celia Smedley', trailing, single, tube and sepals rich rose, corolla vivid red; *F.* 'Checkerboard', upright, single, tube deep red, sepals white with red base, corolla red with white base; *F.* 'Chillerton Beauty', upright, single, tube and sepals pale pink, corolla purple with pink veins, outdoor; *F.* 'Cloverdale Pearl', upright, bushy, single, tube white, sepals rich pink, corolla white with pink veins; *F.* 'Dark Eyes', upright, double, tube and sepals deep red, corolla deep blue-violet; *F.* 'Eva Boerg', loosely upright, semi-double, tube green-white, sepals white flushed pink, corolla pink-purple with pink flecks; *F.* 'Flash', upright, single, tube and sepals pale red, corolla red, a small, outdoor variety; *F.* 'Garden News', upright, double, tube and sepals pink,

above *Fuchsia* 'Mrs Popple'. One of the oldest but still one of the best and most freely flowering among hardy fuchsias.

left *Fuchsia* 'Celia Smedley' is one of the best new bush fuchsias of recent years, raised by the British breeder George Roe.

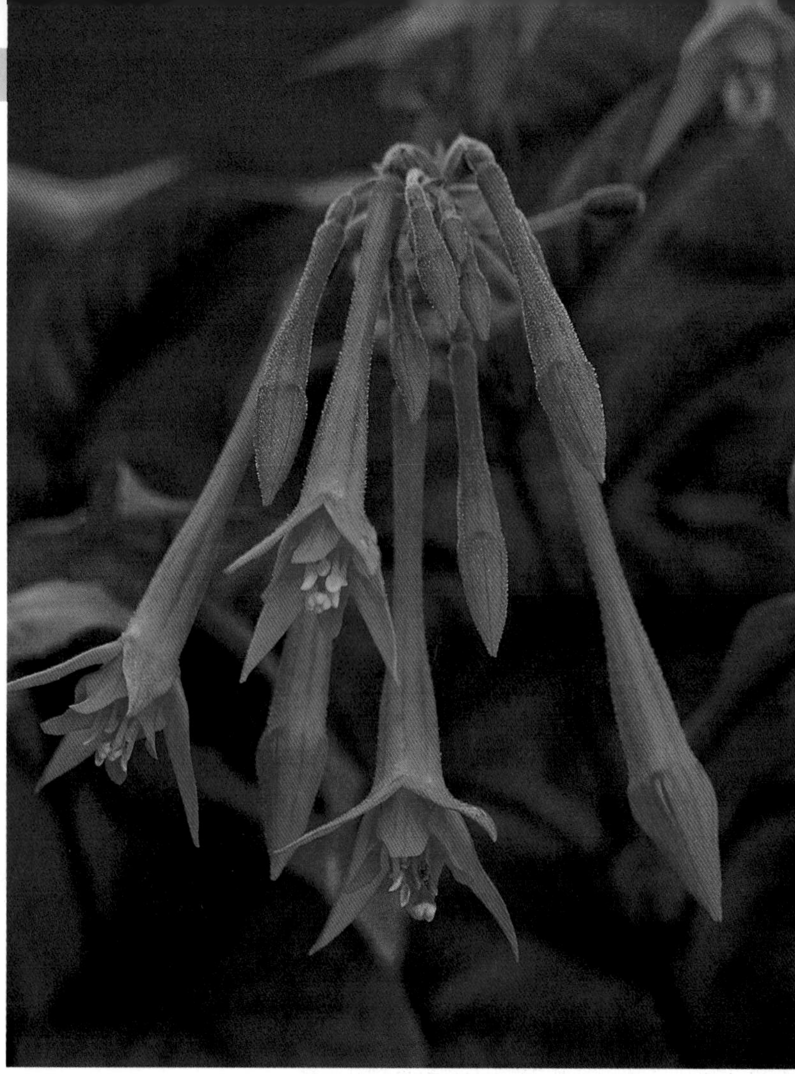

above *Fuchsia fulgens.* The species fuchsias have a very special appeal and this Mexican plant is a particularly fine example.

corolla rose and pink; *F.* 'Genii', upright, single, lime-green leaves, tube and sepals cerise, corolla violet at first, later purple-red, I find this one of the most reliable outdoor fuchsias for cold areas; *F.* 'Golden Marinka', trailing, single, green to yellow leaves, tubes and sepals deep red, corolla darker red; *F.* 'Heidi Ann', upright, double, tube crimson, sepals cerise crimson, corolla lilac purple; *F.* 'Jack Shahan', trailing, single, tube and sepals rich rose, corolla rose pink; *F.* 'La Campanella', lax, upright, semi-double, tube and sepals white with pink flush, corolla deep purple, fading with age; *F.* 'Lady Thumb', upright, semi-double, tube and sepals carmine, corolla white with pink veins; *F.* 'Lena', lax, upright, semi-double, tube soft pink, sepals paler pink, corolla white with pink veins, ageing to pink, one of the most reliable outdoor varieties; *F.* 'Lye's Unique', upright, single, tube and sepals white, corolla orange-salmon; *F.* 'Madame Cornélissen', upright, semi-double or double, tube and sepals crimson, corolla white with crimson veins; *F.* 'Margaret', upright, double, tube and sepals carmine red, corolla violet-purple; *F.* 'Marinka', trailing, single, tube and sepals red, corolla darker red; *F.* 'Mrs Popple', probably the best known outdoor fuchsia, upright, single, tube and sepals scarlet, corolla violet-purple; *F.* 'Phyllis', upright, semi-double, tube and sepals rose-red, corolla darker rose-red; *F.* 'Riccartonii', the favourite hedging variety, upright, single, tube and sepals crimson, corolla rich rose; *F.*'Royal Velvet', upright, double, tube and sepals cerise, corolla purple with red veins; *F.* 'Swingtime', loosely upright, double, tube and sepals scarlet, corolla white with scarlet veins; *F.* 'Tennessee Waltz', upright, semi-double, tube and sepals rose, corolla lilac-flecked pink; *F.* 'Thalia', upright, triphylla, tube and sepals rich orange red, corolla scarlet orange; *F.* 'Tom Thumb', upright, small flowers, single to semi-double, tube and sepals carmine, corolla mauve purple; *F.* 'Winston Churchill', upright, double, tune and sepals pink, corolla lavender with pink veins.

Species

F. arborescens (syn. *F. arborea*), upright evergreen shrub or small tree, more or less lance-shaped leaves, dark green, panicles of very small flowers, tube rose to magenta, sepals rose-pink, corolla pale mauve, in summer, purple fruit, 2m/1.7m (6½ft/5½ft); *F. corymbiflora*, arching, oblong to lance-shaped pale to mid-green leaves, veined with pink, tube, sepals and corolla crimson, summer to early autumn, a wonderful plant that is very easy to raise from seed, 1.2-1.8m/60-90cm (4-5¾ft/2-3ft); *F. denticulata* (syn. *F. serratifolia*), upright shrub, dark green leaves, sepals pink to pale red, petals bright orange, 4m/1.5m (13ft/5ft); *F. fulgens*, upright shrub, oval to heart-shaped leaves, pendent clusters of flowers, tubes pink to dull red, sepals pale red, tinged yellow-green near edges, corolla bright red, 1.5m/80cm (5ft/2½ft); *F. magellanica*, upright shrub, oval to elliptic, toothed or scalloped, hairless leaves, small flowers, tubes red, sepals deep red, sometimes pale pink or white, corolla purple, 3m/2-3m (10ft/6½-10ft); *F. m.* var. *gracilis*, narrower leaves and more slender flowers; *F. m.* var. *g.* 'Variegata', leaves edged cream-yellow, 60cm/60cm (2ft/2ft); *F. m.* var. *molinae*, light green leaves, sepals white, petals pale lavender; *F. m.* var. *m.* 'Sharpitor' (syn. *F.* 'Overbecks'), grey-green leaves, edged white, 75cm/60cm (2½ft/2ft); *F. m.* var. *m.* 'Versicolor' (syn. *F.* 'Versicolor), grey-green leaves; *F. microphylla*, dwarf, bushy, dark green narrow leaves, purple-red flowers, 60cm/60cm (2ft/2ft); *F. procumbens*, trailing shrub, easy and charming plant, heart-shaped leaves, tubes green-yellow to pale orange, sepals green, tipped purple, stamens with bright blue pollen, no corolla; *F. thymifolia*, deciduous, lax shrub, pale green leaves, sparse, minute green-white flowers, later purple-pink, black fruit; 1m/1m (3ft/3ft).

Gaillardia Asteraceae

Small annuals, biennials and perennials. Barely hardy to hardy and very good for hot and sunny borders where their flowers are eye-catching; but not plants for the cold and wet. Basal rosettes of toothed, often lobed, hairy leaves. Red, orange or yellow daisy-like flowers with red, yellow or darker centres, sometimes with contrasting margins, in summer. Flowers are good for cutting. Sow seed in warmth in spring or divide established plants. ❀ *G.* 'Burgunder' (syn. 'Burgundy'), large, deep red flowers with dark red centres, 50-60cm (20-2ft); *G.* 'Goblin' (syn. *G.* 'Kobold'), dwarf, rich red flowers, yellow-tipped, red centres, 30cm (1ft); *G.* 'Golden Goblin' (syn. *G.* 'Goldkobold'), dwarf, compact, abundant gold flowers, darker gold centre, 25cm (10in); *G.* 'Lollipops', dwarf half-hardy annual, grey-green leaves, yellow, cream and red globular flowers, 30cm (1ft); *G.* 'Monarch', perennial, mixed bright colours, 60-90cm (2-3ft); *G.* 'Red Plume', erect, bushy, compact dwarf, abundant double, deep red flowers, 30cm (1ft); *G.* 'Sherbet Plumes', dwarf, double flowers, 30cm (1ft).

Galanthus *Snowdrop* Amaryllidaceae

Small bulbous ornamentals. Hardy. Much loved plants for the late winter and suitable for borders, naturalizing in grass, beneath trees and in wasteland. Bulbs may cause skin irritation; all parts are toxic if eaten. Strap-shaped to more or less lance-shaped leaves. Small, white, pendent, six-part flowers, three longer outer sepaloid parts and three shorter inner petaloid parts; inner 'petals' usually have a small green mark. Flowers often scented (although this is seldom appreciated), late winter to spring, sometimes in autumn. Thrive in moist, well-drained soil enriched with humus, in partial shade. Divide established clumps as soon as flowers fade; snowdrops establish much less satisfactorily from dormant bulbs. The size varies considerably but most of those below, unless otherwise mentioned are 8-15cm/3-5cm (3-6in/1-2in). ❀ *G.* 'Atkinsii', narrow glaucous leaves, the best of the tall varieties in my experience, 10-15cm/8cm (4-6in/3in); *G. caucasicus*, wide glaucous leaves; *G. elwesii*, wide grey-green leaves, sometimes twisted, honey-scented, elongated flowers with two green marks on inner petals, best in rather dry, alkaline soil; *G. ikariae*, glossy bright green leaves, large green marks on inner petals; *G. i.* Latifolius Group, broad green leaves, V-shaped mark on inner petals; *G.* 'Lady Beatrix Stanley', glaucous leaves, double; *G. nivalis*, good for naturalizing, grey-green, strap-shaped leaves, honey-scented flowers, single green marks on inner petals; *G. n.* 'Flore Pleno', double; *G. n.* 'Lady Elphinstone', double, sometimes with yellow marks; *G. n.* 'Pusey Green Tip', double, green-tipped outer petals, plain white inner petals; *G. n.* 'Sandersii' (syn. 'Lutescens'), small flowers with yellow marks on inner petals and yellow ovaries; *G. n.* 'Viridapicis', bold green marks on outer petals; *G.* 'S. Arnott' (syn. 'Sam Arnott'), grey-green leaves, large almond-scented, rounded flowers, marked with V-shape on inner petals, 25cm/8cm (10in/3in); *G.* 'Straffan', narrow glaucous leaves, flower with inverted V-shaped marks.

left *Galanthus* 'Atkinsii'. I find that many snowdrop varieties are not especially distinctive but there's no doubting the singularity of this majestically tall and reliable variety.

Galega *Goat's Rue* Papilionaceae

Large hardy herbaceous perennials. Very hardy. Best for naturalizing in larger, wild gardens; I find it too robust for the border. Pinnate, light green or blue-green leaves, oval to oblong leaflets, unpleasant smelling when crushed. Erect spikes of blue, white, lilac or bicoloured pea-like flowers in summer, followed by rounded seedpods. Sow seed in a cold-frame in spring or divide established plants in winter. ❀ *G. bicolor*, abundant lilac-blue and white flowers, mid-summer to autumn, 1.5m (5ft); *G.* x *hartlandii* 'Alba', clump-forming, dark green divided leaves, white, summer; *G. officinalis*, clump-forming, bushy, light green pinnate leaves, pointed leaflets, clusters of purple-mauve, white or bicoloured flowers, summer to early autumn, 30-150cm/90cm (1-5ft/3ft); *G. o.* 'Alba', white, 1-1.5m/60-100cm (3-5ft/2-3ft).

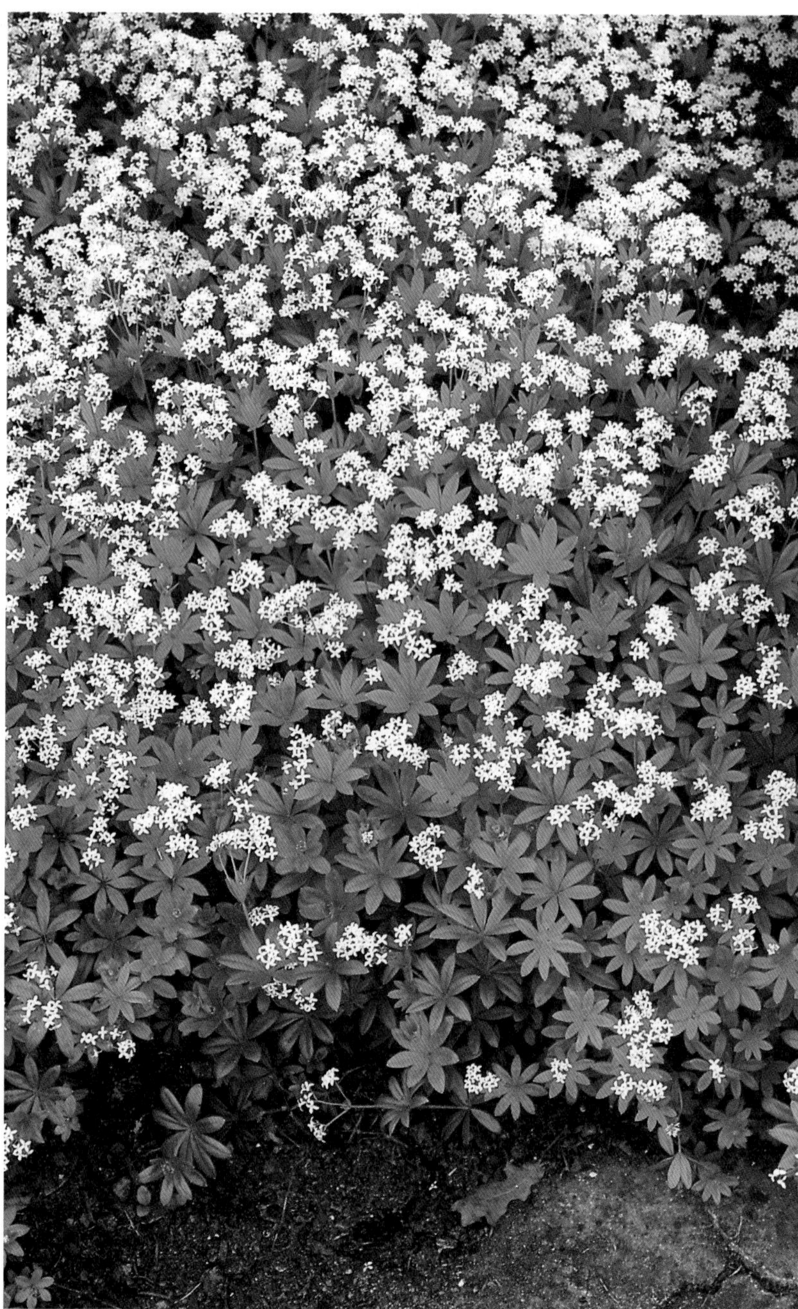

above *Galium odoratum* is an essential species for any native plant garden; but do give it room to spread.

Galium *Bedstraw* Rubiaceae

Climbing, scrambling or erect annuals, biennials and herbaceous perennials and including the familiar weed goose-grass with its tiny, spherical, clinging fruits. Barely hardy to moderately hardy. Characteristic whorls of linear leaves, minute white, pink or yellow flowers, singly or in clusters, in spring. Sow ripe seed in a cold-frame, divide established perennials in autumn or early spring. ❀ *G. mollugo* (Hedge Bedstraw), erect, hardy herbaceous perennial, small lance-shaped leaves, clusters of tiny star-like flowers, spotted purple, summer, 1.5m/1m (5ft/3ft); *G. odoratum* (syn. *Asperula odorata*) (Sweet Woodruff), carpeting hardy herbaceous perennial, elliptic emerald green leaves, sweetly-scented of coumarin (freshly mown hay), clusters of white star-shaped flowers, late spring to mid-summer, prefers partial shade, can be invasive, 45cm (1½ft)/indefinite; *G. vernum* (Lady's Bedstraw), spreading perennial, linear, glossy dark green leaves, clusters of bright yellow flowers, summer to early autumn, 1.2m (4ft)/indefinite.

Galtonia Hyacinthaceae

Medium bulbous ornamental. Barely hardy to moderately hardy. Suitable for growing in containers and borders and valuable as few other bulbs flower at the same time. In cold areas, best lifted in autumn and stored over winter. Linear to lance-shaped glossy, stiff, fleshy basal leaves, loose clusters of pendent, tubular or trumpet-shaped white flowers, summer. Sow ripe seed in a cold-frame or divide established clumps in spring. ❀ *G. candicans* (Summer Hyacinth), semi-erect, bright green, narrowly pointed, slightly glaucous leaves, waxy white flowers on tall stems, late summer, 1m/60cm (3ft/2ft); *G. princeps*, wide grey-green strap-shaped leaves, green waxy flowers tinged white, slightly earlier than *G. candicans*, 75cm (2½ft); *G. viridiflora*, grey-green strap-shaped leaves, open bell-shaped pale green flowers, early to mid-autumn, 60cm/60cm (2ft/2ft).

Garrya *Tassel Bush* Garryaceae

Large evergreen shrub or small tree. Moderately hardy. Suitable for coastal sites, shrub-borders or growing against a wall; not my favourite shrub – its catkins are too sombre to be really appealing. Oval to elliptic leaves, petal-less flowers carried on catkins, male and female on separate plants, catkins followed on female plants by purple-brown fruits. No routine pruning. Sow seed in a cold-frame in spring or summer or take semi-ripe cuttings in summer. ❀ *G. elliptica*, erect, glossy or matt oblong-elliptic to oval leaves, grey-green to dark green, grey beneath, with wavy edges, silver-green catkins, midwinter to early spring, purple-brown fruit in autumn, 4m/4m (13ft/13ft); *G. e.* 'James Roof', dark green leaves, silver-grey catkins, male catkins supposedly to 20cm (8in) in length but there appears to be some doubt whether there really is a distinctive form; possibly some individuals are better than others; *G.* x *issaquahensis* 'Glasnevin Wine', a better plant with deep mauve male catkins that later turn golden.

Gaultheria Ericaceae

Small/medium evergreen shrubs. Moderately hardy to very hardy. Suitable for containers and rock gardens, smaller species for ground cover; grown commercially for the essential oil, oil of wintergreen, and in gardens mainly for their striking, although often poisonous, fruits. Dark green leathery leaves, sprays of waxy, urn-shaped pendent flowers, similar to those of lily-of-the-valley. Requires moist, acidic soil in partial shade. No routine pruning. Take semi-ripe cuttings in late summer, replant suckers or layer. ❀ *G. cuneata*, dwarf, compact shrub, narrow leaves, white flowers, late spring to early summer, smell of antiseptic when crushed, 30cm/1m (1ft/3ft); *G. mucronata* (syn. *Pernettya mucronata*), female form of a suckering shrub, glossy, dark green leaves, pointed, abundant small white flowers, late spring to early summer, followed by clusters of round white, pink or purple fruits when male form is present; varieties are distinguished mainly by fruit colour, 1.2m/1.2m (4ft/4ft); *G. m.* 'Bell's Seedling', hermaphrodite form, dark shiny leaves, large dark red fruits; *G. m.* 'Crimsonia', white flowers, large crimson fruits; *G. m.* 'Pink Pearl', lilac-pink fruits; *G. m.* 'Sneeuwwitje', (syn. 'Snow White'), white fruits, faintly spotted with pink; *G. procumbens*, moderately hardy, carpeting, aromatic, glossy dark green elliptic leaves, solitary, pendent white flowers, sometimes flushed pink, summer, followed by red holly-like fruits, late summer to autumn, 15cm/1m (6in/3ft) or more; *G. shallon*, carpeting, leathery leaves, flushed red-purple, white or pink-white flowers, late spring to early summer, followed by large clusters of dark purple fruits; 1.2m/1.5m (4ft/5ft); *G.* x *wisleyensis*, 'Pink Pixie', dwarf, suckering shrub, white flowers flushed pink, in late spring, followed by clusters of purple-red fruits, 30cm/45cm (1ft/1½ft).

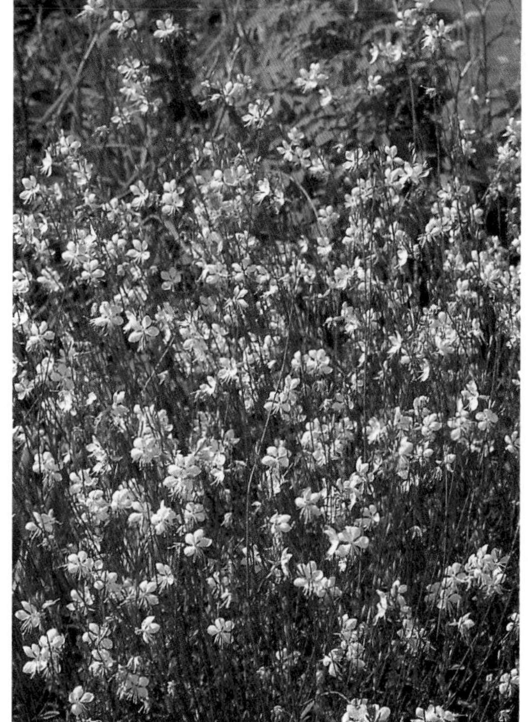

left When I first decided to grow *Gaura lindheimeri*, many years ago, hardly anyone knew it. I'm delighted that it has become more widely available.

Gaura Onagraceae

Medium/large annuals, biennials, herbaceous perennials and sub-shrubs. Hardy. Lance-shaped to more or less lance-shaped or elliptic, willow-like leaves, graceful but fragile-looking spikes of irregularly star-shaped, white tubular flowers, sometimes pink or red. Sow seed in autumn, divide established plants in spring, or take basal or softwood cuttings in spring, heeled semi-ripe cuttings in summer. ❀ *G. lindheimeri*, bushy perennial, a plant that gardeners have been rediscovering in recent years, green leaves, open clusters of tubular white flowers, fading to pink, mid-summer to autumn, 1.5m/90cm (5ft/3ft); *G. l.* 'The Bride', white flowers; *G. l.* 'Whirling Butterflies', grey-green leaves, white flowers with red sepals, 60-75cm (2-2½ft).

Gazania Asteraceae

Small annuals and evergreen perennials. Tender to barely hardy; the perennial hybrids are widely grown as half-hardy summer bedding annuals. They are especially successful in coastal gardens and are usefully tolerant of drought but must have hot, dry summers; a gazania in a wet summer is a very sad thing. Rosettes of lance-shaped, sometimes downy leaves, deeply lobed or pinnate, brightly coloured solitary, daisy-like flowers with darker centres, sometimes darker beneath, summer. Sow seed in warmth in late winter or early spring, take basal cuttings in late summer or early autumn, or semi-ripe cuttings in late autumn. ❀ *G.* 'Chansonette', dwarf, spreading, glossy green leaves, silver beneath, flowers orange, rose,

far left *Gaultheria mucronata* 'Pink Pearl'. This is one of many varieties with very attractive and distinctive, although unfortunately poisonous fruits.

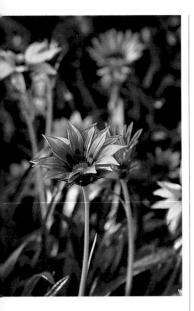

above *Gazania* 'Chansonette'. Gazanias are plants for the sun and so the recent succession of warmer summers may encourage their popularity to increase.

salmon-pink, bronze or yellow, with zones of contrasting colour, dark centres, 20cm/25cm (8in/10in); *G.* 'Daybreak Bright Orange', spreading, silver leaves, orange flowers with darker basal ring, early summer, 20-25cm (8in/10in); *G.* 'Ministar' Series, a range of valuable compact varieties, tufted, toothed, silver leaves, orange, gold, white, beige, bright pink or bronze flowers, single colours or mixed, sometimes with contrasting colours, 20 cm (8in); *G.* 'Orange Surprise', smooth, lance-shaped leaves, orange flowers, 15cm (6in); *G.* 'Talent', dwarf, silver leaves, yellow, orange, brown, and pink flowers, summer, 25cm/25cm (10in/10in); *G.* 'Sundance', large flowers, bronze, red and orange shades, 30cm (1ft); *G.* 'Sunshine', orange, red, cream, yellow and bicoloured flowers, mid-summer to mid-autumn, 23-30cm (9in-1ft).

Genista *Broom* Papilionaceae

Small/large hardy deciduous shrubs related to *Cytisus* and *Spartium*, both of which are also called brooms. Good for ground cover, rock gardens, shrub-borders and specimen plants, although the flowering season is short and the site requirements specific: they must have full sun and are quite intolerant of cold and wet soils. Simple or palmate leaves, some species almost leafless with only very reduced leaves. Yellow flowers, singly or clusters, summer. No routine pruning and severe pruning may lead to die-back. Sow seed in a cold-frame in spring or autumn, take semi-ripe cuttings in summer or hardwood cuttings in winter. ❀ *G. aetnensis* (Mt. Etna Broom), a magnificent sight in full flower, a large spreading shrub or small tree, light green weeping branches, sparse mid-green, linear leaves, loose clusters of gold-yellow fragrant flowers in summer, 8m/8m (25ft/25ft); *G. hispanica* (Spanish Gorse), erect shrub, deep green linear to lance-shaped leaves on flowering branches, abundant gold-yellow flowers in summer, 75cm/1.5m (2½ft/5ft); *G. lydia*, dwarf evergreen, linear grey-green leaves, abundant clusters of bright yellow flowers, late spring to early summer, 60cm/1m (2ft/3ft); *G. pilosa*, dwarf semi-evergreen, elongated oval mid-green leaves, small yellow flowers, late spring to summer, 40cm/1m (1½ft/3ft); *G. p.* 'Vancouver Gold', spreading, mound-forming, dwarf shrub, gold-yellow flowers, 45cm (1½ft); *G. tinctoria*, deciduous shrub, slender, erect or prostrate, dark green linear to lance-shaped leaves, clusters of deep yellow flowers, early to late summer, 60-90cm/1m (2-3ft/ 3ft); *G. t.* 'Flore Pleno' (syn. 'Pleno'), semi-prostrate dwarf, deep yellow double flowers, 35cm (1¼ft).

Gentiana *Gentian* Gentianaceae

Small to large annuals, biennials, deciduous, semi-evergreen and evergreen perennials. Moderately hardy to hardy. One of the most glorious and much loved genera of alpines although some are very tricky to induce into flowering. Simple leaves, most in basal rosettes. Bell-, urn- or trumpet-shaped flowers, mostly (and much better) in shades of blue, some white or yellow, rarely red, spring to autumn. Thrive in light, moist, well-drained soil enriched with humus, in full sun where summers are cool and damp, some in partial shade. Autumn-flowering species and varieties generally require lime-free soil. Sow ripe seed in an open-frame, divide established plants or replant offsets in spring. ❀ *G. acaulis* (syn. *G. kochiana*) (Trumpet Gentian), mat-forming evergreen that is particularly reluctant to flower, glossy, leathery, oval mid-green to dark green leaves, solitary trumpet-shaped, brilliant deep blue flowers, spotted green, late spring to early summer, 8cm/30cm (3in/1ft); *G. asclepiadea* (Willow Gentian), herbaceous perennial, the easiest I find of all to grow

right *Genista lydia*. Probably the most striking and intensely yellow among a group of floriferous yellow shrubs.

left *Gentiana x macauleyi* 'Kingfisher'. The best form of one of the finest of all gentians; however, few of them make easy garden plants.

successfully, willow-like oval, mid-green leaves on arching stems, clusters of deep blue flowers, variously striped and spotted white and green, sometimes purple, mid- to late summer, requires damp, partial shade, 60-75cm/45cm (2-2½ft/1½ft); *G. a.* var. *alba*, white flowers tinged green; *G.* Inshriach Hybrids, a good free-flowering range of plants related to *G.* x *macauleyi* 'Kingfisher', carpeting plants with clear 'gentian blue' flowers; *G.* 'Inverleith', trailing semi-evergreen, mid-green linear leaves, solitary trumpet-shaped sky-blue flowers with darker stripes on the outside, autumn, 10cm/30cm (4in/1ft); *G. lutea* (Great Yellow Gentian), a completely unexpected plant, an erect, clump-forming herbaceous perennial, blue-green basal leaves, oval to elliptic, ribbed leaves, clusters of small star-shaped yellow flowers, mid-summer, 1.2m/60cm (4ft/2ft); *G.* x *macauleyi*, compact, low-growing, mid-green linear leaves, trumpet-shaped deep blue flowers with darker stripe, autumn, 8cm/20cm (3in/8in); *G.* x *m.* 'Kingfisher', deep blue flowers up to 7cm (2in) long; *G. saxosa*, mat-forming evergreen, spoon-shaped to lance-shaped leathery deep green leaves, sometimes tinged purple-brown, bell-shaped white flowers, solitary or in clusters, summer and early autumn, 7cm/10cm (2in/4in); *G. septemfida*, very variable, spreading, oval, pointed mid-green leaves, clusters of bell-shaped flowers, purple-blue or bright blue, with dark stripes, white throat, late summer, must have full sun, 15-20cm/30cm (6-8in/1ft); *G. sinoornata*, trailing, mid- to pale green pointed leaves, trumpet-shaped blue flowers, striped darker blue, autumn, reliable but intolerant of lime, 8cm/40cm (3in/1½ft); *G. s.* 'Angel's Wings', deep green leaves, white flowers, blue-flushed; *G. s.* 'Edith Sarah', deep blue flowers with white stripes; *G.* 'Strathmore', mid-green linear leaves, sky-blue trumpet shaped flowers, striped silver-white, in autumn, 75cm/25cm (2½ft/10in); *G. verna* (Spring Gentian), ssp. *balcanica*, mat-forming evergreen, probably the trickiest of all to flower, keep moving it until it responds, dark green, oval leaves, solitary tubular sky-blue flowers, usually with white throats, spring to early summer, 60cm/10cm (2ft/4in).

Geranium Geraniaceae

Annuals, biennials, herbaceous, semi-evergreen and evergreen perennials. Tender to moderately hardy. To my mind, one of the very best of all herbaceous perennials, their value limited only by restricted colour range and short flowering season. Palmate lobed leaves, round or pointed, often aromatic, sometimes colouring well in autumn. Saucer-shaped or star-shaped flowers, pink, white, blue, or purple, solitary or in clusters, spring to early autumn. Thrive in most fertile, well-drained soils, in full sun or partial shade; tolerant of alkalinity. Sow seed in a cold-frame when ripe or in spring, divide established plants in spring, or take basal cuttings in early to mid-spring. ❀ *G.* 'Ann Folkard', trailing herbaceous perennial, leaves lemon-yellow at first, later dark green, saucer-shaped magenta flowers with darker centres, black veining, summer to autumn, 60cm/1m (2ft/3ft); *G. asphodeloides*, evergreen perennial, mid-green basal leaves, clusters of star-shaped, pink or white flowers with darker veining, early summer, 30-45cm/30cm (1-1½ft/1ft); *G.* 'Brook-side', divided leaves, bowl-shaped dark blue flowers with white centres, early to late summer, 30cm/30cm (1ft/1ft); *G.* x *cantabrigiense*, mat-forming, compact evergreen, aromatic, glossy, toothed, light green divided basal leaves, good autumn colour, clusters of purple-pink or white flowers, early to mid-summer, 30cm/60cm (1ft/2ft); *G.* x *c.* 'Biokovo', white flowers tinged pink; *G.* x *c.* 'Cambridge', abundant bright pink flowers, late spring to summer, good autumn colour, 15cm/45cm (6in/1½ft); *G. cinereum* 'Apple Blossom', dwarf, evergreen perennial, grey-green basal leaves, clear pale pink flowers; *G. c.* 'Ballerina', dwarf, carpeting, purple-pink with darker veins and centre, forming a wide mat, one of the best *Geranium* hybrids ever raised; *G. c.* 'Lawrence Flatman', purple-red flowers with dark red veining, dark centres, 15cm/30cm (6in/1ft); *G.* x *c.* var. *subcaulescens*, dark green leaves, brilliant magenta flowers with black centres, so vivid it's hard to blend with anything else; *G.* x *c.* var. *s.* 'Giuseppii',

above *Geranium himalayense*. A lovely species, and much prettier, I think, than its more familiar double flowered form.

very similar but lacking black basal spot; *G. clarkei* 'Kashmir Pink', carpeting herbaceous perennial, finely cut leaves, saucer-shaped, veined, pink flowers, early to mid-summer, 50cm (1¾ft)/indefinite; *G.* 'Kashmir White', white flowers, lilac veining, 45cm (1½ft); *G. dalmaticum*, dwarf, creeping, evergreen perennial, glossy light green leaves, red-orange in autumn, clusters of bright pink flowers in summer, 15cm/50cm (6in/1¾ft); *G. d.* 'Album', white flowers; *G. endressii*, mat-forming or clump-forming semi-evergreen, divided toothed leaves, bright pink flowers, late spring to autumn, 45cm/60cm (1½ft/2ft); *G. gracile*, light green leaves, pale pink funnel-shaped flowers with darker veining, late spring to summer, 50cm/20cm (1¾ft/8in); *G. himalayense* (syns. *G. grandiflorum*, *G. meeboldii*), probably my favourite among medium-sized geraniums, mat-forming, densely cut mid-green basal leaves with conspicuous veins, good autumn colour, clusters of large cup-shaped violet-blue flowers with white centres, tinged red-purple, early summer to early autumn, 30-45cm/60cm (1-1½ft/2ft); *G. h.* 'Gravetye' (syn. *G. grandiflorum* var. *alpinum*), larger flowers and smaller leaves, flowers more strongly tinged red-pink, 30cm (1ft); *G. h.* 'Irish Blue', pale blue flowers, centres flushed red-purple; *G. h.* 'Plenum' (syn. 'Birch Double'), shades of rose, blue-purple, very popular but also very prone to insect damage, 23cm (9in); *G. ibericum*, clump-forming, hairy herbaceous perennial, toothed, lobed basal leaves, cup-shaped violet-blue flowers, darker veins, early summer, 50cm/60cm (1¾ft/2ft); *G.* 'Johnson's Blue', spreading herbaceous perennial, mid-green finely cut leaves, saucer-shaped, almost luminous blue flowers, paler centres, summer, 30-45cm/60cm (1-1½ft/2ft); *G. libani*, fairly hardy to moderately hardy, clump-forming, dormant in summer, new glossy, rounded lobed mid-green leaves arise in autumn, clusters of violet-blue flowers in spring, 40cm/45cm (1½ft/1½ft); *G. macrorrhizum*, rhizomatous semi-evergreen, light green aromatic leaves, scalloped edges, sometimes coloured in autumn, magenta flowers, late spring to early summer, 30-60cm/30cm (1-2ft/1ft); *G. m.* 'Album', very pale shell-pink flowers with coral calyces; *G. m.* 'Bevan's Variety', vivid magenta-pink flowers; *G. m.* 'Czakor', leaves purple tinted in autumn, magenta flowers; *G. m.* 'Ingwersen's Variety', glossy light green leaves, soft pink flowers; *G. m.* 'Variegatum', leaves grey-green with cream variegation, pink-purple flowers, 30cm/45cm (1ft/1½ft); *G. maculatum*, clump-forming herbaceous perennial, mid-green, lobed, toothed leaves, leaves fiery in cold autumns, clusters of saucer-shaped pure lilac flowers, late spring to mid-summer, 60-75cm/45cm (2-2½ft/1½ft); *G. maderense*, a glorious plant, the biggest geranium, barely hardy, best grown in a container and moved to protection over winter, shiny green, fern-like, rounded leaves, purple-pink flowers with crimson centres early spring to early summer, monocarpic (dies after flowering), 1.2-1.5m/1.2-1.5m (4-5ft/4-5ft); *G.* x *magnificum*, clump-forming herbaceous perennial, dark green leaves, good autumn colour, clusters of violet-blue flowers with darker veining, mid-summer, 60cm/60cm (2ft/2ft); *G. malviflorum*, tuberous, dormant in summer, in autumn new dark green, deeply cut leaves, clusters of saucer-shaped, pink to violet-blue flowers with red veins, early to mid-spring, 22-30cm/45cm (8in-1ft/1½ft); *G.* x *monacense*, clump-forming herbaceous perennial, lobed basal leaves, saucer-shaped purple-red flowers, white and violet at bases, late spring to early summer, 45cm/60cm (1½ft/2ft); *G.* x *m.* 'Muldoon', quite superb, dark green leaves, spotted purple, 60cm (2ft); *G.* 'Nimbus', mounds of lacy, finely-cut leaves, star-shaped blue-purple flowers; *G. nodosum*, rhizomatous, bright green maple-shaped leaves, light purple flowers with paler centres, crimson veins, late spring to early or mid-autumn, 30-50cm/50cm (1-1¾ft/1¾ft); *G. orientalitibeticum* (syn. *G. stapfianum* var. *roseum*), dwarf, spreading, tuberous, lobed toothed basal leaves, very beautifully marbled dark and pale green, purple-pink cup-shaped flowers with white centres, summer, 30cm/1m (1ft/3ft); *G.* x *oxonianum* 'A T Johnson', semi-evergreen, dark green leaves, funnel-shaped flowers light pink at first, later darker, dark veins, in summer, 75cm/75cm (2½ft/2½ft); *G.* x *o.* 'Claridge Druce', (syn. *G.* 'Claridge Druce'), rose-pink flowers with darker veining, notched petals, late spring to mid-summer, self-seeds wickedly, 45cm/75cm (1½ft/2½ft); *G.* x *o.* 'Southcombe Double', double pink flowers, 40cm (1½ft); *G.* x *o.* 'Thurstonianum', very narrow petals, rich purple, early summer to early autumn, 1m (3ft); *G.* x *o.* 'Walter's Gift', shiny green leaves, red-brown in centre, pink flowers with darker veining; *G.* x *o.* 'Wargrave Pink', flowers cream-pink to salmon-pink, 38cm (1½ft); *G. phaeum*, clump-forming herbaceous perennial, sombre but impressive, soft green basal leaves, sometimes marked purple-brown, small, pendent, silky purple flowers, late spring to early summer, suitable for damp shade, 80cm/45cm (2½ft/1½ft); *G. p.* 'Album', white, gold anthers; *G. p.* var. *lividum*, plain leaves, pale lilac or pink flowers; *G. pratense*, clump-forming herbaceous perennial, lobed, toothed basal leaves, usually divided, saucer-shaped white or violet-blue flowers, darker veining, early to mid-summer, 60cm/60-90cm (2ft/2ft-3ft); *G. p.* f. *albiflorum*, white flowers, 1m (3ft); *G. p.* 'Mrs Kendall Clark', pearl-grey flowers tinged pink; *G. p.* 'Striatum', umbrella-like cut leaves, single clear blue or white flowers, mid-summer; *G. procurrens*, prostrate, cut leaves, excellent ground cover, coarsely toothed mid-green basal leaves, clusters of small purple to purple-pink flowers, darker centres and veins, mid-summer to early autumn, 45cm/1m (1½ft/3ft); *G. psilostemon*, deeply cut leaves, flushed crimson in spring, red in autumn, brilliant magenta-pink flowers with indigo eyes, early to late summer, 60-120cm/60cm (2-4ft/2ft); *G. pylzowianum*, spreading, tuberous, very pretty kidney-shaped or semi-round leaves, deeply cut, clusters of trumpet-shaped deep rose-pink flowers with darker veins, 5-25cm/25cm (2-10in/10in); *G. renardii*, clump-forming, quilted sage-green leaves with scalloped edges, off-white flowers with purple veining, early summer, 30cm/30cm (1ft/1ft); *G.* x *riversleaianum* 'Mavis Simpson', trailing herbaceous perennial, deeply divided grey-green leaves with toothed lobes, loose clusters of funnel-shaped clear to light pink flowers with paler centres, 30cm/1m (1ft/3ft); *G.* x *r.* 'Russell Prichard', clump-forming, grey-green leaves, light magenta-pink flowers, summer to autumn; *G. robertianum*, 'Celtic White', annual or biennial, a white form of the native Herb Robert, hairy, aromatic bright green basal leaves, clusters of star-shaped white flowers, summer to autumn, 10-40cm/30cm (4in-1½ft/1ft); *G. sanguineum*, clump-forming herbaceous perennial, finely cut leaves, dark green, vivid magenta flowers, summer to winter, 20cm/30cm (8in/1ft); *G. s.* 'Album', white flowers; *G. s.* 'Glenluce', large soft pink flowers; *G. s.* 'Shepherd's Warning', shocking pink flowers; *G. s.* var. *striatum* (syn. *G. s.* var. *lancastrense*), pale pink flowers with crimson centres and veins; *G. sylvaticum* 'Album', clump-forming, toothed mid-green leaves, deeply cut, white flowers, spring to early summer, 75cm/60cm (2½ft/2ft); *G. s.* 'Mayflower', flowers light purple at first, later violet-blue; *G. thunbergii*, scrambling, abundant small white flowers, sometimes flushed pink in summer, 30cm (1ft); *G. tuberosum*, tuberous, spreading, dormant in summer, new leaves, mid-green, lobed, toothed, in autumn, cup-shaped flowers, bright purple-pink, darker veins, purple shading, mid-spring, 20-25cm/30cm (8-10in/1ft); *G. versicolor* (syn. *G. striatum*), clump-forming, semi-evergreen, toothed, light green basal leaves, usually marked brown, funnel-shaped

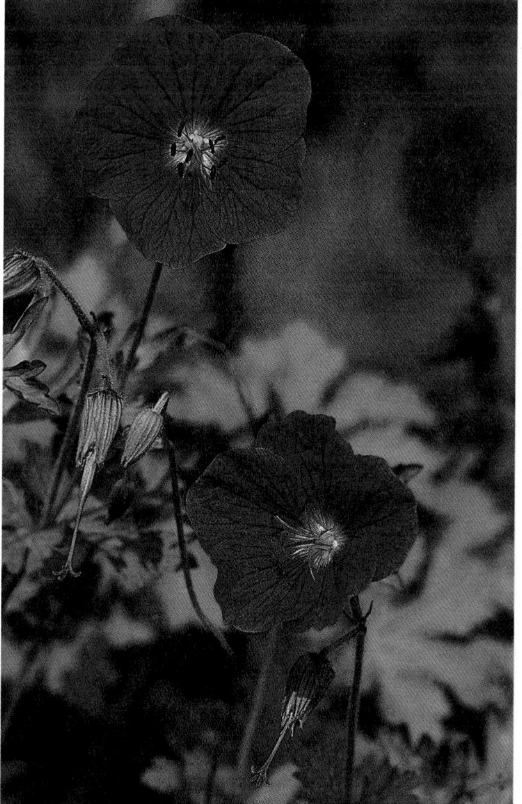

left *Geranium orientalitibeticum*. A notable instance of the value of geraniums for foliage as well as flower appeal.

right *Geum rivale* 'Leonard's Variety'. Geums have many fans although, pretty as they are, I still think their flowers are a bit too small.

white flowers, magenta veining, late spring, then into autumn, 45cm/45cm (1½ft/1½ft); *G. wallichianum* 'Buxton's Variety', trailing, mid-green, dark mottled leaves, rich blue flowers, white centres, 30cm/1.2m (1ft/4ft); *G. wlassovianum*, clump-forming, hairy dark green basal leaves, brown flushed, red in autumn, funnel shaped purple-pink or pink flowers with darker veins, mid-summer, 60cm/60cm (2ft/2ft).

Gerbera *Transvaal Daisy* Asteraceae

Small evergreen or herbaceous perennials. Tender to barely hardy. In cold areas best grown in containers. Basal rosettes of pinnate or lobed, lance-shaped dandelion-like leaves, sometimes toothed, solitary, single or double, daisy-like flowers, in red, purple, pink, orange or yellow, sometimes with white or yellow centres. Sow seed in warmth in early spring or autumn, take basal cuttings in summer or divide established plants in early spring. ❀ *G.* 'Dwarf Frisbee', compact, rounded leaves, flowers in mixed colours, 18-25cm (7-10in); *G. jamesonii*, clump-forming, deeply lobed, more or less lance-shaped, deep green leaves, downy beneath, orange, yellow or scarlet flowers with yellow centres, 30-45cm/60cm (1-1½ft/2ft); *G.* 'Mardi Gras' F1, wide range of colours, early flowering, 45-60cm (1½-2ft).

below *Gerbera jamesonii*. The numbers of South African daisies seem limitless; and like many others, gerberas are best grown with some shelter.

Geum *Avens* Rosaceae

Small/medium herbaceous or evergreen perennials. Moderately hardy. Suitable for rock gardens or herbaceous borders. Basal rosettes of crinkled, toothed or scalloped, pinnate to deeply divided leaves, cup-shaped or globular flowers, sometimes pendent, in a variety of colours and shades, including red, yellow, pink, orange and cream – although I always think there is rather too much leaf for the size of the flowers. Thrive in well-drained, fertile soil in full sun. Apart from *G. rivale*, will not tolerate waterlogged soil in winter. Sow seed in a cold-frame or divide established plants in spring or autumn. ❀ *G.* 'Borisii', clump-forming, rounded hairy leaves, rich green, single flowers, bright orange-red, summer, some in late summer, 30cm (1ft); *G.* 'Coppertone', clump-forming, fresh green leaves, pale apricot flowers, mid-summer, 30cm (1ft); *G.* 'Georgenburg', compact, saucer-shaped single orange flowers flushed gold, bright green leaves, late spring to early summer, 25cm/30cm (10in/1ft); *G.* 'Lady Stratheden', hairy leaves, semi-double yellow flowers throughout summer, 40-60cm/60cm (1½-2ft/2ft); *G.* 'Lionel Cox', pale green leaves, pendent, bell-shaped flowers, cream-flushed apricot, 45cm/20-60cm (1½ft/8in-2ft); *G. montanum* (Mountain Avens), clump-forming, dark green leaves, single, cup-shaped deep gold-yellow flowers, sometimes in clusters, followed by fluffy seedheads, red at first, later brown, 15cm/30cm (6in/1ft); *G.* 'Mrs J Bradshaw', hairy leaves, semi-double scarlet flowers in clusters, early to late summer, 40-60cm/60cm (1½-2ft/2ft); *G. rivale* (Water Avens), erect, clump-forming, rhizomatous, mid- to deep green basal leaves, bell-shaped pendent flowers, single pink or cream flowers with purple-brown calyces, followed by fluffy seedheads, grows well in moist, damp cool sites in shade or full sun, 20-60cm/20-60cm (8in-2ft/8in-2ft); *G. r.* 'Album', white flowers with green calyces in early summer, 30cm (1ft); *G. r.* 'Leonard's Variety', round, deeply cut basal leaves, rose bell-shaped flowers with maroon calyces on mahogany stems, mid- to late summer, 45cm (1½ft); *G. urbanum* (Herb Bennett), erect, clump-forming, rhizomatous, dark green toothed leaves, saucer-shaped pale yellow flowers, summer to early autumn, can be invasive, 60cm/40cm (2ft/1½ft).

Ginkgo *Maidenhair Tree* Ginkgoaceae

Medium/large deciduous tree. Hardy to very hardy. The famous 'living fossil' tree, the sole survivor of a prehistoric family and a quite beautiful specimen for a larger garden. Uniquely characteristic fan-shaped leaves with central split; glorious rich yellow autumn colour. Male and female flowers on separate trees, females producing evil-smelling nuts though this is rare in Britain. No routine pruning. Sow seed in a cold-frame in autumn. ❀ *G. biloba*, the only species, 25m/8m (80ft/25ft); 'Fastigiata', a rare form but worth searching for, narrowly upright.

Gladiolus Iridaceae

Moderately hardy to fairly hardy, small or medium corm-forming perennials, valuable for the mixed border although the larger hybrids are more commonly grown away from ornamental beds for use as cut flowers. Best in moist but very well-drained, fairly rich, neutral or slightly acidic soil and full sun with shelter from cold winds. Narrow, flattened, ribbed, sword-like leaves arise from the base of the stem, flowers tubular or funnel-shaped with the upper petal extended, cowl-like, flowers in most colours and often streaked or blotched with contrasting colour. Tall hybrids require staking. Lift corms after first autumn frosts (even if foliage not blackened) and store dry overwinter to replant in spring. Remove daughter corms and grow on in pots. ❀ Species and near-species: *G. callianthus* 'Murieliae' (syn. *Acidanthera murielae*), up to ten fragrant white flowers with deep purple throat, a beautiful plant, late summer, 75cm (21/2ft); *G. cardinalis*, up to 12 scarlet flowers with white streaks on lower petals, 60cm-1m (2ft-3ft); *G.* 'The Bride', three to six 5 cm (2 in) white flowers, early spring to summer; *G. communis* ssp. *byzantinus*, up to 20 red-purple flowers with pale markings on lower petals, one of the hardiest and earliest, late spring, 60cm-1m (2ft-3ft); *G. illyricus*, purple with white or pale streaks on lower petals, mid-summer, 30-50cm (1-1¾ft); *G. natalensis*, variable, usually lilac or purple but other colours occur also with streaks of varying and contrasting colour on lower petals, 1-1.5m (3-5ft); *G. papilio*, five to ten yellow flowers with purple flush on outside and often on lower petals, 50-90cm (1¾-3ft); *G. tristis*, up to 20 fragrant white to pale cream flowers with green and red-brown flush, mid to late summer, 50cm-1.5m (1¾-5ft).

above *Gladiolus* 'Butterfly Mixed'. The Butterfly varieties display the characteristic gladiolus flower form but have little of its vulgarity.

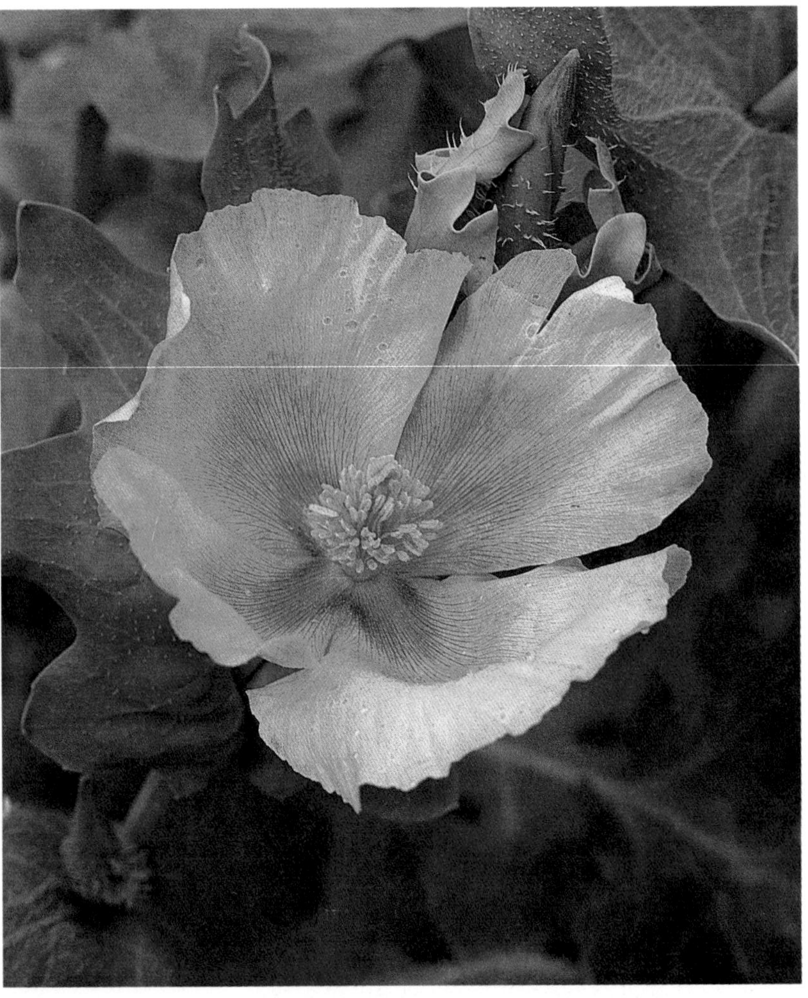

above *Glaucium flavum*. Pretty enough in flower, the really striking feature of this native plant comes from its hugely elongated, horn-like seed pod.

Hybrids: *Gladiolus* hybrids, like many other bulbous plants, come and go rather quickly and individual varieties are often only available from one or two nurseries. There is no universally agreed classification but the following are the main and important groups:

Grandiflora, summer flowering, includes most border varieties, with up to 28 flowers, subdivided on flower size (width of largest expanded floret) and height from Giant (flowers 14cm (5¼in)) and over, height 1.4-1.9m (4-6ft) to Miniature (flowers less than 6cm (2¼in)), height 90cm-1.3m (3-4ft).

Primulinus, flowers well spaced, up to 23 per spike, up to 9cm (3in), with small basal petals, mid to late summer, 90cm-1.4m (3-4ft).

Butterfly, among the best for general use with a mass of very pretty small flowers in a wide range of colours and also good for cutting, to my mind, far and away the best gladioli for general use, summer, 60cm-80cm (2-2½ft).

Nanus, up to seven flowers per spike, flowers up to 5cm (2in), among the hardiest hybrids, early summer, height 60cm-80cm (2-2½ft).

Glaucidium — Glaucidiaceae

Rhizomatous ornamental. Moderately hardy and a lovely woodland plant for moist, slightly acidic soil. Palmate, lobed leaves, poppy-like flowers. Sow seed in an open-frame in spring or divide established plants in early spring. ❀ *G. palmatum*, toothed, veined and crinkly light green leaves, solitary lilac-pink or mauve flowers, gold stamens, spring to early summer, 45cm/45cm (1½ft/1½ft).

Glaucium *Horned Poppy* — Papaveraceae

Small/medium annuals, biennials and perennials. Moderately hardy. Divided, softly hairy or hairless leaves, oval to rounded, poppy-like papery flowers in summer, followed by long, curved seedpods. Roots are toxic if eaten. Sow seed in growing position in early summer. ❀ *G. corniculatum* (syn. *G. phoenicium*), hairy annual, pinnate, glaucous, grey-green leaves, clusters of orange to red flowers, some with darker spots in the centre, early summer, 30-40cm/30-40cm (1-1½ft/1-1½ft); *G. flavum* (Yellow Horned Poppy), perennial, sometimes grown as a biennial, rosettes of blue-grey ruffled leaves, lemon-yellow flowers, 30-90cm/45cm (1-3ft/1½ft); *G. f.* f. *flavum*, rosettes of deeply cut grey-blue leaves, orange flowers, late summer to late autumn, followed by the characteristic horn-like seedpods, 60cm (2ft).

Glechoma — Lamiaceae

Small rhizomatous perennial. Moderately hardy. Suitable for the edges of borders, as ground cover, and in containers, especially hanging baskets and window boxes. Can be invasive and foliage causes allergic reaction in many people when handled. Toothed leaves, flowers variable, two-lipped, usually violet-blue, summer. Take softwood cuttings in late spring or divide established plants in spring or early autumn. ❀ *G. hederacea* (Ground Ivy), mat-forming, round, dark green leaves, purple-blue or lavender flowers mid- to late summer, 15cm/90cm (6in/3ft); *G. h.* 'Variegata' (syn. *Nepeta glechoma* 'Variegata'), less invasive, trailing evergreen or semi-evergreen, kidney-shaped leaves with scalloped margins, dark green with cream-white edges, mauve flowers in summer, 15cm/2m (6in/6½ft)or more.

Gleditsia — Caesalpiniaceae

Large deciduous trees. Moderately hardy. Tolerant of atmospheric pollution but brittle twigs prone to wind damage. Spiny, some with formidable thorns, pinnate or bi-pinnate fern-like leaves, inflorescences of insignificant grey-white flowers, followed by large pendent seedpods. Thrives in any well-drained, fertile soil in full sun. No routine pruning. Easy to raise from seed but doesn't come true and commercially is grafted. ❀ *G. triacanthos* (Honey Locust), spreading, pinnate, frond-like, glossy dark green leaves, yellow in autumn, 20m/5m (60ft/16ft); *G. t.* 'Rubylace', leaves dark bronze-red at first, later dark bronze-green, 10m (33ft); *G. t.* 'Sunburst', spreading, thornless branches, leaves gold-yellow at first, later pale green, then yellow in autumn, scorches in direct sun, 12m/4m (40ft/13ft).

Globularia *Globe Daisy* Globulariaceae

Small evergreen/semi-evergreen alpines. Moderately hardy but need full sun. Leathery, sharply toothed leaves, clusters of tiny flowers in dense, round pompon-like inflorescences. Sow seed in a cold-frame in winter, divide established plants in spring or take softwood or semi-ripe cuttings of woody species in mid- to late summer. ❀ *G. cordifolia*, mat-forming evergreen, basal rosettes of glossy, deep green, spoon-shaped leaves, solitary mauve- or lavender-blue flowers, summer, 5cm/20cm (2in/8in); *G. meridionalis* (syns. *G. bellidifolia, G. pygmaea*), mat-forming evergreen, solitary, lavender-purple flowers, lance-shaped, glossy leaves, summer, 2.5cm/15cm (1in/6in).

Glyceria *Sweet Grass* Poaceae

Medium perennial grasses. Tender to hardy. Suitable for bog gardens, marshy areas, near streams and ponds, although it will also grow satisfactorily in normal borders if you are prepared for the constant chopping back needed. Can be invasive. Divide in spring. ❀ *G. maxima* var. *variegata* (Gardeners' Garters), arching, broad strap-shaped leaves, striped white and yellow or cream, flushed pink in spring, 80cm (2½ft)/indefinite.

Gomphrena Amaranthaceae

Small/medium half-hardy annuals and herbaceous perennials all generally grown as annuals. Lance-shaped or oval leaves, clover-like inflorescences, summer to early autumn. Sow seed in warmth in early spring. ❀ *G. globosa*, annual, oval to oblong leaves, pink, purple or white inflorescences, 30-60cm/30cm (1-1¾ft/1ft); *G. g.* 'Buddy', deep purple, 15cm (6in); *G. g.* 'White Gnome', white.

above *Gomphrena globosa* 'White Gnome'. The inflorescence of *Gomphrena* is remarkably like that of clover although the plants are totally unrelated.

left *Globularia cordifolia*. Surprisingly, not among the best known alpines although they are relatively easy to grow.

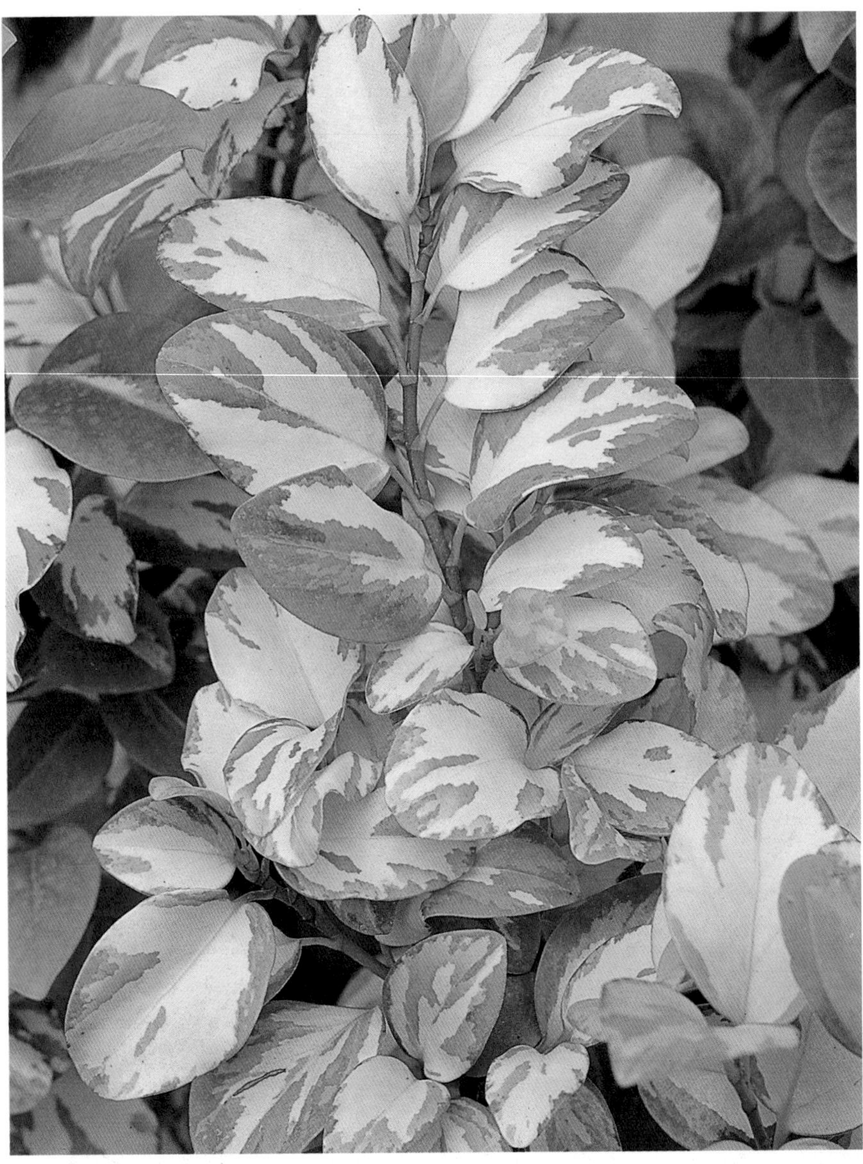

above *Griselinia littoralis* 'Bantry Bay'. A truly glorious shrub but appropriately named for it requires mild areas like Bantry Bay in Southern Ireland in which to flourish.

Griselinia — Cornaceae

Medium/large evergreen shrubs or small trees. Barely to fairly hardy but an excellent and beautiful foliage shrub for coastal gardens. Glossy green leaves, clusters of insignificant small green flowers in late spring. No routine pruning, but cut out green shoots on variegated plants. Take semi-ripe cuttings in early summer. ❀ *G. littoralis*, erect shrub, glossy green leaves, 8m/5m (25ft/16ft); *G. l.* 'Bantry Bay', leaves marked cream-white; *G. l.* 'Variegata', cream-white variegation, principally on the leaf margins.

Gunnera — Haloradigaceae

Rhizomatous, herbaceous, deciduous or evergreen perennials. Barely hardy to moderately hardy and crowns should be protected in winter in cold areas. Wonderful plants for damp areas near water or in rock gardens. Variable in size and habit, from small mat-forming plants to species with gigantic leaves. Leaves oval, sometimes heart-shaped. Large spikes of insignificant flowers, usually green-yellow, followed by fruit. Sow ripe seed in warmth, take cuttings of basal buds in spring or divide small species in spring. ❀ *G. magellanica*, mat-forming, dark green kidney-shaped, toothed leaves, with wavy margins, green-yellow flowers followed by red fruit, 20cm/1m (8in/3ft); *G. manicata*, huge umbrella-like leaves, brown at first, later green, insignificant green-red flowers in cone-shaped inflorescences, red fruit, a plant for the largest water gardens only, 2.5m/3-4m (8ft/10-13ft); *G. tinctoria* (syn. *G. scabra*), leaves more rounded, deeply lobed, club-shaped seed heads, 1.5m/2m (5ft/6½ft).

Gypsophila — Caryophyllaceae

Annuals, herbaceous, evergreen or semi-evergreen perennials. Barely hardy to moderately hardy. Good plants for borders, smaller perennials for rock gardens but resent disturbance. Lance-shaped to linear leaves, usually small star-shaped flowers, singly or in clusters, giving cloud effect, in summer. Sow seed in flowering position in spring (annuals), in warmth in winter or in a cold-frame in spring; take root cuttings in late winter. ❀ *G. cerastioides*, mat-forming semi-evergreen perennial, hairy grey leaves, panicles of shallow trumpet-shaped flowers, white, flushed pale pink, spring to summer, 50cm/50cm (1¾ft/1¾ft); *G. paniculata* (Baby's Breath), 'Bristol Fairy', fairly short-lived herbaceous perennial, linear to lance-shaped, usually hairless leaves, panicles of large double white flowers, 1.2m/1.2m (4ft/4ft); *G. p.* 'Compacta Plena', double pale pink to white flowers, 20-30cm/60cm (8in-1ft/2ft); *G. p.* 'Flamingo', tiny grey-green leaves, abundant double pink flowers, 75-90cm/90cm (2½-3ft/3ft); *G. repens*, mat-forming semi-evergreen, linear leaves, mid-green or blue-green, panicles of star-shaped white or pink flowers, 20cm/30-50cm (8in/1-1¾ft); *G. r.* 'Dorothy Teacher', blue-green leaves, flowers pale pink at first, later darker, 5cm/40cm (2in/1½ft); *G. r.* 'Dubia' (syn. *G. dubia*), mat-forming, leaves tinted silver-grey on dark red stems, white flowers flushed pink, late spring to early summer, 8cm (3in); *G. r.* 'Rosea', dark rose-pink buds open to bright pink flowers; *G.* 'Rosenschleier' (syn. 'Rosy Veil'), mound-forming semi-evergreen, blue-green leaves, dense clouds of tiny pale pink double flowers, mid- to late summer, 40-50cm/1m (1½-1¾ft/3ft).

Haberlea — Gesneriaceae

Small evergreen perennials. Moderately hardy. Requires cool, shady conditions. Basal rosettes of dark green, more or less oval leaves with scalloped edges, clusters of pendent trumpet-shaped flowers spring to early summer. Sow seed in warmth in spring or divide established plants in early summer. ❀ *H. rhodopensis*, oval to oblong hairy leaves, umbels of lavender-lilac flowers on short stems, 15cm/25cm (6in/10in).

Hacquetia — Apiaceae

Moderately hardy rhizomatous ornamental. Suitable for damp shade and among my favourite small woodland species. Like *Euphorbia*, it offers an example of the remarkable beauty that can be achieved from green and yellow. ❀ *H. epipactis* (syn. *Dondia epipactis*), clump-forming, glossy emerald-green leaves, star-shaped, tiny yellow flowers, surrounded by lime-green, petal-like bracts, late winter to early spring, 5cm/15-30cm (2in/6in-1ft).

Hakonechloa — Poaceae

Perennial grass. Moderately hardy. Suitable for front of borders, rock gardens and containers. Divide established plants in spring. ❀ *H. macra* 'Alboaurea', clump-forming, ribbon-like leaves, variegated cream and gold with bronze tinges, one of the best of all variegated grasses, 35cm/40cm (1¼ft/1½ft); *H. m.* 'Aureola', narrow leaves, light green striped with cream, 35cm/40cm (1¼ft/1½ft).

Halesia — Styracaceae

Large deciduous shrubs and small trees for lime-free soils. Moderately hardy. Oval to elliptic or oblong leaves, good autumn colour, abundant bell-shaped, pendent flowers, followed by curious winged, egg-shaped fruit. Strangely neglected as they offer much all-round interest. No routine pruning. Sow seed in warmth in spring, take off wood cuttings in summer or layer in spring. ❀ *H. carolina* (syn. *H. tetraptera*), large shrub or small tree, mid-green elliptic, toothed leaves, yellow in autumn, white flowers on bare branches in late spring followed by green fruit, 8m/10m (25ft/33ft); *H. monticola*, small tree, oval, downy mid-green leaves, hairy at first, yellow in autumn, clusters of four-winged flowers on bare branches or as leaves emerge, followed by four-winged green fruit, 12m/8m (40ft/25ft); *H. m.* var. *vestita*, larger white flowers than species, sometimes flushed pink.

x Halimiocistus — Cistaceae

Small evergreen shrub. Barely hardy to moderately hardy and good for large rock gardens, shrub or mixed borders in full sun; tolerate poor soil. Oval, linear or elliptic leaves, saucer-shaped flowers resembling rock rose (*Helianthemum*). No routine pruning. Take semi-ripe cuttings in late summer. ❀ x *H.* 'Ingwersenii' (syn. *Cistus ingwerseniana*), spreading, dark green, linear to lance-shaped leaves, clusters of saucer-shaped white flowers, late spring to late summer, 45cm/90cm (1½ft/3ft); x *H. sahucii* (syn. *Cistus sahucii*), mound-forming or spreading; inversely lance-shaped to linear dark green leaves, clusters of white flowers, in summer, 45cm/90cm (1½ft/3ft); x *H. wintonensis* (syn. *Cistus wintonensis*), spreading, elliptic to oval, lance-shaped downy grey-green leaves, clusters of saucer-shaped white flowers, yellow stamens and dark crimson-maroon marks at

above *Hacquetia epipactis*. Like *Euphorbia*, this is another example of the beauty of green and yellow flowers.

below *x Halimiocistus* 'Ingwersenii'. A hybrid genus of great merit for larger rock gardens.

bases of petals, 60-90cm (2-3ft); x *H. w.* 'Merrist Wood Cream', cream-yellow flowers, yellow centres, red bands.

Halimium

Cistaceae

Small evergreen shrubs. Barely hardy to fairly hardy. Suitable for mild, sunny gardens, large rock gardens, coastal situations. Any plant with 'hal' in the name, implying something connected with salt, is likely to be a good coastal species. Light green to grey-green leaves. Saucer-shaped yellow flowers resembling single roses have dark blotches at the base of the petals. Sow seed in warmth in spring or take semi-ripe cuttings in late summer. ❀ *H. lasianthum* (syn. *Cistus formosus*), spreading, oval or oblong grey-green leaves, golden-yellow flowers with crimson blotches, 1m/1.5m (3ft/5ft); *H. ocymoides* (syn. *Cistus algarvensis*), erect shrub, downy, inversely lance-shaped grey-green leaves, golden-yellow flowers with chocolate-brown blotches, 60cm/1m (2ft/3ft); *H.* 'Susan', spreading, bright yellow semi-double flowers, oval grey-green leaves, red-purple blotches, 45cm/60cm (1½ft/2ft).

below *Hamamelis x intermedia* 'Pallida' originated from a neglected Dutch nursery in the early years of the 20th century but took half a century more to become widely appreciated.

Hamamelis

Witch Hazel Hamamelidaceae

Large deciduous shrubs or small trees. Moderately hardy. Hazel-like, oval to more or less oval leaves, good yellow in autumn. Clusters of fragrant, small spidery yellow or red flowers on bare branches from early winter to spring. Thrives best in moist, well-drained slightly acidic soil enriched with organic matter, in light shade or full sun. Intolerant of heavy clay; needs protection from cold winds and frosts. No routine pruning. Sow ripe seed in a cold-frame. ❀ *H.* x *intermedia* 'Arnold Promise', spreading bush, bright yellow flowers, 4m/4m (13ft/13ft); *H.* x *i.* 'Diane', leaves red in autumn, dark red flowers mid- to late winter; *H.* x *i.* 'Jelena', spreading shrub, hairy leaves, orange and red in autumn, clusters of yellow flowers flushed copper-red, early to midwinter; *H.* x *i.* 'Pallida', (syn. *H. mollis* 'Pallida'), still the best form, leaves yellow in autumn, strongly fragrant yellow flowers mid- to late winter; *H. mollis*, erect shrub, rounded, hairy mid-green leaves, yellow in autumn, abundant clusters of gold-yellow flowers, sweetly fragrant, mid- to late winter, 4m/4m (13ft/13ft).

Hebe

Shrubby Veronica Scrophulariaceae

Small/medium evergreen shrubs. Barely hardy to moderately hardy. Especially good in coastal gardens; also containers and shrub borders. In cold areas varieties must be chosen carefully and less hardy types given protection in winter. Those described below are all barely to fairly hardy unless stated otherwise. Lance-shaped, round or oval leaves, some tiny, scale-like, resembling cypress (whipcord hebes). Clusters of small purple, white, red, or blue flowers, spring to autumn. Thrive in moist, well-drained neutral to slightly alkaline soil, in full sun or partial shade; container-grown plants require loam-based compost. No routine pruning. Sow ripe seed in a cold-frame or take semi-ripe cuttings in late summer or autumn.
❀ *H. albicans*, mound-forming, lance-shaped grey-green, glaucous leaves, white flowers, early to mid-summer, 60cm/90cm (2ft/3ft); *H.* 'Amy', erect, rounded leaves tinted bronze-purple at first, later glossy dark green, violet-purple flowers, summer, 1.5m/1.5m (5ft/5ft); *H. armstrongii* (syn. *H. lycopodioides* 'Aurea'), whipcord type, oval yellow-green leaves, scale-like, small white flowers, late spring to early summer, 90cm/90cm (3ft/3ft); *H.* 'Autumn Glory', bushy, small round leaves tinted purple-red, intense violet flowers, summer to late autumn, 60cm/90cm (2ft/3ft); *H.* 'Blue Clouds',

leaves dark glossy green, purple in winter, blue-mauve flowers in long spikes, summer to autumn, 1m/1.2m (3ft/4ft); *H.* 'Caledonia' (syns. *H.* 'E B Anderson', *H.* 'Knightshayes'), erect, rounded, long, pointed leaves with purple-red margins and midribs, abundant spikes of violet flowers, 60cm/60cm (2ft/2ft); *H.* 'County Park', spreading, oval grey-green leaves, with red margins, spikes of violet flowers, early to mid-summer, 20cm/48cm (8in/1¾ft); *H. cupressoides* 'Boughton Dome', moderately hardy whipcord type, domed, pale green scale-like leaves on cypress-like branchlets, flowers, lilac-blue, are infrequent, 30cm/60cm (1ft/2ft); *H.* 'Emerald Green' (syns. *H.* 'Emerald Gem, *H.* 'Green Globe'), moderately hardy, rounded, bright green leaves, white flowers are infrequent, 35cm/35cm (1¼ft/1¼ft); *H.* x *franciscana* 'Blue Gem', thick, light green leaves, lilac or deep violet flowers, early summer to mid-autumn, 1.5m/1.5m (5ft/5ft); *H.* x *f.* 'Variegata', shiny, dark green leaves, flushed pale green, broad cream-yellow margins, lilac flowers, mid-summer to mid-autumn; *H.* 'Glaucophylla Variegata', rounded, lance-shaped, grey-green leaves with cream margins, pale lilac-blue flowers, 1m/1m (3ft/3ft); *H.* 'Great Orme', glossy, mid-green, oblong to lance-shaped leaves, dark purple shoots, spikes of large pink flowers fading to white, mid-summer to mid-autumn, 1.2m/1.2m (4ft/4ft); *H. hulkeana*, erect, oblong, elliptic to oval toothed glossy mid-green leaves with red edges, sprays of white, blue or lilac flowers, mid- to late spring, 60cm/60cm (2ft/2ft); *H. macrantha*, erect dwarf, bright green, thick, leathery, more or less oval to elliptic toothed leaves, white flowers 2-3cm (¾-1¼ in) in diameter, early summer, 60cm/90cm (2ft/3ft); *H.* 'Mrs Winder' (syn. *H.* 'Waikiki'), oblong to elliptic leaves, purple at first, later dark green, violet-blue flowers, late summer, 1m/1.2m (3ft/4ft); *H.* 'Nicola's Blush', dwarf, green leaves flushed purple, flowers pink, fading to white, mid-summer, sometimes later in autumn, 75cm/75cm (2½ft/2½ft); *H. ochracea* 'James Stirling', the best whipcord type, scale-like ochre-yellow leaves, white flowers, late spring to early summer, 45cm/60cm (1½ft/2ft); *H. odora* (syn. *H. anomala*), glossy dark green, elliptic to oval dark green leaves, white flowers, early to mid-summer, 1m/1.5m (3ft/5ft); *H.* 'Pewter Dome' (syn. *H. albicans* 'Pewter Dome'), dome-shaped, grey-green leaves, white flowers, mid- to late summer, 40cm/60cm (1½ft/2ft); *H. pimeleoides* 'Quicksilver', silver-grey leaves, paler flowers, 30cm (1ft); *H. pinguifolia* 'Pagei', moderately hardy, semi-prostrate, leathery blue-green leaves, abundant spikes of white flowers, late spring to early summer, 30cm/90cm (1ft/3ft); *H. rakaiensis*, dome-shaped, elliptic to more or less oval, glossy bright green leaves, white flowers, early to mid-summer, a wonderful plant, although its old name of *alpina* implies something small. 1m/1.2m (3ft/4ft); *H. recurva*, compact, spreading, lance-shaped, curved blue-green leaves, spikes of white flowers, summer, 60cm/60cm (2ft/2ft); *H.* 'Red Edge' (syn. *H. albicans* 'Red Edge'), grey-green leaves, red margins, young leaves and leaf buds pink in winter, pale violet-blue flowers, 45cm/60cm (1½ft/2ft); *H. salicifolia*, moderately hardy and very reliable, lance-shaped, bright green leaves, white flowers, sometimes flushed lilac, early to late summer, 2.5m/2.5m (8ft/8ft); *H. topiaria*, dome-shaped, yellow-green leaves, white flowers, summer, 60cm/80-90cm (2ft /2½ft-3ft); *H. vernicosa*, moderately hardy, compact, rounded, bright green glossy leaves, white flowers, sometimes pale lilac at first, 60cm/1.2m (2ft/4ft); *H.* 'Youngii' (syn. 'Carl Teschner'), moderately hardy, mat-forming, small dark green leaves, abundant violet flowers with white throats, early to mid-summer, 20cm/60cm (8in/2ft).

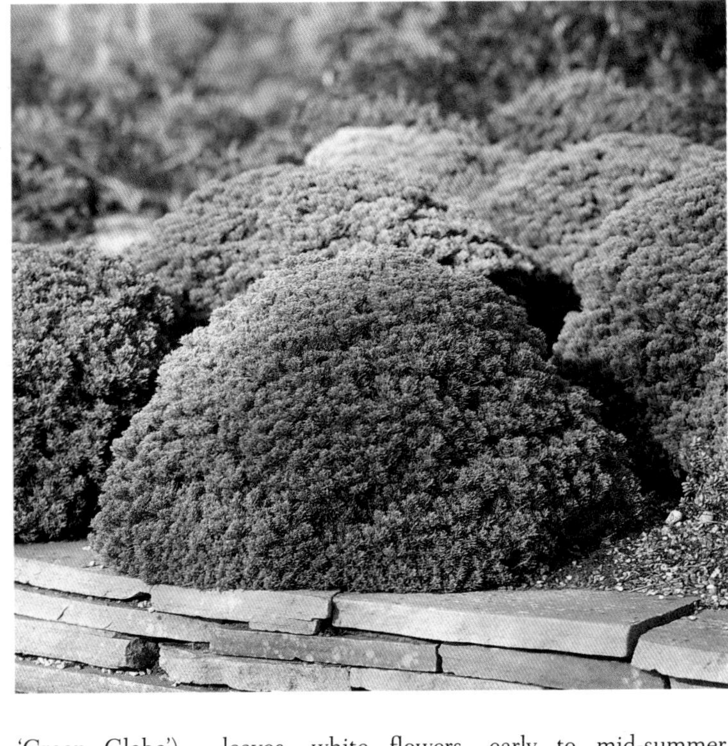

left: *Hebe cupressoides* 'Boughton Dome'. One of the neatest among the whipcord hebes, whose foliage so remarkably resembles that of the cypresses.

right *Helenium* 'Moerheim Beauty'. The rich spicy fragrance of heleniums has few equals among the late summer border daisies.

Hedera *Ivy* Araliaceae

Small/large evergreen climbers. Fairly hardy to hardy. Ivies are among the most undervalued and unjustifiably disregarded of garden plants. They are suitable for ground cover, screening and topiary, in addition to their traditional use on walls and other supports. Glossy green leaves, variously shaped, various sizes, sometimes variegated, hairy beneath, usually entire on mature plants, three-to-five lobes on young leaves. Clusters of insignificant, yellow-green flowers, followed by usually black but sometimes red, orange or cream fruits on mature shoots and when they reach the top of their support. Thrive in rich, moist, soil in full sun or fairly deep shade; best protected from cold winds. No routine pruning but will tolerate clipping. Take semi-ripe cuttings in summer or remove natural layers. ❀ *H. canariensis* 'Gloire de Marengo' (syn. *H. algeriensis* 'Gloire de Marengo'), leaves light green with silver-grey variegation, white margins, 4m (13ft); *H. colchica* 'Dentata Variegata', bright green leaves, cream-yellow margins at first, later cream-white, 5m (16ft); *H c.* 'Sulphur Heart' (syn. 'Paddy's Pride'), pale green leaves heavily splashed with yellow, 5m (16ft); *H. helix* 'Adam', light green leaves with silver margins, 5m (16ft); *H. h.* 'Buttercup', leaves bright yellow at first, later yellow-green to pale green, 2m (6½ft); *H. h.* 'Caecilia', leaves cream-yellow and green, with frilled edges, 1m (3ft); *H. h.* 'Conglomerata', small, hummock-forming, good in rock garden, erect stems, dark green leaves with wavy margins, 1m (3ft); *H. h.* 'Duckfoot', good for neat, limited ground cover, mid-green leaves resemble a duck's foot, 45cm (1½ft); *H. h.* 'Erecta', dwarf non-climber with short upright stems, arrow-shaped leaves, 1m (3ft); *H. h.* 'Glacier', leaves marbled silver-grey, narrow white margins, the best with this colour blend, 2m (6½ft); *H. h.* 'Goldchild', young leaves bright green, pale green centres, gold-yellow margins, later blue-green, grey-green with cream-yellow edges, 1m (3ft); *H. h.* 'Green Ripple', leaves mid-green with conspicuous veins, wavy margins, 2m (6½ft); *H. h.* 'Ivalace', small, compact, good as limited ground cover, leaves bright green, wavy margins, pale green veining, 1m (3ft); *H. h.* 'Kolibri', leaves dark green, speckled cream-white, 45cm (1½ft); *H. h.* 'Little Diamond', bushy, dwarf, diamond-shaped leaves, mottled silver, grey and green, cream margins, 30cm (1ft); *H. h.* 'Oro di Bogliasco' (syn. *H. h.* 'Goldheart'), leaves green with yellow centres, a strong, vigorous plant but reverted green-leaved shoots must be cut out, 8m (25ft); *H. h.* 'Parsley Crested' (syn. *H. h.* 'Cristata'), leaves puckered, light green, sometimes rounded, 1.2m (4ft); *H. h.* 'Sagittifolia', leaves dark green, arrow-shaped, deeply cut, 1.2m (4ft); *H. h.* 'Spetchley', good as rock garden plant and in containers, leaves tiny, dark green, arrow-shaped, 15cm (6in); *H. h.* 'Très Coupé', leaves arrow-shaped, deep green, deeply lobed, 1m (3ft); *H. hibernica*, good ground cover, mid-green leaves, slightly heart-shaped, 10m (33ft).

below *Hedera helix* 'Buttercup'. With the availability of so many variegated ivies, this older yellow variety has unjustifiably been forgotten.

Helenium Asteraceae

Annuals, biennials and perennials; all those I recommend here are herbaceous perennials. Barely hardy to moderately hardy and good plants for sunny borders; good for cutting. Oval to inversely lance-shaped, mid-green leaves. Daisy-like spice-scented flowers with prominent centres, yellow, bronze, red or orange, with yellow or brown centres, are among the most welcome sights of my autumn borders. Require fertile, moist, well-drained soil in full sun. Take basal cuttings of named varieties in spring or divide in autumn. ❀ *H. autumnale*, mid-green, lance-shaped leaves, yellow flowers with brown centres, late summer to mid-autumn, 1.2m-1.5m/45cm (4-5ft/1½ft); *H.* 'Butterpat', rich yellow, late summer to early autumn, 1m/30cm (3ft/1ft); *H.* 'Coppelia', rich orange and copper-red flowers, 1m/30cm (3ft/1ft); *H. hoopesii*, clump-forming, grey-green lance-shaped basal leaves, yellow or orange flowers, yellow-brown centres, in early summer, 1m/45cm (3ft/1½ft); *H.* 'Moerheim Beauty', bronze or crimson flowers, dark brown centres, early to late summer, 90cm/60cm (3ft/2ft); *H.* 'Pumilum Magnificum', erect, gold-yellow flowers, yellow-brown centres, late summer to mid-autumn, 90cm/60cm (3ft/2ft); *H.* 'Rotgold' (syn 'Red and Gold'), red and yellow bicoloured flowers, brown centres, late summer to early autumn, 1.2m/60cm (4ft/2ft); *H.* 'The Bishop', clear yellow flowers, late summer, 1m/30cm (3ft/1ft); *H.* 'Waldtraut', light orange-brown flowers with brown centres, late summer to early autumn, 80-100cm/60cm (2½-3ft/2ft); *H.* 'Wyndley', yellow and copper flowers, dark brown-orange centres, early to late summer, 80-100cm/60cm (2½-3ft/2ft).

Helianthemum *Rock Rose* Cistaceae

Small evergreen or semi-evergreen shrubs. Barely hardy to moderately hardy. Suitable for rock gardens and edging sunny borders. Small oval leaves, sometimes with rolled margins, four- to five-petalled flowers, white and a range of pinks, reds, yellows, with prominent stamens, usually yellow. Requires well-drained soil in full sun, protected from dry winds. No routine pruning. Sow seed in a cold-frame in autumn or winter, or take semi-ripe cuttings in mid-summer. The following recommended varieties are low-growing and mat-forming, 20-40cm (8in-1½ft). ❀ *H.* 'Amy Baring', grey-green leaves, yellow flowers with orange centres; *H.* 'Ben Ledi', dark green leaves, rich rose flowers; *H.* 'Boughton Double Primrose', dark green leaves, double primrose-yellow flowers; *H.* 'Cerise Queen', dark green leaves, double, cerise-red flowers; *H.* 'Fire Dragon', grey-green leaves, bright orange-scarlet flowers; *H.* 'Georgeham', pink and yellow flowers; *H.* 'Henfield Brilliant', grey-green leaves, brick-red flowers; *H.* 'Jubilee', double primrose-yellow flowers; *H.* 'Mrs D W Earle', dark green leaves, double red flowers; *H.* 'Praecox', silver-grey leaves, lemon-yellow flowers; *H.* 'Raspberry Ripple', dark green leaves, rich red-and-pink flowers edged with white; *H.* 'Rhodanthe Carneum', silver-grey leaves, carmine-pink flowers with orange centres; *H.* 'Rose of Leeswood', deep green leaves, double pink flowers; *H.* 'The Bride', silver-grey leaves, cream flowers; *H.* 'Wisley Primrose', grey-green leaves, primrose-yellow flowers.

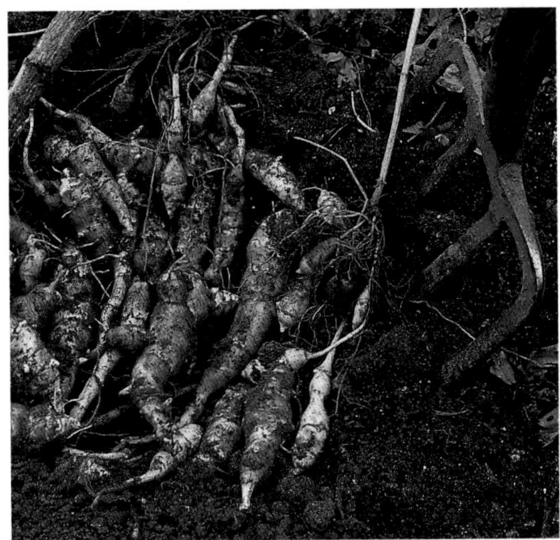

left Jerusalem artichoke 'Fuseau'. A more or less smooth variety that has made peeling these curious vegetables so much less of a chore.

Helianthus *Sunflower, Jerusalem Artichoke* Asteraceae

Medium/large hardy annuals and herbaceous ornamental perennials and also one vegetable. Large, bristly, simple leaves, contact with which may irritate the skin. Large daisy-like flowers, usually yellow but also red, orange or cream, with yellow, brown or purple centres, singly or in clusters. Grows well in any moderately fertile, well-drained soil, in full sun or partial shade. Tolerates dry soil but best in moist conditions. Tall species need support in windy locations and to obtain truly giant specimens, liquid feeding is essential. Sow seed of annuals in growing positions in mid-spring; sow perennials in a cold-frame in spring, divide established plants in early spring or late autumn, or take basal cuttings in spring.

❀ **Annual**: *H. annuus* (Sunflower), 'Giant Single', heart-shaped leaves, yellow flowers with brown or purple centres, 5m (16ft) or more; 'Music Box', dwarf, branching, cream, yellow and red flowers, some bicoloured, with black centres, 70cm (2¼ft); 'Pacino', dwarf, branching, single gold-yellow flowers, 60cm (2ft); 'Russian Giant', one of the tallest, yellow flowers, 5m (16ft) or more; 'Sunbeam' F 1, early, yellow flowers with green centres, 'Sungold' (syn. 'Soleil d'Or'), large double yellow; 'Teddy Bear', dwarf, compact, double yellow, 60cm (2ft); 'Velvet Queen', dark velvet-red flowers, darker centres, late summer, 1.5m (5ft).

Perennial: *H.* 'Monarch', semi-double gold flowers with yellow-brown centres, quilled petals, early to mid-autumn; *H. decapetalus* 'Triomphe de Gand', lance-shaped to oval mid-green leaves, hairy beneath, deep gold-yellow flowers with quilled centres, 1.5m (5ft); *H.* 'Capenoch Star'. lemon-yellow flowers, quilled, slightly darker yellow centres, 1.5m (5ft); *H.* 'Loddon Gold', gold-yellow double flowers, 1.5m (5ft); *H.* 'Lemon Queen', rhizomatous, oval dark green leaves with prominent veining, pale yellow flowers, darker centres, late summer to mid-autumn, 1.7m (5½ft); *H. salicifolius* 'Lemon Queen', narrow, willow-like leaves, loose clusters of yellow flowers in early autumn, 2.5m (8ft).

Jerusalem artichoke (*H. tuberosus*)

Tuberous perennial. Hardy. The edible tuber is knobbly in most varieties, with a light brown to cream-white skin and white flesh. Tall plant with stiff stems, bright green leaves that die down in winter, sometimes small sunflowers form. Tubers are harvested after the top growth has died down, but can remain in the ground until needed and the plants can be used as a windbreak. Requires fertile soil. *H. t.* 'Dwarf Sunray', crisp, tender flesh, peeling unnecessary, 1.5-2.1m (5-6½ft); *H. t.* 'Fuseau', long smooth tubers, easily peeled; preparing the old knobbly varieties is a real chore.

below *Helichrysum milfordiae. Helichrysum* is a very diverse genus and the hot fiery bedding varieties contrast markedly with the cool charm of this mat-forming perennial.

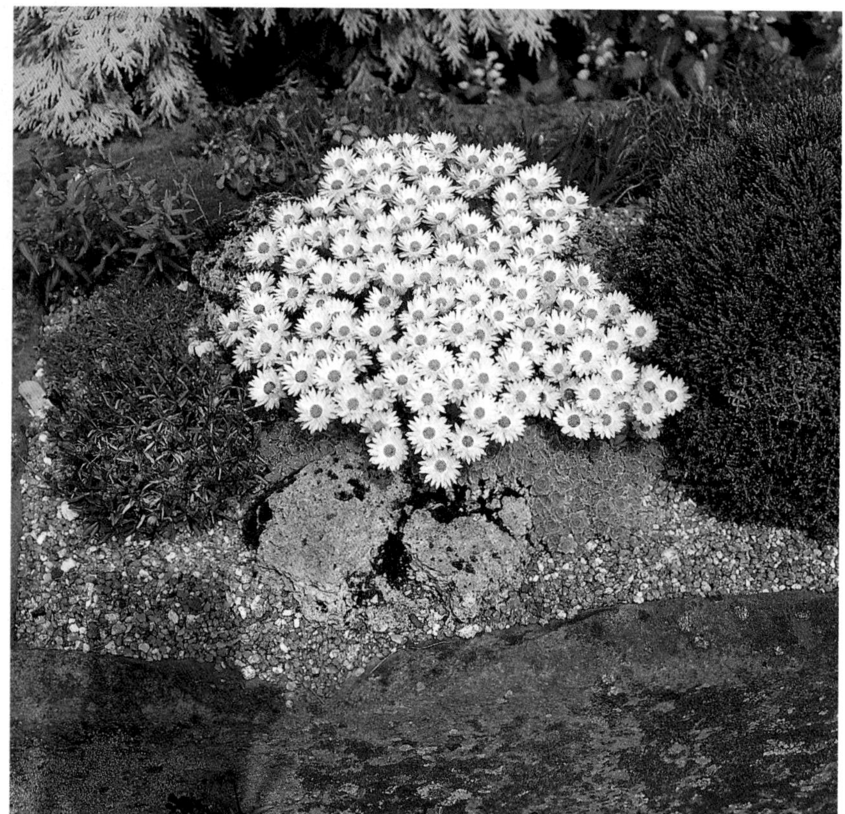

Helichrysum Asteraceae

Annuals, evergreen or herbaceous perennials, evergreen sub-shrubs or shrubs. Tender to hardy. Suitable for rock gardens, annual beds and containers; flowers of some are very good for drying. Silver-green leaves in basal rosettes, sometimes aromatic. Flowers daisy-like, with papery bracts, singly or in clusters, in a range of colours. Requires well-drained soil in full sun. Sow seed in warmth in early spring or in flowering position in mid-spring, take semi-ripe cuttings in summer or divide established perennials in spring. ❀ *H. bellidioides*, carpeting evergreen sub-shrub, tiny oval or round leaves, dark green, silver-white undersides, brilliant white flowers late spring to summer, 15cm/60cm (6in/2ft); *H. bracteatum* (syn. *Bracteantha bracteata*) (Strawflower), short-lived deciduous perennial grown as an annual, lance-shaped grey-green leaves, papery bright white, yellow, red or pink flowers, 1-1.5m/3m (3-5ft/10ft); *H. b.* 'Bright Bikini', double flowers, white and in shades or pink, red, orange, yellow, 30cm (1ft); *H. b.* 'Hot Bikini', dwarf, abundant gold and scarlet flowers, mid-summer to late autumn, 30cm (1ft); *H. b.* 'Pastel', soft shades of pink, apricot, yellow and salmon-pink, 1m (3ft); *H. italicum*, hardy evergreen sub-shrub, narrow grey-white leaves with a strong curry fragrance on woolly stems, clusters of small mustard-yellow flowers summer to autumn, 60cm/1m (2ft/3ft); *H. i.* ssp. *microphyllum*, dwarf, small green-and-silver leaves, spicy fragrance, 20cm (8in); *H. milfordiae*, mat-forming evergreen perennial, barely hardy, rosettes of silver leaves, white flowers with crimson bracts, early summer, 5-10cm/15-30cm (2-4in/6in-1ft); *H. petiolare* (syn. *H. petiolatum*), tender, mound-forming or trailing, evergreen sub-shrub, invaluable as foliage in hanging baskets and other containers, oval, woolly grey leaves, clusters of insignificant flowers cream-white, mid-summer to late autumn, 50cm/2m (1¾ft/6½ft); *H. splendidum*, compact evergreen sub-shrub, grey oblong leaves, woolly white shoots, clusters of tiny yellow flowers in mid-summer, 1.2m/1.2m (4ft/4ft).

Helictotrichon *Oatgrass* Poaceae

Medium to large deciduous/evergreen perennial grasses. Moderately hardy. Flat, linear, ribbed or folded mid- to light green leaves, oblong spikelets in erect panicles. Sow seed in a cold-frame in spring or divide established plants in spring. ❀ *H. sempervirens*, clump-forming, evergreen, arching blue-green leaves, oat-like blue-green plumes. early to mid-summer, 1.4m/60cm (4¾ft/2ft).

Heliotropium

Heliotrope, Cherry Pie Boraginaceae

Half-hardy annuals, evergreen shrubs and sub-shrubs. Extensively used in Victorian gardens as bedding plants and returning to popularity. Simple, wrinkled, hairy, mostly entire leaves, fragrant tiny tubular flowers, blue, purple, or white, in summer. Sow seed in warmth in spring, take semi-ripe or stem-tip cuttings in summer. ❀ *H. arborescens*, evergreen shrub usually grown as an annual; *H. a.* 'Chatsworth', leathery, elliptic or oval green leaves, clusters of tiny, bright, deep purple flowers, 1.2m/45cm (4ft/2ft); *H. a.* 'Dwarf Marine', wrinkled dark green leaves, very fragrant, deep purple flowers, 30cm (1ft); *H. a.* 'Marine', similar to 'Dwarf Marine', flowers deep violet-blue, 45cm (1½ft); *H.* 'Princess Marina', violet-green, crinkly leaves, fragrant, rich purple flowers, 60cm/45cm (2ft/1½ft); *H.* 'White Lady', buds flushed pink, opening to white flowers, 30cm (1ft).

Helipterum *Strawflower* Asteraceae

Small half-hardy annuals. Smooth or hairy linear leaves, papery daisy-like flowers, in summer, excellent for drying. Sow seeds in flowering positions or in warmth in mid-spring. ❀ *H. humboldtianum*, hairy, pale silver-grey, almost white leaves, gold-yellow flowers, mid- to late summer, 40cm/20cm (1½ft/8in); *H. roseum* 'Goliath', grey-green, pointed leaves, dark semi-double cerise flowers with dark brown-yellow centres, mid- to late summer, 45cm/25cm (1½ft/10in).

Helleborus Ranunculaceae

Medium hardy evergreen or deciduous more or less rhizomatous ornamentals. Leathery light to dark green, divided leaves, cup- or saucer-shaped flowers, white, green or purple, some spotted, late winter to mid-spring. Sap may irritate skin; all parts are toxic if eaten. Require moist, fertile soil enriched with humus, in dappled shade or full sun; most grow best in neutral to alkaline soil, a few prefer acidic conditions. Hellebores have become among the most valued and important of garden perennials. Sow ripe seed in a cold-frame or divide in early spring or late summer. ❀ *H. argutifolius* (syn. *H. corsicus*) slightly prickly, leathery dark green leaves, apple green cup-shaped flowers in clusters, midwinter to spring, 1.2m/90cm (4ft/3ft); *H. foetidus*, evergreen, dark green or grey-green leaves, deeply divided, clusters of pendent, green, cup-shaped flowers edged with purple, faintly unpleasant scent but shouldn't detract from an excellent plant, spring, 75cm/ 60cm (2½ft/2ft); *H. f.* Wester Flisk Group, stems, leaves and flower stalks strikingly flushed red; *H. lividus*, fairly hardy, mid-green leaves marbled pale green, purple beneath, bowl-shaped cream-green flowers, flushed pink-purple, mid-winter, *H. niger* (Christmas Rose), evergreen dark green leaves, saucer-shaped pendent flowers, white flushed pink with age, protruding stamens, early winter to early spring, some strains do flower at Christmas, 30cm/45cm (1ft/1½ft); *H. n.* 'Potter's Wheel', large, white flowers with green centres; *H. orientalis* (Lenten Rose), very variable, hairy, sometimes hairless, perennial, leathery dark green basal leaves, saucer-shaped white to green-cream flowers, 45cm/45cm (1½ft/1½ft); *H. o.* 'Pink', pink flowers; *H. o.* "purple", purple flowers, *H. o.* "white", white flowers; *H. o.* ssp. *guttatus*, white or cream flowers, spotted red-purple. *H.* x *sternii*, clump-forming, entire to spiny leaves, three lobed, cream-white flowers with pink-purple veining, late winter to early spring, 30cm/30cm (1ft/1ft); *H.* x *s.* Blackthorn Group, grey-green leaves with bold veining, green flowers stained pink or purple; *H. torquatus*, clump-forming deciduous, mid-green leaves, violet-purple, saucer-shaped dark-veined flowers. sometimes green inside, appear before leaves, midwinter to early spring, 20-40cm/30cm (8in-1½ft/1ft); *H. viridis*, clump-forming,

left *Heliotropium* 'Princess Marina'. The gardeners of the 19th century loved these plants; perhaps those of the 21st century will similarly appreciate their merits.

above *Helleborus foetidus* Wester Flisk Group. A startling plant for those gardeners familiar with the native green form of this valuable winter perennial.

above *Helleborus viridis.* another very good advertisement for native plants although one I think with a slightly sinister feel.

right *Hemerocallis fulva* 'Green Kwanzo'. There are now so many Day Lily varieties but I find this one of the more charming.

deciduous, dark green basal leaves, clusters of saucer-shaped pendent green flowers, spring, 20-40cm/ 45cm (8in-1½ft/1½ft).

Hemerocallis

Day Lily Hemerocallidaceae

Small/medium evergreen, semi-evergreen and herbaceous perennials. Most moderately hardy, a few barely hardy. Suitable for mixed and herbaceous borders, wild and coastal gardens, smaller species for containers. Some, especially the older varieties, can be very invasive. Leaves strap-shaped, arching mid- to dark green. Flowers mainly trumpet- or lily-shaped, some oval, double, ruffled, or spider-shaped, in a variety of colours that has increased greatly in recent years, including cream-white, yellow, orange, purple, very dark red-black. Most last individually for only a day but are produced over relatively long periods and appear to hang above the border on their thin but tough stems. Require fertile, well-drained soil in full sun, a few preferring some shade. Divide established plants in autumn or spring, evergreen species in spring. The species and varieties listed below are herbaceous perennials.

❀ *H.* 'Anzac', trumpet-shaped, rich red with orange stripes, 76cm (2½ft); *H.* 'Black Magic', star-shaped, mahogany-red, 1m (3ft); *H.* 'Bonanza', trumpet-shaped, pale orange-yellow flowers with brown centres, 85cm (2¾ft); *H.* 'Burning Daylight', flaring, ruffled flowers, rich orange, slightly flushed crimson, 75cm (2½ft); *H.* 'Cartwheels', open trumpet-shaped, glowing orange, 75cm (2½ft); *H.* 'Catherine Woodbery', wide, lightly ruffled, pale lavender-pink, 75cm (2½ft); *H.* 'Cherry Cheeks', deep pink, tinted bright pink, white midribs, yellow throat, black anthers, 1m (3ft); *H.* 'Chicago Sunrise', semi-evergreen, gold-yellow, round, ruffled, green throat, 65cm (2¼ft); *H.* 'Corky', lily-shaped, pale yellow sepals, mahogany-brown on petal backs, flowers open two days, 85cm (2¾ft); *H.* 'Cream Drop', ruffled, trumpet-shaped, cream-yellow, chartreuse throat, 43cm (1½ft); *H. dumortieri*, star-shaped, red-brown buds open to orange-yellow flowers, 50cm/45cm (1¾ft/1½ft); *H.* 'Frans Hals', rust-red, orange sepals, cream midribs, 60cm (2ft); *H.* 'Gentle Shepherd', semi-evergreen, slightly tender, round, ruffled, cream-white flowers, 73cm (28in); *H.* 'Golden Chimes', red-brown buds opening to rich yellow bell-shaped flowers, 61cm (2ft); *H.* 'Hyperion', narrow trumpet-shaped, fragrant, lemon-yellow, 90cm (3ft); *H. fulva* (syn. *H. lilioasphodelus*), semi-evergreen, rhizomatous, double tawny-orange flowers, 60-75cm (2-2½ft); *H. f.* 'Green Kwanzo', as the species, with red-eye zone; *H. f.* 'Kwanzo Variegata', leaves have white margins; *H.* 'Little Wine Cup', trumpet-shaped, wine-red, chartreuse throats, 50cm (1¾ft); *H.* 'Luxury Lace', frilly star-shaped pink-lavender, green throat, 80cm (21/2ft); *H.* 'Marion Vaughn', very fragrant, lily-shaped, pale lemon-yellow, 84cm (2¾ft); *H.* 'Michele Coe', oval, pale apricot, lavender-pink midribs, 1m (3ft); *H.* 'Pink Damask', star-shaped, rose-pink, tinged buff, yel-

low throat, cream-pink midribs, 95cm (3ft); *H.* 'Sammy Russell', trumpet-shaped, dark red, 70cm (2¼ft); *H.* 'Stafford', tapering lily-shaped, scarlet, green-yellow throat, 70cm (2¼ft); *H.* 'Stella de Oro', fragrant, bell-shaped, brassy yellow, 28cm (10½in); *H.* 'Stoke Poges', pink, deeper pink eye zone 60cm (2ft); *H.* 'Summer Wine', trumpet-shaped, light wine-red, chartreuse throat, 60cm (2ft); *H.* 'Whichford', trumpet-shaped, fragrant, delicate yellow, green throat, 70cm (2¼ft).

Hepatica Ranunculaceae

Small herbaceous/evergreen perennials. Moderately hardy. Ideal for shady woodland gardens and among the loveliest early season woodland plants. Simple toothed, kidney-shaped dark green leaves, sometimes marbled silver-white beneath; disappear by early summer. Star-shaped or bowl-shaped flowers, late winter to early spring. Sow ripe seed in an open-frame or divide established plants in spring. ❀ *H. acutiloba*, evergreen, dark green leaves, lavender-blue, sometimes pink or white flowers, late winter to early spring, 8cm/15cm (3in/6in); *H. nobilis* (syn. *H. triloba*), evergreen, kidney-shaped leaves, sometimes with grey, pink or dark green marbling and purple beneath, white, purple, blue or pink flowers, single, sometimes double, late winter to early spring, 10cm/15cm (4in/6in); *H. transsilvanica* (syn. *H. angulosa*), pale green, hairy leaves with scalloped edges, bowl-shaped very pale pink, blue or white flowers, early spring, 15cm/20cm (6in/8in).

Hermodactylus
Snake's Head Iris Iridaceae

Tuberous ornamental. Moderately hardy. Linear leaves, solitary, fragrant, iris-like flowers in spring, Divide established plants in early summer. ❀ *H. tuberosus* (syn. *Iris tuberosa*), grey-green or blue-green leaves, fragrant, strikingly unusual green-yellow flowers, black-brown outer petals, 20-40cm/5cm (8in-1½ft/2in).

Hesperis
Sweet Rocket, Dame's Violet Brassicaceae

Medium hardy annuals and hardy herbaceous short-lived perennials. Narrow mid-green leaves, fragrant white, pink and purple flowers, very attractive to butterflies, spring or summer. Sow seed in flowering positions in spring or divide established plants in spring. ❀ *H. matronalis*, perennial, sometimes grown as a biennial, rosettes of elliptic to oval or oblong, toothed leaves, dark green, clusters of lilac or white flowers, sometimes pale lilac or white, late spring to mid-summer, 90cm/45cm (3ft/2ft); *H. m. albiflora*, white flowers; *H. m.* var. *a.* 'Alba Plena', double white flowers; *H. m.* 'Lilacina Flore Pleno', double lilac flowers.

above *Hermodactylus tuberosus*. An excellent eye-catching and readily naturalising bulb that inevitably arouses comment from those unfamiliar with it.

Heuchera *Alum Root* Saxifragaceae

Small/medium evergreen and semi-evergreen perennials. Barely hardy to hardy. Make excellent ground cover in borders or light woodland gardens, flowers good for cutting. Clumps or mounds of heart-shaped, lobed or scalloped leaves, sometimes toothed. Clusters of small tubular or bell-shaped flowers, sometimes petal-less, with prominent calyces. Thrive in fertile, well-drained neutral soil, in full sun or partial shade and tolerant of deep shade if given moist conditions. Sow seed in a cold-frame in spring, or divide established plants in autumn. ❀ *H. americana*, mound-forming, rosettes of oval to heart-shaped,

above *Heuchera micrantha* 'Palace Purple'. What heucheras lack in spectacular flowers, they make up for in lovely foliage colours.

right *Hibiscus syriacus* 'Oiseau Bleu' is arguably the best of all the hardy forms of *Hibiscus* and comes as a revelation to people who thought they were all tender.

glossy, leathery leaves, marbled and veined brown at first, later deep green flushed copper-green, brown-green flowers in early summer, 45cm/30cm (1½ft/1ft); *H. cylindrica* 'Greenfinch', dark green, heart-shaped leaves, olive-green flowers on tall stems, early to mid-summer, 90cm/60cm (3ft/2ft); *H.* 'Green Ivory', clump-forming, rounded, kidney-shaped, lobed, toothed leaves, dark green marbled pale green, abundant cream, green tipped, bell-shaped flowers in early summer, 75cm/75cm (2½ft/2½ft); *H.* 'Leuchtkäfer' (syn. *H.* 'Firefly'), mat-forming, rounded leaves, fragrant, scarlet flowers, 75cm/30cm (2½ft/1ft); *H. micrantha* var. *diversifolia* 'Palace Purple', clump-forming, copper-purple, heart-shaped, irregularly lobed leaves with a metallic sheen, light magenta-pink beneath, sprays of feathery, tiny white flowers on wiry dark stems, followed by rose-bronze seedpods, summer to autumn, probably the best variety overall, 90cm/45cm (3ft/1½ft); *H.* 'Pewter Moon', purple leaves beautifully marbled silver-grey, bell-shaped pale pink flowers, 40cm/30cm (1½ft/1ft); *H.* 'Rachel', clump-forming, round or kidney-shaped, dark green leaves flushed purple, sprays of coral-pink, bell-shaped flowers, 30cm/30cm (1ft/1ft); *H.* 'Snow Storm', round, lobed, dark green leaves marbled silver-white, flushed pink in winter, cerise bell-shaped flowers, 45cm/30cm (1½ft/1ft).

x Heucherella — Saxifragaceae

Small evergreen perennials. Moderately hardy. Oval, lobed, sometimes hairy green leaves, with conspicuous veining, flushed brown when young, red-brown in autumn. Clusters of bell-shaped white or pink flowers, spring to autumn. Remove off-sets in autumn or divide established plants in spring. ❀ *H. alba* 'Bridget Bloom', clump-forming, toothed, mid-green lobed leaves, marbled brown along veins, clusters of tiny white flowers with pink calyces, 40cm/30cm (1½ft/1ft); *H. a.* 'Rosalie', light green lobed leaves, marbled tan, fluffy heads of pink flowers, mid to late spring; *H. tiarelloides*, stoloniferous, rounded, toothed lobed light green leaves, sometimes marbled brown when young, tiny pink flowers mid-spring to early summer, 45cm/45cm (1½ft/1½ft).

x Hibanobambusa — Poaceae

Bamboo. Moderately hardy. Suitable for borders as an isolated specimen or for growing in a large container if repotted every two to three years. Divide established plants in spring. ❀ *H. tranquillans* 'Shiroshima', broad green leaves striped pale yellow at first, later white, thick culms (stems), 3m/1m (10ft/3ft).

Hibiscus — Malvaceae

Half-hardy annuals, herbaceous perennials and deciduous/evergreen shrubs or small trees. Tender to moderately hardy. Hardier species and varieties are suitable for shrub, herbaceous or mixed borders but shouldn't be confused with the tender forms of *H. rosa-sinensis* sold as houseplants. Toothed, grey-

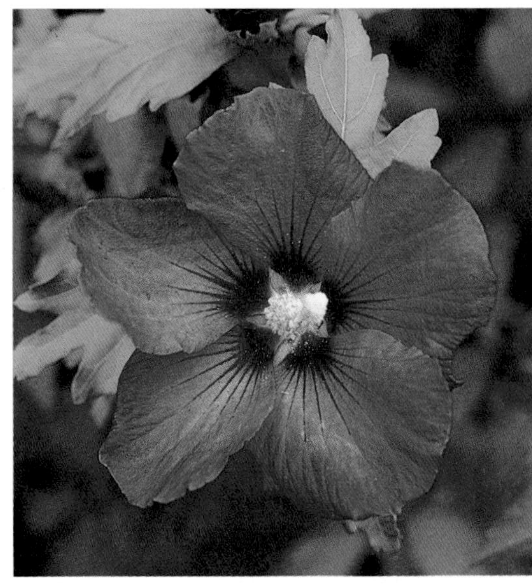

green leaves, usually with good autumn colour. Trumpet-shaped, usually single flowers, sometimes semi-double or strikingly double, in yellow, orange, white and shades of red, pink, blue and mauve, sometimes with darker centres. Requires light, rich, well-drained soil in full sun or light shade. No routine pruning. Sow seed in warmth in late winter (annuals), take semi-ripe cuttings in late summer.

Shrubs

H. syriacus 'Ardens', deciduous, deep green, oval, toothed leaves, double rose flowers with violet tints, 3m/2m (10ft/6½ft); *H. s.* 'Diana', pale green lobed leaves, white flowers with crumpled margins, 3m/2m (10ft/6½ft); *H. s.* 'Hamabo', pale pink flowers with crimson centres, mid-summer to mid-autumn, 3m/2m (10ft/6½ft); *H. s.*'Meehanii', low-growing, leaves with cream-yellow margins, lavender flowers with maroon centres, 3m/2m (10ft/6½ft); *H. s.* 'Oiseau Bleu' (syn. 'Blue Bird'), single violet-blue flowers with darker centres, mid- to late summer, a superb variety, 3m/2m (10ft/6½ft); *H. s.* 'Pink Giant', pink flowers with deep red centres; *H. s.* 'William R Smith', white flowers with crinkled petals; *H. s.* 'Woodbridge', rose-crimson flowers with darker throat, mid-summer to mid-autumn.

Types grown as half-hardy annuals

H. grandiflora 'Rose Mallow' pink flowers, with darker spot at base, 50cm (13/4ft); *H. manihot* 'Cream Cup', narrow, toothed lobed leaves, cream flowers with dark maroon centres, late summer until autumn, 2-2.5m (6½ft-8ft); *H. moscheutos* 'Disco Belle', dwarf, pink, red and white flowers, 50cm (1¾ft); *H. trionum* 'Vanilla Ice', erect, toothed, deeply divided leaves, cream flowers with chocolate centres, followed by bladder-like seed capsules, 75cm/60cm (2½ft/2ft); *H. t.* 'Simply Love', dwarf, bell-shaped cream-yellow flowers with darker centres, followed by seed capsules, 50cm (1¾ft); *H. t.* 'Sunny Day', lemon-yellow flowers with dark purple centres, late summer to early autumn, 40cm (1½ft).

Hieracium *Hawkweed* Asteraceae

Small hardy herbaceous or evergreen perennials, including some common, though not serious, weeds. Moderately hardy. Suitable for wild flower gardens, some for rock gardens; enticingly pretty but some are very invasive. Rosettes of lance-shaped to linear or more or less oval, sometimes toothed, pale to dark green, dandelion-like flowers followed by fluffy seedheads. Sow seeds in an open-frame in autumn or spring, or divide established plants. ❀ *H. lanatum* (syn. *H. welwitschii*), clump-forming, grey-green, oval to lance-shaped woolly leaves with white margins, deep yellow flowers, 45cm/20cm (1½ft/8in); *H. maculatum*, evergreen, toothed, oblong deep leaves marked with purple, clusters of yellow flowers, 40cm/30cm (1½ft/1ft); *H. villosum*, evergreen, oblong, woolly, silver-white leaves, sulphur yellow flowers, 30cm/20cm (1ft/8in).

Himalayacalamus Poaceae

Large perennial bamboo. Barely hardy. Linear blue-green leaves on glossy, sometimes striped, canes. Divide in early spring. ❀ *H. falconeri* (syn. *Arundinaria falconeri*), clump-forming, olive-green canes, blue-green leaves, purple patterning around nodes of culms (stems), outer canes arching, 9m (30ft); *H. f.* 'Damarapa', purple mottling, pink and yellow streaks on culms.

below *Himalayacalamus falconeri* 'Damarapa'. Most bamboos have had their names changed in recent years so this may sound unfamiliar but it remains one of the best varieties for milder gardens.

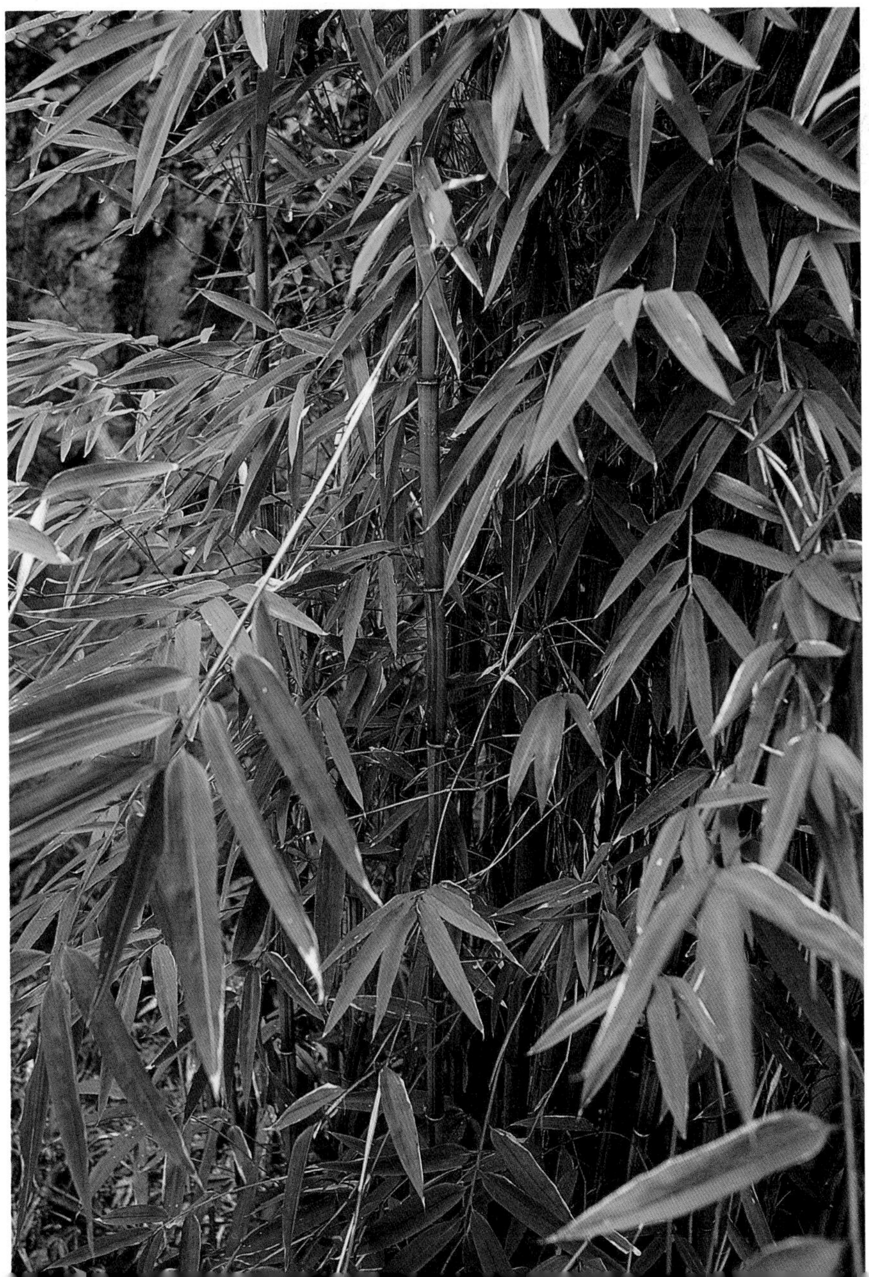

Hippocrepis Papilionaceae

Annuals, perennials and shrubs. Moderately hardy. Unspectacular but pretty plants for rock and wild gardens. Pinnate light to mid-green leaves, small pea-like flowers. Sow seed in a cold-frame in spring or autumn, take cuttings of non-flowering shoots in summer. ❀ *H. comosa* (syn. *Coronilla comosa*), creeping perennial, mid-green leaves, clusters of lemon-yellow flowers, 40cm/40cm (1½ft/1½ft); *H. emerus* (syn. *Coronilla emerus*), deciduous shrub, small bright green leaves, clusters of fragrant flowers, yellow marked brown, early to mid-summer, followed by long brown seedpods, 1.2m (4ft).

right *Hippophae rhamnoides*. A familiar enough native shrub in its natural sand-dune habitat but not seen as commonly as it might be in gardens.

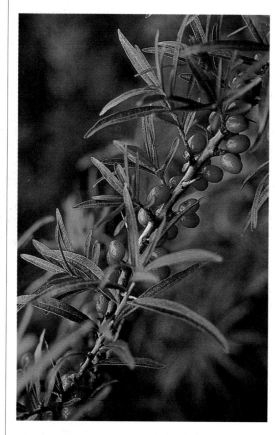

Hippophae *Sea Buckthorn* Elaeagnaceae

Large deciduous shrubs and small trees. Moderately hardy. Suitable for mixed or shrub borders, ideal for informal hedging in coastal gardens but can be grown inland too. Linear or linear to oblong leaves, variously mid-green, grey-green or silver-green. Inconspicuous yellow-green male and female flowers produced on separate plants, followed on female plants by attractive orange fruits in autumn and winter. No routine pruning. Sow seed in an open-frame when ripe or in spring, take semi-ripe cuttings in summer, hardwood cuttings in late autumn, or layer in autumn. ❀ *H. rhamnoides*, large shrub or small tree, linear grey-green leaves with silver to bronze scales, spiny shoots, clusters of yellow-green flowers, followed by bright orange fruits, 6m/6m (20ft/20ft).

Hoheria *Lacebark* Malvaceae

Large deciduous/evergreen shrubs or small trees. Barely hardy and in cold areas need protection from frosts and cold dry winds. Toothed, lance-shaped or oval grey-green to dark green leaves, often with metallic sheen when young. Beautiful cup-shaped, honey-scented white flowers, singly or in clusters. No routine pruning. Sow seed in a cold-frame in autumn or take semi-ripe cuttings in late summer or autumn. ❀ *H. glabrata*, deciduous tree, dark green leaves with scalloped edges, white hairs, yellow in autumn, clusters of white flowers with purple anthers, in mid-summer, 7m/1m (23ft/3ft); *H.* 'Glory of Amlwch', semi-evergreen tree, glossy toothed, oval bright green leaves, large white flowers, mid- to late summer, 7m/6m (23ft/20ft); *H. lyallii* (syn. *Plagianthus lyallii*), deciduous tree, very hairy, oval, toothed grey-green leaves, hairs white, clusters of white flowers with purple anthers, mid-summer, 7m/7m (23ft/23ft); *H. sexstylosa*, evergreen, sharply toothed, rich green leaves, lance-shaped, glossy white flowers, mid- to late summer, 8m/6m (25ft/20ft).

Holcus Poaceae

Annual and perennial grasses. Moderately hardy. Most are invasive weeds but the one I recommend here is safe. Linear, mid-green or blue-green, flat or folded, flowers in panicles, in summer. Divide in spring. ❀ *H. mollis* (Creeping Soft Grass), 'Albovariegatus', rhizomatous, green leaves striped white, open, white oblong to oval panicles, early summer, 30cm/45cm (1ft/1½ft).

Holodiscus Rosaceae

Large deciduous shrubs. Moderately hardy. Oblong to rounded, divided, lobed leaves, usually hairy, abundant small, cup-shaped cream-white flowers in feathery panicles, mid- to late summer. No routine pruning. Sow ripe seed in an open-frame, take semi-ripe cuttings in summer or layer in summer or autumn. ❀ *H. discolor* (Ocean Spray), dark green leaves, hairy beneath, sharply toothed, branching clusters of white, cream, and pale brown flowers, 4m/4m (13ft/13ft).

Hordeum *Barley* Poaceae

Small annual and perennial grasses. Moderately hardy and includes the important cereal crop. Linear mid-green or blue-green leaves, sometimes with rolled margins, feathery flower spikelets in larger panicles. Divide in spring or autumn. ❀ *H. jubatum* (Fox-Tail Barley), light green leaves, light green spikelets with long silky pendent bristles, flushed red or purple, summer, 50cm/ 30cm (1¾ft/1ft).

Hosta *Plantain Lily* Hostaceae

Small/large herbaceous perennials, most rhizomatous, some stoloniferous. Moderately hardy. Suitable for ground cover, containers, mixed and herbaceous borders and water-side plantings. Hostas have become hugely popular and important and have also come to be recognised as both diverse and very versatile; not simply plants for the water garden. Heart-shaped or lance-shaped leaves, green, blue-grey, yellow, yellow-green, often variegated, sometimes puckered, wavy-margined. Spikes of funnel- or bell-shaped flowers followed by pale brown seed capsules. Thrive in fertile, preferably, although not essentially, moist but well-drained soil in full sun or partial shade. Sow seed in a cold-frame in spring, or divide established plants in late summer or early spring. Particularly susceptible to damage by slugs and snails. ❀ *H.* 'August Moon', rounded or heart-shaped, cupped and puckered leaves, pale green at first, later gold-yellow, bell-shaped grey-white flowers, 50cm/75cm (1¾ft/2½ft); *H.* 'Big Daddy', rounded, cupped, intensely blue leaves, puckered, pale lavender-white flowers, early to mid-summer, 60cm/90cm (2ft/3ft); *H.* 'Blue Angel', arching, pointed, blue-grey, smooth leaves, slightly cupped, with wavy margins, 1m/1.2m (3ft/4ft); *H. crispula*, lance-shaped to heart-shaped leaves, mid- to dark green, with wavy margins, twisted tips, edged irregularly with white, funnel-shaped, lavender-white flowers, 75-90cm/ 50cm (2½-3ft/1¾ft); *H. fortunei*, oval, pointed, dark green leaves edged irregularly with cream at first, later white, funnel-shaped mauve flowers, 55cm/80cm (1¾ft/2½ft); *H. f.* var. *albopicta*, narrow, heart-shaped, cream-yellow leaves, dark green edges, 75-90cm/1m (2½-3ft/3ft); *H. f.* var. *a.* f. *aurea*, broad, pointed, pale yellow leaves at first, later light green, fine green veins giving a quilted effect, 60cm (2ft); *H. f.* var. *aureomarginata*, heart-shaped to oval, leathery, veined, olive-green leaves, with irregularly edged yellow to cream, 1m (3ft); *H. f.* var. *hyacinthina*, oval to heart-shaped, puckered, grey-green leaves with wavy margins, white and blue-grey beneath, violet flowers, summer, 60cm/1m (2ft/3ft); *H.* 'Francee', flat, heart-shaped, dark olive-green leaves, irregularly edged with white, lavender flowers, mid- to late summer, 60cm/1m (2ft/3ft); *H.* 'Frances Williams', (syns. *H.* 'Golden Circle', *H.* 'Eldorado'), heart-shaped, puckered, cupped blue-green leaves, irregularly edged green-yellow, bell-shaped grey-white flowers, in early summer, 60cm/1m (2ft/3ft); *H.* 'Ginko Craig', dark green, lance-shaped, flat leaves with clear white margins, funnel-shaped, deep purple to violet flowers, summer, 25cm/45cm (10in/1½ft); *H.* 'Golden Prayers', deep yellow, oval to heart-shaped leaves, smooth at first, later puckered, pale lavender to white flowers, early to mid-summer, 30cm/50cm (1ft/ 1¾ft); *H.* 'Golden Tiara', neat, compact, oval to heart-shaped green leaves, irregularly edged white, deep lavender flowers striped purple, mid- to late summer, 30cm/60cm (1ft/2ft); *H.* 'Honeybells', oval to heart-shaped, pale green leaves with prominent veining, slightly wavy margins, fragrant, bell-shaped white, sometimes

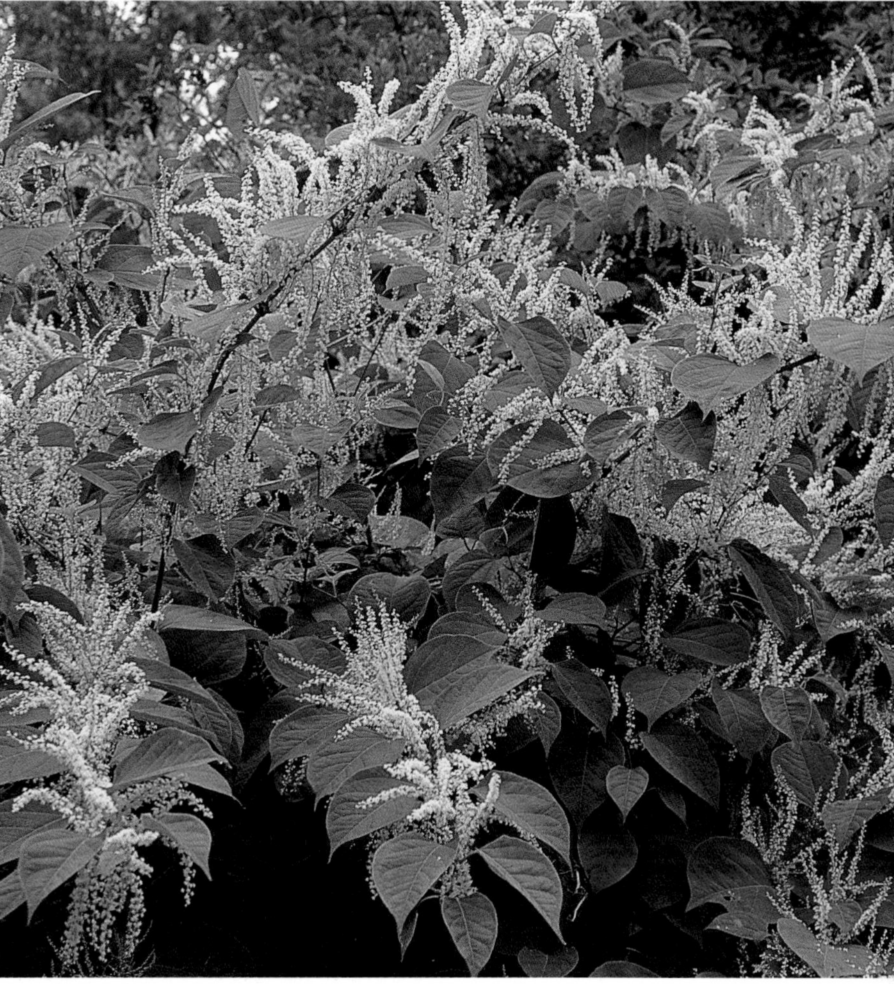

above *Holodiscus discolor.* It takes some imagination to believe that this feathery leaved shrub actually belongs to the rose family; but it is an easy and rewarding plant nonetheless.

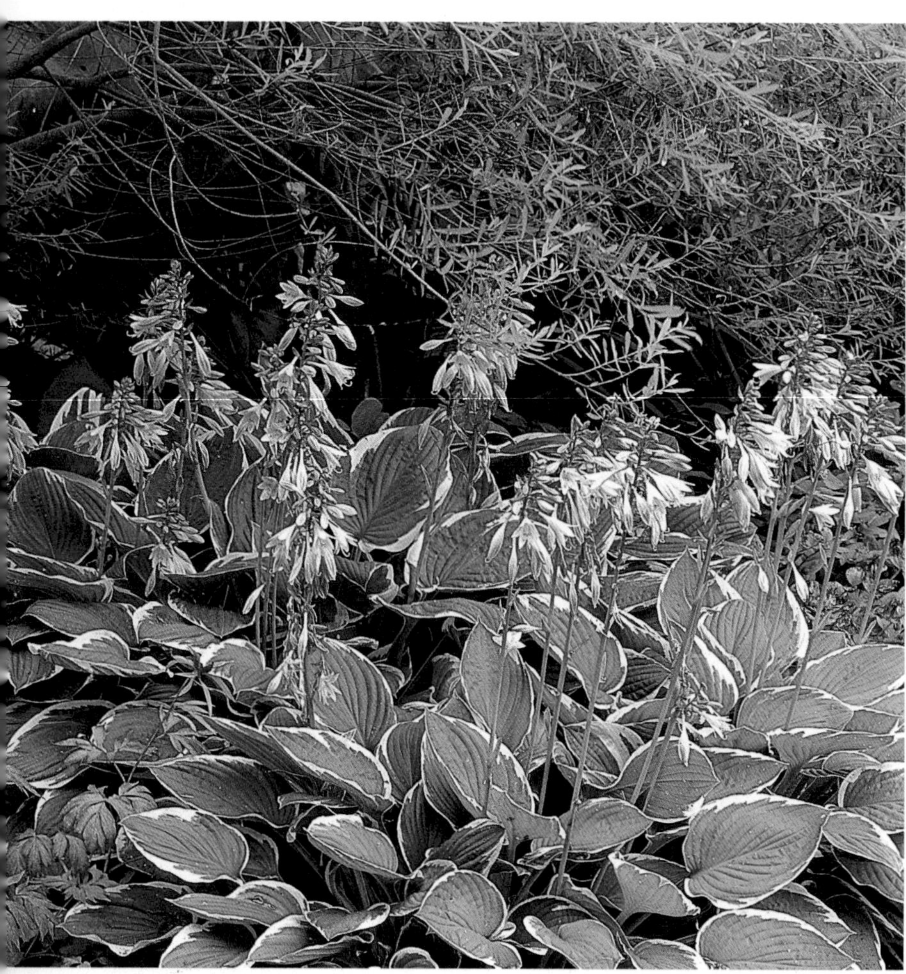

above *Hosta* 'Francee' is a variety that belies the perception of hostas as foliage plants only.

lavender-blue, flowers, 75cm/1.2m (2½ft/4ft); *H.* 'Krossa Regal', oval to lance-shaped blue-green leaves with prominent veining, bell-shaped pale lilac flowers, summer, 70cm/75cm (2¼ft/2½ft); *H. lancifolia*, narrow, lance-shaped, glossy dark green leaves, funnel-shaped deep purple flowers, late summer, 45cm/75m (1½ft/2½ft); *H.* 'Royal Standard', oval to heart-shaped, ribbed, glossy bright green leaves, funnel-shaped fragrant white flowers, late summer, 60cm/1.2m (2ft/4ft); *H.* 'Shade Fanfare', light or mid-green, heart-shaped leaves with wavy cream margins, later white, funnel-shaped lavender-blue flowers, summer, 45cm/60cm (1½ft/2ft); *H. sieboldiana*, oval to heart-shaped, cupped and puckered leaves, grey-green or blue, paler beneath, bell-shaped, flowers pale lilac-grey at first, later white tinted lilac, or white, early summer, 1m/1.2m (3ft/4ft); *H. s.* var. *elegans*, intense blue-green leaves; *H.* 'Sum and Substance', flat, heart-shaped, glossy yellow or yellow-green leaves, smooth at first, later puckered, bell-shaped pale lilac flowers, mid-summer to early autumn, 75cm/1.2m (2½ft/4ft); *H.* Tardiana Group 'Blue Moon', heart-shaped, pointed, deep blue-green leaves, puckering with age, bell-shaped, pale mauve-grey flowers, mid-summer, 10cm/30cm (4in/1ft); *H.* Tardiana Group 'Halcyon', smooth heart-shaped, silver-blue leaves, grey-lavender flowers, early to mid-summer, 50cm/1m (1¾ft/3ft); *H. tokudama*, heart-shaped to rounded, cupped, puckered, deep blue-green, bell-shaped flowers, grey-white, early to late summer, 35cm/1m (1¼ft/3ft); *H. undulata* var. *albomarginata*, matt green leaves, irregularly edged white, lavender flowers, in mid-summer, 35cm/45cm (1¼ft/1½ft); *H. u.* var. *undulata*, matt green leaves, narrow white central variegation; *H. venusta*, smooth, green leaves, oval to heart-shaped, deep lavender flowers, 8cm/10cm (3in/4in); *H.* 'Wide Brim', heart-shaped, cupped and puckered leaves, mid-green, cream-white margins, pale lavender to near white flowers, 60cm/1m (2ft/3ft); *H.* 'Zounds', heart-shaped, puckered, yellow-gold leaves, slightly twisted, sometimes striped green, pale lavender, nearly white flowers, early to mid-summer, 10cm/75cm (4in/2½ft).

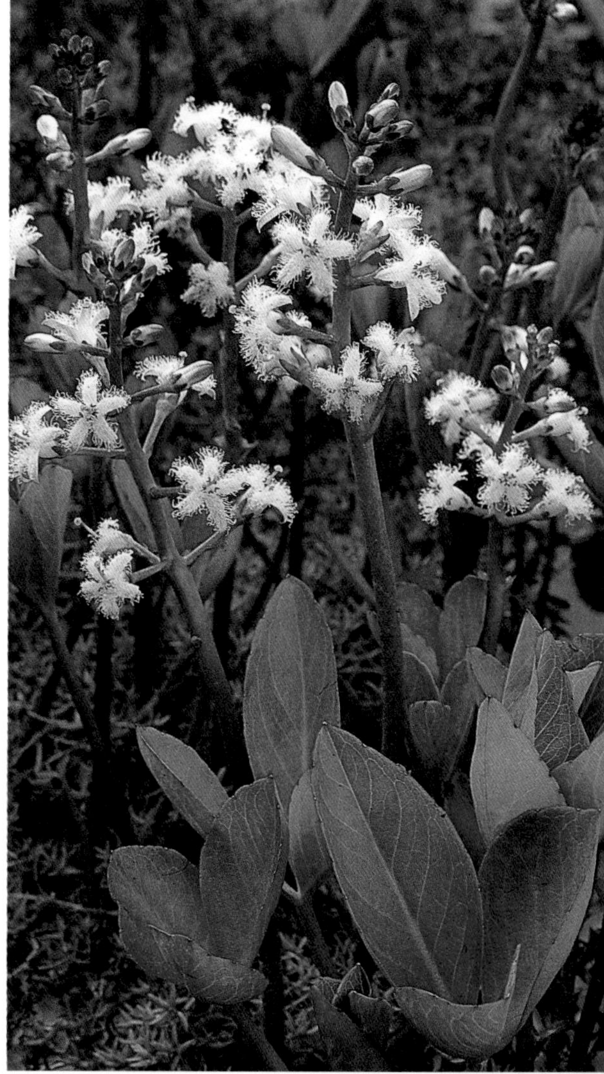

right *Hottonia palustris.* Some remarkable things float on water and this unusual member of the primula family is among them.

Hottonia Primulaceae

Small submerged or floating perennial. Barely hardy to moderately hardy. Suitable for both small and large ponds. Feathery, pinnate, light green leaves. Clusters of white to violet primrose-like flowers, spring. Sow seed in spring, take cuttings or divide established plants in spring or autumn. ❀ *H. palustris* (Water Violet), light green leaves with linear leaflets, dish-like white, pale violet or lilac flowers held above the water, in spring, 30-90cm (1ft-3ft)/indefinite.

Houttuynia Saururaceae

Small, rhizomatous ornamental. Moderately hardy Suitable as ground cover especially for water-side plantings. Sow seed in a cold-frame when ripe, take softwood cuttings or divide established plants. Can be invasive. ❀ *H. cordata*, 'Chameleon', heart-shaped blue-green leaves, with very assertive darker green, cream and red patterning, spikes of insignificant flowers surrounded by white bracts, early to mid-summer, 15-30cm (6-1ft)/indefinite; *H. c.* 'Flore Pleno', leaves patterned red and cream, double flowers.

Humulus *Hop* Cannabaceae

Large herbaceous perennial climber. Barely hardy to moderately hardy. Suitable for training over arches, fences, up trees and through hedges. Palmate, lobed leaves, male and female flowers on separate plants, the female flowers in cone-like clusters, males in panicles. Cut back to soil level in late autumn. Take softwood cuttings in spring, best forms don't come true from seed. ❀ *H. lupulus*, twining, light green toothed leaves, fragrant female flowers, green at first, pale green-yellow or light straw, 6m (20ft); *H. l.* 'Aureus', green-yellow to gold-yellow leaves, much the best garden form; *H. l.* 'Fuggle', commercial hop for flavouring beer.

Hyacinthoides *Bluebell* Hyacinthaceae

Small bulbous ornamentals. Moderately hardy. Excellent and beautiful for naturalizing in wild gardens, in grass and under trees but notoriously invasive. Strap-shaped basal leaves, erect clusters of bell-shaped blue, white or pink flowers, spring. Sow ripe seed in a cold-frame or remove and replant daughter bulbs at any time. ❀ *H. hispanica* (syns. *Endymion hispanicus, Scilla campanulata*) (Spanish Bluebell), erect, glossy, strap-shaped dark green leaves, unscented blue, pink or white flowers with reflexed tips and blue anthers, 40cm/10cm (1½ft/4in); *H. non-scripta* (syn. *Endymion non-scriptus*) (Bluebell), linear to lance-shaped, glossy, dark green leaves, pendent, fragrant, bell-shaped mid-blue flowers, sometimes white, with cream anthers, reflexed tips, 20-40cm/8cm (8-1½ft/3in).

above *Humulus lupulus* 'Aureus'. The golden hop may not flavour much beer but it is one of the best among that small group of herbaceous deciduous climbers.

Hyacinthus *Hyacinth* Hyacinthaceae

Small bulbous ornamentals. Moderately hardy. Often thought of only as indoor plants but suitable for borders and containers outdoors. Treated bulbs grown indoors can be planted later outside but the flowers will be smaller and won't of course again appear prematurely. Glossy, usually strap-shaped, dark or bright green channelled leaves. Spikes of bell-shaped flowers in spring. Thrives in moderately fertile, well-drained soil, in full sun or partial shade; container-grown plants are best in loam-based compost. Best allowed to proliferate naturally rather than dividing clumps. ❀ *H. orientalis* 'Anna Marie', linear to lance-shaped, bright green leaves, tubular to bell-shaped pale pink flowers, 20-30cm/8cm (8in-1ft/3in); *H. o.* 'Ben Nevis', double, ivory white flowers; *H. o.* 'Blue Jacket', dark blue flowers with purple veining; *H. o.* 'City of Haarlem', primrose-yellow; *H. o.* 'Delft Blue', light lilac-blue; *H. o.* 'Gipsy Queen', salmon-pink to orange; *H. o.* 'Hollyhock', double, bright red; *H. o.* 'L'Innocence', ivory-white; *H. o.* 'Ostara', deep blue; *H. o.* 'Pink Pearl', deep pink; *H. o.* 'Violet Pearl', violet-purple.

below *Hydrangea aspera* Villosa Group. Having seen most of the hydrangeas that are available to gardeners, I still return to this as the most beautiful.

Hydrangea — Hydrangeaceae

Medium/large deciduous/evergreen shrubs and climbers. Barely hardy to moderately hardy. Suitable for containers as well as shrub borders and as specimen plants; flowers are good for drying. Oval or lance-shaped, toothed leaves, inflorescences of small, insignificant fertile flowers and larger sterile flowers. Flowers of *H. macrophylla* are either of lacecap or hortensia (mophead) type, the former particularly beautiful with flattened inflorescences of fertile flowers surrounded by a few sterile ray florets, the latter with rounded inflorescences composed almost entirely of sterile flowers. Don't make the common mistake of imagining that *H. macrophylla* represents the extent of the genus *Hydrangea*. Require fairly fertile, moist, well-drained soil enriched with humus, in full sun or partial shade. In acidic soils, most forms of *H. macrophylla* will have blue flowers; in alkaline soils, the flowers turn pink, a process that can to some extent be reversed with commercial 'blueing powder' (aluminium sulphate). Sow seed in a cold-frame in spring, take semi-ripe cuttings in summer or hardwood cuttings in winter. Mopheads and lacecaps may be pruned back by one-third in late spring; routine pruning is unnecessary in other varieties. The species and varieties described below are all moderately hardy and deciduous unless otherwise stated. ❀ *H. anomala* ssp. *petiolaris* (syn. *H. petiolaris*), deciduous climber, best on a shady wall, oval, pointed, serrated, rich dark green leaves, pale green, downy beneath, yellow in autumn, attractive reddish flaking bark when mature, flat inflorescences of cream-white fertile and sterile flowers, summer, 15m (50ft); *H. arborescens* 'Annabelle', oval leaves, dark green, paler beneath, dull white, mainly fertile flowers, summer, 2.5m/2.5m (8ft/8ft); *H. aspera*, lance-shaped to oval dark green leaves, flat inflorescences of blue to white fertile flowers, with white or lilac-pink (purple on acidic soil) sterile flowers, mid-summer, tolerant of alkaline and drier soils, 3m/3m (10ft/10ft); *H. a.* ssp *sargentiana*, oval, bristly, dark green leaves, flattened inflorescences of fertile flowers, purple or blue, surrounded by white sterile flowers, often purple tinged, late summer to autumn, 3m/2.2-2.5m (10ft/6¾ft-8ft); *H. a.* Villosa Group (syn. *H. villosa*), lance-shaped to oval, felted dark green leaves, inflorescences of blue or purple-blue fertile flowers and rose or white sterile flowers, the most beautiful of all hydrangeas, 1-4m/1-4m (3-13ft/3-13ft); *H. involucrata*, oblong to oval, bristly dark green leaves, domed inflorescences of small blue fertile flowers, white, pink or blue sterile flowers, 1m/2m (3ft/6½ft); *H. i.* 'Hortensis', extremely pretty double pale pink sterile flowers; *H. macrophylla* 'Altona', mophead, glossy, oval, toothed green leaves, rich pink to dark purple-blue flowers, mid- to late summer, 1m/ 1.5m (3ft/5ft); *H. m.* 'Ami Pasquier', mophead, dark crimson or purple-blue flowers, mid- to late summer, 1.5m/2m (5ft/6½ft); *H. m.* 'Ayesha', mophead, glossy leaves, flattened, slightly fragrant, pale pink or mauve to blue, mid- to late summer, 1.5m/2m (5ft/6½ft); *H. m.* 'Europa', mophead, deep pink (purple-blue on acidic soil), in late summer, 1.8m (5¾ft); *H. m.* 'Générale Vicomtesse de Vibraye', mophead, matt, pale green leaves, bright pink flowers, crimson tinged in autumn (sky-blue on acidic soil), mid- to late summer, 1.5m (5ft); *H. m.* 'Geoffrey Chadbund', lacecap, small, red fertile flowers surrounded by brick-red sterile flowers, retains colour in acidic soils, 1.5m (5ft); *H. m.* 'Hamburg', mophead, dark pink (dark blue on acidic soil), 1.5-2m (5-6½ft); *H. m.* 'Lanarth White'. lacecap, blue or pink fertile flowers surrounded by white sterile flowers, in mid-summer, 1.5m (5ft); *H. m.* 'Madame Emile Mouillère', mophead, leaves brown-russet and crimson flushed in autumn, white inflorescences, later pink-tinged especially in full sun, mid-summer to mid-autumn, 1.8m (5¾ft); *H. m.* 'Mariesii', lacecap, bright green, pointed leaves, flattened inflorescences of blue-tinted fertile flowers (rich blue in very acidic soil) surrounded by rose-pink sterile flowers, mid- to late summer, 1.8m (5¾ft); *H. m.* 'Mariesii Perfecta', lacecap, inflorescences of rich blue (acidic soil) or pink or mauve (alkaline soil) sterile flowers, fertile flowers a darker shade than the sterile flowers, 1.8m (5¾ft); *H. m.* 'Nigra', mophead, rose-pink flowers (blue on acidic soil), 1.8m (5¾ft); *H. m.* 'Parzifal', mophead, dark pink (deep blue on acidic soil), 1.2m (4ft); *H. m.* 'Pia', slightly flattened, bright carmine-red flowers, mid- to late summer, 60cm (2ft); *H. m.* 'Tricolor', lacecap, variegated leaves, yellow, green-white and mid-green, mauve-pink to white flowers, in late summer, 2.4m (6¾ft); *H. m.* 'Veitchii', lacecap, white flowers, crimson-red in autumn, good on alkaline soils, 1.8m (5¾ft); *H. m.* 'White Wave', lacecap, flattened inflorescences of blue or pink fertile flowers surrounded by white sterile flowers with toothed edges; *H. paniculata* 'Grandiflora', green, tapering leaves, conical inflorescences of sterile flowers, white at first, later purple-pink, a wonderful woodland plant, 3m (10ft); *H. p.* 'Kyushu', glossy leaves, white flowers, late summer to mid-autumn; *H. p.* 'Praecox', abundant flowers, white at first, later purple-pink, fertile flowers at the top and centre, sterile below and at bottom; *H. p.* 'Tardiva', large inflorescences of small sterile flowers, late summer to mid-autumn, 2.4m/1.2m (6¾ft/4ft); *H. p.* 'Unique', densely packed sterile flowers, white at first, later purple-pink, mid-summer to mid-autumn, 4m (13ft); *H.* 'Preziosa', mophead, young leaves and stems red-brown, salmon-pink sterile flowers, later red, mid-summer to early autumn, 1m/75cm (3ft/2½ft); *H. quercifolia*, huge dark green, toothed, wrinkled and lobed leaves with rich red autumn colour, the most beautiful foliage of any hydrangea, conical inflorescences of cream-white sterile and fertile flowers, later orange-pink or purple, 1.5m/1.5m (5ft/5ft); *H. q.* 'Snow Flake', arching inflorescences of double sterile white flowers, later pink; *H. seemannii*, evergreen climber, elliptic to lance-shaped mid-green, leathery leaves, domed inflorescences of green-white fertile flowers surrounded by sterile flowers, 10m (33ft); *H. serrata* 'Bluebird' (syn. *H. s.* 'Acuminata'), pointed, oval mid-green leaves, red in autumn, flattened inflorescences of rich blue fertile flowers surrounded by pale blue sterile flowers, 1.2m/1.2m (4ft/4ft); *H. s.* 'Grayswood', lacecap, small mauve fertile flowers, white at first, later dark red, 2m/2m

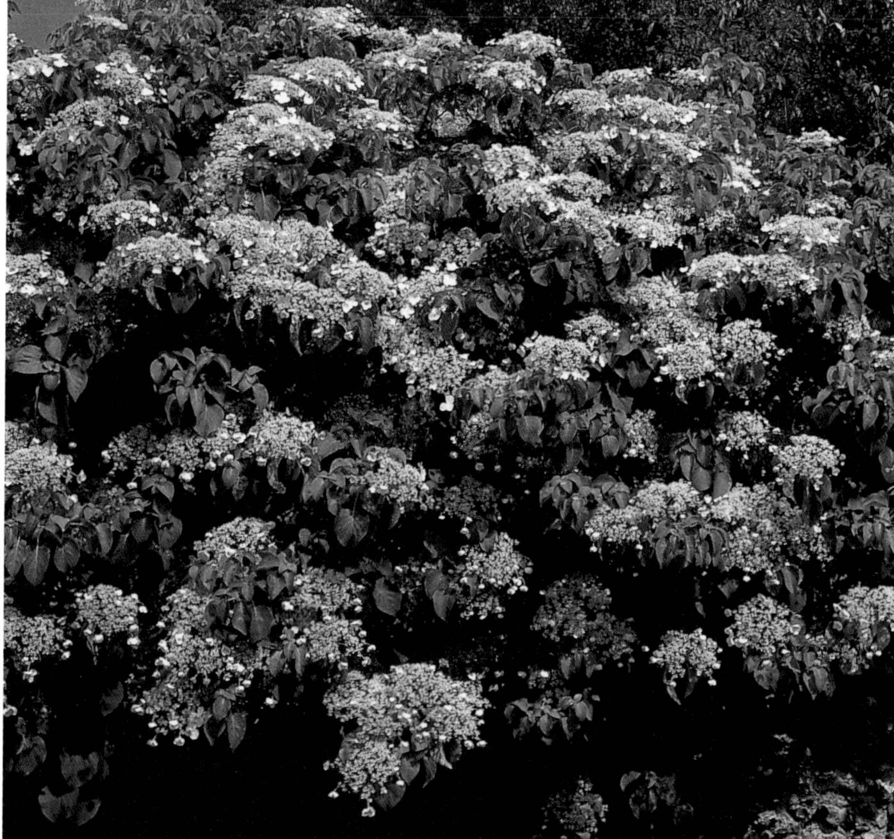

above *Hydrangea anomala petiolaris.* Much the best known of the climbing hydrangeas and a beautiful, if ultimately large plant.

left *Hydrangea macrophylla* 'Mariesii Perfecta'. One of the many hydrangeas of this type that display strikingly different colours on different soils.

(6½ft/6½ft); *H. serratifolia* (syn. *H. integerrima*), barely hardy self-clinging evergreen climber, leathery, elliptic, dark green leaves, sharply toothed at first, white fertile flowers, sterile flowers infrequent, a superb and neglected plant for sheltered places, 15m (50ft).

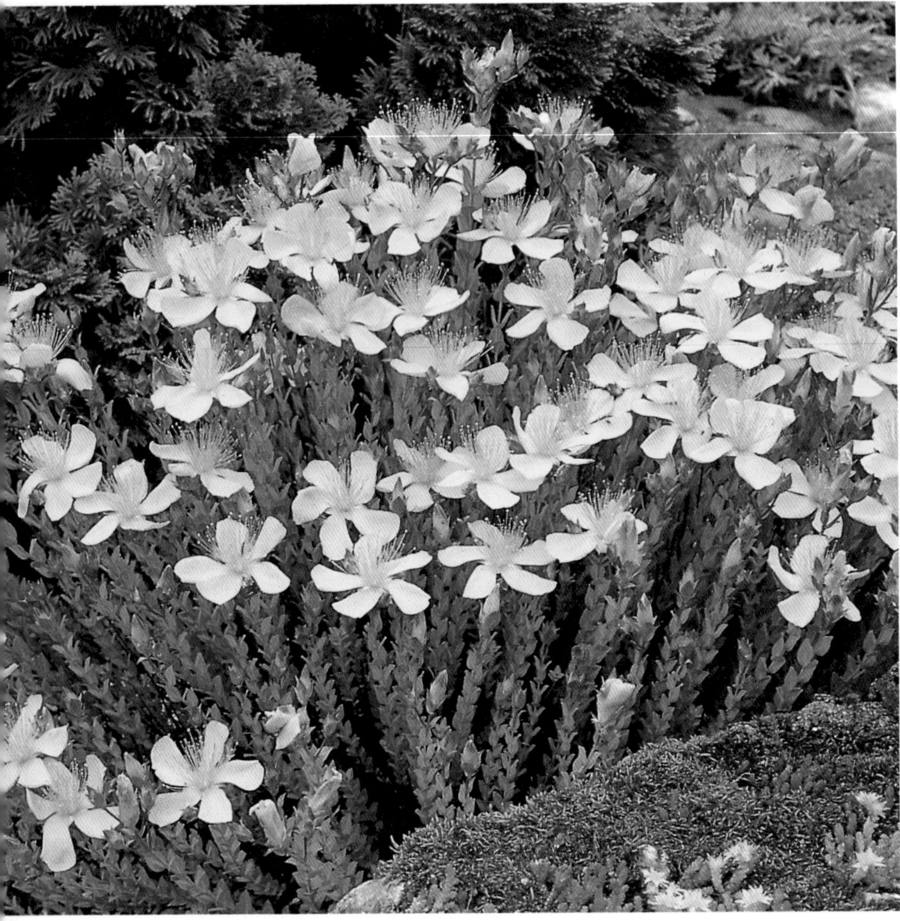

above *Hypericum olympicum*. The flowers of hypericums are remarkably constant among a genus that displays a considerable range of overall form.

Hypericum *St. John's Wort* Clusiaceae

Evergreen and deciduous shrubs, trees and perennials. Tender to very hardy. A good 'workhorse' genus of yellow flowered shrubs; never exciting but some are valuable, if occasionally invasive, ground cover. Leaves variable, some species with good autumn colour. Cup- or star-shaped flowers, usually bright yellow with conspicuous stamens, singly or in clusters, summer. Thrive in most well-drained soils, in sun or partial shade; dwarf species require a position in full sun in well-drained soil. No routine pruning. Sow seed in a cold-frame in autumn, take semi-ripe cuttings in summer or hardwood cuttings in winter. ❀ *H. aegypticum*, evergreen, oblong mid-green leaves, clusters of small, star-shaped, pale yellow flowers, 50cm/90cm (1¾ft/3ft); *H. androsaemum*, hardy, deciduous, oval, stalkless mid-green red-tinged leaves, heart-shaped at base, small fluffy flowers with prominent anthers, followed in autumn by fruit-like seed capsules, red at first, later black, 75cm/90cm (2½ft/3ft); *H. balearicum*, evergreen, barely hardy, oval to oblong leathery, dark green leaves with wavy margins, star-shaped bright yellow flowers, 25cm/25cm (10in/10in); *H. calycinum* (Rose of Sharon), dwarf evergreen, very hardy, large golden-yellow flowers, red anthers, can be invasive, but nonetheless a valuable plant for covering wild, difficult areas, 60cm (2ft)/indefinite; *H. cerastioides*, spreading perennial, moderately hardy, oblong to oval grey-green leaves, deep yellow star-shaped flowers, 15cm/40cm (6in/1½ft); *H.* 'Hidcote', semi-evergreen, fairly hardy, triangular to lance-shaped leaves, pale green, dense net-veining beneath, gold-yellow saucer-shaped flowers in mid-summer to mid-autumn, probably the best ornamental *Hypericum*, 1.2m/1.5m (4ft/5ft); *H.* x *inodorum* 'Elstead', deciduous or semi-evergreen, stalkless leaves, small yellow flowers followed by large fruit, pink-red when ripe, late summer to early autumn, 1.2m/1.2m (4ft/4ft); *H.* x *moserianum*, dwarf, deciduous, fairly hardy, gold-yellow flowers with red anthers, red arching stems, mid-summer to mid-autumn, 30cm-60cm (1-2ft); *H.* x *m.* 'Tricolor', semi-evergreen, oval leaves variegated white, pink and green, arching shoots flushed red, clusters of yellow cup-shaped flowers, 30cm/60cm (1-2ft); *H. olympicum*, dwarf deciduous sub-shrub, small oblong, elliptic or lance-shaped green leaves, clusters of bright yellow flowers in summer, 25cm/60cm (10in/2ft); *H. o.* f. *minus*, mound-forming, pointed leaves on blue-green stems, rich yellow flowers, 15cm/20cm (6in/8in); *H. o.* f. *uniflorum* 'Citrinum', elliptic to more or less oval blue-green leaves, clusters of pale sulphur-yellow flowers, 25cm/30cm (10in/1ft); *H. perforatum*, perennial, mid-green linear, elliptic to oblong leaves, clusters of star-shaped, bright yellow flowers, 60-110cm/60cm (2-3ft/2ft).

Hypsela Campanulaceae

Barely hardy to moderately hardy perennials. Mid- to dark green toothed or entire leaves, tubular flowers, can be invasive and create a multitude of problems in rock gardens. Sow seed in warmth during spring or divide established plants. ❀ *H. reniformis* (syn. *H. longiflora*), creeping, fleshy, rounded to kidney-shaped, bright green leaves, solitary pale pink or white flowers with red veining, late spring to summer, 2cm (¾in)/indefinite.

Iberis *Candytuft* Brassicaceae

Hardy annuals, perennials and sub-shrubs, the smaller species ideal for rock gardens, the larger for the front of a border. Annual candytuft is arguably the easiest of all plants to grow and excellent for children. Tolerates most soils but generally best in slightly alkaline conditions. Sow seed in growing positions in spring (annuals) or in a cold-frame in autumn. ❀ *I. amara* (Common Candytuft), tufted, bushy plant, heads of small fragrant white, pink or lilac flowers, spring to autumn, self-seeds freely, 30cm/15cm (1ft/6in); *I. a.* Hyacinth Flowered Series, tall, dense heads of superficially hyacinth-like flowers in white, pink or lilac, good for cutting, 40cm (1½ft); *I. sempervirens*, spreading evergreen sub-shrub, broad heads of tiny white flowers, spring to early summer, 30cm/60cm (1ft/2ft); *I. s.* 'Schneeflocke', masses of brilliant white flowers and rich green foliage, 25cm (10in); *I. s.* 'Weisser Zwerg' (syn. 'Little Gem'), shorter, more compact, 15cm (6in).

Ilex *Holly* Aquifoliaceae

Small/large evergreen and deciduous shrubs and trees. Hardy to very hardy; a few are tender. Vastly under-appreciated genus; to think of holly as a prickly, red-berried evergreen is to miss an enormous amount of good horticulture. Spiny, entire or toothed leaves, some with scalloped edges, in a wide range of green shades, some variegated. Small cup-shaped flowers, mainly white or cream, sometimes pink, green or lavender blue, are followed by red, black or yellow fruits. Male and female flowers usually produced on separate plants. Thrive in fertile, moist, well-drained loamy soil, in full sun or partial shade; good for woodlands. Sow in a cold-frame in autumn (germination may take two years), or layer in autumn. Fruits are mildly toxic if eaten. ❀ *I. x altaclarensis* (Highclere Holly), 'Camelliifolia', large tree, female, camellia-like usually spineless leaves, red-purple at first, later glossy, dark green, deep red fruits, 14m (42½ft); *I.* x *a.* 'Golden King', large shrub or medium tree, female, almost spineless green leaves with bright yellow margins, small white flowers followed by abundant bright red fruits, 6m (20ft); *I.* x *a.* 'Lawsoniana', large shrub or medium tree, female, green leaves splashed yellow at the centre, may revert to entire green, dull red fruits, 6m (20ft); *I. aquifolium* (Common Holly), shiny dark green leaves, pale beneath, with wavy margins, usually spiny, red fruits, 25m/8m (80ft/25ft); *I. a.* 'Argentea Marginata', female, leaves pink to purple at first, later green with white margins, abundant red fruits, 15m/4m (50ft/13ft); *I. a.* 'Argentea Marginata Pendula', small tree, female, weeping branches, leaves green with white margins, red fruits, 4m/3m (13ft/10ft); *I. a.* 'Aurea Marginata', female, gold-edged leaves, red fruits, 5m/3m (16ft/10ft); *I. a.* 'Bacciflava', female, dark green leaves, abundant yellow fruits, 15m (50ft); *I. a.* 'Ferox' (Hedgehog Holly), male, thick, leathery leaves, twisted and curled; *I. a.* 'Ferox Argentea', male, silver-edged leaves on purple twigs, 8m/4m (25ft/13ft); *I. a.* 'Golden Milkboy', male, spiny-edged dark green leaves with gold splashes in the centre, 6m/4m (20ft/13ft); *I. a.* 'Golden Queen', male, dark green spiny leaves, shaded pale green and grey, with broad yellow margins, 10m/6m (33ft/20ft); *I. a.* 'Golden van Tol', female, green leaves with yellow margins, few fruits, 4m/3m (13ft/10ft); *I. a.* 'Handsworth New Silver', slow-growing shrub, female, deep green leaves with grey mottling, broad cream margins, very spiny, bright red fruits, 8m/5m (25ft/16ft); *I. a.* 'Hascombensis', narrow, small dark green leaves, sharply spined, 1.2m/60cm (4ft/2ft); *I. a.* 'J C van Tol', female, self-

left *Ilex aquifolium* 'Ferox Argentea'. The hedgehog hollies, both plain-leaved and variegated, have some of the most prickly leaves of any garden shrub.

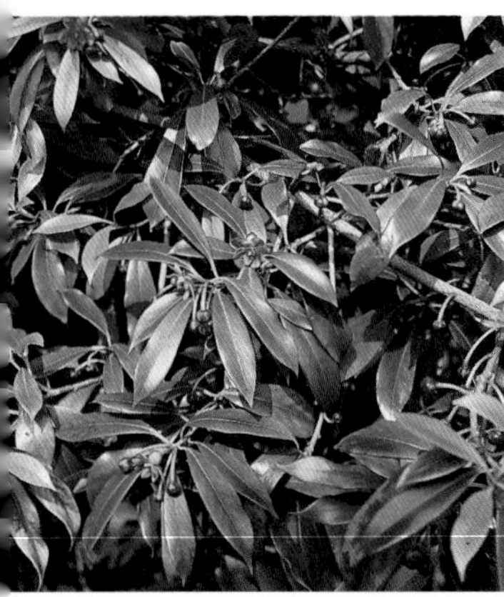

above Unfamiliar to many gardeners but *Illicium floridanum* is a quietly distinguished plant for mild acidic gardens.

right *Impatiens* New Guinea Group. Busy Lizzies are among the outstanding bedding plants of modern times; and especially so for their shade tolerance.

fertile, dark glossy leaves, nearly spineless, red fruits, 6m/4m (20ft/13ft); *I. a.* 'Madame Briot', female, very spiny green leaves with dark yellow margins and mottling, sometimes completely gold-yellow, deep red fruits, 10m/5m (33ft/16ft); *I. a.* 'Myrtifolia Aurea Maculata', male, compact, dark green spiny leaves, shaded pale green, gold splashed at centre, 5m/2.5m (16ft/8ft); *I. a.* 'Pyramidalis', female, self-fertile, glossy bright or dark green leaves, slightly spiny, red fruits, 6m/5m (20ft/16ft); *I. a.* 'Silver Queen' male, leaves pink at first, later dark green with pale grey marbling, cream margins, 10m/4m (33ft/13ft); *I. crenata* 'Convexa', female, slow-growing, small rounded leaves, few spines, dark green glossy, puckered leaves, small black fruits, 2.5m/2m (8ft/6½ft); *I. c.* 'Fastigiata', narrowly upright, small dark green leaves, small black fruits, 2.5m/1m (8ft/3ft); *I. c.* 'Golden Gem', female, best in partial shade, pale green-yellow leaves, few spines, some yellow variegation, small black fruits, 1.1m/1.2-1.5m (3ft/4-5ft); *I.* x *meservae*, 'Blue Angel', female, dark glossy blue-green leaves, red fruits, 4m/2m (13ft/6½ft); *I.* x *m.* 'Blue Princess', female, glossy blue-green leaves, red fruits, 3m (10ft).

Illicium
Illiciaceae

Medium evergreen shrubs and trees. Tender to barely hardy plants for sheltered gardens with slightly acidic soil. Glossy, aromatic leaves, oval to lance-shaped, beautiful fragrant star-shaped flowers with long thin petals, followed by star-shaped fruit. Take semi-ripe cuttings in summer or layer. ❀ *I. floridanum*, evergreen shrub, glossy, leathery, dark green leaves, pendent flowers late spring to early summer, followed by red to red-purple or maroon fruit, 2m/2m (6½ft/6½ft).

Impatiens
Balsam, Busy Lizzie Balsaminaceae

Annuals, evergreen perennials and sub-shrubs. Tender to moderately hardy. A large genus but the Busy Lizzies for summer bedding and containers surpass all others in their importance. Especially valuable as much the best bedding plants for shaded places. Fleshy leaves, semi-succulent stems, five-petalled, cup-shaped or open, flat flowers, singly or in clusters; upper petals often hooded. Require moist, well-drained soil enriched with humus in partial shade; container-grown plants are best in loam-based compost in dappled light. Stems are brittle so protect from wind. Sow seed in warmth in early spring or take softwood cuttings (*I. walleriana* and New Guinea Group varieties) in spring or early summer. ❀ *I. balfourii*, annual, finely toothed fleshy leaves, loose heads of white flowers with pink flushes and yellow lower petals, 50cm/25cm (1¾ft/10in); *I. balsamina* (Balsam), Camellia Flowered Series, lance-shaped leaves, double, open, flat pink or red flowers mottled white, summer to early autumn, 75cm/45cm (2½ft/1½ft); *I. b.* 'Extra Dwarf Tom Thumb', drought tolerant, double camellia-flowered, purple-rose, scarlet, carmine, pink and white flowers 30cm/20cm (1ft/8in); *I.* New Guinea Group (New Guinea Hybrid Busy Lizzies), 'Fire Lake', tender perennials, usually grown as annuals, lance-shaped leaves, red or bronze, some yellow, variegated with pink midribs and dark green edges, brightly coloured orange flowers, late spring to early autumn, 60cm/40cm (2ft/1½ft); *I.* New Guinea Group 'Spectra' F1, lance-shaped, toothed, mid-green leaves, open, flat, lavender, pink, scarlet, rose-pink or white flowers, some bicoloured, summer to autumn, 35cm/30cm (1¼ft/1ft); *I.* New Guinea Group 'Tango' F1, toothed, lance-shaped, dark bronze-green leaves, open, flat tangerine flowers, summer to autumn, 35cm/30cm (1¼ft/1ft); *I. tinctoria*, half-hardy tuberous perennial, dark green oblong, toothed leaves, fragrant, white or pink hooded flowers, with purple marks on the throats, late summer to early

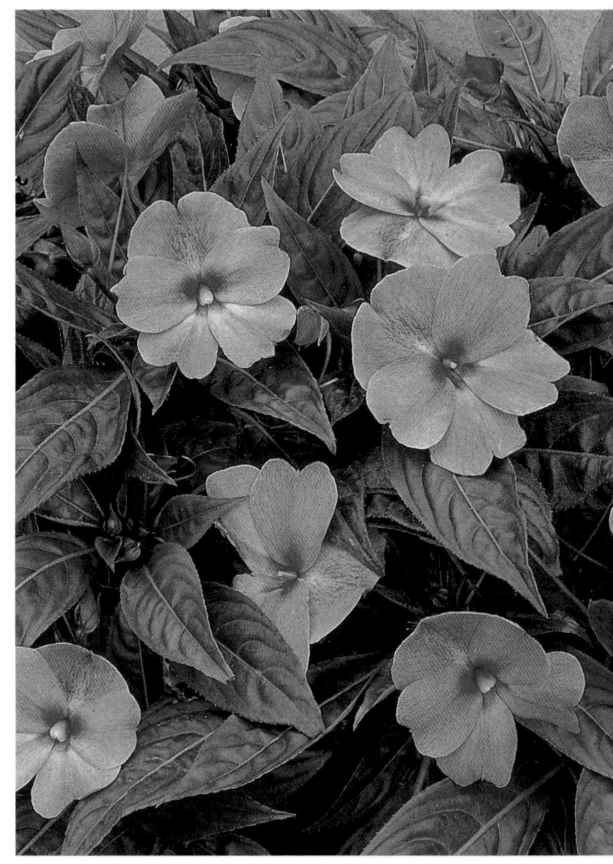

autumn, 2.2m/1m (6¾ft/3ft); *I. walleriana* (syn. *I. sultani*) (Busy Lizzie), perennials grown as half-hardy annuals, varieties come and go very quickly and it pays to check each year's seed catalogues for the latest introductions; commonly one or two colours from particular series stay for a few years; *I. w.* Accent Series F1, compact, flowers white and shades of pink, orange, crimson, wine-red, violet and lavender-blue, some with central stars; *I. w.* Blitz Series F1, dark green leaves, orange, pink, red, violet and white flowers, 35cm (1¼ft); *I. w.* 'Blue Pearl', pale green, oval, succulent leaves with serrated edges, pale lilac flowers, 20-30cm (8in-1ft); *I. w.* 'Cleopatra' F1, flowers with silky sheen, many shades of red, lilac, pink, mauve and white, 15-25cm (6-10in); *I. w.* Double Confection Series F1, double, sometimes semi-double, red, white, pink and purple flowers, 25cm (10in); *I. w.* 'Mosaic Lilac' F1, lilac, flushed white, 45cm (1½ft); *I. w.* 'Novette star', dwarf, lilac, red and pink flowers with white star-shaped patterning, 15-20cm (6-8in); *I. w.* 'Rosette', double pink 20cm (8in); *I. w.* 'Starbright' F1, violet, pink, red, orange flowers with central white star, 20cm (8in); *I. w.* 'Tempo Pastel' F1, pastel shades of salmon-apricot and pink, 20-25cm (8-10in).

Imperata — Poaceae

Medium perennial grasses. Fairly hardy. Linear pointed leaves, panicles of spikelets in summer. Divide in spring or autumn. ❀ *I. cylindrica*, clump-forming, leaves mid-green at first, later deep red along most of their length, silver-white flower spikelets in late summer, 60cm/30cm (2ft/1ft); *I. c.* 'Rubra' (Japanese Blood Grass), ribbon-shaped leaves flushed deep maroon.

Incarvillea — Bignoniaceae

Small/large hardy herbaceous perennials for herbaceous or mixed borders or rock gardens but many with very assertive colours so need placing carefully. Pinnate leaves, with toothed leaflets, trumpet-shaped flowers with flared mouths. Sow seed in a cold-frame in spring or autumn. ❀ *I. delavayi*, rosettes of mid-green leaves with toothed leaflets, clusters of flaring trumpet-shaped rose-pink to purple flowers with yellow throats, early to mid-summer, 60cm/30cm (2ft/1ft); *I. d. alba*, white flowers; *I. mairei*, dark green wrinkled leaves, clusters of trumpet-shaped crimson or purple flowers with yellow throats, in early summer, 15-30cm/30cm (6in-1ft/1ft); *I. sinensis* 'Alba', narrowly elongated, toothed leaves, white flowers; *I.* 'Snowtop', purple/white flowers tinged with green.

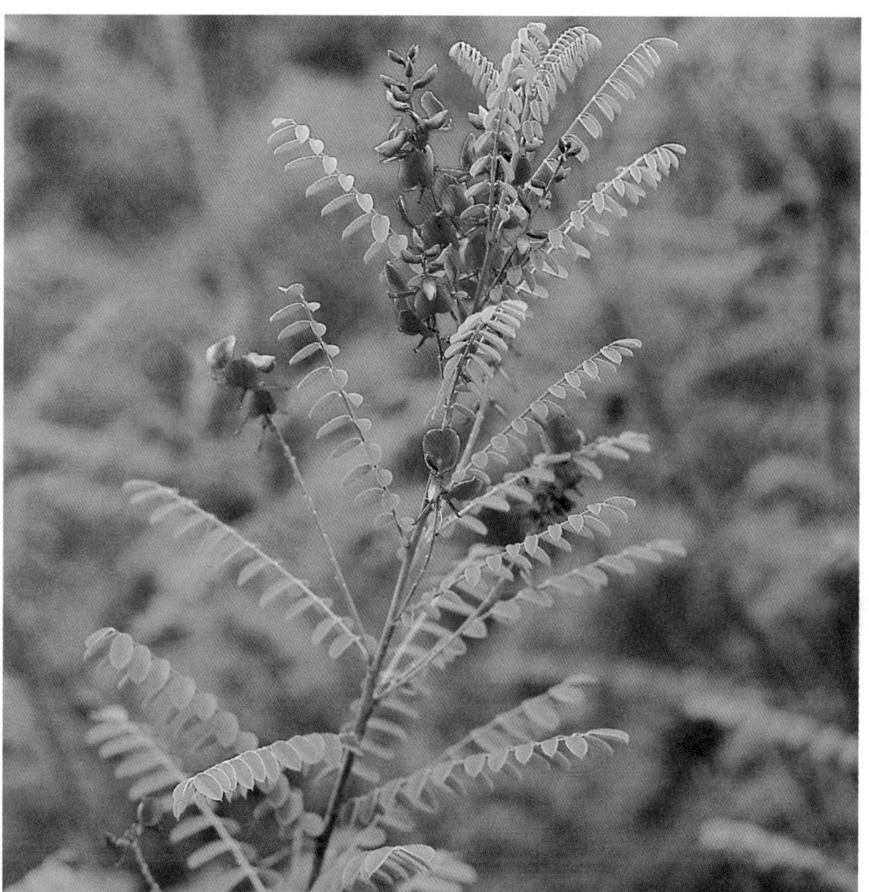

above *Indigofera heterantha.* More than simply an interesting ornamental, the name betrays the fact that this plant has been an important source of the dye indigo.

Indigofera — Papilionaceae

Annuals, herbaceous perennials and evergreen/deciduous shrubs and trees for shrub-borders and training against walls; smaller species for rock gardens. Barely hardy to moderately hardy. Finely divided leaves, clusters of pea-like flowers. No routine pruning. Sow seed in a cold-frame in autumn, take basal cuttings in spring or softwood cuttings in late spring. ❀ *I. amblyantha*, moderately hardy deciduous shrub, hairy grey-green leaves, clusters of pale pink flowers, summer to early autumn, 2m/2.5m (6½ft/8ft); *I. heterantha* (syn. *I. gerardiana*). moderately hardy deciduous shrub, grey-green leaves, clusters of purple-pink flowers, 2-3m/2-3m (6½-10ft/6½ft-10ft).

Indocalamus — Poaceae

Small evergreen bamboo. Moderately hardy. Good as a specimen in a container and a splendid plant for a 'Japanese' courtyard garden. Long leaves on single branches arising from each node. Divide in spring. ❀ *I. latifolius*, thin, felted culms (stems) and leaves, 1.5m/60cm (5ft/2ft); *I. tessellatus*, low-growing and mound-forming, thin arching culms, long leaves to 60cm (2ft), 1m/1m (3ft/3ft).

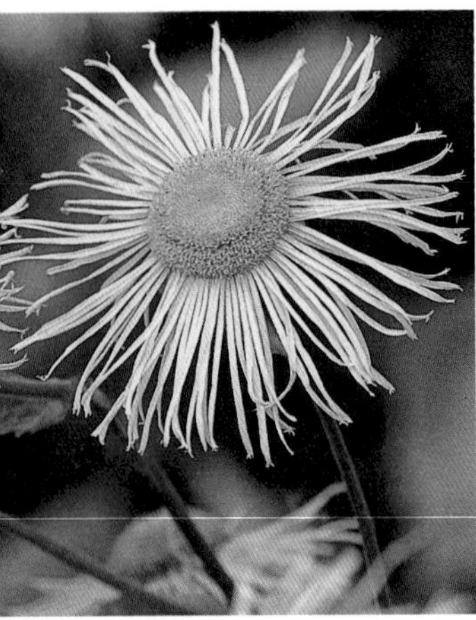

above *Inula magnifica.* A quite fascinating perennial that is fully hardy, despite its exotic appearance.

Inula — Asteraceae

Small/large annuals, biennials, and hardy herbaceous perennials. Barely hardy to moderately hardy. Lance-shaped or oval leaves, daisy-like flowers. I think they are among the prettiest and most dainty of the perennial yellow-flowered daisies.Their spidery petals have a special charm and confer an exotic feel that is usually associated with much more tender plants. Sow seed in a coldframe in spring or autumn or divide established plants. Those described here are all hardy herbaceous perennials. ❀ *I. ensifolia*, mid-green leaves with prominent veining and hairy margins, gold-yellow flowers, orange-yellow centres, mid- to late summer, 25-60cm/30cm (10in-2ft/1ft); *I. helenium*, oval to oval-elliptic, toothed mid-green leaves, hairy beneath, clusters of bright yellow flowers, mid- to late summer, 90-120cm/90cm (3-4ft/3ft); *I. hookeri*, clump- forming, oval to oblong, finely serrated, hairy mid-green leaves, solitary, soft yellow flowers, late summer to mid-autumn, can be invasive, 60-75cm/60cm (2-2½ft/2ft); *I. magnifica*, clump- forming, oval, deep green leaves on hairy stems, clusters of spidery yellow flowers, late summer to mid-autumn, can be invasive but probably the prettiest, 60-75cm/60cm (2-2½ft/2ft); *I. orientalis* (syn *I. glandulosa*), toothed, hairy, oval leaves, woolly buds open to solitary orange-yellow flowers, in summer, 60-90cm/60cm (2-3ft/2ft).

Ipheion — Alliaceae

Small bulbous ornamental. Fairly hardy but best in a sheltered spot in colder areas. One of my favourite early spring bulbs. Grass-like basal leaves emerge in autumn well before the flowers, smell of garlic when crushed, six-petalled, star-shaped flowers, often honey-scented. Sow seed in a coldframe when ripe or in spring, or divide established plants in summer. ❀ *I.* 'Rolf Fiedler' (syn. *Tristagma* 'Rolf Fiedler'), blue-green or grey-green leaves, clumps of blue flowers, in spring, 10-12cm (4-5in); *I. uniflorum*, (syn. *Tristagma uniflorum*), narrow, pale green leaves, fragrant white flowers tinted violet-blue, 15-20cm (6-8in); *I. u.* 'Album', white flowers; *I. u.* 'Froyle Mill', violet flowers, the best form; *I. u.* 'Wisely Blue', violet-blue flowers.

Ipomoea
Morning Glory — Convolvulaceae

Half-hardy annuals and herbaceous perennials, tender evergreen shrubs and trees; the most familiar are climbing or trailing species. Toothed, lobed or finely dissected leaves, short-lived tubular or funnel-shaped flowers, open in the morning, closed by early afternoon, summer to early autumn. The common climbers are like brilliantly coloured bindweeds but, not being hardy, they are never threatening. Sow seeds in warmth in spring, take semi-ripe cuttings in summer or soft-

right *Ipheion uniflorum* 'Froyle Mill'. How such a lovely plant has been overlooked by so many gardeners for so long is a total mystery to me.

wood cuttings in spring or summer. ❀ *I. coccinea*, half-hardy annual climber, heart-shaped light green pointed leaves, clusters of tubular, fragrant scarlet flowers with yellow throats, summer to mid-autumn, 2-4m (6½ft-13ft); *I.* x *hederacea* 'Roman Candy', half-hardy annual climber, green and white leaves, hideously lurid cerise and white flowers, 1.2m (4ft); *I. indica* (syns. *I. acuminata, I. learii*), half-hardy herbaceous perennial climber, mid-green, pointed, heart-shaped leaves, blue or purple flowers, singly or in clusters, 6m (20ft) or more; *I. purpurea*, half-hardy annual climber, oval or round mid-green leaves, flowers purple, fading with age, or pink, magenta or white, sometimes colours are in stripes on a white background, singly or in clusters, 2-3m (6½ft-10ft). *I. p.* 'Cardinal', half-hardy annual climber, trumpet-shaped cardinal-red flowers, 2.4m (6¾ft); *I. nil* 'Early Call', annual climber, white flowers with scarlet lobes, 5m (16ft); *I. n.* 'Platycodon Flowered', single or semi-double flowers in red, white or purple, 5m (16ft); *I. n.* 'Scarlet Star', cerise flowers with clear white star-shaped centre; *I. n.* 'Scarlet O'Hara' bright red flowers; *I. tricolor* 'Flying Saucers', annual or short-lived perennial, flowers marbled white and purple-blue, 3-4m (10-13ft); *I. t.* 'Heavenly Blue', azure-blue flowers with white throats, probably the best form.

Iresine *Bloodleaf* Amaranthaceae

Annuals, evergreen perennials and sub-shrubs, some erect, others climbing. Tender and often seen as houseplants but foliage is valuable for summer carpet bedding. Colourful, entire, simple leaves. Spikes of insignificant white or green flowers. Take stem-tip cuttings at any time or softwood cuttings in late winter or early spring. ❀ *I. herbstii*, erect annual or short-lived perennial, rounded to oval, waxy maroon leaves with prominent veining in lighter red, 1.5m/90cm (5ft/3ft).

Iris Iridaceae

Small/medium bulbous and rhizomatous ornamentals. Tender to moderately hardy. A huge genus of important and diverse garden plants, subdivided most usefully into two main groups, bulbous and rhizomatous. These are further divided into subgroups: rhizomatous irises into bearded and beardless, and bulbous irises into Xiphium, Juno and Reticulata, some of which are further subdivided (see below). The characteristic and readily identifiable flowers comprise six segments, linked by a short tube: the outer three are reflexed petals known as falls; the inner three are usually erect and are known as standards. Three lipped structures, the petal-like styles, arise between the standards and the falls and in bearded irises the falls have a 'beard' of fleshy hairs. All parts of irises should be considered toxic. Cultivation requirements vary between groups but, generally, most irises require well-drained neutral to slightly acidic or slightly alkaline soil in full sun. Sow seed in a cold-frame in autumn or spring, divide clumps of established plants or replant offsets between mid-summer and autumn. The varieties that I recommend here are only a small selection of more than 300 species and many more varieties currently available (many of which, especially among the border irises, are each offered by only a few nurseries).

above *Iris pumila*. The miniature dwarf bearded varieties are perhaps the least appreciated among the bearded iris groups.

Bearded Irises

Miniature Dwarf Bearded, flower mid-to late summer: *I. attica*, yellow flowers tinged green, 5-10cm (2-4in); *I. pumila*, flowers purple, yellow or yellow tinted brown, 10cm (4in).

Standard Dwarf Bearded, flower late spring: *I.* 'Blue Denim'; *I.* 'Cherry Garden'; *I.* 'Pogo'.

Intermediate Bearded, flower mid-to late spring: *I.* 'Florentina', white flowers flushed blue, 40cm (1½ft); *I. germanica*, blue-purple to violet flowers with white beards, 70cm (2¼ft); *I.* Langport Series, wide variation in flower colour, from purple-blue through buttercup-yellow and red-orange to blue and copper-bronze.

above *Iris* Pacific Coast hybrids. Probably the loveliest of all the smaller, non-bulbous Iris groups.

Tall Bearded, flower late spring to early summer: *I.* 'Berkeley Gold'; *I.* 'Blue Rhythm', mid-blue flowers; *I.* 'Blue Shimmer'; *I.* 'Jane Phillips', pale blue; *I.* 'Kent Pride', yellow or pink with wine, brown or pink stippling; *I. pallida* 'Variegata', bright green leaves with gold-yellow stripes, fragrant, soft blue, 1.2m (4ft); *I.* 'Party Dress', flamingo pink with tangerine beard; *I.* 'Pearly Dawn'; *I.* 'Titan's Glory', deep purple; *I.* 'White City'.

Beardless Irises

Pacific Coast (Californian) irises, low-growing, beautiful and under-appreciated, usually evergreen, flowers in a range of colours, most with distinctive veins: *I. innominata*, deep green leaves, bright yellow to cream flowers with rich brown veins, early summer, 15-25cm (6-10in); *I.* Broadleigh Series, range of colours including clear blue and pink.

Water Irises (Laevigata Irises), require damp soil, blue, pink, red, purple, white or yellow flowers: *I. ensata* (syn. *I. kaempferi*), conspicuous midribs on the leaves, purple or red-purple flowers, mid-summer, 90cm (3ft); *I. e.* 'Moonlight Waves', white flowers with lime-green centres; *I. e.* 'Variegata', white and green variegated leaves, wine-purple flowers; *I. laevigata*, for pond margins and other damp places, pale green leaves with black patterning, blue flowers, early to mid-summer, 80cm (2½ft); *I. pseudacorus*, for margins of large ponds and lakes, grey-green ribbed leaves, yellow flowers with brown or violet patterning, darker yellow on each fall, 90-150cm (3-5ft); *I.* 'Holden Clough', arching, sometimes evergreen grey-green leaves, yellow flowers with purple veining, late spring, 50-90cm (1¾ft-3ft); *I. versicolor*, slightly arching leaves, violet, purple or lavender-blue flowers, purple area on each fall veined white, 20-80cm (8in-2½ft); *I. v.* 'Kermesina', red-purple flowers.

right *Iris bucharica*. This has long been one of my favourites although when the leaves first appear, you could be forgiven for thinking this could not possibly be an iris.

Sibirica Irises, require damp but not waterlogged soil and are suitable for damp borders or close to pools: *I. sibirica*, narrow, grass-like leaves, blue-violet flowers with dark veining, in early summer, 50-120cm (1¾ft-4ft). *I. s.* 'Dreaming Yellow', white standards, slightly ruffled cream-white falls, 80cm (2½ft); *I. s.* 'Papillon'. soft pale blue; *I. s.* 'Perry's Blue'.

Chrysographes irises, related to Sibirica Irises but require more moisture: *I. chrysographes*, best in rich, moist, organic soil, standards not erect, but an at angle of 45 degrees, drooping falls, deep blue or red-purple, almost black, with gold veining on falls, 40-50cm (1½-1¾ft); *I. forrestii*, leaves glossy on one surface, grey on the other, yellow flowers with brown-purple streaks on falls, early summer, 35-40cm (1-1½ft).

Spuria irises, tolerant of a variety of conditions, including very wet and very dry, full sun or shade, flowers with narrow, erect standards, oval falls, glossy mid-green, slender leaves, 15cm-1.8m (6in-5¾ft): *I. graminea*, grassy leaves, blue-purple flowers, in early summer, 20-40cm (8-1½ft); *I. orientalis*, leaves remain throughout winter, white flowers with yellow centres on falls, early to mid-summer, 90cm (3ft).

Other rhizomatous irises: *I. foetidissima*, evergreen, dark glossy foliage, malodorous when crushed, insignificant flowers, slate-grey flushed pink and brown, in early summer, followed by seedpods that split in autumn to reveal bright orange fruits, an invaluable plant tolerant of dry shade, 50cm (1¾ft); *I. f. citrina*, cream-yellow flowers; *I. f.* 'Variegata', silver leaves with white marks; *I. setosa*, linear mid-green leaves, blue or purple-blue falls and bristle-like standards, 15-90cm (6in-3ft); *I. unguicularis* (syn. *I. stylosa*) (Winter-flowering Iris), grass-like evergreen leaves, fragrant pale lavender to deep violet flowers with contrasting veins, yellow stripe on falls, late winter to early spring, must be placed where it receives hot sun in summer, 30cm (1ft); *I. u.* 'Mary Ballard', bright violet flowers in mid-winter.

Crested irises, evergreen, not all are reliably hardy, mid-green linear leaves, flowers with crest resembling cock's comb, on falls, early to mid-summer: *I. confusa*, best grown with shelter, white flowers with yellow crest, early to mid-summer, 1m (3ft); *I. cristata*, lavender flowers, white patch and white crest tipped with orange, in spring, sometimes at other times in the summer, 10cm (4in).

Bulbous Irises
Short-lived and often grassy foliage that may elongate untidily after flowering, flower winter to early summer.
Reticulata group, tubular four- to eight-sided leaves, skin on bulbs netted (reticulated): *I.* 'Cantab', pale blue flowers, paler at tips, yellow crest and white rims, 15cm (6in); *I. danfordiae*, yellow, honey-scented flowers with tiny standards, green-yellow marks on falls, not reliable at flowering after the first year and best grown as an annual, 8-15cm (3-6in); *I.* 'Harmony', deep royal-blue flowers, 15cm (6in); *I.* 'J S Dijt', purple-red flowers, 15cm (6in); *I.* 'Katherine Hodgkin', blue-green standards, yellow-green falls grey-blue veining on yellow patches, 12cm (5in); *I. reticulata*, deep purple-blue flowers, orange flash on falls, late winter to early spring, 10-15cm (4-6in).
Juno group, broadly lance-shaped glossy green leaves, flowers arise from leaf axils: *I. bucharica*, a strikingly different plant and good in a container, sweetly-scented cream-white flowers with bright yellow falls, 20-40cm (8in-1½ft).
Xiphium Group, hybrids divided into Dutch, Spanish and English irises, all with long-lived but sparse deep green leaves, sometimes with grey bloom: Dutch irises, colours range from blue, yellow and white to purple, early summer, 38-60cm (1½-2ft); Spanish irises, lance-shaped leaves, flowers in mid-summer range from blues, mauves, purples to brown and white, with orange or yellow patterning on each fall, 60cm (2ft); English irises, narrow lance-shaped, silver-green leaves, flowers are white, pink, purple, blue, usually flecked, mid- to late summer, 25-60cm (10in-2ft).

Itea — Escalloniaceae

Small to medium deciduous/evergreen shrubs. Barely hardy to moderately hardy. In cold areas, less hardy species are best grown against a warm sunny wall or in a warm, lightly shaded position. Soft, rather holly-like leaves; deciduous species give good autumn colour. Narrow catkin-like spikes of pendent, fragrant, green-white, cream or white flowers, summer. Sow ripe seed in an open-frame, taking semi-ripe cuttings in spring or semi-ripe cuttings in summer; ❀ *I. ilicifolia*, evergreen, glossy leaves, honey-scented, green-white flowers, late summer, 3-5m/3m (10-16ft/10ft); *I. virginica*, deciduous, bright green narrow oval leaves, orange or red in autumn, white flowers, mid-summer.

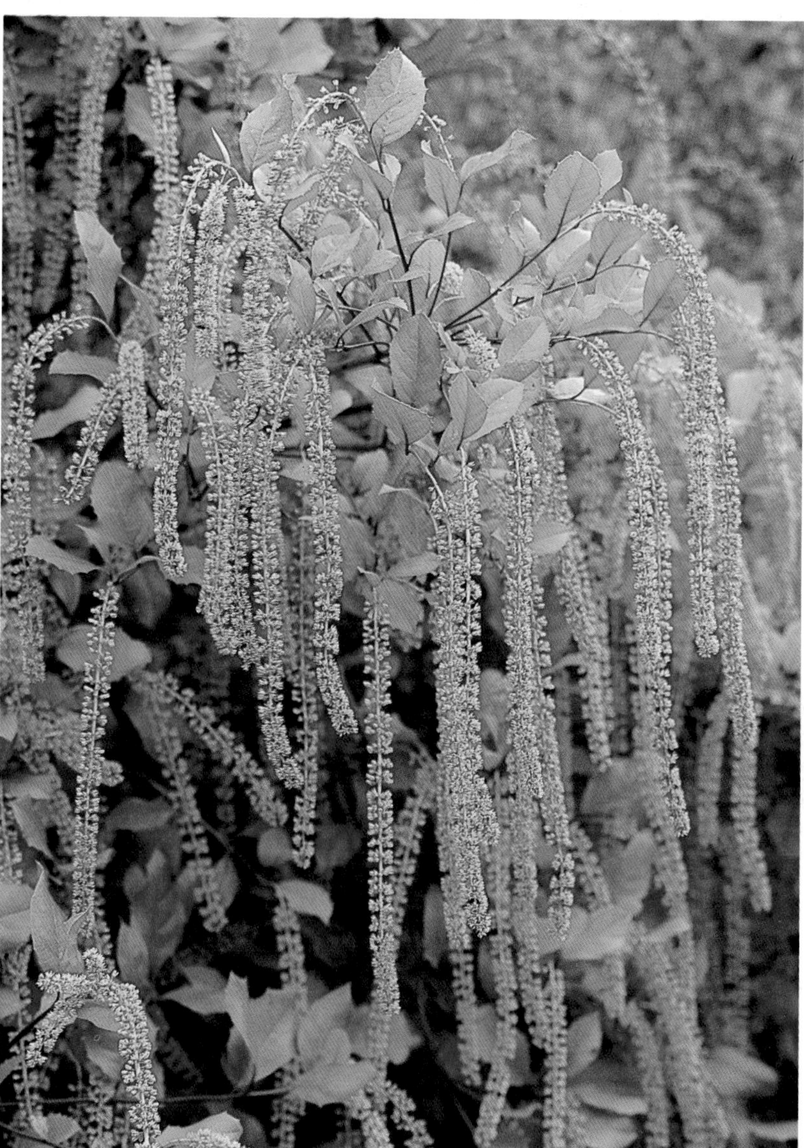

above *Itea ilicifolia* possesses some of the most dainty and pretty of all catkin-like flowers and perhaps a slight tenderness is the reason for its relative unfamiliarity.

Ixia — Iridaceae

Small half-hardy corm-forming ornamentals. Narrow, sword-like leaves, clusters of six-petalled, bowl-shaped flowers on thin, wiry stems. Sow ripe seed in a cold-frame, or replant offsets in late summer. Named varieties not usually available and unnamed hybrid mixtures are sold in a range of colours, from white, cream-white, through orange, yellow and brown-red to blue, purple and pink, often with darker centres, some with contrasting marks on the petals.

above *Jasione heldreichii*. Lovers of native wild plants will adore this plant for although not itself a native, it is very similar to its relatives of light pasture land.

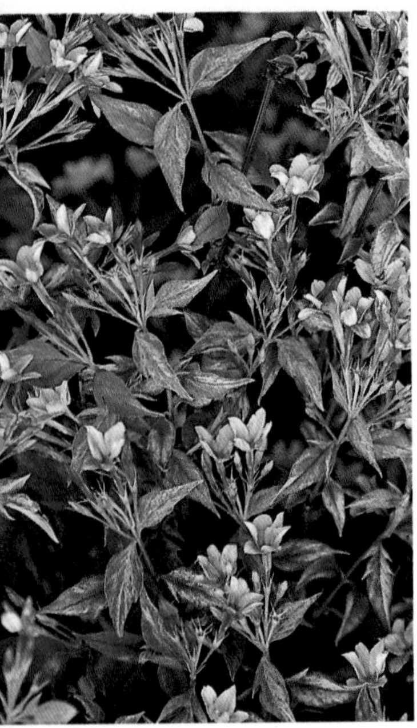

above *Jasminum* x *stephanense*. A lovely hybrid between *J. beesianum* and *J. officinale* dating from around 1920.

Jasione *Sheep's Bit* Campanulaceae

Annuals, biennials and perennials. Moderately hardy; the native species are among the characteristic plants of light alkaline grassland and they merit a role in gardens too. Mid- to deep green simple leaves, pompon-like inflorescences, usually blue, with conspicuous stamens, surrounded by ruffs of green bracts. Sow seed in a cold-frame when ripe or in autumn; replant self-sown seedlings. ❀ *J. heldreichii* (syn. *J. jankae*), herbaceous perennial or biennial, narrow, pointed, hairy leaves, deep blue flowers, summer, 10-20cm/15cm (4-8in/6in); *J. laevis* 'Blaulicht' (syn. 'Blue Light'), herbaceous perennial or biennial, cushion-forming, rosettes of narrow, oval, slightly toothed leaves, dark blue flowers with narrow petals, mid-summer to autumn, 20-30cm/20cm (8in-1ft/8in).

Jasminum *Jasmine* Oleaceae

Small to medium deciduous/evergreen shrubs and climbers. Barely hardy to moderately hardy. Includes the best loved and certainly most delightfully fragrant of summer shrubs and also the most reliable of all winter-flowering plants. Simple to pinnate, sometimes fern-like leaves, clusters of small, fragrant, usually tubular, flowers, sometimes followed by black fruits. Requires a position in full sun, preferably against a wall; tolerant of most soils if not waterlogged. *J. nudiflorum* is tolerant of poor soils and shade. Cut back the oldest third of the stems of the summer-flowering forms to soil level every spring. *J. nudiflorum* may be treated similarly or the dead flower shoots and any frost-damaged shoots may be cut back to new wood after flowering. Alternatively, if grown against a wall or as a hedge, Winter Jasmine may be clipped to shape with shears after flowering. Take semi-ripe cuttings in summer, hardwood cuttings in winter, or layer. ❀ *J. beesianum*, deciduous or evergreen climber, oval to lance-shaped dark green leaves, small red flowers, late spring to early summer, followed by abundant, glossy black fruits, 5m (16ft); *J. humile* (syn. *J. reevesii*) 'Revolutum', semi-evergreen shrub, erect or arching, deep green pinnate leaves, large deep yellow flowers, slightly fragrant, in domed inflorescences, late spring to early summer, 2.5m/3m (8ft/10ft); *J. mesnyi* (syn. *J. primulinum*), barely hardy evergreen shrub, best given some support, glossy, deep green leaves, bright yellow semi-double flowers, singly or in small clusters, summer, 3m/1-2m (10ft/3-6½ft); *J. nudiflorum* (Winter-flowering Jasmine), slender, arching deciduous shrub, best grown against a wall or used as cover on a bank, pinnate leaves, bright yellow flowers, late autumn to late winter, 3m/3m (10ft/10ft); *J. officinale* (Common Jasmine), lax shrub, pinnate leaves with elliptic leaflets, sharp point, clusters of very fragrant white flowers, summer, 12m (40ft); *J. o.* 'Argenteo-variegatum' (syn. *J. o.* 'Variegatum'), grey-green leaves with cream-white margins; *J. parkeri*, dwarf deciduous shrub for rock gardens, small, pinnate, sharply pointed leaves, tiny yellow flowers, in summer, followed by green-white fruits, 30cm/40cm (1ft/1½ft); *J.* x *stephanense*, scrambler or climber, oval to lance-shaped or pinnate leaves, often flushed cream-yellow when young, later dull green, fragrant, pink-white flowers, early to mid-summer, 5m (16ft).

Juglans *Walnut* Juglandaceae

Deciduous trees and some shrubs. Barely hardy to hardy. The walnuts are definitely trees for the largest of gardens only. Ash-like leaves, usually toothed, sometimes with good autumn colour. Male and female flowers, sometimes on separate plants; male flowers form pendent catkins, female flowers form inconspicuous short spikes, followed by green fruit containing edible nuts. Good fruiting forms don't come true from seed and it is only worth buying a grafted plant of a known fruiting strain. ❀ *J. nigra* (Black Walnut), large, aromatic, pinnate glossy dark green leaves with oblong to oval leaflets, gold-yellow in autumn, round fruit, in pairs, 30m/20m (100ft/60ft); *J. regia* (Common Walnut), aromatic, pinnate, light to mid-green leaves, with elliptic to oval leaflets, green, round fruit, 30m/15m (100ft/60ft).

Juncus *Rush* Juncaceae

Small evergreen or deciduous superficially grass-like perennials. Very hardy. Narrow, flattened or cylindrical leaves. Small green or brown flowers in spikes, in mid-summer, some on twisted stems. Divide established clumps in spring or autumn. ❀ *J. effusus* (Common Rush), 'Spiralis', evergreen, cylindrical, green stems, twisted into spirals, like a corkscrew, tiny brown flowers in loose clusters, 45cm/60cm (1½ft/2ft); *J. e.* 'Zebrinus', horizontal green and white bands.

Juniperus *Juniper* Cupressaceae

Small/large evergreen alpines, shrubs and trees. Barely hardy to hardy. Huge range of varieties for use as specimen shrubs or trees and for hedging; smaller forms for ground cover or in rock gardens. Blue, green, grey or yellow foliage, adult leaves usually fleshy, scale-like or linear; juvenile foliage pointed needles, usually sharp. Leaves can cause skin irritation. Clusters of tiny flowers on tips of branches. Male and female cones on separate plants; fleshy, ovoid and fruit-like. Grows best in moist, well-drained, deep, rich loam in full sun or light shade, sheltered from cold winds. No routine pruning but hedges should be clipped twice each year. Sow ripe seed in a cold-frame, take semi-ripe cuttings in summer or hardwood cuttings in spring.

❀ *J. chinensis* 'Expansa Variegata' (syn. *J. davurica* 'Expansa Albopicta'), dwarf, slow-growing, grey-green juvenile needles, splashed with cream, dark green, scale-like, diamond-shaped adult needles with pungent scent, violet to brown fruits marked with outlines of scales 1m/3m (3ft/10ft); *J. c.* 'Pyramidalis', slow-growing, blue-green prickly needles, most of which are juvenile, fruits green at first, then glaucous blue, black when ripe, 60cm/30cm (2ft/1ft); *J. communis* 'Compressa', slow-growing, dwarf, compact with very neat, dense habit, very prickly needles, silver beneath, blue-green at first with white stripe, may later revert to green, 80-100cm/45cm (2½-3ft/1½ft); *J. c.* 'Depressa Aurea', dwarf, almost prostrate, gold-yellow leaves, greener in winter; *J. c.* 'Hibernica', compact, very slow-growing, grey-blue to silver-blue needles, 3-5m/30cm (10-16ft/1ft); *J. c.* 'Repanda', dwarf, carpeting, grey-green needles, usually bronze in winter, 30cm/2m (1ft/6½ft); *J. horizontalis* 'Bar Harbor', prostrate, grey-green, glaucous, scale-like, smooth needles, purple in winter, 30cm (1ft)/ indefinite; *J. h.* 'Blue Chip', bright blue foliage throughout the year, 30cm (1ft); *J. h.* 'Hughes', mat-forming, radiating branches, grey-green to silver-blue foliage, 30cm (1ft); *J.* x *pfitzeriana* (syn. *J.* x *media*), 'Old Gold', compact, dark gold, scale-like needles retain colour in winter, dark purple fruits, later paler, 90cm/2m (3ft/6½ft); *J.* x *p.* 'Pfitzeriana Aurea', foliage mainly of the juvenile type, with bright gold-yellow, pointed needles, later yellow-green, 90cm/2m (3ft/6½ft); *J. procumbens* 'Nana', small tree, bright green, prickly, overlapping needles, brown-black fruits, 60cm/1.2m (2ft/4ft); *J. sabina* 'Tamariscifolia', prostrate, mainly juvenile needles, blue-green to dark green, have a pungent smell when crushed, brown-black fruits with white bloom, 1-2m/1.5-2m (3-6½ft/5-6½ft); *J. scopulorum* 'Skyrocket', narrow tree but opens out with age, green to blue-grey, fleshy, scale-like needles, blue-black fruits, 6m/50-60cm (20ft/1¾-2ft); *J. squamata*, 'Blue Carpet', semi-prostrate, bright, intensely blue-green sharply pointed needles, ovoid, glossy black fruit probably the best and most reliable of the prostrate 'blue' conifers, 30cm/1.2m (1ft/4ft); *J. s.* 'Blue Star', low-growing, hummock-forming, silver-blue needles, 40cm/1m (1½ft/3ft); *J. s.* 'Holger', small, spreading, needles cream-yellow at first, later green-green to blue, sometimes all three colours together, 2m/2m (6½ft/6½ft); *J. virginiana* 'Grey Owl', wide-spreading, soft silver- grey, scale-like needles, blue fruits with white bloom, 2-3m/3-4m (6½-10ft/10-13ft); *J. v.* 'Sulphur Spray', semi-prostrate, pale sulphur-yellow needles, sometimes mottled, 2m/2m (6½ft/6½ft).

above *Juniperus communis* 'Compressa'. I always think this, one of my favourite junipers, is more like a chess piece than anything living.

left *Juncus effusus* 'Spiralis'. Quite literally, one of the more curious twists that the rush family can take.

right *Kalmiopsis leachiana* 'Marcel le Piniec'. A pretty and endearing plant, if you can persuade it not to die after two or three years.

below *Kirengeshoma palmata*. A rather unfamiliar member of the *Hydrangea* family, gaining its unusual name from an ancient Japanese name for the plant.

Kalmia — Ericaceae

Small/large evergreen shrubs. Moderately hardy. Lovely flowering shrubs for acidic soils in woodland gardens. Leathery leaves, large cluster of cup-, bowl- or saucer-shaped flowers, summer. Requires acidic, moist soil enriched with humus in partial shade, although tolerant of full sun if the soil is kept moist. No routine pruning. Sow seed in warmth in spring, take semi-ripe cuttings in late spring, or layer. ❀ *K. angustifolia* f. *rubra* (Sheep Laurel), mound-forming, dark green oblong to elliptic leaves, small cup- or bowl-shaped red-purple flowers, early summer, 60cm/1.5m (2ft/5ft); *K. latifolia* (Calico Bush), glossy yellow-green, leathery leaves, cone-shaped, crimped, often deep red or pink buds open to white, red, purple or pink flowers, late spring to mid-summer, 60cm/1.5 (2ft/5ft); *K. l.* 'Ostbo Red', bright red buds open to pale pink flowers.

Kalmiopsis — Ericaceae

Evergreen alpine shrub, like a miniature *Kalmia*. Moderately hardy. Requires lime-free soil; a challenging and notoriously short-lived plant. Sow seed in warmth in spring or take semi-ripe cuttings in summer. ❀ *K. leachiana*, dwarf, bright green, oval, pointed leaves, sticky beneath, clusters of bell-shaped rose-pink flowers tinged purple, spring to early summer, 30cm/30cm (1ft/1ft).

Kerria — Rosaceae

Deciduous shrub. Hardy and extremely easy for a shrub border or against a wall. Simple leaves, cup- or saucer-shaped yellow flowers, spring. No routine pruning but periodically thin out congested stems. Take semi-ripe cuttings in summer, divide in autumn or remove natural layers. ❀ *K. japonica*, narrow, dull green oval leaves, finely toothed, small, solitary rose-like flowers, 3-5cm (1-2in) in diameter, mid- to late spring, 2m/2.5m (6½ft-8ft); *K. j.* 'Golden Guinea', large single flowers, 5-6cm (2in) in diameter; *K. j.* 'Picta' (syn. *K. j.* 'Variegata'), grey-green leaves with cream-white margins, flowers less abundant than other varieties, 1.5m/2m (5ft/6½ft); *K. j.* 'Pleniflora', double pompom-like gold-yellow flowers, still the best form, 3m/3m (10ft/10ft).

Kirengeshoma Hydrangeaceae

Medium rhizomatous ornamentals. Moderately hardy. Requires lime-free soil in a shaded position and an imposing feature in early autumn. Maple-like leaves, tubular, waxy yellow flowers on wiry stems. Sow seed in a cold-frame when ripe or divide established plants in spring. ❀ *K. palmata*, clump-forming, irregularly cut leaves on dark purple stems, shuttlecock-like flowers, waxy, pale yellow, late summer to autumn, 60-120cm/175cm (2-4ft/5½ft).

Knautia *Scabious* Dipsacaceae

Medium/large annuals and hardy perennials. Moderately hardy and essential plants for the wild flower garden on light soil. Rosettes of simple or divided basal leaves, cup-shaped inflorescences with prominent stamens, surrounded by bristly-haired bracts. Sow seed in a cold-frame in spring or take basal cuttings. ❀ *K. arvensis* (syn. *Scabiosa arvensis*) (Field Scabious), pale green hairy leaves, blue-violet flowers on tall hairy stems, mid-summer to early autumn, 1.5m/30cm (5ft/1ft); *K. macedonica* (syn. *Scabiosa rumelica*), clump-forming, pinnate mid-green basal leaves, crimson to purple-red flowers on curving stems, mid- to late summer, 60-80cm/45cm (2ft-2½ft/1½ft).

Kniphofia
Red Hot Poker Asphodelaceae

Small/large evergreen or deciduous rhizomatous ornamental. Tender to moderately hardy. An essential plant for the herbaceous or mixed border. Light to mid-green or blue-green lance-shaped or strap-shaped leaves, sometimes thin and grass-like. Dense, erect spikes of tubular or cylindrical usually pendent flowers on long stout stems, in red, orange, cream, white, yellow, green-white or green. Divide established plants in late spring. Tie up leaves loosely in winter to protect crown. No routine pruning. ❀ *K.* 'Alcazar', bright red flowers, 1.5m (5ft); *K. caulescens*, grey, toothed, strap-shaped leaves, orange-red buds open to silver-yellow flowers with conspicuous stamens, in summer, 1.2m/60cm (4ft/2ft); *K. galpinii*, small, red-orange flowers in late summer, 60cm/30cm (2ft/1ft); *K.* 'Little Maid', grass-like leaves, narrow, tubular flowers, green buds open to ivory-white flowers, late summer to autumn, 60cm/45cm (2ft/1½ft); *K.* 'Percy's Pride', green flowers flushed with yellow, late summer to early autumn, 1.2m/60cm (4ft/2ft); *K.* 'Royal Standard', bright vermilion buds open to yellow flowers, mid- to late summer, 90-100cm/60cm (3ft/2ft); *K. thomsonii* var. *snowdenii*, barely hardy, erect linear leaves, curved, yellow-orange to coral pink, mid-summer to late autumn, 90cm/45cm (3ft/1½ft).

Koelreuteria Sapindaceae

Small/medium deciduous trees. Barely hardy to moderately hardy. Pinnate leaves, large clusters of bowl-shaped flowers followed by inflated seed capsules. This plant is a glorious sight in full flower. No routine pruning. Sow seeds in a cold-frame in autumn or take root cuttings in late winter. ❀ *K. paniculata* (Golden Rain Tree), pinnate leaves, pink-red at first, later mid-green, yellow in autumn, small yellow flowers in large erect panicles, mid- to late summer, bladder-like, green seed capsules flushed red or pink, 10m/10m (33ft/33ft).

Kolkwitzia
Beauty Bush Caprifoliaceae

Deciduous shrub. Moderately hardy. Simple leaves, masses of charming bell-shaped pink flowers in dense clusters, late spring to early summer. No routine pruning. Take semi-ripe cuttings between late spring and early summer, or remove suckers in spring. ❀ *K. amabilis*, small, oval dark green leaves, clusters of pink flowers with orange to yellow speckled throats on arching branches, 3m/4m (10ft/13ft); *K. a.* 'Pink Cloud', a better form with deeper pink flowers, 2m/2m (6½ft/6½ft).

left *Kniphofia* 'Percy's Pride'. There's no better variety than this for demonstrating that red hot pokers need not be red.

right *Lactuca sativa* 'Red Salad Bowl'. The range of lettuce varieties has multiplied enormously in recent seasons; and some are now very good ornamentals.

+ Laburnocytisus Papilionaceae

Deciduous tree. Moderately hardy. Dark green palmate leaves with three leaflets, pea-like flowers resembling those of *Laburnum* and *Cytisus*, of two colours and two types at the same time, late spring to early summer. An extraordinary plant, a graft hybrid produced by grafting *Laburnum* onto *Cytisus*. The effect is an acquired taste that I have never acquired. ❀ + *L.* 'Adamii', erect tree, long sprays of yellow pea-like flowers and purple-pink *Cytisus*-like flowers, usually on separate branches, late spring to early summer, sometimes intermediate, pea-like flowers of copper-pink on all branches, 8m/6m (25ft/20ft).

above + *Laburnocytisus adamii*. Quite the oddest tree that most gardeners are ever likely to see.

Laburnum Papilionaceae

Small deciduous trees. Hardy. Good for small gardens, particularly as a specimen tree, but not with young children as all parts of the plant are toxic, most particularly the seedpods. Small leaves comprising three leaflets, pendent clusters of bright yellow pea-like flowers, late spring to early summer, followed by seedpods. Thrives in fairly fertile well-drained soil in full sun. The best forms do not come true from seed and are grafted. ❀ *L. alpinum* 'Pendulum', glossy dark green leaves, paler beneath, narrow clusters of bright yellow, slightly fragrant flowers, 8m/8m (25ft/25ft); *L.* x *watereri* 'Vossii', shiny pale green leaves, huge, trailing clusters of gold-yellow flowers, 8m/8m (25ft/25ft).

Lactuca *Lettuce* Asteraceae

Leafy salad crop. Grown as half-hardy and hardy annuals. Different varieties are suitable for growing throughout the year, even in cold areas, if plants are raised in warmth in winter. Extremely varied in leaf form and texture, and generally divided into four groups: butterhead (also called smooth or cabbage), crisphead, cos and loose leaf. A fifth type, stem lettuce, is sometimes included, as here (see below). Thrives in well-drained moist soil enriched with humus, in full sun. Rather intolerant of acidic soil. Sow seed in warmth from late winter to early spring, also in autumn with cloche or other protection for harvesting winter to spring, and during spring and summer for harvesting from summer to autumn.

Butterhead lettuces (firm round hearts, smooth leaves): 'All The Year Round', hardy, slow to bolt, sow spring to summer; 'Tom Thumb', compact, early dwarf variety, long standing, sow spring to summer.

Crisphead lettuces (firm hearts, crinkly crisp leaves): 'Arctic King', very hardy, sow autumn outdoors, harvest in spring; 'Avoncrisp', mildew resistant, sow in summer; 'Avondefiance', dark green leaves, resistant to mildew and root aphid, sow in summer; 'Lakeland', solid, crisp, resistant to mildew and root aphid, sow spring to late summer; 'Webb's Wonderful', curly leaves, dark green, slow to bolt, sow spring to late summer.

Cos lettuces (elongated leaves, erect habit): 'Little Gem', dwarf cos, a superb modern lettuce, tight hearts, sow spring to late summer; 'Lobjoits Green Cos', large, tall, sweet, crisp, green leaves, sow spring to late summer; 'Valmain', large, mildew resistant, sow summer and autumn; 'Winter Density', semi-cos, crisp hearts, dark green leaves, slow to mature and bolt, resistant to cold, sow autumn.

Loose leaf lettuces (curly, crinkly leaves, can be cut as needed, make very attractive edging to kitchen garden, sow early spring to summer): 'Lollo Bionda', pale green, indented leaves; 'Lollo Rossa', red-tinged very curly, crisp leaves; 'Red Salad

Bowl', oak-like leaves tinged red; 'Salad Bowl', slow to bolt, green oak-like leaves.

Stem lettuce, a Chinese vegetable that grows on a stem to 30cm (1ft), sow spring to late summer for harvesting in autumn, both stems and leaves are eaten but grown mainly for swollen stems: 'Celtuce'.

Lagurus *Hare's tail Grass* Poaceae

Annual grass. Moderately hardy. Linear to lance-shaped pale green leaves, ovoid, fluffy green-white, finely hairy, silky inflorescences, sometimes tinged purple at first, later cream; good for cutting for small dried arrangements. Sow seed in a cold-frame or cool greenhouse in late summer or early autumn, or in growing positions in spring. ❀ *L. ovatus*, arching tufts of lance-shaped green leaves, inflorescences borne on slender stems, early summer to early autumn, 50cm/30cm (1¾ft/1ft).

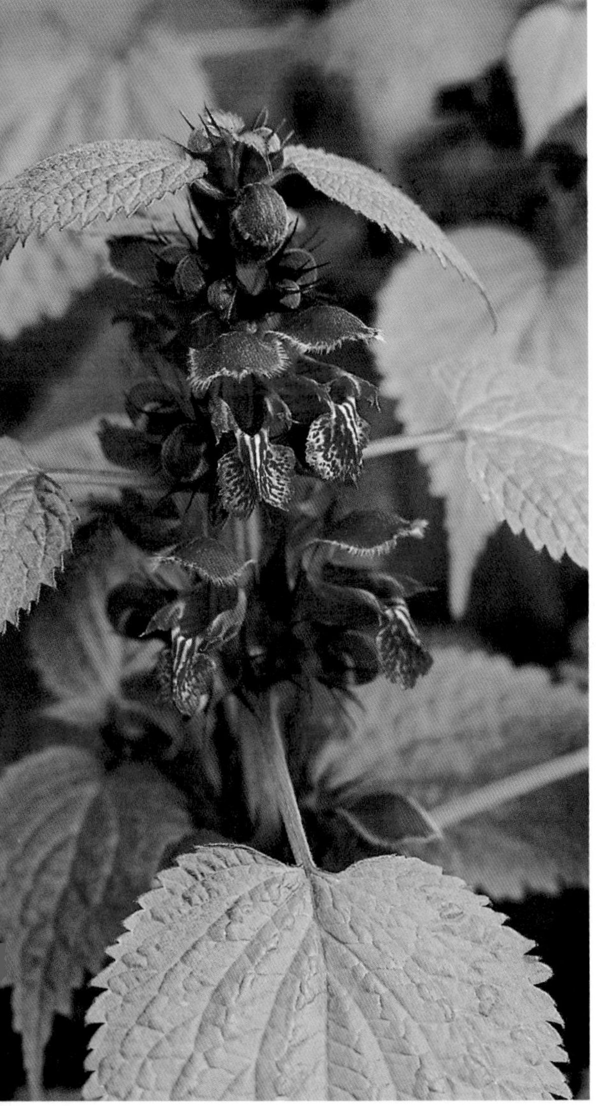

left *Lamium orvala*. A lovely demonstration of what a commonplace genus such as *Lamium* is capable.

Lamium *Dead-nettle* Lamiaceae

Small annuals and mainly evergreen perennials. Hardy. Suitable as ground cover and also good for containers, especially hanging baskets. The fact that some species are weeds shouldn't deter you. Narrow, aromatic oval to lance-shaped, toothed leaves, often variegated. Tubular, two-lipped, solitary flowers late spring to summer. Grows best in fertile, moist soil in shade, but tolerates poor, dry conditions in full sun. Sow seed in a cold-frame in winter, divide established plants in spring or autumn or take semi-ripe cuttings in summer. ❀ *L. galeobdolon*, mat-forming, oval, toothed, dark green leaves with silver patterning, yellow flower spikes, red-brown marks on lower lip, in summer, very invasive, 60cm (2ft)/indefinite; *L. g.* 'Florentinum', leaves have red-purple or bronze tints in winter, *L. g.* 'Hermann's Pride', narrow, oval leaves streaked with silver; *L. g.* 'Silberteppich' (syn. 'Silver Carpet'), silver leaves with green net pattern, yellow flowers in spring, less invasive than other varieties of this species; *L. maculatum* 'Aureum', triangular to oval green-yellow leaves with white centres, tinged silver, pink flowers, 40cm/1m (1½ft/3ft); *L. m.* 'Beacon Silver', dwarf, strikingly coloured silver leaves with narrow green margins, pale pink flowers, becomes disappointingly untidy as it ages, 10cm (4in); *L. m.* 'Pink Pewter', silver leaves, crinkly green edges, pale pink flowers, 20cm (8in); *L. m.* 'White Nancy', silver leaves, narrow green edges, ivory-white flowers, 13cm (5in); *L. orvala*, clump-forming, oval to triangular toothed, hairy, pointed dark green leaves with prominent veining, tubular, pink, white or dark purple flowers, mid- to late spring, 60cm/30cm (2ft/1ft).

Lantana *Shrub Verbena* Verbenaceae

Small, tender, evergreen perennials and shrubs grown under protection but also, rather valuably, as summer bedding plants. Toothed, simple leaves, sometimes crinkled. Abundant clusters of tiny, tubular flowers in summer which give a very distinctive and unique appearance as different colours appear simultaneously. Contact with leaves may cause skin irritation; all parts toxic if eaten. Sow seed in warmth in spring or take semi-ripe cuttings in summer. ❀ *L. camara*,. small shrub, oval, mid-green wrinkled leaves, sometimes strongly scented but not exactly pleasant, flower clusters usually yellow at first, later red, also may be white, lilac or wholly yellow with darker centres, sometimes with more than one colour on the plant, 1-2m/1-2m (3-6½ft/3-6½ft); *L. camora* is available in several

above *Lantana montevidensis*. This species has the characteristic *Lantana* flower form but not the expected range of colours.

right *Larix kaempferi* 'Nana'. I find the dwarf larches very pretty but much more tricky than other dwarf conifers to satisfy.

colour selections, including 'Brasier', bright red, 'Cloth of Gold', bright yellow, 'Feston Rose', deep pink and yellow and 'Snow White', cream-white; *L. montevidensis*, mat-forming shrub, oval to lance-shaped, toothed mid-green leaves, clusters of pink-purple flowers with yellow centres, in summer, 20-100cm/60-120cm (8in-3ft/2-4ft).

Lapageria
Chilean Bell Flower Philesiaceae

Small/medium evergreen climbers. Barely hardy. In mild areas can be grown against a sheltered wall. Leathery, oval dark green leaves, quite glorious waxy, pendent oblong or bell-shaped flowers, singly or in small clusters, summer to late autumn. One of the most stylish of climbing plants, the national flower of Chile. No routine pruning. Sow seed in warmth in spring, take semi-ripe cuttings in summer or layer in late autumn or winter. ❀ *L. rosea*, erect, twining, dark green, oval, pointed leaves, pink to red flowers, sometimes followed by pink flowers, 5m (16ft); *L. r.* 'Nash Court', pale pink flowers with darker pink or red mottling.

Larix *Larch* Pinaceae

Large deciduous coniferous trees. Hardy. Leaves are soft, flat needles, blue-green, pale or bright green, with glorious orange, red or yellow colours in autumn. Thimble-shaped flowers are followed by female and male cones. Male cones spherical to ovoid, pink or yellow; female cones cylindrical, ovoid or conical, usually purple at first, later brown. One of the loveliest of conifers but not plants for small gardens. ❀ *L. decidua* (European Larch), soft, pale green leaves on drooping branches, rich yellow in autumn, twigs off-white or buff, flowers red at first, later purple, female cones red or pale green, then brown, male cones yellow, 30m/4-6m (100ft/13-20ft); *L. kaempferi* (Japanese Larch), linear, grey-green or blue-green leaves, bright green at first, russet in autumn, twigs reddish, pink flowers, sometimes soft lime-green, 30m/4-6m (100ft/13-20ft); *L. k.* 'Blue Dwarf', shrubby, blue-green leaves, 1m/1.5m (3ft/5ft); *L. k.* 'Nana', dwarf, bright green leaves, 50cm/50cm (1¾ft/1¾ft); *L. k.* 'Pendula', weeping branches, leaves orange and yellow in autumn, deep red flowers 25m/6.8m (80ft-26ft).

Lathyrus Papilionaceae

Small/large annuals and herbaceous and evergreen perennials. Barely hardy to moderately hardy. Many are climbers for growing up netting, trellis or stick pyramids; others are bushy and clump-forming, suitable for rock gardens and borders, with some small species suitable for containers. Pinnate leaves, fragrant, pea-like flowers. Seeds are toxic if eaten. Require fertile, well-drained soil enriched with humus, in full sun or light shade. Intolerant of poor soil or deep shade. Flowering of sweet peas is prolonged if deadheaded regularly. Sow seed, after soaking, in a cold-frame in early spring or in growing positions in mid-spring; alternatively, may be sown in autumn in a cold-frame or in growing positions in mild areas.

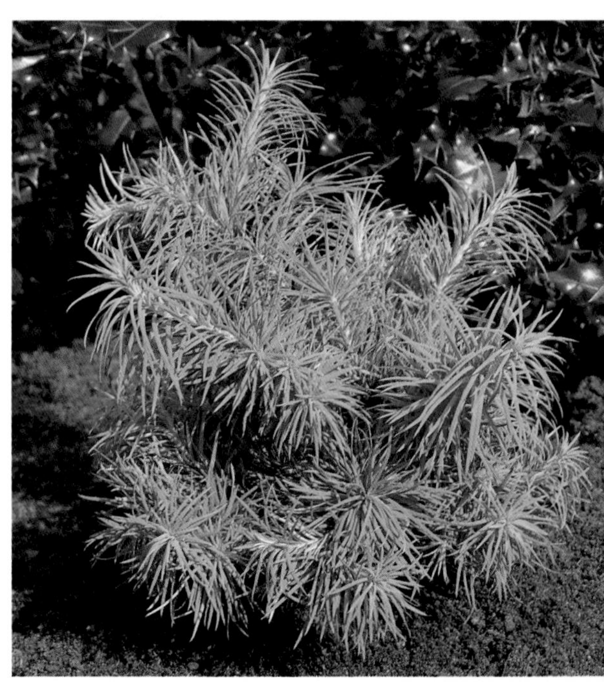

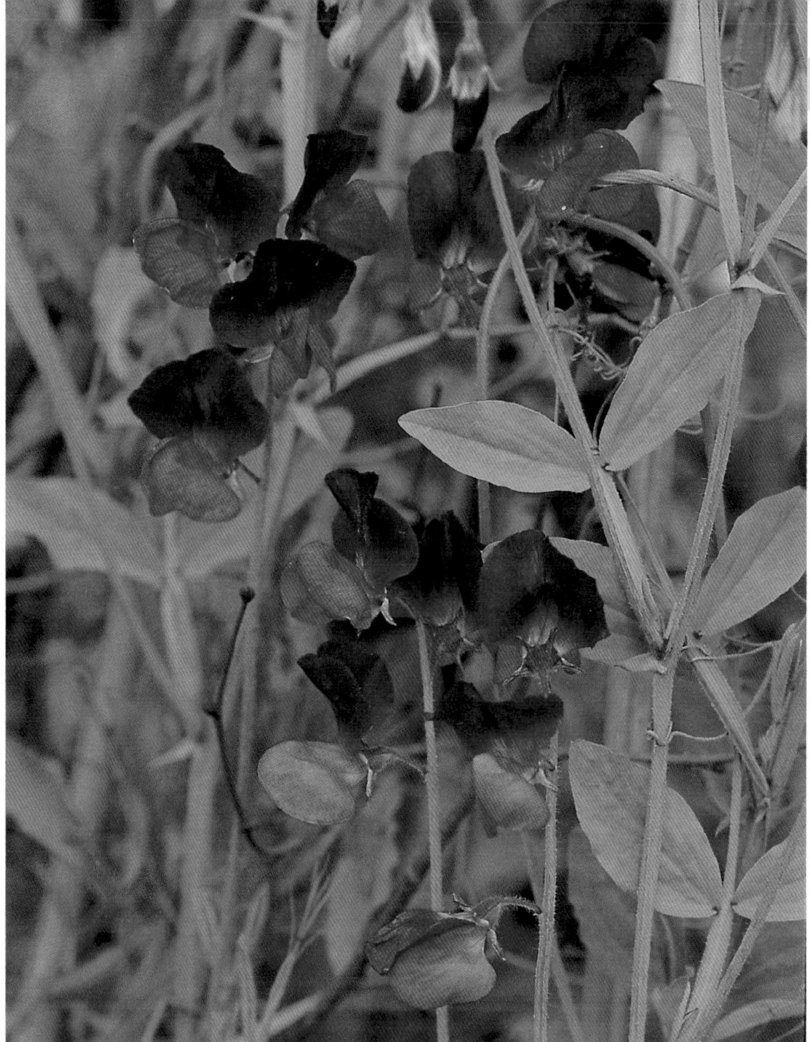

Perennial Sweet Peas

❀ *L. aureus* (syn. *L. luteus* 'Aureus'), clump-forming herbaceous perennial, dark green leaves with elliptic to oval leaflets, clusters of yellow-orange flowers, gold-yellow at first, late spring to early summer, 60cm/30cm (2ft/1ft); *L. grandiflorus*, scrambling herbaceous perennial, mid-green leaves, clusters of bicoloured flowers in pink and maroon, mid-summer, the best of the perennial sweet peas, 2m (6½ft); *L. latifolius*, climbing herbaceous perennial, blue-green leaves, with oblong to elliptic leaflets, clusters of magenta-pink flowers, summer to early autumn, 2m (6½ft); *L. l.* 'White Pearl', white flowers; *L. nervosus*, climbing herbaceous perennial, barely hardy, leathery grey-green leaves, oval to elliptic leaflets, clusters of fragrant red and purple flowers summer to early autumn, 5m (16ft); *L. vernus*, clump-forming herbaceous perennial, pale to mid-green leaves with sharp-pointed, oval leaflets, clusters of purple-blue flowers, mid- to late spring, 20-40cm/45cm (8-1½ft/1½ft); *L. v.* 'Alboroseus', rose-pink and white bicoloured flowers.

Annual Sweet Peas

L. odoratus, smooth, oval mid-green leaflets with tendrils at ends of leaf stalks, fragrant flowers in most colours except yellow, early summer to early autumn. Varieties are divided according to height and flower type.

Tall varieties: Spencer Varieties, good for both exhibition and garden, flower from early summer to autumn, four to five flowers on each stem, 2m (6½ft) but with feeding and re-training downwards then up again, can be at least double this; 'Blue Danube', blue-mauve; 'Brian Clough', red; 'Champagne Bubbles', very fragrant cream-pink; 'Cream Southbourne', fragrant, frilled cream; 'Midnight', glorious dark maroon; 'Royal Wedding', white, fragrant, long stemmed; 'Sally Unwin', pink; 'The Doctor', mauve; 'White Leamington', white, sweetly fragrant.

Galaxy Varieties, up to eight waved flowers per stem, usually in mixed colours, salmon-pink, rose-pink, scarlet, lavender-blue and white, 2-2.5m (6½-8ft).

Intermediate varieties, from 60-100cm (2-3ft): 'Continental', semi-climbing, up to five flowers per stem, slightly waved wing petals, white and shades of pink, blue, red, 1-1.1m (3ft); 'Jet Set', bushy, up to five flowers per stem, red, blue, pink, white, with slightly waved petals; 'Snoopea', up to four flowers per stem, waved, red, blue, pink and white, lacks tendrils, does not need supporting, 60-75cm (2-2½ft); 'Supersnoop', as 'Snoopea', but slightly more vigorous.

Dwarf varieties, 15-45cm/15cm (6in-1½ft/6in), less self-supporting: 'Bijou', bushy, slightly fragrant flowers, up to four per stem, pink, blue, red or white, require only a little support, 45cm (1½ft); 'Cupid', spreading, abundant, large fragrant flowers in mixed colours, good for containers; 'Patio', well-scented, in mixed colours.

Other variety: 'Matucana' climber, wonderful very old type, the one that I would not be without, very strong fragrance, small deep blue and purple flowers, 2m (6½ft).

above *Lathyrus* 'Matucana'. There's is absolutely no question in my mind that this ancient variety has the richest fragrance of any sweet pea I have ever grown.

Laurentia — Campanulaceae

Small half-hardy annuals and herbaceous perennials. Those described here are perennials usually grown as annuals. Probably the best bell-flowers for summer bedding and containers. Lobed to divided, linear, oval or oblong leaves, solitary, star-like tubular flowers with five narrow petals. Sow seed in warmth in mid-winter or take semi-ripe stem cuttings in late summer. ❀ *L. axillaris* (syns. *Isotoma axillaris, Solenopsis axillaris*), narrow, dark green leaves with toothed lobes, fragrant, lavender-blue flowers, early summer to early autumn, 30cm/30cm (1ft/1ft); *L. a.* 'Blue Stars', sky-blue flowers; *L. a.* 'Shooting Stars', white flowers.

below *Laurentia axillaris* 'Blue Stars'. This is a plant that has become almost indispensable in recent years for hanging baskets.

Laurus *Bay* Lauraceae

Large evergreen shrubs and small trees. Moderately hardy. Good for topiary and growing in containers, in both formal and informal situations. Tolerant of salt spray but need protection from cold, drying winds. Aromatic, narrow, elongated dark green, rather glossy leaves with slightly wavy margins. Inconspicuous green-yellow male and female flowers on separate plants, in spring and early summer, followed on female trees by purple-black fruits. No routine pruning but may be clipped twice each year or cut back hard to rejuvenate if necessary. Sow seed in a cold-frame in autumn, take semi-ripe cuttings in summer, or layer in early autumn. ❀ *L. nobilis* (Bay Laurel, Sweet Bay), slow-growing evergreen tree or large shrub. Oval, leathery, pointed dark green leaves, clusters of green-yellow flowers with prominent stamens, in spring, followed on female plants by oval black fruits, 12m/10m (40ft/33ft); *L. n.* 'Aurea', rather sickly looking gold-yellow leaves.

Lavandula *Lavender* Lamiaceae

Small evergreen shrubs and sub-shrubs. Barely hardy to moderately hardy. Many of the lavenders commonly sold are not fully hardy and are best overwintered in containers in a greenhouse in cold areas, or grown at the base of a warm, sunny wall. Leaves simple, entire to toothed, pinnate, with rolled margins. spikes of tubular two-lipped flowers, usually (but not invariably) very fragrant, in spring and summer. Require fertile, well-drained soil in full sun. Clip after flowering to just below base of flower stems. Take semi-ripe cuttings in summer. ❀ *L. angustifolia* (syn. *L. officinalis*) (Old English Lavender), moderately hardy, linear, oblong leaves, grey-green at first, greener later, pale grey-blue flowers, late spring to late summer, 1m/1.2m (3ft/4ft); *L. a.* 'Alba', grey-green leaves, white flowers, mid- to late summer, 50cm (1¾ft); *L. a.* 'Hidcote', compact, silver-grey leaves, dark purple flowers, 60cm/75cm (2ft/2½ft); *L. a.* 'Imperial Gem', grey leaves, excellent small variety, dark purple flowers; *L. a.* 'Nana Alba', very compact, white flowers, in mid-summer, 30cm/30cm (1ft/1ft); *L.* x *intermedia* 'Grappenhall', grey-green, oblong leaves, slightly fragrant, pale purple flowers, mid- to late summer, 50cm/80cm (1¾ft/2½ft); *L. lanata*, bushy, linear to inversely lance-shaped, white woolly leaves, fragrant dark purple flowers, in late summer, 75cm/90cm (2½ft/3ft); *L. stoechas* (French Lavender), barely hardy, compact, bushy, grey-green linear leaves, fragrant dark purple flowers with conspicuous rose-purple bracts in tufts at tips of flower spikes, late spring to summer, 60cm/60cm (2ft/2ft); *L. viridis*, barely hardy, pale green leaves, small white flowers with green bracts at the tip of the flower spike, mid- to late summer, 60cm/75cm (2ft/2½ft).

below *Lavandula angustifolia* 'Imperial Gem'. I think this is the best new lavender variety to appear for many years.

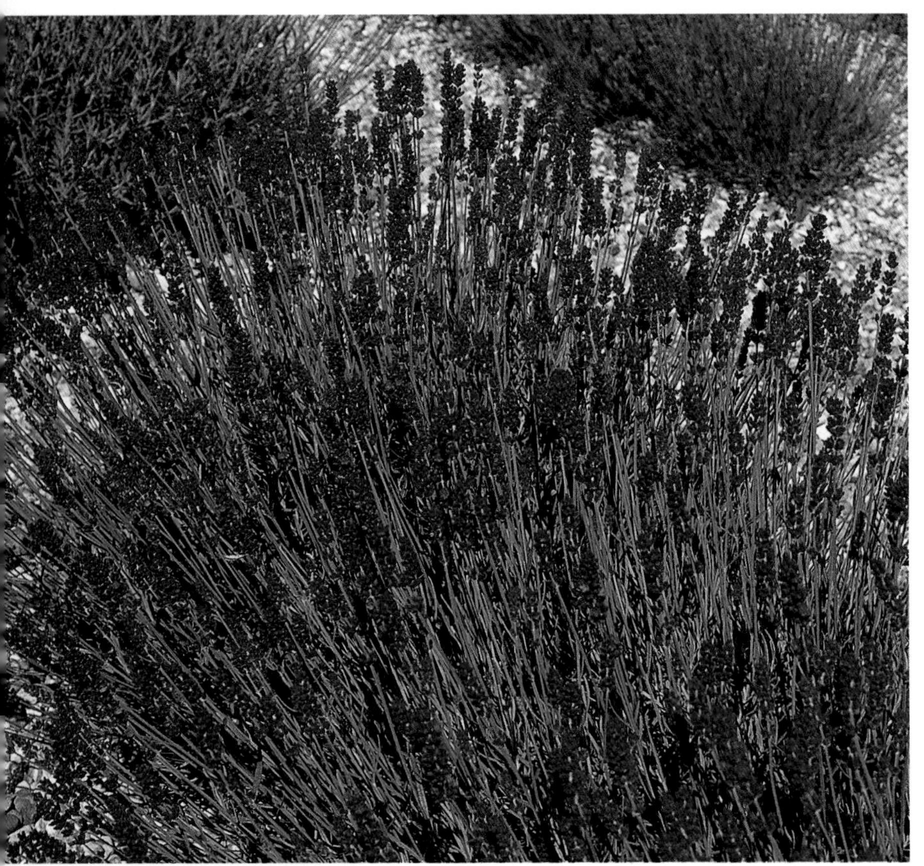

Lavatera *Tree Mallow* Malvaceae

Annuals, biennials, evergreen or herbaceous perennials, deciduous, evergreen or semi-evergreen shrubs and sub-shrubs. Barely hardy to hardy. Suitable for summer bedding and herbaceous borders; annuals, perennials and biennials make good cut flowers. Leaves mainly light green or grey-green, heart-shaped to triangular. Saucer- or funnel-shaped, five-petalled pink or white flowers, sometimes with characteristic dark veining, mid-summer to mid-autumn. Prune shrubby forms hard in spring. Sow seed of shrubs and perennials in a cold-frame in mid-summer, sow seed of biennials and *L. trimestris* in growing positions in mid-spring; take semi-ripe cuttings in early summer or hardwood cuttings in winter. ❀ *L.* 'Barnsley', semi-evergreen perennial or sub-shrub, mystifyingly popular and far too over-planted in gardens, downy green leaves, abundant funnel-shaped white flowers with red centres, summer to autumn, 2m/2m (6½ft/6½ft);

L. 'Burgundy Wine', semi-evergreen perennial or sub-shrub, grey-green leaves, funnel-shaped pink flowers with darker veining, summer, 2m/2m (6½ft/6½ft); *L. maritima*, small evergreen shrub, downy, grey-green leaves, rose, pink, lilac or white flowers with purple veins, deep purple centres, summer, 1.5m/1m (5ft/3ft); *L.* 'Rosea', semi-evergreen sub-shrub, grey-green leaves, abundant clusters of rose-pink flowers, 2m/2m (6½ft/6½ft); *L. thuringiaca* 'Ice Cool', perennial, downy grey-green basal leaves with heart-shaped bases, abundant, funnel-shaped white flowers, singly or in clusters, 1.5m/1.5m (5ft/5ft); *L. trimestris* 'Mont Blanc', dwarf hardy annual, dark green lobed leaves, funnel-shaped white flowers, 50cm/45cm (1¾ft/1½ft); *L. t.* 'Pink Beauty', pale pink flowers with darker veining, purple centres, 60cm/45cm (2ft/1½ft); *L. t.* 'Silver Cup', abundant funnel-shaped, silver-pink flowers with darker veining, throughout summer, an excellent if assertive bedding plant, 75cm/45cm (2½ft/1½ft).

Leontopodium *Edelweiss* Asteraceae

Small deciduous alpines. Very hardy. Simple entire leaves. Brown button-like inflorescences surrounded by narrow, long white downy bracts, late spring to mid-summer. Sow seed when ripe or in late winter or early spring in a cold-frame, or divide established plants between early spring and early summer. ❀ *L. alpinum*, tufts of linear to lance-shaped grey-green leaves, downy beneath, clusters of white inflorescences surrounded by woolly white bracts although a popular and instantly recognisable plant, it isn't easy to care for as those woolly leaves trap moisture, 20cm/10cm (8in/4in).

Lepidium *Cress* Brassicaceae

Small leafy salad crop. Moderately hardy, but often grown indoors together with mustard (or, more commonly, rape), to be picked at the seedling stage and used in salads or as a garnish. Quick growing, therefore good for children to grow. Small, bright green linear leaves. Sometimes produces white flowers followed by red-brown seeds. Sow seed in warmth throughout the year or in a cold-frame or seedbed outside. ❀ *L. sativum* (Garden Cress), strongly aromatic, deeply cut linear leaves, small white flowers and red -brown seeds in round, flattened pod. 'Curled' varieties can be grown outdoors as a cut-and-come-again salad crop; 'Greek', peppery taste, usually cut when young.

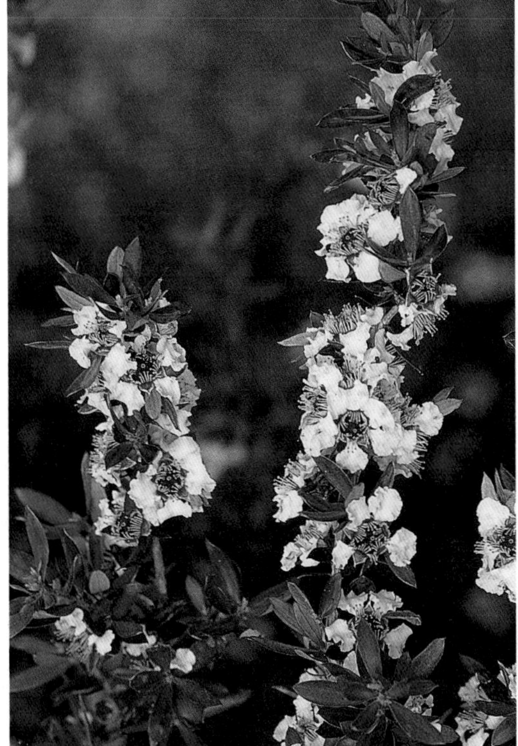

left *Leptospermum lanigerum*. Despite its English name, this is not the source of tea as we know it and is in fact an Australian species.

Leptospermum *Tea Tree* Myrtaceae

Small/large evergreen shrubs or small trees. Tender to moderately hardy. Suitable for coastal areas; in cold areas less hardy species and varieties may survive outdoors in very sheltered positions but are best grown in containers and given winter protection. Small, usually aromatic, purple-green leaves. Small, rose-like cup-shaped to star-shaped white, pink or red flowers, singly or in clusters, early to mid-summer. No routine pruning. Sow seed in warmth in autumn or spring, or take semi-ripe cuttings in summer. ❀ *L. lanigerum*, barely hardy erect shrub or small tree, more or less oval to oblong or oval, aromatic green or silver leaves with silky hairs, may be bronze in autumn, cup-shaped white flowers with conspicuous red-brown calyces, 3-5m/1.5m (10-15ft/5ft); *L. rupestre* (syn. *L. humifusum*), moderately hardy prostrate shrub, glossy dark green, elliptic or more or less oval, aromatic leaves on red stems, sometimes bronze-purple in autumn, saucer- to star-shaped white flowers, singly or in pairs, late spring to summer, 25cm-1.5m/1-1.5m (10in-5ft/3-5ft); *L. scoparium*, tender, compact aromatic shrub, narrow oblong, pointed leaves, dark green, young leaves often with silver hairs, abundant solitary cup-shaped to saucer-shaped white flowers, sometimes tinged pink, late spring to early summer, 3m/3m (10ft/10ft); *L. s. nanum* 'Kiwi', dwarf shrub, immature leaves tinged purple, abundant deep crimson-pink flowers, 1m/1m (3ft/3ft); *L. s.* 'Nichollsii', fairly hardy small shrub, purple-bronze leaves, crimson flowers, 2m/1m (6½ft/3ft); *L. s.* 'Red Damask', fairly hardy, dark green, purple-flushed leaves, double, deep red flowers, 2m/1m (6½ft/3ft).

above *Leucanthemum* x *superbum* 'Wirral Supreme'. One of the oldest and best forms of what used to be called Shasta daisies.

Leucanthemopsis Asteraceae

Small hardy evergreen perennials. Pinnate leaves, daisy-like flowers in summer. Sow seed when ripe, in spring, divide established plants or take basal cuttings. ❀ *L. alpina* (syn. *Chrysanthemum alpina*), mat-forming, oval to spoon-shaped silver-grey leaves, white flowers, sometimes pink later, with yellow centres, 10cm/20cm (4in/8in).

Leucanthemum Asteraceae

Small/medium annuals and herbaceous perennials. Barely hardy to moderately hardy. Suitable for rock and wild gardens, good cut flowers. Basal rosettes of dark green, entire, toothed, pinnate leaves with scalloped or lobed edges. Daisy-like, single, semi-double or double flowers, usually white with yellow centre. Sow seed in warmth in late winter, in flowering positions in spring (annuals), or in a cold-frame in spring or autumn (perennials), or divide established plants between early spring and late summer. ❀ *L.* x *superbum* (syn. *Chrysanthemum maximum* 'Aglaia') (Shasta Daisy), clump-forming perennial, inversely lance-shaped, toothed leaves, white, double or semi-double flowers with yellow centres, 60cm/50-60cm (2ft/1¾-2ft); *L.* x *s.* 'Phyllis Smith', single flowers, with finely cut petals, 90cm/60cm (3ft/2ft); *L.* x *s.* 'Wirral Supreme', double flowers, usually with a central disk of erect tubular florets, 90cm/75cm (3ft/2½ft); *L. vulgare*, variable rhizomatous perennial, usually spoon-shaped, toothed silver-green leaves, solitary silver-white flowers with gold-yellow centres, late spring to mid-summer, 30-90cm/60cm (1-3ft/2ft).

Leucojum *Snowflake* Amaryllidaceae

Small bulbous ornamentals. Barely hardy to hardy. Good for naturalizing in grass, for rock gardens and borders and to take over the white flower theme as snowdrops fade. Strap-shaped to linear basal leaves, bell-shaped white flowers. Sow seed when ripe or divide clumps as the flowers fade. ❀ *L. aestivum* (Summer Snowflake), bright green, erect, strap-like leaves, waxy white flowers edged with green, late spring, 45-60cm/8cm (1½-2ft/3in); *L. a.* 'Gravetye Giant', very imposing large flowers up to 4cm (1in) long on tall stems, much the best variety, 90cm (3ft); *L. autumnale* (Autumn Snowflake), mid-green narrow, grass-like leaves, bell-like flowers flushed pink, early to mid-autumn, 10-15cm/5cm (4-6in/2in); *L. nicaeense*, fairly hardy, narrow linear leaves, waxy bell-shaped white flowers, spring to early summer, 10cm/5cm (4in/2in); *L. vernum* (Spring Snowflake), fairly hardy, glossy, strap-shaped dark green leaves, waxy white, cup-shaped flowers with prominent green spots on each petal, sometimes flushed purple or pink, winter and early spring, 20-30cm/8cm (8-1ft/3in).

right *Leucojum aestivum* 'Gravetye Giant'. The giant among leucojums, named appropriately after the garden of William Robinson, a giant among gardeners.

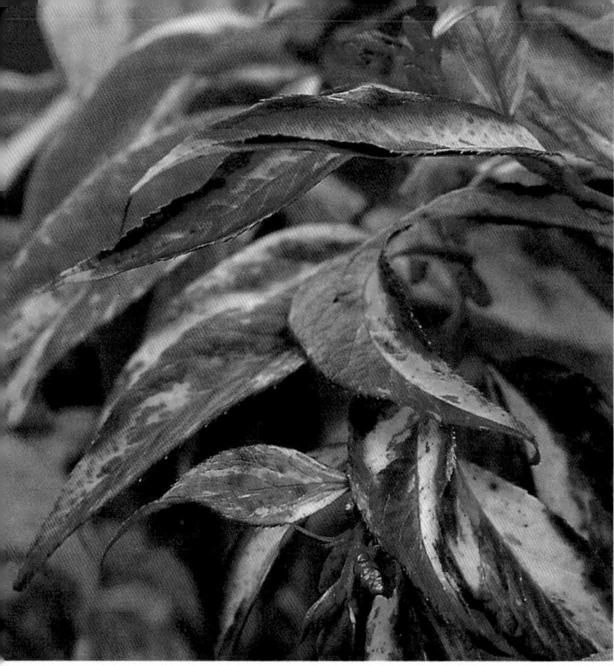

left *Leucothoe walteri* 'Rainbow'. This is a popular shrub but one that I find has too many colours for its own good.

Leucothoe Ericaceae

Small deciduous, evergreen or semi-evergreen shrubs. Barely hardy to moderately hardy. Good for woodland or rock gardens. Glossy, dark green, simple leaves of variable shape, clusters of tiny, urn-shaped flowers in summer. Thrives in acid, moist soil enriched with humus, in partial or deep shade. No routine pruning. Sow seed in a cold-frame in spring, take semi-ripe cuttings in summer or divide suckering, established plants in spring. ❀ *L.* 'Scarletta' evergreen, lance-shaped leaves, rich scarlet at first, later green, flushed red in winter, white flowers on pendent stems, 1.2m/3m (4ft/10ft); *L. walteri* (syn. *L. fontanesiana*) 'Rainbow', leaves flushed pink when young, later with white variegation, white flowers, in late spring, 1.5/2m (5ft/6½ft).

Levisticum *Lovage* Apiaceae

Perennial herb. Moderately hardy. Pinnate, dark green leaves, clusters of star-shaped flowers, in mid-summer. The whole plant smells strongly of celery. All parts may cause irritation when skin is exposed to the sun. Sow seed when ripe or divide established plants in spring. ❀ *L. officinale*, smooth leaves, up to 70cm (2¼ft) long, tiny yellow-green flowers in summer, followed by tiny, aromatic seeds, 2m/1m (6½ft/3ft).

Lewisia Portulacaceae

Small hardy, evergreen or herbaceous alpines. Suitable for borders, rock or wall crevices and rock gardens. Rosettes of fleshy leaves of variable shape. Saucer- or bowl-shaped flowers in spring or summer. These are among the best-loved alpines although they aren't especially easy to grow and some of the flower colours are almost luminous. Thrive in fertile, very well-drained neutral to acidic soil enriched with humus, evergreen species in full sun, herbaceous species in partial shade. They are very prone to rotting from moisture collecting around the neck and are best planted vertically in walls or crevices to minimize this. Sow seed in a cold-frame in autumn or remove offsets of evergreens in autumn. Those species and varieties described below are all moderately hardy or hardy unless otherwise specified. ❀ *L. brachycalyx*, rosettes narrow, lance-shaped, grey-green or deep green leaves, white to pale pink flowers, early to mid-spring, 8cm/8cm (3in/3in); *L. cotyledon*, evergreen, leathery, thick, strap-shaped dark green leaves, sometimes with wavy margins, funnel-shaped, cream-white to pink flowers with yellow or orange stripes, or pink flowers with purple stripes, late spring to late summer, 30cm/25cm (1ft/10in);

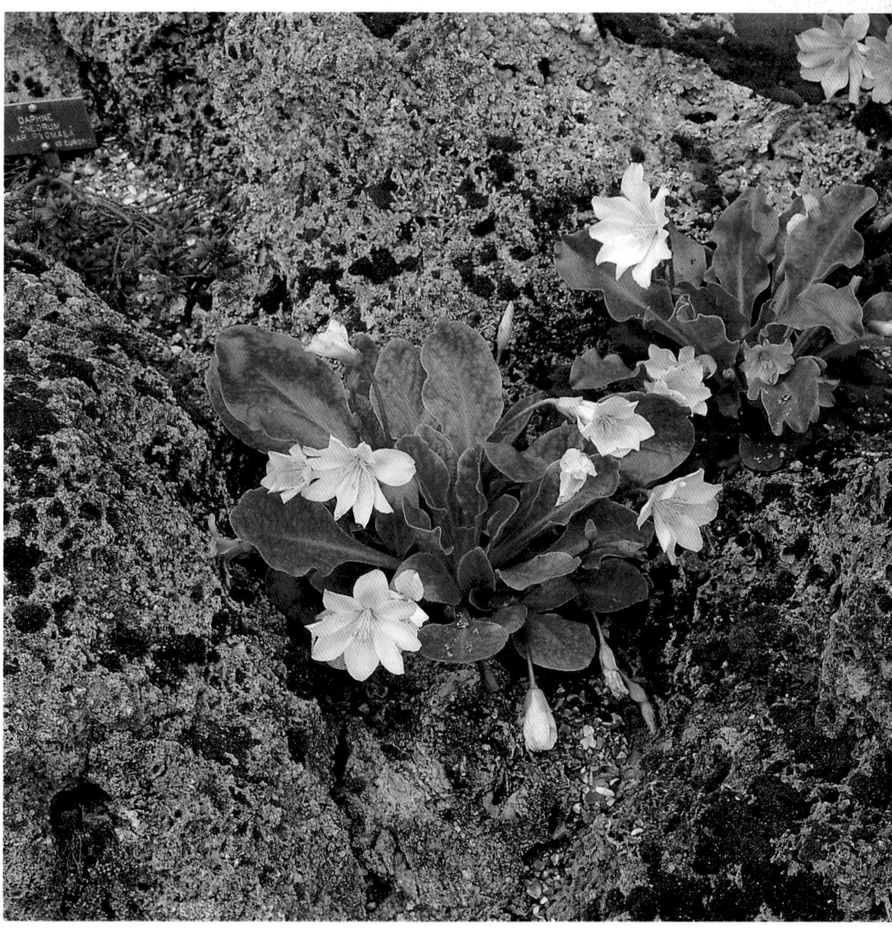

above *Lewisia tweedyi*. Probably the best loved and most distinctive of all alpines.

L. c. f. *alba*, white flowers, *L. c.* Crags Hybrids, clump-forming, evergreen, mid- to dark green leaves, clusters of funnel-shaped flowers in pink, orange, yellow, magenta, late spring to summer, 15-30cm/20-40cm (5in-1ft/8in-1½ft); *L. longipetala*, bright green rosettes of thick, strap-

above *Ligularia* 'Gregynog Gold'. Despite its rather unattractive name, I find this is a richly rewarding plant.

below *Liatris spicata* 'Floristan Violett'. I always think *Liatris* are better as cut flowers than as garden perennials.

shaped leaves, pale rose-pink, fragrant flowers, late spring to early summer, 10cm/10cm (4in/4in); *L. nevadensis*, mid-green strap-shaped to oblong leaves, white flowers, sometimes flushed pink, late spring to early summer, 10cm/10cm (4in/4in); *L. rediviva*, dark green, linear or club-shaped leaves, clusters of white to pink, sometimes carmine flowers, late spring to early summer 5cm/10cm (2in/4in); *L. tweedyi*, evergreen, leathery, more or less oval, deep green leaves, funnel-shaped, white to pink flowers, spring to early summer, 20cm/30cm (8in/1ft).

Leycesteria *Himalayan Honeysuckle, Pheasant Berry* Caprifoliaceae

Medium deciduous shrubs. Moderately hardy. Heart-shaped, pointed leaves, long, pendent spikes of five-petalled small white flowers with red bracts, early summer to early autumn, followed by glossy purple fruits. Prune all growth to just above soil in spring. Sow seed in a cold-frame in autumn or take softwood cuttings in summer. ❀ *L. formosa*, moderately hardy, oval, tapering dark green leaves, immature shoots blue-green, white flowers with claret bracts, followed by red-purple fruits, 2m/2m (6½ft/6½ft).

Liatris Asteraceae

Large hardy herbaceous perennials for borders. Strikingly different flower form although with some extraordinarily bright colours. Flowers are good for cutting. Rosettes of linear to lance-shaped leaves, tubular flowers on bottlebrush-like spikes. Sow seeds in a cold-frame in autumn or divide established plants in spring. ❀ *L. spicata*, linear to lance-shaped basal leaves, linear stem leaves, mauve flowers, summer, 1.5m/45cm (5ft/1½ft); *L. s.* 'Alba', white, *L. s.* 'Floristan Violett', purple; *L. s.* 'Floristan Weiss', white.

Libertia Iridaceae

Medium evergreen rhizomatous ornamentals for early summer borders. Barely hardy to moderately hardy. Leathery, linear basal leaves, clusters of six-petalled blue or white flowers, late spring to late summer, followed by glossy, light brown seed capsules. Sow seed when ripe or divide in spring. ❀ *L. caerulescens*, leathery, linear leaves, clusters of sky-blue flowers, late spring, 60cm/30cm (2ft/1ft); *L. formosa*, deep green leaves, dense clusters of white flowers, early to mid-summer, 90cm/60cm (3ft/2ft); *L. grandiflora*, linear, leathery leaves, open sprays of white flowers, early to mid-summer, followed by red-brown seed capsules, 90cm/60cm (3ft/2ft); *L. peregrinans*, white flowers, early to mid-summer, followed by yellow-orange seed capsules, 50cm/1m (1¾ft/3ft).

Ligularia *Leopard Plant* Asteraceae

Medium/large hardy perennials. Good for waterside or bog garden plantings or for borders if given protection from strong winds and provided the soil is moist; they will suffer in dry conditions. Kidney-shaped, elliptic or oval-oblong leaves, clusters of daisy-like flowers. Sow seed outside in autumn or spring, or divide established plants in spring. ❀ *L. dentata* 'Desdemona', clump-forming, round, brown-green leaves, maroon beneath, clusters of orange flowers with brown centres, on red stalks, mid-summer to early autumn, 1m (3ft); *L.* 'Gregynog Gold' (syn. *Senecio* 'Gregynog Gold'), clump-forming, toothed, rounded leaves, clusters of conical spikes of orange flowers with brown centres, late summer to early autumn, 1.8m/1m (5¾ft/3ft); *L.* x *palmatiloba*, rounded leaves, with deeply cut margins, pale orange flowers, 90cm-120cm (3-4ft); *L. przewalskii* (syn. *Senecio przewalskii*) and *L.* 'The Rocket', large rounded leaves with serrated margins, long cylindrical spikes of small yellow flowers on tall black stems,

left *Ligustrum lucidum* 'Tricolor'. This is a fine example of a plant for those gardeners who think of *Ligustrum* simply as boring hedges.

late summer, 1.8m/1m (5¾ft/3ft); *L. veitchiana*, clump-forming, triangular to heart-shaped leaves, wavy, toothed margins, triangular clusters of yellow flowers with brown centres, mid- to late summer followed by purple-brown fruit, 1.8m/1.2m (5¾ft/4ft).

Ligustrum *Privet* Oleaceae

Medium/large deciduous and evergreen shrubs and small trees. Barely hardy to hardy. Too many gardeners think only of privet as a rather dull hedge but in truth the genus includes some fine species that are appropriate in shrub-borders and as specimen plants in well-drained soil in full sun or partial shade. All parts are toxic if eaten. No routine pruning but clip hedges at least twice each year. Take semi-ripe cuttings in summer or hardwood cuttings in winter. ❀ *L. japonicum* (Japanese Privet), 'Rotundifolium', rounded, dark green, leathery leaves, clusters of fragrant white flowers, mid-summer to early autumn, 1.5m/1m (5ft/3ft); *L. lucidum*, evergreen, dark green, oval glossy leaves, clusters of white flowers, late summer to early autumn, followed by blue-black fruit, 10m/10m (33ft/33ft); *L. ovalifolium*, evergreen or semi-evergreen, glossy, oval, rich green leaves, clusters of fragrant (some people find unpleasantly so) tubular cream flowers with cross-shaped lobes, in summer, followed by black fruits, 3m/4m (10ft/13ft); *L. o.* 'Argenteum', leaves edged with cream-white; *L. o.* 'Aureum' (syn. Aureomarginatum'), leaves have bright yellow margins, much the best of the 'boring' hedge privets; *L. quihoui*, deciduous, glossy, mid-green, oval to more or less oval leaves, clusters of fragrant white flowers, late summer to early autumn, followed by glossy purple-black fruit, 2.5m/2.5m (8ft/8ft).

Lilium *Lily* Liliaceae

Small/large bulbous ornamental. Fairly hardy to moderately hardy. Lilies are among the truly classic garden bulbs, suitable for borders and especially, I think, for growing in containers. Mid- to dark green, often glossy, linear to lance-shaped leaves. Flowers vary in shape, from funnel-, bowl- and trumpet-shape to the type known descriptively as Turk's cap, which has recurved petals. The flowers, often richly fragrant, are borne singly or in clusters at the top of the stems. Thrive in fertile, well-drained soil enriched with humus, in partial shade or full sun. Most prefer neutral to acidic soil; some will not tolerate alkaline soil, others prefer it. Container-grown plants are best in loam-based compost with added grit and leaf mould. Species that produce roots along their stems (stem-rooting) should be planted deeply. Sow seed when ripe in a cold-frame or in warmth (half-hardy species), remove and replant offsets or stem bulbils in summer or remove and pot up bulb scales. Lily growing has unfortunately been limited in recent years in

below *Lilium pardalinum*. The variety available among both lily species and varieties is now enormous.

some areas by the spread of the bright red lily beetle. Of more than 100 species and innumerable varieties, the following are essentially plants recommended from personal experience.

❀ African Queen Group, linear to elliptic leaves, large trumpet-shaped, orange or yellow flowers, mid- to late summer, 1.5m (5ft); *L. auratum*, stem-rooting, lance-shaped deep green leaves, clusters of fragrant bowl-shaped white flowers, petals recurved at tips, with central yellow band, sometimes scattered with crimson flecks, in late summer, good container plant, 50cm-1.5m (1¾ft-5ft); *L. candidum* (Madonna Lily), inversely lance-shaped, bright green basal leaves, clusters of funnel-shaped, fragrant, white flowers with yellow anthers, early to mid-summer, requires very shallow planting, 1-1.8m (3-5¾ft); *L.* 'Casa Blanca', clusters of very fragrant, waxy, wide bowl-shaped flowers, petals recurved at tips, conspicuous orange-brown anthers, mid- to late summer, often grown as container plants, 1-1.2m (3ft); *L.* 'Connecticut King', clump-forming, clusters of star-like bright yellow flowers, early to mid-summer, good for containers, 1m (3ft); *L.* 'Enchantment', clump-forming, narrow, oval leaves, clusters of star-shaped, rich orange flowers, spotted black inside, 60-100cm (2-3ft); *L. formosanum* var. *pricei*, barely hardy, stem-rooting, dark green, linear to oblong to lance-shaped leaves, trumpet-shaped, fragrant, white flowers flushed crimson-purple on the outside, late summer, 60cm (2ft); *L. hansonii*, stem-rooting, dark green inversely lance-shaped to elliptic leaves, Turk's cap orange-yellow flowers, with purple-brown spotting, mid-summer, 1-1.5m (3-5ft); *L. henryi*, stem-rooting, dark green, lance -shaped to oval lance-shaped leaves, clusters of Turk's cap deep orange flowers, black spotted, with red anthers, best in neutral to alkaline soil, an imposing plant in good soil, 1-3m (3-10ft); *L. lancifolium* (syn. *L. tigrinum*) (Tiger Lily), clump-forming, stem-rooting, lance-shaped leaves, clusters of Turk's cap flowers, orange with dark purple spots, late summer to early autumn, thrives in moist, acidic soil, but tolerates some lime, 60-150cm (2ft-5ft); *L. l.* 'Flore Pleno', double flowers; *L. longiflorum*, barely hardy, stem-rooting, oblong to lance-shaped glossy dark green leaves, very fragrant, white, trumpet-shaped flowers with yellow anthers, mid- to late summer, good for containers, 40-100cm (1½ft-3ft); *L. mackliniae* (Manipur Lily), stem-rooting, small, linear to lance-shaped elliptic, deep green leaves, clusters of semi-pendent bowl-shaped rose-pink flowers, flushed purple, with purple anthers, early summer, 30-60cm (1-2ft); *L. martagon* (Martagon Lily), dark green, lance-shaped leaves, Turk's cap, unpleasantly scented, waxy mauve-pink pendent flowers with darker spots, lime tolerant, good for naturalizing, 1-2m (3-6½ft); *L. m.* var. *album*, small pure-white flowers; *L. monadelphum* (syn. *L. szovitsianum*), clump-forming, stem-rooting, bright green, inversely lance-shaped or oval leaves, clusters of Turk's cap yellow, fragrant flowers with dark red or purple spotting, mid-summer, 1-1.5m (3-5ft); *L.* 'Mont Blanc', large star-shaped cream-white flowers, early to mid-summer, good in containers, 60-70cm (2-2¼ft); *L. nanum* (syn. *Nomocharis nana*), linear leaves, solitary fragrant, bell-shaped pink flowers, sometimes with dark spots, early summer, 6-30cm (2in-1ft); *L. oxypetalum* var. *insigne*, linear to linear-lance-shaped leaves, semi-pendent, funnel-shaped, yellow, green-white or green-yellow flowers flecked or spotted with red-purple, singly or in clusters, requires acidic soil and partial shade, 60-100cm (2-3ft); *L. pardalinum* (Panther Lily), clump-forming, rhizomatous, inversely lance-shaped to elliptic, deep green leaves, clusters of Turk's cap flowers, crimson to red-orange, spotted maroon and maroon and yellow, lime tolerant, 1.5-2.5m (5-8ft); *L. pyrenaicum*, stem-rooting, bright green, linear to lance-shaped leaves, bright yellow Turk's cap flowers with purple spots, malodorous, good for naturalizing, requires neutral to alkaline soil,

above *Lilium* 'Star Gazer'. Not perhaps the most subtle of colours but one of the most popular varieties.

left *Limnanthes douglasii.* The origin of the common name of poached egg plant is self-evident.

30-100cm (1-3ft); *L. regale*, the most glorious of all lilies, one of the plant collector Ernest Wilson's greatest treasures, shiny dark green linear leaves, stem-rooting, very fragrant, trumpet-shaped white flowers, flushed purple or pink outside, with yellow centres and anthers, mid-summer, 60cm-2m (2-6½ft); *L. r.* 'Album', white flowers with orange anthers; *L. speciosum* var. *album*, stem-rooted, lance-shaped to oval leaves, fragrant, pendent Turk's cap flowers on purple stems, waxy, smooth petal with faint green band, late summer to early autumn, best in acidic soil 1-1.7m (3-5½ft); *L. s.* var. *rubrum*, carmine-red flowers on brown-purple stems; *L.* 'Star Gazer', clusters of large, very fragrant, star-shaped red flowers, recurved at tips, with darker crimson spots, a very good container plant, 1-1.5m (3-5ft).

Limnanthes
Limnanthaceae

Small hardy annual. Self-seeds freely. Suitable for edging paths, borders and rock gardens. Bright green, pinnate leaves, saucer- or cup-shaped very distinctive yellow flowers edged with white, in summer. Sow seed in autumn or spring in growing positions, protecting autumn-sown seedlings with cloches in cold areas. ❀ *L. douglasii* (Poached Egg Plant), spreading, glossy, finely divided and toothed yellow-green leaves, abundant cup-shaped flowers spring to autumn, this has become a popular species with organic gardeners who use it to attract beneficial insects to the garden. 15cm/15cm (6in/6in).

Limonium
Statice, Sea Lavender Plumbaginaceae

Small/medium annuals, biennials and herbaceous/evergreen perennials and sub-shrubs. Tender to hardy. Good for borders and rock gardens, also for cutting and drying. Basal rosettes of entire or pinnate leaves, panicles of small papery flowers and bracts, usually borne on one side of the flowering stem, in summer and autumn. Sow seed in warmth (annuals) in spring or in containers outside in spring (perennials), or by division in spring. ❀ *L. bellidifolium* (syn. *Statice bellidifolium*), evergreen perennial, deep green leathery leaves, abundant trumpet-shaped, blue to mauve flowers in loose sprays, in early summer, 15cm/15cm (6in/6in); *L. platyphyllum* (syn. *L. latifolium*), perennial, rosettes of spoon-shaped to elliptic, mid- to dark green leaves, panicles of tiny tubular lavender-blue flowers, late summer to early autumn, 60cm/45cm (2ft/1½ft).

Linaria
Toadflax Scrophulariaceae

Small/medium annuals, biennials, alpines and herbaceous perennials. Barely hardy to moderately hardy. Grey-green, oval or linear to lance-shaped leaves, irregular, very pretty

below *Linaria alpina* is a plant that demonstrates how the *Linaria* flower shape is so appropriate to the neat alpine habit.

two-lipped flowers, like small antirrhinums, in white, red, yellow, pink, purple or orange. Sow seeds in growing positions in spring (annuals) in a cold-frame in early spring (perennials) or divide established plants or take softwood cuttings in spring. ❀ *L. alpina* (Alpine Toadflax), trailing, short-lived perennial, blue-green linear-lance-shaped leaves, clusters of violet flowers with yellow or orange patterning at the mouth, late spring to summer, I think the prettiest member of the whole charming group. 8cm/15cm (3in/6in); *L. dalmatica*, erect perennial, oval glaucous leaves, clusters of yellow flowers, 1m/60cm (3ft/2ft); *L. maroccana* 'Fairy Bouquet', erect annual, linear, light green leaves, tiny two-lipped flowers, salmon-pink, rose-pink, orange, carmine, lavender, white and yellow, in summer, 23cm/15cm (9in/6in); *L. m.* 'Fairy Lights', mixed colours, similar to those of 'Fairy Bouquet', but with white throats; *L. m.* 'Northern Lights', flowers as 'Fairy Bouquet', but larger, 60cm/15cm (2ft/6in); *L. purpurea* (Purple Toadflax), erect semi-evergreen perennial, narrow mid- to grey-green leaves, violet flowers, summer to early autumn, self-seeds freely, 90cm/30cm (3ft/1ft); *L. p.* 'Springside White', grey-green leaves, white flowers; *L. triornithophora*, erect semi-evergreen perennial, mid-green lance-shaped to oval leaves, purple-and-yellow flowers, early summer to early autumn, 90cm/60cm (3ft/2ft).

above *Linum narbonense*. The blue flowers of flax have become familiar as farmers have turned to growing linseed; however, this species is simply one to look at.

Linum *Flax* — Linaceae

Annuals, biennials, deciduous/evergreen and semi-evergreen perennials, shrubs and sub-shrubs. Tender to moderately hardy. Simple leaves, shallowly funnel-shaped flowers, individually short-lived but produced over a long period in summer. Sow seed in flowering positions (annuals) or in a cold-frame (perennials and sub-shrubs) in spring or autumn, take stem-tip cuttings (perennials) in early summer, or semi-ripe cuttings (shrubs and sub-shrubs) in summer. ❀ *L. flavum* 'Gemmell's Hybrid', evergreen perennial, elliptic, grey-green leaves, rich yellow flowers, early to mid-summer, 15cm/20cm (6in/8in); *L. narbonense*, herbaceous or semi-evergreen perennial, narrow to lance-shaped grey-green leaves, pale to deep blue flowers, late spring to early summer, usually self-seeding, 30-60cm/40cm (1-2ft/1½ft); *L. n.* 'Heavenly Blue', abundant, intensely blue flowers with white centres; *L. perenne* (syn. *L. sibiricum*), herbaceous perennial, grass-like, deep green leaves, abundant pale blue flowers, summer to early autumn, 10-30cm/60cm (4in-1ft/2ft); *L. p.* 'Blau Saphir' (syn. *L. p.* 'Blue Sapphire'), sky-blue flowers, 30cm (1ft); *L. p.* 'White Diamond', white flowers, 30cm (1ft).

Liquidamber — Hamamelidaceae

Small/large deciduous trees. Barely hardy to moderately hardy. Ideal as specimen trees or in woodland, where their maple-like leaves display brilliant autumn colours. Inflorescences of inconspicuous yellow-green flowers, followed on female

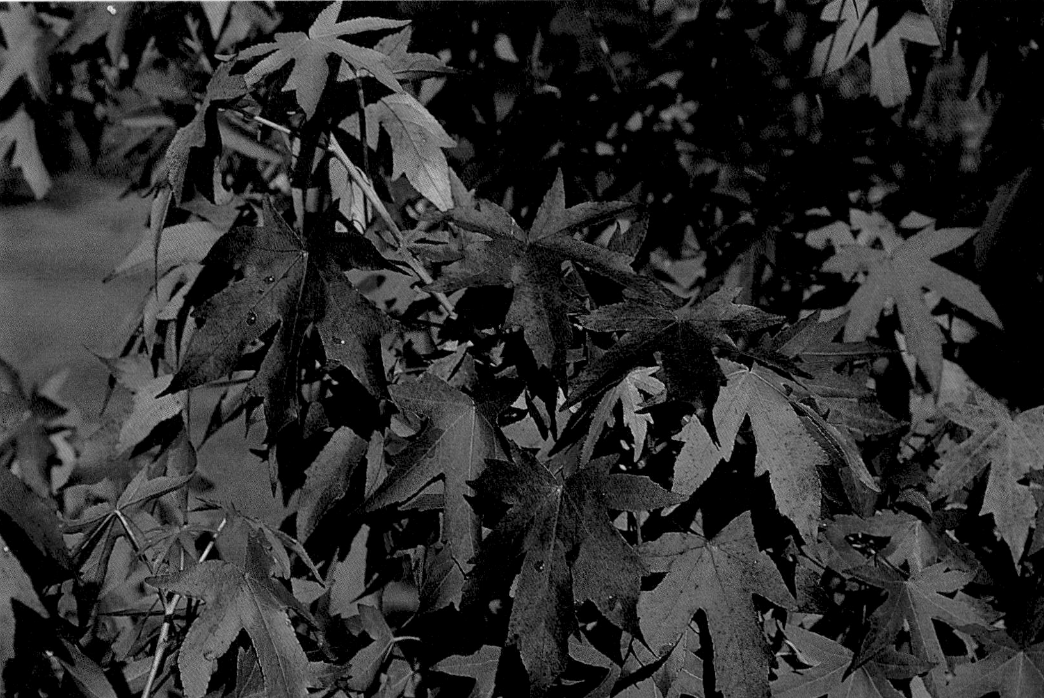

right All of the liquidambers display fine autumn colours; *Liquidamber styraciflua* 'Worplesdon' has the added advantage of a purple tint before the yellow appears.

plants by spherical fruit. No routine pruning. Sow seed in a cold-frame in autumn or take semi-ripe cuttings in summer. ❀ *L. styraciflua*, glossy, mid-green leaves, purple, red or orange in autumn, 25m/12m (80ft/40ft); *L. s.* 'Lane Roberts', leaves dark red in autumn, *L.* 'Worplesdon', autumn leaves purple at first, later orange-yellow.

Liriodendron *Tulip Tree* Magnoliaceae

Large deciduous trees. Moderately hardy. Magnificent plants as specimens for large gardens although they will not flower until mature. Square-shaped leaves, exquisite cup-shaped flowers followed by cone-like fruit. No routine pruning. Sow seed in a cold-frame in autumn; will not strike from cuttings; bought plants are grafted. ❀ *L. tulipifera*, silver-grey bark, dark green leaves, yellow in autumn, yellow-green cup-shaped flowers with conspicuous stamens and orange patterning, 30m/15m (100ft/50ft); *L. t.* 'Aureomarginatum', yellow edged leaves, a beautiful plant, even when too young to flower, 20m/10m (60ft/33ft); *L. t.* 'Fastigiatum', columnar, otherwise as species, 20m/1m (60ft/3ft).

Liriope *Lily Turf* Convallariaceae

Small rhizomatous and tuberous ornamentals. Moderately hardy. Unusual as a bulbous plant in making good ground cover; hence the English name. Arching grass-like leaves, spikes of spherical to round flowers, followed by black fruits. Sow seeds in cold-frame or divide established plants in spring. ❀ *L. muscari* (syn. *L. graminifolia*), dark green leaves, clusters of dark mauve, bell-like flowers, late summer to late autumn, 30cm/45cm (1ft/1½ft); *L. m.* 'Gold-banded', arching leaves edged with gold; *L. m.* 'Monroe White', white flowers; *L. m.* 'Variegata', green leaves edged with gold, 30cm/30cm (1ft/1ft).

Lithodora Boraginaceae

Small evergreen shrubs or sub-shrubs. Barely hardy to moderately hardy. Hairy leaves vary from elliptic to more or less oval, linear to lance-shaped, funnel-shaped bright blue or white flowers, usually in summer. Sow seeds in warmth in winter or early spring, or take semi-ripe cuttings in late summer. ❀ *L. diffusa* (syn. *Lithospermum diffusum*), mat-forming sub-shrub, narrow elliptic leaves, clusters of bright blue flowers in early summer in acidic soil, in alkaline soil flowers usually purple-blue, leaves yellow-green, 30cm/50cm (1ft/1¾ft); *L. d.* 'Grace Ward', deep blue flowers; *L. d.* 'Heavenly Blue', trailing shrubs, deep green leaves, azure-blue flowers; *L. oleifolia* (syn. *Lithospermum oleifolia*), semi-erect shrub, grey-green oblong to oval leaves, silky hairs beneath, pink-flushed buds open to sky-blue flowers, early summer, best in alkaline soil, 20cm/30cm (8in/1ft).

Lobelia Campanulaceae

Small/large hardy and half-hardy annuals, herbaceous perennials and sub-shrubs. For many years, extremely popular for hanging baskets and other containers, also summer bedding, although tending to be replaced now by more reliable species. A few are good water garden marginals while some are taller perennial species for herbaceous borders. Simple, stalkless leaves, tubular two-lipped

above *Lithodora diffusa* 'Heavenly Blue'.

below *Liriodendron tulipifera* 'Aureomarginatum' is one of the most glorious of foliage trees.

above *Lobelia tupa*. Superficially more like a lily than a lobelia; an interesting rather than spectacular plant.

flowers. Requires fertile, moist, well-drained soil in full sun or partial shade. Keep container-grown plants out of full sun. Sow seed in small clusters in warmth in late winter (annuals) or when ripe (perennials), divide established perennials in spring, aquatic perennials in summer, or take bud cuttings of *L. cardinalis* in mid-summer. ❀ *L. cardinalis*, clump-forming, short-lived hardy perennial, basal rosettes of narrow, toothed mid- to bright green leaves, scarlet tubular flowers on long spikes, summer to autumn, 90cm/30cm (3ft/1ft); *L.* 'Dark Crusader', hardy herbaceous perennial, maroon leaves and stems, velvety deep red flowers, mid- to late summer, 60-90cm/30cm (2-3ft/1ft); *L. erinus* 'Crystal Palace', compact, low-growing perennial, usually raised as half-hardy annual, dark bronze-green leaves, with oval bases, narrowing towards the tip, deep blue flowers, 15cm/15cm (6in/6in); *L. e.* 'Mrs Clibran', compact, brilliant blue flowers with white centres, 10-15cm/10-15cm (4-6in/4-6in); *L. e.* 'Cambridge Blue', light blue flowers; *L. e.* Cascade Series, pink, white, violet, blue and lilac flowers, usually with white centres; *L. e.* 'Rosamund', compact, red flowers with white centres, 10-15cm/10-15cm (4-6in/4-6in); *L. laxiflora* var. *angustifolia*, spreading rhizomatous perennial, barely hardy but striking, linear leaves on arching red-flushed stems, tubular, semi-pendent red and yellow flowers, late spring to early summer, 60cm/45cm (2ft/1½ft); *L.* 'Pink Flamingo', clusters of rose-pink flowers, 120cm (4ft); *L.* 'Queen Victoria', clump-forming, short-lived perennial, lance-shaped, purple-red leaves on purple-red stems, rich scarlet flowers, late summer to mid-autumn, 45cm/30cm (1½ft/1ft); *L. siphilitica*, clump-forming perennial, lance-shaped, oval to oblong leaves, toothed, light green, tubular bright blue flowers, late summer to mid-autumn, 60-120cm/30cm (2-4ft/1ft); *L. tupa*, clump-forming perennial, red-purple stems, downy, lance-shaped, grey-green leaves, red to orange-red flowers, summer to mid-autumn, 2m/90cm (6½ft/3ft).

Lobularia Brassicaceae

Small annuals and perennials. Moderately hardy. Linear to lance-shaped, usually mid-green leaves, four-petalled cross-shaped flowers, sometimes fragrant, in summer. The only important plant is the freely self-seeding bedding annual formerly called *Alyssum*. Sow seed in the flowering position or cold-frame in late spring. ❀ *L. maritima* (Bedding Alyssum), 'Carpet of Snow' (syn. *L. m.* 'Snow Carpet'), low-growing annual or short-lived perennial, slightly hairy grey-green leaves, abundant, slightly fragrant, tiny white flowers, 10cm/20-30cm (4in/8in-1ft); *L. m.* 'Little Dorrit', spreading, white flowers, 10cm/20-30cm (4in/8in-1ft); *L. m.* 'Violet Queen', violet flowers.

Lonicera *Honeysuckle* Caprifoliaceae

Small/large deciduous and evergreen shrubs and climbers. Barely hardy to hardy. Although usually thought of only as climbers, there are also some wonderful shrubby honeysuckles for mixed and shrub borders. The climbers are best for scrambling into large shrubs and small trees rather than formal positions against house walls. Simple leaves, tubular, bell- or funnel-shaped flowers, two-lipped or with five spreading lobes, often

left *Lonicera* x *purpusii* 'Winter Beauty'. A fine early flowering hybrid between *Lonicera fragrantissima* and *L. standishii.*

fragrant, usually followed by small fruits. Thrive in well-drained soil in full sun or partial shade. Climbers require fertile, moist and well-drained soil enriched with humus. No routine pruning but thin out old or very congested stems in spring. Sow seed when ripe in a cold-frame, take semi-ripe cuttings in summer, hardwood cuttings in autumn, or layer. Those species and varieties described below are all moderately hardy unless stated otherwise.

Climbing Honeysuckles: ❀ *L.* x *americana*, deciduous, dark green oval leaves, fragrant yellow, two-lipped flowers flushed purple-red, summer to early autumn, followed by red fruits, 7m (23ft); *L.* x *brownii* 'Dropmore Scarlet', hardy deciduous or semi-evergreen climber, blue green, oval leaves, slightly fragrant trumpet-shaped orange-scarlet flowers, in summer, sometimes followed by orange-red fruits, 4m (13ft); *L. caprifolium* (Fly Honeysuckle), deciduous, cup-like, grey-green leaves, pink flowers flushed with cream, heavily fragrant, mid-to late spring, followed by clusters of orange-red fruits, 6m (20ft); *L. etrusca*, deciduous or semi-evergreen, mid-green more or less oval or oval leaves, fragrant two-lipped tubular yellow flowers, flushed red, with red fruits, 4m (13ft); *L. e* 'Superba', flowers cream at first, later orange; *L.* x *heckrottii*, deciduous or semi-evergreen, oval to oblong or elliptic dark green leaves, blue-green beneath, tubular two-lipped fragrant flowers, pink, orange-yellow inside, sometimes red fruits, 5m (16ft); *L henryi*, fairly hardy to moderately hardy, evergreen, oblong to lance-shaped glossy, dark green leaves, small orange-yellow flowers, flushed pink, early to mid-summer, purple black fruits, 10m (33ft); *L.* x *italica*, deciduous, maroon buds opening to pink and yellow fragrant flowers, followed by orange-red fruits, 2m/2m (6½ft/6½ft); *L. japonica* 'Aureoreticulata', evergreen or semi-evergreen, elliptic to oval, deeply lobed dark green leaves, tubular two-lipped fragrant white flowers flushed pink at first, later yellow, spring to late summer, followed by blue-black fruits, 10m (33ft); *L. j.* 'Halliana', flowers white at first, later deep yellow; *L. j.* var. *repens*, leaves and shoots tinged purple, white, fragrant flowers flushed purple on outside; *L. periclymenum* 'Belgica', deciduous, flowers pink-red at first, later yellow, late spring to early summer, and late summer, fruits orange in late summer then red in autumn, 7m (23ft); *L. p.* 'Graham Thomas', flowers white at first, later yellow; *L. p.* 'Serotina', leaves tinted bronze, cream-white flowers with purple and red streaks, mid-summer to early autumn; *L.* x *tellmanniana*, deciduous, elliptic to oblong deep green leaves, pale blue beneath, tubular two-lipped, copper-orange flowers, late spring to

below *Lonicera x brownii* 'Dropmore Scarlet'. I'm inclined to think this one of the most spectacular of the hardy climbing honeysuckles.

above *Lotus berthelotii.* A mouthful of a name for one of the most spectacular of hanging basket plants.

mid-summer, 5m (16ft); *L. tragophylla*, deciduous, slightly hairless, tinted bronze at first, gold-yellow flowers, tinted red above, in early summer, 6m (20ft).

Shrubby Honeysuckles: *L. fragrantissima*, deciduous or semi-evergreen, dark green oval leaves, blue-green beneath, very fragrant tubular two-lipped flowers, cream white, winter to early spring, followed by dull red fruits, 2m/3m (6½ft/10ft); *L. maackii*, erect, deciduous, tapering dark green leaves, tubular two-lipped fragrant flowers, white at first, later yellow, in early summer, followed by dark red fruits, a glorious plant but, alas, barely hardy, 5m/5m (16ft/16ft); *L. nitida*, evergreen, glossy, oval leaves. dark green above, paler beneath, tubular cream-white flowers, glossy blue-purple fruits, 3.5m/3.5m (11ft/11ft); *L. n.* 'Baggesen's Gold', arching shoots, oval bright yellow-green leaves, 1.5m/1.5m (5ft/5ft); *L. involucrata*, deciduous, oval to oblong or lance-shaped, mid-green leaves, tubular dark yellow flowers, sometimes flushed red, surrounded by bracts, red at first, later green glossy black fruits, late spring to summer, 3m (10ft); *L. pileata*, low-growing evergreen suitable for ground cover, glossy, dark green leaves with conspicuous veining, funnel-shaped cream-white flowers, in late spring, purple-blue fruits, 60cm/2.5m (2ft/8ft); *L.* x *purpusii*, semi-evergreen, bristly leaves, cream flowers with heavy fragrance, late winter to mid-spring, red fruits, 1.5m/1.5m (5ft/5ft); *L.* x *p.* 'Winter Beauty', deciduous or semi-evergreen, oval, dark green leaves, very fragrant white, two-lipped tubular flowers, with prominent yellow anthers, late winter to early spring, a considerable improvement on the older form 2m/2.5m (6½ft/8ft); *L. standishii*, erect deciduous or semi-evergreen, bristly dark green, oblong to lance-shaped leaves, tubular, two-lipped cream-white flowers, sometimes tinged pink, late autumn to early spring, red fruits, 2m/2m (6½ft/6½ft).

Lotus Papilionaceae

Annuals, perennials, deciduous/evergreen and semi-evergreen sub-shrubs. Tender to moderately hardy. One species has become important as a hanging basket plant. Palmate or pinnate leaves, pea-like flowers. Sow seed in warmth in spring, or take semi-ripe cuttings in summer. ❀ *L. berthelotii* (Parrot's Beak), tender, trailing evergreen sub-shrub, palmate silver-grey leaves, beak-like scarlet flowers with black centres, 20cm (8in)/indefinite.

Lunaria *Honesty* Brassicaceae

Small/medium hardy biennials and herbaceous perennials. Oval to heart-shaped toothed leaves, cross-shaped flowers, purple, white or red-purple, followed by rounded or elliptical seedpods much appreciated in flower arrangements. Sow seeds in spring or early summer or divide established plants in spring. ❀ *L. annua*, biennial, mid-green, toothed heart-shaped leaves, fragrant purple flowers late spring to summer, followed by flat, round silver seedpods, 90cm/30cm (3ft/1ft); *L. a.* var. *albiflora*, white flowers; *L. rediviva*, clump-forming, short-lived perennial, triangular heart-shaped leaves, fragrant pale lilac-white flowers, early spring to early summer, followed by white elliptic papery seedpods, 60-90cm/30cm (2-3ft/1ft).

Lupinus *Lupin* Papilionaceae

Small/large hardy and half-hardy annuals, herbaceous perennials and sub-shrubs. Suitable for herbaceous borders, shrubby species for wild gardens. Palmate leaves, columnar spikes of pea-like flowers, yellow, orange, blue, purple, red, cream. Thrive in neutral to slightly acid, light sandy soil, in sun or partial shade. The herbaceous perennial, early summer-flowering lupins wax and wane in popularity; presently, whilst there are some good new hybrids available, many gardeners find the problems caused by aphids and mildew to be insurmountable. Sow seeds in flowering positions in spring (annuals) or in a cold-frame in spring or autumn, or take basal cuttings (perennials) in spring. ❀ *L. chamissonis*, low-growing shrubby, evergreen perennial, silver-grey leaves, blue-and white flowers with yellow blotches, late summer, 1m/1.5m (3ft/5ft); *L.* 'Chandelier', clump-forming perennial, bright yellow flowers, 90cm/75cm (3ft/2½ft); *L.* 'Lulu', dwarf hardy perennial, usually available in mixed colours, 60cm (2ft); *L.* 'My Castle', clump-forming perennial, deep rose-pink flowers, 90cm/75cm (3ft/2½ft); *L.* 'Noble Maiden', clump-forming perennial, cream-white flowers, early to mid-summer, 90cm/75cm (3ft/2½ft); *L.* Russell Hybrids, bicoloured flowers in mixed colours, including deep blue and white, ivory-white and white, rose-lilac and white, 90cm (3ft); *L.* 'The Chatelaine', clump-forming perennial, bicoloured pink and white flowers, 90cm/75cm (3ft/2½ft); *L.* 'The Governor', clump-forming perennial, bicoloured deep blue and white flowers, 90cm/ 75cm (3ft/2½ft).

Lychnis *Catchfly* Caryophyllaceae

Medium, hardy biennials and herbaceous perennials for borders and for cutting; small species for rock gardens. Simple, sometimes hairy, leaves, dish-shaped, tubular or star-shaped flowers, white and shades of red or purple, solitary or in clusters. Sow seed in a cold-frame when ripe or in spring, divide established plants or take basal cuttings in spring. ❀ *L. alpina* (Alpine Catchfly), dwarf perennial, dark green linear to spoon-shaped leaves, clusters of deep rose-pink flowers with notched petals, late spring to summer, 15cm/15cm (6in/6in); *L.* x *arkwrightii*, clump-forming, short-lived perennial, dark red-flushed leaves, scarlet flowers, summer, 40cm/20cm (1½ft/8in); *L. chalcedonica*, pale green lance-shaped to oval leaves, clusters of scarlet flowers with notched petals, early to mid-summer, 1-1.2m/30cm (3-4ft/1ft); *L. c.* 'Flore Pleno', double red flowers; *L. coronaria* (Rose Campion), erect biennial or short-lived perennial, silver-grey woolly, oval to lance-shaped leaves, clusters of red-purple flowers, summer, 80cm/45cm (2½ft/1½ft); *L. c.* Alba Group, white flowers; *L. c.* Atrosanguinea Group, pale grey leaves, deep pink flowers; *L. floscuculi* (Ragged Robin), spreading perennial, blue-green basal leaves, dark green pointed stem leaves, bright pink flowers with deeply cut petals, summer to early autumn, 75cm/80cm (2½ft/2½ft); *L. flos-jovis*, mat-forming perennial, downy, white, lance to spoon-shaped leaves, clusters of white, purple or pink flowers, summer, 20-60cm/45cm (8in-2ft/ 1½ft); *L. f.* 'Hort's Variety', rose-pink flowers; *L. viscaria* (Sticky Catchfly), mat-forming or tufted perennial, elliptic, dark green leaves on sticky stems, red-purple flowers, summer, 45cm/45cm (1½ft/1½ft); *L. v.* 'Splendens Plena', double, bright magenta flowers.

Lycopersicon *Tomato* Solanaceae

Annual or short-lived perennial vegetable fruit. Tender to barely hardy. The genus contains around ten species, which include both dwarf and tall varieties with small to large fruit, suitable for indoor and outdoor cultivation. The fruit of cultivated tomatoes ranges widely in size from tiny currant

below *Lychnis flos-jovis.* Like many members of its family, a plant with a wide range of flower colours.

tomatoes to huge beefsteak types. They may be yellow, red, red-orange, orange, green, brown or almost black, most are spherical (although some very irregularly so), but some plum- or pear-shaped. Varieties raised outdoors require fertile, well-drained, moisture-retentive soil in a warm, sunny, sheltered position. Those raised in warmth require loam-based compost. All tomatoes must be given supplementary liquid fertilizer. Sow seed in warmth between late winter and early spring for transplanting at six weeks of age. There are two main groups of tomato varieties: Indeterminate or Cordon tomatoes, which are tied to a vertical support and their side shoots removed; and Determinate or Bush varieties, which form a mound of growth and are not side-shooted. In the following lists, all Cordon varieties may be grown in cool or heated greenhouses or outdoors unless stated otherwise; Bush varieties should be grown outdoors: ❀ 'Ailsa Craig', cordon, medium-sized fruit; 'Alicante', cordon, medium-sized fruit, the best all-round medium-sized tomato in my experience; 'Big Boy' F1 cordon, large, round, smooth fruit; 'Buffalo', cordon, large beefsteak type fruit, greenhouse; 'Dombito' F1, cordon, large beefsteak-type fruit, greenhouse, or outdoors in milder areas; 'Gardeners' Delight', cordon, small fruit with very sweet flavour; 'Golden Sunrise', cordon, medium-sized yellow fruit; 'Incas', cordon, plum fruit, outdoors; 'Moneymaker', cordon, medium-sized fruit; 'Outdoor Girl', cordon, outdoors; 'Red Alert', bush, small fruit, outdoors; 'Shirley' F1, cordon, medium-sized fruit, greenhouse; 'Sleaford Abundance' F1, bush, medium-sized fruit, outdoors; 'Sungold' F1, cordon, small sweet yellow fruit with taste; 'Sweet 100' F1, cordon, very small fruit; 'Tigerella', cordon, medium-sized red fruit with yellow stripes; 'The Amateur' bush, medium-sized fruit, outdoors; 'Tumbler' F1, trailing, tiny fruit, ideal for containers; 'Yellow Perfection', cordon, medium-sized yellow fruit.

above Tomato 'Gardener's Delight'. Despite recent claimants, this remains for me the tomato with the finest flavour.

right Tomato 'The Amateur'. This is the best and most reliable bush variety that I have grown.

Lysichiton

Bog Arum, Skunk Cabbage Araceae

Medium/large hardy rhizomatous ornamentals for damp conditions and therefore suitable for bogs or pond margins. Oval to oblong, glossy mid- to dark green basal leaves, striking large yellow spathe and inner spiky spadix of insignificant flowers, usually heavily scented of musk. Sow seed in a cold-frame when ripe, or replant offsets in summer or autumn. ❀ *L. americanus*, leathery ribbed leaves, yellow spathe, spadix green at first, later yellow, 1m/1.2m (3ft/4ft); *L. camtschatcensis*, prominently ribbed leaves, white spathe, fragrant, pale green spadix, 75cm/75cm (2½ft/2½ft).

Lysimachia *Loosestrife* Primulaceae

Small to large hardy herbaceous and evergreen perennials and shrubs. A diverse group with plants suitable for moist herbaceous borders and the edges of ponds and streams. Simple, entire leaves or toothed leaves, sometimes scalloped, hairy. Cup-, saucer- or star-shaped flowers, singly or in panicles, usually white or yellow. Sow seed in spring or divide established plants in spring or autumn. ❀ *L. ciliata*, herbaceous perennial, oval leaves, hairy mid-green leaves, star-shaped, pendent flowers, singly or in pairs, red-brown centres, mid-summer, 1.2m/60cm (4ft/2ft); *L. c.* 'Fire-cracker', purple leaves, 75cm/45cm (2½ft/1½ft); *L. clethroides*, herbaceous perennial, oval to lance-shaped, pointed, mid-green leaves, white flowers on arching stems, late summer, 90cm/60cm (3ft/2ft); *L. ephemerum*, clump-forming herbaceous perennial, grey-green leaves, saucer-shaped white flowers on arching spikes, mid- to

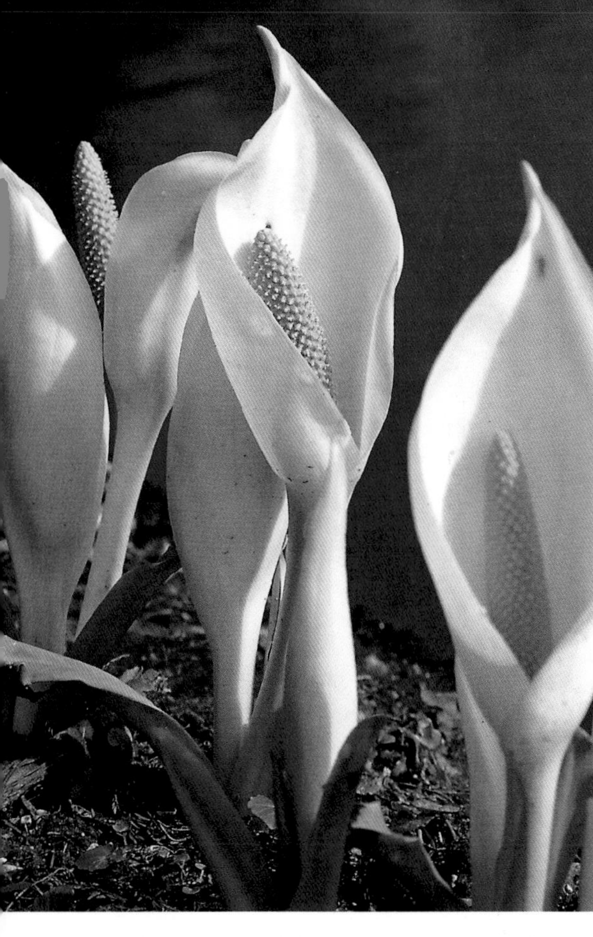

late summer, 1m/30cm (3ft/1ft); *L. minoricensis*, dark green leaves marbled white, 30cm/75cm (1ft/1½ft); *L. nummularia* (Moneywort, Creeping Jenny), prostrate evergreen creeping perennial, round to oval bright green leaves, cup-shaped, shiny bright yellow flowers, early summer, an extremely pretty plant for the water garden, 5cm (2in)/indefinite; *L. n.* 'Aurea' bright gold leaves, prettier still; *L. punctata*, herbaceous perennial, dark green, elliptic, pointed leaves with hairy margins, erect spikes of bright yellow cup-shaped flowers, summer, can be invasive but still a useful plant given room, 1m/60cm (3ft/2ft); *L. vulgare*, lance-shaped, bright green leaves, star-shaped pale yellow flowers, mid-summer, 1.2m/1m (4ft/3ft).

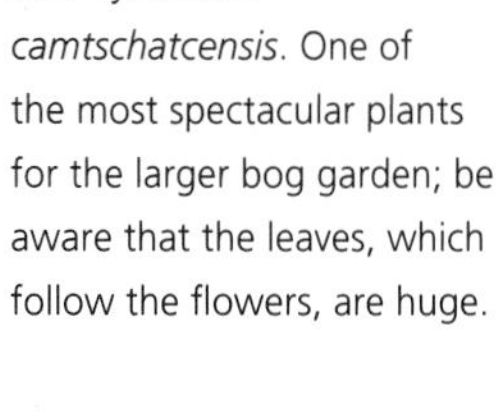

left *Lysichiton camtschatcensis*. One of the most spectacular plants for the larger bog garden; be aware that the leaves, which follow the flowers, are huge.

Lythrum *Loosestrife* Lythraceae

Medium hardy annuals and perennials for growing near water margins and in other sites where the soil is moisture-retentive. Oval to lance-shaped linear leaves, funnel-shaped or star-shaped flowers, single, in clusters or in spikes, purple-pink or pink, rarely, white. Sow seed in warmth in spring, divide established plants in spring or take basal cuttings in spring or early summer. ❀ *L. salicaria* (Purple Loosestrife), clump-forming perennial, downy, lance-shaped leaves, red-purple flowers, mid-summer to early autumn, indispensable for the wild flower garden, the name 'loosestrife' derives from the old use of tying bunches to the harnesses of farm horses to drive away flies and so 'lessen the strife' between the animals. 1.2m/45cm (4ft/1½ft); *L. s.* 'Feuerkerze' (syn. *L. s.* 'Firecandle'), rose-pink flowers; *L. s.* 'Robert', bright pink flowers; *L. virgatum* 'Rosy Gem' clump-forming perennial, purple flowers flushed pink, 90cm/45cm (3ft/1½ft).

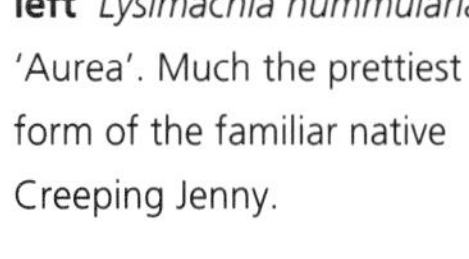

left *Lysimachia nummularia* 'Aurea'. Much the prettiest form of the familiar native Creeping Jenny.

far right *Magnolia campbellii*. A wonderful sight in early spring, especially against a clear blue sky.

Macleaya *Plume Puppy* Papaveraceae

Large moderately hardy rhizomatous ornamentals for water-side plantings and big herbaceous borders. Broad, long, shiny mid-green palmate leaves with notched margins, downy white undersides, on erect, glaucous stems. Tiny petal-less tubular flowers in clusters resembling feathered plumes. Magnificent screening plants but they really are huge and can be invasive. Sow seed in a coldframe in spring, divide established plants in spring or late autumn, or replant suckers. ❀ *M. cordata*, rounded, deeply lobed leaves, cream-white flowers in large plumes, in summer, followed by seed capsules, 2.5m/1m (8ft/3ft); *M. c.* 'Flamingo', grey-green leaves, pink buds open to cream-white and apricot pink flowers; *M. microcarpa* 'Kelway's Coral Plume', rounded, deeply cut, grey-green leaves, grey-white beneath, fluffy panicles of coral-yellow to red flowers, pink in bud, the best form, 3m/1m (10ft/3ft).

Magnolia Magnoliaceae

Small/large deciduous and evergreen trees. Tender to hardy. Magnificent plants, best grown as specimens; some are best against walls in cooler areas. Leaves usually more or less oval, large flowers, sometimes fragrant, have six to nine petals (actually petal-like structures called tepals), of variable shape, including saucer-, cup-, goblet- and star-shaped. Flowers may be followed in autumn by cone-shaped fruit with red seeds. Most require moist, well-drained, neutral to acidic soil enriched with humus in full sun or partial shade, protected from strong winds; species tolerating some lime include *M. acuminata, M. delavayi, M. grandiflora, M. kobus, M.* x *loebneri, M. stellata*, and *M. wilsonii*, although they usually benefit from the addition of rich organic matter. Sow seed in autumn, take semi-ripe cuttings in late summer or layer. No routine pruning and generally to be discouraged. All of the following, except *M. grandiflora*, are deciduous. ❀ *M. campbellii*, fairly hardy, elliptic oval to elliptic more or less oval, mid-green leaves, cup-and-saucer-shaped crimson, rose-pink or white flowers, late winter to early spring on bare branches, 15m/10m (50ft/33ft); *M. denudata* (syn. *M. heptapeta*), moderately hardy, mid-green. more or less oval leaves, cup-shaped white flowers on bare branches, spring 10m/10m (33ft/33ft); *M. grandiflora*, fairly to moderately hardy evergreen, usually grown against a wall but will survive better in the open than many gardeners imagine though prone to snow damage, leathery, glossy, dark green leaves, often with red-

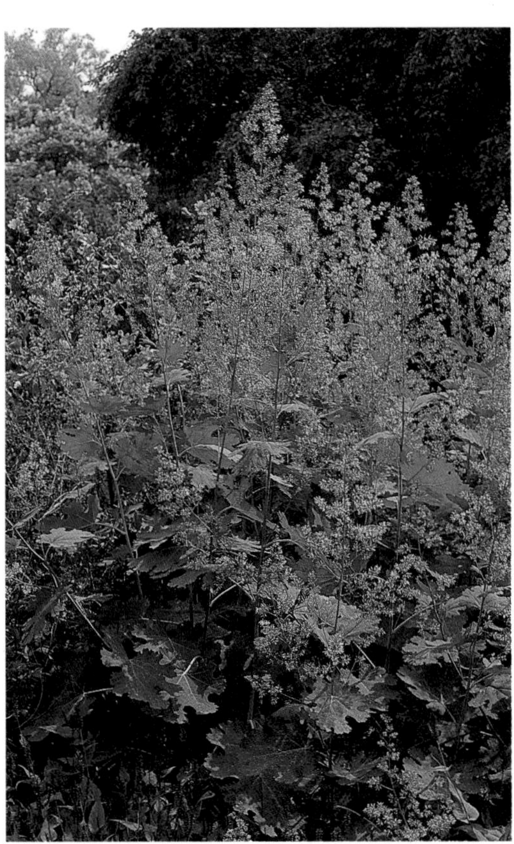

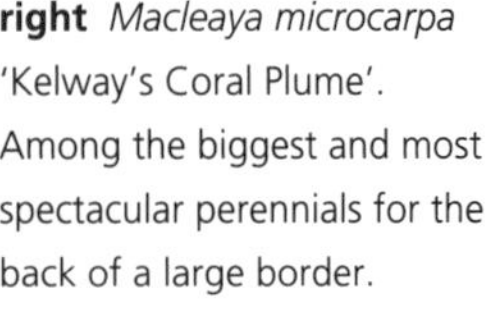

right *Macleaya microcarpa* 'Kelway's Coral Plume'. Among the biggest and most spectacular perennials for the back of a large border.

brown downy undersides, magnificent, large, very fragrant cup-shaped cream-white flowers to 25cm (10in) in diameter over many weeks, summer to autumn, 6-18m/15m (20-56ft/50ft); *M. g.* 'Exmouth', hardier than species and flowering at an earlier age, narrow, oval, light green leaves; *M. g.* 'Goliath', like 'Exmouth', flowers early, leaves slightly twisted, undersides lack down, flowers 20-30cm (8in-1ft) in diameter; *M.* 'Heaven Scent', moderately hardy, small/medium, glossy, mid-green leaves, heavily fragrant, cup-shaped pink flowers with deep rose-pink flush at base of petal, magenta-pink stripe on back, mid- to late spring, 10m/10m (33ft/33ft); *M.* 'Iolanthe', moderately hardy small/medium, mid-green more or less oval leaves, abundant large cup-and-saucer-shaped, rose-pink flowers, cream inner petals, 25cm (10in) in diameter, spring, 10-12m/8m (33-40ft/25ft); *M. kobus*, hardy, aromatic, more or less oval mid-green leaves, white, slightly fragrant flowers, vase-shaped at first, later goblet- or saucer-shaped, sometimes pink-tinged at base, mid-spring, 12m/10m (40ft/33ft); *M. liliiflora* 'Nigra' (syn. *M. quinquepeta* 'Nigra'), hardy, elliptic to more or less oval dark green leaves, goblet-shaped, slightly fragrant dark purple-red flowers, cream-white tinged purple inside, early summer, some later until autumn, 3m/4m (10ft/13ft); *M.* x *loebneri* 'Leonard Messel', moderately hardy, small, mid-green, more or less oval leaves, star-shaped, fragrant pale lilac-pink flowers, in mid-spring, 8m/6m (25ft/20ft); *M.* x *l.* 'Merrill', large white fragrant flowers, goblet-shaped at first, opening to star-shaped, 8m/8m (25ft/25ft); *M. sargentiana* var. *robusta*, moderately hardy, light green oblong-oval leaves, goblet- to cup-shaped rose-pink flowers, cream inside, sometimes pendent, on bare branches, early to mid-spring, 15m/10m (50ft/33ft); *M. sieboldii*, moderately hardy, oblong to oval-elliptic, dark green leaves, downy grey-green beneath, fragrant, cup-shaped flowers, erect at first, later slightly pendent, late spring to late summer, followed by clusters of crimson fruit, 8m/12m (25ft/40ft); *M.* x *soulangeana*, hardy, tolerant of heavy clay soils, dark green, more or less oval leaves, goblet-shaped flowers, varying in shape, size and colour, from white to deep pink-purple, from 8-30cm (3in-1ft) in diameter, early and late spring, before and with leaves, 6m/6m (20ft/20ft); *M.* x *s.* 'Alba Superba' (syn. *M.* x *s.* 'Alba'), white, goblet-shaped flowers tinged purple at bases; *M.* x *s.* 'Lennei', goblet-shaped, dark purple-pink flowers, cream-white inside flushed pale purple, 10cm (4in) in diameter; *M.* x *s.* 'Rustica Rubra' (syn. *M.* x *s.* 'Rubra'), oval leaves, rich rose-red flowers; *M. stellata*, hardy, good for containers, mid-green, more or less oval-oblong to inversely lance-shaped leaves, slightly fragrant, white, star-shaped flowers of some 12-15 petals, sometimes flushed pink, early to mid-spring, on bare branches, 3m/4m (10ft/13ft); *M. s.* 'Royal Star', large flowers, 12cm (5in) in diameter, of some 25-30 petals, tinged pink in bud, opening to white; *M. s.* 'Waterlily', white flowers of up to 32 petals; *M.* 'Susan', moderately hardy, oval, mid-green leaves, fragrant, goblet-shaped, red-purple flowers, paler inside, mid-spring, 4m/3m (13ft/10ft); *M. tripetala*, hardy, dark green, more or less oval to inversely lance-shaped leaves, cup-shaped, cream-white, strongly pungent flowers, late spring to early summer, followed by clusters of red cone-shaped fruit, 10m/10m (33ft/33ft); *M. wilsonii*, hardy, dark green, elliptic or oval to lance-shaped leaves, downy red-brown beneath, fragrant, pendent white flowers with crimson stamens, early summer, 6m/6m (20ft/20ft).

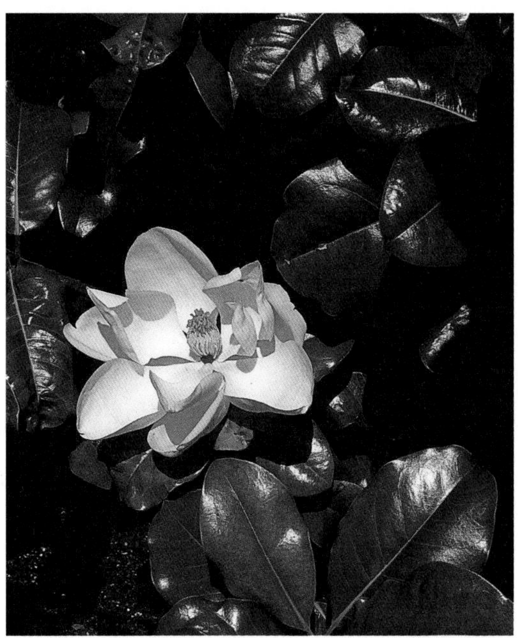

left *Magnolia grandiflora* 'Goliath'. I grow this variety simply because it flowers very well at a very early age.

Mahonia Berberidaceae

Medium/large evergreen shrubs. Fairly hardy to hardy. Some make wonderful specimens for early season flowers; others are good ground cover. Dark green, leathery, glossy, pinnate or trifoliate leaves with spiny margins. Fragrant yellow flowers, in spreading racemes or dense clusters, sometimes both, autumn to spring, some followed by fruits. Thrive in moist, fertile, well-drained soil enriched with humus, most in full or partial shade although some will tolerate sun. No routine pruning. Sow seed in autumn or when ripe, or take semi-ripe cuttings between late summer and autumn.

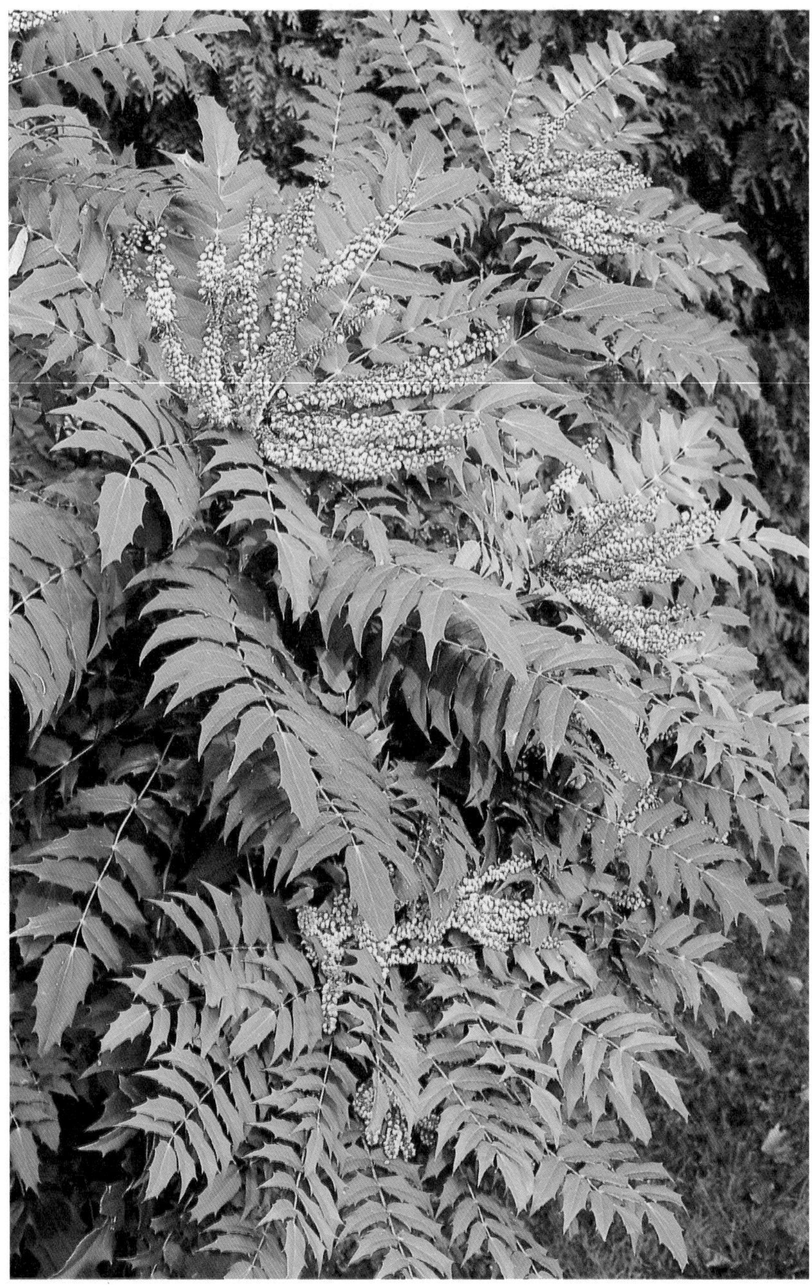

above *Mahonia* x *media* 'Charity'. According to most opinions, the finest hybrid mahonia ever raised; not surprisingly better than its stable-mates 'Faith' and 'Hope'

right *Malcolmia maritima*. The stocks are a confusing group of fragrant cottage garden plants; if Virginian Stock is your choice, then this is it.

❀ *M. aquifolium* (Oregon Grape), hardy to very hardy, glossy, dark green pinnate leaves, often purple or red tinged in winter, clusters of rich yellow flowers produced in racemes in spring, followed by blue-black fruits, 1m/1.5m (3ft/5ft); *M. a.* 'Apollo', low-growing, deep green leaves on red-brown stems, flowers in large clusters, the best form; *M. japonica*, hardy to very hardy, pinnate, dark green leaves, sharply toothed leaflets, clusters of pendent racemes of lemon-yellow flowers with fragrance reminiscent of lily-of-the-valley, late autumn to early spring, 2m/3m (6½ft/10ft); *M. j.* Bealei Group (syn. *M. bealei*), broad, blue-green leaflets, erect racemes; *M. lomariifolia*, fairly hardy, needs protection from strong, cold winds, dark green, thick, leathery, pinnate leaves, sharply toothed leaflets, rich yellow, slightly fragrant flowers in clusters of erect racemes, winter, 3m/2m (10ft/6½ft); *M.* x *media* 'Buckland', moderately hardy, dark green pinnate leaves, tinted red in autumn, arching racemes of slightly fragrant, bright yellow flowers, winter, 5m/4m (16ft/13ft); *M.* x *m.* 'Charity', erect and spreading racemes of slightly fragrant, deep yellow flowers, late autumn to midwinter, probably the best hybrid *Mahonia* its name deriving from the fact that among a group of these seedling varieties, it managed to surpass the two others which, with political inspiration, were named 'Faith' and 'Hope'; *M.* x *m.* 'Lionel Fortescue', erect racemes of bright yellow, fragrant flowers; *M.* x *wagneri* 'Undulata', moderately hardy, glossy, wavy, dark green leaves, red-purple in autumn, deep yellow flowers, spring, 2m/2m (6½ft/6½ft).

Malcolmia — Brassicaceae

Hardy annuals and perennials for cottage gardens. Leaves variable, from linear-oblong to pinnate, white, red or purple, cross-shaped flowers, spring to autumn. Sow seed in flowering positions in late spring. ❀ *M. maritima* (Virginian Stock), low-growing annual, grey-green elliptic leaves, clusters of lilac, rose, white or red flowers with sweet fragrance, throughout summer, 20-40cm/10-15cm (8in-1½ft/6in).

Malope — Malvaceae

Small/medium hardy annuals. Bright green oval leaves, sometimes lobed, trumpet-shaped, papery pink or violet flowers, sometimes white, deeply veined. Sow seed in warmth or in flowering positions in spring. Self-seeds freely. ❀ *M. trifida* 'Pink Queen', pointed, lobed leaves, shell-pink flowers with deeper veining and centres, 60-90cm/23cm (2-3ft/9in); *M. t.* 'Vulcan', bright magenta flowers with green centres, metallic sheen, summer, 65cm/23cm (2¼ft/9in); *M. t.* 'White Queen', white flowers, 60-90cm/23cm (2-3ft/9in).

Malus — Rosaceae

Small, moderately to very hardy tree. A hugely important genus because it includes all types of apple but also several beautiful spring-flowering ornamental forms with blossom, fruit and/or autumn foliage appeal and all with the unique advantage among ornamental trees of being obtainable in a range of ultimate sizes, achieved by buying plants grafted onto one of the growth-restricting apple rootstocks (see Table below). Tolerant of most soils and only really likely to fail in very heavy, wet conditions. No routine pruning for ornamental types; the pruning of fruiting apples is described in the companion volume. Most do not come true from seed and are difficult to strike from cuttings.

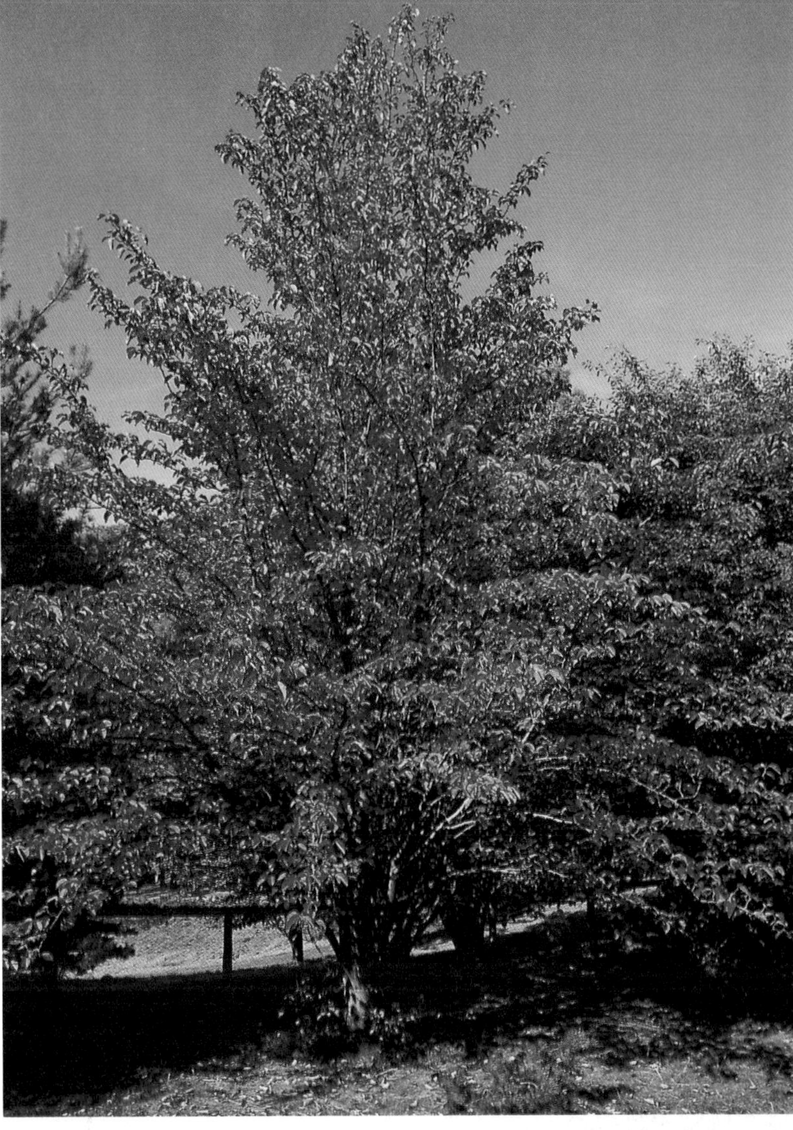

above *Malus tschonoskii.* Probably the best all round ornamental *Malus* species.

Effects of growth-restricting apple rootstocks

Rootstock	*Height of free-standing tree after ten years (m/ft)*
M.27	1.5 (5)
M.9	2 (6½)
M.26	2.5 (8)
M.106	3-4 (10-13)
M.111	5 (16)

❀ *M. floribunda*, distinctive, broadly spreading habit, bright green leaves, red buds, white or very pale pink flowers, small yellow fruits; *M. hupehensis*, prolific small white flowers, huge numbers of small, clear red fruits, a very lovely plant; *M.* 'John Downie', easily the best for crab-apple jelly, white flowers, red-orange fruits; *M.* x *moerlandsii* 'Profusion', my favourite among darker coloured *Malus*, rich, deep red flowers contrasting with dark red-purple foliage, very dark red fruits, tending to be lost among the foliage; *M.* x *robusta* 'Red Sentinel', white flowers, large numbers of shiny red fruits; *M.* x *schiedeckeri* 'Red Jade', white flowers, masses of rounded, bright fruits, vies with 'Red Sentinel' as the best red fruited variety; *M. tschonoskii*, superb autumn colours of red, yellow, orange and purple, easily the best autumn colour in the genus, white, pink-flushed flowers, yellow-green fruits with red shades; *M.* x *zumi* 'Golden Hornet', white flowers, masses of small, rounded golden-yellow fruits that usually persist until well into the winter.

Apples

Tree fruit. Apples are the toughest of all garden tree fruit and those most likely to thrive in cold, exposed areas, although the provision of some shelter and the use of restricted training methods (such as cordons or espaliers) will also help to ensure a good crop whilst making optimum use of limited space. Although a slightly acidic soil is ideal, you should obtain at least some fruit from trees grown on any soil likely to be found in the British Isles. You can choose the ultimate size of the trees by selecting an appropriate rootstock onto which your chosen fruiting variety is grafted (see Table). By growing the plants as cordons or espaliers, you can also have many more varieties than you might

above Apple 'Golden Noble'. A cooking apple, probably from the late 18th century and less acidic than 'Bramley's Seedling'.

right Apple 'Ashmead's Kernel'. First raised around 1700 and still widely regarded for its sweet flavour although low yielding.

imagine in your available space. It's also possible to buy 'family' trees, where more than one variety has been grafted onto the same rootstock. This neatly circumvents another complication: most apples are not self-fertile so another, compatible variety (or, in the few cases of triploid trees, two additional varieties) are needed in order for pollination and fruit set to occur. Garden apple varieties fall roughly into three main types: the crab (see above), the dessert or eating apple and the more acidic culinary apple or cooker (a fourth group, the very acidic cider apple, is rarely grown in gardens). Some varieties are called dual purpose and are useful in limited space for they cook well but are not so acidic that they can't be eaten fresh. With well over 2,000 existing varieties and probably around 100 readily available, choosing apples is difficult. It is compounded because many varieties will not thrive well in all areas and because the taste, even of familiar commercially grown types, may vary when grown in different parts of the country. The list that I have given therefore makes no attempt to describe flavour but includes some varieties for extremes of climate and covers most requirements in respect of use, time of maturing and keeping qualities. They are listed in cropping sequence from early to late and it should be noted that this is also a pretty accurate indication of their keeping qualities. Among early apples, 'Discovery' is an exception in keeping fairly well. In general too, varieties that crop at similar times also flower at similar times and are likely to be good pollinators for each other.

Cooking varieties: 'Emneth Early', 'Grenadier', 'Reverend W Wilks', 'Lord Derby', 'Peasgood's Nonsuch', 'Bramley's Seedling', 'Golden Noble', 'Howgate Wonder', 'Lane's Prince Albert'.

Dessert varieties: 'Beauty of Bath', 'Devonshire Quarrenden', 'Discovery', 'Epicure', 'George Cave', 'Irish Peach', 'Lord Lambourne', 'Sunset', 'Cox's Orange Pippin', 'Egremont Russet', 'Ellison's Orange', 'Fiesta', 'Fortune', 'Greensleeves', 'James Grieve', 'Katja', 'Red Devil', 'Worcester Pearmain', 'Ashmead's Kernel', 'Allington Pippin', 'Court Pendu Plat', 'Gala', 'Golden Delicious', 'Jonagold', 'Laxton's Superb', 'Orleans Reinette', 'Ribston Pippin', 'Rosemary Russet', 'Suntan', 'Spartan'.

Dual purpose varieties: 'Blenheim Orange', 'Charles Ross', 'Newton Wonder'.

Malva *Mallow* Malvaceae

Medium to large herbaceous or semi-evergreen annuals, biennials, perennials and sub-shrubs. Moderately hardy to very hardy and good, if unexciting, plants for informal borders and wild gardens, rather successful in coastal areas. Bright green, deeply cut basal leaves, usually rounded, sometimes heart- or kidney-shaped. Saucer-shaped flowers with five heart-shaped petals, lavender, pink, white, or purple, singly or in clusters, from late summer to autumn. Thrives best in free-draining soils, in sun or light shade, but needs protection from strong cold winds. Intolerant of

wild flower garden. Sow seed in spring or summer. Self-seeds freely. ❀ *M. recutita* (syn. *M. chamomilla*) (Scented Mayweed) flowers sweetly scented, in clusters, late spring to late summer, 50cm/30cm (1¾ft/1ft).

left *Malva moschata*. This is a tough, reliable, fairly pretty but never spectacular perennial.

Matteuccia Aspidiaceae

Medium deciduous ferns. Very hardy. Vase-shaped clumps of lance-shaped, pinnate, light green sterile fronds, yellow in autumn, with fertile dark brown inner fronds from mid- to late summer. Replant offsets between early spring and mid-autumn. Beautiful but invasive. ❀ *M. struthiopteris*, pale green, lacy shuttlecock-like clumps of gold-green sterile fronds, shorter, darker, inner fertile fronds, brown in late summer, 1.7m/1m (5½ft/3ft).

below *Matricaria recutita*. A sweetly scented little daisy, related to several common weeds.

heavy clay or highly acidic soil. Sow seed in warmth in early spring or in growing positions in late spring or early summer, divide established plants between mid-autumn and mid-spring, or take basal shoot cuttings in spring. Self-seeds freely. ❀ *M. alcea* var. *fastigiata*, erect perennial, pale green leaves, pink flowers, from late summer until autumn, 80cm/60cm (2½ft/2ft); *M. moschata*, very hardy erect, herbaceous perennial, pale green, kidney-shaped, finely cut leaves with musk scent, pink or white flowers, early summer to early autumn, 90cm/60cm (3ft/2ft); *M. m.* f. *alba*, abundant silky, white saucer-shaped flowers, summer, 46cm (1½ft); *M. sylvestris*, hardy biennial or short-lived perennial, erect or trailing, rounded, lobed dark green leaves, usually with a darker basal mark, pink-purple flowers, notched petals with darker veining, early summer to autumn, 45-90cm/60-90cm (1½-3ft/2-3ft); *M. s.* 'Primley Blue', prostrate evergreen shrub, rounded, green leaves, lavender-blue flowers with conspicuous darker blue veining, summer to early autumn, 20cm/30-60cm (8in/1-2ft); *M. s.* Zebrina', erect, shiny white flowers with deep purple veining, 90cm (3ft).

Matricaria *Mayweed* Asteraceae

Small hardy annuals, biennials and short-lived perennials, including some common weeds. Bright green, finely cut feathery leaves, white daisy-like flowers with yellow, button-like centres. Very aromatic, with a fragrance similar to camomile (*Chamaemelum nobile*) and good plants for the

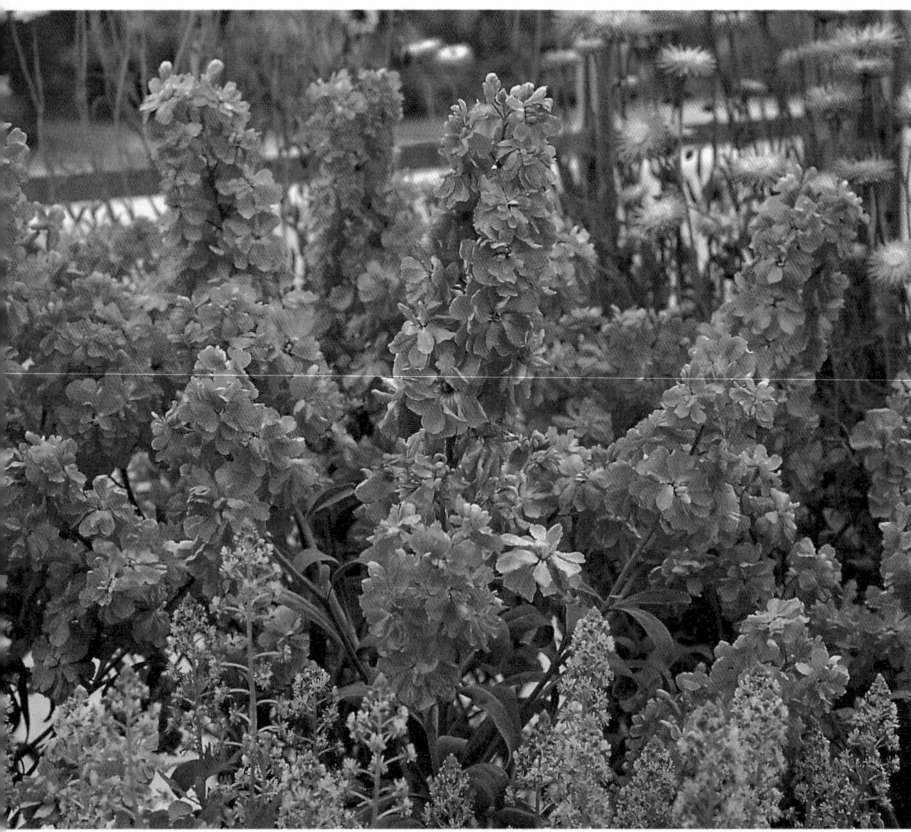

above *Matthiola incana* Brompton Stock. Among the best loved of old cottage garden flowers.

right *Meconopsis cambrica*. This plant self-seeds in my garden under a large yellow shrub rose; the combination is delightful.

Matthiola *Stock* Brassicaceae

Half-hardy or hardy annuals, perennials and subshrubs and long grown in cottage gardens and as cut flowers for their rich fragrance. Grey-green to mid-green lance-shaped, divided or shallowly lobed leaves, spikes of single or double, cross-shaped, highly perfumed flowers, usually in white and shades of red, pink and purple. Thrive in moderately fertile, moist, well-drained soil enriched with humus, preferably neutral to slightly alkaline; best in full sun. Sow half-hardy annuals for summer bedding in warmth in early spring and biennials in mid-summer in a cold-frame; perennials in a cold-frame in spring or summer. ❀ *M. incana*, grey-green or white, hairy leaves, fragrant mauve, white, violet, purple or pink flowers, from late spring to summer, 80cm/40cm (2½ft/1½ft). Varieties of *M. incana* are usually divided into two main groups, half-hardy annuals and biennials.

Annual stocks have single or double flowers, most in white and shades of crimson, lavender, lilac, mauve and pink, from early to mid-summer: 'Beauty of Nice', multi-coloured, on branched stems, 60cm/40cm (2ft/1½ft); Column Series, unbranched, usually double flowers, pink, pale blue, red or white, 30cm/75cm (1ft/2½ft); Ten Week stocks, branched, crimson, pink, lavender, purple and white flowers, usually double, produced about ten weeks after sowing, 30cm/25cm (1ft/10in); Trisomic Seven Week stocks, flowers similar to the above but produced about seven weeks after sowing, 45cm/30cm (1½ft/1ft).

Biennial varieties of *M. incana* are fairly hardy and are divided into two groups, Brompton stocks and East Lothian stocks. Both have single and double flowers in white and shades of crimson, lavender, lilac, mauve and pink, the former growing to 50cm/30cm (1¾ft/1ft), the latter to 30cm/30cm (1ft/1ft).

M. longipetala (syn. *M. bicornis*) (Night Scented Stock), annual, linear or pinnatifid grey-green leaves, clusters of rather unexciting pink, purple or mauve flowers, with a wonderful fragrance on summer nights, 30-35cm/23cm (1-1¼ft/9in).

Mazus Scrophulariaceae

Small annuals and herbaceous perennials and alpines. Fairly hardy. Lance-, spoon-shaped or linear toothed leaves, flattened tubular, two-lipped flowers resembling antirrhinums, the bottom lip with three lobes, from late spring to summer. Sow seeds in a cold-frame in spring or autumn, replant rooted sections or divide established plants in spring or autumn. ❀ *M. reptans*, dwarf, mat-forming, creeping perennial, toothed green, lance-shaped leaves, purple-blue flowers, lower lips spotted yellow, or red, yellow and white, in spring and summer, 5cm/30cm (2in/1ft).

left *Meconopsis* x *sheldonii*. Among the most admired yet challenging of garden flowers are the Asiatic blue poppies.

Meconopsis Papaveraceae

Annuals, biennials and evergreen/herbaceous perennials. Moderately hardy. Most celebrated for the Asiatic blue poppies, which must have moist, organic, slightly acidic soil in light shade, *Meconopsis* also includes other valuable and much easier garden species. Basal rosettes of pinnate or simple leaves, cup- or saucer-shaped, pendent, silky, poppy-like flowers with conspicuous stamens, singly or in clusters. Some perennial species are monocarpic (die after flowering). Sow seed when ripe or in spring in a cold-frame, or divide established plants after flowering. Perpetuate monocarpic forms by replanting off-sets. ❀ *M. betonicifolia* (syn. *M. baileyi*), herbaceous perennial, oblong, hairy leaves, heart-shaped at base, bright sky-blue, sometimes purple or white flowers on bristly, stiff stems, from early to mid-summer, followed by bristly, oval seedpods, 1.2m/45cm (4ft/1½ft); *M. cambrica*, herbaceous perennial, lobed, pale blue-green leaves, sometimes hairless, lemon-yellow, cup-shaped flowers, from mid-spring to mid-autumn, self-seeds freely but readily controlled and a lovely plant, 45cm/25cm (1½ft/10in); *M. c. flore-pleno*, double flowers; *M. c.* 'Frances Perry', scarlet flowers, rather misses the point I always feel; *M. chelidonifolia*, clump-forming deciduous perennial, pale green hairy leaves, pale yellow, pendent, saucer-shaped flowers, mid- to late summer, 1m/60cm (3ft/2ft); *M. grandis*, deciduous perennial, mid- to dark green, toothed leaves with red-brown hairs, pendent, cup-shaped flowers, vivid blue, white or deep red-purple, in early summer, 1-1.2m/60cm (3-4ft/2ft); *M. quintuplinervia*, clump-forming herbaceous perennial requiring acidic soil, rosettes of inversely lance-shaped or lance-shaped mid- to dark green leaves, with yellow or red-brown hairs, pendent, cup-shaped purple-blue or lavender-blue flowers, from early to late summer, 45cm/30cm (1½ft/1ft); *M.* x *sheldonii*, clump-forming herbaceous perennial, toothed, dark green basal leaves, cup-shaped blue flowers, flushed green, late spring to early summer, 1.2-1.5m/60cm (4-5ft/2ft); *M.* x *s.* 'Slieve Donard', rich, deep blue flowers, long pointed petals, probably the best of the blue poppies overall, 1m/60cm (3ft/2ft).

Melissa
Bee Balm, Lemon Balm Lamiaceae

Medium herbaceous perennials. Very hardy. Small oval, somewhat heart-shaped, wrinkled yellow-green leaves with lemon fragrance. Small tubular yellow-white or white flowers, summer to early autumn. Very attractive to bees. Sow seed in a cold-frame in spring, take semi-ripe cuttings in summer, or divide in spring or autumn. ❀ *M. officinalis*, bushy, erect, oval, toothed leaves, clusters of pale yellow flowers in summer, sometimes to autumn, 60-120cm/30-40cm (2-4ft/1-1½ft); *M. o.* 'Aurea', hairy, toothed leaves with gold-yellow variegation when young, fading during summer, white flowers, the most beautiful of all herbs in spring but rather a let-down later, 30-60cm/30-45cm (1-2ft/1-1½ft).

Melittis *Bastard Balm* Lamiaceae

Small/medium herbaceous perennials. Very hardy. Oval, pointed and toothed mid-green leaves with strong honey fragrance, tubular, two-lipped, hooded white, pink or purple flowers, often bicoloured, late spring to early summer. Sow seed in a cold-frame when ripe or in autumn, or divide established plants in spring, after flowering, or in autumn. ❀ *M. melissophyllum*, hairy, wrinkled leaves with conspicuous veining, abundant clusters of white flowers, sometimes pink, purple or white, with purple lower lip, along entire length of stem, late spring to early summer, 20-70cm/50cm (8in-2¼ft/1¾ft).

Mentha *Mint* Lamiaceae

Small to large strongly aromatic perennial herbs. Very hardy and among the indispensable herbs although most are invasive and must be confined in

right *Menyanthes trifoliata*. Although it has nothing to do with real broad beans, the foliage resemblance is striking.

some way. Lance-shaped or rounded leaves in shades of green, sometimes variegated. Clusters of two-lipped small tubular to bell-shaped flowers from summer to early autumn. Thrive in poor, moist soil in full sun or partial shade, some species tolerate damp or wet conditions near or in water. Best forms do not come true from seed; divide established plants in spring or autumn. ❀ *M. aquatica* (Water Mint), for pool margins and bog gardens, grey-green, peppermint-scented oval, hairy, toothed leaves on red-purple stems, lilac flowers, 15-90cm/1m (6in-3ft/3ft); *M.* x *gracilis* (Ginger Mint), erect, oval to lance-shaped leaves, lilac flowers, sweetly scented of ginger, 30-90cm (1-3ft)/indefinite; *M.* x *g.* 'Variegata', dark green leaves splashed and striped yellow, makes good ground cover, 30cm/1m (1ft/3ft) or more; *M. longifolia* (Horse Mint), stalkless, coarse, lance-shaped, toothed grey-green leaves, spearmint scent, white, mauve or lilac flowers, from mid- to late summer, best in full sun, 1.2m/1m (4ft/3ft) or more; *M.* x *piperita* (Peppermint), dark green, smooth, lance-shaped leaves, sometimes tinged purple, lilac-pink flowers, in summer, 30-90cm (1-3ft)/indefinite; *M.* x *p. citrata*, (Eau de Cologne Mint, Orange Mint), oval dark bronze-purple leaves on purple runners, lavender aroma, mauve flowers, the finest aromatic foliage in the herb, or any other garden. 50cm/1m (1¾ft/3ft) or more; *M. pulegium* (Pennyroyal), prostrate or erect stems, pungent peppermint-scented, elliptic to oval leaves, sometimes toothed, lilac flowers, summer, can cause adverse effects when ingested, 10-40cm/50cm (4in-1½ft/1¾ft); *M. requienii*, (Corsican mint) carpet-forming, tiny, strongly scented oval to round leaves, minute lilac flowers, summer, wonderful among damp paving, 1cm (½in)/indefinite; *M. spicata* (Spearmint), bright green, sweetly-scented, wrinkled, lance-shaped leaves, lilac, white or pink flowers, summer, the best with new potatoes, 1m (3ft)/indefinite; *M. s.* 'Crispa' (Curled Spearmint), leaves crinkled at edges, 30-100cm (1-3ft)/indefinite; *M. s.* 'Moroccan', used in Moroccan mint tea, white flowers, in summer, 60cm (2ft); *M. suaveolens* (Apple Mint), oblong-oval or rounded, wrinkled, hairy, toothed grey-green leaves, white or pink flowers, the best for mint sauce; *M. s.* 'Variegata' (Pineapple Mint), broad cream streaks on leaves and along margins, woolly leaves sometimes entirely white, pink flowers rather rarely, good for dark damp corners, 40-100cm (1½-3ft)/indefinite; *M.* x *villosa alopecurioides* (Bowles' Mint), oval, toothed, hairy apple-scented leaves, pink flowers, 30-90cm (1-3ft)/indefinite.

below *Mentha* x *piperita citrata*. One of the loveliest foliage fragrances in the entire garden.

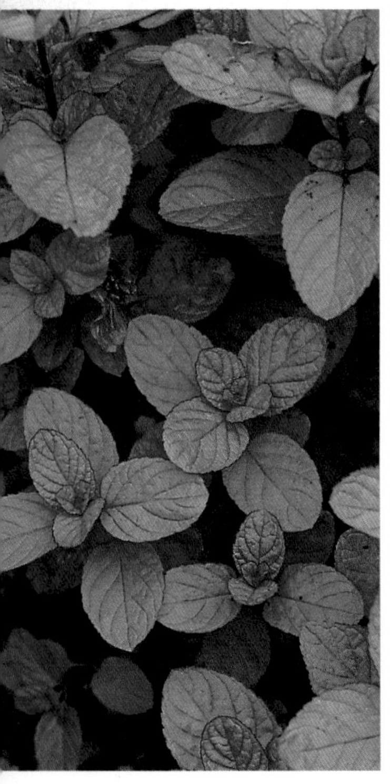

Menyanthes

Bog Bean Menyanthaceae

Small water marginal. Hardy to very hardy. Floating, tripalmate pale green leaves of elliptic to oval or more or less oval leaflets, resembling those of the broad bean. Spikes of white-fringed, star-shaped flowers, from late spring to summer, followed by globular fruit. Divide established plants in spring, or take softwood cuttings in spring or summer. Can be invasive and not for small pools. ❀ *M. trifoliata*, erect perennial, blue-green trifoliate leaves on fleshy stems, erect spikes of pink buds opening to white flowers, spring to summer, sometimes to autumn, 20-30cm (8in-1ft)/ indefinite.

Menziesia

Ericaceae

Small hardy deciduous shrubs. Oval to elliptic or oblong leaves, clusters of small, tubular, bell- or urn-shaped waxy flowers, cream-white, purple or pink, sometimes bicoloured, late spring. A striking small shrub for acidic soil. Sow seeds in warmth in late winter, take softwood cuttings in summer or divide established plants in early spring but has a reputation for being difficult to propagate. ❀ *M. ciliicalyx* var. *multiflora*, oval leaves edged with fine hairs, pale flowers with yellow-green base, purple-pink lobes, 60cm/60cm (2ft/2ft).

Mertensia Boraginaceae

Small/medium moderately hardy herbaceous deciduous and semi-evergreen perennials, most for slightly shaded borders. Blue-green or grey elliptic leaves, clusters of pendent, bell-shaped or tubular blue flowers, spring to early summer. Sow ripe seed in a cold-frame, divide established plants in early spring or take root cuttings of *M. pulmonarioides* from late summer to autumn. ❀ *M. pulmonarioides*, (syn. *M. virginica*) (Virginian Cowslip), deciduous, requires damp conditions, soft, fleshy blue-green leaves, clusters of pendent, deep blue flowers, tubular, flaring at the mouth, mid to late spring, 90cm/30cm (3ft/1ft); *M. simplicissima* (syn. *M. maritima* ssp. *asiatica*), rosettes of glaucous, more or less oval leaves, flared tubular, turquoise-blue flowers, spring to early autumn, 90cm/30cm (3ft/1ft).

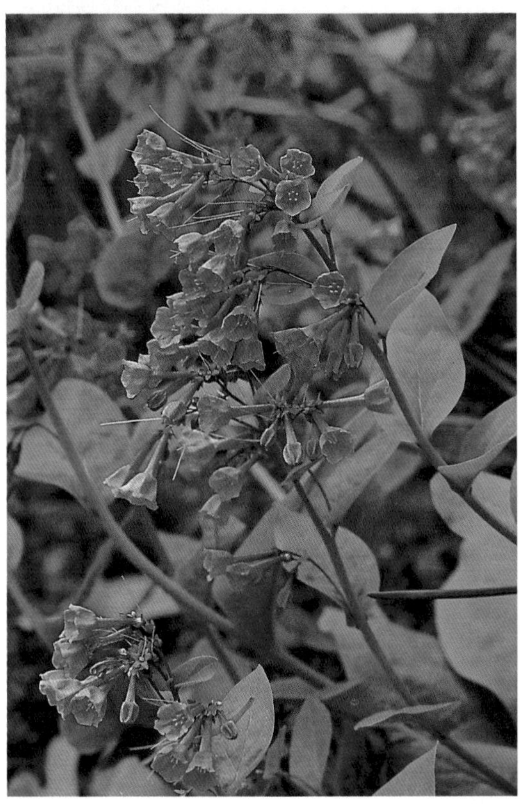

Mespilus *Medlar* Rosaceae

Large, moderately hardy deciduous shrub or small tree. Usually considered for its fruit, which is an acquired taste, but the blossom and autumn foliage colours are good enough for it to be grown as an ornamental. Thrives in fairly fertile, moist, well-drained soil, in full sun or partial shade. No routine pruning. Named varieties can only be propagated by grafting. ❀ *M. germanica*, dull green oblong leaves, hairy beneath, yellow-brown in autumn, stout spines on branches, five-petalled, white flowers, sometimes tinged pink, late spring to early summer, followed by apple-like fruit, green at first, later brown, edible when partly over-ripe in late autumn after frosts, 6m/8m (20ft/25ft). *M. g.* 'Nottingham', practically spineless, with larger flowers and fruit.

Metasequoia
Dawn Redwood Taxodiaceae

Hardy deciduous tree that makes a fine specimen in large gardens; tolerant of atmospheric pollution and best in damp, acidic soils. Too many gardeners with small gardens are seduced by its appeal however and live to regret their choice. Shredding, cinnamon brown bark, soft, linear leaves borne in rows, giving the appearance of a divided, feathery leaf. Sow seed in autumn, take hardwood cuttings in winter or semi-ripe cuttings in mid-summer. ❀ *M. glyptostroboides*, bright green leaves, double banded in light green beneath, tawny pink, orange and gold in autumn, clusters of yellow male flowers, smaller clusters of yellow-green female flowers followed by round or cylindrical light brown female cones, ovoid, pendent, spherical male cones, 20-40m/5m (8in-1½ft/16ft).

Microbiota Cupressaceae

Evergreen moderately hardy coniferous shrub that can be successful as ground cover; tolerates most soils. Scale-like leaves, male and female cones. Sow seed in autumn or take semi-ripe cuttings during the spring. ❀ *M. decussata*, low, mound-forming, dark green leaves in flattened sprays, bronze in winter, sometimes brown, insignificant flowers in spring, followed by tiny male and female berry-like brown cones with leathery scales, 1m/1.5m (3ft/5ft).

Milium Poaceae

Small annual and perennial grasses, many are weeds and only one a good garden plant. Moderately hardy. Light green or yellow-green, linear to lance-shaped leaves, clusters of single-flowered spikelets, late spring to mid-summer. Sow seed in growing positions in spring, or divide established plants in early spring or early autumn. ❀ *M. effusum* 'Aureum' (Bowles' Golden Grass), perennial, tufts of flat, gold-yellow, arching leaves, colour best in spring, tiny gold spikelets of bead-like flowers, on pendent panicles, early summer, 60cm/30cm (2ft/1ft).

left *Mertensia pulmonarioides.* An intriguing plant with the flower form of a real cowslip but with a colour true to its own family.

above *Milium effusum* 'Aureum'. This is justifiably one of the best known and most popular of all coloured grasses.

above *Mimulus moschatus*. One of the oddest stories in botany attaches to this plant as the species lost its fragrance world-wide around 1914.

right *Miscanthus sinensis* 'Gracillimus'. The various forms of *Miscanthus* are among the prettiest, as well as the largest, of all ornamental grasses.

below *Mirabilis jalapa*. The Four o'clock Plant because its flowers open in late afternoon.

Mimulus
Monkey Flower Scrophulariaceae

Small/medium tender to moderately hardy annuals, perennials and evergreen shrubs for damp or boggy areas; smaller species in moisture-retaining rock gardens. Pale green or grey-green, linear to rounded, toothed or entire leaves, funnel-, trumpet-shaped or tubular, two-lipped, antirrhinum-like flowers, many spotted with contrasting colours, spring to autumn. Flowers are attractive to insects, including bees, but not to all people; I think they are very much an acquired taste. Sow seed in a cold-frame in spring or autumn, less hardy species in warmth in spring or divide established plants in summer. All those described below are hardy herbaceous perennials. ❀ *M. cardinalis*, light green downy, toothed, oval to oval-elliptic leaves, tubular scarlet flowers with yellow throat, summer, 90cm/60cm (3ft/2ft); *M. cupreus* 'Whitecroft Scarlet', short-lived, low-growing, spreading, mid-green, oval leaves, abundant clusters of trumpet-shaped, bright vermilion flowers, early to late summer, 10cm/15cm (4in/6in); *M. guttatus* (syn. *M. langsdorfii*), bright green, toothed, more or less oval to rounded leaves, bright gold-yellow flowers with purple-brown or red spots on lower lip, 30cm/50-120cm (1ft/1¾-4ft); *M. g.* Highland Series, trumpet-shaped flowers in various colours, including yellow, often with only a few spots, 20cm/30cm (8in/1ft); *M. luteus* (Monkey Flower), spreading, toothed mid-green, oval to oblong leaves, bright yellow flowers, summer, 30cm/60cm (1ft/2ft); *M. moschatus* (Musk Flower), spreading, mat-forming, small, pale yellow flowers scented of musk, summer, 20cm/30cm (8in/1ft); *M. ringens* (Allegheny Monkey Flower), erect, toothed, oblong, lance-shaped or inversely lance-shaped mid-green leaves, long clusters of tubular violet, white, blue-violet or, rarely, pink flowers, summer, 90cm/30cm (3ft/1ft).

Mirabilis
Nyctaginaceae

Annuals and tuberous ornamentals. Tender to barely hardy. In cold areas grown as half-hardy annuals for summer bedding. Oval leaves, clusters of large, sometimes scented, narrow, trumpet-shaped flowers in summer, followed by fruit. Sow seed in warmth in early spring or in flowering positions in late spring following the last frost, or divide established plants in spring. ❀ *M. jalapa* (Marvel of Peru, Four o'clock Plant), bright green leaves, richly fragrant, bright crimson, yellow, purple or orange flowers sometimes all on the same plant, sometimes striped, flowers open in the afternoon and fade by morning and are followed by small green fruit, 60cm/60cm (2ft/2ft).

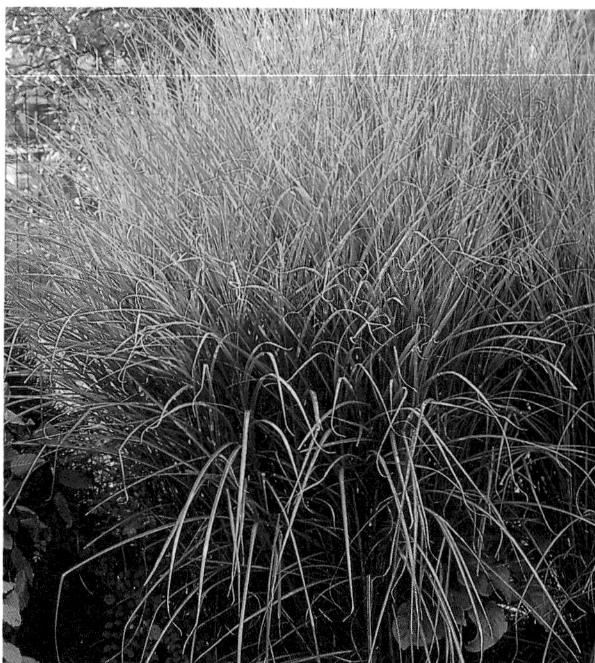

Miscanthus
Poaceae

Small/large deciduous or evergreen perennial grasses. Barely hardy to moderately hardy plants that make superb specimens in borders or moist but well-drained soil beside water; larger species of limited value as windbreaks. Narrow, lance-shaped or linear leaves on reed-like stems, panicles of silky feathery spikelets, late summer to autumn. Sow seed in a cold-frame in spring or divide established plants in spring. ❀ *M. sacchariflorus*, clump-forming, deciduous, ribbon-like pale green, arching leaves on bamboo-like stems, hairy, fan-shaped panicles may form but only after hot summers, 1.5-2.2m/1.5m (5-6½ft/5ft); *M. sinensis* 'Silberfeder' (syn. *M.* 'Silver Feather'), deciduous, narrow, linear, blue-green leaves, silver to pale pink-brown feathery plumes, early to mid-autumn, 2.5m/1.2m (8ft/4ft); *M. s.* 'Gracillimus', clump-forming, deciduous, narrow, curling, blue-green leaves with white midribs, leaves pale straw to bronze in autumn, silky, plume-like panicles, autumn, 1.3m/1.2m (4ft/4ft); *M. s.* 'Kleine Silberspinne', loose, spidery panicles, red tinged with white at first, later silver, late summer to autumn, 1.2m/1.2m

(4ft/4ft); *M. s.* 'Morning Light', very narrow, arching leaves with silver veins, 1.2m/1.2m (4ft/4ft); *M. s.* var. *purpurascens*, narrow, green leaves, with pink midribs, purple-green in summer, later red and orange tinges in autumn, narrow brown-pink panicles, mid-autumn, 1.2/1.2m (4ft/4ft); *M. s.* 'Undine', very narrow leaves with white veining, fluffy plumes, tinted purple, 1.5m/1.2m (5ft/4ft).

Molinia Poaceae

Small/large hardy perennial grasses. Narrow, linear leaves with good autumn colour, erect panicles of flower spikelets. A very good grass for wet, acidic soils. Sow seed in a cold-frame or divide established plants in spring. ❀ *M. caerulea* ssp. *caerulea* 'Variegata' (Purple Moor Grass), clump-forming, short tufts of linear to oblong, green and cream leaves on ochre stems, feathery purple plumes, both leaves and plumes pale buff in autumn, 45-60cm/40cm (1½-2ft/1½ft).

Molucella Lamiaceae

Half-hardy bedding annuals and short-lived perennials. Strikingly distinct pale green, oval to rounded, toothed or scalloped-edged leaves, long clusters of two-lipped, hooded tubular flowers surrounded by bell-shaped calyces, from summer to autumn. Sow seed in warmth in early spring or in flowering positions in late spring after the frosts. ❀ *M. laevis* (Bells of Ireland), scalloped, pale green leaves, tiny white or pale purple, fragrant flowers within pale green calyces, produced in clusters on tall erect stems, late summer, calyces later white, papery, a very good cut flower for preserving in glycerine, 60-90cm/20cm (2-3ft/8in).

Monarda *Bergamot* Lamiaceae

Medium annuals and moderately hardy herbaceous perennials, often grown in herb gardens but also very good border plants and especially attractive to butterflies. Mid- to dark green or purple-green, aromatic, lance-shaped to oval, pointed, sometimes toothed leaves on square stems, clusters of narrow, tubular, two-lipped flowers surrounded by pointed bracts, in summer. All the varieties described below are clump-forming herbaceous perennials. Sow seed in a cold-frame in autumn or spring, divide established plants or take basal cuttings in spring. ❀ *M.* 'Aquarius', dark green leaves, light mauve flowers, mid- to late summer, 90cm/45cm (3ft/1½ft); *M.* 'Beauty of Cobham', purple-green leaves, pale pink flowers with dark purple-pink bracts, late summer to autumn, 90cm/45cm (3ft/1½ft); *M.* 'Cambridge Scarlet', hooded, sage-like scarlet-red flowers, brown-red calyces, the best variety, 90cm/45cm (3ft/1½ft); *M.* 'Croftway Pink', similar to 'Cambridge Scarlet' but with clear rose-pink flowers, 90cm/45cm (3ft/1½ft); *M. punctata*, biennial or short-lived perennial, sometimes grown as a half-hardy annual, lance-shaped, mid-green leaves, yellow flowers marked with purple, with yellow or purple bracts, 1m/40cm (3ft/1½ft); *M.* 'Schneewittchen' (syn. 'Snow Witch'), white flowers, green bracts, mid-summer to autumn, 90cm/45cm (3ft/1½ft).

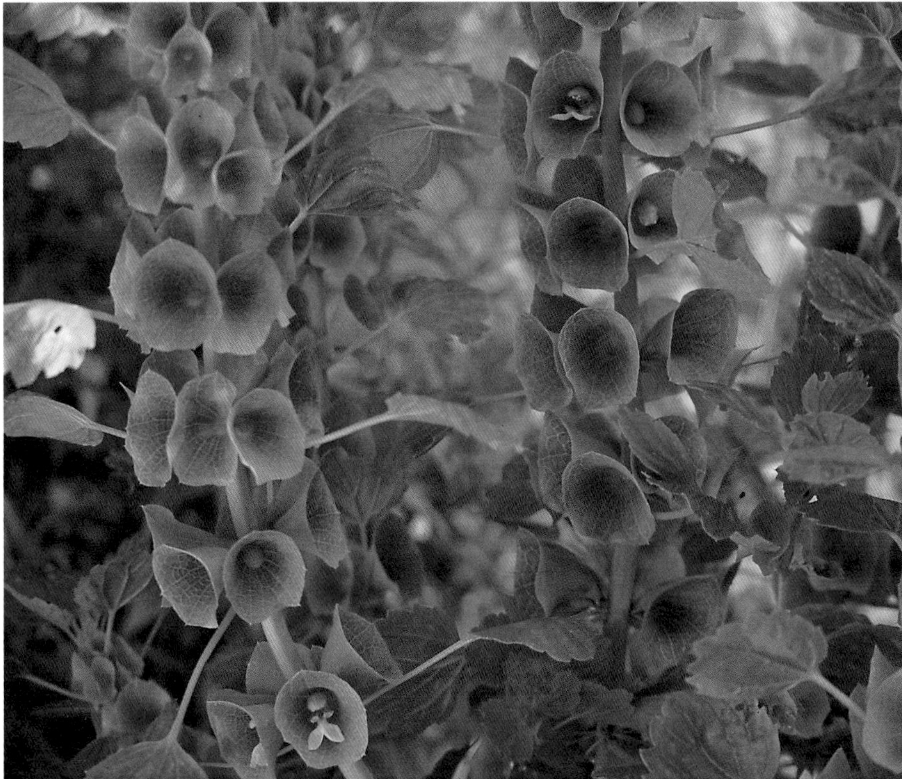

above *Molucella laevis*. Among the few annuals with green flowers, always popular with flower arrangers.

Morina Morinaceae

Large/medium hardy evergreen short-lived perennials, superficially like thistles. Eye-catching plants but ones that I find tricky; they must have good growing conditions. Rosettes of glossy, lance-shaped, prickly, dark green leaves, spikes of tubular pink, red, white or yellow flowers encircling stems, above which are spiny bracts in whorled clusters, all at intervals up the stem. Sow seed in a cold-frame when ripe, or take root cuttings in winter. ❀ *M. longifolia* (Whorflower), dark green, aromatic, wavy-margined, spiny basal leaves, waxy flowers white at first, then pink, deepening to crimson, from early summer, 90cm/30cm (3ft/1ft).

below *Morina longifolia*. A very frustrating plant, like a thistle in leaf although with very different flowers; one that simply will not grow for me.

above *Morus nigra*. Mulberries are plants of the old cottage garden and their fruits are wonderfully tasty and juicy.

Morus
Mulberry Moraceae

Deciduous shrubs and small trees. Tender to moderately hardy. They are best grown against a warm wall in cold areas. Don't plant close to a garden seat; the fruit stain notoriously. Light to dark green, toothed, oval to rounded leaves, sometimes with heart-shaped bases. Tiny, pale green cup-shaped male and female flowers, followed by sweet, raspberry-like fruit, edible and delicious on *M. nigra*. Thrives in moist, fairly fertile, well-drained soil in full sun, protected from dry, cold winds. Sow seeds when ripe or in spring, take semi-ripe cuttings in summer or hardwood cuttings in autumn. ❀ *M. alba* (syn. *M. bombycis*) (White Mulberry), glossy, bright green, oval to heart-shaped leaves, irresistible to silkworms, yellow in autumn, fruit white at first, later red or nearly black, late summer, 10m/10m (33ft/33ft); *M. a.* 'Pendula', weeping, 3m/5m (10ft/16ft); *M. nigra* (Black Mulberry), coarse, heart-shaped, dark green leaves, gold-yellow in autumn, red-black fruit, late summer, 12m/15m (40ft/50ft).

Muehlenbeckia
Polygonaceae

Small/large tender to fairly hardy deciduous and evergreen shrubs and climbers for ground cover, arches, pergolas and trellises. Linear to rounded leaves, fragrant, tiny cup-shaped flowers, singly or in clusters. Sow seed in warmth when ripe or take semi-ripe cuttings in summer. ❀ *M. complexa* (syn. *M. axillaris*), fairly hardy, twining deciduous climber or mat-forming shrub, more or less rounded leaves on thin, dark stems, clusters of green-white flowers in autumn, followed by fleshy small white fruit, 3m (10ft).

Muscari
Grape Hyacinth Hyacinthaceae

Small barely hardy to moderately hardy bulbous ornamentals for sunny or lightly shaded borders or rock gardens, but plant with care as some are invasive. Mid-green, fleshy leaves, usually linear to inversely lance-shaped, in basal clusters. Clusters of tiny bell-shaped, tubular or round flowers on leafless stalks, in spring or autumn. Sow seed in a cold-frame in autumn, divide clumps in summer. ❀ *M. armeniacum*, narrow, semi-upright mid-green leaves, clusters of purple-blue flowers with white mouths, mid-spring, 20cm/5cm (8in/2in); *M. a.* 'Blue Spike', double, dark blue flowers with green-yellow mouths; *M. aucheri* (syn. *M. tubergenianum*), spoon- to sickle-shaped, mid-green leaves, conical or oval clusters of rounded flowers, bright blue with white mouths, usually paler blue, sterile flowers at the top, early spring, 10-15cm/5cm (4-6in/2in); *M. azureum*, grey-green, inversely lance-shaped leaves, conical or oval clusters of bell-shaped, pale to bright blue flowers with darker stripe, early spring, 10cm/5cm (4in/2in); *M. comosum* 'Plumosum' (syn. *Leopoldia comosum*) (Tassel Hyacinth), linear mid-green leaves, large clusters of very eye-catching thread-like, blue-mauve, sterile flowers, spring, 20-60cm/5cm (8in-2ft/2in); *M. latifolium*, inversely-lance-shaped, mid-green leaves, fragrant, dark violet-blue flowers at base, pale blue flowers at the top, mid to late spring, 20cm/5cm (8in/2in).

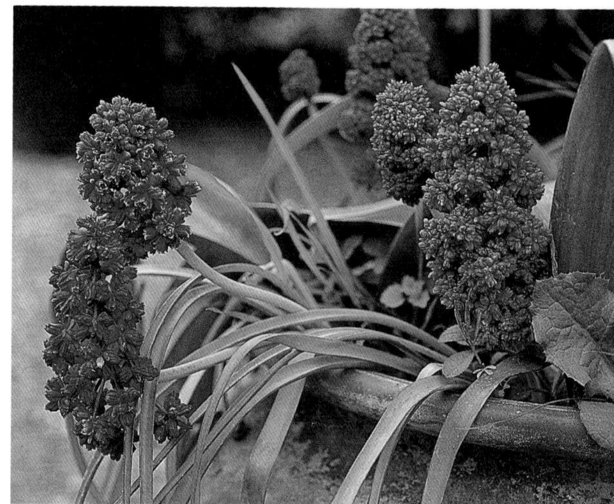

right *Muscari comosum* 'Plumosum' Some muscaris are troublesome and invasive; this one isn't.

Myosotis
Forget-Me-Not Boraginaceae

Small hardy annuals, biennials and short-lived perennials. These are much loved and very easy plants for borders, beds and rock gardens; *Myosotis scorpioides* requires moisture and is best grown as a water marginal or in other moist sites. Hairy, variable leaves, tiny dish- or funnel-shaped, blue, white or yellow flowers. Sow seed in flowering positions in spring or in a cold-frame in early summer (annuals and biennials), in a cold-frame in spring (perennials) or divide established plants in spring. ❀ *M. colensoi*, mat-forming perennial, oval to lance-shaped leaves, white flowers, singly or in clusters, in early summer, 5cm/20cm (2in/8in); *M. scorpioides* (syn. *M. palustris*), evergreen perennial, long, spoon-shaped, mid-green leaves, sky-blue flowers with yellow centres, in early summer, 15-30cm/30cm (6in-1ft/1ft); *M. s.* 'Mermaid', compact, shiny dark green leaves, small bright blue flowers, 15-23cm/30cm (6-9in/1ft); *M. sylvatica*, biennial, masses of tiny blue flowers in loose heads, spring to summer; numerous cultivated forms, self-seeds freely, 30cm/15cm (1ft/6in); *M. s.* 'Blue Ball', intense blue, compact, 15cm (6in); *M. s.* 'Royal Blue', very deep blue flowers, 3cm (1in).

Myrica — Myricaceae

Medium/large, barely hardy to hardy, deciduous and evergreen shrubs and small trees. Oval to lance-shaped, aromatic dark green leaves, clusters of insignificant flowers in the form of male and female catkins, in spring and summer, produced on the same or separate plants. Sow ripe seed in cold-frame, layer or take semi-ripe cuttings between early and mid-summer. ❀ *M. gale* (Bog Myrtle), hardy, deciduous branching shrub, lance-shaped, glossy, toothed, sweetly scented dark green leaves, gold-brown catkins in late spring or early summer, followed by yellow-brown fruit, now a rather rare plant in the wild and especially valuable as bog shrubs are few and far between, 1.5m/1.5m (5ft/5ft).

Myrrhis *Sweet Cicely* — Apiaceae

Hardy herbaceous perennial herb for a moist but well-drained position in a herb garden, mixed border or wild garden, and near ponds and streams. Finely divided, fern-like leaves, umbels of tiny white flowers. Sow ripe seed in a cold-frame or divide established plants in spring or autumn. ❀ *M. odorata*, bright green, pinnate leaves, star-shaped white flowers, early summer, followed by shiny brown fruit, 2m/1.5m (6½ft/5ft).

Myrtus *Myrtle* — Myrtaceae

Medium/large evergreen shrubs and small trees. Barely hardy to fairly hardy. Myrtles are good for coastal areas but will survive in sheltered spots in much colder places than is imagined. They also make good container plants to be taken under cover in winter. Aromatic leaves, fragrant flowers, spring to autumn, followed by fruit. Flowers and fruit are only produced in hot, dry summers. No routine pruning. Sow seed in warmth in early or mid-summer, or in a cold-frame in autumn, or take semi-ripe cuttings in late summer. ❀ *M. communis* (Common Myrtle), oval, deep green leaves, abundant white flowers with prominent white stamens, mid- to late autumn, followed by purple-black fruits, 3m/3m (10ft/10ft); *M. c.* ssp. *tarentina*, (syn. *M. c.* 'Jenny Reitenbach'), a superb, compact plant with small, narrow, elliptic leaves, white flowers tinged pink, white fruits; *M. c.* 'Variegata' cream-white margined leaves.

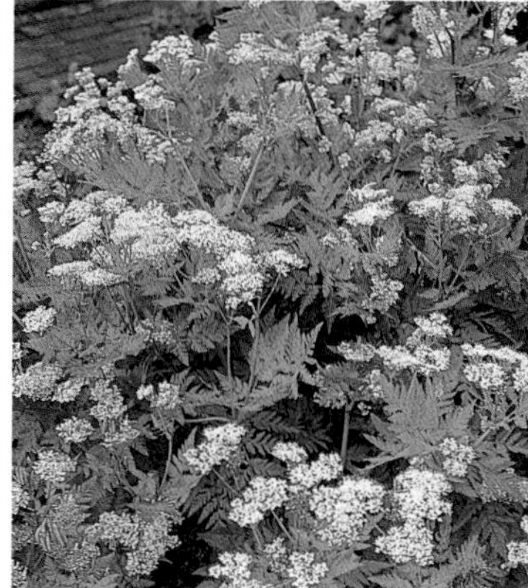

above *Myrrhis odorata* are equally valuable in the large herb bed or water garden.

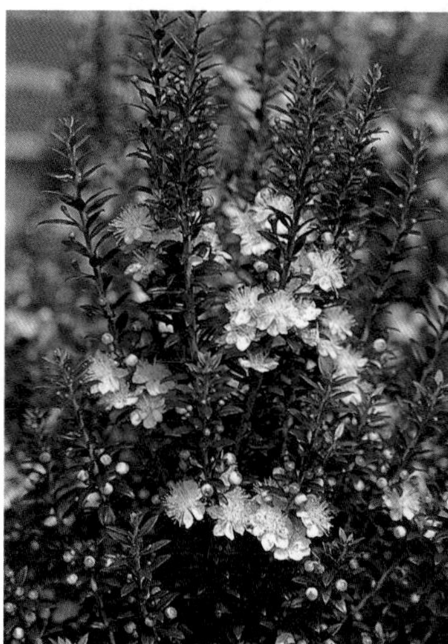

above *Myrtus communis tarentina*. One of my gardening pleasures of recent years has been the discovery that myrtles are not as tender as I had believed.

left *Myrica gale*. This is one of a small and valuable group of ornamental bog garden shrubs.

above *Narcissus* 'Professor Einstein'. The contrast here between the orange of the cup and the white of the petals is really among the most striking of any variety.

Nandina

Sacred Bamboo Berberidaceae

Semi-evergreen/evergreen shrub. Fairly hardy and a very good plant for Oriental-style gardens in cold areas where real bamboos are unreliable; but does need full sun. Low-growing varieties are good ground cover. Pinnate leaves, white flowers followed by fruit. No routine pruning. Sow seed in a cold-frame when ripe or take semi-ripe cuttings in summer. ❀ *N. domestica*, bamboo-like shrub, pinnate green leaves with lance-shaped leaflets, flushed purple-red in spring and autumn, sprays of small, star-shaped flowers with prominent yellow anthers, mid-summer, followed in hot summers by spherical, bright-red fruits, 2m/1.5m (6½ft/5ft); *N. d.* 'Firepower', dwarf, compact, yellow-green leaves turn red-purple in autumn, 45cm/60cm (1½ft/2ft).

Narcissus *Daffodil* Amaryllidaceae

Small/medium bulbous ornamentals. Barely hardy to moderately hardy and perhaps the most indispensable spring bulbs. Spring wouldn't be spring without the display of daffodils and narcissi. Different species and varieties are suitable for borders, naturalizing in grass, woodland plantings, containers, rock gardens and for cutting; but do remember that not all are appropriate for all purposes. Strap-shaped leaves, flowers singly or in clusters at the top of a leafless stem, have a central trumpet or cup (corona) surrounded by six petals. Colours usually yellow or white, with white, yellow, orange, red or pink petals. Species and their many varieties are usually divided into 12 groups on the basis of their flower shape. Thrive in fairly fertile, well-drained soil, moist in the growing season, in full sun or light shade. Some species are best in a neutral or acidic soil, others prefer alkalinity. Sow seed (species) in a cold-frame when ripe; divide clumps when dormant. After flowers fade, feed plants and don't cut down foliage for at least six weeks. The commonest problem is blindness (lack of flowers), most often caused by planting too shallowly.

Trumpet Daffodils Single flower per stem, with trumpet as long as, sometimes longer than, petals, planting distance usually 8-16cm (3¼in/6½in). ❀ 'King Alfred', gold-yellow, smooth, broad petals, still the best large golden daffodil for naturalizing, 40cm (1½ft); 'Mount Hood', cream-white trumpet, off-white, overlapping petals, mid-spring, the outstanding white daffodil, 45cm (1½ft); 'Rijnveld's Early Sensation', large yellow flowers, 9cm (3½in) in diameter, early spring, 25-50cm (10in-1¾ft); 'Spellbinder', sulphur-yellow, trumpet fading to cream, white-green mouth, mid-spring, 50cm (1¾ft); 'W P Milner', pendent, pale cream-yellow trumpet, forward-pointing cream petals, early to mid-spring, 23cm (9in).

right It's very hard to pick a favourite among the tiny flowered Tazetta group but *Narcissus* 'Minnow' has performed delightfully for me over many years.

Large-cupped Daffodils Single flower per stem, cup more than one-third the length of, but less than the petals, planting distance usually 16cm (6½in). ❀ 'Carlton', pale yellow, frilled cup, mid-spring, very good for forcing; 'Ice Follies', frilled cup, lemon-yellow at first, later off white, cream-white petals, mid-spring, 40cm (1½ft); 'Professor Einstein', frilled vivid orange cup, white petals, a striking and splendid variety; 'Saint Keverne', gold-yellow, cup indented at rim, mid-spring, resistant to basal rot, 45cm (1½ft); 'Salmon Trout', buff-yellow cup, white petals, mid-spring; 'Salomé', large pink-orange cup, waxy pure white or cream petals, mid-spring, the best pink, 45cm (1½ft).

Small-cupped Narcissi Single flower per stem, cup no more than one-third the length of the petals, planting distance usually 16cm (6½in). ❀ 'Barrett Browning', deeply frilled orange-red cup, smooth white petals, early to mid-spring, a very fine plant; 'Purbeck', goblet-shaped yellow cup tinged green at throat, fringed orange band, white petals, mid-spring, 45cm (1½ft).

Double Daffodils and Narcissi One or more flowers per stem, fully double or with either double outer or inner petals, some fragrant, planting distance usually 16cm (6½in). ❀ 'Cheerfulness', scented, fully-double cream and pale yellow, one to three neat flowers per stem, mid-spring, 40cm (1½ft); 'Golden Ducat', fully-double, gold-yellow, pointed central segments, mid-spring, 45cm (1½ft); 'Petit Four', fully-double, apricot centre, white outer petals, early spring; 'Rip van Winkle' (syn. *N. minor* var. *pumilus* 'Plenus'), fully double, green-yellow, pointed petals, early spring, 30cm (1ft); 'Unique', large double flowers, 10cm (4in) in diameter, yellow centre, white outer petals, mid-spring, 50cm (1¾ft); 'Yellow Cheerfulness', fragrant, yellow fully-double flowers, three or four per stem, mid-spring, 45cm (1½ft).

Triandrus Narcissi Two to six pendent flowers per stem, often with recurved petals and short cups, planting distance usually 5-8cm (2-3¼in); ❀ 'Hawera', three to five small flowers per stem, pale yellow, slightly recurved petals, late spring, 18cm (7in); 'Liberty Bells', lemon-yellow, mid-spring, my favourite of the group, 30cm (1ft); 'Thalia', two star-like white flowers per stem, twisted, slightly recurved petals, mid-spring, 35cm (1¼ft).

Cyclamineus Narcissi Single pendent flower per stem, long trumpet-shaped cups, recurved petals, planting distance usually 8cm (3¼in). ❀ 'February Gold', gold-yellow petals, darker cup, late winter to early spring, 30cm (1ft); 'Jack Snipe', short yellow cup, white petals, mid-spring, long-lasting, good for naturalizing, 20cm (8in); 'Jenny', cup lemon-yellow at first, later cream, cream-white petals, mid-spring, 30cm (1ft); 'Jetfire', yellow flowers, cup later bright orange, early spring, very long-flowering period, to my mind, the best new narcissus for years, 20cm (8in); 'Little Witch', gold-yellow, early to mid-spring, 22m (72ft); 'Peeping Tom', gold-yellow, cup flared at tip.

above *Narcissus bulbocodium conspicuous*. The foliage of this quite charming plant emerges weeks in advance of the flowers, a promise of the pleasure to come.

Jonquilla Narcissi One to five flowers per stem, stems rounded, mid- to dark green leaves, fragrant flowers, spreading petals, not recurved, planting distance usually 8cm (3½in); ❀ 'Pipit', lemon-yellow petals, paler cup, two to three flowers per stem, mid- to late spring, 25cm (10in); 'Quail', gold-yellow, two to three flowers per stem, mid-spring, 40cm (1½ft); 'Suzy', orange cup, primrose-yellow petals, one to two flowers, mid-spring, 40cm (1½ft); 'Sweetness', gold-yellow, mid-spring, 40cm (1½ft).

Tazetta Narcissi Small flowers, sometimes fragrant, dark green, broad leaves, many are half-hardy and are best grown in a greenhouse, planting distance usually 8cm (3½in). ❀ 'Canaliculatus', tiny flowers, yellow cups, white petals, grey leaves; 'Cragford', hardy, fragrant white and orange flowers, early spring, 50cm (1¾ft); 'Geranium', hardy, shiny white petals, orange-red cup, flowers 5.5cm(2in) in diameter, mid- to late spring, excellent cut flower, 35cm (1¼ft); 'Minnow', hardy, cream petals, cup yellow at first, later cream, mid-spring, 18cm (7in); *N. papyraceus* (syn. 'Paper

above I have no hesitation is saying that I find *Narcissus* 'Jetfire' to be the finest new *Narcissus* variety that I have grown for a very long time.

White'), barely hardy and often grown indoors, glossy, mid-green leaves, clusters of up to ten fragrant white flowers, late winter to early spring, 35cm (1¼ft).

Poeticus Narcissi Most have a single flower per stem, small, flat, disc-shaped, red-rimmed cup or eye, pure white spreading petals, planting distance usually 16cm (6½in). ❀ 'Actaea', large, round, very fragrant flowers, wavy petals, yellow, red-rimmed eye, late spring, 45cm (1½ft); 'Cantabile', round flowers, pure white petals, red-rimmed, green eye, late spring, 25cm (10in).

Species and closely related forms Wild daffodil species and their closely related varieties, many best grown in an alpine house; planting distance usually 5-8cm (2-3¼n) for small bulbs, 16cm (6½in) for larger bulbs. Perhaps the most charming group of all. ❀ *N. asturiensis*, glaucous leaves, pale yellow flowers, late winter, 8cm (3¼in); *N. bulbocodium* (Hoop Petticoat Daffodil), hardy, grass-like dark green leaves, tiny, funnel-shaped, deep yellow flowers with narrow petals, round, expanded trumpets, mid-spring, good for naturalizing in a moist, grassy site that is dry in summer, often said to require acidic soil but thrives well in my own neutral soil, 10-15cm (4-6in); *N. b.* var. *conspicuus*, gold-yellow flowers, the best form; *N. cantabricus* ssp. *cantabricus* narrow, funnel-shaped white flowers, tiny pointed petals, expanded trumpets, winter, 15-20cm (6-8in); *N. cyclamineus*, hardy, bright green, keeled leaves, gold-yellow, pendent flowers with narrow, recurved petals, long trumpets, early spring, 15-20cm (6-8in); *N. jonquilla*, hardy, narrow leaves, fragrant, gold-yellow flowers, up to five per stem, tiny flat cups, late spring, best in well-drained alkaline soil in full sun, 30cm (1ft); *N. poeticus* var. *recurvus* (Pheasant's Eye Narcissus), strap-shaped, channelled leaves, single flowers, flat, red-rimmed, yellow cup, usually frilled, shiny white recurved petals, late spring, 35cm (1¼ft); *N. pseudonarcissus* (Wild Daffodil, Lent Lily), strap-shaped, glaucous leaves, pendent flowers, yellow trumpets, narrow, twisted cream petals, early spring, requires moist site, good for naturalizing, 15-30cm (6in-1ft); *N. p.* ssp. *obvallaris* (syn. *N. obvallaris*) (Tenby Daffodil), gold-yellow flowers, very good for naturalizing, 30cm (1ft).

Split Corolla Narcissi Single flower per stem, cup split for at least one-third of its length, planting distance usually 16cm (6½in). Sometimes called Orchid-Flowered Narcissi. ❀ 'Cassata', pendulous flowers with yellow inner petals over white outer petals, in mid-spring, 40cm (1½ft); 'Chanterelle', white flowers yellow centres; 'Dolly Mollinger', orange.

Other Narcissi This group includes all narcissi not placed in any of the above groups; planting distance 5-8cm (2-3¼in) for small bulbs, 16cm (6½in) for larger bulbs. ❀ 'Jumblie', pendent flowers with yellow, recurved petals, pale yellow cups with orange rims, up to three flowers on each stem, many stems produced from one bulb, early spring, 17cm (6½in); 'Tête-à-Tête', gold-yellow slightly recurved petals, deeper yellow cups, mid-spring, a perpetual favourite, 15cm (6in).

Nectaroscordum — Alliaceae

Medium/large moderately hardy bulbous ornamentals. Large, linear, garlic-scented leaves, clusters of pendent bell-shaped flowers. A very effective and eye-catching plant, best in very light shade, a bulb that I wouldn't be without. Sow seed

right Few easy-to-grow bulbous plants have taller stems or more strikingly unusual flowers than *Nectaroscordum siculum*.

in a cold-frame in spring or autumn or divide clumps in summer. *N. siculum*, strap-shaped basal leaves, clusters of pale green-cream flowers, flushed with green-red, mid- to late spring, followed by erect seedpods, 1.2m/10cm (4ft/4in).

Nemesia — Scrophulariaceae

Small half-hardy to hardy annuals, herbaceous perennials and sub-shrubs, extensively grown as summer bedding plants although the perennials are also valuable for cutting; in cold areas the perennials are best grown in a greenhouse. Linear to lance-shaped, sometimes toothed, leaves, trumpet- shaped flowers. Sow seed in warmth between early and late spring, take semi-ripe cuttings in late summer or softwood cuttings in early spring. ❀ *N. caerulea* (syn. *N. foetens*), half-hardy perennial, pale green, entire or toothed leaves, lilac flowers with yellow centres, early summer to early autumn, 60cm/30cm (2ft/1ft); *N. c.* 'Joan Wilder', dark lavender-blue flowers; *N. denticulata*, hardier than most other species, pale green leaves, pink-purple flowers, 25m/30cm (80ft/1ft); *N. strumosa* 'Blue Gem', annual, lance-shaped, fairly hairy, toothed or entire leaves, bright blue flowers with white stamens, 18-30cm/10-16cm (7in-1ft/4-6½in); *N. s.* Carnival Series, cream, pink, orange, white, purple and yellow flowers with purple veining; *N. s.* 'KLM', blue-and-white bicoloured flowers with yellow throats; *N. s.* 'Mello Red and White', red-and-white bicoloured flowers.

Nemophila — Hydrophyllaceae

Small hardy annuals for rock gardens, borders and containers. Mid-green or grey-green, toothed, variously shaped leaves, saucer- or bell-shaped flowers, summer. Sow seed in flowering positions in spring or autumn. Self-seeds freely. ❀ *N. maculata*, pinnate, oblong or oval leaves, saucer-shaped flowers, white with a blue spot on each of the five petals, sometimes flushed or veined violet-blue, 15-30cm/15-30cm (6in-1ft/6in-1ft); *N. menziesii*, oval to oblong, pinnate, toothed, grey-green leaves, saucer-shaped, blue flowers with a white centre, marked with dark blue or purple spots, 20cm/30cm (8in/1ft); *N. m.* 'Penny Black', dark purple flowers edged with white.

Nepeta — Lamiaceae

Small/medium half-hardy annuals and hardy, often fragrant herbaceous perennials for borders and rock gardens. Ovate to lance-shaped, entire, toothed or scalloped, sometimes hairy, aromatic leaves, small, tubular, two-lipped, hooded flowers, white, blue or purple, usually in long spikes or racemes. Sow seeds in a cold-frame in late summer or early autumn, take softwood cuttings in late spring, or divide established plants in early spring. ❀ *N. cataria* (Catmint, Catnip), hairy, grey-green leaves, white flowers with violet markings, in summer, irresistibly attractive to cats which will roll in it, 1m/60cm (3ft/2ft); *N. c.* 'Citriodora', lemon-scented leaves, light blue flowers; *N. govaniana*, ovate to oblong-elliptic, pale green, pointed leaves, spikes of pale yellow flowers, mid-summer to early autumn, 90cm/60cm (3ft/2ft); *N. grandiflora* 'Dawn to Dusk', clump-forming, erect, matt green, scalloped, hairy leaves, pale pink-lipped flowers,

above It's a pity that more gardeners don't explore the genus *Nepeta* beyond the Common Catmint and have the delight of discovering the Himalayan species *Nepeta govaniana*.

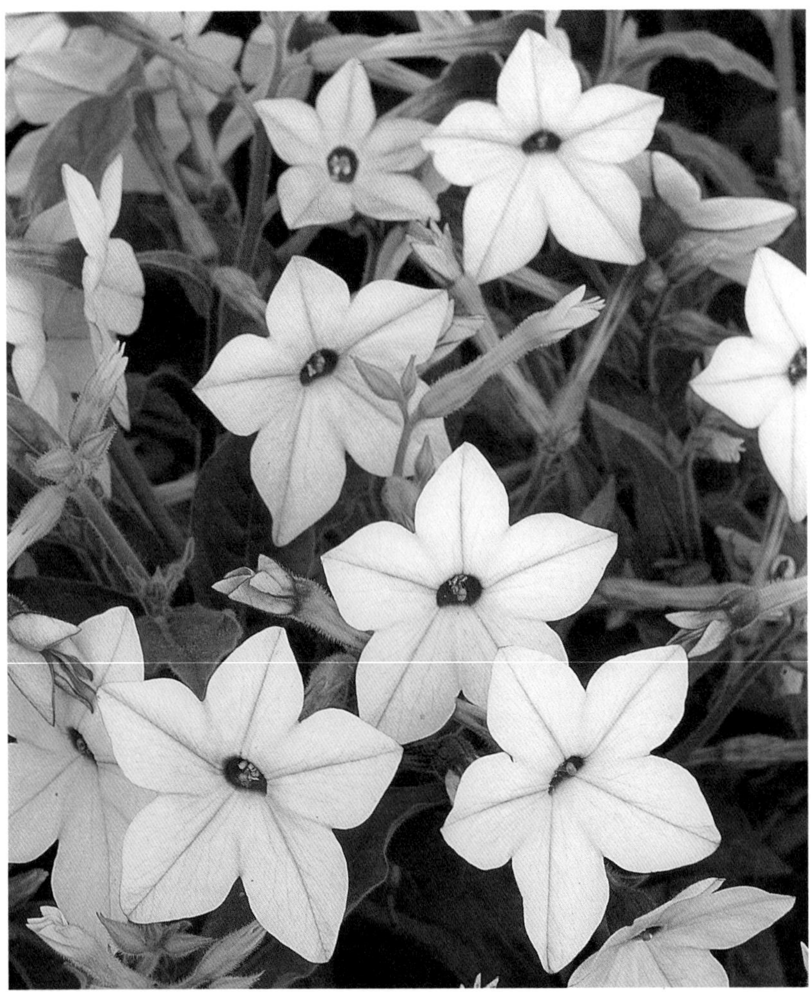

above *Nicotiana* Domino Series Salmon Pink. There's no denying that the newer forms of *Nicotiana* like the Domino series are easy to grow and very easy on the eye; but they do lack that delicious old style fragrance.

pink-brown tube-shaped calyces, mid-summer to late summer, 75cm/30cm (2½ft/1ft); *N. racemosa* (syn. *N. mussinii*) 'Snowflake', ovate, hairy, scalloped mid-green leaves, white flowers, summer, 30cm/45cm (1ft/1½ft); *N. sibirica*, (syn. *N. macrantha, Dracocephalum sibirica*), narrow, dark green leaves, long spikes of lavender-blue flowers, mid-summer, 90cm/45cm (3ft/1½ft); *N. subsessilis*, clump-forming, toothed, ovate, dark green leaves, clusters of bright blue flowers, mid-summer to early autumn, 90cm/30cm (3ft/1ft).

Nerine Amaryllidaceae

Small herbaceous/evergreen bulbous ornamentals. Barely hardy to moderately hardy and suitable for warm sunny places in borders and containers. Many gardeners fail with nerines, most commonly because the bulbs are planted far too deeply; just below the surface is ideal. Strap-shaped, mid-green leaves, wavy-margined, usually trumpet-shaped, lily-like flowers, autumn. Sow seed in warmth when ripe or divide established clumps after flowering. *N. bowdenii*, moderately hardy, umbels of slightly scented, funnel-shaped pink flowers, 45cm/8cm (1½ft/3¼in); *N. b.* 'Pink Triumph', deep pink flowers.

Nicotiana *Tobacco Plant* Solanaceae

Small/large annuals, biennials and perennials. Tender to fairly hardy. Most are grown as half-hardy annuals and now that tobacco growing has fallen from favour, they are much better known as ornamentals for borders and containers. Leaves usually oval, large, mid-green, tubular, five-petalled flowers, some very fragrant (but choose carefully: the popular Domino series is scentless), summer. Sow seed in warmth in mid-spring. ❀ *N. alata* (Flowering Tobacco), sticky, rather unappealing large leaves, fragrant white elongated funnel-shaped flowers, 1m/40cm (3ft/1½ft); Domino Series, available in the following mixed colours or separately, red, pink, white, crimson, with white eyes, salmon-pink or white with rose-pink edges, 30-35cm/30cm (1-1¼ft/1ft); *N. a.* 'Havana Apple Blossom' F1, flowers rose-pink inside, pale pink outside, 35cm (1¼ft); *N. a.* 'Havana Lime Rose' F1, flowers yellow-green outside, rose-pink inside, 35cm (1¼ft); *N. a.* 'Lime Green', yellow-green flowers, 1m (3ft); *N. langsdorfii*, annual, sticky leaves and stems, ovate leaves in basal rosette, pendent clusters of apple-green flowers, 1.5m/35cm (5ft/1¼ft).

Nierembergia *Cup Flower* Solanaceae

Annuals, herbaceous perennials and shrubs. Tender to moderately hardy. Those described here are hardy herbaceous perennials. Spoon-shaped leaves, tubular-, cup-shaped or bell-shaped flowers, summer. Sow seed in warmth in autumn or spring, take stem cuttings or divide established plants in summer. ❀ *N. caerulea* (syn. *N. hippomanica*), 'Mont Blanc', pointed, mid-green leaves, cup-shaped white flowers, summer, 20cm/20cm (8in/8in); *N. c.* 'Purple Robe', violet-blue flowers.

Nigella Ranunculaceae

Small hardy annuals. Feathery, pinnate leaves. Blue, pink or white, sometimes yellow flowers, singly or in pairs, with five petal-like sepals, two-lipped petals, sometimes surrounded by ruff of thread-like bracts, in summer, followed by decorative inflated seedpods which are valuable dried for indoor arrangements. Self-seeds fairly freely but never invasive. Sow seed in flowering positions in mid-spring or autumn. *N. damascena* (Love-in-a-Mist), 'Dwarf Moody Blue', oval, finely divided bright green leaves, saucer-shaped flowers, violet at first, later sky-blue, surrounded by fine bracts, summer, 20cm/15cm (8in/6in). *N. d.* 'Miss Jekyll', sky-blue flowers, 45cm (1½ft); *N. d.* 'Persian Jewels', sky blue, violet-blue, white, deep pink or rose-pink flowers 40cm/23cm (1½ft/9in).

Nuphar Nymphaeaceae

Large deciduous water plants. Tender to very hardy. Large leathery leaves, single yellow globular flowers, summer, followed by ovoid to flask-like fruit. Divide established plants in spring. Invasive and certainly not a plant for small garden pools, but fine if you have a lake. ❀ *N. lutea* (Yellow Water Lily, Brandy Bottle), very hardy, thick, oval to rounded, deep green floating leaves, 40cm (1½ft) long, pale green submerged leaves, waxy, yellow, evil-smelling flowers held above water surface, 6cm (2¼in) in diameter, 2m (6½ft).

Nymphaea *Water Lily* Nymphaeaceae

Small/large deciduous tender to very hardy water plants and the indispensable plants for any garden pool. Variable in size and flower colour and variety choice is critical; a vigorous variety in a small pool will create havoc. Some smaller species and varieties are suitable for growing in large containers such as barrel-pools. Rounded or oval, mid-green floating leaves, sometimes variegated, sometimes with wavy margins. Waxy, single or double star- or cup-shaped white, pink, red or yellow flowers (the ever-appealing blue flowers are only on tender tropical species), sometimes fragrant, appear a few at a time throughout the summer. Thrive in still water, in special aquatic compost or loam-based soil, and in sun; depth of planting depends on size (see below). Divide established plants in late spring. Those species and varieties described below are hardy unless specified otherwise.

Large water lilies: for water depth 30cm-1m (1ft/3ft); surface spread up to 1.5m (5ft). ❀ *N.* 'Colonel A J Welch', mid-green, slightly spotted leaves, semi-double, star-shaped yellow flowers with yellow stamens; *N.* 'Gladstoneana', large, rounded leaves with wavy margins, bronze at first, later dark green, fragrant, double, white, star-shaped flowers; *N. alba* (White Water Lily), dark green leaves, usually red beneath, double cup-shaped, white, slightly fragrant flowers with yellow stamens.

Medium water lilies: for water depth 20-60cm (8-2ft); surface spread up to 1m (3ft). ❀ *N.* 'Conqueror', leaves purple at first, later green, semi-double flowers, copper or deep rose; *N.* 'Moorei', dark green leaves, blotched purple, semi-double, star-shaped pale yellow flowers with yellow stamens; *N.* 'Escarboucle', rounded leaves red-green first, later green, fragrant, semi-double crimson flowers, cup-shaped at first, later star-shaped, red stamens tipped yellow, finest red water lily ever raised; *N.* 'Gonnère', mid-green leaves, double, cup-shaped white flowers with gold-yellow stamens, pale green sepals; *N.* 'Madame Wilfon Gonnère', rounded mid-green leaves with overlapping lobes, double, cup-shaped pink flowers, deep rose-pin at centre, with gold stamens; *N.* 'Marliacea Carnea', leaves purple-green at first, later dark green, flowers, vanilla scented, pale pink at first, darker pink later, yellow stamens; *N.* 'Marliacea Chromatella', leaves dark spotted brown, semi-double, cup-shaped yellow flowers with gold stamens; N. odorata, leaves purple at first, later pale green, fragrant, single, white star- shaped with gold stamens. *N.*

left *Nigella damascena* 'Miss Jekyll'. The good Gertrude Jekyll gave her name to several plants but I find it hard to imagine she could have been more happy than with this fine form of a cottage garden favourite.

above *Nymphaea* 'Escarboucle'. Red water lilies just don't come any better than this fantastic variety raised in 1909 by the great French water lily breeder and innovator Joseph Latour-Marliac.

odorata, leaves purple first, later pale green, fragrant, single, white star-shaped with gold stamens.

Small water lilies: for water depth 15-45cm (6-1½ft); Surface spread up to 60cm (2ft). ❀ *N.* 'James Brydon', rounded, dark green to purple-green leaves, flecked red, semi-double to double, cup-shaped crimson flowers, red stamens with gold tips; *N. odorata* var. *minor*, smaller than *N. odorata*, soft green leaves and smaller white flowers; *N.* 'Sioux', green-bronze leaves mottled brown, rich brown beneath, semi-double, star-shaped flowers, yellow at first, then orange, later rich red, yellow stamens.

Very small water lilies: for water depth 10-30cm (4in-1ft); Surface spread up to 30cm (1ft). ❀ *N.* 'Pygmaea Helvola' (syn. *N.* x *helvola*), oval to heart-shaped, olive-green leaves, single, star-shaped, yellow flowers with orange stamens; *N.* 'Ellisiana', oval, mid-green leaves, single, star-shaped flowers pale red at first, darker later, yellow stamens; *N.* 'Laydekeri Liliaceae', glossy green leaves sparsely flecked brown, single flowers, soft pink at first, later deep rose-pink.

Nymphoïdes

Floating Heart Menyanthaceae

Medium deciduous water plants. Very hardy. Floating, circular to heart-shaped, mid-green leaves, similar in appearance to those of water lilies, single yellow flowers, summer. Divide established plants in spring. Invasive and not for small pools. ❀ *N. peltata* (Yellow Floating Heart, Water Fringe), ovate to rounded, mottled bright green leaves, funnel-shaped, bright gold-yellow flowers, summer, 60cm/60cm (2ft/2ft); *N. p.* 'Bennettii' (syn. *Villarsia benettii*), leaves mottled brown, a very striking plant.

right *Nymphoïdes peltata*. This striking plant appears to be a close relative of the water lilies although its true affinities lie with the Bog Bean. It is probably a native species but certainly not a plant for small pools.

left *Ocimum basilicum purpurascens.* Varieties of basil are multiplying by the season but this old and distinctive form should be in every collection.

Ocimum *Basil* Lamiaceae

Small annuals, evergreen perennials and shrubs. Tender to barely hardy. A genus of increasing importance as wider ranges of varieties of the herb basil become available for raising from seed. All are pleasantly aromatic, some with very ornamental foliage; but it will be a curious cuisine that finds a culinary role for some of them. The basils are ideal for small containers dotted around the herb and kitchen garden. Oval to linear, usually green or red, aromatic leaves. Clusters of small tubular, usually white flowers. Sow seed in warmth in early spring or in growing positions in early summer.

❀ *O. basilicum* (Basil, Sweet Basil), annual or short-lived perennial, glossy bright green leaves, fresh, spicy flavour, clusters of small, two-lipped white flowers, late summer, 30-60cm/30cm (1-2ft/1ft); *O. b.* 'Cinnamon' (Cinnamon Basil), unique cinnamon-like aroma, rose-pink flowers, 45-74cm (1½-2½ft); 30-45cm (1-1½ft); *O. b.* var. *citriodorum* (Lemon Basil), narrow, ovate, lemon-scented leaves, white flowers, followed by lemon-flavoured seeds, 45-69cm/25-35cm (1½-4ft); *O. b.* 'Green Ruffles', ornamental, leaves heavily ruffled and fringed, 30cm (1ft); *O. b.* 'Horapha' (Thai Basil, Anise Basil), leaves flushed mulberry, pale pink flowers, red stems and bracts, anise fragrance, 40cm (1½ft); *O. b.* var. *minimum* (Bush Basil, Greek Basil), compact dwarf, small, ovate, pointed leaves, flavour weaker than other basils, clove-scented, 15-30cm/15-30cm (6in-1ft/6in-1ft); *O. b.* 'Napolitano' (Lettuce-Leaf Basil), large, crinkled leaves, particularly good flavour, 45cm/15-30cm (1½ft/ 6in-1ft); *O. b.* 'Purple Ruffles', mainly ornamental, aromatic, glossy leaves, dark purple, almost black, with curly, fringed edges, pink-purple flowers, 45-60cm/45-60cm (1½-2ft/1½-2ft); *O. b.* var. *purpurascens* (Red Basil, Purple Basil), ruffled, dark red-purple leaves, 45cm/15-30cm (1½ft/6in-1ft).

Oenothera
Evening Primrose Onagraceae

Small/large annuals, biennials and herbaceous perennials. Barely hardy to moderately hardy. Intriguing rather than beautiful plants with herbal/medicinal interest for the herb garden, wild flower garden and in borders. Light to mid-green, simple, lance-shaped or pinnate, entire or toothed leaves, sometimes in basal rosettes, white, yellow or pink, usually fragrant, saucer- or cup-shaped, individually short-lived flowers with five heart-shaped petals, some opening at sunset, early summer to early autumn. Sow seed in a cold-frame in early spring, or in flowering positions in autumn or late spring, take softwood cuttings in early summer or divide established plants in early spring or autumn. ❀ *O. biennis*, annual or biennial, but usually raised as a biennial, basal rosettes of lance-shaped to oblong, glossy, bright green leaves, spikes of fragrant flowers, pale yellow at first, later dark gold-yellow, opening at dusk, summer to autumn, 1-1.5m/60cm (3-5ft/2ft); *O. fruticosa* 'Fyrverkeri' (syn. *O. fruticosa* 'Fireworks'), biennial or perennial, glossy, mid-green, lance-shaped to ovate toothed leaves, flushed purple-brown, on red-tinged stems, red buds open to cup-shaped, deep yellow flowers, late spring to late summer, 30-90cm/30cm (1-3ft); *O. macrocarpa* (syn. *O. missouriensis*), moderately hardy, pale to mid-green, lance-shaped to ovate, toothed, hairy leaves with white mid-ribs, sometimes on red-flushed stems, lemon-yellow, cup-shaped, fragrant flowers, late spring to early autumn, followed by broad-winged fruit, 15cm/50cm (6in/1¾ft); *O. speciosa* 'Pink Petticoats', moderately hardy short-lived perennial, mid-green elliptic leaves, very fragrant, saucer-shaped flowers, pale pink with paler veins and slightly frilled petals, 30cm/30cm (1ft/1ft).

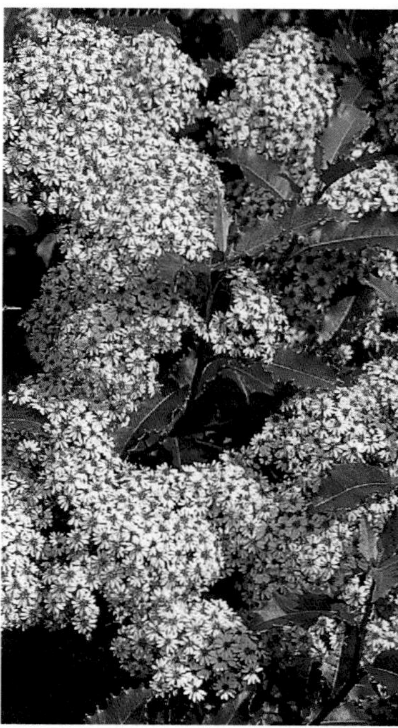

above *Olearia macrodonta.* One of New Zealand's finest exports to European coastal gardens but rarely as successful inland and so rarely seen there.

Olearia *Daisy Bush* Asteraceae

Small/large evergreen shrubs, small trees, and herbaceous perennials. Tender to moderately hardy and always a reminder for me of what I miss by not living on the coast; shrubby daisies are generally too tender for me. Very suitable for hedging, borders and, especially, coastal sites; resistant to wind and salt. Leathery, grey-green to sea-green leaves, downy white or silver beneath. Clusters of white, sometimes blue, cream or mauve daisy-like flowers, in summer. No routine pruning. Take semi-ripe or softwood cuttings between early and mid-summer. ❀ *O. macrodonta*, moderately hardy shrub or small tree, toothed, grey-green or sage green holly-like leaves, fragrant white flowers, summer, 6m/5m (20ft/16ft); *O. phlogopappa* (syn. *O. gunniana*), barely hardy erect shrub, glossy oval, toothed mid-green leaves, grey-white beneath, with wavy margins, abundant clusters of white flowers, mid- to late summer, 2m/2m (6½ft/6½ft); *O. p.* 'Comber's Pink', pink flowers; *O. solandri*, barely hardy shrub or small tree, heather-like dark green leaves, downy beneath, sticky, hairy yellow shoots, fragrant pale yellow flowers, summer to autumn, 2m/2m (6½ft/6½ft).

below *Onopordum acanthium*. This truly is a giant among thistles but it's curious to discover that so much stem and so much leaf is needed for such small flower heads.

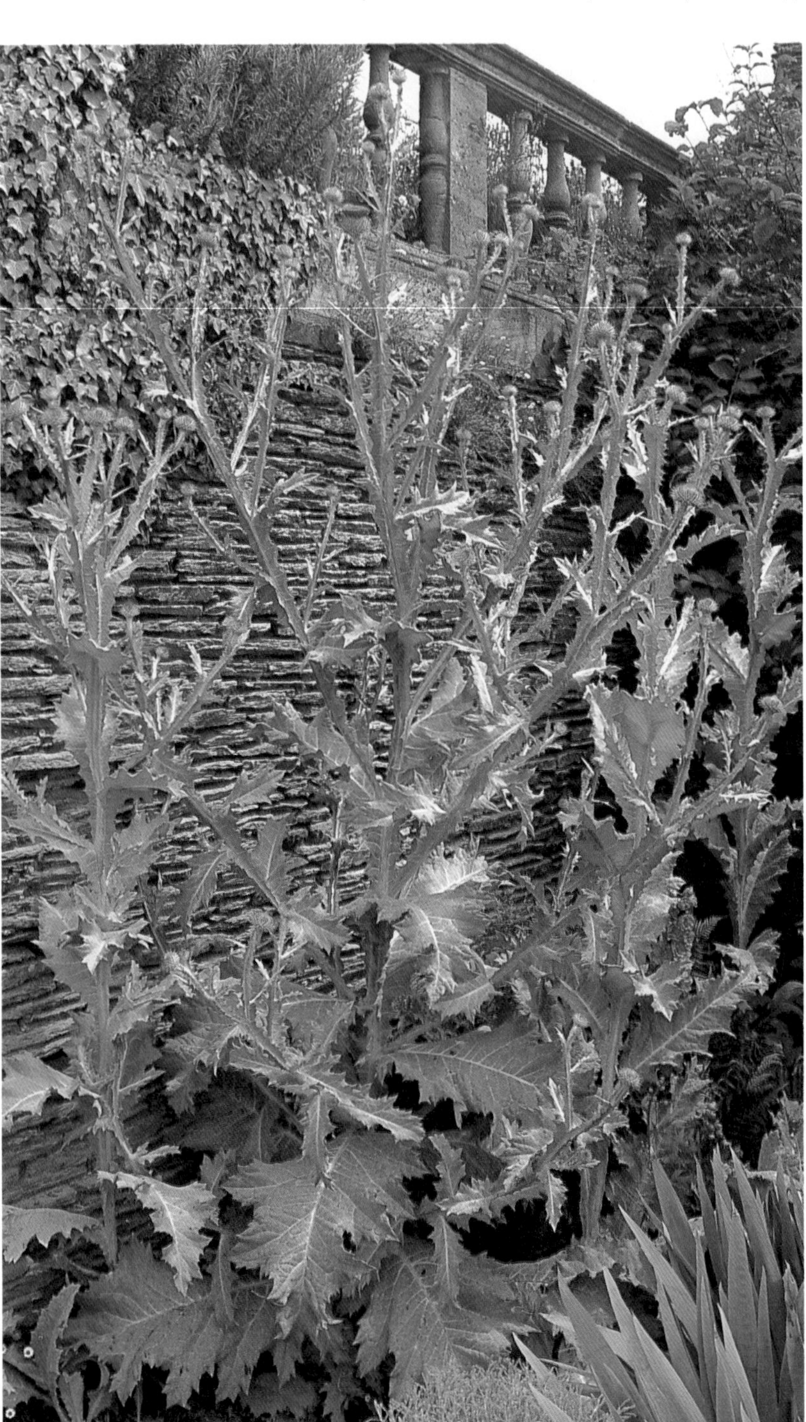

Omphalodes *Navelwort* Boraginaceae

Small hardy annuals, biennials and perennials, sometimes evergreen/semi-evergreen. I have, I hope, been responsible for this being in a great many gardens, where it makes lovely ground cover, especially in wooded places or large rock gardens. Simple leaves, blue or white flowers, singly or in clusters, resemble forget-me-nots. Sow seed in a cold-frame in spring or in flowering positions, take basal cuttings in early summer or divide established plants in spring. ❀ *O. cappadocica*, evergreen, bright green, slightly crinkled leaves, clusters of electric-blue flowers with white eyes, early spring, the best form by far, 25cm/40cm (10in/1½ft); *O. c.* 'Cherry Ingram', compact, larger, deep gentian-blue flowers, 26cm (10½in); *O. c.* 'Starry Eyes', larger flowers, pale lilac with white stripe of each petal, sometimes dark blue star at centre; *O. verna* (Blue-Eyed Mary), semi-evergreen spreading perennial, pointed, oval, dark green basal leaves, clusters of bright blue flowers, early to late spring, 20cm/30cm (8in/1ft) or more; *O. v.* 'Alba', pure white starry flowers, spring, 20cm (8in).

Onoclea Aspidiaceae

Small/medium deciduous fern. Moderately hardy. Moisture-loving and a good plant for a water garden, mid-green, pinnate sterile fronds, bipinnate fertile fronds, late summer. Divide established plants in spring. ❀ *O. sensiblis* (Sensitive Fern), triangular fronds pink-bronze at first, later green, sterile fronds die back after first frosts of autumn, fertile ones persist longer, turning brown, 60cm (2ft)/indefinite.

Onopordum Asteraceae

Large hardy biennials. Simple to pinnate, silver-grey or silver-green, spiny-toothed leaves with soft hairs, characteristic thistle flowers, large, round, singly or in clusters. Among the most spectacular thistles and, in reality, among the most spectacular of all herbaceous perennials – but for big borders only. Sow seed in a cold-frame or in flowering positions in spring or autumn. ❀ *O. acanthium* (Scotch Thistle, Cotton Thistle), rosettes of large, silver-grey, downy lobed leaves, pale pink-purple or white inflorescences, singly or in clusters, mid-summer to autumn, 3m/1m (10ft/3ft).

Ophiopogon *Lily Turf* Convallariaceae

Small evergreen perennials. Barely hardy to moderately hardy. Curious plants, often erroneously thought to be grasses, hence the common name. Linear leaves, clusters of tiny bell-shaped white or purple flowers, summer, followed by round glossy, black or blue fruit. Sow seed in a cold-frame when ripe, or divide established plants in spring. ❀ *O. jaburan*, barely hardy, dark green, strap-shaped, leathery leaves, bell-shaped white flowers, sometimes flushed purple, followed by blue-black fruit, 20-30cm/30cm (8in-1ft/1ft); *O. planiscapus*, clump-forming, strap-shaped, dark green leaves, purple-white flowers, in summer, followed by dark blue-black fruit, 20cm/30cm (8in/1ft); *O. p.* 'Nigrescens' (syn. *O.* 'Black Dragon'), the closest that any plant comes to having black leaves.

Origanum
Oregano, Marjoram Lamiaceae

Small herbaceous perennials and deciduous/evergreen sub-shrubs, including important culinary herbs which are not only useful but very pretty too. Barely hardy to moderately hardy. Suitable not only for herb gardens but also rock gardens, herbaceous borders, and containers. Small, simple, aromatic leaves, funnel-shaped or tubular two-lipped flowers, mid-summer to autumn. Sow seed in warmth in spring or in a cold-frame in autumn, take basal cuttings in late spring or divide established plants in spring. Those species and varieties described below are moderately hardy unless otherwise specified. ❀ *O. amanum*, evergreen sub-shrub, ovate, bright green leaves, funnel-shaped pink flowers, with small, spreading lobes, set in green bracts that later turn purple-pink, summer to autumn, 10-20cm/30cm (4-8in/1ft); *O.* 'Barbara Tingey', mound-forming, semi-evergreen, rounded, blue-green, hairy leaves, purple beneath, pendent, tubular, pink hop-like flowers, bracts green at first, later deep pink, 10cm/20cm (4in/8in); *O. laevigatum*, clump-forming perennial, rosettes of non-aromatic, ovate to elliptic, blue-green leaves on red, wiry stems, clusters of small, two-lipped light purple flowers in purple bracts, late spring to autumn, 50-60cm/45cm (20-2ft/1½ft); *O. l.* 'Herrenhausen', immature leaves tinged purple, flowers larger, 45cm (1½ft); *O. l.* 'Hopleys', large deep pink flowers, large bracts in narrow whorls, 60cm (2ft); *O. majorana* (Sweet Marjoram), barely hardy evergreen sub-shrub or perennial herb, sometimes grown as an annual, grey-green, softly hairy elliptic to ovate leaves, tubular white or pink flowers, grey-green bracts, early to mid-summer, 80cm/45cm (2½ft/1½ft); *O.* 'Rosenkuppel', purple-tinged green, oval leaves, clusters of maroon buds opening to tiny, wine-red flowers, mid- to late summer, 60cm/30cm (2ft/1ft); *O. rotundifolium*, woody perennial or deciduous sub-shrub, smooth, blue-green leaves, rosettes of tubular, pale pink flowers, apple-green bracts, late summer to autumn, 10-30cm/30cm (4-1ft/1ft); *O. vulgare* (Oregano, Common Marjoram), spreading perennial, the culinary herb oregano or wild marjoram, rounded to ovate, highly aromatic, dark green leaves, clusters of tubular deep to pale pink or white flowers, purple-tinged bracts, can be invasive, 30-90cm/30-90cm (1-3ft/1-3ft); *O. v.* 'Aureum', bright yellow-green leaves, lavender-pink flowers, less invasive than species and extremely pretty in spring, 30cm/30m (1ft/100ft); *O. v.* 'Gold Tip' (syn. *O. v.* 'Variegatum'), more spreading habit than species, green leaves with yellow flush at tip, 40cm (1 1/2ft).

above *Origanum vulgare* 'Aureum'. Much the prettiest form of this familiar and important culinary herb.

Ornithogalum Hyacinthaceae

Small/large bulbous ornamentals. Moderately hardy but plants to choose and place with care as some (although not the form I recommend) can be very invasive. Narrow, strap-shaped leaves, white or white-green, usually star-shaped flowers, sometimes on tall conical spikes, spring and summer. Sow seed in warmth when ripe or divide clumps in late summer. ❀ *O. nutans*, moderately hardy, semi-erect, bright green strap-shaped basal leaves, semi-pendent, one-sided racemes of white flowers with conspicuous green mid-rib, mid- to late spring, 20-60cm/5cm (8-2ft/2in).

above *Orontium aquaticum*. Some people find it hard to understand why I consider this North American member of the arum family one of my favourite water plants; but just look at those delightful little 'candles'.

Orontium
Golden Club Araceae

Small, hardy deciduous water marginal; probably my favourite water plant for its curious flower spikes. Submerged, aerial or floating leaves, club-like spadices. In summer, sow seed when ripe in a cold-frame or divide established plants. ❀ *O. aquaticum*, oblong to oval, blue-green submerged, floating or aerial leaves, pencil-like spikes of tiny flowers, chrome-yellow at the tip, white towards the base, late spring to mid-summer, 30-40cm/60-75cm (1-1½ft/2-2½ft).

Osmanthus
Oleaceae

Medium/large evergreen shrubs and small trees. Moderately hardy to hardy and good, reliable plants for woodland gardens and shrub borders, some species for hedging and topiary. Lance-shaped to oval leaves, clusters of small tubular white flowers, sometimes yellow or orange, usually fragrant, often followed by oval, blue-black fruit. No routine pruning. Sow seed in a cold-frame when ripe or in spring, take semi-ripe cuttings in summer or layer. ❀ *O.* x *burkwoodii* (syn. x *Osmarea burkwoodii*), hardy, compact, glossy, dark green, oval, leathery, slightly toothed leaves, abundant clusters of fragrant white flowers, spring, 3m/3m (10ft/10ft); *O. delavayi*, moderately hardy, small shrub, finely toothed, glossy, leathery, dark green leaves, clusters of fragrant, white, jasmine-like flowers, mid- to late spring, 2-6m/4m (6½-20ft/13ft); *O. heterophyllus*, large shrub or small tree, glossy, dark green, finely or coarsely spiny-toothed (sometimes spineless on older plants), holly-like leaves, clusters of fragrant, tubular white flowers, late summer to autumn, followed by oval, blue-black fruit, 5m/5m (16ft/16ft); *O. h.* 'Goshiki', medium shrub, leaves bronze tinged when young, later green mottled with cream-yellow; *O. h.* Variegatus', medium shrub, leaves edged with cream.

Osmunda
Osmundaceae

Medium/large deciduous fern. Moderately hardy and the largest native fern; wonderful in gardens but must have the correct, moist conditions; they are water-side plants. Lance-shaped, triangular or ovate pinnate, green, sterile outer fronds, yellow or gold-brown in autumn, light to mid-green fertile inner fronds. Divide established plants in early spring or autumn. ❀ *O. regalis* (Royal Fern), erect, lance-shaped bipinnate sterile fronds, brown at first, later green, yellow in autumn, partially fertile, rust-brown fronds with tasselled tips in summer, 2m/4m (61/2ft/13ft); *O. r.* 'Purpurascens', fronds red-purple in spring, a lovely form.

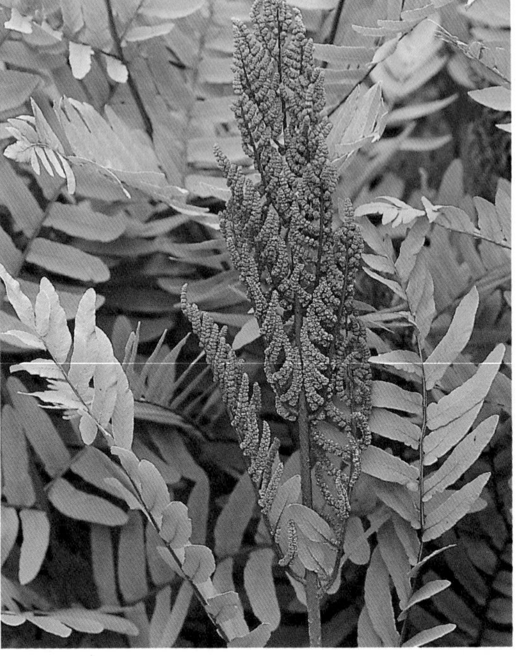

right *Osmunda regalis* 'Purpurascens'. There is no finer form than this of a plant that is unarguably our most imposing native European fern.

Osteospermum
Asteraceae

Small/medium annuals, perennials and evergreen sub-shrubs. Fairly hardy to moderately hardy. Linear to more or less ovate, daisy-like flowers, pink, yellow or white, white flowers sometimes flushed purple, usually with contrasting centres, often remaining closed in dull weather. Among the most striking of summer daisies but they must have full sun. Sow seed in warmth in late winter, or take semi-ripe cuttings in late summer. With the exception of *O. jucundum*, the species and varieties described below are all sub-shrubs. ❀ *O.* 'Buttermilk', fairly hardy, inversely lance-shaped, slightly toothed, mid-green leaves, white flowers flushed primrose-yellow, petals bronze-yellow beneath, dark blue-mauve centres, late spring to autumn, 60cm/60cm (2ft/2ft); *O.* 'Cannington Roy', fairly hardy, prostrate, spreading sub-shrub, more or less ovate, slightly toothed, mid-green leaves, white flowers, petals purple-tipped at first, later mauve-pink, late spring to autumn, 15cm/60cm (6in/2ft); *O.* 'Nairobi Purple' (syn. *O.* 'Tresco Purple'), barely hardy, bright green, more or less ovate to spoon-shaped, slightly toothed leaves, dark purple flowers, flushed white beneath, black centres, late spring to summer, 15cm/90cm (6in/3ft); *O.* 'Pink Whirls', pink flowers with quite remarkable spoon-shaped petals, rather like propeller blades, mauve beneath, mauve centres, 60cm/60cm (2ft/2ft); *O.* 'Silver Sparkler', leaves variegated cream and green, white flowers, purple centres, 60cm/60cm (2ft/2ft); *O.* 'Whirligig' (syn. *O.* 'Tauranga'), inversely lance-shaped, grey-green, toothed leaves, white flowers with spoon-shaped, propeller-like petals, blue-grey beneath, blue-grey centres, 60cm/60cm (2ft/2ft).

Oxalis — Oxalidaceae

Small bulbous, rhizomatous or tuberous ornamentals. Moderately hardy. Palmate, clover-like leaves, five-petalled, bowl-, cup- or funnel-shaped flowers, singly or in clusters, usually closing in dull weather. Some are wonderful woodland or rock garden species; some (not included here) are devilish weeds. Sow seed in warmth in late winter or early spring, or divide established plants in spring. ❀ *O. adenophylla*, blue-grey leaves, heart-shaped leaflets, pink flowers with darker pink centres, purple veining, early summer, one of the best plants for a shaded rock garden, 10cm/15cm (4in/6in); *O. purpurea* 'Ken Aslet', barely hardy, dark green leaves with white, silky hairs, bright, deep yellow flowers, autumn to winter, 10cm/15cm (4in/6in); *O. tetraphylla* (syn. *O. deppei*), barely hardy, clump-forming, mid-green leaves, strap-shaped to inversely triangular, sometimes notched, leaflets, funnel-shaped, red-purple flowers with green throats, early to late summer, 15cm/15cm (6in/6in); *O. t.* 'Iron Cross', V-shaped, purple bands across each of the four leaflets, forming a cross shape.

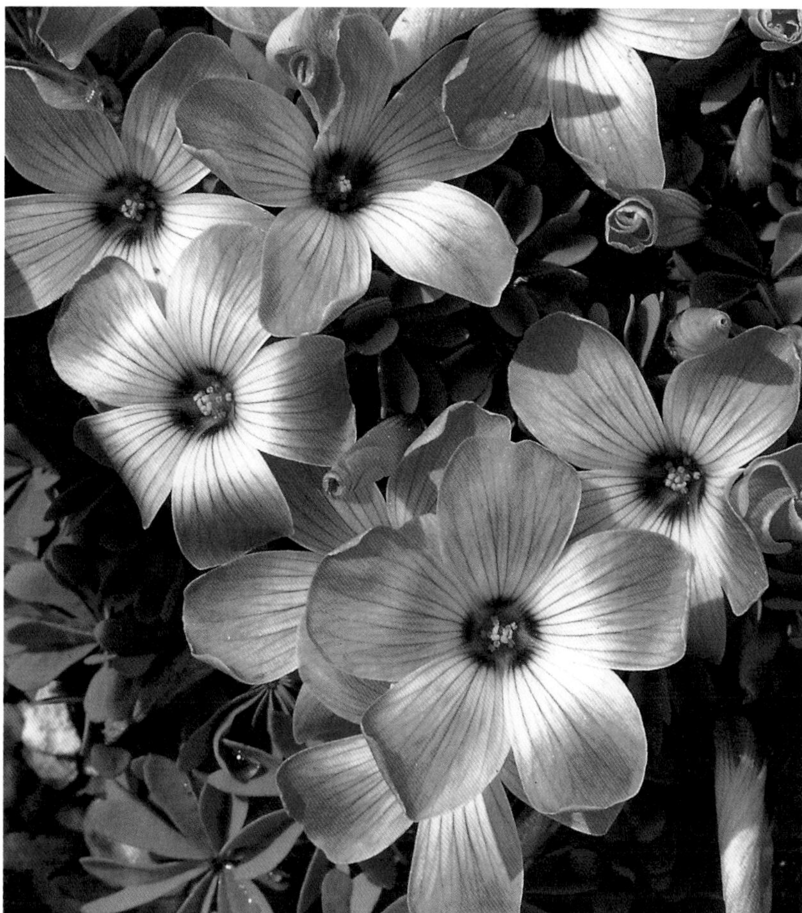

above *Oxalis adenophylla.* I have a soft spot for this little Andean plant as it was the first Alpine that I ever grew. And I have never stopped since, as much as anything because it is unusually tolerant of light shade.

Ozothamnus — Asteraceae

Small perennials and medium/large evergreen shrubs. Fairly hardy to moderately hardy and among my favourite Antipodean plants for a warm, sunny place. They look for all the world like some form of heather rather than daisies. Small, heath-like leaves, white flowers. No routine pruning. Sow seed when ripe or take semi-ripe cuttings in summer. ❀ *O. ledifolius* (syn. *Helichrysum ledifolius*) (Kerosene Bush), compact shrub, aromatic, oblong-linear dark green leaves with recurved margins, downy beneath, clusters of bright red buds open to white flowers in early summer, 1m/1m (3ft/3ft); *O. rosmarinifolius* (syn. *Helichrysum rosmarinifolius*), compact, erect shrub, bright green, needle-like leaves on white, woolly branchlets, clusters of purple-pink buds opening to a dense mass of white flowers, early to mid-summer, 2-3m/1.5m (6½-10ft/5ft); *O. r.* 'Silver Jubilee', the best form, silver-grey leaves.

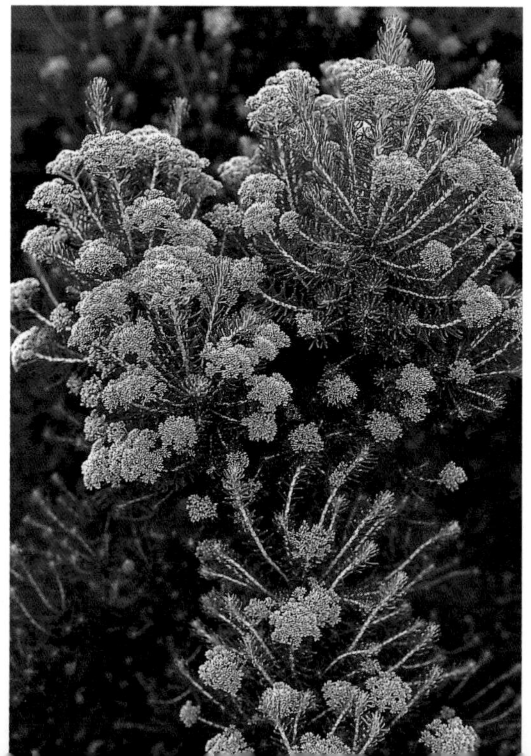

left *Ozothamnus rosmarinifolius* 'Silver Jubilee'. A well-established plant of this beautiful species, in a good year, can be so covered with flowers as for its foliage almost to vanish from view.

Pachysandra Buxaceae

Small semi-evergreen/evergreen hardy perennials and sub-shrubs for woodland gardens, borders, and often recommended as ground cover although I find them over-rated; they just don't grow quickly enough to do the job properly. Intolerant of alkaline soils. Ovate to more or less oval, grey-green to dark green, entire or toothed leaves, clusters of small, petal-less male and female flowers on the same plant, spring or early summer. Divide established plants in early or late spring. ❀ *P. terminalis*, carpeting, evergreen perennial, rosettes of rich green, glossy leaves, spikes of fragrant, insignificant white flowers, both male and female flowers together, male flowers with conspicuous stamens, spring, 20cm (8in)/indefinite; *P. t.* 'Variegata', leaves edged with cream, even slower growing, 25cm/60cm (10in/2ft).

Paeonia *Paeony* Paeoniaceae

Medium herbaceous perennials, deciduous shrubs and sub-shrubs ('tree paeonies'). Barely hardy to moderately hardy. Paeonies are among the classic garden flowers but never easy to position as their flowering season is very short and their foliage not particularly attractive. Dotted in groups of three among other plants in a mixed border is as effective as anything although 'tree paeonies' should be placed towards the back. Flowers are good for cutting. Compound or lobed, usually mid- to dark green leaves, single, semi-double or double cup-, saucer- or bowl shaped flowers, sometimes fragrant, late spring to summer. Thrive in fertile, moist, well-drained soil enriched with humus, in full sun or partial shade. Protect tree paeonies from cold, dry winds. Sow seed in autumn or early winter (species), divide established perennials in spring, just as growth is beginning, take root cuttings in winter or semi-ripe cuttings (tree paeonies) in summer.

below *Paeonia delavayi ludlowii*. Although this lovely shrub never produces as many flowers as I hope for, it is certainly the easiest of the so-called 'tree paeonies' for most gardens.

❀ *P. cambessedessi*, barely hardy herbaceous perennial, glossy, dark green leaves of lance-shaped leaflets, purple-red veins, purple beneath, single, bowl-shaped, rose-pink flowers, yellow stamens with red filaments, mid- to late spring, 45-55cm/45-55cm (1½-1¾ft/1½-1¾ft); *P. delavayi*, moderately hardy deciduous shrub, deeply cut, dark green leaves, blue-green beneath, horizontal or pendent, cup-shaped, single dark red flowers, 2m/1.2m (6½ft/4ft); *P. d.* var. *ludlowii* (syn. *P. lutea* var. *ludlowii*), bright green leaves, bright yellow flowers, the easiest and most rewarding of the large species, very easy from seed, 2.5m/2.5m (8ft/8ft); *P. lactiflora* 'Bowl of Beauty', herbaceous perennial, mid-green leaves, large, semi-double, anemone-like carmine-red flowers, tinged pink, cream-white centres of narrow petal-like structures (petaloids), one of the most popular varieties but I can never understand why, 80-100cm (2½-3ft); *P. l.* 'Duchesse de Nemours', large, double, fragrant pure white flowers with ruffled, yellow inner petals, buds flushed green, 70-80cm/70-80cm (2¼-2½ft/2¼-2½ft); *P. l.* 'Félix Crousse', double fragrant, crimson-pink flowers, ruffled petals with silver margins, dark crimson centres, 70-75cm/70-75cm (2¼-2½ft/2¼-2½ft); *P. l.* 'Festiva Maxima', double, fragrant flowers with pure white outer petals, white inner petals with crimson blotch at base, 90-100cm/90-100cm (3-3ft/3-3ft); *P. l.* 'Président Poincaré', leaves red in autumn, large, fragrant, double crimson flowers, ruffled central petals, 90-100cm/90-100cm(3-3ft/3-3ft); *P. l.* 'Sarah Bernhardt', very large, fragrant, double pale pink flowers, petals ruffled at margins, the classic old variety, 90-100cm/90-100cm(3-3ft/3-3ft); *P. mlokosewitschii*, moderately hardy herbaceous perennial, soft blue-green leaves of broad, oval leaflets with red edges, single, bowl-shaped, lemon-yellow flowers, pale yellow stamens, 65-90cm/65-90cm (21/4-3ft); *P. officinalis* 'Rubra Plena', glossy, bright green divided leaves, double crimson flowers with ruffled, satin petals, 70-75cm/70-75cm (2¼-2½ft/2¼-2½ft); *P. suffruticosa* (Tree Paeony), moderately hardy deciduous shrub, 2.2m/2.2m (6¾ft/6¾ft); *P. s.* 'Godaishu', semi-double, white; *P. s.* 'Howki', semi-double, bright red; *P. s.* 'Lord Selbourne', semi-double, pale pink; *P. s.* 'Mrs William Kelway', double white.

Papaver *Poppy* Papaveraceae

Small/medium half-hardy and hardy annuals, biennials and herbaceous evergreen perennials. Poppies as a group are very versatile and although all have individually fragile, short-lived flowers, they can give bright splashes of colour for long periods in summer in mixed or herbaceous borders, some of the small species are good for rock gardens. Simple, toothed or pinnate leaves, cup-, bowl- or saucer-shaped flowers, usually four-petalled, followed by pepper-pot seedpods ringed with open pores. Sap or latex, exuded from stems, may cause skin irritation. Thrive in fertile, well-

left *Papaver alpinum.* The name shouldn't mislead you into imagining that this is only a rock garden plant. In reality, it is rather short-lived to be reliable there and is much better grown in small groups elsewhere in the garden as an annual.

drained soil in full sun; *P. rupifragum* is best in partial shade. Sow seed in early autumn or early spring in a cold-frame. Divide established plants of *P. orientale* or take root cuttings when flowering has finished.

❀ *P. alpinum* (Alpine Poppy), hardy short-lived evergreen perennials often grown as annuals, finely divided green or grey-green leaves, single, cup- or saucer-shaped white, yellow, orange or salmon-pink flowers, late spring to mid-summer, self-seeds freely, 15-20cm/10cm (6-8in/4in); *P.* 'Fireball' (syn. *P.* 'Nanum Flore Pleno'), hardy herbaceous perennial, lance-shaped, mid-green, hairy-bristly leaves, single semi-double to double orange flowers, 30cm/30cm (1ft/1ft); *P. nudicaule* (Iceland Poppy), 'Champagne Bubbles', annual or short-lived evergreen perennial, deeply divided yellow or grey-green basal leaves, large flowers, 12cm (5in) in diameter, in pastel shades including apricot-yellow, pink, bronze-yellow and red, 45cm/15cm (1½ft/6in); *P. n.* Garden Gnome Group, dwarf, flowers in various colours, including white, bright orange, red, pink, salmon and yellow, summer, 30cm (1ft); *P. n.* 'Oregon Rainbows', single or semi-double flowers in all the usual poppy colours, including bicolours and picotees with darker or pale margins; *P. n.* 'Red Sails', orange-scarlet flowers, summer, 60-75cm (2-2½ft); *P. orientale* (Oriental Poppy), 'Allegro', clump-forming hardy herbaceous perennial, deeply divided bristly, oblong to lance-shaped, mid-green to deep green leaves, bright scarlet flowers, each petal with a bold black blotch at the base, early to mid-summer, 45-90cm/60-90cm (1½-3ft/2-3ft); *P. o.* 'Black and White', white flowers with a crimson-black blotch at the base of each petal; *P. o.* Goliath Group, rich, ruby-red flowers, 75-90cm (2½-3ft); *P. o.* Goliath Group 'Beauty of Livermere', large, crimson-scarlet flowers, 20cm (8in) in diameter, black basal blotch, 90-120cm/90cm (3-4ft/3ft); *P. o.* 'Mrs Perry', soft salmon-pink flowers, black basal blotch; *P. o.* 'Perry's White', white flowers with deep purple centres; *P. rhoeas* (Field Poppy), hairy annual, downy, light green, lobed leaves with narrow segments, red flowers, sometimes white or pale pink, sometimes with dark basal blotch, 90cm/30cm (3ft/1ft); *P. r.* 'Shirley Singles' (Shirley Poppies), single flowers in rose, salmon, pink, crimson, yellow and white, unmarked petals, 60cm/30cm (2ft/1ft); *P. r.* 'Shirley Doubles', double flowers in the above colours; *P. rupifragum*, clump-forming herbaceous perennial, grey-green deeply divided leaves, brilliant red, bowl-shaped flowers on branched stems, 45cm/20cm (1½ft/8in); *P. somniferum* (Opium Poppy), smooth, glaucous annual, single, cup-shaped white, mauve or purple flowers, each with a dark basal blotch, 1m/30cm (3ft/1ft); a range of double and semi-double forms is available from time to time, mostly in white or pink; most commonly seen are *P. s.* 'Hens and Chickens', very large seedpods with clusters of smaller seedpods; *P. s.* 'Paeony Flowered', large double flowers in the usual poppy colours and with large seedpods; *P. s.* 'White Cloud', very large double white.

above *Parthenocissus tricuspidata*. The various forms of Parthenocissus are confusing to identify. This close clinging species with the most vivid red autumn colours is the best known but despite its common name of Boston Ivy, it is an Oriental plant.

Parahebe — Scrophulariaceae

Small evergreen/semi-evergreen subshrubs. Moderately hardy. Mid- to dark green, sometimes blue-green, ovate, toothed leaves, clusters of small saucer- or cup-shaped flowers, summer to autumn. Excellent and under-utilized plants for warm sunny positions. Sow seed in a cold-frame when ripe or take softwood cuttings in early spring or mid-summer. ❀ *P.* x *bidwillii* 'Kea', moderately hardy, mat-forming, leathery, oval, green leaves, indented margins, white flowers with crimson veining, 10cm/15cm (4in/6in); *P. catarractae*, toothed, pointed, dark green leaves, light blue flowers with red-purple eye, summer and again in autumn, 30cm/30cm (1ft/1ft); *P. c.* 'Delight', lightly bronzed leaves, violet-blue flowers, purple veining, red-purple eye, 25cm (10in); *P. lyallii*, moderately hardy semi-evergreen, slightly toothed, dark green, leathery leaves, white flowers with red veins and centres, summer, 25cm/50cm (10in/1¾ft); *P. perfoliata*, fairly hardy, slightly leathery, ovate blue- or grey-green leaves, pendent clusters of blue flowers, late summer, 60-75cm/45cm (2ft/1½ft).

Parrotia

Persian Ironwood — Hamamelidaceae

Small hardy deciduous tree to grow as a specimen or in woodland plantings for its rich autumn colour and winter flowers. Peeling bark, rich green leaves, petal-less flowers with bright red stamens, mid-winter to early spring. Sow seed in a cold-frame in autumn, take semi-ripe cuttings in mid- or late summer, or layer in autumn. ❀ *P. persica*, glossy, more or less oval, rich green leaves, crimson and gold in autumn, flowers are clusters of crimson stamens, from late winter to early spring, on bare branches, 8m/10m (2ft/33ft).

Parthenocissus — Vitaceae

Large hardy deciduous self-clinging climbers for covering large walls and fences or (although this isn't seen very often) for growing into large trees. Palmate leaves, excellent, sometimes breathtaking, autumn colour, clusters of inconspicuous five-petalled green flowers, in late spring or summer, sometimes followed by black or blue-black, grape-like (but toxic) fruits. Some are twining, others cling by means of adhesive pads on leaf tendrils. Thrive in fertile, well-drained soil enriched with humus (and tolerant of alkalinity), in sun or partial shade and among the most attractive ways of covering a bare wall, although, like all self-clinging plants, will damage old crumbly bricks and mortar. Sow seed in a cold-frame in autumn, take semi-ripe cuttings in late summer or early autumn, hardwood cuttings in late autumn, or layer in autumn. ❀ *P. henryana* (syns. *Vitis henryana, Ampelopsis henryana*), moderately hardy, self-clinging (by adhesive suckers), large three- to four-lobed palmate, dark green toothed leaves, prominent silvery veins, sometimes flushed pink in the centre, bright red and silver in autumn, the most dramatic of all the species, 10m (33ft); *P. quinquefolia* (syn. *Vitis quinquefolia*) (Virginia Creeper), moderately hardy, self-clinging, dull mid-green palmate leaves with five oval, toothed leaflets, brilliant red in autumn, 15m (50ft); *P. tricuspidata* (Boston Ivy), moderately hardy, firmly self-clinging, bright green, deeply toothed, ovate leaves with three ovate leaflets, red to purple in autumn, 20m (60ft); *P. t.* 'Beverley Brook', leaves tinged purple in summer, brilliant red in autumn.

right *Parrotia persica*. Although almost always seen as a free-standing tree grown for autumn colour, I have seen this species trained rather effectively against a wall.

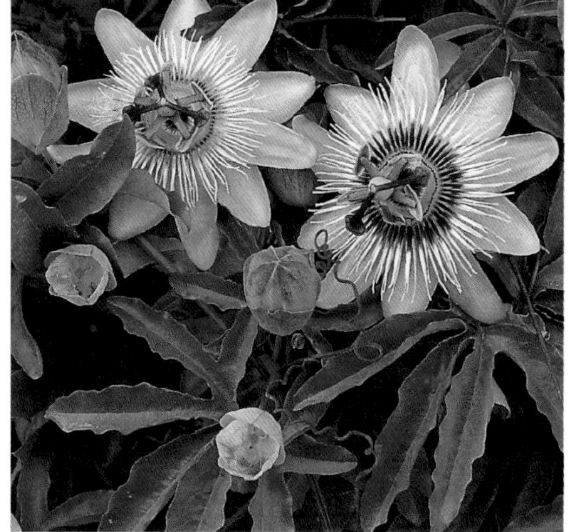

Passiflora

Passion Flower Passifloraceae

Mainly deciduous/evergreen climbers, some perennials, annuals, shrubs and trees. Tender to moderately hardy. The more hardy climbers are excellent for growing up trellis and walls although, sadly, only one is really reliable in our climate. Elliptic to rounded or ovate lobed leaves, fantastically exotic looking flowers with tubular bases, flat or recurved petals, sometimes cup-shaped, with central fleshy filaments, singly or in clusters. Flowers are followed by rounded, edible fleshy fruit. Thrives in moderately fertile, well-drained moist soil, in full sun or partial shade but requires protection from cold, drying winds. Container plants require loam-based compost. Sow seed in warmth in spring, take semi-ripe cuttings in summer, or layer. ❀ *P. caerulea* (Blue Passion Flower), fairly hardy evergreen, deep green, five- to seven-lobed leaves, slightly fragrant, white or pink-tinged flowers with purple, pink or white zoned filaments, followed by rounded fruit, white and woolly at first, later orange or yellow with darker stripes, 4m (13ft); *P. c.* 'Constance Elliot', fragrant white flowers, pale blue or white filaments, a lovely form, certainly no less hardy.

Pastinaca

Parsnip Apiaceae

Root vegetable, a biennial grown as an annual. Thrives in most soils in full sun or light shade. Sow seed in growing position, mid- to late spring for harvesting from autumn onwards; germination is slower and more erratic than that of any other vegetable. ❀ *P. sativa*, 'Avonresister', highly resistant to all forms of parsnip canker, the commonest disease; 'Exhibition Long'; 'Gladiator' F1; 'Hollow Crown'; 'Javelin' F1; 'Tender and True', traditional variety with very long roots and little core, much prized for exhibition; 'White Gem'.

Paulownia

Scrophulariaceae

Small/medium moderately hardy deciduous trees. Ovate or lobed, hairy to velvety leaves, mid- to yellow-green, erect clusters of bell- or trumpet-shaped flowers similar to foxgloves, produced in bud in autumn, open on bare branches in spring. A tree in full flower is a glorious sight but they are only reliable in milder localities. No routine pruning. Sow seed in warmth in spring. ❀ *P. tomentosa* (Foxglove Tree), silver-grey bark, ovate, hairy, bright green leaves, more densely hairy beneath, fragrant, pink-lilac flowers, dotted purple and yellow inside, in late spring, 12m/10m (40ft/33ft).

left *Passiflora caerulea* 'Constance Elliott'. Although the blue passion flower is the only really hardy species for our gardens, you can obtain some variation by also growing this quite lovely white flowered form of it.

above *Paulownia tomentosa*. This is a real head-turning tree when in full flower and although it only blooms reliably in warmer areas, that it should do so at all in our climate is something to be astonished at.

Pelargonium

Geraniaceae

Small/medium evergreen perennials, succulents, sub-shrubs and shrubs. Tender to moderately hardy. Overall the variety available for summer borders and containers has never been greater. Mainly palmate lobed leaves, sometimes aromatic. Clusters of funnel-, star-, trumpet-, or saucer-shaped petals; some, described as butterfly-shaped, have two large upper petals and three smaller lower petals. Perennial pelargoniums, grown as half-hardy annuals, are among the mainstays of summer colour in our gardens. The older varieties, perpetuated by cuttings, have given way in mass production to seed-raised F1 hybrids but the pendulum has begun to swing back a little in recent years with long-forgotten types becoming obtainable once more. They require fertile, ideally neutral to slightly alkaline, well-drained soil, preferably in full sun, although Regal varieties benefit from partial shade and some Zonal varieties are tolerant of some shade. Container plants do well in loamless or loam-based compost in a well-ventilated, light position out of direct sun. Sow seed in warmth in autumn or in late winter (species and zonal F1 varieties) or take softwood cuttings in late summer or late winter. Pelargoniums are subdivided in various ways but the scheme I've adopted here is probably the most generally accepted.

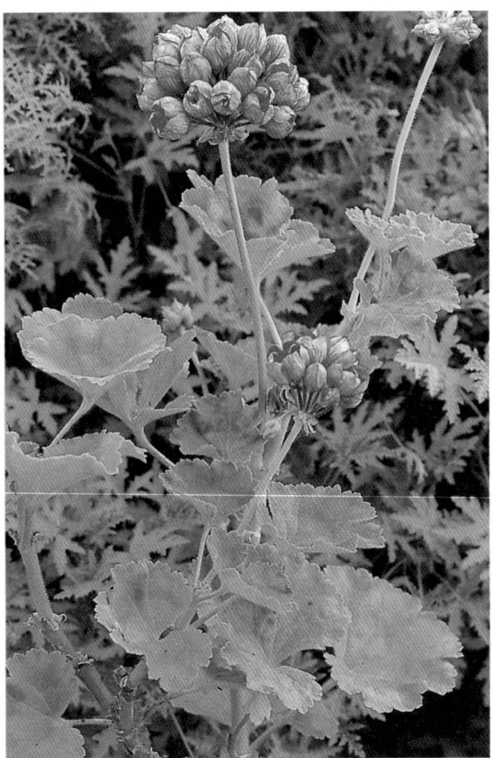

above *Pelargonium* 'Patricia Andrea'. Among the many very pretty forms of pelargonium, few flower types elicit as much comment as the tulip-flowered varieties.

Zonal singles Zonal pelargoniums are evergreen perennials with succulent stems, rounded plain leaves, or leaves marked with zones of dark bronze-green or maroon. They are raised either from seed or from cuttings. Single varieties usually have five-petalled flowers. Most are 20-30cm/20-25cm (8in-1ft/8-10in): ❀ 'Ashfield Serenade', lavender-pink; 'Edward Humphris', white; 'Paul Crampel', scarlet.

Zonal singles raised from seed Divided into four groups: Standard or Specimen types with few, large heads, most around 45cm/30cm (1½ft/1ft); Cascading types, semi-trailing, with stems arching outwards from the base, mostly 30cm/40cm (1ft/1½ft); Multibloom (Floribunda) types, with ten or more flowers in a compact, rounded head, about 35cm/25cm (1¼ft/10in); and Dwarf (Bedding) types, small varieties, about 20cm/15cm (8in/6in). ❀ Standards: Century Series, early flowering, white or shades of red or pink; 'Hollywood Star', pink; 'Orange Appeal', bright orange; Orbit Series, very early, fine zoning, large clusters, white or shades of orange, red, pink. Cascading types: Breakaway Series, a flat spreading habit that branches from the base, red or salmon-pink. Multibloom types: Sensation Series, very early flowering, tolerant of poor weather conditions, red, pink or orange shades, some with white eyes, some in mixtures, early. Dwarf types: Vista Series F2 , four single colours.

Zonal doubles with plain leaves Range between 30-90cm/25-30cm (1-3ft/10in-1ft). ❀ 'Ashfield Monarch', semi-double, bright red; 'Gustav Emich', bright red; Deacon Series, around 30 varieties in the full colour range; Highfield Series, sturdy, compact plants with large flower heads and a good colour range, mainly in pinks; the series also includes singles and semi-doubles; 'Pink Rosebud', extremely pretty, very tight double blooms, prone to weather damage; 'Patricia Andrea', salmon-pink, tulip-shaped flowers.

Zonal pelargoniums with fancy leaves Most are around 45cm/30cm (1½ft/1ft): ❀ 'Caroline Schmidt', leaves edged silver-white, bright red flowers; 'Dolly Varden', leaves variegated cream, red and green, scarlet flowers; 'Freak of Nature', green leaves with white central markings, white trailing stems up to 20cm (8in) long, red flowers; 'Happy Thought', rounded leaves with light yellow centres, lightly scalloped edges, star-like crimson flowers; 'Miss Burdett Coutts', green, white and pink leaves, red leaves; 'Mr Henry Cox', rounded, gold-yellow leaves marked red, green and purple, pink flowers with white eyes.

Stellar-flowered pelargoniums Single or double flowers, irregularly star-shaped, pointed leaves, sometimes with zonal markings, size varies from 13-45cm/15-30cm (5¼in-1½ft/6in-1ft): ❀ 'Arctic Star', white; 'Golden Ears', vermilion, pale green foliage with brown blotch; 'Grenadier', double crimson.

Cactus-flowered pelargoniums Single or double flowers similar to those of cactus dahlias, with petals twisted into quills. Size varies up to about 45cm/30cm (1½ft/1ft): ❀ 'Mrs Salter Bevis' double, pale pink; 'Star of Persia', double, magenta.

right *Pelargonium* 'Lilian Pottinger'. Forced to grow only one of the scented leaf pelargoniums, this deliciously fresh fragrant variety would be my choice.

Angel pelargoniums Rounded, sometimes scented, leaves, clusters of small pink, mauve, purple or white flowers resembling violas. Most are about 25-30cm/10-15cm (10in-1ft/4-6in): ❀ 'Catford Belle', compact, mid-green, lobed leaves, semi-double pink-mauve flowers with dark mauve blotches on upper petals; 'Spanish Angel', lilac lower petals, dark purple upper petals with picotee edge; 'Tip Top Duet', soft pale pink flowers with mauve veining and margins on lower petals, upper petals feathered with red-purple blazing, a very striking plant.

Unique pelargoniums Lobed or rounded mid-green leaves, sometimes aromatic when crushed, single, trumpet-shaped flowers are white, pink, red, orange or purple and similar to the Regal type (see below). Size varies up to about 45cm/60cm (1½ft/2ft): ❀ 'Crimson Unique', deep crimson with very dark markings; 'Golden Clorinda', bright pink, gold and green foliage; 'White Unique', white.

Dwarf pelargoniums These are small forms of most of the most other Pelargonium groups. Size up to 20-30cm/10-20cm (8in-1ft/4-8in): ❀ 'Bird Dancer', dark zoned leaves, single flowers, pale pink lower petals, salmon-pink upper petals, a dwarf Stellar variety; 'Emma Jane Read', double, deep mauve pink, dark green foliage; 'Rosita', double scarlet, dwarf rosebud type; 'Vancouver Centennial', bronze and gold leaves, star-shaped, bright red flowers.

Miniature varieties Smaller even than the dwarf varieties, most of these little plants are small Zonals. Size range around 13-20cm/10-15cm (5¼in-8in/4-6in). ❀ 'Bridal Veil', white, golden foliage with white zone; 'La France', semi-double, mauve, a miniature ivy-leaved type; 'Red Black Vesuvius', very dark green, almost black leaves, bright red single flowers; 'Snowflake', white.

Scented-leaved pelargoniums A very diverse group, all with some interesting fragrance in the foliage when crushed, all with small flowers and all too often thought of only as houseplants; they are excellent outdoors in containers in light shade in the summer: ❀ 'Attar of Roses', rose-scented leaves, clusters of mauve flowers, 50-60cm/25-30cm (1¾in-2ft/10in-1ft); 'Chocolate Peppermint', peppermint-scented, soft green leaves with dark brown central zone, soft mauve-pink flowers, 90cm/75cm (3ft/2½ft); 'Citriodorum', heart-shaped leaves with lime scent, clusters of star-shaped mauve-pink flowers, 60cm/45cm (2ft/1½ft); Fragrans Group, grey-green leaves, pine-scented, clusters of white flowers, 20-25cm/15-20cm (8-10in/6-8in); 'Graveolens', slightly rough, lobed, mid-green leaves, lemon-rose scent, clusters of mauve flowers, 45-60cm/20-40cm (1½-2ft/8in-1½ft); 'Lady Plymouth', green leaves with silver margins, lemon scent, lavender-pink flowers, 30-40cm/15-40cm (1-1½ft/6in-1½ft); 'Lilian Pottinger', toothed, irregularly lobed leaves, nutmeg-pine scent, clusters of white flowers, my favourite and one that I wouldn't be without, 20-25cm/12-15cm (8-10in/5-6in); 'Prince of Orange', small, rounded leaves, orange-scented, clusters of mauve flowers, 25-30cm/15-20cm (10in-1ft/6-8in).

Ivy-leaved pelargoniums Stiff, fleshy trailing leaves, often mid-green, single to double flowers are white, or shades of mauve, purple, red and pink. Size ranges from trailing dwarf varieties to plants with stems 90cm (3ft) or more in length: ❀ 'Crocketta', semi-double, white flecked with crimson; 'Decora Lilas', lavender-pink; 'Hederinum Variegatum' (syn. 'Duke of Edinburgh'), deep pink,

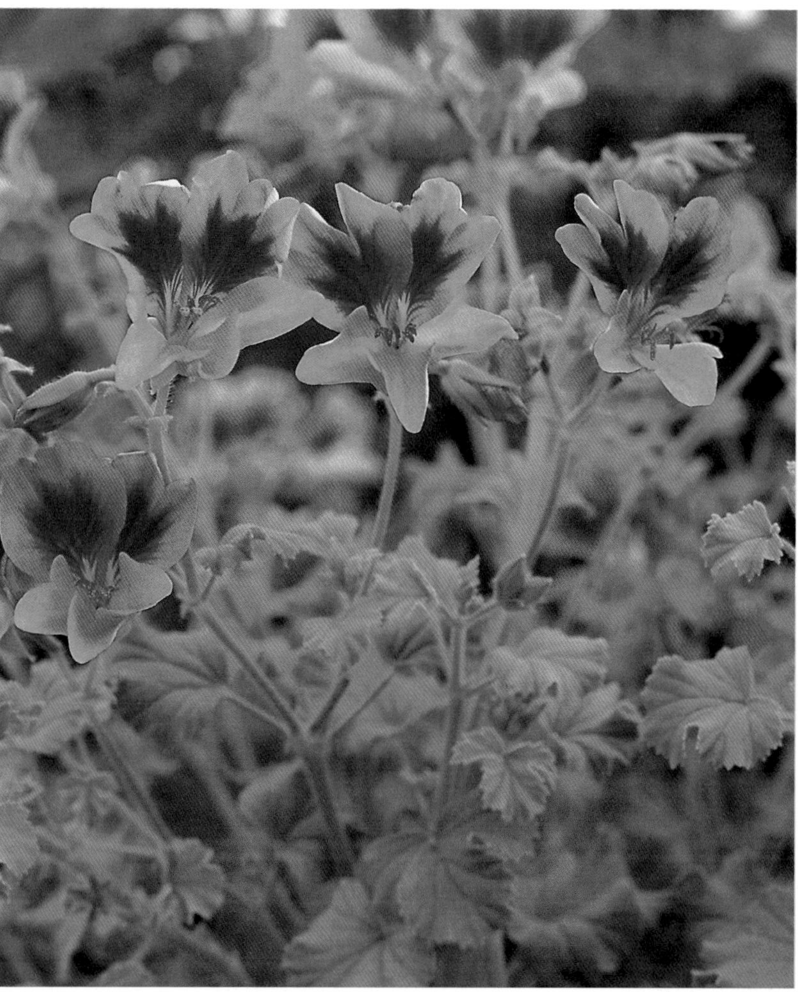

above *Pelargonium* 'Catford Belle'. The Angel pelargoniums would in some ways be more appropriately called Viola-flowered varieties for it is small violas that their very attractive little flowers most resemble.

right *Penstemon* 'Port Wine'. Remember that penstemons are best when treated as shrubs rather than perennials and the beautifully rich coloured varieties like this one will then flower reliably for many years.

variegated foliage; 'L'Elégante', silver-green leaves, sometimes turning mid-green with cream variegation in dry conditions, single white flowers; 'Rouletta', semi-double flowers, clusters of crimson and white bicoloured flowers, sometimes entirely crimson in hot summers; 'Summer Showers', single flowers in mixed colours lavender-blue, rose-pink, plum-pink and white, raised from seed.

Regal pelargoniums Rounded, mid-green, sometimes partially toothed or lobed leaves, white, red, mauve or purple single, rarely double, flowers. Size 30-45cm/20-45cm (1-1½ft/8in-1½ft): ❀ 'Askham Fringed Aztec', white with purple markings, fringed petals; 'Brown's Butterfly', very dark brown, almost black with mahogany flecks; 'Lavender Grand Slam', mauve flowers, purple markings on upper petals, black-purple feathering; 'Lord Bute', pink-edged, dark crimson flowers; 'White Glory', white, sometimes with red markings.

Species pelargoniums ❀ *P. tomentosum*, a scented-leaf pelargonium with mid-green, heart-shaped lobed leaves with peppermint fragrance, butterfly-shaped white flowers, 75-90cm/60-75cm (2¼-3ft/2-2½ft).

Pennisetum — Poaceae

below *Pennisetum alopecurioïdes*. This Oriental and Southern Hemisphere species is on my list of indispensable ornamental grasses; and like many of them, it is especially pretty when growing through gravel.

Small/large fairly hardy annual and perennial grasses. Linear leaves, clusters of very attractive bristly/feathery, oblong to lance-shaped spikelets, summer to autumn. Sow seed in growing positions in early spring or divide established plants in late spring or early summer. ❀ *P. alopecurioides* (Fountain Grass, Swamp Foxtail Grass), clump-forming perennial, arching, stiff, bright green leaves, hairy, brown spikelets resembling bottle-brushes, on wiry stems, early autumn to late autumn, followed by spikes of red-brown seeds, 60-150cm/60-120cm (2-5ft/2-4ft); *P. a.* 'Hameln', smaller form, 60cm (2ft); *P. orientale*, hummock-forming perennial, fine, arching, narrow dark green leaves, pendent, bristled, pink bottle-brush spikelets, 60cm/75cm (2ft/2½ft).

Penstemon — *Scrophulariaceae*

Small/large half-hardy and moderately hardy herbaceous or evergreen perennials and alpines. These lovely plants are making a justified return to favour for borders, the smaller species for rock gardens, more compact varieties for containers. Linear to lance-shaped leaves, clusters of two-lipped, tubular or bell-shaped, open-mouthed flowers, spring to autumn. Thrive in well-drained soil in full sun or partial shade; alpines require gritty, well-drained, poor to moderately fertile soil in full sun. Treat penstemons as shrubs rather than perennials. Don't cut down the top growth until the spring, and take some cuttings as a precaution against winter loss. Growing them in containers and overwintering them in a cold-frame also makes sense in cooler areas. Sow seed in a cold-frame (alpines) or in warmth (perennials) in late winter or spring, divide established plants in spring, take softwood cuttings in early summer or semi-ripe cuttings mid-summer. ❀ Alpine types: *P. campanulatus* (syn. *P. kunthii*), erect semi-evergreen, toothed, linear to lance-shaped dark green leaves, clusters of pink-purple or violet flowers, early summer, 30-60cm/45cm

(1-2ft/1½ft); *P. heterophyllus*, half-hardy to hardy evergreen, blue-green or mid-green linear to lance-shaped leaves, funnel-shaped pink-blue flowers, summer, 30-50cm/30-50cm (1-1¾ft/ 1-1¾ft); *P. pinifolius*, low-growing, shrubby, hardy, light green, needle-like leaves, spikes of vivid orange-red flowers, 25cm/30cm (10in/1ft); *P. p.* 'Mersea Yellow', yellow flowers. Perennial Border varieties: *P.* 'Alice Hindley', large pale lilac-blue flowers flushed mauve, white inside, mid-summer to mid-autumn, 90cm/45cm (3ft/ 1½ft); *P.* 'Andenken an Friedrich Hahn', low-growing, narrow, dark green leaves, garnet-red tubular flowers, summer to late autumn, 75cm (2½ft); *P.* 'Apple Blossom', narrow, fresh green leaves, small pink and white tubular-bell-shaped flowers, white throats, mid-summer to autumn, 45-60cm/45-60cm (1½-2ft/1½-2ft); *P.* 'Burgundy' (syn. *P.* 'Burford Seedling'), broad bell-shaped flowers, wine-red, paler veins in white-red throat, mid-summer to autumn, 90cm/45cm (3ft/1½ft); *P.* 'Catherine de la Mare', oval to lance-shaped leaves, spikes of foxglove-like blue-purple flowers, 30-40cm (1-1½ft); *P.* 'Evelyn', very narrow leaves, small, slender tubular pale pink flowers, light pink inside with darker lines, mid-summer to autumn, 45-60cm/30cm (1½-2ft/1ft); *P.* 'Osprey', large cream-white tubular flowers with pink edges, summer, 40-60cm/30-60cm (1½-2ft/1-2ft); *P.* 'Pennington Gem', narrow leaves, tubular-bell-shaped flowers, pink with white throats, purple anthers, mid-summer to autumn, 75cm/45cm (2½ft/1½ft); *P.* 'Port Wine', deep red-purple flowers, summer to autumn, 60-90cm/ 60cm (2-3ft); *P.* 'Rubicundus', less hardy than most, I find, large tubular crimson-scarlet flowers with a white throat, summer to autumn, 60-75cm (2-2½ft); *P.* 'Schoenholzeri', compact, pink-red flowers, summer to autumn, 60-90cm/60cm (2-3ft/2ft); *P.* 'Sour Grapes', a very choice plant but less hardy than many, large, tubular-bell-shaped, grey-blue flowers flushed purple, tinged green, mid-summer to autumn, 60cm/45cm (2ft/1½ft); *P.* 'Stapleford Gem', lilac-purple flowers, upper lips pale pink, throat and lower lips white with purple stripes, mid-summer to autumn, 60cm/ 45cm (2ft/1½ft); *P.* 'White Bedder' (syn. *P.* 'Snow Storm'), large leaves, tubular-funnel-shaped flowers, white at first, later flushed pink, mid-summer to autumn, 60cm/45cm (2ft/1½ft).

Perovskia *Russian Sage* Lamiaceae

Large deciduous moderately hardy sub-shrubs and quite excellent plants for mixed borders; they blend very well with yellows. Narrow, oval leaves, deeply cut, with white hairs, scented of sage, tubular, two-lipped blue flowers, late summer to early autumn. Cut back top growth in spring. Take basal cuttings or divide in spring. ❀ *P. atriplicifolia*, erect, deeply cut lobed, grey-green leaves, tall clusters of violet-blue flowers, late summer to early autumn, 1.2m/1m (4ft/3ft); *P. a.* 'Blue Spire', silver-grey leaves, abundant tubular, violet-blue flowers on tall spikes, 1.2m/1m (4ft/3ft).

above *Perovskia atriplicifolia* 'Blue Spire'. A plant that I was first introduced to when I rescued it from an over-grown border in a garden many years ago. I have never been without its lovely pastel colours since.

Persicaria *Knotweed* Polygonaceae

Small/large annuals, evergreen, semi-evergreen or deciduous perennials and sub-shrubs. Moderately hardy. The fact that the group includes some unappealing weeds shouldn't detract from many valuable plants for borders or naturalizing in grass or woodland, with several low-growing, spreading species suitable as ground cover. Variously shaped leaves, usually with prominent veins, on fleshy stems. Panicles or spikes of small funnel-, bell- or cup-shaped flowers, sometimes followed by brown-red fruit. Sow seed in a cold-frame in spring, or divide established plants in spring or autumn. ❀ *P. affinis* (syn. *Polygonum affine*), 'Darjeeling Red', dark green, lance-shaped leaves, russet-brown in autumn, spikes of cup-shaped pink-red flowers, brown in autumn, 25cm/60cm (10in/2ft); *P. a.* 'Donald Lowndes', compact, salmon-pink flowers, darkening with age; *P. a.* 'Superba' (syn. *P.* 'Dimity'), leaves rich brown in autumn, pale pink flowers, deep pink-red calyces; *P. amplexicaulis* (syns. *Bistorta amplexicaulis*,

above *Not merely a curious weed, Petasites fragrans can provide ideal ground cover in wild and difficult places.*

below *Petunia Surfinia Series. These very floriferous trailing varieties have been among the most exciting new hanging basket plants in recent years.*

Polygonum ·*amplexicaule*), clump-forming, semi-evergreen, pointed, mid-green ovate to lance-shaped leaves, downy beneath, crinkled above, narrow, long tapering spikes of bell-shaped, soft pink or purple flowers, mid-summer to early autumn, 1.2m/1.2m (4ft/4ft); *P. a.* 'Atrosanguinea', slender spikes of tiny, crimson flowers, late summer to autumn; *P. bistorta* 'Superba' (syn. *Polygonum bistorta*), clump-forming, semi-evergreen perennial, ovate, pointed, conspicuously veined mid-green leaves, cyclamen-pink poker-like spikes of tiny, bell-shaped flowers, early summer to mid-autumn, 90cm/90cm (3ft/3ft); *P. vacciniifolia* (syn. *Polygonum vacciniifolium*), creeping, semi-evergreen perennial, glossy, leathery, pointed leaves, red in autumn, spikes of heather-pink flowers, late summer to autumn, 20cm/50cm (8in/1¾ft); *P. virginiana* 'Painter's Palette', (syn. *Tovara filiformis*), low-growing perennial, large oval leaves with cream and green marbling, flushed pink, with a V-shaped mark, red at first, later black-brown, yellow splashes and deep pink-red tints, red mid-ribs and stalks, cream-white, sometimes pink-tinged flowers, late summer, 40-120cm/60-140cm (1½-4ft/2-4¾ft).

Petasites
Butterburr, Sweet Coltsfoot Asteraceae

Small/medium rhizomatous ornamentals. Fairly hardy to moderately hardy. Suitable as ground cover, particularly near water, or for wild flower gardens; rather ungainly but interesting plants that can be invasive. Kidney- to heart-shaped basal leaves, small, daisy-like flowers. Divide established plants in spring or autumn. ❀ *P. fragrans* (Winter Heliotrope), rounded, dark green basal leaves, grey beneath, clusters of fragrant, pale lilac or purple flowers, late winter or early spring, emerging before leaves, 30cm/1.2m (1ft/4ft); *P. japonicus* var. *giganteus*, huge glossy, light green round leaves, 1m (3ft) in diameter, neat clusters of green and white flowers, late winter to early spring, 1m/2.4m (3ft/6¾ft); *P. j.* var. *g.* 'Variegatus', yellow streaks and blotches on leaves, pale yellow flowers.

Petroselinum *Parsley* Apiaceae

Small moderately hardy biennial herb. Parsley is far too often simply wasted; it is a very attractive plant, suitable for edging borders, herb gardens and containers. Triangular, pinnate mid-green aromatic leaves with toothed leaflets, umbels of tiny, star-shaped, white or yellow-green flowers in the second year, followed by small, round fruit. Thrives in fertile, moist, well-drained, preferably slightly alkaline, soil in light or partial shade and is best protected by cloches overwinter in colder areas. Sow seed in growing positions in spring and again in late summer. ❀ *P. crispum* (Curled Parsley), leaves curled at margins, yellow-green flowers in summer followed by tiny, ribbed, ovoid fruit, much the best for edging and other ornamental uses, 30-80cm/30cm (1-2½ft/1ft); *P.* 'Champion Moss Curled', *P.* 'Curlina' and *P.* 'Moss Curled' are seed company selections, probably little different from each other; *P. c.* var. *neapolitanum* (Italian Parsley), plain-leafed or flat-leafed parsley, flat, dark green leaves, strongly flavoured and the parsley for the gourmet, hardier and more weather resistant then many other varieties; *P. c.* var. *tuberosum* (Turnip Rooted Parsley, Hamburg Parsley), large, edible roots and edible leaves, similar to leaves of curly-leafed parsley, roots are cooked and eaten like parsnip and one of the most shade-tolerant vegetables 35cm/30cm (1¼ft/1ft).

Petunia Solanaceae

Small half-hardy annuals and short-lived tender perennials grown as annuals for summer bedding, mixed borders and all types of containers. They have suffered in the past from rain damage but modern forms are much more weather tolerant. Mid- to dark green, ovate to lance-shaped leaves, saucer- or trumpet-shaped, single or double, five-petalled flowers, summer to autumn. Thrive in light, well-drained soil in full sun; container-grown plants are best in loam-based potting compost. Protect from wind and dead-head regularly to encourage more flowers. Modern petunias are complex hybrids, generally called simply *P.* x *hybrida* and the range of varieties is changing and extending every year. They tend to be divided into three main groups: Multifloras, Grandifloras and Millifloras, although the name Floribundas is sometimes used for ranges such as the Mirage Series F1 and Reflections Series F1 that combine the large flowers of the Grandiflora types with the multiplicity of flowers associated with the Multifloras.

Multiflora petunias Bushy plants with abundant small flowers, more weather resistant than varieties in other groups: ❀ Carpet Series F1, compact, spreading, colours include cream-white, strong reds and oranges, makes good ground cover; Celebrity Series F1, compact, early flowering, blues, pinks, reds, paler shades or yellow and pink, some with darker veining, 30-90cm (1ft/3ft); 'Pink Wave' F1, and 'Purple Wave' F1, rose-pink and purple flowers respectively on trailing plants for window boxes and hanging baskets or as ground cover; 'Plum Pudding', purple flowers with lace-like veining; 'Purple Wave' F1, spreading, vibrant magenta flowers, 45cm/30-90cm (1½ft/1-3ft); Surfinia Series, vigorous, branching and trailing, wide range of colours, tolerant of wet weather, propagated from softwood cuttings, much the best for hanging baskets where they can be spectacular, 23-40cm/30-90cm (9in-1½ft/1-3ft).

Grandiflora petunias Less abundant, larger flowers, more susceptible to damage by wind and wet weather than others: ❀ Daddy Series, large flowers, colours include plum, burgundy, and pastel pink, salmon-pink, purple and lavender-blue, with darker veining, 35cm/30-90cm (1¼ft/1-3ft); Falcon Series F1; compact, bushy plants with very large flowers in white, salmon, reds and blue; Storm Series, claimed to have particularly good weather resistance, lavender, pink, white and salmon are available; Supercascade Series, spreading, huge long-flowering blooms in white, blue, lilac-pink, rose-pink, salmon-pink and deep red.

Milliflora petunias Small flowers, only 3cm (1¼in) in diameter: ❀ Fantasy Series, much the best of a limited number of varieties, dwarf, compact, colours include blues, rose-pink, rose-red, deep blue and scarlet-red.

Phalaris Poaceae

Medium/large hardy annual and perennial grasses. Linear, flat, pale to mid-green leaves, ovate spikelets comprising three to four flowers. Divide established plants between mid-spring and mid-summer. ❀ *P. arundinacea* (Gardeners' Garters, Reed Canary Grass), var. *picta* 'Feesey', clump-forming perennial, ribbon-shaped leaves striped white and green, sometimes with purple flush, spikelets pale green at first, later buff, an attractive grass but one to plant with thought as it is invasive, 1.5m (5ft)/indefinite; *P. a.* var. *p.* 'Picta', white striped leaves, 1m (3ft).

above *Phalaris arundinacea picta* 'Picta'. A very pretty but very invasive ornamental grass to be planted with caution.

Phaseolus *Bean* Papilionaceae

Half-hardy annual and tender perennial vegetables. The genus contains two species of edible beans: the perennial climber *P. coccineus* (Runner Bean) (the only perennial garden pea or bean), and the annual *P. vulgaris* (French Bean, Dwarf Bean, Kidney Bean). Runner beans thrive in most deep, rich soils in a sunny position, and can be grown in the same place for several years; French beans and related beans do best on a light, well-drained soil. Sow seed in warmth in spring or, and I think better, in growing positions in mid- or late spring.

Runner beans Twining perennial usually grown as an annual. Flowers, scarlet, white or, rarely, bicoloured, are followed by green edible seedpods, which are harvested between mid-summer and early autumn, sometimes until late autumn. Varieties are divided into string types, which have a tough fibrous edge to the pods which must be removed before cooking, and stringless, which lack this fibre but tend to be less strongly flavoured. Seed colour varies widely and attractively: ❀ 'Achievement', red flowers, string, purple seeds;

above Dwarf Bean 'Mont d'Or'. The many varieties of attractively coloured bean can add a great deal to the ornamental appeal of any kitchen garden.

right *Philadelphus* 'Manteau d'Hermine'. No-one denies that mock oranges are glorious to behold, but so many of them grow too large for small gardens. This compact double flowered variety is the answer.

'Desirée', white flowers, stringless, large white seeds; 'Enorma', red flowers, string; 'Hammonds Dwarf Scarlet', dwarf, non-climbing variety, red flowers, string; 'Kelvedon Marvel', red flowers, string; 'Painted Lady', very old variety, red-and-white flowers, string, pink-brown seeds with darker marks, coarse pods; 'Polestar', red flowers, the best stringless variety; 'Prizewinner', red flowers, string; 'Red Knight', red flowers, string; 'Scarlet Emperor', red flowers, string; 'White Emergo, white flowers, string.

French beans, dwarf and kidney beans Most of these are dwarf varieties, although some are climbing, which give heavier crops but need support. Pods are flattened or round (pencil-podded), green, purple or yellow although the colour of the darker-podded types tends to be lost on cooking. French beans that are left to mature and then dried supply haricot beans. Dwarf French beans are also known as kidney beans. ❀ Dwarf varieties: 'Masterpiece Stringless', stringless, flat green pods; 'Mont d'Or' (syn. 'Golden Butter'), stringless, yellow, slightly flat, waxy pods, erect or semi-climbing; 'Purple Queen', stringless, round, dark purple pods; 'Purple Tepee', slightly curved round, purple pods; 'Royalty', purple, curved round pods; 'Tendergreen', stringless, round, green pods; 'The Prince', dark green flat pods, still probably the best dwarf variety. Climbing varieties: 'Blue Lake White Seeded', stringless, round green pods, white seeds, good haricot beans when ripe; 'Hunter', stringless, flat green pods; 'Purple Podded Climbing'.

Phegopteris

Beech fern — Thelypteridaceae

Small deciduous fern. Moderately hardy. Delicate-looking pinnate, bipinnate or finely divided fronds. A lovely small fern for the edge of woodland in moist, preferably slightly acidic, soil. Divide in spring. ❀ *P. connectilis* (syn. *Thelypteris phegopteris*), lime-green, triangular, pinnate fronds, 30cm (1ft)/indefinite.

Philadelphus

Mock Orange — Hydrangeaceae

Medium deciduous shrubs. Moderately hardy and quite indispensable for early summer flowers and fragrance in borders and as specimen plants. Ovate, mid-green leaves, sweetly fragrant, cup- or bowl-shaped, usually four-petalled flowers, semi-double, double or single, singly or in clusters, summer. Thrive in any moderately fertile, well-drained soil in full sun or partial shade. Although no pruning is essential, philadelphus benefit from having up to one third of the oldest branches cut out each spring. Take softwood cuttings in summer, hardwood cuttings in autumn or spring. ❀ *P.* 'Beauclerk', medium, toothed leaves, single, cup-shaped, milk-white flowers flushed cerise around

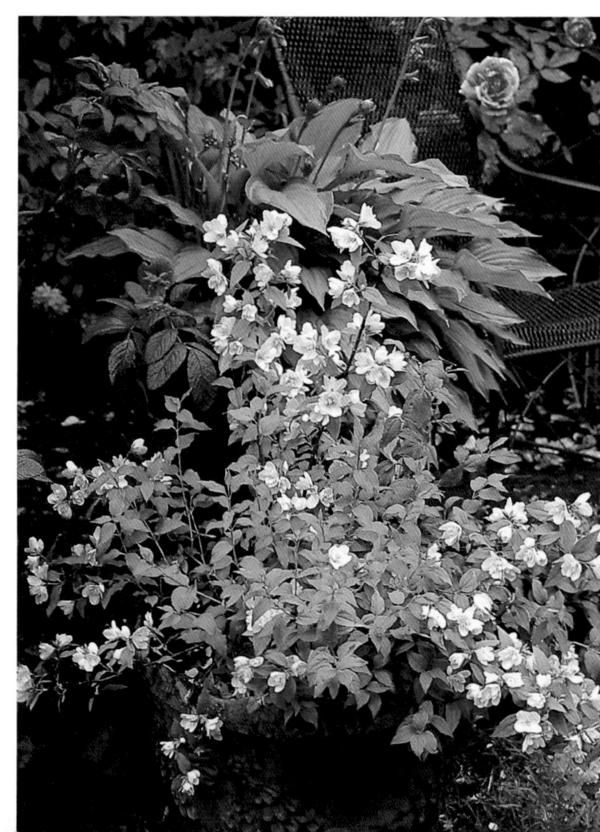

the stamens, mid- to late summer, a manageably sized plant, 2.5m/2.5m (8ft/8ft); *P.* 'Belle Etoile', compact, single, fragrant white flowers, flushed maroon at the centre, 1.2m/2.5m (4ft/8ft); *P. coronarius* 'Aureus', leaves bright yellow at first, later green-yellow, cream-white flowers are richly fragrant though fewer and less conspicuous against the foliage than in other varieties, early summer, 3m/2.5m (10ft/8ft); *P. c.* 'Variegatus', leaves edged cream-white; *P.* 'Innocence', medium, ovate leaves, sometimes edged with cream, abundant cream-white, fragrant single flowers, in early or mid-summer, 3m/2m (10ft/6½ft); *P.* 'Manteau d' Hermine', dwarf, compact, pale to mid-green leaves, fragrant, cream, double flowers, early to mid-summer, the best small form, 75cm/1.5m (2½ft/5ft); *P.* 'Sybille', small shrub, abundant single, almost square, orange-scented flowers, prominently marked purple in the centre, from early to mid-summer, 1.2m/2m (4ft/6½ft); *P.* 'Virginal', clusters of strongly scented double, pure white flowers, 5m/2.5m (16ft/8ft).

Phlomis — Lamiaceae

Herbaceous perennials and evergreen shrubs or sub-shrubs. Barely hardy to moderately hardy and widely grown in herbaceous borders, the smaller species in rock gardens although I find they have too much stem and leaf and not enough flower. No routine pruning. Sow seed in warmth in spring, take softwood cuttings in summer, or semi-ripe cuttings in autumn. ❀ *P. fruticosa* (Jerusalem Sage), low-growing, rather ungainly, moderately hardy evergreen shrub, oval to lance-shaped dull, mid-green leaves, clusters of bright yellow flowers, from early to mid-summer, 1m/1.5m (3ft/5ft); *P. italica*, barely hardy evergreen shrub, dull green, rough, lance-shaped leaves, pink or purple flowers, mid-summer, 30cm/60cm (1ft/2ft); *P. lanata*, dwarf evergreen shrub, rounded, sage-green, woolly leaves, gold-yellow flowers, summer, 50cm/75cm (1¾ft/2½ft); *P. russeliana* (syn. *P. samia*), moderately hardy perennial, rough, heart-shaped, grey-green leaves, clusters of hooded, pale yellow flowers, late spring to early autumn, 90cm/75cm (3ft/2½ft).

Phlox — Polemoniaceae

Small/large half-hardy and hardy bedding annuals, herbaceous or evergreen perennials and shrubs. A diverse and highly individual group of North American plants for herbaceous and summer borders and woodland plantings, the smaller species for rock gardens and edging. Linear to ovate, light to dark green leaves, dish-shaped to funnel-shaped flowers, with tubular bases opening to five ovate petals, in terminal inflorescences, in summer. Thrive in fertile, well-drained soil in full sun, light or partial shade; smaller species in rock gardens require gritty, well-drained, poor to moderately fertile soil in full sun. Sow seed in warmth in early spring (annuals); sow seed in a cold-frame when ripe, divide in spring or autumn, take root cuttings in winter (perennials); take softwood cuttings between early and mid-summer (alpines). The species and varieties described below fall into four groups: border perennials, other, lower growing perennials, alpines, and annuals.

above *Phlox subulata* 'Amazing Grace'. This was the first of the North American alpine *Phlox* species to reach European gardens, soon after its discovery in 1745. It has spawned a great many colourful varieties since.

Herbaceous border perennials *P. maculata* 'Alpha', linear to ovate leaves, fragrant, dish-shaped lilac-pink flowers, early to mid-summer, 90cm/45cm (3ft/1½ft); *P. m.* 'Omega', white flowers, small lilac eye; *P. paniculata* 'Amethyst', toothed, narrow, ovate to lance-shaped or elliptic leaves, fragrant, violet flowers, summer to autumn, 1.2m/60-100cm (4ft/2-3ft); *P. p.* 'Brigadier', deep pink flowers flushed orange; *P. p.* 'Eventide', pale mauve-blue flowers; *P. p.* 'Fujiyama', long clusters of white flowers, 75cm (2½ft); *P. p.* 'Mother of Pearl', white flowers flushed pink, 75cm (2½ft); *P. p.* 'Nora Leigh', white variegated leaves, lilac flowers, 90cm (3ft); *P. p.* 'Prince of Orange', orange-red flowers, 80cm (2½ft); *P. p.* 'Starfire', deep red flowers, 90cm (3ft); *P. p.* 'White Admiral', pure white flowers, 90cm (3ft).

Other perennials *P. adsurgens* 'Wagon Wheel', spreading, evergreen, ovate leaves, dish-shaped salmon-pink flowers with very narrow petals, resembling a wheel, late spring to early summer, 30cm/30cm (1ft/1ft); *P. carolina* 'Bill Baker', erect, spreading, bright green leaves, dish-shaped pink flowers, early summer, 45cm/30cm (1½ft/1ft); *P. divaricata* 'Blue Dreams', erect, semi-evergreen, hairy, ovate leaves, deep blue buds opening to soft, light blue flowers, 35cm/50cm (1¼ft/1ft); *P. d.* ssp. *laphamii* 'Chattahoochee', compact, wide clusters of silky flowers, rich lilac-blue at first, later pale blue, with dark purple eyes; *P. d.* 'May Breeze', pale, ice-blue flowers.

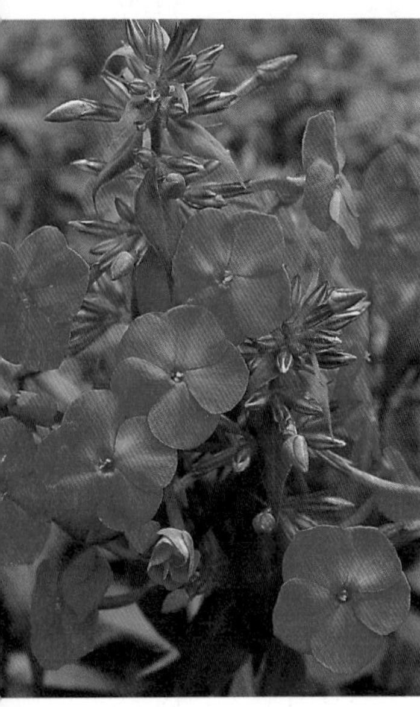

above *Phlox maculata* 'Alpha'. One of the two most important border species, this is a plant that has curiously given rise to far fewer varieties than its compatriot *Phlox paniculata*.

Alpines *P. douglasii* 'Boothman's Variety', mound-forming evergreen, dark green, lance-shaped leaves, pale lilac flowers with thin purple ring at the centre, 20cm/30cm (8in/1ft); *P. d.* 'Crackerjack', compact, magenta-red flowers, 12cm/20cm (5in/8in); *P. d.* 'Red Admiral', deep crimson flowers; *P.* x *procumbens* 'Variegata', mat-forming semi-evergreen, glossy green leaves variegated cream and flushed with pink, vivid rose-pink flowers, 10cm/30cm (4in/1ft); *P.* x *p.* 'Blue Ridge', clear lavender-blue flowers; *P. subulata* 'Amazing Grace', cushion or mat-forming evergreen, hairy, bright green linear to elliptic leaves, pink flowers with purple eyes, from late spring to early summer, 5-15cm/50cm (2-6in/1¾ft); *P. s.* 'G F Wilson', deep lavender-blue flowers; *P. s.* 'McDaniel's Cushion', large, bright pink flowers; *P. s.* 'Tamaongalei', deep magenta flowers.

Annuals *P. drummondii*, glossy, oval to lance-shaped leaves, clusters of flowers in white and a variety of shades including blues, purple, pinks, with contrasting eyes, some flowers multi-coloured, mid-summer to early autumn, 10-45cm/25cm (4in-1½ft/10in); *P. d.* 'African Sunset', dusky to deep red flowers; *P. d.* 'Brilliancy Mixed', mixed colours; *P. d.* 'Fantasy Mixed', bushy plant, flowers in clear, pure colours; *P. d.* 'Tapestry Mixed', fragrant flowers in numerous colour combinations, including self-colours, picotees and bicolours, *P. d.* 'Twinkle', tiny star-shaped flowers in a variety of shades including salmon-pink and rose-pink, picotees, petals sometimes fringed, 15cm (6in).

Phormium *Flax Lily* Agavaceae

Small/large evergreen perennials. Fairly hardy and, I find, hardier than is often appreciated, although in very cold areas should be given winter protection. Suitable for herbaceous and shrub borders and as specimen plants, especially in coastal gardens. Sword-shaped, keeled leaves with V-shaped bases and sharply pointed tips, leaves sometimes finely striped or variegated. Clusters of small tubular flowers, summer. Divide established plants in spring. ❀ *P.* 'Bronze Baby', dwarf, bronze, pointed leaves, 60-80cm/60-80cm (2-2½ft/2-2½ft); *P. cookianum* (syn. *P. colensoi*), pale to dark green leaves, yellow or green-and-orange flowers, late summer, followed in autumn by narrow, pendent, curved and twisted seedpods, 1.2m/30cm (4ft/1ft); *P. c.* ssp. *hookeri* 'Tricolor', leaves edged with cream, yellow and red; *P.* Maori Series, varieties with strikingly variegated leaves, including 'Maori Chief', bronze leaves striped pink and red, and 'Maori Sunrise', leaves striped apricot and pink and edged in bronze; *P.* 'Sundowner', bronze-green leaves, tipped pink and purple, clusters of yellow-green flowers, summer, 2m/2m (6½ft/6½ft); *P. tenax* (New Zealand Flax), erect, tough, linear dark green leaves with orange or red margins and mid-ribs, blue-green beneath, tubular, red flowers in red-purple panicles, summer, 4m/2m (13ft/6½ft); *P. t.* Purpureum Group, leaves in shades of purple; *P.* 'Yellow Wave', bright yellow-and-green leaves.

right *Phormium* 'Maori Sunrise'. Not surprisingly, many of the beautifully coloured varieties of New Zealand Flax have New Zealand names; and some are remarkably hardy in Europe.

Photinia Rosaceae

Large deciduous and evergreen shrubs and small trees. Moderately hardy and essential members of any shrub planting although the deciduous forms require acidic soils. Suitable for shrub borders, woodland gardens and as specimens. Mid- to dark green, lance-shaped to ovate leaves: on evergreens, leaves are glossy and sometimes red when young; deciduous leaves often brightly coloured in autumn. Clusters of small five-petalled flowers in summer, followed by rounded, usually red fruit; in cold areas flowers and fruit produced rarely on evergreen species. No routine pruning. Sow seed in a cold-frame in autumn or take semi-ripe cuttings in summer. ❀ *P. davidiana*, moderately hardy large evergreen shrub or small tree, leathery, dark green lance-shaped leaves, mature leaves turning bright red in autumn, small white flowers, summer, followed by clusters of pendent, brilliant crimson fruit, 8m/6m (26½ft/20ft); *P. d.* 'Palette', slow-growing, leaves blotched cream-white, tinged pink when young, 5m/3m (16ft/10ft); *P.* x *fraseri* 'Red Robin', fairly hardy compact, evergreen shrub, elliptic, leathery, sharply toothed dark green

leaves, brilliant red when young, justifiably the most popular, 5m/5m (16ft/16ft); *P.* 'Redstart', moderately hardy large evergreen shrub or small tree, bright red when young, white flowers, summer, followed by orange-red fruit, flushed yellow, 5m/3m (16ft/10ft).

Phuopsis Rubiaceae

Hardy perennial for large rock gardens, edging and ground cover in full sun. A pretty plant if you can tolerate the strong, foxy smell. Elliptic leaves, clusters of tiny, tubular-funnel-shaped flowers. Sow seed in autumn, divide established plants or take stem cuttings in late spring. ❀ *P. stylosa* (syn. *Crucianella stylosa*), mat-forming, pointed, pale green, musk-scented leaves, clusters of tiny pink flowers, summer, 15cm/50cm (6in/1¾ft); *P. s.* 'Purpurea', deep purple-pink flowers.

Phygelius Scrophulariaceae

Small barely hardy evergreen shrubs and sub-shrubs and generally best grown as herbaceous perennials. Toothed, oval to lance-shaped, dark green, pointed leaves, tubular, *Penstemon*-like flowers, summer to autumn. Cut back to soil level in spring. Sow seed in a cold-frame or take semi-ripe cuttings in mid- to late summer. ❀ *P. aequalis*, small sub-shrub, pale dusky pink to red flowers, yellow at the throat, late summer to early autumn, 1m/1m (3ft/3ft); *P. a.* 'Yellow Trumpet', wide, bright green leaves, pale cream-yellow flowers; *P. capensis* (Cape Figwort), small shrub, pendent, tubular, orange-red to deep red flowers, yellow at the throat, turning back towards the stem, summer, 1.2/1.5m (4ft/5ft); *P.* x *rectus* 'African Queen' (syn. 'Indian Chief'), pendent, pale red flowers with straight tubes, 1m/1.2m (3ft/4ft); *P.* x *r.* 'Devil's Tubes', deep pink flowers, turning back towards the stem; *P.* x *r.* 'Moonraker', small shrub, yellow, straight-sided flowers; *P.* x *r.* 'Winchester Fanfare', pendent, straight tubular flowers, dusky red-pink with scarlet lobes.

x Phylliopsis Ericaceae

Dwarf moderately hardy evergreen sub-shrub for a peaty or similar acidic soil bed. Richly glossy, dark green leaves, bell-shaped flowers. No routine pruning. Take semi-ripe cuttings in late summer or autumn. ❀ x *P.* 'Coppelia', pink flowers, mid- to late spring, 20cm/40cm (8in/1½ft); x *P. hillieri* 'Pinocchio', small, glossy green leaves, deep pink flowers, spring, second flush in autumn, 20cm/30cm (8in/1ft).

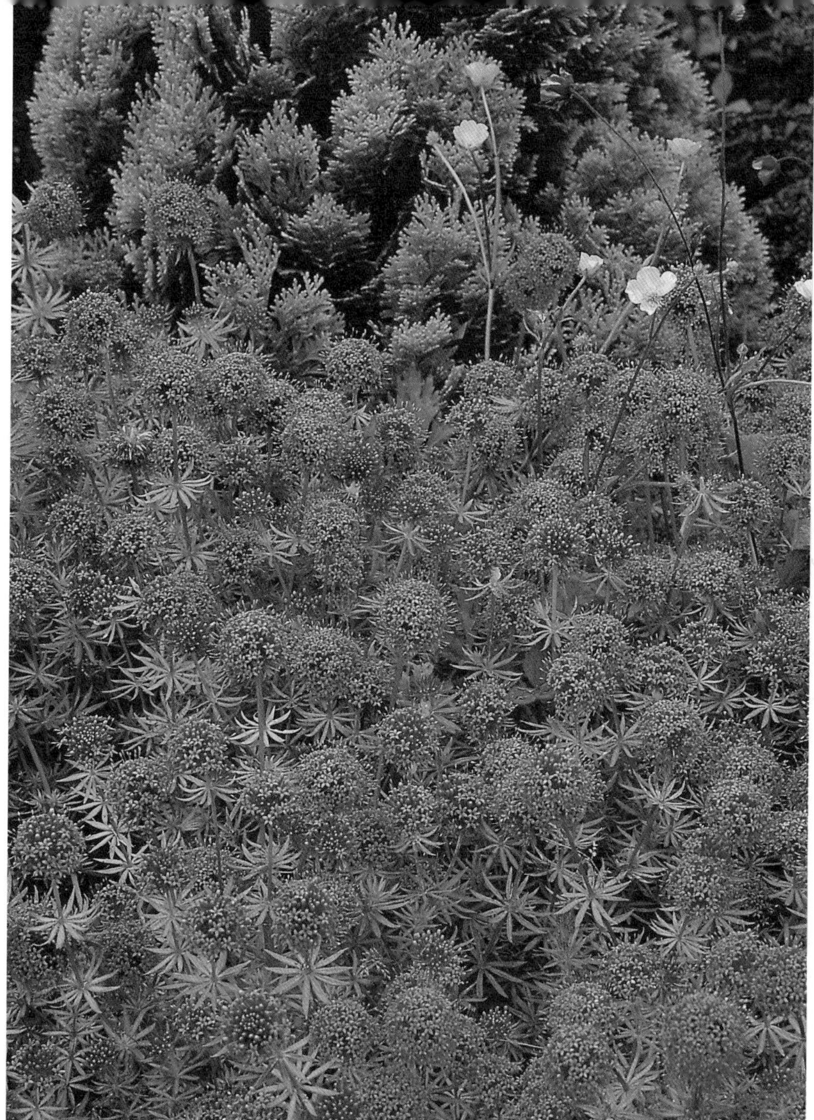

above Few plants have as distinctive or curious a smell as *Phuopsis stylosa*.

Phyllodoce
Mountain Heather Ericaceae

Small evergreen shrubs and sub-shrubs. Hardy to very hardy plants for the rain-soaked alpine garden on acidic soil. Leathery, linear toothed leaves with rolled edges, felted beneath, pendent clusters of large, bell-, urn- or pitcher-shaped flowers. No routine pruning. Take semi-ripe, heeled cuttings in mid-summer. ❀ *P. caerulea*, dwarf, cushion-forming, glossy, dark green narrow leaves, pitcher-shaped purple-blue flowers, late spring to early summer. 15-22cm/30cm (6-8½in/1ft); *P. empetriformis*, mat-forming, glossy, toothed, bright green leaves, downy beneath, bell-shaped, rose-red flowers, late spring to early summer, 30cm/40cm (1ft/1½ft).

Phyllostachys Poaceae

Medium/large evergreen bamboos. Moderately hardy. Yellow-green to light green, narrow leaves on hollow, grooved culms (canes); look particularly effective in containers. Divide established plants in spring. ❀ *P. aurea*, clump-forming, erect,

below *Phyllodoce empetriformis.* I am mystified why this charming North American heather isn't grown more widely in gardens, at least in cooler, wetter areas.

right *Picea abies* 'Nidiformis'. Big spruces are not good garden plants; small and distorted forms like this 'bird's nest' variety are however rather appealing.

lance-shaped gold-green to yellow-green leaves, culms bright green at first, later brown-yellow, with cup-shaped swellings under each node, 2-10m (6½-33ft)/indefinite; *P. nigra*, clump-forming, slender, arching culms become shiny black with age, dark green, glossy lance-shaped leaves, 3-8m (10-26½ft)/indefinite; *P. viridiglaucesens*, clump-forming, culms green at first, later yellow-green, leaves brilliant green above, blue, bloom beneath, 4-6m/1m (13-20ft/3ft).

above *Physalis peruviana*. This curious South American plant has become very popular in recent years, its sweet fruit served with coffee at fashionable restaurants. It is nonetheless, easy to grow in a greenhouse, if vigorous.

Physalis Solanaceae

Small/medium annuals and herbaceous perennials. Tender to moderately hardy. Two common and recognizably related types, one grown as an edible annual, the other a perennial ornamental. Entire or pinnate, mid-green leaves, inconspicuous, bell-shaped flowers singly or in clusters, followed by spherical fruit contained within an inflated papery calyx. Sow seed in growing positions (annuals) or in a cold-frame (perennials), or divide established plants in spring. ❀ *P. alkekengi* (Bladder Cherry, Winter Cherry), perennial, diamond-shaped or triangularly ovate leaves, pendent cream flowers, mid-summer, followed by inflated, orange-scarlet, papery calyces enclosing edible, orange-red fruits, 60-75cm/90cm (2-2½ft/3ft); *P. a.* var. *franchetii* (Chinese Lantern), larger than species with broad, ovate leaves, tiny cream-white flowers, vivid, orange-red calyx much prized by flower arrangers; *P. peruviana* (syn. *P. edulis*) (Cape Gooseberry), edible, pale orange fruit enclosed in inflated calyces, green at first, later gold-brown, 1.8m (5¾ft).

Physocarpus *Ninebark* Rosaceae

Medium/large hardy deciduous shrubs for foliage effect in mixed plantings. Peeling bark, mid- to dark green, ovate to round or kidney-shaped lobed leaves, clusters of small, white, cup-shaped flowers, early summer. No routine pruning. Sow seed in a cold-frame in late autumn or early spring, take semi-ripe cuttings between early and mid-summer, or hardwood cuttings in late autumn. ❀ *P. opulifolius* 'Dart's Gold', three-lobed leaves, bright yellow at first, later dull green, clusters of white flowers, pink-tinged, followed by bladder-like, red fruits flushed green, 3m/5m (10ft/16ft); *P. o.* 'Luteus', leaves pure yellow.

Physostegia Lamiaceae

Small/large rhizomatous ornamentals for middle of the border. Moderately hardy. Variable leaves, sometimes toothed, tall spikes, up to 20cm (8in) long, of two-lipped, tubular flowers, from summer to autumn. Sow seed in a cold-frame in autumn or divide established plants between autumn and spring. ❀ *P virginiana*, narrow, tapering bright green leaves, tubular red, rather assertive rose or white flowers on tall spikes, late summer to early autumn, 1.2m/60cm (4ft/2ft); *P. v.* 'Alba', white flowers on spikes 30cm (1ft) long; *P. v.* 'Red Beauty'; *P. v.* ssp. *speciosa* 'Variegata', grey-green leaves, pale lavender-pink flowers; *P. v.* 'Summer Snow', pure white flowers on spikes 30cm (1ft) long; *P. v.* 'Vivid', claret-pink flowers, 30-60cm/30cm (1-2ft/1ft).

Picea *Spruce* Pinaceae

Large evergreen trees. Hardy to very hardy. Spruces are among the most frequently misplaced of trees and are really suitable as specimens only in large gardens, when some species can look magnificent, although dwarf or compact forms can be very attractive and useful in smaller areas. Short needles, forward pointing, usually grey or green, in whorls around the stems; sometimes pendulous branches. Tiny insignificant male and female flowers, from late winter to spring, followed by cones, females cylindrical or ovoid, usually green or red at first, later purple or brown; male cones ovoid, usually yellow to purple-red. Thrive in fertile, neutral to acidic, moist, well-drained soil and always makes best shape in full sun. No routine pruning. Sow seed in warmth in late winter. ❀ *P. abies* (Norway Spruce, Christmas Tree), 'Little Gem', dwarf, slow-growing, rounded shrub, sharply pointed, short dark green needles, pale green when young, lacks cones, 20cm/20cm (8in/8in); *P. a.* 'Nidiformis', dwarf, very slow-growing flat-topped shrub with a depressed centre, short, yellow-green or light green needles, 50cm-1.8m (1¾-5¾ft); *P. breweriana* (Brewer's Spruce), a very beautiful tree when well grown, spreading or downward-curving branches with pendent slender branchlets, shining dark blue-green leaves, double-banded in white beneath, cones green at first, later purple, needs protection from cold winds, 25m/8m (80ft/26½ft); *P. glauca* (White Spruce), var. *albertiana* 'Alberta Globe', dwarf, slow-growing rounded bush, grey-green needles, lacks cones, 1m/1.2m (3ft/4ft); *P. g.* var. *a.* 'Conica', slow-growing cone-shaped tree, dusky green needles, new leaves bright, light green, 4m/2m (13ft/6½ft); *P. g.* 'Echiniformis', a striking, dwarf, slow-growing globe-shaped bush, prickly, grey-green needles; *P. mariana* 'Nana', dwarf, slow-growing, mound-forming bush with flattened top, blunt, blue-green needles, lacks cones, 75cm/3m (2½ft/10ft); *P. orientalis* (Oriental Spruce, Caucasian Spruce), 'Aurea', slow-growing tree, glossy, dark green blunt needles, young growth cream-yellow, then pale green, purple cylindrical cones ripen to brown, 30m/10m (100ft/33ft); *P. pungens* (Colorado Blue Spruce), 'Globosa', dwarf, flat-topped, globe-shaped bush, vivid blue leaves, lacks cones, 80cm/80cm (2½ft/2½ft); *P. p.* 'Hoopsii', blue-white needles, 5m/1.5m (16ft/5ft); *P. p.* 'Koster', slow-growing, narrow, conical tree, silver-blue needles, 3m/1m (10ft/3ft).

Pieris — Ericaceae

Small/large evergreen shrubs. Moderately hardy and very popular and important for shrub borders and woodland gardens on acidic soil; also effective in large containers. Glossy, lance-shaped to more or less ovate or oblong, mid- to dark green leaves, sometimes red when young. Clusters of small, urn-shaped flowers in spring, often opening from buds that have formed in autumn and rather prone to late frost damage. Leaves are toxic if eaten. Thrives in fertile, well-drained, moist acidic soil enriched with humus, in full sun or light shade. Benefits from protection of young shoots and flower buds. No routine pruning. Sow seed in warmth in spring or autumn, take semi-ripe cuttings in late summer or layer. ❀ *P.* 'Flaming Silver', leaves bright red at first, later green with pink margins that become silver-white when mature, cream-white flowers; *P.* 'Forest Flame', justifiably the most popular form, hardy, compact, erect, leaves red, then pink and cream-white, later green, pendent clusters of white flowers, mid- to late spring, 4m/2m (13ft/6½ft); *P. formosa* var. *forrestii* 'Wakehurst', hardy, erect, glossy, finely toothed oblong leaves, dark green, brilliant red when young, later pink, then green, glistening, slightly fragrant white flowers, mid- to late spring, 5m/4m (16ft/13ft); *P. japonica* 'Firecrest', moderately hardy, glossy, oval to lance-shaped leaves, red at first, then pink, cream or white-yellow, later mid-green, pendent clusters of white, pink or sometimes pink-red flowers, early to mid-spring, 4m/3m (13ft/10ft); *P. j.* 'Little

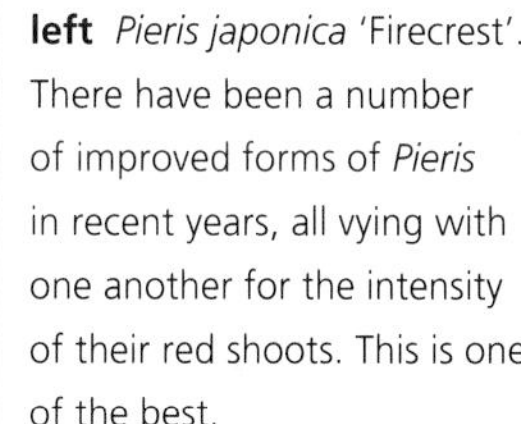

left *Pieris japonica* 'Firecrest'. There have been a number of improved forms of *Pieris* in recent years, all vying with one another for the intensity of their red shoots. This is one of the best.

right *Pinus montezumae*. The Aztec ruler of Mexico has many legacies, but this quite splendid pine is certainly one of the more enduring.

Heath', dwarf, compact, young leaves bronze-red, silver-white margins; *P. j.* 'Mountain Fire', leaves deep red at first, later chestnut-brown; *P. j.* 'Purity', compact, pale green leaves, erect clusters of white flowers, 1m/1m (3ft/3ft); *P. j.* 'Variegata', slow-growing, white variegated leaves, white flowers.

Pimpinella — Apiaceae

Hardy annuals, biennials, perennials and herbs. Simple or pinnate leaves on hairy stems, umbels of tiny, star-shaped flowers, followed by rounded fruit. Sow seed in growing positions or divide established plants in spring. ❀ *P. anisum* (Aniseed, Anise), annual, kidney-shaped to ovate, divided or toothed leaves, tiny off-white flowers, summer, followed by fruit containing aromatic ribbed seeds, green at first, ripening to grey, may not produce seed during cool summers, particularly in cold areas, 45cm/25cm (1½ft/10in); *P. major* 'Rosea', perennial ornamental, mid-green, divided, fern-like leaves with ovate to lance-shaped leaflets, umbels of tiny pink flowers, early to mid-summer, 1.2m/60cm (4ft/2ft).

below *Pinus sylvestris* 'Fastigiata'. Some fastigiate forms of trees are so totally different from the wild species as to be quite unrecognisable. This Scots pine is a particularly impressive example.

Pinus *Pine* — Pinaceae

Small/large evergreen shrubs and trees. Moderately hardy to hardy. As with other important coniferous genera like *Picea*, the pines as full-sized trees are suitable only for large gardens, when the long-needled forms can be superb. Some species are also valuable as shelter and windbreaks, particularly in coastal areas. Some of the dwarf varieties are nonetheless suitable for small gardens. Needles, either short or long, depending on species, and in bundles of two, three or five, insignificant male and female flowers in separate clusters, male flowers comprise catkin-like cones, female flowers resemble small immature cones. Cones vary in size and shape, from rounded through conical to elongated and curved, and are often an important contributor to the appeal of mature trees. Thrive in well-drained, ideally acidic soil in full sun, although some will tolerate neutral to alkaline soil. Most are intolerant of shade and smoke-polluted air. No routine pruning. Sow ripe seed in cold-frame or outdoors. ❀ *P. contorta* (Lodgepole Pine), two-needled, hardy tree, yellow-green, forward-pointing twisted needles, long, spiny, brown to yellow-brown female cones, 25m/8m (80ft/26½ft); *P. heldreichii* var. *leucodermis* (Bosnian Pine), 'Compact Gem', two-needled, hardy tree, dark, rigid, erect needles, almost black-green, forward pointing, conical female cones, cobalt-blue at first, later brown, 15-20m/5-6m (50-60ft/16-20ft); *P. h.* var. *l.* 'Schmidtii', dwarf, compact form that I have grown for many years, 3m/1.5m (10ft/5ft); *P. montezumae* (Montezuma Pine), usually five-needled, barely hardy tree, blue-grey, rough, sharp, pendent needles, 30cm (1ft) long, on red-brown stems, ovoid to ovoid-conical, prickly female cones, blue-purple at first, later rust to yellow-brown, in clusters, singly on young trees, a fantastic tree for a mild garden, 15-30m/6-9m (50-100ft/20-30ft); *P. mugo* (Mountain Pine), two-needled, 'Gnom', small, compact, slow-growing, hardy tree, deep green needles, pointed, oval dark brown female cones, erect or in drooping clusters, singly on young trees, 3.5m/5m (11ft/16ft); *P. m.* 'Mops', dwarf, rounded, mop-headed, resinous buds in winter, 1m/1m (3ft/3ft); *P. m.* 'Ophir', dwarf, shrubby, bun-shaped, flat-topped, gold-yellow needles, slightly twisted, light green in summer, 60cm/30cm (2ft/1ft); *P. m.* var. *pumilio*, very dark green needles, pure white, resin-covered winter buds, tiny, rounded female cones, 2.5cm (1in) long, purple at first, later dark brown, 2m/3m (6½ft/10ft); *P. nigra* (Austrian Pine), two-needled, hardy, large tree, rigid, dark green needles, long, ovoid, yellow-brown cones, 30m/6-8m (100ft/20-

25ft); *P. parviflora* (Japanese White Pine) 'Adcock's Dwarf', five-needled, hardy, slow-growing, compact, erect shrub, grey-green needles in dense bunches, 2.4m/1.2m (6¾ft/4ft); *P. p.* f. *glauca*, blue-green needles, 12m (40ft); *P. pumila* (Dwarf Siberian Pine), five-needled, 'Glauca', hardy, very slow-growing, dark green needles with blue-green inner stripe, on upward-sweeping branches, give an overall blue-grey appearance, clusters of rounded cones, purple-violet at first, later dull brown, 2m/1m (6½ft/3ft); *P. radiata* (Monterey Pine), three-needled, hardy, fast-growing tree, glossy, bright green needles, ovoid, yellow-brown, glossy female cones, 25-40m/8-12m (80-130ft/26½-40ft); *P. strobus* (White Pine), 'Radiata', five-needled, dwarf, very slow-growing, compact bush, blue needles with grey-white inner surface, held upwards at the tips, 1.5m/1.5m (5ft/5ft); *P. sylvestris* (Scots Pine), two-needled, hardy tree, best suited to very large gardens or parks, very fast-growing when young, long, stiff, twisted, grey-green or blue-green needles, radially arranged, egg-shaped cones, green at first, later brown, 35m/4m (115ft/13ft); *P. s.* 'Aurea', bright gold-yellow in winter; *P. s.* 'Fastigiata', narrow tree, smaller than species and suited to medium to large gardens, 15m (50ft); *P. s.* 'Watereri', dwarf, erect, conical when young, later rounded, stiff, slightly twisted blue-grey needles, 4m/4m (13ft/13ft); *P wallichiana* (Bhutan Pine), five-needled, a sumptuous hardy tree, blue-green, slender needles, becoming pendent with age, banana-shaped female cones, green, later brown, with forward-pointing scales, 30m/8m (100ft/26½ft).

Pisum *Pea* Papilionaceae

Half-hardy to hardy climbing annual vegetable. White flowers, followed by seedpods, usually stiff with parchment-like walls containing edible seeds; seedpods of some varieties (sugar-pod or mangetout varieties) are tender enough to be edible. Thrives in light, well-drained but rich and moisture-retentive soil in sun or very light shade. Sow seed of hardiest varieties in growing positions in autumn or other varieties from early spring to mid-summer; only smooth-seeded types are hardy enough for autumn or early spring sowing; wrinkled-seeded varieties are less hardy. Round-Seeded First Early Varieties, for harvesting from late spring to early summer after autumn, or early spring sowing with cloches: ❀ 'Douce Provence'; 'Feltham First'; 'Fortune'; 'Meteor'. Wrinkled-Seeded First Early varieties, for harvesting early summer after spring sowing: 'Early Onward'; 'Kelvedon Wonder'; 'Pioneer'. Second Early Varieties, for harvesting around and shortly after mid-summer: 'Hurst Green Shaft'; 'Onward'. Maincrop varieties for harvesting late summer and early autumn: 'Alderman'; 'Cavalier'. Other Varieties (sow as maincrop): 'Markana', semi-leafless; 'Oregon Sugar Pod', dwarf sugar pod; 'Sugar Bon', dwarf sugar pod; 'Sugar Snap', tall sugar pod; 'Waverex', petit pois.

Pittosporum Pittosporaceae

Large evergreen shrubs and small trees. Barely hardy to moderately hardy and among the loveliest shrubs that I am unable to grow in my own garden. In milder areas, they are splendid as specimen plants and, in coastal areas especially, as hedging. Glossy, sometimes leathery leaves, fragrant, five-petalled flowers, singly or in clusters, followed by rounded fruit. Thrive in fertile, well-drained soil in full sun. No routine pruning but hedges should be clipped lightly once each year. Sow seed in a cold-frame when ripe or in spring, take semi-ripe cuttings in summer or layer. ❀ *P.* 'Garnettii', large shrub, oblong to elliptic, grey-green leaves with pink markings, cream margins, bell-shaped red flowers, late spring to early summer, brown fruit, probably the best, 3-5m/2-4m (10-16ft/6½-13ft); *P. tenuifolium*, large shrub or small tree, wavy-

below Pea 'Sugar Bon' The sugar snap pea varieties have appealing, crunchy, edible pods; unfortunately, many are very tall growing although 'Sugar Bon' and others are dwarf varieties.

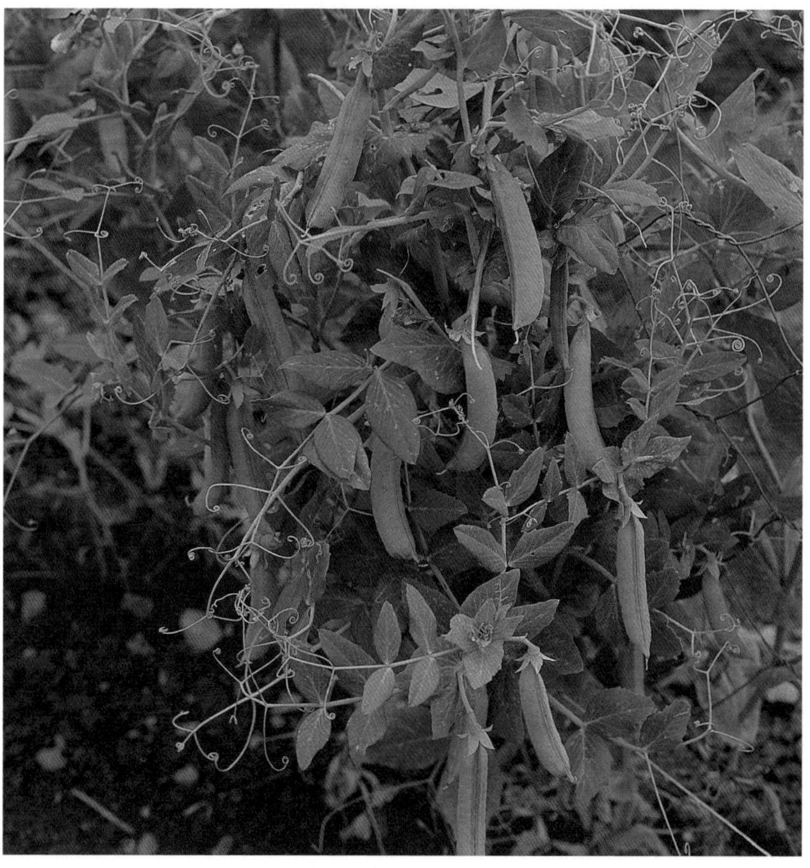

edged, glossy, pale green to mid-green leaves on black branches, dark red-purple flowers, scented of honey, grey-black fruit, late spring to early summer, 4-10m/2-5m (13-33ft/6½-16ft); *P. t.* 'Irene Paterson', leaves cream at first, later green with white marbling, pink tinged in winter, dark red flowers, 1.2m/60cm (4ft/2ft); *P. t.* 'Tom Thumb', dwarf, leaves green at first, later red-purple, dark red flowers with yellow anthers, 1m/60cm (3ft/2ft); *P. tobira*, large shrub or small tree, glossy, bright green leaves, paler beneath, recurved margins, clusters of fragrant, bell-shaped, cream-white flowers, late spring to early summer, rounded yellow-brown fruit, 2-10m/1.5-3m (6½-33ft/5-10ft); *P. t.* 'Variegatum', grey-green leaves with cream margins.

above *Plantago major* 'Rubrifolia'. This really is rather an impressive plant; one scarcely to be associated with its normal green-leaved weedy relative.

Plantago
Plantain Plantaginaceae

Annuals, biennials, evergreen perennials and shrubs but maligned and neglected because some are troublesome weeds, especially on lawns. Moderately hardy. Grown for their foliage, they are suitable for herbaceous borders, smaller species for rock gardens or wall crevices. Rosettes of linear or lance-shaped leaves, clusters of tiny, mainly insignificant, tubular flowers, in summer. Sow seed in a cold-frame in autumn, or divide established plants in spring. ❀ *P. asiatica* 'Variegata', perennial, variegated, lance-shaped leaves, minute, green flowers in slender spikes often likened, rather unfortunately, to rats' tails, 15cm/20cm (6in/8in); *P. major* 'Rosularis', leathery, oval or heart-shaped leaves, green flowers form *Zinnia*-like inflorescences, mid- to late summer, 25cm/25cm (10in/10in); *P. m.* 'Rubrifolia', large, broad, deeply veined, dark maroon-red leaves, clusters of green flowers, later green-brown, spiky brown seedheads, 30cm/25cm (1ft/10in).

Platanus *Plane Tree* Platanaceae

Large hardy deciduous trees but much too big for any except the largest gardens. Palmate-lobed green leaves, gold-brown in autumn, inconspicuous flowers followed by fruit. No routine pruning. Sow seeds in autumn or take hardwood cuttings in winter. ❀ *P.* x *hispanica* (syn. *P.* x *acerifolia*) (London Plane), mottled grey-brown to olive-green, flaking bark, bright green leaves, spherical green, then dark brown, pendent fruit, remaining on the tree throughout winter, 30m/20m (100ft/60ft).

Platycodon
Balloon Flower Campanulaceae

Hardy perennial. Toothed, ovate to ovate-lance-shaped leaves, clusters of bell-shaped flowers, very obviously related to *Campanula*. Generally easy but intolerant of heavy or wet soils. Sow seed in flowering positions in spring or divide established plants in summer. ❀ *P. grandiflorus*, clump-forming, blue-green leaves, large, angular, inflated buds open to pale blue flowers, late summer, 60cm/30m (2ft/100ft); *P. g. albus*, white flowers, sometimes flushed blue; *P. g. apoyama*, dwarf perennial, large violet-blue flowers, 20cm (8in); *P. g.* 'Fuji Pink', pale pink; *P. g.* 'Fuji White', white flowers; *P. g.* 'Hakone', double, deep blue flowers; *P. g. mariesii*, very dark blue flowers; *P. g. m. albus*, pure white flowers; *P. g.* 'Park's Double Blue', double, violet-blue flowers.

Pleioblastus Poaceae

Small/large hardy evergreen bamboos and perhaps the most reliable bamboo for European gardens. Linear to lance-shaped leaves, sometimes with bristly margins, on hollow or solid woody culms (canes). Divide established plants in spring. ❀ *P. auricomus* (syn. *Arundinaria auricoma, A. viridistriata*), pale green leaves, striped yellow, canes downy at first, sometimes tinged purple, 1.2m/60cm (4ft/2ft); *P. humilis* var. *pumilus*, (syn. *Arundinaria pumila*), bright green leaves on branched canes, 1m/1m (3ft/3ft); *P. pygmaeus* (syn. *Arundinaria pygmaea*), spreading, mid-green canes, usually solid, downy, mid-green leaves, 40cm/1m (1½ft/3ft); *P. variegatus* (syn. *Arundinaria variegata*), downy leaves, green with white stripes, 1m/1m (3ft/3ft).

Pleione Orchidaceae

Small barely hardy orchids but successful outdoors in rock gardens in milder areas. Among the easiest of terrestrial orchids. Mid-green, pleated, linear to lance-shaped leaves (sometimes only one) from swollen, bulb-like stems (pseudobulbs), most purple or green and pear-shaped. Flowers with central tube have a large lower lip, surrounded by five petals, singly or in clusters. Divide in spring.

left *Pleione formosana.* The only orchids hardy outdoors in our climate are the terrestrial species; and most are very tricky to grow. The pleiones are among the easiest of them.

❀ *P. formosana*, single, white or rose-lilac flowers, white lips with red and yellow ridges and markings, 15cm/30cm (6in/1ft); *P. f.* 'Oriental Splendour', two purple-rose flowers with paler lip, yellow and brown markings; *P. forrestii*, single, pleated lance-shaped leaf, large flowers, singly, ranging in colour from pale to deep orange-yellow, lips dotted with red and brown blotches, 15cm/30cm (6in/1ft).

Plumbago *Leadwort* Plumbaginaceae

Annuals, perennials, evergreen shrubs and climbers. Barely hardy but perfectly successful outdoors in summer in containers. Simple, entire leaves, clusters of five-petalled blue flowers (although less appealing red and white flowered forms also exist). Cut back previous year's growth by half in early spring. Sow seed in warmth in spring or take semi-ripe cuttings in summer. ❀ *P. auriculata* (syn. *P. capensis*), evergreen shrub, usually grown as a climber, narrow, oblong to more or less lance-shaped green leaves, sometimes tinged blue, clusters of slender, long-tubed sky-blue flowers, summer to autumn, 3-6m/1-3m (10-20ft/3-10ft).

Polemonium
Jacob's Ladder Polemoniaceae

Small/medium hardy annuals and perennials for mixed borders. Pinnate basal leaves, leaflets in pairs, funnel-, bell-, saucer-shaped or narrow, tubular flowers, spring and summer. Sow seed in autumn or divide established plants in spring. Self-seed freely and need watching carefully. ❀ *P. caeruleum*, bipinnate leaves, with oblong-lance-shaped leaflets, clusters of lavender-blue flowers with yellow stamens, in early summer, 30-90cm/30cm (1-3ft/1ft); *P. c.* ssp. *caeruleum* f. *album*, white flowers; *P. carneum*, clump-forming, divided, pinnate leaves with elliptic to ovate leaflets, bell-shaped, silky, salmon-pink, yellow or purple-lavender flowers, with yellow stamens, early summer, 10-40cm (4in-1½ft); *P. pauciflorum*, short-lived perennial, pinnate leaves with elliptic-lance-shaped leaflets, clusters of soft yellow, tubular flowers, sometimes flushed red-pink, early to late summer, 50cm/50cm (1¾ft/1¾ft); *P. reptans*, clusters of pendent, tubular, pale blue flowers, 45cm/45cm (1½ft/1½ft).

left *Polemonium carneum.* I find the flowers of this North American species have the most beautiful texture in the genus.

above *Polygonatum verticillatum*. All of the polygonatums are good plants for shaded borders but the foliage of this species is particularly attractive and it is unjustifiably neglected.

Polygala *Milkwort* Polygalaceae

Annuals, evergreen perennials and hardy rock garden shrubs with striking bicoloured little flowers that always arouse comment. Linear to rounded, sometimes leathery leaves, clusters of pea-like flowers, in spring and summer. No routine pruning. Sow seeds in autumn or take heeled softwood cuttings in early summer. ❀ *P. chamaebuxus*, small, spreading, evergreen shrub, dark green, leathery, oval to lance-shaped leaves, flowers with bright yellow or white lips, wings bright yellow at first, later brown, singly or in pairs, 5-15cm/30cm (2-6in/1ft); *P. c.* var. *grandiflora*, yellow lip, deep purple-pink wings.

Polygonatum
Solomon's Seal Convallariaceae

Small/large moderately hardy or hardy rhizomatous ornamentals and excellent plants for shady places; if the attacks of the Solomon's Seal sawfly don't create havoc with the foliage. Linear to elliptic or ovate leaves on arching stems, pendent to erect bell-shaped flowers, singly or in clusters, followed by red or black fruits. All parts of the plant are toxic if eaten. Sow seed in a cold-frame in autumn, or divide established plants in early spring. ❀ *P. falcatum*, clump-forming, lance-shaped or sickle-shaped, narrow green leaves, small white pendent flowers beneath erect stems, early summer, small fruits, 1m/45cm (3ft/1½ft); *P. f.* 'Variegatum', oval leaves edged with cream-yellow, on stems flushed with pink, 90cm/45cm (3ft/1½ft); *P. hookeri*, spreading, mid-green, lance-shaped leaves on erect stems, short-stemmed tubular, white or pink flowers with spreading petals, late spring to early summer, followed by rounded black fruits, 10cm/30cm (4in/1ft); *P.* x *hybridum* (syn. *P. multiflorum*), ovate to lance-shaped, mid-green leaves on slightly arching stems, tubular to bell-shaped white flowers, flushed green, hang beneath the stems in late spring, followed by spherical blue-black fruits, 1.5m/30m (5ft/100ft); *P. odoratum* 'Variegatum', oval or lance-shaped leaves with cream-white margins, on arching stems flushed with red, fragrant white, green-tipped pendent flowers in spring, spherical black fruits, 85cm/30cm (2¾ft/1ft); *P. verticillatum*, erect perennial, mid-green, narrow, pointed lance-shaped leaves, pendent, bell-shaped, green-white flowers, late spring to mid-summer, small red fruits, 20-90cm/25cm (8in-3ft/10in).

Polypodium *Polypody* Polypodiaceae

Small hardy deciduous/evergreen ferns and a genus that includes some of the most valuable hardy garden species as they are both lime and dryness tolerant. Suitable for rock gardens, mixed borders and plantings in open, sunny places. Lance-shaped, simple to finely divided or pinnate fronds. Divide established plants in spring or early summer. ❀ *P. cambricum* (syn. *P. australe*) (Welsh Polypody), deciduous, mid-green, lance-shaped to triangular-ovate, pinnate fronds, slightly toothed, fertile fronds are produced in late summer, 15-60cm (6in-2ft)/indefinite; *P. interjectum* 'Cornubiense', mat-forming, bright green, ovate-triangular, deeply lobed fronds, good for ground cover and I think the loveliest form, 40cm/60cm

(1½ft/2ft); *P. vulgare* (Common Polypody), evergreen, thin to leathery, lance-shaped to oblong, deeply divided leaves, suitable for growing on rocks and trees, 30cm (1ft)/indefinite; *P. v.* 'Cornubiense Grandiceps', three-pinnate fronds, with terminal crests.

Polystichum *Holly Fern* Aspidiaceae

Small/medium hardy deciduous or evergreen ferns for rock gardens or shaded borders. Lance-shaped, pinnate to tri-pinnate fronds, usually forming shuttlecock-shaped crowns. Divide established plants in spring. ❀ *P. aculeatum*, evergreen, glossy, dark green, leathery, lance-shaped pinnate or bipinnate fronds, 50cm/30cm(1¾ft/1ft); *P. polyblepharum*, evergreen, spreading, lance-shaped, bipinnate, slightly toothed, glossy dark green fronds, 60-80cm/90cm (2-2½ft/3ft); *P. setiferum*, the species that I believe includes some of the best all-round garden ferns, evergreen, bipinnate, dark green, bristly toothed fronds, 1.2m/90cm (4ft/3ft); *P. s.* Acutilobum Group, lance-shaped-ovate leaflets, fronds slightly horizontal; *P. s.* Congestum Group, tightly rolled fronds giving a congested but very attractive clump; *P. s.* Divisilobum Group, spreading, three-pinnate fronds, bulbils sometimes form along the mid-ribs, 50-70cm (1¾-2¼ft); *P. s.* Plumosum Group, very feathery, bright green fronds, pale chestnut-brown scales beneath, 60cm (2ft); *P. tsussimense*, evergreen lance-shaped bipinnate, dark green fronds, 40cm/40cm (1½ft/1½ft).

Populus *Poplar* Salicaceae

Large moderately hardy to very hardy deciduous trees. Poplars make very good windbreaks and are good in coastal sites but almost all are trees for large gardens only and their high water demand means they should not be placed near to buildings. Ovate, ovate-triangular or diamond-shaped leaves, sometimes aromatic when young. Tiny insignificant male and female flowers form catkins on separate trees, on bare branches in early spring. Male catkins are red, green female catkins are followed by strings of green seed capsules. No routine pruning and tend to produce suckers when cut back. Take hardwood cuttings in winter. ❀ *P. alba* (White Poplar), ovate to rounded, deeply lobed, maple-like, dark green leaves, white, woolly beneath, yellow in autumn, 20-40m/15m (60-130ft/50ft); *P.* x *canadensis* (Canadian Poplar), 'Aurea', (syn. *P.* x *c.* 'Serotina Aurea') pale, clear yellow, triangular to ovate leaves with scalloped edges, gold in autumn, 20m/10m (60ft/33ft); *P.* x *candicans* 'Aurora', the best poplar for gardens, white, pink and cream variegated, pine-scented leaves, ovate with heart-shaped bases, 30m/15m (100ft/50ft); *P. lasiocarpa* (Chinese Necklace Poplar), rounded or heart-shaped to triangular leaves, bright green with red veining, yellow-green catkins, usually with both male and female flowers, in mid-spring, 20m/12m (60ft/40ft); *P. nigra* var. *italica* (Lombardy Poplar), male, tapered, although opening out with age, triangular to ovate, glossy leaves, bronze when young, later dark green, yellow in autumn, 30m/10m (100ft/33f); *P. tremula* (Aspen), toothed, ovate leaves, bronze when young, later dark green, clear butter yellow in autumn, trembling in the breeze, 20m/7m (60ft/23ft).

above *Polysitchum setiferum* 'Divisilobum'. Perhaps the most variable of all ferns, but one of the easiest.

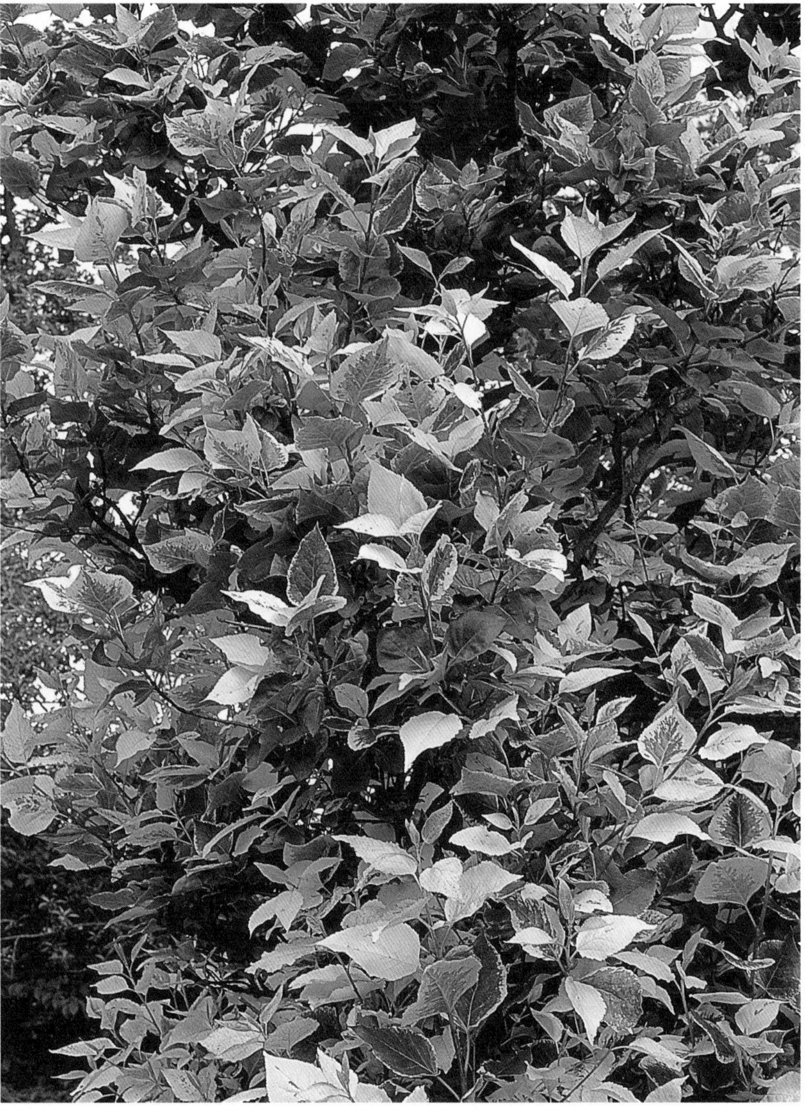

below Few poplars make good garden trees, but *Populus x candicans* 'Aurora' is an exception.

right *Potentilla fruticosa* 'Manchu'. My favourite, I think, among a large group of long-flowering summer shrubs.

Portulaca *Purslane* Portulacaceae

Small half-hardy annuals and perennials for summer bedding and containers. Most species are succulent or semi-succulent. Small, fleshy, rather moss-like leaves, cup-shaped flowers, closing in dull weather. Sow seed in warmth in mid-spring. ❀ *P. grandiflora* 'Double Mixed', cylindrical, bright green leaves on red stems abundant semi-double, saucer-shaped ruffled flowers, white and shades of red, pink, or orange, mid-summer to early autumn, 10-20cm/15cm (4-8in/6in); *P. g.* 'Sundial' F1, large double flowers in a variety of colours, including cream, pink, orange, scarlet, yellow and white with pink stripes, drought resistant, 10-15cm (4-6in); *P. g.* 'Peppermint', double white flowers with pink stripes; *P. g.* 'Cloudbeater', double flowers, white and shades of red, pink, or orange, more likely to remain open in dull weather.

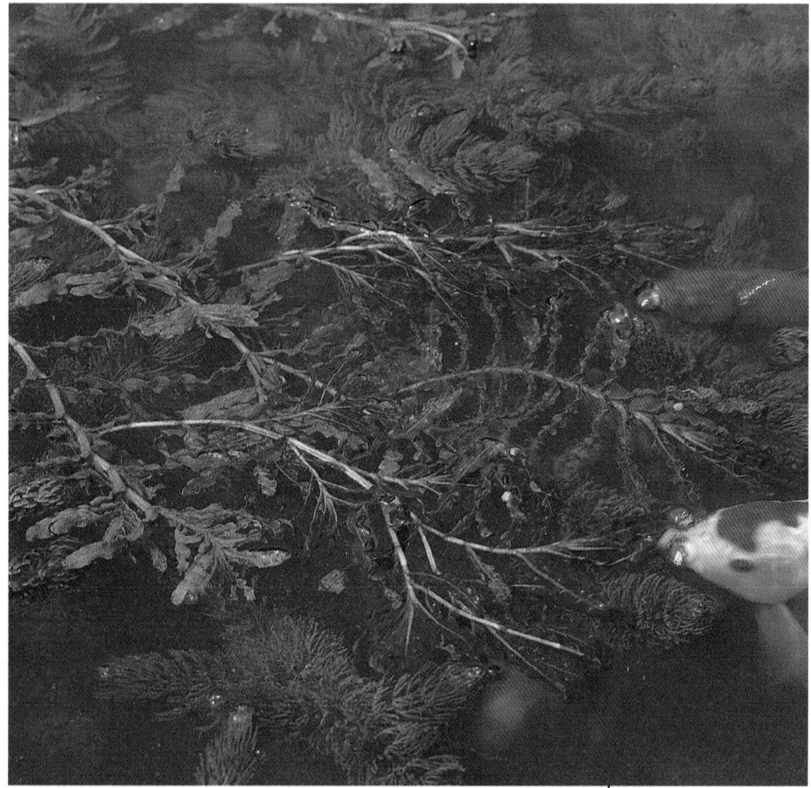

above *Potamogeton crispus*. Not many people would consider this among the most beautiful of water plants but its foliage is rather appealing and it is easy to grow to the point almost of invasiveness.

Potamogeton *Pondweed* Potamogetonaceae

Medium, deciduous submerged water plant. Very hardy. Suitable for large pools and lakes. Strap-like, wavy-edged, dark green leaves, spikes of small, green-white flowers held above the water surface, summer. Divide established plants in spring. ❀ *P. crispus*, narrow, grass-like leaves with wavy edges, spread 1-2m (3-6½ft).

Potentilla *Cinquefoil* Rosaceae

Hardy annuals, biennials, herbaceous perennials, alpines and shrubs and one of the most valuable genera in a very valuable family. Suitable for herbaceous and shrub borders, hedging or rock gardens. Pinnate or palmate leaves, sometimes wrinkled, saucer- cup- or star-shaped flowers, in white, pink, orange, red or yellow. Thrive in well-drained, poor to fairly fertile soil, but do need full sun. Species suitable for rock gardens require gritty, well-drained soil. No routine pruning. Sow seed in a cold-frame in spring (annuals and perennials); divide established plants in early spring (perennials and alpines); take semi-ripe cuttings in late spring or summer or layer (shrubs). ❀ *P. alba*, low-growing, clump-forming perennial, palmate, dark green leaves, silver-grey beneath, white, saucer-shaped flowers with yellow centres, mid-summer, 8cm/30cm (3¼in/1ft); *P. atrosanguinea*, clump-forming perennial, dark green, palmate, toothed, hairy leaves, clusters of yellow, orange and red flowers, summer to autumn, 45-90cm/60cm (1½-3ft/2ft); *P. a.* var. *argyrophylla*, yellow or orange-yellow flowers; *P. cuneata* (syn. *P. ambigua*), mat-forming perennial, small, mid-green, palmate leaves, bright yellow flowers, 10cm/20cm (4in/8in); *P. eriocarpa*, small, bright green to blue-green toothed leaves, cup-shaped, deep yellow flowers, singly or in clusters, early summer, 8cm/30cm (3¼in/1ft); *P. fruticosa* 'Abbotswood', compact deciduous shrub, dark blue-green pinnate leaves with oblong leaflets, saucer-shaped white flowers, 75cm/1.2m (2½ft/4ft); *P. f.* 'Daydawn', cream or peach-pink flowers; *P. f.* 'Elizabeth', grey-green leaves, large canary yellow flowers; *P. f.* 'Goldfinger', dwarf, blue-green leaves, large, rich yellow flowers; *P. f.* 'Manchu', (syn. *P.* 'Mandshurica'),dwarf, spreading, grey-green leaves, pure white flowers, probably the most undervalued of the shrubby forms, an excellent plant; *P. f.* 'Primrose Beauty', grey-green leaves, pale primrose-yellow flowers on arching branches; *P. f.* 'Tangerine', low-growing, large, copper-yellow flowers; *P. f.* 'Tilford Cream', deep green leaves, large cream-yellow flowers; *P. megalantha* (syn. *P. fragiformis*), clump-forming perennial, glossy, palmate, mid-green leaves, rich yellow flowers, summer, 45cm/60cm (1½ft/2ft); *P. neumanniana* 'Nana' (syn. *P. verna* 'Pygmaea'), compact, mat-forming perennial, bright green palmate leaves with toothed leaflets, clusters of saucer-shaped yellow flowers, spring to late summer, 8cm/15cm (3¼in/6in); *P. n.* 'Miss Willmott', rose-pink flowers with a darker pink centre, 30-45cm (12-1½ft); *P. recta pallida* (syn. *P. r.* var. *sulphurea*), clump-forming perennial, hairy, grey-green to mid-green palmate leaves, pale yellow flowers, mid-summer, 60cm/45cm (2ft/1½ft); *P. rupestris*, rosettes of pinnate, toothed leaves, white flowers, 45cm/30cm (1½ft/1ft); *P.* x *tonguei*, clump-forming perennial, palmate, dark green leaves, clusters of bow-shaped apricot flowers with deep red eyes, 10cm/30cm (4in/1ft).

Pratia — Campanulaceae

Small evergreen hardy alpines. Ovate to rounded leaves, sometimes toothed, abundant two-lipped, star-shaped flowers. Divide established plants in spring or autumn. ❀ *P. pedunculata* (syn. *Lobelia pedunculata*), prostrate, creeping, toothed, ovate to rounded leaves, star-shaped, pale blue flowers, summer, invasive, 2cm (¾in)/indefinite; *P. p.* 'County Park', fragrant, violet-blue flowers.

Primula — Primulaceae

Half-hardy and hardy or very hardy herbaceous and evergreen perennials and alpines. *Primula* has been described as the most valuable genus of garden ornamentals and there are species suitable for a wide variety of habitats, from rock gardens to borders, woodland and water-side plantings and containers. Basal rosettes of light to dark green linear to ovate to more or less oval leaves, bell- or funnel-shaped, tubular or dish-shaped flowers, singly or in clusters of varying and characteristic form. Among the commonest types, the Primroses have flowers borne more or less individually on their stems, the Candelabra primulas have the flowers in distinct whorls along the stem and the Polyanthas a multiple head of small, characteristically primrose-like flowers. Leaves, stems and flowers of some species are covered with a silvery mealy wax called farina. Cultural requirements vary; in general, alpine species require well-drained, gritty soil enriched with humus, in partial shade; species and varieties grown in containers require peat-or loam-based compost with added leaf mould and grit; border primulas are best in most fertile, moisture-retentive soils in full sun or partial shade (depending on species). Sow ripe seed on surface of compost at cool temperatures (germination is suppressed above 20°C (68°F)) or divide established plants after flowering. ❀ *P. allionii*, evergreen alpine, grey-green, inversely-lance-shaped, sticky, hairy leaves, sometimes scalloped or toothed, umbels of white, pink or red-purple dish-shaped flowers with white centres, late winter to early spring, requires alkaline soil, 5-7cm/20cm (2-2¾in/8in). This species has given rise to a large number of varieties, with flowers ranging from white to shades of violet, pink, purple and red, many with contrasting eyes. *P. auricula* (Auricula), evergreen alpine, rosettes of leathery, oblong, entire or toothed, sometimes mealy, mid-green pointed leaves, trumpet-shaped flowers with a white mealy eye, 20cm/25cm

below *Primula* 'Wanda Jack-in-the-Green'. The inflated green calyx form called 'Jack-in-the-Green' has been known in the primrose for many centuries and occurs also in the popular related hybrid 'Wanda'.

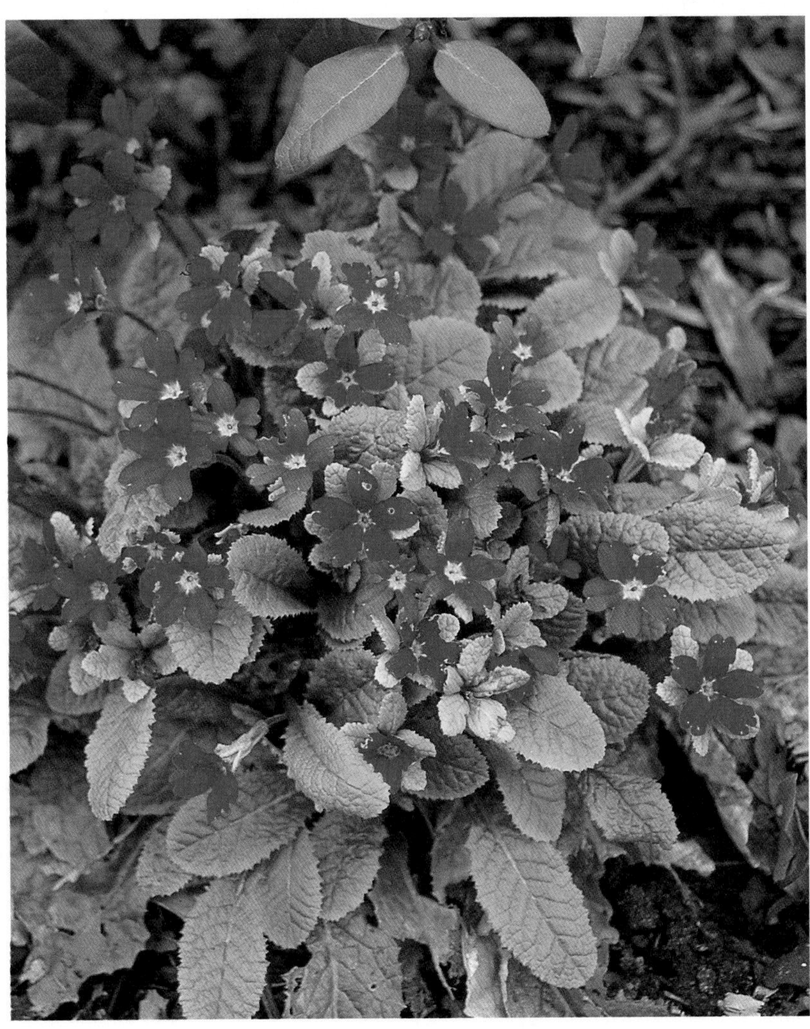

above *Primula* Gold Laced Group. Perhaps the most appealing of all the Polyantha types is this lovely form, surprisingly easy to raise from seed.

(8in/10in). Varieties derived from *P. auricula* form a complex group. They are hardy but, apart from the border auriculas, must be protected by growing in warmth; the flowers usually have several circlets of colour and a velvety appearance. The amount of farina increases from little in the border auriculas, though a moderate amount in the alpine auriculas, to a thick covering in the cosseted indoor show auriculas. *P. beesiana*, semi-evergreen candelabra, inversely lance-shaped to elliptic toothed leaves, mealy clusters of deep rose flowers with a yellow eye, 60cm/25cm (2ft/10in); *P. bulleyana*, semi-evergreen candelabra, mealy stems, rosettes of ovate to ovate-lance-shaped, toothed, mid-green leaves, red buds opening to gold-yellow flowers, summer, 60cm/25cm (2ft/10in); *P. chionantha*, deciduous, mid-green, toothed or entire inversely lance-shaped leaves, dark purple, tubular flowers on a mealy stem, late spring to early autumn, 30cm/15cm (1ft/6in); *P. cockburniana*, deciduous and sadly short-lived candelabra, oblong, to oblong-ovate mid-green leaves, orange-red flowers on mealy stems, summer, 3cm/15cm (1¼in/6in); *P.* 'Dawn Ansell', semi-evergreen primrose, double white flowers enclosed in a ruff of green leaves, early to mid-spring, 10-15cm/25cm (4-6in/10in); *P. denticulata*, deciduous, rosettes of finely toothed, slightly hairy, oblong-ovate or spoon-shaped, mid-green leaves, round clusters of pink to purple flowers on relatively tall stems, early spring to early summer, 45cm/25cm (1½ft/10in); *P. d.* var. *alba*, white flowers; *P. elatior* (Oxlip), semi-evergreen or evergreen, toothed, hairy, prominently veined ovate to oblong or elliptic mid-green leaves, clusters of funnel-shaped yellow flowers down one side of the stem, spring and summer, 25cm/20cm (10in/8in); *P. farinosa* (Bird's-Eye Primrose), deciduous, rosettes of inversely lance-shaped slightly mealy mid-green leaves, sometimes toothed, umbels of saucer-shaped, pink-purple flowers with yellow eyes, summer, 25cm/20cm (10in/8in); *P.* Gold Laced Group, polyantha, green leaves edged with gold, very dark brown-purple flowers, deep gold eye, 15-20cm/25cm (6-8in/10in); *P. japonica*, deciduous candelabra, pale green, toothed, more or less oval, oblong or spoon-shaped leaves, red-purple, white or pink flowers with a darker eye, on green or red-green stems leaves, late spring to early summer, 45cm/30cm (1½ft/1ft); *P. j.* 'Miller's Crimson', dark red flowers; *P. j.* 'Postford White', large white flowers, yellow eye; *P. juliae*, creeping, stoloniferous semi-evergreen, toothed, rounded leaves, deep magenta flowers with a yellow eye, mid- to late spring, a parent of many modern primrose varieties, 15cm/20cm (6in/8in). *P. marginata*, evergreen or semi-evergreen, rosettes of leathery, oblong to more or less oval, toothed mid-green leaves, mealy on the edges, umbels of fragrant, tubular to funnel-shaped flowers on mealy stems, lavender-blue with white mealy eyes, 15cm/30cm (6in/1ft). There are numerous varieties in a range of colours, including 'Kesselring's Variety', deep lavender-blue flowers, and 'Holden Variety', funnel-shaped dark blue flowers; *P.* 'Marie Crousse', primrose, double violet flowers with white margins; *P.* 'Miss Indigo', primrose, double, deep blue flowers with white margins; *P. polyneura*, deciduous, dark green, ovate to rounded hairy leaves, umbels of pale pink to crimson flowers, green-yellow eye, early summer, 40cm/20cm (1½ft/8in); *P. prolifera* (syn. *P. helodoxa*), evergreen candelabra, diamond-shaped, toothed, dark green leaves, slightly pendent,

right *Primula cockburniana*. My only wish is that this delightful little Chinese species was longer lived.

fragrant, mealy, yellow flowers, 75cm/20cm (2½ft/8in); *P.* x *pubescens*, evergreen perennial, rosettes of more or less oval to spoon-shaped mid-green leaves, umbels of dish-shaped flowers; numerous varieties in various shades of red, white, brown, purple, yellow and pink, spring, 15cm/30cm (6in/1ft); *P. pulverulenta*, large, deciduous candelabra, rosettes of inversely lance-shaped leaves, tubular, red or red-purple flowers with darker eyes, from late spring to summer, 1m/60cm (3ft/2ft); *P. rosea*, deciduous, rosettes of glossy, oval leaves, clusters of large, vivid rose flowers, yellow eyes, late spring, good for bog gardens and water margins, 15cm/20cm (6in/8in); *P. sieboldii*, deciduous, pale green, oval, hairy leaves, with toothed, wavy margins, flowers in shades of pink and purple, with white eyes; a range of varieties thrive in moist, shady conditions, 20cm/20cm (8in/8in). *P. sikkimensis*, deciduous, oval, pale green leaves, pendent clusters of tubular, yellow or cream flowers, late spring to early summer, 40cm/20cm (1½ft/8in); *P.* 'Val Horncastle', semi-evergreen primrose, double cream and yellow flowers, from early to mid-spring, 10-15cm/25cm (4-6in/10in); *P. veris* (Cowslip), evergreen or semi-evergreen, dull green leaves, loose heads of up to 16 nodding yellow flowers, best in light, drier soils, late spring to summer, 30cm/15cm (1ft/6in); *P. vulgaris* (Primrose), evergreen or semi-evergreen, bright green leaves, scalloped with prominent veining, hairy beneath, clusters of dish-shaped, sometimes fragrant, pale yellow flowers, best in heavier, slightly shaded places, early winter to early summer, 20cm/35cm (8in/1¼ft). *P. vulgaris* has produced numerous varieties, many with double flowers, including 'Double Sulphur', yellow flowers, 'Double White', white flowers, and 'Jack in the Green', single yellow flowers surrounded by green bracts; these varieties must all be divided frequently to maintain their vigour; *P.* 'Wanda', primrose, very dark leaves, very deep red-purple flowers, early to late spring, 15-20cm/25cm (6-8in/10in).

Prunella *Self Heal* Lamiaceae

Small hardy herbaceous ground cover perennials. Oval to linear-lance-shaped leaves, sometimes toothed or lobed, two-lipped, tubular, white, purple or pink flowers. Many people have a skin allergy to the foliage. Sow seed in warmth in spring or divide established plants in spring or autumn. ❀ *P. grandiflora*, spreading, slightly toothed, oval, deep green leaves, clusters of violet flowers, with darker lips, summer, 15cm/1m (6in/3ft); *P. g.* 'Loveliness', pale violet-blue flowers, *P. g.* 'White Loveliness', white flowers; *P. vulgaris* (syn. *P. incisa*), creeping, deeply cut, oblong-oval, toothed leaves, clusters of deep purple flowers, summer to autumn, 50cm (1¾ft)/indefinite.

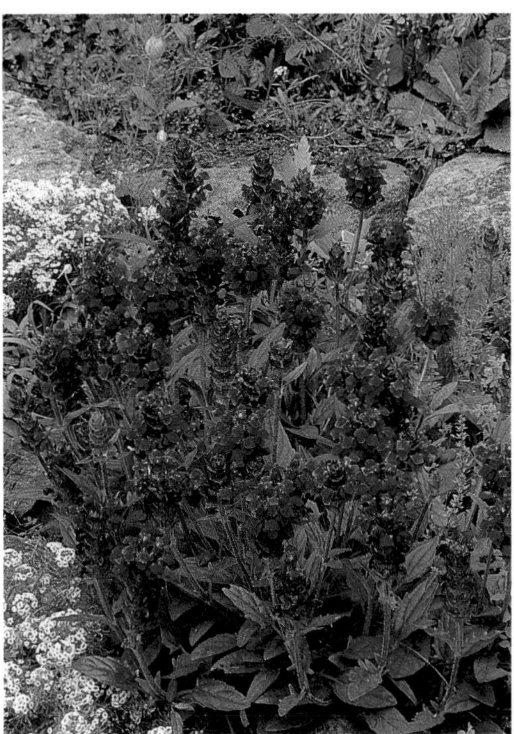

left *Prunella grandiflora*. An aptly named, and very much grander relative of the familiar native self-heal.

Prunus Rosaceae

Deciduous or evergreen shrubs and trees. Barely hardy to hardy. This is a hugely important genus of ornamental and fruiting plants, although their popularity as ornamentals has declined as many varieties have been discovered to age rather unappealingly, and some are prone to bacterial diseases. Most of the popular blossom cherries are also rather dull when out of flower although some have very good autumn leaf colour and a few have very attractive bark. Leaves elliptic, oblong, more or less oval or lance-shaped, sometimes toothed. Single, semi-double or double, cup-, bowl- or saucer-shaped white, pink, sometimes red, flowers are followed by fleshy, spherical fruit. Evergreen species and varieties thrive in moderately fertile, moist, well-drained soil in full sun or partial shade, deciduous species and varieties are generally best in full sun. No routine pruning apart from formative pruning of fruiting trees and maintenance pruning of wall-trained fruits; details are given in the companion volume. Evergreen species grown as hedges should be clipped twice each year. Many *Prunus* species respond to pruning by producing masses of twiggy growth. Sow seed in a cold-frame in early spring or take semi-ripe cuttings in early

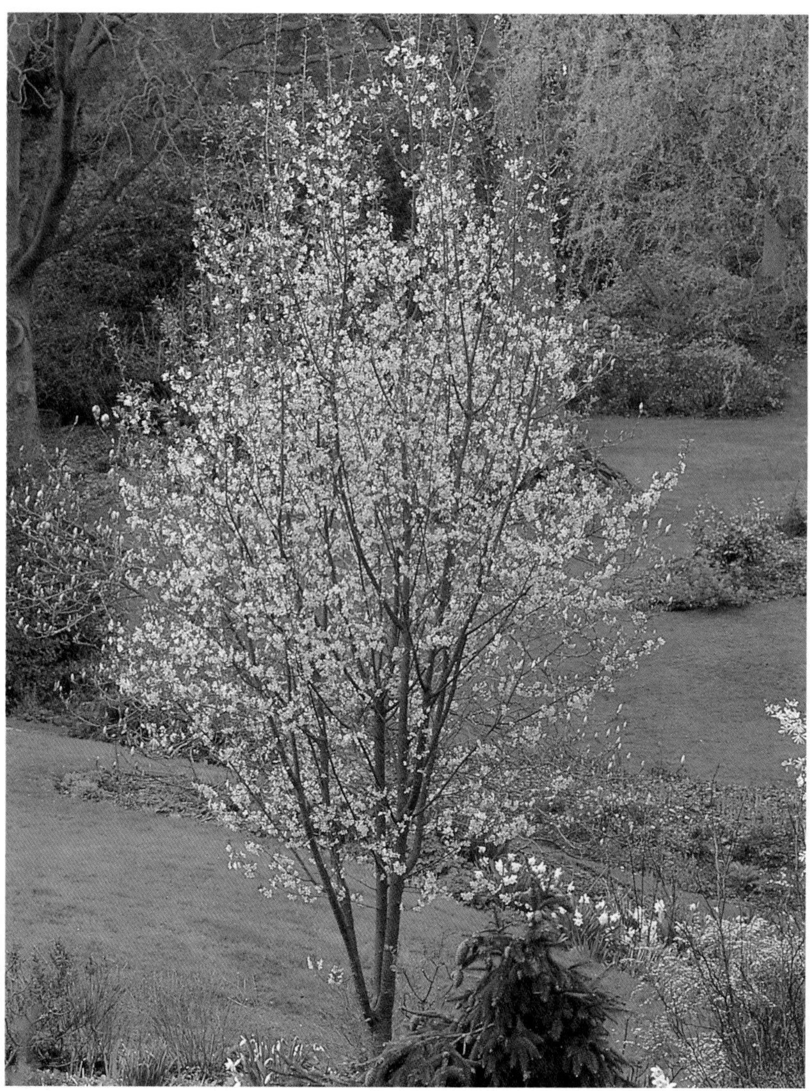

above *Prunus* 'Spire'. One of the best among the newer, upright forms of flowering cherry and a plant that has replaced 'Amanogawa' in many gardens.

summer; most fruiting and ornamental varieties do not come true from seed or strike readily from cuttings and in consequence are grafted but there are no growth-limiting rootstocks with the dwarfing effect of those used with apples.

Ornamentals–Deciduous

The deciduous blossom trees within this group are generally referred to as flowering or ornamental cherries, although strictly some are derived from plums, almonds or other *Prunus* species: ❀ *P.* 'Accolade', spreading, tapering, dark green, oblong leaves with serrated edges, clusters of deep pink buds open to pendent, semi-double, pale pink flowers, early to mid-spring, 8m/8m (26½ft/26½ft); *P.* 'Amanogawa', columnar-fastigiate but opening out with age, more or less oval, toothed leaves, bronze-yellow at first, later mid-green, red, green and yellow autumn colours, erect clusters of slightly fragrant, semi-double shell-pink flowers, late spring, 8m/4m (26½/13ft); *P. cerasifera* (Cherry Plum, Myrobalan), 'Nigra', spreading, more or less oval leaves, red at first, later dark purple, single bowl-shaped, pink flowers, fading to pale pink, early spring on bare branches, sometimes followed by edible red or yellow fruit, 10m/10m (33ft/33ft); *P.* x *cistena* (syn. *P.* 'Crimson Dwarf'), erect shrub, oval leaves, red at first, later red-purple, single white flowers, mid-spring, followed by black-purple fruit, 1.5m/1.5m (5ft/5ft); *P. glandulosa* (Dwarf Flowering Almond), 'Alba Plena', rounded shrub, narrow, elliptic or oval, pale green leaves, abundant pure white double flowers, singly or in pairs, late spring, followed by dark red fruit, 1.5m/1.5m (5ft/5ft); *P.* 'Kiku-shidare-zakura' (syn. *P.* 'Cheal's Weeping'), weeping, the best weeping cherry, lance-shaped, glossy mid-green leaves, bronze-green at first, on arching branches, abundant clusters of double, deep pink flowers, before or with the leaves, mid- to late spring, usually grafted as a standard, 3m/3m (10ft/10ft); *P. sargentii*, spreading, elliptic leaves, bronze-red at first, later dark green, brilliant orange and crimson in autumn, single pink flowers, early spring, 15m/6m (50ft/20ft); *P. serrula*, spreading, wonderful shiny bark, red-brown, resembling polished mahogany, peels off in strips, lance-shaped, dark green leaves, yellow in autumn, fairly insignificant small, single white flowers, late spring, followed by small fruit, 10m/6m (33ft/20ft); *P.* 'Shirofugen', spreading, oblong leaves, bronze-red at first, later dark green, orange-red in autumn, pink buds open to clusters of fragrant, double white flowers, later purple-pink, late spring, 10m/10m (33ft/33ft); *P. spinosa* (Blackthorn, Sloe), erect tree or shrub with very sharp spines, more or less oval to elliptic, dark green leaves, small, white single flowers, on bare branches, early spring, followed by small edible fruit, blue with white bloom at first, later black, 5m/4m (16ft/13ft); *P.* 'Spire' (syn. *P. hillieri* 'Spire'), vase-shaped, conical when young, dark green, more or less oval leaves, bronze at first, orange and red in autumn, clusters of single, so-pink flowers, mid-spring, a fine tree for smaller gardens, better in many ways than 'Amanogawa', 10m/6m (33ft/20ft); *P.* x *subhirtella* 'Autumnalis' (Winter Flowering Cherry), spreading, oval or elliptic, toothed leaves, bronze at first, later dark green, yellow in autumn, clusters of semi-double white flowers tinged pink, between autumn and spring except during periods of hard frost, an attractive tree but rather big and planted too often in tiny gardens, 10m/8m (33ft/26½ft); *P.* x. s. 'Autumnalis Rosea', double blue-pink flowers; *P.* 'Taihaku' (Great White Cherry), spreading, tapering, serrated leaves with thread-like points, copper-green at first, later mid-green, abundant clusters of very large white flowers, mid-spring, 8m/5m (26½ft/16ft); *P. tenella* (Dwarf Russian Almond), 'Fire Hill', bushy, shrub, glossy, dark green, more or less oval to inversely lance-shaped leaves, rose-red flowers, singly or in clusters, mid- to late spring, followed by velvety, grey-yellow, almond-like fruit, 1.5m/1.5m (5ft/5ft); *P. triloba* (Flowering Almond), tree or shrub, mid-green elliptic leaves, paler, hairy beneath, pink flowers, singly or in clusters, early to mid-spring, followed by red fruit, 3m/3m (10ft/10ft).

left *Prunus laurocerasus* 'Otto Luyken'. The best form of this rather useful if rarely spectacular hedging plant.

Ornamentals–Evergreen

❀ *P. laurocerasus* (Cherry Laurel), spreading shrub, glossy, leathery, oblong mid-green leaves, 20cm (8in) long, pale green beneath, erect inflorescences of cup-shaped, fragrant white flowers, mid- to late spring, followed by small, cherry-like fruit, red at first, maturing to black, toxic if eaten, intolerant of chalk soils, prune in mid-spring, 8m/6m (26½ft/20ft); *P. l.* 'Otto Luyken', dense shrub, deep glossy green leaves, up to 10cm (4in) long, white flowers, excellent as a small hedge, 1.5m/1.5m (5ft/5ft).

Fruiting

P. armeniaca (Apricot), hardy, in cold areas best against a sunny wall, although it is hardy enough to be grown as a free-standing tree in many places, oval, glossy, mid- to dark green leaves, clusters of saucer-shaped, five-petalled white flowers, sometimes flushed pink, late winter or early spring, followed by round yellow fruit, flushed red, late summer, 2.5m/3.5m (8ft/11ft); *P. a.* 'Moor Park', the most reliable in most areas.

P. avium (Sweet Cherry, Bird Cherry, Gean), grown as free-standing or fan-trained trees or espaliers, best when grafted on to 'Colt' rootstock which limits trees to about 4m (13ft), must be netted against birds, most are not self-fertile. *P. a.* 'Early Rivers', red-black fruit, early summer, vigorous; *P. a.* 'Merton Glory', yellow-red fruit, early—mid-season; *P. a.* 'Stella', self-fertile, the best for garden use, late, red or dark red fruit.

P. domestica (Plum), grown as bush trees, half-standards or fan-trained trees, usually grafted on to 'St Julien A' or more dwarfing 'Pixie' rootstocks, which limit trees to about 5m (16ft) or 4m (13ft) respectively, oval leaves, green-white flowers, all those I recommend here are self-fertile. *P. d.* 'Cambridge Gage', small, round green-yellow plum, self-fertile but for good crops best planted with another variety such as 'Czar', good for desserts or preserving, harvest late summer; *P. d.* 'Czar', rounded, egg-shaped red fruit with waxy blue bloom, golden flesh, red juice, good cropper, harvest late summer, susceptible to silver leaf; *P. d.* 'Marjorie's Seedling', oval, purple fruit, yellow flesh, all-round variety, heavy cropper; *P. d.* 'Oullins Golden Gage', rounded yellow-gold fruit with brown flecks; *P. d.* 'Victoria', bright red, sometimes flushed yellow, good cropper, excellent dessert and preserving variety, harvest late summer to early autumn, susceptible to silver leaf disease but still the best all-round garden plum; *P. d.* 'Warwickshire Drooper', marked drooping habit, egg-shaped yellow fruit with brown flecks, late.

P. dulcis (Almond), more or less lance-shaped, toothed leaves, pink or white flowers, singly or in pairs, on bare branches, fruits unreliably in all except milder areas, 8m/5m (26½ft/16ft).

P. insititia (Damson, Bullace), *P. i.* 'Merryweather', black, good for dessert and preserving, self-fertile, harvest late summer early autumn, much the best damson for garden use; *P. i.* 'Prune Damson', smaller and less sweet than 'Merryweather', never sweet enough to eat uncooked.

P. persica (Peach), lance-shaped, tapering leaves, white to pale pink flowers, singly or in pairs, spring, in cold areas best grown fan-trained against a warm south or south-west wall, 8m/6m (25ft/20ft). *P. d.* 'Peregrine', large, crimson fruit; *P.* 'Rochester' late flowering, hardier than 'Peregrine'; *P. p.* var. *nectarina* (Nectarine), a smooth skinned variant of the peach, grown in the same way; *P. n.* 'Lord Napier', large, pale yellow, flushed brown, white aromatic flesh, reliable, self-fertile; *P. n.* 'Pineapple', later and better in warmer areas for its longer season.

below *Prunus x cistena.* One of the best small *Prunus* hybrids for growing in gardens with limited space.

right *Psylliostachys suworowii.* Quite one of the loveliest of all annuals and I am amazed year after year that seed companies don't make more of it.

Pseudotsuga Pinaceae

Small/large evergreen trees. Moderately hardy to very hardy. Magnificent trees when well grown but only as specimens in the largest gardens; in the forest, the tallest trees in Britain; be warned. Pointed, scaled buds open to linear to oblong aromatic needles. Insignificant male and female flowers, followed by cones. No routine pruning. Sow seeds in a cold-frame in spring. ❀ *P. menziesii* (Douglas Fir), bark smooth at first, later corky, with deep fissures, needles soft, dark green, in pairs, with two silver-white stripes beneath, erect, red female flowers, followed by pendent female cones, pointed bracts, 25-50m/6-10m (80-165ft/20-33ft); *P. m.* 'Glauca Pendula', small, weeping, silver-blue needles, 10m (33ft).

Psylliostachys Plumbaginaceae

Small half-hardy and hardy annuals. Oblong to lance-shaped, light to mid-green leaves, elongated inflorescences of tiny, tubular flowers, spring to summer. Sow seed in warmth in spring. ❀ *P. suworowii* (syns. *Statice suworowii, Limonium suworowii*), half-hardy, rosettes of light green, slightly lobed basal leaves, branching spikes of rose-pink flowers, summer to autumn, a wonderful plant, far too little known, 30-45cm/30cm (12in-1½ft/1ft).

below *Pulmonaria* 'Mawson's Blue'. Among the finest coloured forms in a popular genus of early spring flowering perennials.

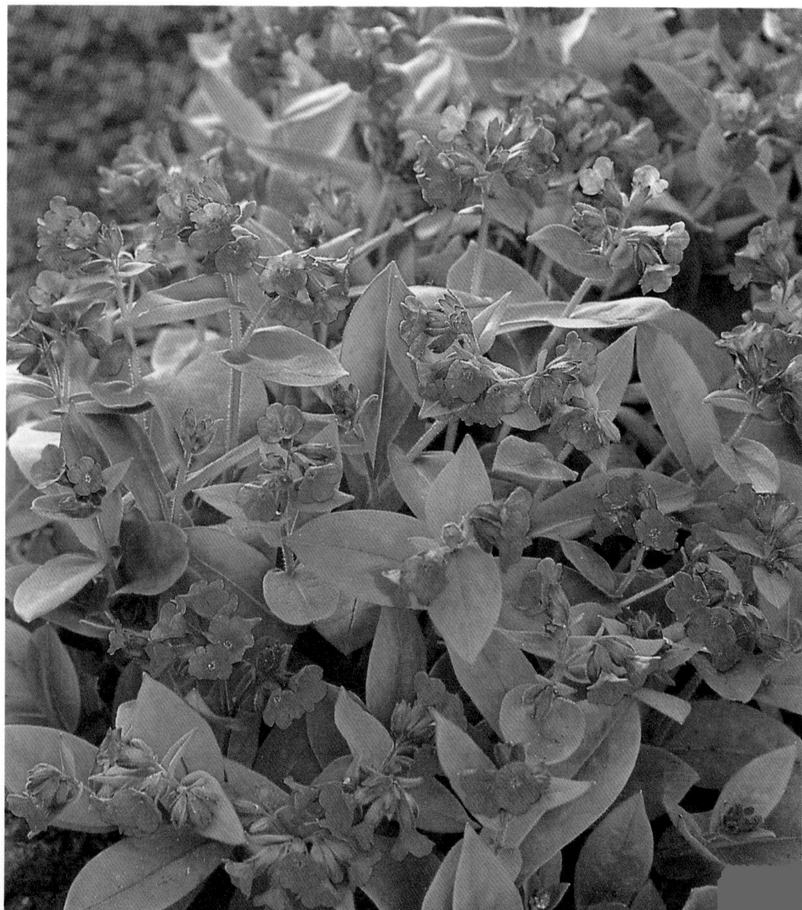

Pulmonaria *Lungwort* Boraginaceae

Small hardy herbaceous/evergreen perennials. Suitable for ground cover in shady or partially shaded borders, in woodland plantings and shaded corners of a wild garden. Among the most valuable accompaniments to spring flowering bulbs, but do choose varieties carefully: some of the seed-raised plants are extremely dull. Oval to elliptic basal leaves, frequently spotted with white or silver, blue funnel-shaped, five-lobed flowers, white and shades of blue and pink, throughout spring unless stated otherwise. Thrives in fertile, well-drained, moist soil enriched with humus, best in light shade; will tolerate full sun but only if soil is constantly moist. Sow seed when ripe, divide established plants in late autumn, or take root cuttings in mid-winter. ❀ *P. angustifolia*, clump-forming, herbaceous, mid- to dark green, lance-shaped leaves lack spotting, abundant clusters of deep blue flowers, 25-30cm/45cm (10in-1ft/1½ft); *P. a.* ssp. *azurea*, bright blue flowers; *P. a.* 'Munstead Blue', flowers red-violet at first, later blue, arguably the best blue of all though 'Mawson's Blue' is close behind; *P. longifolia*, clump-forming, herbaceous, long, narrow, lance-shaped, dark green leaves, silver-white spots, blue to blue-purple flowers, late winter to late spring, 30cm/45cm (1ft/1½ft); *P. l.* 'Bertram Anderson', more compact, leaves longer, narrower, more vividly marked, brighter blue flowers; *P.* 'Mawson's Blue', spreading, herbaceous, elliptic or oval, hairy, dark green leaves, lack spotting, dark blue flowers, 35cm/45cm (1¼ft/1½ft); *P. officinalis*, clump-forming, evergreen, oval leaves with heart-shaped bases, bristly, bright green with white spots, deep pink buds open to pink flowers, later violet-blue, in dense clusters, 30cm/45cm (1ft/1½ft); *P. o.* Cambridge Blue Group, leaves silver-spotted, flowers pink at first, later pale blue, 30cm/45cm (1ft/1½ft); *P. o.* 'Sissinghurst White', silver-spotted leaves, pale pink buds open to pure white flowers, 30cm/45cm (1ft/1½ft); *P. rubra* 'Barfield Pink', clump-forming, evergreen, elliptic, downy, bright green leaves lack spotting, flowers striped pink-and-white, late winter to mid-spring, 30cm/45cm (1ft/1½ft); *P. r.* 'David Ward', sage-green leaves with cream margins, pale pink flowers; *P. r.* 'Redstart', coral-red flowers, late winter; *P. saccharata*, clump-forming, evergreen, elliptic, mid-green leaves with white spots or blotches, sometimes almost covering the surface, white, red-violet or violet flowers with dark green calyces, late winter to late spring, 30cm/60cm (1ft/2ft); *P. s.* Argentea Group, narrow leaves, silver-white with mottled green margins, flowers red at first, later dark violet; *P. s.* 'Mrs Moon', pink buds open to violet-blue flowers; *P. vallarsae* 'Margery Fish', clump-forming, herbaceous, elliptic to oblong, downy, blotched, bright green leaves with silvery surface and wavy margins, flowers coral-pink to red-violet at first, later violet, 18-28cm/60cm (7-11½in/2ft).

Pulsatilla
Pasque Flower — Ranunculaceae

Small, hardy, mainly herbaceous, perennials for rock gardens and raised beds. Finely cut, feathery leaves, delicious bell- or goblet-shaped downy flowers with six petals and prominent gold stamens, followed by decorative, silky seedheads. They were once classed in *Anemone* and are like regal, noble forms of the familiar spring-flowering anemones. All parts are toxic if eaten; sap may cause skin irritation. Sow seed when ripe or in autumn, or take root cuttings in winter. ❀ *P. alpina* ssp. *apiifolia* (syn. *P. alpina* ssp. *sulphurea*) (Alpine Pasque Flower), clump-forming, bipinnate, mid-green, hairy leaves, cup-shaped, pale yellow flowers, spring, thrives in acidic soil, 15-30cm/20cm (6-1ft/8in); *P. vulgaris* (syn. *Anemone pulsatilla*) (Common Pasque Flower), clump-forming, pinnate, hairy, light green leaves, erect or slightly pendent bell-shaped, pale to dark purple flowers, sometimes white or red, spring, 10-20cm/20cm (4-8in/8in); *P. v. alba*, white flowers; *P. v.* var. *rubra*, red flowers.

Puschkinia
Striped Squill — Hyacinthaceae

Very hardy bulbous ornamental, closely related and similar to *Scilla* but seen much less frequently. Lovely for rock gardens, but also for naturalizing in short grass or for woodland plantings with dappled shade. Erect basal leaves, clusters of bell-shaped flowers, in spring. Sow seed in a cold-frame between late summer and autumn or divide clumps after flowering. ❀ *P. scilloides* var. *libanotica*, linear leaves, small white flowers about 7mm (⅓in) in diameter, with pointed lobes and occasional blue stripes, 20cm/5cm (8in/2in); *P. s.* var. *l.* 'Alba', white flowers.

Pyracantha *Firethorn* — Rosaceae

Large, moderately hardy, evergreen shrubs or small trees, rather prone to cold winter wind damage. Most familiarly grown against walls but equally attractive free-standing in shrub borders or as hedging. Small, toothed leaves on very thorny branches, abundant clusters of white, five-petalled flowers, followed by small red, yellow or orange fruits. Seeds are toxic if eaten. Thrives in fertile, well-drained soil in full sun or partial shade. Fruits may be stripped by birds in some winters. If grown free-standing, no routine pruning but when grown against a wall, prune in spring after flowering, removing sideshoots to within 2cm (¾in) of their base to produce a plant either formally trained to a neat geometric shape or less formally as a simple two-dimensional shrub. Hedges should be clipped lightly after flowering although some loss of fruit will of course be inevitable. Sow seed in a cold-frame in autumn or take semi-ripe cuttings in summer. Some species are particularly prone to scab and fireblight diseases. ❀ *P. coccinea* 'Lalandei', dark green, oval to lance-shaped leaves, small cream-white flowers, in early summer, followed by orange-red fruits, susceptible to scab and fireblight, 3m/2.5m (10ft/8ft); *P. c.* 'Red Column', erect shrub, red shoots, glossy oval to elliptic leaves, scarlet fruits produced early; *P.* 'Mohave', oval, dark green leaves, long-lasting, bright orange-red fruits which seem to be ignored by birds, disease resistant, 3m/2m (10ft/6½ft); *P.* 'Orange Charmer', arching branches, flowers in early summer, followed by deep orange fruits, 3m/3m (10ft/10ft); *P.* 'Orange Glow', glossy, elliptic to more or less oval, glossy leaves, flowers in late spring, bright orange-red fruits, long-lasting, early autumn to winter, 3m/1.5m (10ft/5ft); *P. rogersiana*, erect, later arching, shrub, lance-shaped, bright green leaves, flowers in spring, followed by

above *Pulsatilla vulgaris*. Once classed as an anemone, but in truth, no anemone ever had such rich quality.

above *Pyracantha* 'Teton'. Outstanding among the newer varieties of firethorn, and valuable for its resistance to fireblight disease which has blighted this group.

abundant bright red-orange fruits from mid-summer, 3m/2m (10ft/6½ft); *P.* 'Soleil d'Or', elliptic, glossy dark green leaves on red-tinged shoots, flowers in early summer, followed by large clusters of gold-yellow fruits, 3m/2.5m (10ft/8ft); *P.* 'Teton', erect, glossy, bright green leaves with wavy edges, flowers in early summer, followed by abundant small, orange-yellow fruits, resistant to fireblight, a very good modern variety, 3m/2m (10ft/6½ft).

Pyrus *Pear* Rosaceae

Moderately hardy deciduous shrubs and trees, including a few ornamentals and those grown for their edible fruit. The ornamental varieties are best grown as specimen trees; fruiting pears may be grown free-standing but are often better with the shelter provided by training them as espaliers, cordons or fans. Elliptic, oval to oblong leaves, bowl- or saucer-shaped five-petalled flowers, usually white with red anthers, in spring, followed by characteristically pear-shaped, sometimes spherical, fruit. Pears require fertile, well-drained soil in full sun. In cold areas, fruiting trees are best grown against a wall in a sunny position; pears are not as hardy as apples and the success of fruiting crops is much less predictable in the North. No routine pruning of ornamentals; fruiting trees are pruned similarly to apples, as described in the companion volume. Ornamental pears may be propagated from semi-ripe cuttings taken in summer but fruiting trees should be bought, grafted.

Ornamental *P. calleryana* 'Chanticleer', narrow, conical tree, glossy, oval, toothed or scalloped leathery, dark green leaves with pointed tips, sometimes yellow in autumn, clusters of white flowers, early to mid-spring, sometimes also in summer, followed by spherical, brown, ornamental fruit, 15m/6m (50ft/20ft); *P. salicifolia* (Willow-leaved Pear), 'Pendula', lance-shaped to elliptic, willow-like leaves, white, felted at first, later grey-green, on weeping branches, clusters of cream-white flowers, mid-spring, followed by hard, green, pear-shaped fruit, a charming plant and a sensible alternative to a weeping willow for small gardens, 8m/5m (26½ft/16ft).

Fruiting *P. communis*: the range of reliable pear varieties is much smaller than the range of apples and four varieties dominate garden pear growing: 'Conference', 'Williams' Bon Chrétien', 'Doyenné du Comice' and 'Beurre Hardy'. The others that I recommend are good enough trees but are worth trying only in warmer areas. I have included my suggested pollinators for each variety and have again limited myself to reliable garden varieties. The range of pear rootstocks is also limited and modern trees are almost always grafted on to 'Quince A' or 'Quince C', giving free-standing trees of about 4m (13ft). 'Beth', early, pollinate with 'Williams' Bon Chrétien'; 'Concorde', late, rather like a green-skinned 'Conference', pollinate with 'Doyenné du Comice'; 'Beurre Hardy', mid-season, green-yellow, rather 'clumsy' looking fruit but juicy, pollinate with 'Conference'; 'Conference', mid-season, far and away the best all-round pear, dark green fruit flushed russet, sweet, juicy and will set a good crop on its own, although more reliable when pollinated, use 'Williams' Bon Chrétien' or 'Joséphine de Malines'; 'Doyenné du Comice', late, the best flavoured of all but requires a sheltered position on a warm, sunny site, late flowering, juicy, pale yellow fruit, flushed red or russet, white flesh, pollinate with 'Beth' or 'Conference'; 'Louise Bonne of Jersey', mid-season, green-yellow fruit, flushed deep red, juicy, white flesh, pollinate with 'Joséphine de Malines'; 'Onward', early, very juicy, pollinate with 'Doyenné du Comice'; 'Williams' Bon Chrétien', early, gold-yellow fruit, russet spots, white, sweet, juicy flesh, pollinate with 'Onward' or 'Conference'.

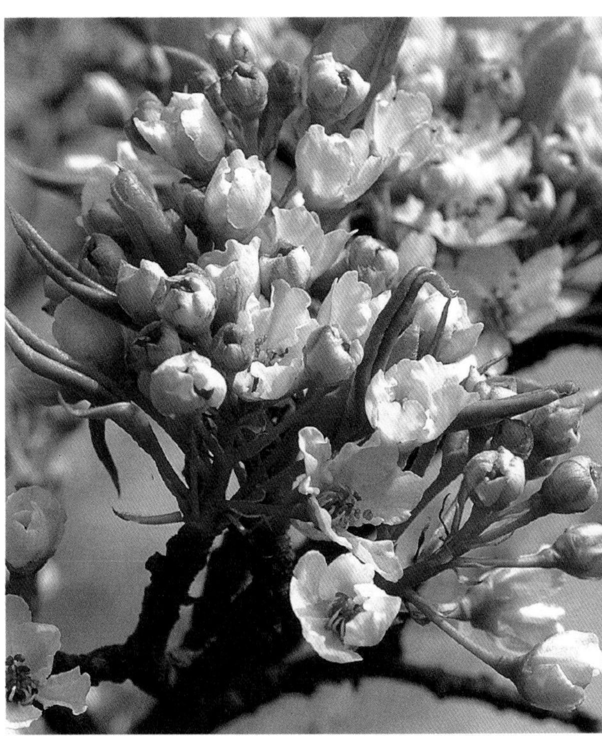

right *Pyrus calleryana* 'Chanticleer'. There are very few ornamental pears, but this is the one to choose above all.

Quercus *Oak* Fagaceae

Large deciduous, semi-evergreen or evergreen trees and a few shrubs. Moderately hardy to very hardy. Oaks are appropriate as specimen trees in large gardens only; although deceptive and slow growing, they will ultimately become very large. Furrowed bark, entire, lobed or toothed leaves, some with good autumn colour. Inconspicuous male and female flowers, male flowers borne on catkins, females singly, in pairs or in clusters, followed by hard brown fruit (acorns) in scaled cups. Sow seed in a cold-frame when ripe. ❀ *Q. coccinea* (Scarlet Oak), 'Splendens', deciduous tree, dark green, deeply lobed toothed leaves, rich scarlet red in autumn, ovoid fruit, needs acidic soil, 20m/10m (60ft/33ft); *Q. ilex* (Holm Oak), evergreen, glossy, dark green, leathery leaves, grey beneath, varying in shape, green fruit, suitable for coastal sites, thrives in mild areas, a sombre tree at the best of times, 25m/15m (80ft/50ft); *Q. petraea* (syn. *Q. sessiliflora*) (Sessile Oak), spreading, deciduous tree, dark green, oblong, oval or more or less oval leaves with lobed margins, stalkless, ovoid fruit, 30m/20m (100ft/60ft); *Q. robur* (Pedunculate Oak, English Oak), f. *fastigiata*, erect, deciduous tree, oval to oblong, dark green leaves with rounded lobes, ovoid fruit, singly or in clusters, 20m/5m (60ft/16ft); *Q. rubra* (syn. *Q. borealis*) (Red Oak), spreading deciduous tree, mid-green, matt, elliptic leaves with bristled lobes, yellow to dull red and orange-yellow autumn, hemispherical fruit, 25m/20m (80ft/60ft).

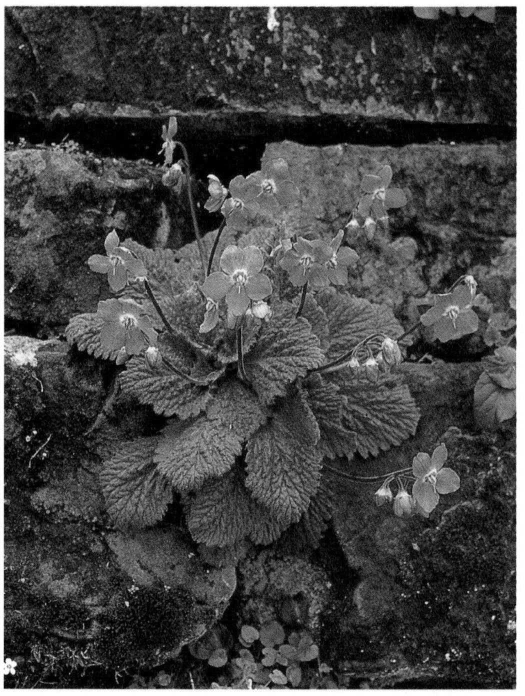

Ramonda Gesneriaceae

Small hardy evergreen perennials and totally unexpected as hardy, outdoor relatives of African violets. Rosettes of wrinkled, hairy leaves, cup-shaped flowers, usually blue or violet, singly or in clusters, late spring to early summer. Sow seed in a cold-frame when ripe, divide established plants in early spring or take leaf cuttings in early autumn. ❀ *R. myconi* (syn. *R. pyrenaica*), dark green leaves, russet-haired beneath, clusters of flat, five-petalled, mauve-blue flowers with yellow anthers, 10cm/20cm (4in/8in).

Ranunculus
Buttercup, Crowfoot Ranunculaceae

Hardy annuals, biennials and herbaceous/evergreen perennials, including some very familiar wild flowers and a few troublesome weeds; but all with endearing flowers. Essential for the wild flower garden and for woodland plantings, rock gardens, borders, bog and water gardens. Entire, toothed, lobed or finely divided leaves, bowl- , cup- or saucer-shaped flowers, usually with five petals, singly or in clusters, spring to autumn. Sap may cause skin irritation. Most species thrive in moist, well-drained soil in sun or partial shade; alpine species require gritty, well drained soil enriched with humus, in full sun; bog or aquatic species thrive in muddy margins of pools and streams or in shallow water at the edges of pools and streams. Sow seed in a cold-frame when ripe, divide established plants in spring or autumn or replant bulbils of tuberous species in spring or autumn. ❀ *R. aconitifolius* 'Flore Pleno', glossy, palmate, dark green, deeply cut and toothed basal leaves, clusters of double button-like white flowers, late spring to early summer, 60cm/45cm (2ft/1½ft); *R. acris* (Meadow Buttercup), 'Flore Pleno' (Bachelor's Buttons), clump-forming, dark green, oval, palmate lobed, toothed basal leaves, clusters of double, saucer-shaped, glossy yellow flowers, early to mid-summer, a delightful variant of a familiar wild flower, 20-90cm/22cm (8in-3ft/8½in); *R. asiaticus* Turban Group, barely hardy, best grown in containers in cold areas, pale green, oval to rounded, hairy basal leaves, double red, pink, yellow or white flowers, with purple-black eyes, late spring and early summer, quite the most unattractive members of the genus, clumsy, vulgar plants, but loved by the Victorians and a few modern gardeners too, 20-45cm/20cm (8in-1½ft/8in); *R. ficaria* (Lesser Celandine), there are numerous double-flowered and other variants of this common weed; all are utterly delightful in early spring:

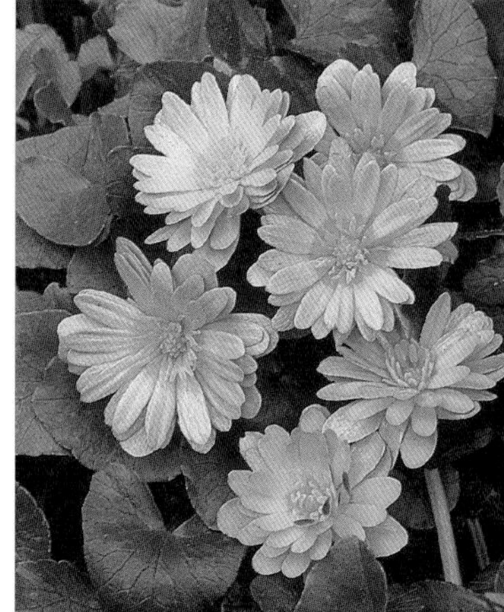

above *Ranunculus ficaria* 'Flore Pleno'. This is but one of numerous double and otherwise aberrant forms of the lesser celandine; and all are utterly delightful.

left *Ramonda myconi*. At first glance, this could be an African violet growing outdoors; in reality, it is a hardy European relative.

'Brazen Hussy', heart-shaped, purple-bronze basal leaves, gold-yellow flowers with oblong petals, with bronze undersides, 5cm/30cm (2in/1ft); *R. f.* 'Collarette', dark green leaves with bronze bands at the centre, double yellow; *R. f.* 'Flore Pleno'; *R. f.* 'Green Petal', pale green flowers; *R. f.* 'Salmon's White', pale green leaves, marked with bronze, cream flowers, undersides tinged purple-blue; *R. lingua* (Greater Spearwort), 'Grandiflorus', dainty water marginal, spear-shaped green leaves, yellow flowers, singly or in small clusters, summer, 1m/25cm (3ft/10in); *R. montanus* 'Molten Gold', mat-forming, glossy, deep green basal leaves with toothed lobes, cup-shaped, glossy, bright gold-yellow flowers, in early summer, 10cm/30cm (4in/1ft); *R. repens* (Creeping Buttercup), var. *pleniflorus*, another lovely double-flowered variant of a 'weed', erect, spreading, mid- to dark green, triangular-oval leaves, glossy bright yellow double flowers, pale yellow sepals, late spring to early summer, invasive, 30-60cm/2m (12in-2ft/6½ft).

Raoulia — Asteraceae

Small evergreen perennials or sub-shrubs. Fairly hardy. Suitable for rock gardens, but not usually successful in very cold areas and need protection from winter wet. Rosettes of beautiful, tiny, overlapping silver-green or green leaves, small inflorescences of disc-shaped flowers. Sow seed in mid-spring or replant rooted shoots in spring. *R. australis*, mat-forming, minute spoon-shaped silver-grey, hairy leaves, star-shaped, bright yellow inflorescences, in summer, 1cm/30cm (½in/1ft); *R. hookeri*, mat-forming, minute oval leaves, fluffy, straw-coloured inflorescences, can be invasive once well established, 2cm/30cm (¾in/1ft).

above *Raoulia hookeri*. Many people see this plant growing in rock gardens and pass it by in the belief that it must be some form of moss. In reality, it is a very charming species with some of the smallest leaves and flowers imaginable.

Raphanus *Radish* — Brassicaceae

Root vegetable. The biennial species *R. sativus* is grown as an annual. Round, cylindrical, globe-shaped or elongated roots, green coarse foliage. Thrives best in fertile, well-drained soil enriched with humus, in full sun. Sow seed in growing positions from early spring to summer; most summer radishes will bolt if sown after early July; winter varieties are sown in growing positions between early and late summer.

Summer salad radishes: 'Cherry Belle', round scarlet root; 'French Breakfast', cylindrical scarlet root with white tip; 'Long White Icicle', cylindrical white roots, harvest when 7-15cm (2¾-6in) long; 'Prinz Rotin' (syn. 'Red Prince'), scarlet globe-shaped root, relatively resistant to bolting and splitting; 'Saxa', (syn. 'Short Top Forcing'), suitable for forcing in frames or under cloches from mid-autumn to late winter, or sowing in growing positions in spring or early summer.

Other radishes: 'Black Spanish Round', a Chinese-type winter radish with a round root having very dark brown, almost black, skin, crisp white flesh, rather like a small turnip; 'China Rose', winter radish, cylindrical root, deep pink skin, white flesh; Mooli type radishes originated in China and Japan, have white skin and are approximately 30cm (1ft) long. Varieties include 'Mino Early', mild flavoured, crisp and tender, for autumn and winter harvesting.

Reseda *Mignonette* — Resedaceae

Small/medium hardy and half-hardy annuals and perennials. Mid-green, entire or toothed leaves with conspicuous veining, tiny, star-shaped, yellow-green or green-white flowers, sometimes fragrant, spring to autumn. Sow seed in warmth in late winter or in flowering positions in spring or autumn. ❀ *R. lutea*, short-lived perennial, best grown as a biennial, lance-shaped, deeply divided leaves, spikes of tiny yellow-green flowers, mid- to late summer, 30cm/15cm (1ft/6in); *R. luteola*, biennial, lance-shaped leaves with wavy margins, spikes of tiny white flowers flushed green-white, mid- to late summer, 1m/45cm (3ft/1½ft); *R. odorata*, annual, oval, lobed leaves, rounded clusters of very fragrant, tiny yellow-green or green-white flowers with orange-brown stamens, mid-summer to autumn, I always sow it hidden among grander things, simply for its fragrance, 30-60cm/23cm (1-2ft/9in).

Rhamnus *Buckthorn* — Rhamnaceae

Large, moderately hardy deciduous/evergreen shrubs or small trees. Suitable for shrub borders, woodland plantings or hedging and invaluable in the native plant garden as food for butterfly and moth caterpillars. Leaves variable, some deciduous species with good autumn colour. Clusters of cup-shaped, unisexual or hermaphrodite flowers, sometimes fragrant, followed by fruit. All parts of the plant are toxic if eaten. Sow seed in a cold-frame when ripe or take semi-ripe cuttings in summer. ❀ *R. alaternus* (Mediterranean Buckthorn), 'Argenteovariegata' (syn. *R. a.* 'Variegata'), barely hardy evergreen shrub, elliptic to oval, grey-green leaves, marbled grey with cream margins, clusters of yellow-green flowers, late spring to early summer, followed by spherical fruits, red at first, later black, 5m/4m (16ft/13ft); *R. cathartica* (Buckthorn), moderately hardy

left *Rhamnus catharticus.* One of the most valuable of native hedgerow plants for its role in providing food for insects of many kinds.

deciduous shrub, elliptic or oval, glossy, dark green leaves on spiny branches, clusters of yellow-white flowers, late spring to early summer, followed by spherical fruits, red at first, later black, 6m/6m (20ft/20ft); *R. frangula* (Alder Buckthorn), moderately hardy deciduous shrub, glossy, deep green, oval to more or less oval pointed leaves, red in autumn, clusters of green flowers, late spring to early summer, followed by fleshy, spherical fruits, orange-red at first, later purple-black, 5m/5m (16ft/16ft).

Rheum *Rhubarb* Polygonaceae

Medium/large rhizomatous ornamentals and perennial vegetable fruit. Moderately hardy. The genus contains the ornamental and edible rhubarbs. Large, rounded, palmate lobed leaves with prominent veins and mid-ribs. Tiny, petal-less flowers on erect spikes, followed by winged fruit. The leaves are toxic if eaten. Thrive in moist soil enriched with humus, in full sun or partial shade. Best forms do not come true from seed; divide established plants in autumn.

Ornamental: *R.* 'Ace of Hearts' (syn. *R.* 'Ace of Spades'), elongated, heart-shaped, mid- to dark green crimson-flushed leaves with red veins, purple-red veins beneath, tiny pink flowers, early to mid-summer, 1.2m/90cm (4ft/3ft); *R. palmatum*, oval, palmate lobed, mid- to blue-green, coarsely toothed leaves, purple-red, hairy beneath, star-shaped dark red to cream-green flowers in tall spikes, 2.5m/2m (8ft/6½ft); *R. p.* 'Atrosanguineum' (syn. *R. p.* 'Atropurpureum'), leaves flushed red; *R. p.* var. *tanguticum*, divided leaves with jagged leaflets, leaves red-green at first, later dark green, sometimes purple tinted, white, pink or crimson flowers on large spikes, 2m (6½ft).

Edible: *R.* x *hybridum* (syn. *R.* x *cultorum*), 'Early Red' (syn. 'Champagne Early); 'Timperley Early', early, thin stalks, red-skin, green flesh, good for forcing and the best all-round rhubarb; 'Victoria', late.

Rhodiola Crassulaceae

Small rhizomatous ornamentals. Moderately hardy and among the best outdoor succulents. Fleshy basal and stem leaves, star-shaped, five-petalled flowers with conspicuous stamens, male and female flowers on separate plants. Sow seed in a cold-frame, divide established plants in spring or autumn, or take cuttings from non-flowering shoots in spring. ❀ *R. rosea* (syns. *Sedum rosea, S. rhodiola*) (Rose Root), clump-forming, oval to inversely lance-shaped, glaucous grey-green leaves, tipped red, on purple fleshy branches, clusters of pink buds open to yellow male or female flowers, summer, 5-30cm/20cm (2in-1ft/8in).

below *Rhodiola rosea.* A strikingly attractive and surprisingly hardy succulent.

right *Rhodochiton atrosanguineum*. Highly individual flowers are the appealing features of this small tender perennial that is best grown outdoors as a half-hardy annual for summer containers.

Rhodochiton Scrophulariaceae

Medium semi-evergreen/evergreen climber. Tender, but in cold areas successful when grown as a half-hardy annual, especially in containers. In mild areas, free from frost, will survive as a perennial and grow large enough for pergolas and arches. Simple, toothed leaves on twining leaf stalks, pendent, tubular flowers with flared calyces. Sow seed in warmth in early spring. ❀ *R. astrosanguineus*, (syn. *R. volubilis*), deep green, heart-shaped leaves, extraordinary maroon to red-purple flowers with pink or mauve, cup-shaped calyces, summer to autumn, 3m (10ft).

far right *Rhododendron* 'Hino-mayo'. Among all of the evergreen hardy azaleas, I have always had a soft spot for this one, brought to the West in 1910 from the Emperor's garden in Tokyo.

Rhododendron (including Azalea)
Ericaceae

Small/large deciduous and evergreen shrubs and trees. Tender to very hardy. Suitable for woodland plantings, specimens, hedging and containers; small, low-growing species are suitable for rock gardens and ground cover. The most characteristic and invaluable plants for any garden on acidic soil. In general, rhododendrons thrive best in light shade, azaleas in full sun. Mid- to dark green, usually lance-shaped leaves. Single or double flowers, sometimes fragrant, solitary or in clusters (trusses), variously shaped, from bell-shaped and tubular through trumpet-shaped, many funnel-shaped, to those known as hose-in-hose (one flower almost inside another). Require moist, well-drained, acidic soil enriched with humus, usually in dappled or partial shade, some in full sun. Plants raised in warmth require ericaceous compost and bright, filtered light. No routine pruning. Sow seed in warmth when ripe or in early spring, or in a cold-frame when ripe (hardy dwarf species and hybrids), take semi-ripe cuttings in late summer or layer. The genus *Rhododendron* is usually divided into several groups, including evergreen rhododendrons, evergreen and deciduous azaleas, Vireya rhododendrons (tropical, evergreen, tender shrubs), and the hybrids known as azaleodendrons. The species and varieties described below are a very small, personal selection of the huge numbers available. I have grouped them in the way that is I think most helpful for gardeners: species, hardy hybrids, evergreen azaleas and deciduous azaleas.

***Rhododendron* species** All the species described below are evergreen unless stated otherwise. ❀ *R. augustinii*, moderately hardy shrub or small tree, mid- to dark green leaves, clusters of funnel-shaped, blue or lavender flowers, blotched green-brown inside, in mid-spring, 3m/3m (10ft/10ft); *R. campylocarpum*, fairly to moderately hardy dwarf shrub, glossy, inversely lance-shaped leaves, clusters of pendent, bell-shaped, white, pink or purple flowers, tolerant of full sun, 75cm/75cm (2½ft/2½ft); *R. davidsonianum*, fairly

hardy to moderately hardy shrub, scaly leaves on arching shoots, clusters of funnel-shaped, pink to lavender flowers, sometimes pink blotched, mid-spring, sun or partial shade, 4m/4m (13ft/13ft); *R. fortunei*, hardy shrub or small tree, oblong leaves, matt, dark green, pale green beneath, clusters of pink or lilac-pink flowers, mid- to late spring, 10m/2.5m (33ft/8ft); *R. impeditum*, moderately hardy dwarf shrub, scaly, aromatic, grey-green leaves, funnel-shaped, purple-blue flowers, mid- to late spring, a superb little plant, 60cm/60cm (2ft/2ft); *R. lepidostylum*, moderately hardy dwarf shrub, oblong or oval leaves, gold-yellow scales beneath, funnel-shaped yellow flowers with dark brown anthers, singly or in pairs, late spring to early summer, 1m/1m (3ft/3ft); *R. lutescens*, moderately hardy semi-evergreen shrub, oval-oblong to lance-shaped leaves, bronze at first, later matt green, paler, with yellow scales, beneath, funnel-shaped pale yellow flowers, early spring, 5m/5m (16ft/16ft); *R. pemakoense*, moderately hardy dwarf shrub, glossy dark green leaves, glaucous beneath, clusters of bell-shaped, pink flowers, early to mid-spring, 60cm/60cm (2ft/2ft); *R. ponticum*, moderately hardy shrub, lance-shaped to elliptic leaves, dark green, paler beneath, funnel-shaped flowers, red-purple, sometimes white, sometimes spotted yellow inside, summer, the naturalized 'weed' species but nonetheless beautiful where space permits, 6-8m/6m (20-26½ft/20ft); *R. williamsianum*, moderately hardy shrub, leaves brown at first, later bright green, glaucous beneath, clusters of bell-shaped flowers, ink, sometimes white, mid- to late spring, charming, 1.5m/1.2m (5ft/4ft); *R. yakushimanum*, very hardy shrub, glossy, lance-shaped, dark green leaves, pale pink, almost white, flowers, in late spring, tolerates full sun, quite lovely, 2m/2m (6½ft/6½ft).

Rhododendron hybrids The following are all evergreen and at least moderately hardy. ❀ *R.* Alison Johnstone Group, blue-green, oval leaves, bell-shaped, amber flowers flushed pink, in late spring, 2m/2m (6½ft/6½ft); *R.* 'Baden-Baden', dwarf, glossy dark green, twisted leaves, deep waxy red flowers, late spring to early summer, 1m (3ft); *R.* Blue Diamond Group, very hardy, dwarf, large clusters of saucer-shaped, violet-blue flowers, mid- to late spring, 1.5m/1.5m (5ft/5ft); *R.* Blue Tit Group, dwarf, compact, clusters of funnel-shaped, lavender-blue flowers, mid-spring, 1m/1m (3ft/3ft); *R.* Bow Bells Group, leaves red-bronze at first, later green, bell-shaped, pink flowers, late spring, 2m/2m (6½ft/6½ft); *R.* 'Britannia', very hardy, pale green leaves, clusters of bright red, bell-shaped flowers, late spring to early summer, 1.5m/2.2m (5ft/63/4ft); *R.* 'Carmen', dwarf, deep green leaves, clusters of waxy, deep red, shiny, tubular flowers, mid- to late spring, 1m/1.2m (3ft/4ft); *R.* 'Chikor', dwarf, abundant saucer-shaped yellow flowers, late spring, 60cm/60cm (2ft/2ft); *R.* Cilpinense Group, fairly hardy dwarf, glossy green leaves, clusters of funnel-shaped pink flowers or white flowers flushed pink, early spring, 1.1m/1.1m (3½ft/3½ft); *R.* 'Cynthia', very hardy, clusters of rose-pink, funnel-shaped flowers, spotted crimson and black, late spring to early summer, 6m/6m (20ft/20ft); *R.* 'Egret', dwarf, hardy, deep green leaves, abundant, tiny, bell-shaped white flowers, late spring, 1m (3ft); *R.* Elizabeth Group, moderately hardy, mid-green leaves, clusters of bright red, trumpet-shaped flowers, mid-spring, sometimes later in autumn, 1m/1m (3ft/3ft); *R.* 'Golden Torch', moderately hardy, clusters of pink buds opening to bell-shaped, pale yellow flowers, 1.5m/1.5m (5ft/5ft); *R.* 'Gomer Waterer', hardy, dark green, leathery leaves, lilac buds opening to fragrant, funnel-shaped white flowers flushed mauve-pink, early summer, 2m/2m (6½ft/6½ft); *R.* Humming Bird Group, compact, rounded, glossy leaves, slightly pendent, bell-shaped red flowers, mid- to late spring, 1.5m/1.5m (5ft/5ft); *R.* 'Loderi King George', large shrub or small trees, large clusters of lily-like pink flowers, late spring to early summer, 4m/4m (13ft/13ft); *R.* 'Percy Wiseman', moderately hardy, clusters of pink-and-cream flowers, late spring, 2m/2m (6½ft/6½ft); *R.* 'Pink Drift', hardy, dwarf, small aromatic

above *Rhododendron* 'Klondyke'. The deciduous azaleas fall into several groups of which the Knap Hill hybrids are among the most celebrated. Even among a striking group, however, I think this stands out as a magnificent plant.

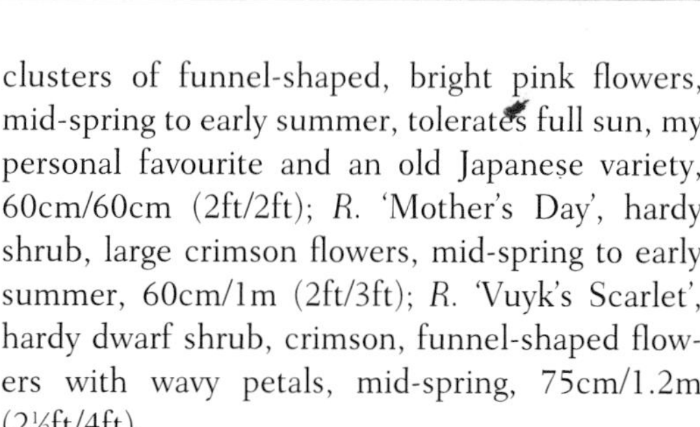

right *Rhododendron impeditum*. From Southern China, and quite simply the best dwarf species I grow; it is covered with flowers in spring.

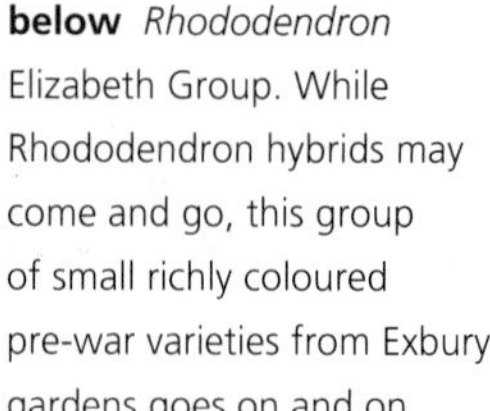

below *Rhododendron* Elizabeth Group. While Rhododendron hybrids may come and go, this group of small richly coloured pre-war varieties from Exbury gardens goes on and on.

leaves, abundant clusters of pink-mauve flowers, late spring, 1m (3ft); *R.* 'Pink Pearl', very hardy, abundant clusters of pink, funnel-shaped flowers, late spring to early summer, 4m/4m (13ft/13ft); *R.* 'Praecox' (syn. *R. praecox*), moderately hardy, aromatic leaves, clusters of rose-purple flowers, early spring, susceptible to frost damage, 1.3m/1.3m (4½ft/4½ft); *R.* 'Princess Anne', dwarf, hardy, leaves bronze at first, later mid- to light green, pale yellow, funnel-shaped flowers, late spring, 75cm-1.2m/75cm-1.2m (2½-4ft/2½-4ft); *R.* 'Purple Splendour', very hardy, funnel-shaped, frilled purple-blue flowers with black markings, 3m/3m (10ft/10ft); *R.* 'Sappho', very hardy, dark, glossy green leaves, clusters of funnel-shaped pure white flowers with purple marks, late spring to early summer, 3m/3m (10ft/10ft); *R.* 'Snipe', dwarf, barely hardy, pale green leaves, abundant lavender-pink flowers, early to mid-spring, 2m/2m (6½ft/6½ft); *R.* 'Surrey Heath', narrow leaves, downy at first, funnel-shaped pink flowers with paler centres, late spring, 2m/2m (6½ft/6½ft); *R.* 'Titian Beauty', moderately hardy, dark green leaves, brown, downy beneath, tubular to bell-shaped red flowers, early summer, thrives in full sun, 2m/2m (6½ft/6½ft); *R.* Yellow Hammer Group, abundant tiny yellow flowers, mid-spring, sometimes also in autumn, tolerant of full sun, 2m/2m (6½ft/6½ft).

Evergreen azaleas These evergreen species and varieties are sometimes referred to collectively as Japanese azaleas, although most modern varieties are, in fact, European. ❀ *R.* 'Addy Wery', moderately hardy dwarf, clusters of funnel-shaped vermilion flowers, mid-spring, 1.2m/1.2m (4ft/4ft); *R.* 'Blaauw's Pink', hose-in-hose salmon-pink flowers, flushed paler pink, mid-spring, 75cm/75cm (2½ft/2½ft); *R.* 'Hinode-giri', moderately hardy dwarf shrub, bright crimson funnel-shaped flowers, mid-spring, at their best in full sun, 60cm/60cm (2ft/2ft); *R.* 'Hino-mayo', hardy dwarf semi-evergreen shrub, abundant clusters of funnel-shaped, bright pink flowers, mid-spring to early summer, tolerates full sun, my personal favourite and an old Japanese variety, 60cm/60cm (2ft/2ft); *R.* 'Mother's Day', hardy shrub, large crimson flowers, mid-spring to early summer, 60cm/1m (2ft/3ft); *R.* 'Vuyk's Scarlet', hardy dwarf shrub, crimson, funnel-shaped flowers with wavy petals, mid-spring, 75cm/1.2m (2½ft/4ft).

Deciduous azaleas ❀ *R.* 'Cécile', moderately hardy, dark salmon-pink buds open to tubular-funnel-shaped, paler salmon-pink flowers with yellow blotches, late spring, 2m/2m (6½ft/6½ft); *R.* 'Gibraltar', deep crimson-orange buds open to clusters of funnel-shaped, vivid orange flowers flushed yellow, wrinkled petals, late spring to early summer, 1.5m/1.5m (5ft/5ft); *R.* 'Klondyke', moderately hardy, leaves copper-red at first, red flushed buds open to large clusters of fragrant, funnel-shaped gold-yellow flowers, red tinged on back, late spring 2m/2m (6½ft/6½ft).

Rhodohypoxis Hypoxidaceae

Small corm-forming ornamentals. Barely hardy to moderately hardy. Hairy, lance-shaped leaves, six-petalled flowers in a wide variety of pastel shades and white, spring to summer. Sow seed in early spring or divide corms of established plants in late spring. ❀ *R. baurii*, barely hardy, clump-forming, dull green leaves, red to white flowers on hairy branches, 10cm/5m (4in/16ft); *R.* 'Douglas', deep, rich red flowers; *R.* 'Fred Broome', broad-petalled, shell-pink flowers; *R. milloïdes*, moderately hardy, clump-forming, bright green linear- to lance-shaped keeled leaves, almost hairless, red, white, pink or magenta flowers, on hairy branches, summer, 15cm/20cm (6in/8in); *R.* 'Picta', large white flowers with white-tipped petals.

Rhus *Sumac* Anacardiaceae

Medium/large deciduous/evergreen shrubs and small trees. Tender to moderately hardy. Suitable for shrub borders, woodland plantings and as specimen trees but invasive by sucker spread, especially if roots are disturbed. Pinnate or palmate leaves provide magnificent autumn colour, clusters of insignificant green flowers in spring. No routine pruning but may be cut back very hard in spring to limit size and promote foliage appeal. Take root cuttings in early winter or replant suckers in spring or autumn. Contact with the leaves of some species can cause skin irritation. ❀ *R. typhina* (Stagshorn Sumac), moderately hardy erect deciduous shrub or tree, pinnate leaves with dark green, lance-shaped leaflets, bright orange-

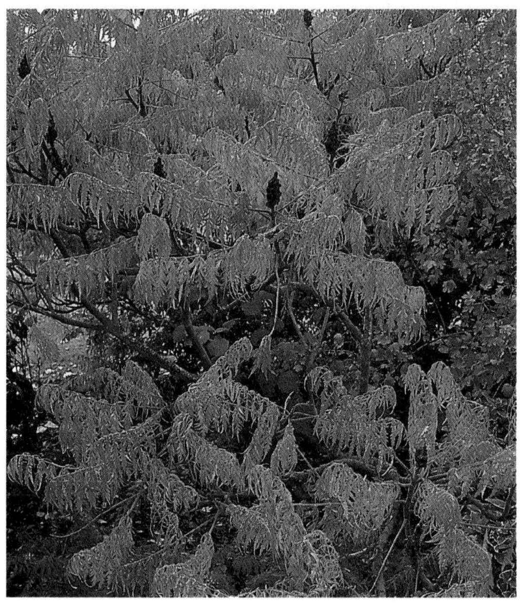

red in autumn, erect clusters of yellow-green flowers, in summer, male and female flowers usually on separate plants, female flowers followed by spherical deep red fruit, 5m/6m (16ft/20ft); *R. t.* 'Dissecta' (syn. *R. t.* 'Laciniata'), female, leaflets finely dissected, 2m/3m (6½ft/10ft).

Ribes
Currant, Gooseberry Grossulariaceae

Medium deciduous/evergreen shrubs. Barely hardy to very hardy and includes both ornamental species and the edible soft fruits, red, black and white currants and gooseberries. Ornamental species are valuable and rather striking for shrub borders and hedging. Usually three to five lobed leaves, tubular, bell- or cup-shaped flowers, singly or in erect or pendent clusters, male and female flowers sometimes on separate plants, followed by edible or inedible fruit. Thrive in moderately fertile, well-drained soil, usually in full sun. Ornamental forms are best pruned by cutting out the oldest third of the shoots each spring; pruning of edible forms varies with growth habit and is described in the companion volume. Take semi-ripe cuttings in summer (evergreens) or hardwood cuttings in winter (deciduous species) but replace edible varieties with new, virus-free stock.

Ornamental species

R. x *gordonianum*, hardy deciduous shrub, aromatic dark green, toothed leaves, pendent clusters of tubular red flowers with yellow centres, early summer, 2m/2.5m (6½ft/8ft); *R. odoratum* (Buffalo Currant), very hardy deciduous shrub, bright green, toothed, oval leaves, red and purple in autumn, pendent clusters of tubular, bright yellow flowers, deliciously clove-scented, mid- to late spring, followed by spherical black fruits, 2m/2m (6½ft/6½ft); *R. sanguineum* (Flowering Currant), 'Brocklebankii', hardy deciduous shrub, three- to five-lobed, gold-yellow leaves, best in partial shade, pendent clusters of pale pink flowers, spring, followed by blue-black fruits, 2m/2m (6½ft/6½ft); *R. s.* 'King Edward VII', compact, dark red flowers; *R. s.* 'Pulborough Scarlet', dark red flowers with white centres, 2.5m/3m (8ft/10ft); *R. s.* 'Tydeman's White', pure white flowers, 2.5m/2.5m (8ft/8ft); *R. speciosum* (Fuchsia Flowered Gooseberry), moderately hardy semi-evergreen shrub, glossy green leaves, abundant clusters of narrow, bell-shaped, fuchsia-like red flowers, from mid- to late spring, followed by bristly red fruits, best grown against a warm sunny wall, a quite wonderful plant, 2m/2m (6½ft/6½ft).

Edible species and varieties

Usually grown as bushes, although red and white currants and gooseberries can be grown as standards, cordons or fans against a wall. All varieties require moist, well-drained soil.

Blackcurrants (*R. nigrum*) require a position that provides shelter from spring frosts: 'Baldwin', compact bush, mid- to late season, medium to large fruits; 'Ben Lomond', mid- to late season, large, juicy fruits, some frost and mildew resistance; 'Ben More', mid- to late season, very large fruit, flowers late, after last frosts, some resistance to mildew; 'Ben Sarek, compact plants, mid-season, exceptionally heavy crops, frost tolerant and mildew resistant, the best garden variety by far; 'Boskoop Giant', very early, old variety, large, sweet, well-flavoured fruit but not a good

left *Rhus typhina* 'Dissecta'. The combination of deeply divided leaves and the most intense of colours make this shrub a particularly arresting sight in autumn.

above *Ribes speciusum*. This is a most unexpected and quite beautiful member of its genus, but it must have a sheltered position.

right *Robinia hispida*. Because its more familiar relatives have yellow flowers, the striking pink blossom of this tree always attracts interest.

cropper; susceptible to frost damage; 'Wellington XXX', mid-season, large fruit.

Red and white currants (*R. rubrum*), thrive on moisture-retentive, ideally slightly acidic, soils in a sheltered position: 'Laxton Number One', early, medium to large red fruits; 'Red Lake', mid-season, large red fruits; 'Redstart', late, a modern, very high yielding red variety; 'Versailles Blanche' (syn. 'White Versailles'), early to mid-season white currant, the only variety likely to be seen.

Gooseberries (*R. uva-crispa* var. *reclinatum*) require similar conditions to red and white currants: 'Careless', early to mid-season culinary, large, downy, oval yellow-green fruits; 'Invicta', early to mid-season, dual purpose, large pale green fruits, mildew resistant; 'Jubilee', early to mid-season, dual purpose, large yellow fruit, mildew resistant; 'Lord Derby', late season dessert, very large dark red fruits; 'Leveller', mid-season dessert, large yellow fruits, susceptible to mildew; 'Whinham's Industry', mid-season, dual-purpose, large dark red fruits, very susceptible to mildew.

Other edible *Ribes* species include *R. divaricatum* (Worcesterberry), which is a cross between a gooseberry and a blackcurrant: late season, small, very dark red fruits.

Robinia Papilionaceae

Large deciduous shrubs and small trees. Moderately hardy to very hardy and popular as specimen trees, although also suitable for shrub borders but need shelter from winds as twigs are brittle. Pinnate leaves, sometimes on thorny or spiny branches, pendent clusters of pea-like flowers, spring to early summer. All parts of the plant are toxic if eaten. No routine pruning. Sow seed in a cold-frame in autumn or take root cuttings in winter. ❀ *R. hispida* (Rose Acacia, Moss Locust), erect shrub, dark green pinnate leaves, pendent clusters of rose-pink flowers, early to mid-summer, followed by bristly, brown seedpods, needs shelter from winds, 2.5m/2m (8ft/6½ft); *R. pseudoacacia* (False Acacia), erect, very hardy thorny tree, pinnate leaves light green above, pale blue-green beneath, slightly fragrant, small white flowers, early summer, followed by smooth round seedpods, 25m/8m (80ft/26½ft); *R. p.* 'Frisia', leaves gold-yellow at first, then yellow-green, orange-yellow in autumn, foliage scorched in hot sun, 15m/6m (50ft/20ft); *R. p.* 'Tortuosa', slow-growing, twisted shoots, 15m/8m (50ft/26½ft).

Rodgersia Saxifragaceae

Medium/large rhizomatous ornamentals. Moderately hardy and among the indispensable plants for the large bog garden or woodland planting with moist conditions. Large palmate or pinnate leaves on long stalks, tall plumes of tiny, star-shaped petal-less flowers, in summer. Sow seed in autumn or divide established plants in spring or autumn. ❀ *R. aesculifolia*, clump-forming, crinkled, deeply lobed, bronze-tinted green leaves, fragrant white flowers, pink tinged, in erect plumes 60cm (2ft) long, mid-summer, 2m/1m (6½ft/3ft); *R. pinnata*, clump-forming, glossy, dark green, pinnate or palmate, crinkled, heavily veined, leaves, plumes of tiny, star-shaped, pink, red or cream-white flowers, mid- to late summer, 1.2m/75cm (4ft/2½ft); *R. p.* 'Elegans', pink-tinged cream flowers; *R. p.* 'Superba', leaves bronze-tinted at first, later green, branched spray of bright pink flowers; *R. podophylla*, palmate leaves crinkled, bronze at first, later smooth, glossy green, copper-tinted in autumn, small, cream-white flowers in erect plumes, from mid- to late summer, 1.5m/1.8m (5ft/5¾ft); *R. sambucifolia*, hairy, palmate leaves with quite prominent veining, dense sprays of white or pink flowers, early to mid-summer, much less frequently seen but I think the best, 90cm/90cm (3ft/3ft).

Romneya

Californian Tree Poppy Papaveraceae

Large perennial sub-shrubs. Barely to fairly hardy. Glorious plant, suitable for sunny borders or growing against a wall but don't underestimate the amount of space that they need. Lobed to finely divided, glaucous leaves, silky, large, poppy-like flowers with bright yellow stamens, in summer. Sow seed in warmth or take basal cuttings in spring, or take root cuttings in winter. ❀ *R. coulteri*, deciduous shrub, glaucous, grey-green leaves, single, large cup-shaped, six-petalled white flowers, 12cm (5in) in diameter, with conspicuous yellow stamens, summer, 1-1.5m (3-5ft)/indefinite.

Rosa Rose

Rosaceae

Deciduous and semi-evergreen fairly hardy to moderately hardy shrubs and climbers. That bald definition embraces the most important genus of ornamental plants in the world, the 150 species having given rise to tens of thousands of varieties suitable for almost every garden. Roses are extremely versatile and suitable for containers, as specimen plants, standards, in mixed and shrub borders, as hedging and ground cover; while climbers and ramblers can be trained up walls or pillars or allowed freely to scramble up walls, into trees and over pergolas, arches and arbours. Leaves composed of five to seven, sometimes toothed, leaflets. Single, semi-double or double flowers, solitary or in clusters. Roses are relatively undemanding and thrive in any moderately fertile, moist, well-drained soil enriched with humus, in full sun, although some will tolerate some shade. Most species and varieties are pruned annually to remove damaged or dead wood and to promote flowering, the method and time of pruning depending on the type of rose. Details for each type are given in the companion volume. Sow seed of species in a cold-frame in autumn, take hardwood cuttings in autumn or bud in summer. The species and varieties that I recommend here represent of course only a small number of the roses that are available but they are all roses that I know and enjoy. I have grouped them along fairly conventional lines. More details of each grouping are given in the companion volume but always bear in mind that if you want a relatively small plant with an abundance of flowers over a long period, a modern bush rose will be most appropriate. Shrub roses, both old and new, tend to be larger plants with a shorter flowering season, generally in early summer.

Species and near-species roses Species roses usually have short-lived single flowers, often with little or no scent. They are the wild roses that have been used to breed the more familiar and popular garden varieties. Most are large shrubs that flower only once each year. They are suitable for medium-sized to large gardens, many of them making excellent hedges. Near-species are varieties that have arisen (often by natural mutation or crossing), but differ only slightly, from their wild parents. ❀ *R. eglanteria* (syn. *R. rubiginosa*) (Sweet Brier), dark green, fern-like, apple-scented leaves, on arching, prickly branches, single pink flowers, summer, followed by bright red, oval hips, 2.5m/2.5m (8ft/8ft); *R.* 'Dunwich Rose', hummock-forming, dark green leaves, abundant single, deliciously fragrant, cream-white flowers with conspicuous yellow stamens, early summer, 1.5m/1.2m (5ft/4ft); *R. primula* (Incense Rose), spicily aromatic, fern-like, long, mid-green leaves with up to 15 leaflets, on erect or arching branches, single, fragrant pale yellow flowers, late spring, sometimes followed by small, spherical red hips, one of the earliest of all roses to flower in most areas, 3m/1.5m (10ft/5ft); *R. xanthina* 'Canary Bird' (syn. *R.* 'Canary Bird'), fern-like, grey-green leaves on arching branches, single yellow, musk-scented flowers borne along the branches, early spring, 3m/2.5m (10ft/8ft).

above *Rosa* 'Fantin Latour'. Forced, as I sometimes am, to name my favourite rose, this glorious old Centifolia is it.

left *Romneya coulteri*. Best known to horticulture students as the classic example of propagation from root cuttings, this is also a plant well worth growing to maturity.

right *Rosa* 'Blairii No 2'. A curiously named Bourbon climber but with a very fine combination of colour and fragrance and a plant that covers the arched entrance to my kitchen garden.

Species and near-species climbers and ramblers ❀ *R. filipes* 'Kiftsgate' (syn. *R.* 'Kiftsgate'), vigorous climber, glossy light green leaves, large, profuse clusters of single, cream-white, sweetly fragrant flowers, early summer, followed by small, orange-red oval hips, a gigantic plant, the most vigorous of all climbing roses, 10m/6m (33ft/20ft); *R.* 'Félicité Perpétue' (syns. *R.* 'Climbing Little White Pet', *R.* 'Félicité et Perpétue'), semi-evergreen rambler, dark green leaves, fragrant, double, white to palest pink pompon flowers, summer, 5m/4m (16ft/13ft).

below *Rosa* 'Aloha'. I have grown this plant as a pillar rose for very many years and still think it the finest modern low climber.

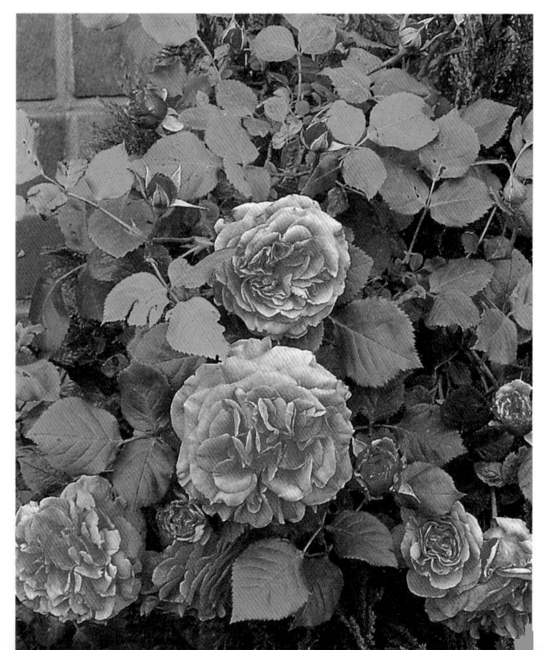

Gallica roses Gallicas usually form relatively short, bushy, leafy shrubs with few thorns and dull, usually dark green, leaves with oval leaflets; the flowers are very fragrant. ❀ *R.* 'Complicata', grey-green leaves on arching branches, large, single pink flowers, 12cm (5in) in diameter, with paler centres and yellow stamens, can be grown as a short climber, ~~2.2m/~~2.5m (6¾ft/8ft); *R.* 'Tuscany Superb', dark green leaves, fragrant double velvety flowers, deep crimson-maroon, fading to purple, with conspicuous yellow stamens, summer, an exquisite plant, 2m/1m (6½ft/3ft).

Centifolia roses Centifolias, also known as Provence roses, have fairly coarse leaves borne on very thorny, arching branches; the flowers are usually large, heavy and very fragrant, with crowded petals. ❀ *R.* 'Fantin-Latour', broad, dark green leaves, fully double, fragrant pale pink flowers, cupped at first, outer petals later reflexed, mid-summer, probably my favourite of all roses, 1.5m/1.2m (5ft/4ft).

Moss roses The sepals and branches of Moss roses are covered in a soft, bristly, moss-like growth. Leaves are dark green with oval leaflets; flowers, in clusters, are either double or semi-double, usually fragrant, and borne around mid-summer. ❀ *R.* 'Mousseline' (syn. 'Alfred de Dalmas'), large, double, cup-shaped pale pink flowers with relatively little light brown moss, fragrant, repeat flowering, good on poorer soils, 1.5m/1.2m (5ft/4ft); *R.* 'William Lobb' (syn. 'Old Velvet Moss'), mid-green leaves on prickly, arching branches, double, velvety dark crimson flowers fading to violet-grey, rich fragrance, summer, may require support, 2m/2m (6½ft/6½ft).

Damask roses Damask roses are renowned for their open habit and tall elegant growth, neatly cut, downy leaves and fragrant flowers. Flowers, single or double, in loose clusters, mainly in summer. ❀ *R.* x *damascena* var. *versicolor* (syn. 'York and Lancaster'), untidy habit, twiggy, dull grey-green leaves on prickly, arching branches, clusters of flat, double flowers, white tinged pink, or deep pink, sometimes both together or with some striped petals, requires rich soil if it is to thrive, 2m/1.2m (6½ft/4ft); *R.* 'Madame Hardy', slightly leathery, light green leaves on very prickly branches, fully double, white flowers are quartered rosettes with a green button eye, outer petals slightly reflexed, fragrant, summer, the favourite of many rose experts, 2m/1.2m (6½ft/4ft).

Alba roses Tall shrubs with grey-green leaves and fragrant flowers are pink, white or white tinged pink. Tolerant of partial shade and varieties that I find useful at the back of the border. ❀ *R.* x *alba* 'Alba Semiplena' (syn. 'White Rose of York'), grey-green leaves, clusters of large, flat, very fragrant semi-double white flowers with conspicuous gold-yellow stamens, summer, followed by elongated, oval, scarlet hips, requires space, 2.2m/1.5m (6¾ft/5ft); *R.* 'Great Maiden's Blush' (syn. 'Cuisse de Nymphe'), glaucous, grey-green leaves on arching branches, fully double, cupped, very fragrant pink-white flowers, petals inwardly folded, early to mid-summer, 2m/1.3m (6½ft/4½ft).

Rugosa roses Medium/large, dense shrub roses with coarse, deeply veined leaves, large flowers, single or fully double. Most will repeat flower in late summer; they are tolerant of poor conditions and are very disease and pest resistant. ❀ *R.* 'Blanche Double de Coubert', spreading, leathery, mid-green leaves, semi-double, cupped or flat, pure white flowers with thin, papery petals and yellow stamens, throughout summer, flowers followed by a few spherical red hips, 1.5m/1.2m (5ft/4ft); *R.* 'Fru Dagmar Hastrup', spreading, leathery mid-green leaves, pointed buds open to single fragrant pink flowers with cream stamens, followed after first flowering by round, deep red hips that appear at the same time as the later flowers, 1m/1.2m (3ft/4ft). *R.* 'Roseraie de l'Hay', leathery, crinkled, apple-green leaves, wine-red buds open to flat or cupped, double, purple-red fragrant flowers, 2.2m/2m (6¾ft/6½ft).

Hybrid musk roses Hybrid musk roses are shrubs with pale, delicate flowers held in large clusters in early summer, and then intermittently. ❀ *R.* 'Buff Beauty', abundant dark green leaves, fully double, warm apricot-yellow flowers, in summer, some later, 1.2m/1.2m (4ft/4ft).

Hybrid musk climbers ❀ *R.* 'The Garland', climber or rambler, clusters of small, cream-salmon flowers with narrow, quilled petals, orange fragrance, summer, followed by small oval, red-orange hips, can also be grown as a large shrub, 4.5m (14¾ft).

China roses China roses are similar to the many groups of old shrub roses, with fine blooms and strong fragrance, but with the significant advantage of repeat flowering. The leaves have much in common with modern roses, but are smaller and more refined. ❀ *R.* 'Pompon de Paris' (also a climbing form that I adore, 'Climbing Pompon de Paris'), tiny, semi-double rose-pink flowers, solitary, repeat flowering.

Bourbon roses Bourbon roses have strongly scented, heavy and opulent flowers, typical of old shrub roses, but their foliage has more in common with that of modern varieties. ❀ *R.* 'Madame Isaac Pereire', arching shrub or climber, large, dark green leaves, fully double, cupped, quartered rosette-shaped, purple-pink flowers, 15cm (6in) in diameter, petals reflexed at the edges, rich fragrance, 2.2m/2.2m (6¾ft/6¾ft).

Bourbon climbers ❀ *R.* 'Blairii No 2' leaves red-green at first, later mid-green, clusters of fully double, deeply cupped flowers, delicious deep pink with paler margins, summer, a few later, 3m/1.5m (10ft/5ft).

above *Rosa* 'Roseraie de l'Hay'. The Rugosa varieties have many highly individual features, including most untypical rose foliage and high levels of pest and disease resistance.

Noisette climbers Noisette climbers have delicate, fragrant flowers, often produced rather later than those of most shrub roses. ❀ *R.* 'Madame Alfred Carriére', pale green leaves, large, cupped double white flowers flushed pink, very sweet fragrance, summer to autumn, 5m/3m (16ft/10ft).

Tea climbers Climbing tea roses have glossy, light or dark green leaves and semi-double to double flowers, singly or in clusters, summer to autumn. They are not as hardy as many other roses and require a position against a warm sunny wall but are exquisitely lovely with exquisitely lovely fragrance. ❀ *R.* 'Sombreuil', flat, quartered rosette-shaped, fragrant flowers, cream-white, sometimes pink at the centre, repeats well and the finest low

above *Rosa* 'English Garden'. The New English Roses, bred by David Austin, uniquely combine the appearance and fragrance of the old varieties with the long flowering period of the more modern forms.

right *Rosa primula*. The earliest flowering rose in my garden is this beautifully fragrant single from China.

growing white climber that I know, 3.5m (11ft); *R.* 'Gloire de Dijon', glossy, dark green leaves, large, quartered rosette-shaped, buff-yellow flowers, sometimes flushed pink and gold, cupped at first, later flat, very fragrant, early summer to autumn, one of the all-time classics of the rose world, 5m/4m (16ft/13ft).

Hybrid perpetual roses Hybrid perpetuals are erect shrubs with dark green leaves on prickly branches and fully double, often fragrant, flowers, singly or in clusters. They flower from summer through until autumn and were the favourite roses of the Victorian garden. ❀ *R.* 'Frau Karl Druschki' (syn. *R.* 'Snow Queen'), mid-green leaves on arching branches, fully double, pure white flowers tinted lemon-green at the centre, from summer to autumn, 1.5m/1.2m (5ft/4ft); *R.* 'Reine des Violettes', grey-green leaves on arching, almost thornless, branches, fully double, fragrant, quartered rosette-shaped, lilac- purple flowers, summer to autumn, suffers in wet weather, 1.5m/1.2m (5ft/4ft).

Polyantha roses Polyanthas are hardy, dwarf, compact roses that flower throughout the summer and most are excellent for growing in containers. Flowers are single or double, usually with little fragrance, and borne in small sprays; small, glossy leaves have lance-shaped leaflets. ❀ *R.* 'Perle d'Or', glossy, dark green leaves, miniature, fragrant, fully-double flowers of the hybrid tea type, light apricot at first, fading to cream, a quite wonderful plant, 1.2m/1m (4ft/3ft); *R.* 'Cécile Brunner' (syns. *R.* 'Sweetheart Rose', *R.* 'Mignon'), dark green leaves, fully-double, light pink flowers, very similar to 'Perle d'Or', summer to autumn, 1m/60cm (3ft/2ft).

Modern shrub roses Modern shrub roses are a diverse group, most of them bred in the latter half of the 20th century. They are often larger than Hybrid Teas and Floribundas, with large or medium-sized leaves composed of lance-shaped or oval leaflets. Flowers are single or double, solitary or in clusters, usually fragrant, borne from summer to autumn. ❀ *R.* 'Nevada', small, light green leaves, abundant fragrant, semi-double, very pale yellow to cream-white flowers, with conspicuous gold stamens produced all along the arching branches in summer and intermittently until autumn, 2.2m/2.2m (6¾ft/6¾ft); *R.* 'Frühlingsgold', matt, light green, toothed leaves on arching branches, fragrant, semi-double, pale yellow flowers with conspicuous yellow stamens, early summer, a few later, 2m/1.5m (6½ft/5ft); *R.* 'Zigeunerknabe', (syn. *R.* 'Gypsy Boy'), coarse, dark green leaves, on prickly branches, fragrant, double, dark violet-purple flowers with conspicuous gold stamens, early summer, disease resistant, more tolerant than most of difficult positions, 2m/1.2m (6½ft/4ft).

New English roses English roses are a group bred by the rose breeder David Austin. The flowers are similar in form and fragrance to those of the old roses, but have the modern characteristic of repeat or continuous flowering throughout the summer. They are invaluable for the modern garden. ❀ *R.* 'English Garden', erect shrub, light green leaves, rosette-shaped flowers, cupped, soft pale apricot-yellow, paler on the outer edges, light fragrance, summer to autumn, 1m/75cm (3ft/2½ft); *R.* 'Mary Rose', matt, mid-green leaves on twiggy branches, loose-petalled, cupped, rose-pink double flowers, 1.2m/1m (4ft/3ft).

Ground cover roses Ground cover roses are relatively low-growing, bushy shrubs with small flowers, most produced in large sprays. They differ from other ground cover plants in that they do not creep along the ground but usually attain a height of 60-100cm (2-3ft). Most of them are modern varieties. ❀ *R.* 'Swany' shiny dark green leaves,

abundant clusters of flat, fully double, white to cream-white flowers, from summer to autumn, 75cm/2m (2½ft/6½ft); *R.* 'Nozomi', lower-growing than most, glossy dark green leaves, very small, pearl pink to white flowers 1cm (½in) in diameter, in summer, does not repeat, can be grown as a small climber, 45cm/1.2m (1½ft/4ft), climber to 1.5m (5ft); *R.* 'Flower Carpet', glossy bright green leaves, clusters of double, cupped flowers, violently rose-pink, summer to autumn, 75cm/2m (2½ft/6½ft).

Miniature and patio roses The miniature roses have tiny flowers and grow to a height of 30-45cm (1-1½ft). They are repeat or continuous flowering but as a group are not as reliably hardy as other roses and are less tolerant of adverse weather conditions. Patio roses have some of the characteristics of miniatures but the flowers are more sculptural in appearance, rather similar to small Floribundas. They are repeat or continuous flowering. ❀ *R.* 'Easter Morning', erect, compact miniature, dark green glossy leaves, ivory-white flowers, resistant to rain damage, the best miniature in my experience, 30cm (1ft); *R.* 'Yellow Doll', miniature, tiny, double soft yellow flowers with narrow petals, light fragrance, 30cm (1ft); *R.* 'Dresden Doll', miniature moss rose, semi-double to double shell-pink flowers with conspicuous stamens, fairly fragrant, moss-covered buds, 35cm (1¼ft); *R.* 'Angela Rippon', miniature, dark green leaves, urn-shaped, fully double rose-pink to salmon-pink flowers, summer to autumn, 45cm/30cm (1½ft/1ft).

Floribunda roses Floribundas, also known as cluster-flowered bush roses, produce flowers in large sprays throughout the summer and autumn, sometimes with a few in early winter. Although not renowned for their fragrance, some are pleasantly scented. They are the most popular and overall probably the most useful roses in the modern garden. ❀ *R.* 'Iceberg' (syns. 'Fée des Neige', 'Schneewittchen'), light green, pointed leaves on almost thornless branches, double, pure white flowers, sometimes pink tinged, light fragrance, 1.2m/60cm (4ft/2ft); *R.* 'Arthur Bell', glossy leaves, large, semi-double flowers, bright yellow fading to cream, strong fragrance, 1m (3ft); *R.* 'Korresia', glossy green leaves, double, bright yellow flowers with wavy edged petals, fragrant, 75cm/60cm (2½ft/2ft); *R.* 'The Queen Elizabeth' (syn. *R.* 'Queen Elizabeth'), very vigorous, large glossy, leathery, dark green leaves, clear pink, globular flowers on long, erect stems, 2.2m/1m (6¾ft/3ft); *R.* 'Masquerade', leathery, dark green leaves, large clusters of small, cupped to flat, semi-double flowers, changing from yellow to flame to pink and red with age, all colours appearing together, light fragrance, 80cm/60cm (2½ft/2ft).

Floribunda climbers ❀ *R.* 'Allgold', a lovely plant with all the merits of the bush form and, since there aren't many good yellow-flowered climbers of any sort, a plant that should be used more widely, 4.5m (15ft); *R.* 'Iceberg', fewer thorns than on the bush form, and more shade tolerant, good for growing on a pillar, 3m (10ft).

Hybrid tea roses Hybrid teas, also known as large-flowered bush roses, usually have solitary flowers, most with a perfect conical shape, that are larger than those of the floribundas. They are grown for their individual blooms; many are fragrant and, if you are content with fewer flowers, you will certainly find them more stylish and elegant than Floribundas. ❀ *R.* 'Pascali', narrow, erect bush, dark green leaves, medium-sized white flowers, sometimes buff at the centre, singly or, rarely, in clusters, slight fragrance, 75cm/50cm (2½ft/1¼ft); *R.* 'The Lady', compact, honey-yellow flowers, edged with pink, 90cm (3ft); *R.* 'Tequila Sunrise', glossy dark green leaves, very striking double yellow flowers with scarlet-edged petals, lightly scented, 75cm/60cm (2½ft/2ft); *R.* 'Peace' (syn. 'Mme A Meilland'), glossy leaves, large, pale yellow flowers tinged pink with wavy-edged petals, summer and autumn, good disease resistance, probably the most famous rose ever raised, 1.2m/1m (4ft/3ft); *R.* 'Mrs Oakley Fisher', bronze-green leaves, flat, single, apricot flowers, fading to pale buff, on spindly stems, 1m/75cm (3ft/2½ft); *R.* 'Madame Butterfly', erect bush, small mid-green leaves, urn- to cup-shaped pale pink flowers with soft yellow centres, fading to cream, fragrant, 1m/60cm (3ft/2ft); *R.* 'Silver Jubilee', glossy dark green leaves, abundant, large, fully-double, deep pink flowers, paler at the centre, salmon-pink at the petal base, singly or in clusters, 1.1m/60cm (3½ft/2ft); *R.* 'Alec's Red', glossy, mid- to dark green leaves, double cherry-red flowers, strong fragrance, 1m/60cm (3ft/2ft); *R.* 'Josephine Bruce', dark green leaves, double dark crimson flowers, 75cm/60cm (2½ft/2ft).

above *Rosa* 'Perle d'Or'. This is one of the prettiest little roses that you will ever see; and I think it even lovelier than the similar and better known white flowered variety 'Cécile Brunner'.

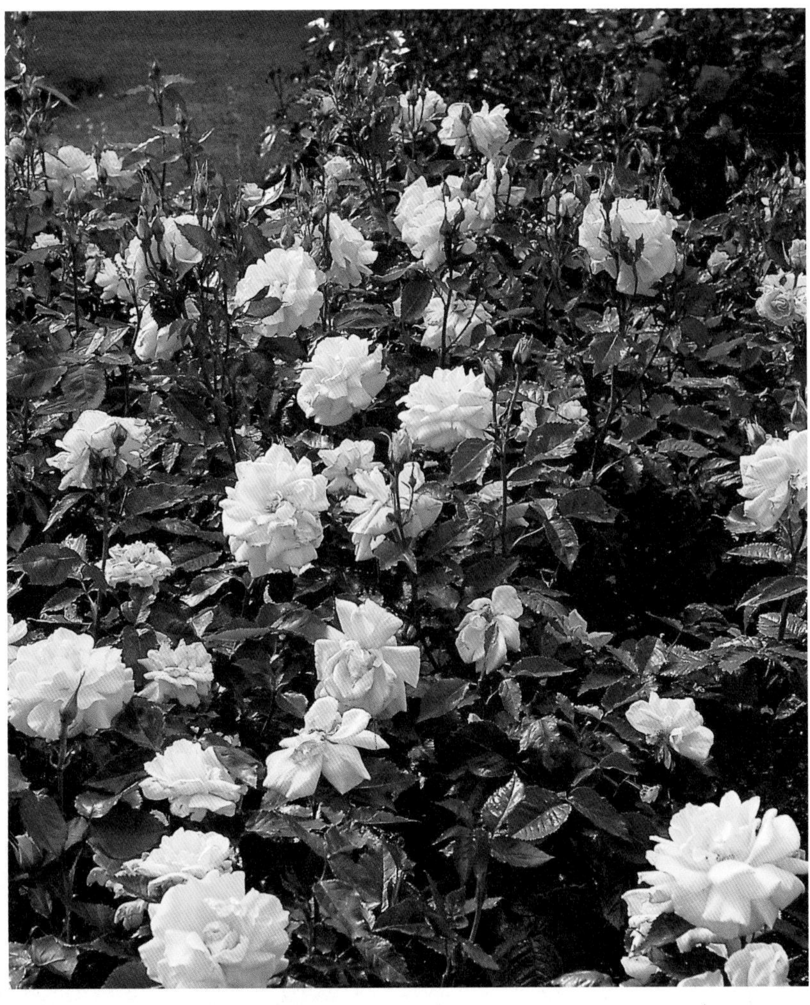

above *Rosa* 'Korresia'. Most yellow-flowered roses suffer from the serious defect of susceptibility to blackspot but this Floribunda from the German breeder Kordes is among the more reliable.

right *Rosa* 'New Dawn'. One of the outstanding climbing roses, although no-one seems quite sure if it is really a climber or a rambler.

Hybrid tea climbers ❀ *R.* 'Mrs Herbert Stevens', large, well-formed double flowers, very fragrant, 6m (20ft); *R.* 'Bantry Bay', erect climber, dark green leaves, clusters of semi-double, deep pink flowers, light fragrance, 4m/2.5m (13ft/8ft); *R.* 'Ena Harkness', mid-green leaves, pendent, double crimson-scarlet, fragrant flowers, summer, some later, shade and weather tolerant, 5m/2.5m (16ft/8ft).

Modern climbers Modern climbers, like their bush relatives, are roses that have been bred relatively recently. Unlike older varieties they repeat flower or flower continuously; most have a tall, lax habit of growth. ❀ *R.* 'Swan Lake', well-formed, fully-double, white hybrid tea flowers, tinged pink at the centre, fragrant, weather tolerant, 2.5m (8ft); *R.* 'Golden Showers', glossy dark green leaves, well-formed buds open to semi-double yellow flowers, fading to cream, suitable for a pillar and for growing as a shrub, will tolerate a north-facing position, 2.5m (8ft); *R.* 'Schoolgirl', large, sparse, glossy leaves, very large double flowers, light orange to apricot, 3m (10ft); *R.* 'Aloha', large, fragrant, cupped clear pink double flowers, flushed orange at the centre, from summer to autumn, disease resistant, arguably the best modern short climbing rose, 2.5m (8ft).

Rambler roses Ramblers are strong-growing roses with long, supple shoots and abundant flowers in large clusters. The flowers are usually small, fragrant, and produced only once in the year, in early summer. They are suitable for covering large areas or growing into trees but most are, sadly, very prone to mildew. ❀ *R.* 'Rambling Rector', grey-green leaves on arching branches, profusion of small, semi-double, cream-white flowers with gold stamens, followed by small, spherical, red hips, strong fragrance, 6m/6m (20ft/20ft); *R.* 'Alberic Barbier', semi-evergreen, fine, glossy, dark green leaves, light apricot-orange buds open to small, cream-white flowers, early summer, rather more resistant to mildew than most, 4.5m (14¾ft); *R.* 'New Dawn' (syn. 'The New Dawn'), glossy mid-green leaves, clusters of cupped, double pale pink, fragrant flowers, summer to autumn, relatively disease resistant and a very beautiful plant, 3m/2.5m (10ft/8ft); *R.* 'Albertine', dark green leaves on arching, prickly branches, abundant clusters of rose-pink buds open to large, double copper-pink flowers, very fragrant, early to mid-summer, very susceptible to mildew, 5m/4m (16ft/13ft); *R.* 'Crimson Shower', small, glossy leaves on lax branches, clusters of small, double crimson flowers, 2.5m/2.7m (8ft/9ft).

Roscoea Zingiberaceae

Hardy to very hardy herbaceous tuberous perennials. Superficially *Iris*-like and suitable for rock gardens, the front of borders and containers. Rather broad, lance-shaped bright green leaves. Flowers at tips of short, leafy or leafless stems, yellow, red, purple, white or bicoloured, throughout summer; plant then dormant until following spring. Much admired whenever seen, which isn't very frequently. Best in rich, acidic, moist soil in sheltered position but with full sun. Sow seed in spring or divide established plants after flowering. ❀ *R. alpina*, single stem with succession of red-purple flowers, 15cm/15cm (6in/6in); *R. auriculata*, up to ten stems, with succession of purple flowers, 40cm/35cm (1½ft/1¼ft); *R. cautleyoïdes*, up to three stems with several yellow flowers in successional groups, 30cm/25cm (1ft/10in); *R. humeana*, single stem with successions of purple or mauve-pink flowers, 30cm/20cm (1ft/8in); *R. purpurea*, single stem with purple, white or bicoloured flowers, 30cm/20cm (1ft/8in).

Rosmarinus *Rosemary* Lamiaceae

Barely hardy to hardy evergreen shrubs grown as herbs and as ornamentals for their richly fragrant foliage and small blue, white or pink summer flowers. Also valuable as dwarf or medium hedging but some forms are browned severely by winter cold. Underestimated but effective as container plants. Upright needle-like leaves, closely flattened to stem with many small, lipped flowers partly hidden among them. Best in fairly rich, well-drained soil in full sun. No routine pruning but old shoots best cut out every two or three years and may be closely clipped twice each year. Take heeled semi-ripe cuttings in summer. ❀ *R. officinalis* (Common Rosemary), dark green, needle-like leaves, white-felted beneath, tiny flowers spring to mid-summer and some in autumn, 1.5-2m/1.5m (5-6½ft/5ft); *R. o. albiflorus*, white flowers; *R. o.* 'Aureus', leaves with yellow markings but reverts and not as attractive as its sounds; *R. o.* 'Benenden Blue', more compact (1m (3ft)), rich blue flowers; *R. o.* 'Majorca Pink', pink flowers, upright habit; *R. o.* 'Miss Jessopp's Upright', upright habit, pale flowers, the best all-round variety; *R. o.* Prostratus Group, prostrate (to 60cm (2ft)), pale blue flowers but only barely hardy; *R. o.* 'Severn Sea', spreading habit, blue-mauve flowers; *R. o.* 'Sissinghurst Blue', upright, rather vigorous, deep blue flowers, the best blue.

Rubus Rosaceae

Moderately hardy to very hardy deciduous or evergreen ornamental and fruiting shrubs. Although including the important soft fruits, raspberries and blackberries, there are also several very attractive and valuable ornamental species grown for their foliage, flowers and especially for their coloured winter stems (canes). Entire, lobed or divided leaves on usually prickly stems, flowers singly or in groups in summer, usually single, white, pink or red followed by characteristic 'raspberry-like' fruits. Best in full sun although will tolerate more shade than other soft fruits; rich, moist but essentially free-draining soil. Fruiting types should be mulched heavily. Pruning varies; ornamentals grown for coloured stems should be pruned hard in spring, other ornamentals require no routine pruning. Fruiting types should have old fruited canes removed after harvest; primocane (autumn) fruiting raspberries should be pruned to soil level in late winter.

below *Rosmarinus* 'Sissinghurst Blue'. There are far more varieties of rosemary than most gardeners imagine and whilst the pink is most striking, this is one of the true blues.

right *Rubus ulmifolius* 'Bellidiflorus'. I don't think that any member of the genus has prettier flowers than this but it is a big, vigorous plant for larger gardens only.

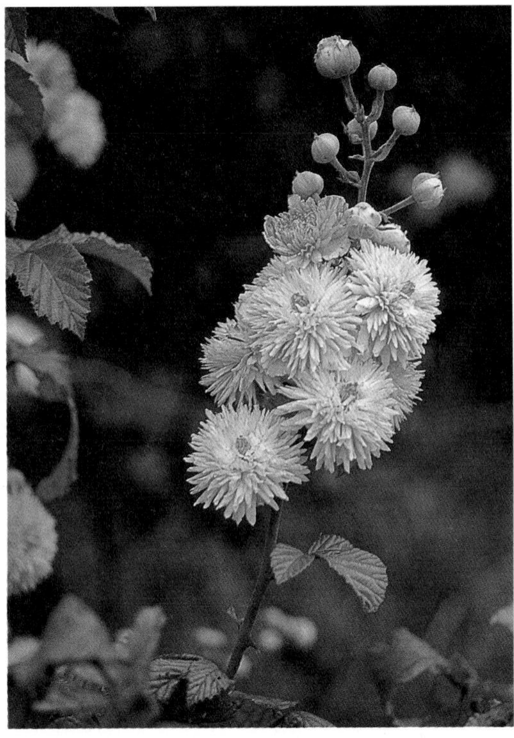

far right *Rumex sanguineus*. A pretty foliage plant for difficult places but one that has inherited the invasiveness of its weed relatives.

Ornamental

R. 'Benenden', deciduous, upright thornless stems with attractive peeling bark, large single white flowers with golden anthers, late spring to summer, 3m/1m (10ft/3ft); *R. cockburnianus*, deciduous, purple shoots with thick white bloom in winter, purple flowers, summer, inedible black fruits, 2.5m/1m (8ft/3ft); *R. thibetanus*, deciduous, purple stems with white bloom in winter, purple flowers, summer, edible black fruits, 2.5m/1m (8ft/3ft); *R. tricolor*, evergreen, ground cover, dark green leaves, thorny stems, white summer flowers, edible red fruits, effective ground cover but severely browned in cold winters, 75cm/3m (2½ft/10ft); *R. ulmifolius* 'Bellidiflorus' (Bramble), deciduous, vigorous, arching, scrambling, very pretty double pink flowers, summer, the best ornamental *Rubus* but must have space; 3m/3m (10ft/10ft).

Edible

***R. fruticosus* (Blackberry, Bramble)**, arching, usually very thorny, stems, large black fruit; *R. f.* 'Ashton Cross', undeniably the best flavour, closest to that of wild brambles; *R. f.* 'Himalayan Giant', very vigorous, for large gardens only; *R. f.* 'Loch Ness', compact variety with upright, raspberry-like canes, ideal for small gardens.

***R. idaeus* (Raspberry)**, upright canes, red fruit, all are summer fruiting varieties unless mentioned otherwise; *R. i.* 'Glen Clova', early-mid-season, big crop but poor pest and disease resistance; *R. i.* 'Malling Delight', early, very heavy crop but poor pest and disease resistance; *R. i.* 'Malling Jewel', mid-season; *R. i.* 'Glen Moy', early, thornless; *R. i.* 'Glen Prosen', mid-season; *R. i.* 'Malling Admiral', mid-late season, vigorous; *R. i.* 'Leo', late; *R. i.* 'Autumn Bliss', autumn fruiting, much the best cropping of any autumn variety but vigorous and invasive.

Hybrid and Species berries 'Boysenberry', derived from cross involving *R. i.* 'Himalayan Giant', large purple fruit; Loganberry Group 'LY 654, raspberry/blackberry cross, large, very dark red fruits; *R. phoenicolasius* (Japanese Wineberry), small orange fruits, very attractive red-brown bristly-hairy stems.

Rudbeckia *Coneflower* Asteraceae

Hardy herbaceous annuals and perennials. Grown for their very pretty late summer yellow or orange daisy flowers with characteristic cone-shaped centres. Excellent plants for the middle or back of mixed borders and best planted in large groups.

Leaves generally mid-green, lance-shaped. Tolerate most good, well-drained soils in full sun. Divide in spring or autumn. All the following are herbaceous perennials. ❀ *R. fulgida deamii*, deep yellow florets with dark central cone, 60cm/45cm (2ft/1½ft); *R. f. speciosa*, larger, more vigorous, 1m (3ft); *R.* 'Goldquelle', double flowers, yellow florets, green central cone; *R.* 'Herbstsonne' (syn. 'Autumn Sun'), single flowers with characteristically floppy yellow florets around green central cone; *R. laciniata*, large flowers, yellow florets, green-yellow central cone, 2m/75cm (6½ft/2½ft); *R. maxima*, golden yellow florets, black central cone, 1.5m/75cm (5ft/2½ft).

Rumex *Dock, Sorrel* Polygonaceae

Moderately hardy to very hardy annuals, biennials, perennials or sub-shrubs and including many pernicious weeds. Dull, often elongated, heart-shaped leaves arising from basal rosette. Flowers are totally unspectacular in dense, often branched, spikes but foliage of some varieties, althought not the weedy species, is valued as a leafy kitchen crop and in a few forms can be attractively coloured. Will grow almost anywhere in any type of soil, including heavy clay, and tolerate partial shade. Take care when growing in kitchen garden as can be invasive and therefore best confined. Sow seed in growing positions in spring or divide plants in spring or autumn. ❀ *R. acetosa* (Sour Dock, Garden Sorrel), leafy kitchen herb, grow as cut-and-come-again crop, 60cm (2ft)/indefinite; *R. sanguineus sanguineus*, foliage ornamental, leaves with striking red or red-purple veins, 1m (3ft)/indefinite; *R. scutatus* (French Sorrel, Garden Sorrel), leafy kitchen herb, leaves with silver stalks, 45cm/30cm (1½ft/1ft); *R. s.* 'Silver Shield', ornamental form, silver leaves.

Ruscus *Butcher's Broom* Ruscaceae

Very hardy evergreen rhizomatous perennial for difficult situations. Admired for its botanical curiosity as much as anything; the true leaves are reduced almost to nought and what appear to be leaves are cladodes, flattened stems. Flowers tiny, green and purple, red fruits follow when male and female plants grown together. Flower arrangers love it. Tolerates dry shade and almost any soil including highly alkaline clay. Sow ripe seed in a cold-frame (slow to germinate) or divide in spring. ❀ *R. aculeatus*, tough, stiff stems with broadly lance-shaped cladodes with apical spines, 1.2m/1m (4ft/3ft).

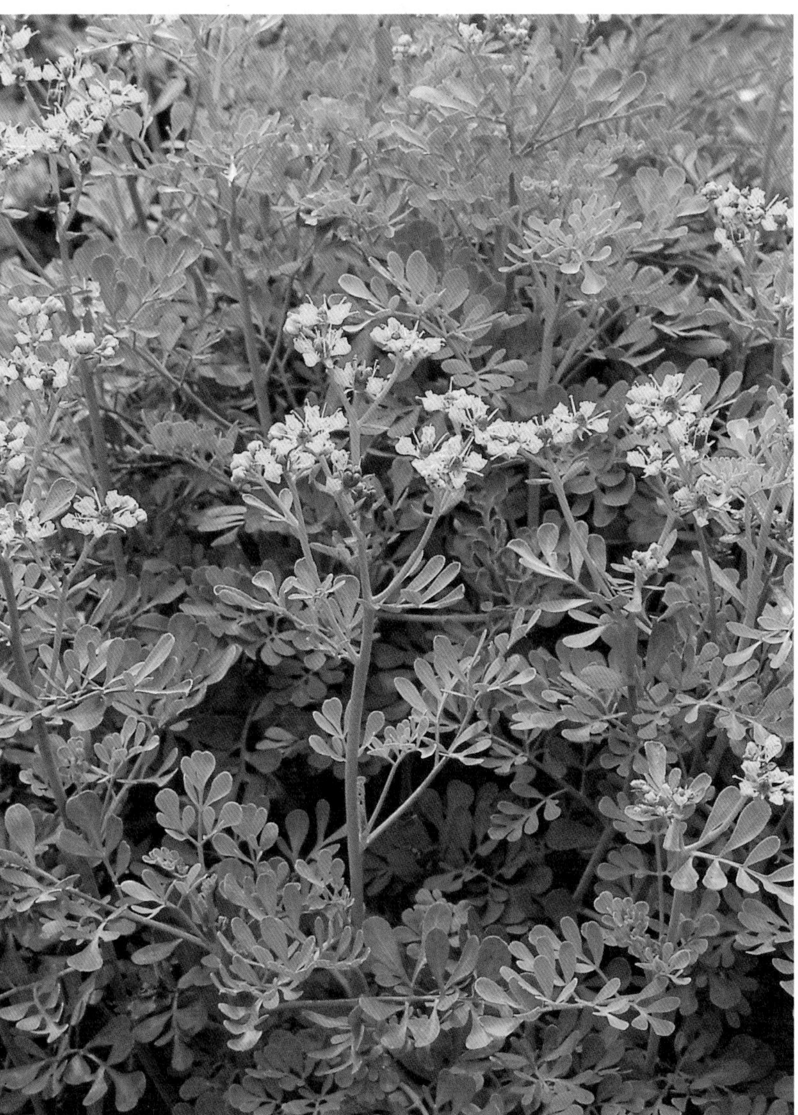

above *Ruta graveolens* 'Jackman's Blue'. Much the best form of this old medicinal herb; the contrast between the yellow flowers and steel-blue foliage is very striking.

Ruta *Rue* Rutaceae

Hardy, evergreen herbaceous perennials or sub-shrubs. Long grown as medicinal herbs but valued now more for their striking foliage form and colour. Finely divided, almost maidenhair fern-like aromatic leaves, groups of small yellow flowers at stem tips in summer. Suitable for herb garden or centre of mixed border. Foliage can cause severe skin irritation in some people in sunlight. Cut back hard, at least to old wood, in spring although plants are best renewed after about five or six years. Take semi-ripe cuttings in summer. ❀ *R. graveolens*, blue-green leaves, contrast vividly with small bright yellow flowers, mid-summer, 45cm/30cm (1½ft/1ft); *R. g.* 'Jackman's Blue', neater, better plant with more intensely coloured leaves; *R. g.* 'Variegata', leaves with cream-white margins, creating a very curious effect.

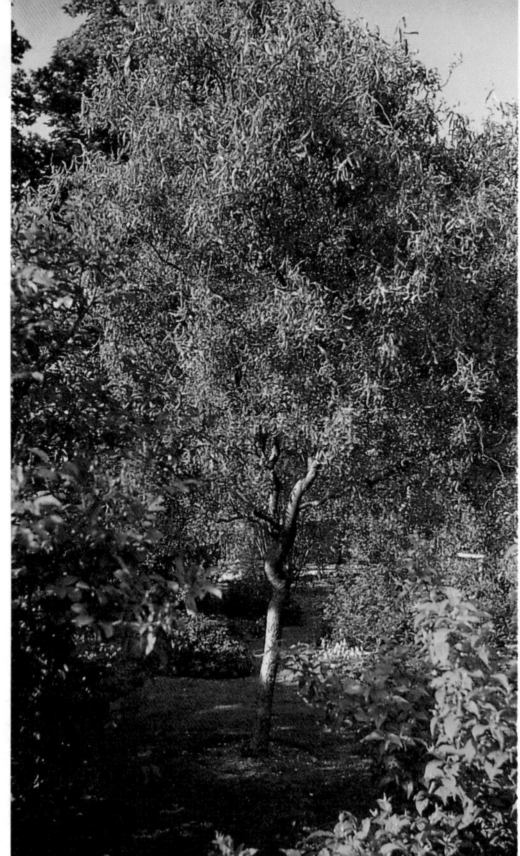

right *Salix babylonica pekinensis* 'Tortuosa'. One of two familiar twisted garden trees (the twisted hazel is the other) that run a life-long gauntlet of flower arrangers' secateurs.

Sagina *Pearlwort* Caryophyllaceae

Small, evergreen herbaceous perennials or alpines. Very hardy. Dense mats or cushions of foliage provide year-round interest on rock gardens, between paving or in troughs, although the plants are often mistaken for moss; and unfortunately treated as such. Minute, white flowers (use magnifying glass) in summer. Require a well-drained, gritty soil of low to moderate fertility and full sun. Sow seed in a cold-frame in autumn or divide plants in spring. ❀ *S. subulata* 'Aurea', yellow-green leaves, 10cm/30cm (4in/1ft).

Sagittaria *Arrowhead* Alismataceae

Medium/large, hardy submerged/marginal plants offering unusual leaves and white flowers in summer and excellent for water-side planting in sun, in water no deeper than 20-30cm (8-12in) by large pools. Sow ripe seed in containers in water or divide plants in spring. ❀ *S. sagittifolia* (syn. *S. japonica*), marginal hardy perennial, arrow-shaped aerial leaves, white flowers, summer, 90cm (3ft)/indefinite; *S. s.* 'Flore Pleno', double-flowers.

Salix *Willow* Salicaceae

Small/large, mostly deciduous trees and shrubs. Very hardy. The willows are a diverse group with species appropriate as specimens or windbreaks, for borders and even for rock gardens and alpine troughs. They offer differing combinations of buds, spring catkins, winter stem colour and summer foliage. Will thrive in most soils except thin alkaline sites and are especially good for wet, heavy places, although alpines need gritty compost. All are best in full sun. The roots of large specimens, especially of the common weeping willow, can invade drains. It is important therefore to avoid this species in all except the largest gardens, and keep it away from buildings. It is important too to know it correctly; its current name is *Salix* x *sepulcralis chrysocoma* but willows change their names remarkably frequently, so don't plant any weeping willow in small gardens that is called simply *S. babylonica*. No routine pruning but all larger willows can be cut back hard and will regrow; sometimes they are pollarded for ornamental effect. Those grown for ornamental bark effect should be pruned very hard in spring to encourage young shoot growth. Semi-ripe or hardwood cuttings root readily. ❀ *S. alba* var. *sericea* (syns. f. *argentea*, 'Sericea', Splendens') (Silver Willow), silver-grey leaves, 6m/4m (20ft/13ft); *S. a.* var. *vitellina* (Golden Willow), strikingly pretty bright yellow shoots, 6m/4m (20ft/13ft); *S. a. v.* 'Britzensis', male clone with bright orange-red shoots; *S. babylonica pekinensis* 'Tortuosa' (syn. *S. matsudana*) (Twisted Peking Willow), upright, fast-growing tree, curiously twisted shoots a winter feature adored by flower arrangers, catkins, 9m/6m (30ft/20ft); *S.* x *boydii*, dwarf, very slow-growing alpine shrub, gnarled branches,

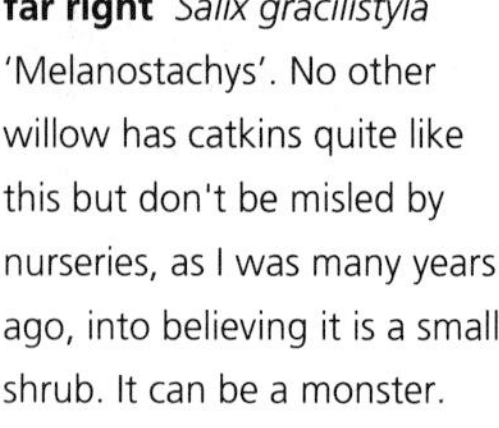

far right *Salix gracilistyla* 'Melanostachys'. No other willow has catkins quite like this but don't be misled by nurseries, as I was many years ago, into believing it is a small shrub. It can be a monster.

grey downy leaves, catkins, 90cm/30cm (3ft/1ft); *S. caprea* 'Kilmarnock' (Kilmarnock Willow), generally sold grafted as a small weeping tree, catkins, 1.5-2m/2m (5-6½ft/6½ft); *S. exigua* (Coyote Willow), large shrub or small tree, forms a thicket, silver-grey leaves, catkins, good in sandy soils, 4m/5m (13ft/16ft); *S. fargesii* (syn. *S. moupinensis*), large, open shrub, red buds in winter, rich red stems, glossy green leaves, catkins, a glorious plant but prone to late frost damage, 3m/3m (10ft/10ft); *S. gracilistyla* 'Melanostachys' (syn. *S. melanostachys*), large, very fast-growing, spreading shrub with purple stems, leaves silky grey then green and smooth, striking black catkins with red anthers, lovely, but don't underestimate its vigour, 3m/4m (10ft/13ft); *S. hastata* 'Wehrhahnii', small shrub, bright green leaves, catkins, 2m/1m (6½ft/3ft); *S. integra* 'Hakuro-nishiki' (syn. 'Albomaculata'), large shrub or small tree, slightly drooping, bright green leaves blotched with white and pink, catkins, 1m (3ft) as a standard; *S. lanata* (Woolly Willow), small shrub, downy, silver-grey leaves, catkins, 1-1.5m/30cm-2m (3-5ft/1-6½ft); *S. repens* (Creeping Willow), small but creeping shrub, grey-green leaves silver-white beneath, catkins, a very variable but splendid plant that I grow in gravel, 30cm/1.5m (1ft/5ft) or more; *S.* x *sepulcralis chrysocoma*, large weeping tree, golden-yellow shoots, bright green leaves, catkins, beautiful but see my remarks above, 15m/15m (50ft/50ft); *S. udensis* 'Sekka' (syn. *S. sachalinensis* 'Sekka'), large shrub or small tree, forms dense thicket, bright green leaves, catkins, a remarkable male form with some flattened and recurved (fasciated) stems, 5m/8m (16ft/26½ft).

Salpiglossis — Solanaceae

Medium half-hardy bedding annuals or short-lived perennials. Particularly effective in containers but useful also as taller summer bedding. Tolerate most soils provided warm and sunny. Stems covered with sticky hairs, pale green leaves. Funnel-shaped flowers in a rich range of blues, oranges, purples, reds and yellows often with gold markings and dark veining, mid-summer to autumn. Sow seed in warmth in mid-spring or late winter to raise bedding plants. All varieties sold as bedding annuals are hybrids derived from *Salpiglossis sinuata* and other species: ❀ 'Bolero' F2, straggly habit, mixture, 60-75cm (2-2½ft); 'Carnival' F2, mixture, 45cm (1½ft); 'Casino' F1, compact, bushy, mixture, 35cm (1¼ft); 'Chocolate Pot' F1, rich brown with gold eye, velvet texture, especially attractive, 30cm (1ft); 'Flamenco' F1, mixture 35cm (1¼ft).

Salvia *Sage* — Lamiaceae

Small/large annuals, biennials, herbaceous perennials (some evergreen), herbs and shrubs. Tender to very hardy. A diverse group, sometimes wrongly judged solely by the vividly coloured annuals. Summer colour from flowers and attractive, sometimes aromatic, foliage. They require a well-drained, moderately fertile soil and full sun or partial shade. Leaves are usually simple, often hairy. Tubular, two-lipped flowers, the upper sometimes elongated to a hood; some have very impressive flower spikes. Bedding salvias derived from *S. fulgens*: sow seed in warmth in early spring. Hardy perennials: divide in spring or autumn, or sow seed in growing positions in spring. Half hardy or tender perennials grown as annuals: take softwood or tip cuttings in summer and keep in greenhouse overwinter or sow seed in warmth in spring.

above *Salvia patens* 'Cambridge Blue'. This is perhaps the loveliest species in the entire genus and it can only be its slightly suspect hardiness that means it isn't grown more widely.

Hardy perennials *S. argentea*, biennial or herbaceous hardy short-lived perennial, basal rosette of silver-grey woolly leaves, branching spikes of white flowers, summer, 90cm/60cm (3ft/2ft); *S. farinacea* 'Blue Victory', violet-blue flowers, 60cm (2ft); *S. nemorosa* 'Ostfriesland' (syn. 'East Friesland'), well-branched habit, mid-green leaves, deep blue-violet flowers, summer to autumn, 45cm/45cm (1½ft/1½ft); *S. officinalis* (Common Sage), medium shrubby evergreen herb, hardy, woolly aromatic leaves of grey-green, lilac-blue flowers, early to mid-summer, to 80cm/1m (2½ft/3ft); *S. o* 'Icterina', yellow and green leaves; *S. o* Purpurascens Group, silver-purple young leaves that darken later; *S. o* 'Tricolor', barely hardy to fairly hardy, beautiful grey-green leaves splashed with cream and pink markings; *S. patens*, medium tuberous ornamental, barely hardy to fairly hardy, mid-green leaves, pale or deep blue flowers, mid-summer to mid-autumn, in mild gardens tubers can be left in the ground but otherwise lift and store over winter or raise from seed, 45-60cm/45cm (1½-2ft/1½ft); *S. p.* 'Cambridge Blue', pale blue flowers; *S. pratensis* Haematodes Group (syn. *S. haematodes*), medium tuberous ornamental, hardy but short-lived, basal rosette of dark green leaves, light lavender-blue flowers, early summer,

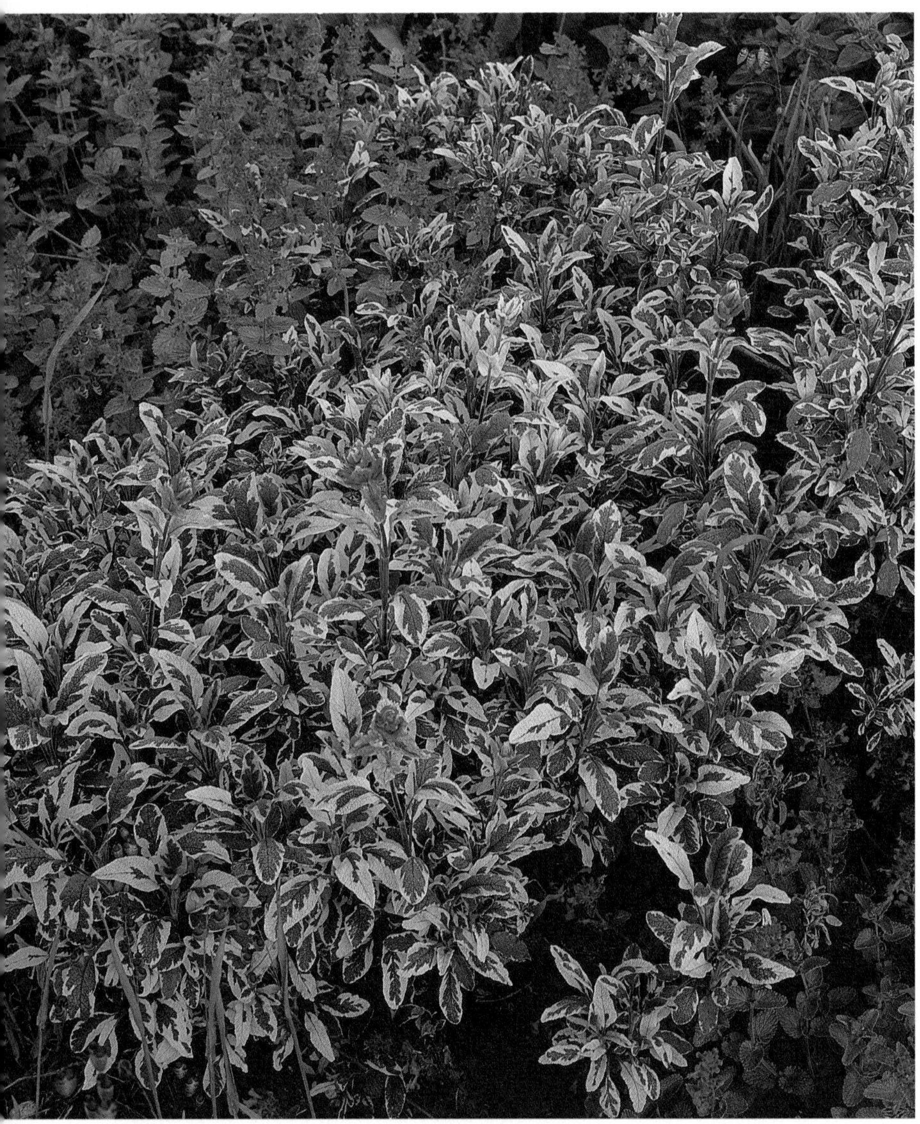

above *Salvia officinalis* 'Tricolor'. Without question, the prettiest variety of all the herb sages; and just as good for culinary use.

right *Sambucus nigra* 'Guincho Purple'. Trees with almost black leaves aren't very common and the contrast between foliage and flowers on this striking form of the wild elderberry is something rather special.

90cm/30cm (3ft/1ft); *S.* x *superba*, mid-green leaves, violet or purple flowers, mid-summer to early autumn, 60-90cm/45-60cm (2-3ft/1½-2ft); *S.* x *sylvestris* 'Blauhügel' (syn. *S. deserta* 'Blue Mound'), mid-green leaves, pure blue flowers, early to mid-summer, 50cm/45cm (1¾ft/1½ft); *S.* x *s.* 'Rose Queen', rose-pink flowers, 75-120cm/60cm (2½-4ft/2ft); *S. verticillata* 'Purple Rain', mid-green hairy leaves, rich violet-blue flowers with purple calyces, 90cm/45cm (3ft/1½ft).

Tender perennials grown as annuals *S. cacaliifolia*, mid-green leaves, loose spikes of deep blue flowers, late summer, 90cm/30cm (3ft/1ft); *S. discolor*, white, woolly branching stems, mid-green leaves with white woolly undersides, very dark indigo flowers, late summer to early autumn, 45cm/30cm (1½ft/1ft); *S. elegans*, mid-green leaves with pineapple scent, bright scarlet flowers, winter to spring, 2m/1m (6½ft/3ft); *S. f.* 'Strata', silver flower spikes, blue flowers with white calyces, 40cm (1½ft); *S. f.* 'Victoria' dense basal branching, deep blue flowers, 50-60cm (1¾-2ft); *S. f.* 'White Victory', silver-white, 60cm (2ft); *S. fulgens* (syn. *S. cardinalis*), green leaves with white woolly hairs on undersides, red flowers, summer, 50-100cm/40-90cm (1¾-3ft/1½-3ft); *S. guaranitica* (syn. *S. concolor*), wrinkled leaves, deep blue flowers, late summer to late autumn, 1.5m/60cm (5ft/2ft); *S. splendens*, pale to dark green leaves, spikes of bright red flowers, summer to autumn, to 40cm/25-35cm (1½ft/10in-1¼ft). 'Flare', deep green leaves, bright scarlet flowers, 45cm (1½ft); 'Blaze of Fire' (syn. 'Fireball'), vivid scarlet, early, 30-45cm (1-1½ft); 'Laser Purple', deep purple, 30-45cm (1-1½ft); 'Lady in Red', loose spikes of light red flowers, early, 30-45cm (1-1½ft).

Sambucus *Elder* Caprifoliaceae

Medium/large hardy or very hardy shrubs or small trees grown for their attractive summer foliage; drinks can be made from fragrant flowers and fruit. Although the golden-leaved varieties make attractive specimens, most elders are best grown in a border or, the native species, in a wild flower garden. Pinnate leaves and serrated leaflets, small white or cream flowers. They tolerate most soils and thrive in alkaline conditions; golden and variegated forms should have full sun to partial shade. No routine pruning, or may be hard pruned in spring to stimulate attractive young foliage. Sow seed in cold-frame in autumn, take hardwood cuttings in winter or semi-ripe heeled cuttings in late summer. ❀ *S. nigra* 'Aurea' (Golden Elder), golden-yellow leaves, full sun for the best leaf colour, 6m/4m (20ft/13ft); *S. n.* 'Guincho Purple', green leaves that deepen to

purple-black in summer then turn red in autumn, pink buds open to white flowers on purple stalks, 6m/4m (20ft/13ft); *S. n.* f. *laciniata*, fern-like leaves, 4m/4m (13ft/13ft); *S. racemosa* 'Plumosa Aurea', fern-like leaves, bronze when young ageing to golden-yellow, foliage can scorch in sun, yellow flowers, 4m/3m (13ft/10ft); *S. r.* 'Sutherland Gold', slightly coarser leaves but less likely to scorch; *S. r.* 'Tenuifolia', slow-growing, fern-like leaves, 1-1.5m/1-1.5m (3-5ft/3-5ft).

Sanguinaria *Bloodroot* Papaveraceae

Small hardy or very hardy rhizomatous ornamental. Lovely when allowed to naturalize in woodland, or planted in shady corners of rock gardens or acidic soil beds, although it requires room as its spreads considerably. Grey-green leaves form a dense canopy after flowers have faded. White flowers in spring. Roots release red sap when cut. Thrives in cool, humus-rich soils in partial shade. Sow seed in cold-frame in autumn or divide plants in autumn. ❀ *S. canadensis*, 30cm/45cm (1ft/1½ft); *S. c.* 'Plena', long-lasting, double, white flowers, much the best form.

Sanguisorba *Burnet* Rosaceae

Medium/large hardy rhizomatous ornamentals and herbs for borders, wild flower meadows and herb gardens for their flowers and foliage. Grey-green leaves. Tiny, spherical flower heads, summer to early autumn. Thrives in any reasonably moist but well-drained soil in sun or partial shade. Sow seed in cold-frame in spring or autumn or lift and divide plants in spring. ❀ *S. minor* (Salad Burnet), cucumber-flavoured foliage, green flower heads with purple tinges, 1m/45cm (3ft/1½ft); *S. obtusa*, nodding rose-pink flowers, 60cm/40cm (2ft/1½ft).

Santolina Asteraceae

Small evergreen sub-shrubs. Barely to fairly hardy and ideal for edging formal beds (such as knot gardens) or rock gardens but become untidy and should be replaced every few years. Aromatic leaves. Button-like flowers of yellow or white in summer. Thrive in well-drained soil in full sun. Take semi-ripe cuttings in summer. ❀ *S. chamaecyparissus* (syn. *S. incana*) (Cotton Lavender), finely-divided, woolly grey-white leaves, bright lemon-yellow flowers, 60cm/60-90cm (2ft/2-3ft); *S. c.* 'Lambrook Silver', silver-grey leaves, more compact; *S. c. nana*, dwarf form, 20cm/20cm (8in/8in); *S. pinnata neapolitana* (syns. *S. neapolitana, S. tomentosa*), feathery mid-green leaves, lemon-yellow flowers, 60cm/90cm (2ft/3ft); *S. p. n.* 'Edward Bowles', grey-green leaves, cream-white flowers, 45cm/50cm (1½ft/1¾ft); *S. rosmarinifolia* 'Primrose Gem', feathery, mid-green leaves, pale primrose-yellow flowers, 60cm/1m (2ft/3ft).

Sanvitalia Asteraceae

Small hardy annuals. Eye-catching flowers and creeping-spreading habit make them ideal for raised beds or containers. Mid-green leaves. Daisy-like flowers in yellow, orange or white, dark centres, mid-summer to early autumn. Thrives in full sun in well-drained soil. Sow seed in mid-spring or autumn in growing positions or in early spring in warmth for containers. ❀ *S. procumbens* 'Mandarin Orange', golden-orange flowers with black centres, 10cm/35cm (4in/1¼ft); *S. p.* 'Yellow Carpet', yellow flowers, dwarf form.

above *Sanguinaria canadensis* 'Plena'. A slowly creeping ground cover plant.

below *Santolina chamaecyparissus* 'Lambrook Silver'. A plant for formal or informal settings.

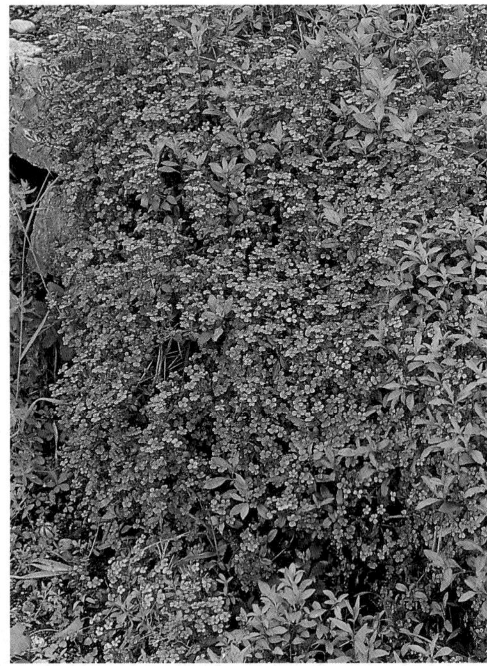

above *Saponaria ocymoides.* I find this is one of the few slightly woody rock garden plants than doesn't very rapidly become straggly.

Saponaria
Caryophyllaceae

Small to medium evergreen herbaceous hardy perennials. Grown for summer flowers in borders; compact types in rock gardens and troughs. Narrow leaves. Flat, small, five-petalled flowers in various shades of pink in summer. Taller, border types will grow in any well-drained, moderately fertile soil; low-growing types need gritty, preferably lime-free, compost. Sow seed in growing position in early summer, take semi-ripe cuttings or divide in spring. ❀ *S. ocymoïdes*, very pretty spreading mat with ovate, hairy leaves of bright green, pink flowers, short-lived but self-seeds, 10cm/45cm (4in/1½ft); *S. officinalis* (Soapwort), upright, mid-green leaves, pink, red or white flowers, summer to autumn, self-seeds and has spreading roots, 80cm/50cm (2½ft/1¾ft); *S. o.* 'Alba Plena', double white; *S. o.* 'Rosea Plena', double pink.

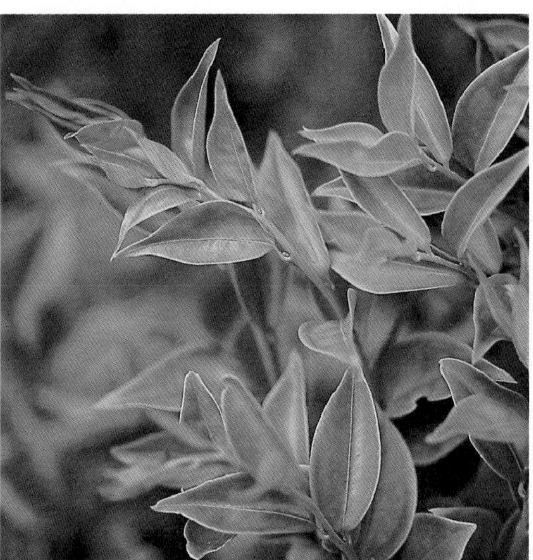

right *Sarcococca ruscifolia.* This unusual rather than beautiful relative of the common box is a valuable addition to the winter garden.

Sarcococca
Christmas Box, Sweet Box Buxaceae

Small hardy evergreen shrubs with attractive foliage, winter flowers and fruits. Narrow, dark green leaves. Clusters of tiny white flowers with sweet fragrance followed by fruits. Ideal for dry shade, although tolerates full sun if soil is moist. All parts of plant toxic if eaten. Transplant rooted suckers or take hardwood cuttings in autumn. ❀ *S. confusa*, glossy dark green leaves, fragrant, cream flowers in winter, black fruits, 1.5m/1m (5ft/3ft); *S. hookeriana* var. *digyna*, bright green leaves, white flowers with pink sepals in winter, black fruits in summer, 1.2m/1.5m (4ft/5ft); *S. h.* var. *humulis*, low-growing form for ground cover, 60cm/60cm (2ft/2ft); *S. ruscifolia*, pointed, dark green leaves, cream-white flowers, late winter to early spring, red fruits in summer, 1m/1m (3ft/3ft).

Satureja *Savory* Lamiaceae

Small/medium annual, perennial and shrubby herbs. Barely hardy to hardy. Grown for their aromatic leaves but also have attractive small flowers in summer. Needs well-drained soil in full sun. Sow seed in growing positions in spring or autumn (summer savory) or sow in warmth in spring or take semi-ripe cuttings in summer (winter savory). ❀ *S. hortensis* (Summer Savory), bushy annual, dark green leaves, slightly spicy flavour, tiny lilac flowers, mid-summer to early autumn, 45cm/30cm (1½ft/1ft); *S. montana* (Winter Savory), hardy evergreen, grey-green leaves, less subtle taste, small, pale rose flowers, mid-summer to mid-autumn, trim back in spring, replace with new plants every 2-3 years, 45cm/30cm (1½ft/1ft).

Saxifraga *Saxifrage* Saxifragaceae

Small hardy to very hardy evergreen perennials or alpines. Arguably the most important genus of rock garden plants (although larger forms are valuable at the front of borders), with a huge range of species and varieties, many only obtainable from specialist nurseries. Vary greatly in habit and leaf form but rosettes or cushion habits are common and small, flat, star-shaped flowers smother plants in spring or summer. Most need, gritty, well-drained, alkaline soil or compost in good light but with protection from hot sun, and many benefit from protection from winter wet. Sow seed in a cold-frame in autumn or divide in spring. Divide herbaceous perennials in spring. Detach rosettes and root as cuttings in late spring to early summer. There are many botanical groups but, for gardening purposes, I find it simplest to reduce these to four. Do be warned however that plants in different groups sometimes have the same name: there are more than one 'Alba' and 'Lutea' for instance, so check carefully when buying. Those I have suggested here are fairly widely obtainable, relatively easy to care for and represent a range of the important and appealing features of the genus.

Encrusted or silver saxifrages Leaves encrusted with particles of lime, best in alkaline soils, thrive in shade and dry conditions. ❀ S. *cochlearis*, rosettes form a cushion, white flowers, early summer, 25cm/15cm (10in/6in); S. 'Minor', compact form of S. *cochlearis*, 10cm (4in); S. 'Southside Seedling', bright green rosettes, white flowers with red spots, 30cm/15cm (1ft/6in); S. 'Lutea' pale yellow 15cm/25cm (6in/10in); S. *paniculata* (syn. S. *aizoon*), silver-green rosettes, cream-white flowers, early summer, 15cm/25cm (6in/10in); S. *p.* var. *baldensis* (syn. 'Baldensis'), dwarf form with red-tinged flower stems, 10cm/15cm (4in/6in); S. 'Rosea', shell-pink; S. 'Tumbling Waters' (syn. S. *longifolia*), justifiably one of the most popular, silver-green rosettes form hummock, white flowers, spring, 75cm/30cm (2½ft/1ft); S. 'Whitehill', violet tints of rosettes, heavy lime encrustation, cream-white flowers, 30cm/40cm (1ft/1½ft).

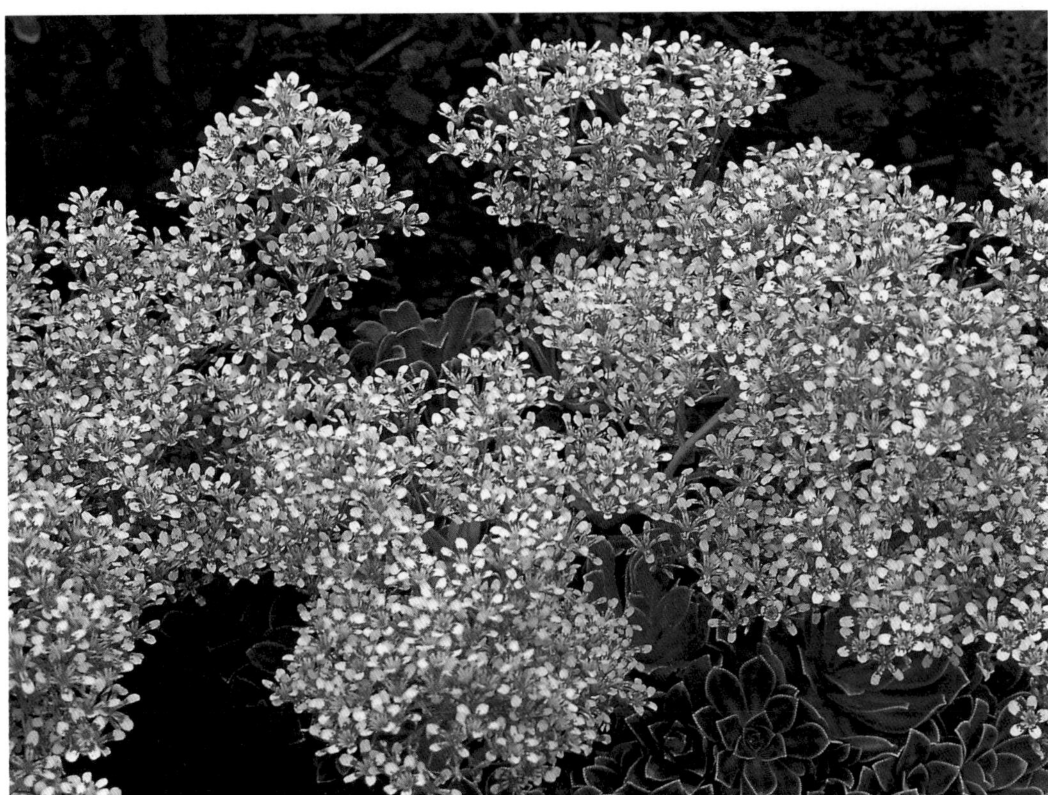

Mossy saxifrages Soft feathery hummocks, most mid-spring flowering. ❀ S. 'Bob Hawkins', leaves variegated green, cream and pink, white flowers, summer, 15cm/30cm (6in/1ft); S. 'Cloth of Gold', slow-growing, rosettes of yellow leaves, white flowers, intolerant of dry spells and hot sun, 3-15cm/15cm (1¼-6in/6in); S. 'Dartington Double', double white flowers; S. 'Elf', carmine, dwarf, early summer, 5-10cm/15cm (2-4in/6in); S. 'Gaiety', deep pink, spring; S. 'Knapton Pink', pink; S. 'White Pixie', white, 5-10cm/15cm (2-4in/6in).

Kabschia or Porophyllum, sometimes called cushion saxifrages Rosettes of leafy shoots, often with lime encrustations. Slow-growing, flowering late winter to early spring. ❀ S. 'Alba', white; S. 'Boston Spa', bright green cushions, yellow flowers, 4cm/20cm (1½in/8in); S. 'Buttercup', slow-growing, glossy rosettes, bright yellow flowers, 6cm/6cm (2¼in/2¼in); S. 'Carmen' (syn. S. x *elisabethae*), dull green cushion, yellow flowers, 5cm/15cm (2in/6in); S. 'Cranbourne' (syns. 'Valborg', 'Valentine', S. x *anglica* 'Cambourne'), dark green rosettes, deep rose-pink flowers fading with age, early summer, 4cm/10cm (1½in/4in); S. 'Gloria', spiky cushion, white, 8cm/8cm (3¼in); S. Gold Dust', golden yellow, 9cm/15cm (3½in/6in); S. 'Gregor Mendel' (syn. S. x *apiculata*), glossy green cushion, primrose-yellow flowers, 15cm/30cm (6in/1ft); S. 'Haagii', dark green rosettes, golden-yellow flowers, 10cm/15cm (4in/6in); S. 'Jenkinsae', dark green cushion, lilac-pink flowers, 5cm/7cm (2in/2¾in); S. *juniperifolia*, bright green cushion, prickly, sparse yellow flowers, 8cm/10cm (3¼in/4in); S. 'Myra' (syn. S. x *anglica* 'Myra'), very slow-growing rosettes form a dark green cushion, deep red-purple flowers, early spring, 2-5cm/8-10cm (¾-2in/3¼-4in); S. 'Penelope', green cushion, amber flowers, 5cm/8cm (2in/3¼in); S. 'Riverslea', grey-green leaves, rich claret flowers, 5cm/8cm (2in/3¼in); S. 'Sulphurea' (syn. S. 'Moonlight'), grey-green mound of rosettes, sulphur-yellow flowers, 15cm/15cm (6in/6in).

Miscellaneous ❀ S. 'Clarence Elliott' (syns. 'Elliott's Variety', S. *primuloïdes*, S. *umbrosa* var. *primuloïdes*), compact rosettes, rose-pink flowers, summer, 15cm/15cm (6in/6in); S. *ferdinandi-coburgi*, grey-green rosettes, golden-yellow flowers, spring, one of the easiest and most reliable, 8cm/10cm (3¼in/4in); S. *fortunei* (syn. S. *cortusifolia* var. *fortunei*), deciduous or semi-evergreen, mid-green leaves with purple tinges, white flowers, late summer to autumn, 30cm/30cm

above *Saxifraga* 'Southside Seedling'. The Encrusted saxifrages, with their lime-embellished foliage are perhaps the most unusual group in this huge and important genus.

below *Saxifraga* 'Wada'. Give this lovely variety a sheltered spot and it will reward you with some of the loveliest foliage colours in the genus.

above *Saxifraga apiculata* 'Alba'. There is only one real problem with the genus *Saxifraga*: you are spoiled for choice.

(1ft/1ft); *S. oppositifolia*, dark green rosettes form a flat mat, pink, red-purple or white flowers, early summer, 3-5cm/20cm (1¼-2in/8in); *S.* 'Ruth Draper', like *S. oppositifolia* but with large flowers of bright rose-pink; *S.* 'Southside Seedling', pale green rosettes forming a mat, white flowers with red spots, late spring to early summer, 30cm/20cm (1ft/8in); *S.* 'Wada' (syn. *S. fortunei* 'Wada's Form'), semi-evergreen, not hardy in cold winters but will thrive in sheltered places, lime-free soil and shade, glossy green leaves age to bronze-red, white flowers on red-brown stems, autumn, 30cm/30cm (1ft/1ft); *S. umbrosa*, best in moist shade, leathery rosettes form a mat of dark green leaves, tiny white flowers with pink centres appear in early summer, 25cm/30cm (10in/1ft); *S. u.* var. *primuloïdes*; neat, mid-green rosettes, white flowers with red spots, summer, 30cm/30cm (1ft/1ft); *S.* x *urbium* (syn. *S. spathularis*) (London Pride), thrives in moist shade, fleshy rosettes form a mat, pale pink flowers, early summer, can be invasive, 25cm/60cm (10in/2ft); *S.* 'Winifred Bevington', requires light soil and partial shade, white flowers with pink centres, early summer, 10cm/20cm (4in/8in).

Scabiosa *Scabious* Dipsacaceae

Small/medium annuals, biennials and perennials. Barely hardy to hardy. Probably most familiar as native flowers but add delicate colour to borders, wild flower gardens or rock gardens. Most have narrow basal leaves and 'pincushion' heads of flowers in blue, pink, white or yellow. Prefer a light, well-drained soil in full sun. Annuals: sow seed in growing positions in early autumn or late spring, protect with cloches over winter. Perennials: divide in early spring. ❀ *S. caucasica*, herbaceous hardy perennial, grey-green leaves, pale blue flowers over a long period in summer, 60cm/60cm (2ft/2ft); *S. c.* 'Clive Greaves', lavender-blue; *S. c.* 'Miss Willmott', white, 90cm (3ft); *S. columbaria* (syn. *S. banatica*), variable, hardy evergreen perennial, grey-green leaves, lilac-blue flowers, late summer, 30-70cm/90cm (1-2¼ft/3ft); *S. c. ochroleuca*, lemon-yellow flowers, late summer, 90cm/90cm (3ft/3ft); *S. lucida*, similar to *S. columbaria* but with pale lilac flowers, 30cm/30cm (1ft/1ft).

Scaevola Goodeniaceae

Tender evergreen perennials used as bedding plants for containers, especially hanging baskets and window boxes where its sprawling nature is seen to best advantage. Fan-shaped flowers in summer. Humus-rich soil or compost in full sun or partial shade. Sow seed in warmth in spring or take softwood cuttings in late spring/early summer. ❀ *S. aemula* 'Blue Fan', purple-blue flowers with white eye, 15cm/1.5m (6in/5ft); a number of new varieties appear each year; 'Saphira' is a new dark blue compact form.

right One of the least appreciated but important container plants to have become popular in recent times. is *Scaevola aemula* 'Blue Fan'.

Schizanthus *Butterfly Flower, Poor Man's Orchid* Solanaceae

Half-hardy bedding annuals grown as summer bedding. Finely-divided leaves and orchid-like flowers in pink, purple, red, white and yellow, often with contrasting throats and markings. Any well-drained but moist soil or compost in full sun. Sow seed in warmth in spring for summer to autumn flowers. ❀ *S. pinnatus* 'Angel Wings', 35cm (1¼ft); *S. p.* 'Hit Parade', large, well-marked flowers, 40cm (1½ft); *S. p.* 'Star Parade', compact plant with large flowers, 30cm (1ft).

Schizophragma Hydrangeaceae

Medium/large deciduous climbers. Very hardy. Summer-flowering climbers for shady walls and, I think, better than their more popular relative, the climbing hydrangea, *Hydrangea anomala petiolaris*. Slow growing at first then vigorous, with self-clinging aerial roots. Best in well-drained, humus-rich soil, tolerates shade but flowers better in sun. No routine pruning. Take softwood or semi-ripe cuttings in summer or layer. ❀ *S. hydrangeoïdes*, dark green, coarse-toothed leaves that turn yellow in autumn, cream-white flowers, 10-12m (33-40ft); *S. integrifolium*, similar but better, larger in size and flower, leaves not so coarsely-toothed, 12m (40ft).

Schizostylis Iridaceae

Medium evergreen rhizomatous ornamentals. Fairly to moderately hardy and valuable for late summer flowers in borders or beside pools. Narrow, sword-shaped leaves of light green. Star-like flowers of pink, red or white borne on slender stems from late summer to early autumn. Need shelter, sun and moist soil and tend to be short-lived in colder areas. Divide in spring. ❀ *S. coccinea*, bright red flowers, 60cm/25cm (2ft/10in); *S. c.* var. *alba*, white flowers, less hardy; *S. c.* 'Jennifer', large pink flowers; *S. c.* 'Major' (syns. *S. c.* 'Gigantea', *S. c.* 'Grandiflora'), many bright red flowers; *S. c.* 'Sunrise' (syn. *S. c.* 'Sunset'), large pink flowers; *S. c.* 'Viscountess Byng', pale pink flowers, mid-autumn, flowers often damaged by early frost.

Scilla *Squill* Hyacinthaceae

Small bulbous ornamental. Most are hardy to very hardy and extremely easy to grow in rock gardens and containers, or to naturalize in grass or under shrubs. Together with *Chionodoxa*, my truly indispensable blue spring bulbs. Glossy mid-green leaves; small star or bell flowers usually in shades of blue or purple in late winter to early spring. Best in well-drained soil enriched with humus, partial shade. Sow seed in early summer or divide clumps after flowering. ❀ *S. bifolia*, fragrant blue-violet flowers, 25cm (10in); *S. mischtschenkoana* (syn. *S. tubergeniana*), pale blue flowers with darker blue stripe, 10cm (4in); *S. peruviana*, barely hardy, needs dry sunny spot and winter mulch, almost evergreen, violet-blue or white flowers, late spring to early summer, 25cm (10in); *S. siberica*, bright blue flowers, 10-20cm (4-8in); *S. s.* 'Alba', white flowers; *S. s.* 'Spring Beauty' (syn. 'Atrocoerulea'), vigorous with deep blue flowers, probably the best and most reliable, 20cm (8in).

Scorzonera Asteraceae

Root vegetable. A hardy perennial usually grown as an annual or biennial. Grows best on a light, free-draining soil free from stones or clods of earth. Sow

above Unlike the climbing hydrangea, far too few gardeners are yet familiar with its even better relative *Schizophragma integrifolia*.

below No garden should be without spring flowering scillas like this *S. mischtschenkoana*.

seed in growing positions in late spring, harvest roots in autumn but may be left in the ground until roots are a suitable size. ❀ *S. hispanica* (Scorzonera), edible roots with black skin and white flesh, milder flavour and broader leaves than salsify, yellow dandelion-like flowers, shoots and buds also edible, 60cm (2ft) (in flower).

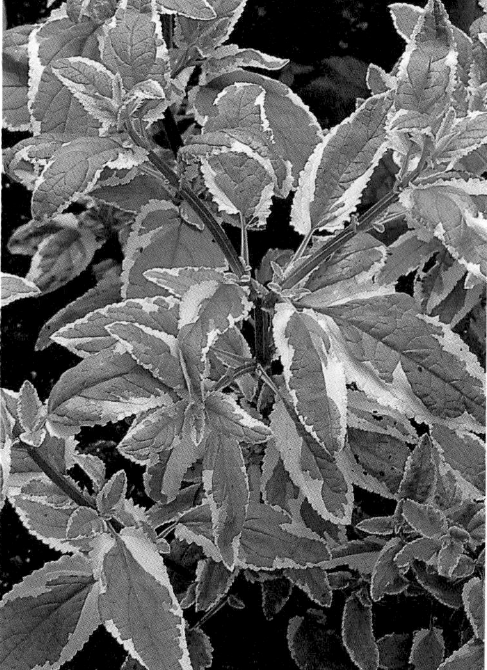

above *Scrophularia auriculata* 'Variegata'. The figworts are familiar if unspectacular native water-side plants but give one variegated foliage and it at once becomes an ornamental of real merit.

Scrophularia
Figwort Scrophulariaceae

Medium/tall herbaceous hardy perennial/water marginal. Unusual plants for the wild flower garden, border or pool side with flowers that seem abnormally small for the amount of stem. Strong-smelling leaves. Foxglove-type flowers in summer. Best in moist soil and partial shade. Divide or take basal cuttings in spring. ❀ *S. auriculata* (syn. *S. aquatica*) (Water Figwort), coarse dark green leaves, flowers yellow-green and maroon, 90cm/60cm (3ft/2ft); *S. a.* 'Variegata', strikingly attractive green and cream leaves, remove flower spikes to produce best foliage effect.

Scutellariaa *Skullcap* Lamiaceae

Small/large herbaceous hardy perennials (some evergreen). Most important species are rock garden plants with antirrhinum-like flowers. Intolerant of dry soil but can be invasive on very fertile soils; sun or partial shade. Sow seeds in cold-frame in autumn, divide plants in spring or take cuttings in late spring. ❀ *S. alpina*, evergreen mid-green leaves, purple flowers with white lower lip, summer, 20cm/30cm (8in/1ft); *S. altissima*, mid-green leaves, cream or pale lilac flowers, mid-summer, 75cm/30cm (2½ft/1ft); *S. incana*, heart-shaped dull green leaves, violet flowers with blue tinges, mid-summer, 1m/60cm (3ft/2ft); *S. scordifolia*, evergreen, can be invasive, blue flowers, summer, 30cm/60cm (1ft/2ft).

Sedum *Stonecrop* Crassulaceae

Small/medium herbaceous hardy to very hardy perennials (some evergreen) and alpines. Sedums are very good drought tolerant plants for late-season colour. Succulent leaves, often coloured. Flowers in pink, purple, red, yellow and white; the taller, late flowering species have a magnetic attraction for late-season butterflies. Suitable for most soils but intolerant of cold, heavy or wet sites. Most require full sun, although a few are better in partial shade. Sow seed in cold-frame in autumn, divide plants in spring or take cuttings of non-flowering shoots in spring. ❀ *S. aïzoon* 'Euphorbioïdes', rich yellow flowers, 35cm/25cm (1¼ft/10in); *S. alboroseum* 'Mediovariegatum', pale green leaves with yellow centres, white flowers, early autumn, tolerates partial shade, 30cm/15cm (1ft/6in); *S.* 'Bertram Anderson', purple-blue leaves, red flowers, 10cm/30cm (4in/1ft); *S. cauticola*, creeping stems, fleshy leaves of blue-green and purple-red, purple flowers in autumn, tolerates partial shade, 10cm/30cm (4in/1ft); *S. c.* 'Lidakense', smaller and neater habit; *S.* 'Herbstfreude' (syn. 'Autumn Joy'), fleshy pale green leaves, flowers green in summer then pink in autumn, ageing to bronze-red, tolerates partial shade, 45cm/45cm (1½ft/1½ft); *S. kamtschaticum* var. *floriferum* 'Weihenstephaner Gold', semi-evergreen, fleshy stems with mid-green leaves, deep yellow flowers, early summer to mid-autumn, 10cm/60cm (4in/2ft); *S. lydium*, evergreen, creeping stems, fleshy leaves of bright green with red tips, white flowers, early to mid-summer, best in partial shade and moist, cool soil, 3cm/15cm (1¼in/6in); *S.* 'Ruby Glow', fleshy leaves of deep green, red-purple flowers, early to mid-autumn, 20cm/60cm (8in/2ft); *S. spathulifolium* 'Cape Blanco' (syn. 'Cappa Blanca'), evergreen, spreading with brittle stems, silver-grey leaves, bright yellow flowers, early summer, a lovely thing but often all but destroyed by

right *Sedum* 'Herbstfreude'. Still more familiar under its name of 'Autumn Joy' this is the plant that attracts more butterflies to my autumn borders than any other.

suppliers. ❀ *S. arachnoïdeum* (Cobweb Houseleek), light green rosettes draped with cobweb-like hairs, rose-red flowers, needs winter protection, 3cm/20cm (1¼in/8in); *S. calcareum*, rosettes blue-green with purple-brown tips, pale pink flowers, 5cm/30cm (2in/1ft); *S. ciliosum borisii*, grey-green rosettes with red tints, lemon-yellow flowers, 5cm/25cm (2in/10in); *S. giuseppii*, bright green rosettes with red tips, red flowers, 8cm/30cm (3¼in/1ft); *S. tectorum*, wide rosettes form large clumps, blue-green leaves with red-purple tints, pink flowers, 8cm/30cm (3¼in/1ft); *S. thompsonianum*, small rosettes with reddish tints, sometimes yellow and pink flowers, needs winter protection, 3cm/15cm (1¼in/6in).

left *Sempervivum arachnoïdeum*. The cobweb houseleek is perhaps the most familiar member of a large and amazingly diverse group of the best hardy foliage succulents.

blackbirds, which tear it to pieces, 10cm/20cm (4in/8in); *S. s.* 'Purpureum', strong spreading habit, plum-red flush to silver-grey leaves in summer; *S. spectabile* (Ice Plant), upright clump, fleshy leaves of pale blue-green, pink flowers, early autumn, the best of all for butterflies, 40cm/40cm (1½ft/1½ft); *S. s.* 'Brilliant', deep rose flowers; *S. s.* 'Iceberg', paler green leaves, white flowers; *S. spurium* 'Schorbuser Blut', semi-deciduous, creeping stems can be invasive, fleshy leaves of dark green ageing to bronze, dark red flowers, 10cm/90cm (4in/3ft); *S. telephium* 'Munstead Red', bright green waxy leaves, dark red flowers, late summer to early autumn, 20cm/30cm (8in/1ft); *S.* 'Vera Jameson', sprawling purple stems, fleshy leaves of purple-pink, pale pink flowers, autumn, 20cm/30cm (8in/1ft).

Sempervivum *Houseleek* Crassulaceae

Small hardy evergreen alpines/perennials. Drought-tolerant plants for rock gardens, walls, containers and almost impossible situations like house roofs. Colourful leaf rosettes and star-like flowers in purple, red, yellow or white in summer; the rosette then dies but offsets live on. Require a well-drained soil or gritty compost in full sun and some need protection from winter wet. Sow seed in cold-frame in spring or detach offsets and root in spring or early summer. Note that apart from the few I have listed here, there's a huge number of 'varieties' and selections, each available from only a few

Senecio Asteraceae

Annuals, herbaceous perennials, climbers and shrubs, although several species have been transferred to other genera (see, for instance, *Brachyglottis*). Tender to very hardy. Cultivation varies with species. ❀ *S. smithii*, large herbaceous hardy perennial, leathery dark green leaves, white daisy flowers with yellow centres appear in summer, moist to boggy soil in partial shade, divide in spring, 1.2m/1m (4ft/3ft); *S. viravira* (syn. *S. leucostachys*), semi-evergreen perennial can be grown as half-hardy annual, deeply divided silver-grey leaves, small pale yellow flowers in summer, needs well-drained soil in sun, sow seed in warmth spring, 75cm/75cm (2½ft/2½ft).

Sidalcea
Prairie Mallow, Checker Mallow Malvaceae

Medium/tall herbaceous perennials. Moderately hardy to hardy. Once popular relatives of mallows for mixed borders and due for a return to favour. Mid-green basal leaves. Funnel-shaped flowers in shades of pink or white in mid-summer and sometimes again in autumn. Thrive in moist soil in a sunny, sheltered spot. Sow seed of species in cold-frame in autumn/spring. Divide named varieties in spring or autumn. ❀ *S. candida*, white flowers, 75cm/50cm (2½ft/1¾ft); 'Elsie Heugh', fringed pale pink flowers, 60cm/50cm (2ft/1¾ft); 'Party Girl', rose-pink flowers 90cm/50cm

(3ft/1¾ft); 'Sussex Beauty', clear pale pink flowers, 90cm/50cm (3ft/1¾ft); 'William Smith', bright rose-pink flushed with salmon-pink, 90cm/50cm (3ft/1¾ft).

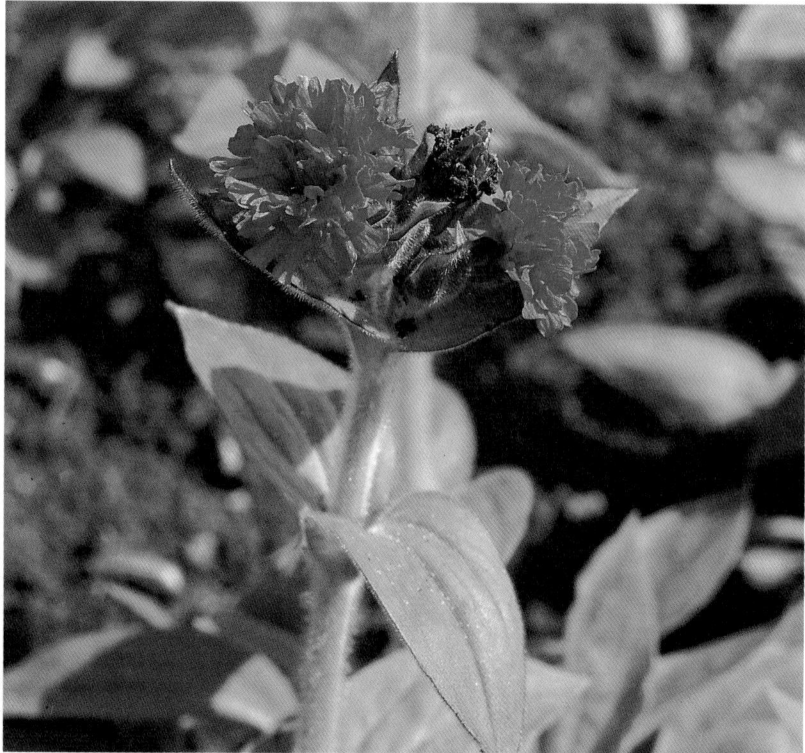

above *Silene dioica* 'Flore Pleno'. This is one of those native plants that tends to be overlooked in a massed planting such as a wildflower meadow but, seen on its own, it really does have an individual charm.

right *Sisyrinchium* 'Quaint and Queer'. The varietal name is a mystery to me but the genus is a pretty if unspectacular one for warm summer gardens.

Silene
Campion, Catchfly Caryophyllaceae

Small annuals and perennials (some evergreen). Half-hardy to hardy. Easy plants, although probably better known as wild flowers than in gardens and most need some protection from winter wet. Most prefer a well-drained, fertile soil in sun but a few are better in partial shade. Perennials: sow seed in a cold-frame in autumn or root basal cuttings in spring. ❀ *S. acaulis*, evergreen, bright green leaves, pale pink to deep rose-pink flowers, late spring, 5cm/15cm (2in/6in); *S. alpestris*, evergreen, light green leaves, white flowers, early to mid-summer, 30cm/20cm (1ft/8in); *S. dioica* 'Flore Pleno', bright green leaves, red double flowers, early summer, thrives in partial shade, 60cm/30cm (2ft/1ft); *S. d.* 'Rosea Plena', dark green leaves, double rose-pink flowers, 80cm/45cm (2½ft/1½ft); *S. schafta*, semi-evergreen, pale green leaves, light pink flowers, mid-summer to mid-autumn, 15cm/30cm (6in/1ft); *S. uniflora* (syn. *S. maritima*), grey-green leaves, white flowers, late spring, 10cm/15cm (4in/6in); *S. u.* 'Druett's Variegated', cream leaf margins; *S. u.* 'Robin Whitebreast' (syn. 'Flore Pleno'), double flowers.

Silybum
Asteraceae

Large annuals or biennials. Hardy. A specimen plant for a large border or wild garden, where its spines can do no harm and its thistle-like flowers can be properly admired. Best in full sun in a well-drained soil with low fertility. Sow seed in growing positions in late spring to early summer. ❀ *S. marianum* (Our Lady's Milk Thistle, Holy Thistle, Blessed Thistle), biennial with leaf rosette in the first season and flowers in the next, glossy dark green leaves with white veins and spiny margins, purple flowers, late spring to early summer, can be invasive, 1.5m/1m (5ft/3ft).

Sinapis
Brassicaceae

Small/medium annual herb grown for its hot spicy flavour, for its seeds and also as one of the commonest 'green manure' crops. Any moist, well-drained, fairly rich soil in full sun. ❀ *S. alba* (White Mustard), moderately hardy and may be sown in growing positions in spring; also often grown indoors with *Lepidium sativum*, as 'mustard and cress' although today, rape is commonly used instead of true mustard, 30-60cm/15-20cm (1-2ft/6-8in).

Sisyrinchium
Iridaceae

Small/medium herbaceous, usually rhizomatous, perennials. Barely hardy to very hardy. Summer flowers and evidently iris-like sword-shaped leaves which lead you to expect an iris-like flower too – although in this you will be sadly disappointed as they are more like little limp buttercups. Require full sun and well-drained soil; some will spread by self-seeding. Sow seed in a cold-frame or divide plants in spring. ❀ *S. angustifolium* (syns. *S.* x

left *Smilacina racemosa*. An utterly lovely North American woodland plant for reasonably moist spots.

anceps, S. bermudianum) (Blue-Eyed Grass), bright blue flowers with yellow centres, 30cm/25cm (1ft/10in); *S.* 'Biscutella', yellow flowers with purple markings, 35cm/30cm (1¼ft/1ft); *S. californicum* (syn. *S. boreale*), bright yellow flowers, late spring and summer, 45cm/30cm (1½ft/1ft); *S. idahoense* (syn. *S. bellum*), violet-blue flowers with yellow centres, mid-summer, 40cm/30cm (1½ft/1ft); *S. i.* 'Album' (syns. *S. album, S.* 'May Snow'), white flowers with yellow centres; *S.* 'Quaint and Queer', dull purple flowers with yellow centres, 15cm/15cm (6in/6in); *S. striatum*, grey-green leaves, cream to pale yellow flowers, mid- to late summer, 60cm/30cm (2ft/1ft).

Skimmia — Rutaceae

Small evergreen shrubs, most with separate male and female plants; both must be present for females to form fruit. Moderately hardy to hardy. Glossy mid- to dark green leathery leaves. All those I include here have fragrant cream-white flowers in spring although their main appeal comes earlier with the buds or later with the fruit. Best in moist but well-drained acidic soil in shade or partial shade. Sow seed in cold-frame in autumn or take semi-ripe cuttings in late summer. ❀ *S.* x *confusa* 'Kew Green', green leaves, aromatic when bruised, a male form that tolerates sun, 45cm/60cm (1½ft/2ft); *S. japonica* 'Fragrans', male form, 1m/1m (3ft/3ft); *S. j.* ssp. *reevesiana*, dark green leaves, red fruits in late summer, hermaphrodite, intolerant of alkalinity, 75cm/75cm (2½ft/2½ft); *S. j.* 'Rubella', lovely rich red-pink buds all winter, male form, 1.5m/1.5m (5ft/5ft); *S. j.* 'Veitchii' (syn. 'Foremanii'), large bunches of fruit, female form, 1.5m/1.5m (5ft/5ft).

Smilacina

False Solomon's Seal — Convallariaceae

Medium rhizomatous ornamental. Very hardy. A good woodland plant, needing lime-free, moist soil in partial shade. Sow seed in cold-frame in autumn or divide plants in spring. ❀ *S. racemosa*, arching stems, light green leaves that yellow in autumn, frothy cream-white flowers, mid-spring to mid-summer, red fruits, 75cm/75cm (2½ft/2½ft).

Solanum — Solanaceae

A diverse genus of annual and perennial herbaceous plants, shrubs, trees and climbers including some extremely important vegetables together with several ornamentals. Many, including, most famously, the nightshades, are extremely toxic.

Ornamental

Medium half-hardy to fairly hardy semi-evergreen ornamental climbers and scramblers for warm, positions. Dark green leaves, small star-like flowers with yellow centres, very evidently related to potatoes, summer to early autumn. They require a moist, fairly rich well-drained soil in sun. Prune lightly after flowering. Take semi-ripe cuttings from summer to early autumn. ❀ *S. crispum*, barely hardy to fairly hardy, lilac-blue flowers, yellow-white fruits, best in alkaline conditions, 4m/1m (13ft/3ft); *S. c.* 'Glasnevin' (syn. *S. c.* 'Autumnale'), much the best form with deep purple-blue flowers; *S. jasminoides* (Potato Vine), half-hardy to barely hardy white flowers with yellow centres, summer to autumn, black fruits, 3m/60cm (10ft/2ft); *S. j.* 'Album', darker leaves tinged with purple, white flowers.

above *Solanum crispum* 'Glasnevin'. I think this is the prettiest of the climbing 'potato vines' but all must have warmth and all are vigorous plants.

right Potato 'Edzell Blue'. This is one of a number of old and, in some cases, remarkable looking potato varieties that has been 'resurrected' for gardeners to grow in recent years.

Edible

***S. melongena* (Aubergine, Egg Plant)**, half-hardy vegetable fruit. Bushy plants with small mauve, potato-like flowers. Succeed outdoors without cloche protection only in mildest areas. Sow seed in early spring in warmth, plant out into pots or growing bags in greenhouse, feed and water as tomatoes but no side-shooting needed. Up to 1m (3ft). ❀ 'Long Purple', medium-sized, elongated purple fruits; 'Ova' F1, many, small white more or less spherical fruits; 'Moneymaker' F1, many elongated, purple fruits, early; 'Slice Rite' F1, large, almost black fruits, late.

***S. tuberosum* (Potato)**, half-hardy tuberous vegetable, although all green parts of the plant are toxic. Usually grown in rows in garden beds but, on a small scale, may be planted in large containers. Always best in light, humus-rich soil, with plenty of moisture necessary – especially after flowering, when tubers begin to swell. Avoid planting in frost pockets or heavy shade and earth up shoots until danger of frost has receded. Crop rotation is important, especially to minimize build-up of eelworms. Although potatoes can be raised from seed, gardeners invariably plant small ('seed') tubers. These should be bought afresh each year, certified for freedom from virus and planted in spring. 1m/60cm (3ft/2ft). Of the large number of potato varieties available, I have selected some, both old and recent, that I have grown in a wide range of conditions and that have been successful. Many others are worth trying and, increasingly, suppliers are reintroducing many old varieties for gardeners to grow. Some have very good flavour, some are very odd to behold but be aware that whilst they may have passed from commercial favour because of non-uniformity or some other feature unimportant in gardens, it may equally have been because of very poor yields or bad disease susceptibility.

Early varieties

Varieties grown for 'new' potatoes, harvested 100 to 120 days after planting. ❀ 'Accent', first early, light yellow skin and flesh, retains its waxy texture well after boiling; 'Arran Pilot', first-second early, white skin and flesh, waxy texture, good yield; 'Belle de Fontenay', second early or maincrop, smooth cream skin, waxy texture, best as salad potato; 'Charlotte' first early, cream-white skin, cream-yellow flesh, salad and other use, good yield, retains firm flesh when cooked; 'Dunluce', first early, white skin, cream flesh, floury texture, good yield; 'Edzell Blue', second early-maincrop, rough violet skin, superb flavour as a mashing potato from a highly unpromising looking object; 'Estima', second early, cream-white skin, light yellow flesh, waxy texture, very high yield, good boiling variety; 'Home Guard', first early, smooth skin, pale cream-white flesh, not a variety for dry areas, floury when cooked; 'Rocket', first early, white skin and flesh, waxy texture, very high yield; 'Wilja', second early, waxy when cooked, good yield.

Maincrop varieties

Varieties to be used fresh and also stored and used through the winter, harvested after 130 days or more. ❀ 'Cara', red and cream skin, cream flesh, good yield, bakes well; 'Desirée', red skin, cream flesh, reliable in dry conditions, good yield, good for all-round cooking; 'King Edward', red and cream skin, cream-white flesh, moderate yield but this is compensated for by excellent flavour, floury when cooked, very successful as the first crop on new land; 'Maris Piper', cream-white skin and flesh, floury texture, very high yield; 'Pink Fir Apple', late, knobbly, pink skin, cream flesh, long tubers, cook in skins then peel, good salad potato but also a good mashed potato, stores very well.

Soldanella — Primulaceae

Small hardy herbaceous evergreen perennials. Very distinctive and eye-catching spring flowers for rock garden or peat bed. Dark green leaves. Small nodding flowers with characteristically fringed petals. Acidic, well-drained soil, some summer shade, in wet areas protect from winter wet. Sow ripe seed in cold-frame, divide plants or remove runners after flowering. ❀ *S. alpina*, kidney-shaped leaves, 15cm/15cm (6in/6in); *S. carpatica*, leaves have violet undersides, 15cm/20cm (6in/8in); *S. villosa*, veined mid-green leaves, hairy leaves and flower stalks, 25cm/45cm (10in/1½ft).

Solenostemon — Lamiaceae

Tender evergreen perennial usually grown as half-hardy annual for its colourful foliage; also popular as pot plant. Lance-shaped leaves often scalloped or wrinkled, many colours and markings. Small, lipped blue flowers, generally cut off to improve foliage appearance. Best in moist but well-drained soil enriched with humus and a warm position in sun or partial shade. Sow seed in spring in warmth. ❀ *Scutellarioïdes* (Coleus, Painted Nettle), named varieties are sometimes available from specialists and can be propagated by softwood cuttings in spring and summer but almost invariably raised from fancifully named seed mixtures; 60cm/45cm (2ft/1½ft) or more if grown as standards.

Solidago *Golden Rod* — Asteraceae

Small/medium herbaceous perennials. Very hardy. Some are weedy and invasive and have given the plant a bad name but named varieties offer attractive late summer flowers for borders and wild flower areas. Lance-shaped, mid-green leaves. Masses of small bright yellow flowers in elongated fluffy inflorescences on stiff stems. Will tolerate most soils and positions. Remove faded flower stems to prevent self-seeding. Divide plants in spring or autumn. ❀ S. 'Cloth of Gold', 45cm/25cm (1½ft/10in); *S. flexicaulis* 'Variegata' (syn. *S. latifolia*), brown and gold leaves, 60cm/30cm (2ft/1ft); S. 'Goldenmosa', yellow-green leaves, deep golden-yellow flowers, 75cm/45cm (2½ft/1½ft); S. 'Queenie' (syn. 'Golden Thumb'), pale green and gold leaves, 30cm/30cm (1ft/1ft); *S. virgaurea*, 1m/60cm (3ft/2ft).

x Solidaster — Asteraceae

Medium to large hardy herbaceous perennial, a hybrid between *Solidago* and *Aster* and, combining the virtues of both, makes an excellent plant in borders for its late flowers. Upright stems with narrow mid-green leaves. Tiny daisy-like flowers borne in clusters on long stems. Thrives in any well-drained soil in full sun. Divide in spring or autumn or take basal cuttings in spring. ❀ x *S. luteus* (syns. x *S. hybridus, S. hybrida*), golden-yellow flowers, late summer to early autumn, 1m/45cm (3ft/1½ft); *S. l.* 'Lemore', shorter with lemon-yellow blooms.

Sophora — Papilionaceae

Small/large deciduous and evergreen trees and large shrubs. Moderately hardy to hardy. Greatly undervalued plants that should be in many more gardens for the merit of their foliage and hanging clusters of pea-like flowers. Thrives in almost any

above *Soldanella alpina*. It's tricky to provide exactly the right conditions for these quite beautiful alpine plants.

below *x Solidaster luteus* 'Lemore'. An improbable parental combination of golden rod and Michaelmas daisy has produced this hybrid genus.

above *Sorbaria sorbifolia.* It comes as something of a surprise to find flower-heads like these on a tree; they really do look as if they belong to a herbaceous perennial.

fertile, well-drained soil in sun, with shelter from cold winds. No routine pruning. Sow ripe seed in cold-frame, take semi-ripe cuttings in summer or autumn. ❀ *S. japonica* (Pagoda Tree), medium/large tree, cream-white flowers on mature trees, late summer to autumn, 12m/3m (40ft/10ft); *S. microphylla*, large evergreen shrub or small tree, yellow flowers on mature trees, late spring, 6m/2.5m (20ft/8ft); *S. tetraptera* (Kowhai), large shrub or small tree, best grown against a warm wall, bright yellow flowers in late spring before the new leaves, seedpods, 6m/3m (20ft/10ft).

Sorbaria *False Spiraea* Rosaceae

Small to medium very hardy deciduous shrubs. Grown for their striking inflorescences, which look as if they belong to a herbaceous perennial, and attractive foliage, often very successful as a multi-stemmed shrub in borders or beside water. Long, pinnate and alternate leaves. Will grow in most soils but requires full sun for the best flowering. Hard prune in late winter for best flowers and foliage. Sow seed in a cold-frame in autumn, take semi-ripe cuttings in summer or remove rooted suckers in autumn. ❀ *S. sorbifolia*, suckering shrub, leaves up to 30cm (1ft) long, clusters of tiny white flowers in fluffy inflorescences in summer, 1.8m/60cm (5¾ft/2ft).

Sorbus Rosaceae

Small/large mostly hardy trees and shrubs. Among the most important ornamental garden trees, especially for their autumn foliage and fruits which display a surprising range of colours. Pinnate or simple leaves. Small cream or white flowers in late spring to early summer. Thrive in most well-drained soils in sun or partial shade. No routine pruning. Sow seed in cold-frame in autumn, or take semi-ripe cuttings in early summer; some varieties are only successful as grafted plants. ❀ *S. aria* (Whitebeam), multi-stemmed tree, young leaves are silver-white then glossy green with silver-white undersides that flicker in a breeze, gold autumn colour, red fruits, tolerates dry chalk and coastal conditions, 12m/4m (40ft/13ft); *S. a.* 'Lutescens', has a more conical habit; *S. aucuparia* (Rowan, Mountain Ash), multi-stemmed tree, leaves have good autumn colour, cream-white flowers in late spring, abundant red fruits, 10m/2m (33ft/6½ft); *S. a.* 'Aspleniifolia', more deeply cut foliage; *S. a.* 'Sheerwater Seedling', a very good selection, narrow crown, large orange-red fruits; *S. cashmiriana*, small spreading tree, rich green leaves with grey-green undersides, pink flush to flowers, large white fruits, 7m/3m (23ft/10ft); *S. commixta* 'Embley', small upright tree, leaf buds sticky in winter, young leaves copper coloured then glossy green, very good autumn colour, abundant orange-red fruits; *S. hupehensis*, small/medium tree, blue-green leaves with good red autumn colour, extremely pretty white or pink fruits, 10m/3m (33ft/10ft); *S.* 'Joseph Rock', small upright tree,, bright green leaves, duller undersides, excellent autumn colour, pale yellow fruits, overall, one of the most desirable garden trees, 9m/3m (30ft/10ft); *S. reducta*, dwarf multi-stemmed shrub, good autumn colour, small flowers in spring, pink fruits, 60cm/60-100cm (2ft/2-3ft); *S. sargentiana*, medium/large tree, big sticky leaf buds in winter, green leaves up to 30cm (1ft) long provide good autumn colour, white flowers in spring, abundant orange-red fruits, 10m/4m (33ft/13ft); *S.* 'John Mitchell' (syn. *S. aria* 'John Mitchell') large tree, almost round leaves of dark green with silver-grey undersides, autumn colour, green fruits turn yellow to orange in late summer, 20m/3m (60ft/10ft); *S. torminalis* (Wild Service Tree), medium tree, good autumn colour, small brown speckled fruits, an invaluable tree for the native plant garden, 10m/2.5m (33ft/8ft); *S. vilmorinii*, leaves good autumn colour, large shrub or small tree, spreading habit, 4.5m/2.5m (14¾ft/8ft).

right *Sorbus hupehensis.* The genus *Sorbus* contains some of the very best moderately sized trees for fruit and autumn foliage appeal. Many of the finest, like this one, are Chinese.

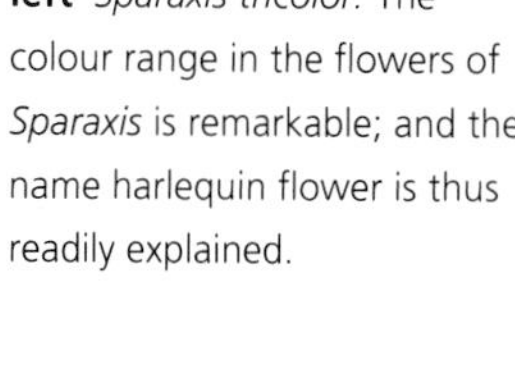

left *Sparaxis tricolor.* The colour range in the flowers of *Sparaxis* is remarkable; and the name harlequin flower is thus readily explained.

Sparaxis Iridaceae

Medium half-hardy corm-forming ornamentals. Grown for their bright, superficially rather star-like spring/early summer flowers. Require a warm sheltered spot in full sun with a well-drained soil or soil-based compost in containers. Plant corms in spring, in autumn apply a dry mulch in mild areas, otherwise lift plants and store corms over winter. Funnel-shaped flowers in bright colours are borne in loose spikes. Sow ripe seed in a cold-frame or remove offsets from dormant corms. ❀ *S. tricolor* (Harlequin Flower), narrow, strap-like leaves, red, orange, yellow or white flowers, spring to early summer, 30cm/30cm (1ft/1ft).

Spartium Papilionaceae

Medium shrub. Moderately hardy and an excellent summer flowering shrub for coastal gardens, although thrives in almost any well-drained soil in an open position in full sun. Will self-seed if not deadheaded. Prune in spring, cutting back all new shoots to within 5cm (2in) of the base to encourage a bushy habit. Sow seed in cold-frame in autumn or spring. ❀ *S. junceum* (Spanish Broom), open habit, dark green rush-like stems, fragrant yellow, pea-like flowers from summer to early autumn, best in sandy or chalky soils, 3m (10ft) but better limited to about 1.5m (5ft) by pruning/1.5m (5ft).

Sphaeralcea
Globe Mallow, False Mallow Malvaceae

Medium/large annuals, perennials and sub-shrubs. Fairly hardy to moderately hardy. Late season, cup-shaped flowers for milder gardens but overall I think rather untidy plants that need space to look their best. A warm, sunny position in a well-drained soil is essential, may need protection from winter wet. No routine pruning. Sow seed of species in spring or divide plants in spring or take basal cuttings in spring or early summer. ❀ *S. fendleri*, fairly hardy sub-shrub, oval, hairy leaves of grey-green, silky, soft orange flowers, late summer to autumn, 45cm-1.2m (1½-4ft)/50cm (1¾ft); *S. munroana*, moderately hardy, heart-shaped grey-green leaves, mid-pink flowers, summer, 45-100cm/50cm (1½-3ft/1¾ft).

Spinacia *Spinach* Chenopodiaceae

Hardy leafy vegetable. A quick-growing plant, grown as a cut-and-come-again crop. Requires full sun and rich, moist but well-drained soils. In light soils, all varieties will run to seed although some do have claimed (real or imagined) bolting resistance. Sow in growing positions from spring to autumn. ❀ *S. oleracea*, 'Broad Leaved Prickly', very hardy winter variety; 'Longstanding Round'; 'Medania', red stems, thick smooth leaves, some resistance to bolting and mildew.

Spiraea Rosaceae

above *Spiraea arguta.* There are few more welcome sights in my shrub borders in spring than these branches, wreathed in blossom.

Small/medium shrubs. Hardy. Grown for flowers, hedging or colourful foliage. There are two distinct groups: the early flowering varieties, blooming on the previous season's growth, and the late-flowering types, blooming on the current season's growth. They are pruned accordingly. All thrive in most soils and are best in full sun but can tolerate very light shade. Cut out weak shoots from spring-flowering types after flowering, prune later-flowering types hard in early spring. Take semi-ripe cuttings in summer, suckering types can be divided. ❀ *S.* 'Arguta' (syn. *S.* x *arguta* 'Bridal Wreath'), dense shrub, bright green leaves, masses of white flowers in spring, much the loveliest plant in the genus and has been in all of my own gardens, 1.8m/1m (5¾ft/3ft); *S. betulifolia* var. *aemiliana*, dwarf plant for the rock garden, red brown shoots, white flowers, early summer, 30cm/30cm (1ft/1ft); *S.* x *cinerea* 'Grefsheim', young leaves grey and downy, masses of white flowers, spring; *S. japonica* var. *albiflora* (syns. *S. albiflora, S. callosa* 'Alba', *S. j.* 'Alba') compact habit, light green leaves, white flowers, summer, 80cm/80cm (2½ft/2½ft); *S. j.* 'Anthony Waterer', twiggy shrub, leaves bizarrely variegated pink and cream, purple buds open to bright crimson flowers that last until autumn, a quite inexplicably popular plant that I find simply ugly, 1.2m (4ft); *S. j.* 'Bullata' (syn. *S. crispifolia*), compact shrub, dark green leaves, crimson flowers, mid-summer, 80cm/80cm (2½ft/2½ft); *S. j.* 'Gold Mound', dwarf habit, bright golden leaves, pale pink flowers in summer, 25cm/25cm (10in/10in); *S. j.* 'Goldflame', bushy shrub, young

right *Stephanandra incisa* 'Crispa'. I'm delighted to have been responsible for introducing this quite lovely ground-covering deciduous shrub into a great many gardens.

leaves red-orange turning to yellow then green, crimson flowers, summer, 1m/1m (3ft/3ft); *S. j.* 'Shirobana', pale green leaves, white and pink flowers, summer, 1.2m/1.2m (4ft/4ft); *S. nipponica* 'Snowmound', dark green leaves, covered with white flowers, early summer, justifiably popular, second best after 'Arguta', 1m/1m (3ft/3ft); *S. thunbergii*, twiggy habit, pale green leaves, white flowers in early spring before leaves; *S.* x *vanhouttei*, multi-stemmed, dark green leaves with blue-green undersides, white flowers, early summer, 1.2m/1.2m (4ft/4ft); *S.* x *v.* 'Pink Ice', pale green leaves with cream variegation, pink shoots and flower buds in spring.

Stachys — Lamiaceae

Medium rhizomatous ornamentals. Moderately hardy to very hardy. Very good, if slightly untidy, foliage plants for ground cover, borders and drought-tolerant plantings. Foliage forms a mat or carpet, many have hairy leaves and some are aromatic. Most are best in well-drained soils in full sun, a few, especially those with hairy foliage, need protection from winter wet. Sow seed in a cold-frame in autumn or spring, divide plants in spring. ❀ *S. byzantina* (syn. *S. lanata*) (Lamb's Tongue, Lamb's Tails, Lamb's Ears), dense mat, thick grey woolly leaves, tiny mauve-pink flowers, summer, 40cm/50cm (1½ft/1¾ft); *S. b.* 'Silver Carpet', velvety silver leaves, no flowers; *S. coccinea*, mid-green leaves, scarlet flowers, summer, 60cm/45cm (2ft/1½ft); *S. macrantha* (syn. *S. grandifolia*), clumped habit, green leaves with scalloped edges, pink-purple flowers, summer to early autumn, needs moist soil, tolerates partial shade, 60cm/25cm (2ft/10in); *S. m.* 'Superba', slight, deeper pink-purple flowers; *S. officinalis* (Wood Betony, Bishop's Wort), mat-forming, mid-green leaves, red-purple, pink or white flowers, mid-summer, tolerates partial shade, 60cm/30cm (2ft/1ft).

below *Stachyurus praecox*. With winter flowering shrubs at such a premium, I'm a little mystified why this very pretty Japanese shrub isn't in more gardens.

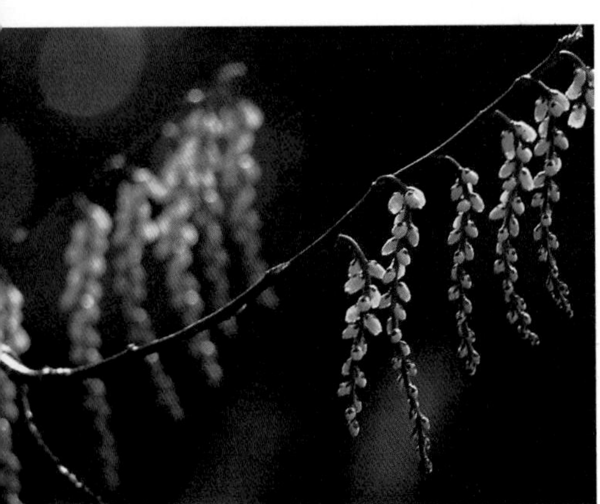

Stachyurus — Stachyuraceae

Medium/large deciduous or semi-evergreen shrubs. Moderately hardy to hardy. Unusual early flowering shrub for woodland or against a wall with a characteristic arching habit. Any well-drained soil enriched with humus in sun or partial shade; benefit from shelter from cold winds. No routine pruning but damaged or feeble shoots should be cut out in spring. Sow seed in cold-frame in autumn, take semi-ripe heeled cuttings in summer or layer. ❀ *S. praecox*, open spreading habit, arching red-brown stems, mid-green leaves, yellow buds form in the autumn, drooping clusters of pale yellow flowers, late winter or early spring, 1.5m/1.8m (5ft/5¾ft).

Stephanandra — Rosaceae

Small/medium deciduous shrubs. Hardy. A wonderful genus that I have introduced on recommendation to many gardens. My chosen forms offer some of the best, most manageable and attractive shrubby ground cover that I know. Alternate toothed or lobed, rather *Crataegus*-like leaves combined with *Spiraea*-like flowers. Will suit a moist but well-drained soil in sun or partial shade. No routine pruning. Remove rooted suckers in dormant season, divide plants in autumn, take semi-ripe cuttings in summer or hardwood cuttings in winter. ❀ *S. incisa* (syn. *S. flexuosa*), dense spreading habit, suckering, leaves have good autumn colour, dense red-brown twiggy branches a valuable winter feature, green-white flowers in early summer, 1.5m/2m (5ft/6½ft); *S. i.* 'Crispa' (syn. *S.* 'Prostrata'), dwarf form for ground cover, the plant to which I am especially attached, 2m (6½ft).

Sternbergia — Amaryllidaceae

Small corm-forming ornamental. Moderately hardy to hardy and a most valuable plant for its remarkably *Crocus*-like flowers in autumn; suitable for rock garden or small sunny border. Arguably the most under-appreciated of all easy to grow bulbous plants. Long, strap-like leaves. Sow ripe seed in a cold-frame or divide plants in spring. ❀ *S. lutea*, yellow funnel-shaped flowers in autumn the same time as the leaves, 8cm (3¼in).

Stewartia Theaceae

Medium/large trees and shrubs (some evergreen). Hardy. Woodland plants with many appealing features including some of the most striking of all white tree-borne flowers, good autumn colour and attractive winter bark. They require a moist, humus-enriched acidic soil and partial shade. No routine pruning. Sow seed in cold-frame in autumn, take cuttings in summer or layer. ❀ *S. pseudocamellia*, medium tree of open habit, fairly hardy, red-brown, flaking bark, bright green leaves, good yellow and red autumn colour, cup-shaped white flowers with yellow anthers, 10m/3m (33ft/10ft).

Stipa *Feather Grass, Needle Grass, Spear Grass* Poaceae

Medium/large perennial grasses. Fairly hardy to moderately hardy. I find this perhaps the most attractive of all the ornamental grass genera, not least for the range of size that it offers. Arching habit and feathery summer flowers. Most require a well-drained soil in full sun; *S. arundinacea* needs a moist, heavier soil and partial shade. Sow seed in a cold-frame in spring or divide plants in spring. ❀ *S. arundinacea* (New Zealand Wind Grass, Pheasant's Tail Grass), rhizomatous, evergreen, leathery dark green leaves with orange brown tints, purple-green inflorescences, summer to autumn, 1m/1.2m (3ft/4ft); *S. calamagrostis*, blue-green leaves, green-brown feathery inflorescences, 1m/1.2m (3ft/4ft); *S. gigantea*, evergreen or semi-evergreen, mid-green leaves, golden inflorescences, 60cm/1.2m (2ft/4ft); *S. tenuifolia*, small clump, pale brown, very feathery, arching inflorescences, 60cm/45cm (2ft/1½ft).

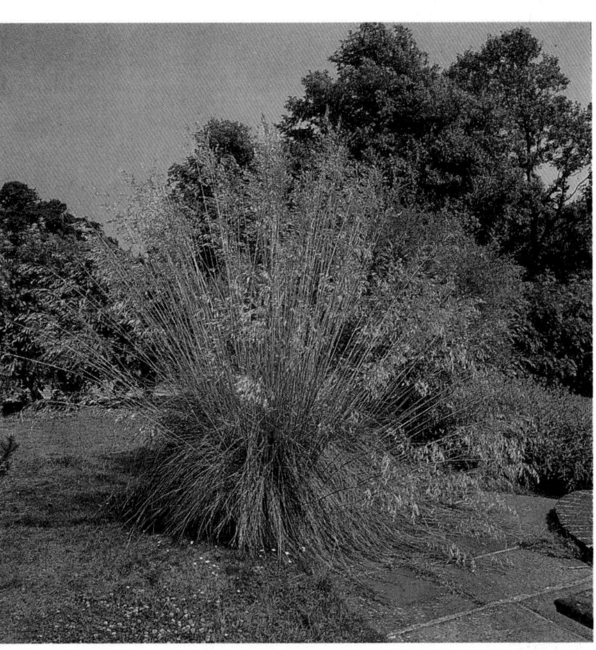

left *Stipa gigantea*. What a pretty and welcome change this plant makes from the more familiar Pampas grasses.

Stokesia *Stokes' Aster* Asteraceae

Medium evergreen herbaceous hardy perennial. Few people can recognise this very striking and pretty plant, although it has long been cultivated and is very easy. Large summer flowers, resembling cornflowers or ragged carnations, above a basal rosette of leaves. Needs a well-drained soil in full sun, intolerant of cold wet soils, may self-seed. Sow seed in cold-frame in autumn, divide plants in spring or take root cuttings in late winter. ❀ *S. laevis*, narrow, mid-green leaves, blue flowers with white centres from mid- to late summer, 60cm/45cm (2ft/1½ft); *S. l.* 'Alba', white flowers; *S. l.* 'Blue Star', deep blue flowers, 45cm/45cm (1½ft/1½ft).

Stratiotes Hydrocharitaceae

Floating/submerged hardy evergreen plant. Vigorous aquatic plant with spiky leaves for still or slow-moving water; can be invasive in small pools and its cultivation is legally restricted in some warm countries. Leaves are submerged but rise to the surface at flowering time. Detach young plants from runners in spring. ❀ *S. aloïdes* (Water Soldier), short runners with stalkless pineapple-like rosettes, narrow, spiny-edged leaves up to 45cm (1½ft) long, small white flowers in mid- to late summer. Spreads indefinitely.

Styrax *Snowbell* Styracaceae

Small deciduous and evergreen trees and shrubs. Barely hardy to hardy. Woodland plants grown for their graceful arching habit; in due course, fragrant, white, bell-shaped summer flowers appear and are well worth the wait, although they are features of mature plants only. Best in moist, lime-free soil in sun or partial shade and a sheltered position. Sow ripe seed or take semi-ripe cuttings in mid-summer. ❀ *S. hemsleyanus*, small tree, rather tender when young so needs a sheltered warm corner if grown in a cold area, pale green leaves with serrated edges, white flowers with yellow anthers, 8m/2m (26½ft/6½ft); *S. japonicus*, large shrub or small tree, spreading habit, hardy, glossy, oval leaves, yellow autumn colour, white flowers with yellow stamens hanging endearingly on the undersides of branches, 8m/2m (26½ft/6½ft); *S. j.* Benibana Group 'Pink Chimes', many pale pink flowers.

Symphoricarpos
Snowberry, Coralberry Caprifoliaceae

Small/medium deciduous shrubs. Very hardy. Easy to grow (often maligned for being too easy) with attractive white, pink or red-purple fruits from autumn to winter, suitable for specimens, hedging or ground cover. Flowers insignificant. Will succeed in any type of soil or position, so valuable in problem areas such as exposed, dry or shady sites. Most produce suckers and require hard pruning in spring to keep them within bounds. Detach rooted suckers or take hardwood cuttings in autumn. ❀ *S. albus laevigatus*, thicket-forming habit, white fruits, *S.* x *chenaultii* 'Hancock', dwarf with spreading, suckering habit, ideal ground cover, deep lilac-pink fruits, 1m/1.5m (3ft/5ft); *S.* x *doorenbosii* 'Mother of Pearl', small dense shrub, white fruits with pink flush, 1.5-2m/4m (5-6½ft/13ft); *S.* x *d.* 'White Hedge', upright but compact growth, ideal for informal hedging, white fruits, 1.5m (5ft).

Symphytum *Comfrey* Boraginaceae

Medium/large very hardy herbaceous perennials, some rhizomatous. Vigorous flowering and foliage plants for wilder parts of the garden; they are some of the roughest and coarsest of all herbaceous perennials. By no stretch of the imagination do they have class. Rough, bristly, oval or lance-shaped leaves. Tubular or bell-shaped flowers usually from late spring to early summer. Will succeed in any soil that retains moisture over the summer, sun or partial shade. Sow seed in a cold-frame in autumn or spring. Divide in spring or take root cuttings in early winter. ❀ *S. caucasicum*, red-purple then blue flowers, early summer, 60cm/60cm (2ft/2ft); *S.* 'Goldsmith', dark green leaves with gold and cream markings, pink, white or blue flowers, early spring, 30cm/45cm (1ft/1½ft); *S.* 'Hidcote Blue', rhizomatous, vigorous, red in bud then pale blue flowers, 45cm/45cm (1½ft/1½ft); *S. ibericum* (syn. *S. grandiflorum*), rhizomatous, red buds open to pale yellow flowers, 40cm/60cm (1½ft/2ft); *S. officinale* (Common Comfrey), vigorous coarse leaves used as compost activator (and you can't have much less class than that), small flowers or yellow-green, pink or purple flowers, 1.2-1.5m/1-2m (4-5ft/3-6½ft); *S. tuberosum*, creeping perennial with tuberous rhizomes, pale yellow flowers in early summer, 50cm/1m (1¾ft/3ft); *S.* x *uplandicum* (syn. *S. peregrinum*) (Russian Comfrey) dark pink buds open to blue-purple flowers, *S.* x *u.* 'Bocking 14', selected form for compost making; *S.* x *u.* 'Variegatum', grey-green leaves with cream margins, often reverts to all-green, pale pink flowers, 1m/45cm (3ft/1½ft).

Syringa *Lilac* Oleaceae

Small/large deciduous shrubs and small trees. Very hardy. Grown for late spring to early summer flowers, which are often very fragrant, but even the most devoted enthusiast must concede that, after the flowers fade, the lilac is sad thing with persisting dead inflorescences and dull foliage. Dark green leaves; small tubular flowers borne in clusters in a wide range of colours. Lilacs thrive in any well-drained soil including alkaline sites and are best in full sun. Remove old flowering wood after flowering; pull away suckers as they arise. Take semi-ripe cuttings in early summer or layer, although most named varieties are grafted. ❀ *S.* x *josiflexa* 'Bellicent', large shrub with large inflorescences of fragrant clear rose-pink flowers, 4m/1.5m (13ft/5ft); *S.* x *laciniata*, small shrub, small inflorescences of lilac flowers; *S. meyeri spontanea* 'Palibin', slow-growing dense shrub, pale lilac-pink flowers, 1.2m/1m (4ft/3ft); *S. pubescens microphylla* 'Superba', masses of fragrant rose-pink flowers from late spring on and off until autumn, 1.8m/1.2m (5¾ft/4ft); *S. vulgaris* (Common Lilac) hybrids grafted on to suckering common lilac rootstock, large shrubs/small trees, fragrant flowers produced two to three years after planting. *S. v.* 'Andenken an Ludwig Späth' (syn. 'Souvenir de Louis Späth'), wine-red flowers; *S. v.* 'Belle de Nancy', purple-red buds open to double lilac-pink flowers; *S. v.* 'Charles Joly', late, double, dark purple-red flowers; *S. v.* 'Katherine Havemeyer', double, purple-lavender flowers that age to pale lilac-pink; *S. v.* 'Madame Lemoine', cream-yellow buds open to double pure white flowers; *S. v.* 'Michel Buchner' , double, pale rose-lilac flowers; *S. v.* 'Sensation', purple-red flowers edged with white, can revert to all-white.

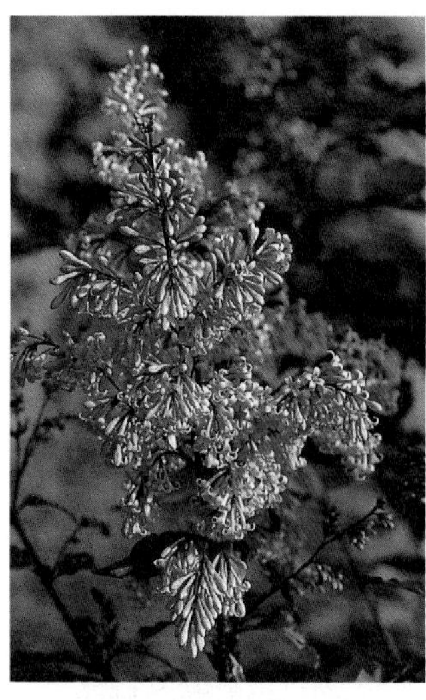

above *Syringa x josiflexa* 'Bellicent'. If you appreciate lilacs, then surely you will enjoy this close relative of the familiar early summer flowering varieties.

right *Styrax japonicus*. A lovely plant, but do remember than the name snowbell refers to the colour of the flowers and not to the time that they appear.

Tagetes *Marigold* Asteraceae

Small/medium half-hardy annuals. Extremely popular and easy to grow bedding plants in bright yellows, oranges and reds. A multiplicity of new varieties appears every year. Finely-divided, dark green leaves with a pungent but rather pleasing, aroma when crushed. Thrive in any well-drained soil in full sun or in soil-based compost in containers. Sow seeds in warmth in spring. Because there are huge numbers of quickly changing varieties in most of the groups, I have listed only the broad types and their characteristics. ❀ *T. erecta* (African Marigold), relatively tall, and often used as 'dot' plants in bedding schemes, fully-double pompon flowers in cream, many shades of yellow or orange; Dwarf double varieties 20-30cm/30cm (8in-1ft/1ft), Tall Double varieties 45cm/30cm (1½ft/1ft). *T. patula* (French Marigold), smaller, more spreading habit than African Marigolds, for containers or for edging beds, masses of small single or double blooms, many shades of yellow, orange, red, many bicolours, 25-45cm/25cm (10in-1½ft/10in), main groups are Carnation Flowered, Crested, (have a crested centre of contrasting colour), Singles, and Super French. Afro-French Marigolds are hybrids between African and French, 35cm/30cm (1¼ft/1ft). *T. tenuifolia* (syn. *T. signata*) (Tagetes), bushy habit with masses of small single flowers, much underappreciated in modern gardening but delightfully simple after their huge cousins, ideally used as edging; 'Golden Gem', golden-yellow; 'Lemon Gem', lemon-yellow; 'Star Fire', a mixture of yellow, red and bicolours.

Tamarix *Tamarisk* Tamaricaceae

Small, moderately hardy to hardy trees and large shrubs. Grown for their attractive feathery foliage and sprays of tiny pink flowers; ideal plants for coastal gardens or dry, exposed places inland. Small scale-like leaves. Need a site with well-drained soil and full sun. Best when pruned fairly hard after flowering to encourage bushy habit. Sow ripe seed in a cold-frame, take semi-ripe cuttings in summer or hardwood cuttings in winter. ❀ *T. ramosissima* (syn. *T. pentandra*), large shrub or small tree, suckering habit, red-brown branches, pale grey-green leaves, feathery pink flowers, late summer, makes a good windbreak, 5m/6m (16ft/20ft); *T. r.* 'Pink Cascade', masses of rich pink flowers obscuring the foliage; *T. tetrandra*, large shrub with open habit, light pink flowers, late spring to early summer, prune after flowering, 4m/4m (13ft/13ft).

above *Tagetes tenuifolia* 'Golden Gem'. I think it a great shame that the small flowering tagetes are seen less commonly now than their giant hybrid relatives the African and French marigolds.

Tanacetum Asteraceae

Small/medium half-hardy to hardy annuals and herbaceous perennials and herbs providing summer flowers for rock gardens, borders, wild areas and herb gardens. Leaves are aromatic, often finely-divided. Daisy-like or button flowers with yellow central disc. Require a well-drained soil in an open, sunny position. Sow seed of species in spring; perennial types can be divided or basal cuttings taken in spring. ❀ *T. balsamita* (Alecost, Costmary), herbaceous perennial herb, aromatic mid-green leaves, white flowers, late summer, 75cm/45cm (2½ft/1½ft); *T. coccineum* (syn. *Pyrethrum roseum*) (Pyrethrum), herbaceous hardy perennial, bright green leaves, white, pink purple or red flowers with yellow centres, late spring to early summer, 75cm/60cm (2½ft/2ft); *T. c.* 'Robinson's Pink', pink flowers; *T. haradjanii*, mat-like evergreen perennial, silver-grey leaves, small yellow flowers in late summer, 30cm/30cm (1ft/1ft); *T. parthenium* (syns. *Chrysanthemum parthenium, Pyrethrum parthenium*) (Feverfew), hardy, short-lived, self-seeding perennial, white flowers, 30cm/50cm (1ft/1¾ft); *T. p.* 'Aureum', bright golden, deeply-cut leaves, flowers best removed to improve the foliage; *T. vulgare*

above *Taxus baccata* 'Fastigiata Aurea'. I really don't think there is a single unattractive variety of the yew in existence, but this form has a particularly individual appearance.

(Tansy), herbaceous hardy perennial for a wild garden (true species is a weed), button-like yellow flowers, late summer to autumn, 1.2m/60cm (4ft/2ft); *T. v.* var. *crispum*, smaller form with fern-like leaves.

Taxus *Yew* Taxaceae

Small/large, very hardy evergreen coniferous trees and shrubs. The finest hedging and topiary plant but also make superb specimens. Tolerant of many problem positions, including dry chalky or acidic soils but not water-logged sites. Will grow in full sun to deep shade, although gold-leaved forms will lose their colour in heavy shade and some scorch in hot sun. Separate male and female plants, the latter produce familiar red fruits. Most parts of yew, especially the seeds, are toxic. Hedges and topiary should be clipped twice each year and may be hard pruned to restore shape; otherwise no routine pruning. Sow ripe seed in a cold-frame or take hardwood cuttings in autumn or softwood cuttings in spring. ❀ *T. baccata* (Common Yew, English Yew), large shrub or small/medium tree, dark green leaves, red fruits, 15m/8m (50ft/26½ft); *T. b.* 'Dovastonii Aurea', small wide-spreading tree, leaves with bright yellow margin, male; *T. b.* 'Fastigiata' (Irish Yew), compact dense column, female; *T. b.* 'Fastigiata Aurea', similar but with yellow margin to leaves, male; *T. b.* 'Repandens', low-growing with long branches, good ground cover, female, 30cm/1m (1ft/3ft); *T. b.* 'Semperaurea', slow-growing, young leaves deep golden-yellow ageing to rust-yellow, male; *T. b.* 'Standishii', slow-growing dense columnar habit, golden-yellow leaves, needs full sun, female.

Tellima *Fringe Cups* Saxifragaceae

Medium semi-evergreen herbaceous hardy perennial. Delightful, undemanding and restrained ground cover, especially for woodland gardens. Basal clump of heart-shaped to kidney-shaped leaves. Small bell-shaped flowers, late spring to mid-summer. Best in a moist soil enriched with humus or leaf mould in partial shade but will tolerate drier soil and full sun. Sow ripe seed in a cold-frame or divide plants in spring. ❀ *T. grandiflora*, light green hairy leaves, small yellow-green flowers turning pink, 75cm/30cm (2½ft/1ft); *T. g.* 'Rubra Group' (syn. 'Purpurea'), purple-red tinges to leaves in winter, 20cm/75cm (8in/2½ft).

Tetragonia Aizoaceae

Leafy vegetable. A tender perennial usually grown as a half-hardy annual and an excellent spinach substitute for warm, dry soils in which spinach runs to seed. Thrives best in a deep sandy soil but can tolerate dry, poor soils without bolting. Sow seed in warmth in spring or sow in growing position after last frosts. Will self-seed and emerge year after year. ❀ *T. tetragonioïdes* (New Zealand Spinach), spreading succulent with spiky leaves, pick young leaves and shoots regularly, discard thicker stems.

Tetragonolobus Papilionaceae

Medium annual. Decorative member of the pea family with edible pods. Requires an open, sunny site and good soil. Sow seed in growing position in late spring. ❀ *T. purpureus* (Asparagus Pea), red flowers, edible winged pods, pick pods when young (3-5cm (1¼-2in) long) and cook whole, 30-45cm/45-60cm (1-1½ft/1½-2ft).

Teucrium
Wood Sage, Germander *Lamiaceae*

Small/large hardy evergreen herbaceous perennials and shrubs (some rhizomatous). Grown for their flowers and usually attractive, aromatic

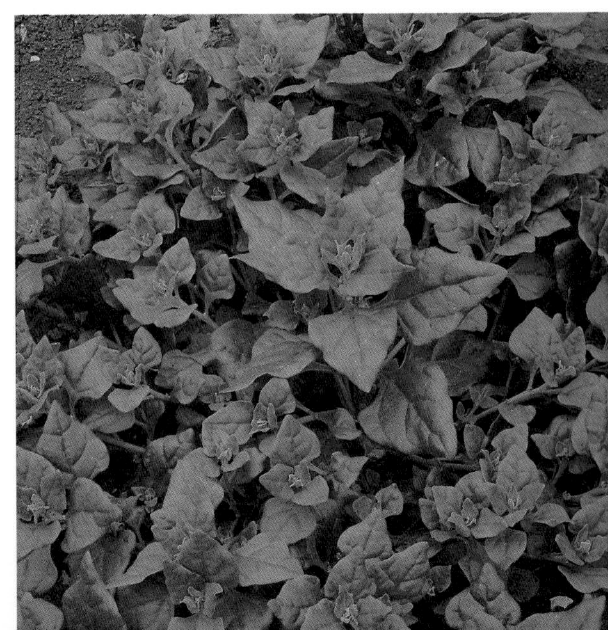

right New Zealand Spinach. An improbable looking but very tasty substitute for spinach for those light dry soils on which the real thing runs to seed.

foliage. They require a well-drained site in full sun but will tolerate poor soils and alkalinity. Sow ripe seed in a cold-frame, take softwood cuttings in early summer or semi-ripe cuttings in mid-summer. ❀ *T. aroanium*, barely hardy, silver-grey leaves, dull purple flowers, 10cm/30cm (4in/1ft); *T. chamaedrys* (Wall Germander), hardy sub-shrub, good ground cover, green holly-like leaves with grey undersides, mauve-pink flowers, 30cm/30cm (1ft/1ft); *T. scorodonia* (Wood Sage), grey-green leaves, green-yellow or white flowers, best in cool, acidic soil, 30cm/45cm (1ft/1½ft); *T. s.* 'Crispum Marginatum', puckered leaf edges of white to pink.

Thalictrum *Meadow Rue* Ranunculaceae

Small/large hardy or very hardy herbaceous hardy perennials (some rhizomatous). Attractive grey-green leaves and summer flowers and suitable for shaded borders and woodland gardens. Tolerate any moist but well-drained soil enriched with humus, in sun or partial shade. Sow ripe seed in a cold-frame or divide plants in spring. ❀ *T. aquilegiifolium*, rhizomatous, delightfully delicate lilac-purple flowers, early summer, 1m/30cm (3ft/1ft); *T. a.* var. *album*, cream-white flowers; *T. delavayi* (syn. *T. dipterocarpum*), rhizomatous, purple (lilac to white) flowers with yellow stamens, mid-summer to early autumn, 1.5m/60cm (5ft/2ft); *T. d.* 'Hewitt's Double', masses of double deep purple flowers, the best form; *T. flavum* ssp. *glaucum* (syn. *T. speciosissimum*), rhizomatous, blue-green leaves, fragrant, tiny pale yellow flowers, summer, 1.5m/60cm (5ft/2ft); *T. kiusianum*, slow, low-growing plant, mid-green leaves, pale pink-mauve flowers, 7cm/20cm (2¾in/8in); *T. minus*, pale green leaves like maidenhair ferns, clouds of small cream-yellow or pale purple flowers, an extremely under-rated ground cover for woodland, 30cm/20cm (1ft/8in); *T. m.* var. *adiantifolium*, grey-green leaves, insignificant purple-green flowers, 1m (3ft).

Thlaspi *Pennycress* Brassicaceae

Small alpines, annuals and perennials. Hardy to very hardy. Good, if unexciting, plants for spring to early summer flowers, suitable for rock gardens or raised beds. Some species have a sweet perfume. Require very well-drained soil and full sun. Sow ripe seed in a cold-frame or divide in spring. ❀ *T. alpinum*, small alpine, mat-like habit, basal rosette of oval leaves, loose spikes of white flowers, 10-15cm/20cm (4-6in/8in).

Thuja *Red Cedar* Cupressaceae

Medium/large hardy evergreen coniferous trees. Among the most valuable yet under-appreciated of conifers for screening. They are most successful in a moist but well-drained soil and don't usually thrive as well in dry sites. Best in full sun but will tolerate light shade; variegated forms usually give their best colour in sun. Needles release sweet fragrance when crushed and may cause skin irritation. Older trees may have attractive red-brown peeling bark. No routine pruning but hedging plants should be clipped twice each year. Sow seed in a cold-frame in autumn or take semi-ripe cuttings in late summer. ❀ *T. occidentalis* 'Danica', dwarf globular bush, needles held vertically in flattened sprays; *T. o.* 'Holmstrup', slow-growing, medium/large bush, needles in vertical sprays; *T. o.* 'Rheingold', slow-growing conical bush, gold/amber needles; *T. o.* 'Smaragd', small tree, narrow conical shape, bright green needles; *T. orientalis* 'Aurea Nana', dwarf globular bush, light yellow-green needles vertically arranged in sprays, a splendid thing; *T. o.* 'Rosedalis', dense bush, soft young needles, bright yellow in early spring, green in summer, purple in winter; *T. plicata*, large tree with spreading branches, fast-growing, glossy green needles, excellent for hedging or screening, tolerates shade and alkalinity, 25m/8m (80ft/26½ft); *T. p.* 'Rogersii',

above *Thalictrum delavayi* 'Hewitt's Double'. This relative of the humble meadow rue has really come a long way from the flower of our meadows.

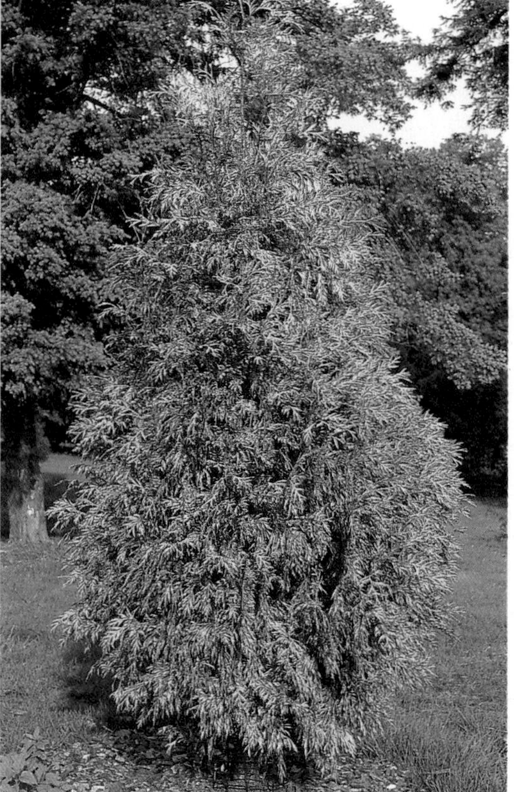

left *Thuja plicata* 'Zebrina'. There's no doubt that thujas are among the least well known of the commoner conifers but in both green leaved and variegated forms, they are among the most attractive.

dwarf conical bush, slow-growing, gold-bronze foliage, 1.2m/1m (4ft/3ft) eventually; *T. p.* 'Stoneham Gold', large bush, slow-growing with narrow conical habit, bright golden needles with copper-bronze tips; *T. p.* 'Zebrina', large tree, conical habit, strong-growing, green needles with cream-yellow bands.

Thujopsis Cupressaceae

Small/medium evergreen coniferous tree. Moderately hardy to hardy. A fine specimen conifer related to *Thuja*. Will thrive in most well-drained soils and tolerates alkalinity; best in a sunny position with shelter from cold winds. Sow seed in a cold-frame from winter to spring or take semi-ripe cuttings in late summer. ❀ *T. dolabrata*, slow-growing, conical habit, glossy dark green leaves with silver-white bands beneath, blue-grey cones, 15m/7m (50ft/23ft); *T. d.* 'Variegata', patches of cream-white on leaves, can revert, 10m/4m (33ft/13ft).

below *Thymus* 'Silver Posie'. Many of the most attractive thymes are of little culinary value. This is a striking exception, being the best flavoured of all.

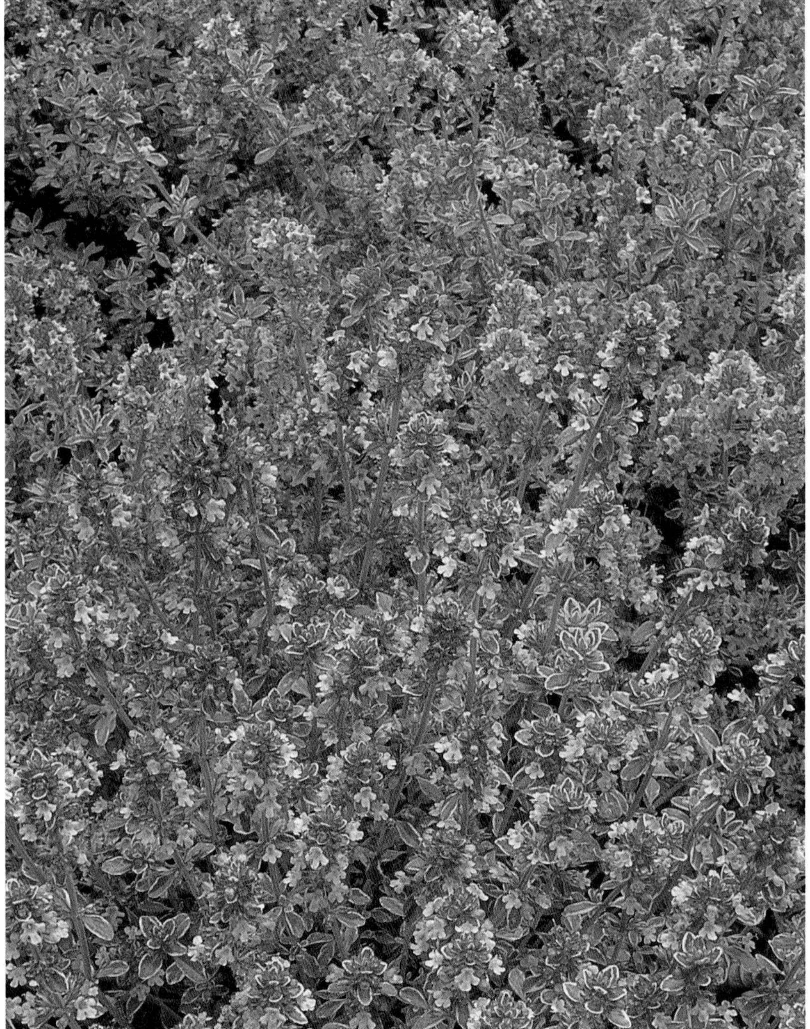

Thunbergia *Clock Vine* Acanthaceae

Small half-hardy annual and perennial climbers. Half-hardy summer climbers are not numerous and this is one of the best; small enough to work well in hanging baskets. Plants grown outside require well-drained, but moist, fertile soil in a sunny position. Sow seed in warmth in early spring. ❀ *T. alata*, tender perennial grown as an annual, dark green leaves, orange, yellow or white flowers, often with brown-purple centres, appear from early summer to mid-autumn, 2m/25cm (6½ft/10in); *T. a.* 'Susie' (and Susie Hybrids), orange-yellow or white flowers with dark centres.

Thymus *Thyme* Lamiaceae

Small evergreen perennials, sub-shrubs and shrubby herbs. Barely hardy to hardy. It is a mistake to think of thyme as just a herb; there are many most attractive ornamental species – although it must also be said that most of the attractive types are of little culinary value. Suitable for the front of sunny borders, rock gardens, containers and among paving (but be sure to use only prostrate forms). Small aromatic leaves, sometimes coloured. Clusters of pink, purple or white flowers in summer. A well-drained soil or gritty compost is essential, they thrive well in alkaline conditions, in a sunny, sheltered position. Shrubby types benefit from light clipping after flowering, replace plants after three or four years. Sow seed in a cold-frame in spring (although many of the best forms do not come true), divide plants in spring or take softwood or semi-ripe cuttings in summer. ❀ *T. caespititius*, prostrate, bright green leaves, purple to pale pink flowers, 5cm/35cm (2in/1¼ft); *T.* x *citriodorus* (Lemon Thyme), upright, mid-green leaves with lemon-scented, lilac flowers, 15cm/15cm (6in/6in); *T.* x *c.* 'Archer's Gold', mid-green leaves with gold-yellow margins; *T.* x *c.* 'Aureus', green leaves with gold markings; *T.* x *c.* 'Bertram Anderson' (syn. *T.* 'Anderson's Gold'), grey-green leaves with yellow; *T.* x *c.* 'Silver Queen', grey and cream-white leaves; *T. doerfleri* 'Bressingham pink', prostrate, grey-green leaves, pink flowers, 10cm/35cm (4in/1¼ft); *T.* 'Doone Valley', mat-like, dark green leaves with yellow spots, red buds open to purple-pink flowers, 10cm/20cm (4in/8in); *T. herba-barona* (Caraway Thyme), mat-like habit, dark green leaves with caraway scent, lilac-pink flowers, 5cm/45cm (2in/1½ft); *T. pseudolanuginosus*, prostrate, very woolly-hairy, self-seeds freely and one of the best for growing between paving, pink-mauve flowers; *T. pulegioïdes*, sub-shrub, dark green leaves, purple to

pink flowers, 8cm/20cm (3¼in/8in); *T. serpyllum* (Wild Thyme), mat-like, dark green leaves, purple or mauve flowers, 5cm/30cm (2in/1ft); *T. s.* var. *albus*, white flowers; *T. s.* 'Annie Hall', pale purple-pink flowers; *T. s. coccineus*, crimson-pink flowers; *T. s.* 'Goldstream', yellow variegated leaves; *T. s.* 'Minimus', dwarf, pink flowers, 5cm/10cm (2in/4in); *T. s.* 'Pink Chintz', grey-green leaves, masses of pink flowers; *T. vulgaris* (Common Thyme), aromatic, dark green leaves, pink or white flowers, variable in size, 15-30cm/30-40cm (6in-1ft/1-1½ft); *T. v.* 'Silver Posie' white margin to the leaves, the best culinary thyme by a long way.

Tiarella *Foam Flower* Saxifragaceae

Small herbaceous evergreen hardy perennials (some rhizomatous). Very hardy. Invaluable and very pretty ground cover for shady areas. Tiny cloud-like masses of white or pink flowers, spring to summer. They prefer a moist soil enriched with humus in a cool, shady position. Sow ripe seed in a cold-frame or divide plants in spring. ❀ *T. cordifolia*, vigorous rhizomes, hairy, lobed leaves of pale green leaves with bronze tint in winter, cream-white flowers, I still think this the best form, 25cm/1m (10in/3ft); *T. polyphylla*, rhizomes, lobed mid-green leaves, cream-white flowers, 20cm/30cm (8in/1ft); *T. wherryi* (syn. *T. collina*), slow-growing clump, palmate leaves of pale green with red tints, pink or white flowers, 15cm/30cm (6in/1ft); *T. w.* 'Bronze Beauty', dark red-bronze leaves, light pink or white flowers.

Tilia *Lime, Linden* Tiliaceae

Large trees. Very hardy. Attractive trees but only for large gardens, as much as anything because they attract aphids and in consequence drip honeydew on to anything placed beneath them. Suitable for all types of fertile soil. Small, fragrant, cream-white flowers are borne in clusters in midsummer; flowers have a narcotic effect on bees. No routine pruning. Stratify seed and sow in cold-frame in spring. Bud in late summer or remove suckers in winter. ❀ *T. cordata* (Small-Leaved Lime), heart-shaped leaves glossy dark green with pale green undersides with red-brown tufts, 25m/8m (80ft/26½ft); *T.* x *euchlora* (Caucasian Lime), semi-pendent habit, heart-shaped leaves, 20m/7m (60ft/23ft); *T.* 'Petiolaris', weeping tree, rounded dark green leaves with white undersides, flowers narcotic to bees, 30m/10m (100ft/33ft).

Tithonia *Mexican Sunflower* Asteraceae

Large half-hardy annual. One of the bigger but least appreciated summer annuals; a wonderful big, bushy plant. A sheltered site in full sun is needed, the soil should be well-drained and enriched with humus. Sow seed in warmth in spring. ❀ *T. rotundifolia* (syn. *T. speciosa*), mid-green leaves, orange flowers, mid-summer to mid-autumn, 3m/1m (10ft/3ft); *T. r.* 'Goldfinger', rich orange flowers with a golden-yellow centre, 75cm/50cm (2½ft/1¾ft); *T. r.* 'Torch', flame-red flowers with a golden-yellow centre, inferior I think to the true species, 1.2m/50cm (4ft/1¾ft).

Tolmieia *Pickaback Plant* Saxifragaceae

Small/medium herbaceous hardy perennials. Fairly hardy to moderately hardy. Fast-spreading, easy ground-cover plants for shade. Best in a moist soil enriched with leaf-mould or compost in shade or partial shade; splendid for the woodland garden. Sow seed in a cold-frame in autumn, divide plants in spring or detach plantlets in summer. ❀ *T. menziesii*, mid-green leaves, nodding green-brown flowers on erect stems, late spring to early summer, 60cm/30cm (2ft/1ft); *T. m.* 'Taff's Gold' (syn. 'Maculata'), pale green leaves mottled with cream and pale yellow.

left *Tithonia rotundifolia* 'Goldfinger'. Among the biggest, most striking and yet least grown of summer daisies, I am so pleased that I discovered this plant many years ago.

below *Tiarella cordifolia*. Among the first plants that I would choose when planting a shaded border, tiarellas have appeal all year round.

right *Trillium grandiflorum*. The wood lilies are not cheap plants but for giving undoubted quality to a moist woodland garden, the investment is well worthwhile.

Trachelospermum
Star Jasmine Apocynaceae

Small evergreen climber. Barely hardy to moderately hardy and one of the plants that I miss most in my present, slightly too cold, garden. Self-clinging climbers grown for their fragrant jasmine-like flowers. Grow on a sunny, sheltered wall. No routine pruning. Take semi-ripe cuttings in summer or layer. ❀ *T. asiaticum*, moderately hardy, glossy dark green leaves, fragrant flowers of cream-white ageing to yellow, 4m/3m (13ft/10ft); *T. jasminoides*, barely hardy, dark green leaves, fragrant white flowers ageing to cream, 3m/3m (10ft/10ft); *T. j.* 'Variegatum', cream-white splashes on the leaves, often red tints in winter.

Tradescantia
Spider Lily, Spiderwort Commelinaceae

Medium evergreen herbaceous perennials. Moderately hardy. Require a fertile moist soil in full sun or partial shade. Divide in spring or autumn. ❀ *T.* Andersoniana Group, untidy, arching narrow leaves of mid-green, flowers composed of three triangular petals, early summer to early autumn (syn. *T.* x *andersoniana*), 40-60cm/45-60cm (1½-2ft/1½-2ft). 'Innocence', pure white flowers; *T.* x. *a.* 'Karminglut' (syn. 'Carmine Glow'), dark red flowers; *T.* x. *a.* 'Osprey', large white flowers with purple-blue stems; *T.* x. *a.* 'Purple Dome', rich purple flowers; several new varieties such as 'Blue 'n' Gold' and 'Chedglow' have golden-yellow leaves; *T. virginiana* 'Caerulea Plena', compact clump of grass-like leaves, double royal blue flowers, 60cm/45cm (2ft/1½ft).

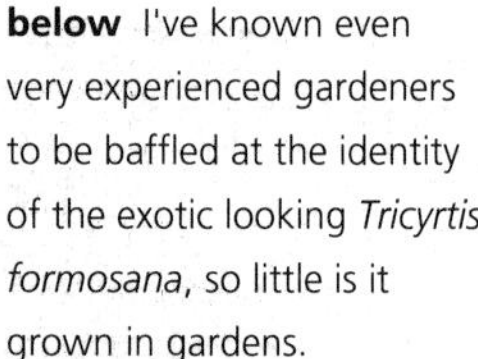

below I've known even very experienced gardeners to be baffled at the identity of the exotic looking *Tricyrtis formosana*, so little is it grown in gardens.

Tricyrtis
Toad Lily Liliaceae

Medium herbaceous rhizomatous hardy perennials. Fairly to moderately hardy and grown for their striking, utterly fantastic spotted flowers. Dark green leaves. Require a soil enriched with humus in sheltered, partially shaded position; ideal plants for the woodland garden. Sow ripe seed in a cold-frame or divide plants in early spring. ❀ *T. formosana*, pink-purple flowers with heavy spotting, early autumn, 60cm/45cm (2ft/1½ft); *T. hirta*, white

flowers with purple spots, late summer to early autumn, 90cm/45cm (3ft/1½ft); *T. h. alba*, white flowers flushed green; *T. h.* 'Miyazaki', flowers spotted lilac-purple, 90cm/45cm (3ft/1½ft); *T. latifolia* (syn. *T. bakeri*), yellow or yellow-green flowers with purple spots, mid-summer, 90cm/45cm (3ft/1½ft); *T. macropoda*, white-purple flowers with purple spots, late summer, 75cm/45cm (2½ft/1½ft); *T.* 'White Towers', upward-facing white flowers, 60cm/30cm (2ft/1ft).

Trifolium *Clover* Papilionaceae

Small hardy annuals, biennials and perennials, a few evergreen. Very hardy. Some are invasive weeds but others can make attractive ground cover. Require an open sunny site with well-drained soil. Sow seed or divide plants in spring, self-seeds freely. ❀ *T. pratense* 'Susan Smith' (syns. 'Dolly North', 'Goldnet'), mat-like perennial, gold veins on leaves, dark pink flowers, early to mid-summer; *T. repens*, semi-evergreen with creeping stems, fragrant, small white flowers, late spring to early autumn; *T. r.* 'Green Ice', two-tone green leaves, cream flowers; *T. r.* 'Purpurascens', red-brown leaves edged with green; *T. r.* 'Purpurascens Quadrifolium', rhizomatous, deep purple centres to leaves, small white flowers, summer, 10cm (4in)/indefinite.

Trillium
Wood Lily, Wake Robin Trilliaceae

Small herbaceous hardy rhizomatous perennials. Moderately hardy to very hardy. These are lovely, if rather costly, woodland plants for moist shade and shelter. Each stem has three leaves and three-petalled flowers that appear in spring. Sow seed in cold-frame or divide established plants after foliage has died down. ❀ *T. chloropetalum*, bright green leaves, white, green-orange, brown or maroon flowers, 45cm/45cm (1½ft/1½ft); *T. erectum*, pale green leaves, deep red flowers, 40cm/30cm (1½ft/1ft); *T. grandiflorum*, white or pink flowers with wavy edge to petals, 45cm/45cm (1½ft/1½ft); *T. luteum* (syn. *T. sessile* var. *luteum*), mid-green leaves with pale green markings, green-yellow flowers, 40cm/30cm (1½ft/1ft); *T. recurvatum*, mottled bronze leaves, red-brown to purple-green flowers, 40cm/30cm (1½ft/1ft); *T. sessile*, leaves marbled with grey, scented dark red-brown flowers, 20cm/30cm (8in/1ft).

Trollius *Globe Flower* Ranunculaceae

Small herbaceous hardy perennials. Easy, colourful plants, buttercup-like, for pool edges or borders where the soil remains moist. Thrive in sun or partial shade. Clumps of deeply divided leaves. Globe or cup-like flowers in yellow, orange or cream appear late spring to early summer. Sow ripe seed in a cold-frame (although may be very slow to germinate) or divide plants in autumn. ❀ *T. chinensis* 'Golden Queen' (syn. *T. ledebourii*), orange flowers; *T.* x *cultorum* 'Canary Bird', lemon-yellow flowers, 75cm (2½ft); *T.* x *c.* 'Earliest of All', clear yellow flowers in mid-spring, 75cm (2½ft); *T.* x *c.* 'Lemon Queen', lemon-yellow, 60cm (2ft); *T. europaeus*, deeply divided bright green leaves, rich yellow flowers, 75cm/45cm (2½ft/1½ft); *T. pumilus*, neat, slow-growing habit, yellow flowers, 25cm/25cm (10in/10in).

Tropaeolum Tropaeolaceae

Annuals, herbaceous perennials and climbers. Tender to barely hardy and grown for their stunningly pretty trumpet-shaped flowers in bright colours of red, pink, orange and yellow. The range of varieties has increased considerably in recent years and these are plants on the crest of a wave of popularity. Full sun is essential, the soil should be moist but well-drained. Sow seed in growing positions in spring; separate tubers in autumn or divide *T. speciosum* in early spring. ❀ *T. majus* (Nasturtium), half-hardy annual, flowers have a long spur, best flowering impact in soils low in nutrients, 2m/2m (6½ft/6½ft); *T. m.* 'Alaska', cream and green variegated leaves, orange, yellow, mahogany or cream flowers, 25cm/25cm (10in/10in); *T. m.* 'Empress of India, dark blue-green leaves, red flowers, 25cm/25cm (10in/10in); *T. m.* 'Hermione Grashoff', semi-double orange-scarlet flowers, propagated by cuttings, 20cm/20cm (8in/8in); *T. m.* 'Jewel of Africa', the first climbing form with variegated foliage, red, yellow, cream, orange and cream-pink flowers, 2m/2m (6½ft/6½ft); *T. m.* 'Strawberry Ice', chrome-yellow flowers with red spots, 25cm/35cm (10in/1¼ft); *T. m.* 'Peach Melba', semi-double, cream-yellow flowers with orange-red centres, grow in container, 25-30cm/45cm (10in-1ft/1½ft); *T. m.* 'Tom Thumb', compact, yellow, orange, pink or red flowers, 25cm/25cm (10in/10in); *T. m.* 'Whirlybird', yellow or red flowers without spurs, 25cm/25cm (10in/10in); *T. peregrinum* (Canary Creeper), half-hardy annual, glaucous leaves, small, vivid yellow spurred flowers, a good plant for big hanging baskets, 3m/1m (10ft/3ft); *T. speciosum* (Flame Creeper, Scots Flame Flower), herbaceous hardy perennial climber, rhizomes, lobed green leaves, bright red flowers, mid- to late summer, sometimes bright blue fruits in autumn, 3m/60cm (10ft/2ft); *T. tuberosum*, half-hardy herbaceous perennial, grey-green leaves, bright orange-scarlet flowers, mid-summer to autumn, 2-4m/1.5m (6½-13ft/5ft).

Tsuga *Hemlock* Pinaceae

Small/medium/large hardy evergreen coniferous trees. Useful shade-tolerant conifers for hedging or elegant specimens of large gardens. Creates probably the densest of all conifer hedges but inexplicably seldom grown. Best in a moist but

below *Tropaeolum majus* 'Jewel of Africa'. Nasturtiums have never been more popular and this is a most valuable recent addition, the first climbing variety with variegated foliage.

well-drained soil enriched with humus in full sun or partial shade, sheltered from cold winds. Sow seed in a cold-frame in spring or take semi-ripe cuttings in late summer. ❀ *T. canadensis* (Eastern Hemlock), 'Jeddeloh', dwarf bush, compact habit, branches arch from a depressed centre, bright green leaves, 1.5m/2m (5ft/6½ft); *T. c.* 'Pendula', low mound of drooping branches, ideal for large rock gardens, 2m/3.5m (6½ft/11ft) (4m/8m (13ft/26½ft)); *T. heterophylla* (Western Hemlock), large tree, fast growing with spreading branches, dark green leaves, not for chalky soils 35m/10m (115ft/33ft).

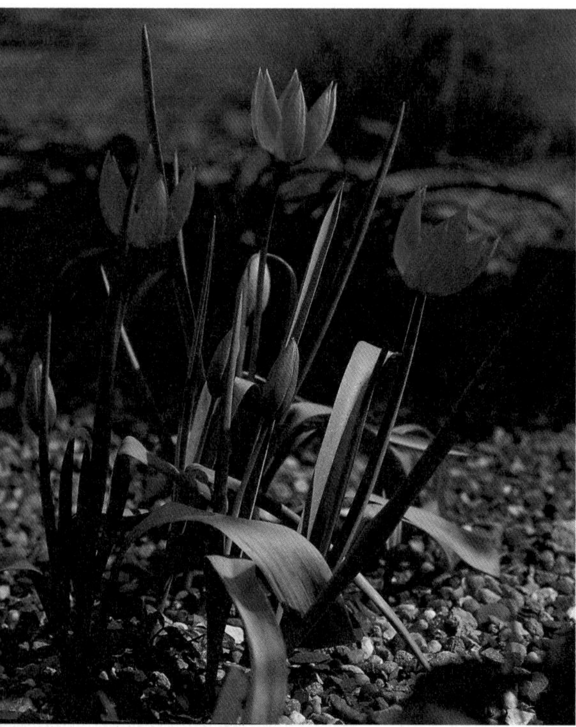

above Tulipa orphanidea Whittalli Group. Not all tulips are happy growing through gravel but I have grown this richly coloured form this way very successfully for many years.

Tulipa *Tulip* Liliaceae

Small/large bulbous ornamentals. Hardy to very hardy. Tulips are grown for their wide range of flower colours and, in recent years, the species and near-species have begun to take as much interest as the tall but wind-susceptible hybrids. Most need sun and a well-drained loam, avoid waterlogged soils. Large-flowered hybrids are best for formal beds and containers; species and related smaller-flowered types for rock gardens, troughs and small, informal beds. Plant bulbs in late autumn or early winter; planting in early autumn leads to premature growth and frost damage. Some types can be lifted but most of the species should be left undisturbed. Many of the large-flowered hybrids deteriorate rapidly and are best considered as annuals. Remove offsets from bulbs after lifting. ❀ *T. aucheriana*, twisted flowers of red or yellow and red, mid-spring, short-lived, 30-40cm (1-1½ft); *T. biflora* (syn. *T. polychroma*), white flowers with yellow eye, early spring, 8-10cm (3¼-4in); *T. clusiana* var. *chrysantha*, yellow flowers with red, mid-spring, 20-30cm (8in-1ft); *T. c.* 'Cynthia', pale cream-yellow flowers; *T. humilis*, sometimes multi-flowered, flowers are various shades of pink with grey-green or blue-black, 25cm (10in); *T. h. pulchella* Violacea Group, large flowers of rich violet-pink with black or yellow centre, late winter to early spring, 15cm (6in); *T. kaufmanniana*, multi-flowered, cream or yellow flowers with pink or red, 25cm (10in); *T. kolpakowskiana*, yellow flowers with red, orange or green, mid-spring; *T. linifolia*, brilliant red flowers, late spring, 13cm (5¼in); *T. l.* 'Batalinii Group' 'Bright Gem', sulphur-yellow flowers, long-lived, 13-20cm (5¼-8in); *T. l.* BG 'Bronze Charm', peach-orange; *T. orphanidea* Whittallii Group, orange flowers with lovely bronze flush, late spring, 15-20cm (6-8in); *T. praestans* 'Fusilier', multi-flowered, red flowers, mid-spring, 30cm (1ft); *T. p.* 'Unicum', very eye-catching with yellow variegated leaves; *T. saxatilis*, stolons, multi-flowered, pink flowers with yellow eye, late spring, best left undisturbed to spread, 30-50cm (1-1¾ft); *T. s.* Bakeri Group, darker pink; *T. s.* BG 'Lilac Wonder', no stolons, shorter than species, single purple-pink flowers; *T. sprengeri*, bright orange-red flowers with yellow-green, late spring, will self-seed, 30cm (1ft); *T. sylvestris*, stolons, yellow flowers with green, mid-spring, a woodland plant, 30cm (1ft); *T. tarda*, multi-flowered, white flowers with green on outside and yellow central eye, mid-spring, very reliable for naturalizing; *T. turkestanica*, multi-flowered, small cream-white flowers with yellow centre and brown-purple anthers, late winter, 15-30cm (6in-1ft); *T. urumiensis*, yellow flowers with lilac, early spring, 15cm (6in).

Large-Flowered Hybrids

Most large-flowered tulip varieties are available for a few years only, to be replaced by others. I have named relatively few individual varieties therefore, concentrating on those that have proved reliable for me for several years, but have described the features of the main Groups.

right *Tulipa praestans* 'Unicum'. I grow this rather remarkable variety beneath a *Magnolia soulangeana*; the flowering times coincide and the flower shapes and colours are a perfect blend.

left *Tulipa* 'Pinnochio'. It's varieties such as this, derived from the low growing species tulips, that have understandably ousted some of the tall hybrids from favour in recent years.

Single Early Flower early spring, valuable as spring bedding, suitable for forcing, 20-35cm (8in-1¼ft). 'Apricot Early', salmon-rose with red; 'General de Wet', bright orange; 'Keizerskroon', yellow with red.

Double Early Flower slightly later than single earlies, large, fully-double blooms, 25-40cm (10in-1½ft). 'Carlton', deep red; 'Orange Nassau', blood-red; 'Peach Blossom', deep rose-pink.

Triumph Flower mid- to late spring, suitable for forcing, 40-50cm (1½-1¾ft). 'Athleet', pure white; 'Kees Nelis', blood-red with orange-yellow; 'Princess Irene' (syn. 'Prinses Irene'), orange-purple; 'Shirley', white with fine purple edge.

Darwin Hybrid Large flowers on tall stems, ideal for cutting. Flower mid- to late spring, traditionally grown with wallflowers and very effective in this combination, 50-60cm (1¾-2ft). 'Apeldoorn', cherry-red with scarlet; 'Golden Apeldoorn', golden-yellow with black anthers.

Single Late Tall tulips that flower mid- to late spring, wide range of colours, 50-70cm (1¾-2¼ft). 'Georgette', multi-flowered, scarlet; 'Queen of Night', deep velvet-maroon.

Lily-Flowered Flowers have pointed or reflexed petals, late spring, 50-60cm (1¾-2ft). 'China Pink', pink with white base; 'White Triumphator', pure white.

Fringed Flower late spring, petals are fringed, often used for cutting, 45-60cm (1½-2ft). 'Fringed Beauty', vermilion with golden-yellow fringed edges, just 25cm (10in) high.

Viridiflora Urn-shaped flowers striped with green, late spring, valuable for cutting, 35-45cm (1¼-1½ft). 'Spring Green', white with green, light green anthers.

Rembrandt Flower late spring, blooms show characteristic mottling and flecking caused by a virus transmitted by aphids.

Parrot Showy tulips that flower mid- to late spring. Petals are fringed and twisted, 50-60cm (1¾-2ft). 'Black Parrot', deep purple with black-purple interior; 'White Parrot', pure white; 'Estell Rijnveld' (syn. 'Gay Presto'), red with white.

Double Late Large, peony-like flowers, late spring. Long-flowering but prone to rain damage, 40-45cm (1½ft). 'Carnival de Nice', white with deep red, leaves have a fine white edge; 'Mount Tacoma', pure white.

Kaufmanniana Early spring, often with bicoloured flowers, some have attractive mottled leaves, small tulips good for containers, 15-20cm (6-8in). 'Shakespeare', carmine-red with yellow, 15cm (6in); 'Showwinner' scarlet with yellow base, mottled leaves.

Fosteriana Taller with larger flowers than the kaufmanniana types, flower mid-spring, 20-40cm (8in-1½ft). 'Madame Lefeber' (syn. 'Red Emperor'), very large fiery red; 'Orange Emperor', orange with pale yellow base; 'Princeps', red with green-bronze base; 'Purissima' (syn. 'White Emperor'), large cream-white flowers.

Griegii Maroon mottling to the leaves, short plants ideal for containers, flower mid- to late spring, 25cm (10in). 'Pinocchio', scarlet with white picotee edge to petals; 'Plaisir', red with pale yellow with a black and yellow base; 'Red Riding Hood', carmine red with a black base, 20cm (8in).

Miscellaneous 'Giuseppe Verdi', carmine with yellow; 'Heart's Delight', carmine-red with pale rose and golden-yellow; 'Johann Strauss', dark red with yellow, mottled leaves.

Typha *Reedmace* Typhaceae

Medium/large rhizomatous water marginal. Very hardy. Most species are only suitable for large pools. Long leaves form dense clumps. Brown flower spikes in summer, male and female flowers on the same spike; lead later to masses of downy seeds. Grow in water to 30-40cm (1-1½ft) deep; be warned that rhizomes can damage flexible liners. Divide rootstock in spring. ❀ *T. angustifolia* (Lesser Reedmace), 1.5m (5ft)/indefinite; *T. latifolia*, 2m (6½ft)/indefinite; *T. l.* 'Variegata', less vigorous, leaves have vertical cream stripe, 1m (3ft); *T. minima*, the only species suitable for smaller pools but although low growing, even this species will spread and need restraining, 75cm/30-45cm (2½ft/1-1½ft).

above *Typha minima*. 'Minima' is a relative term in the genus Typha but nonetheless, this is the only species of reedmace that could even be considered for a small pool

far right *Uvularia grandiflora*. The woodland garden is full of lovely surprises and here is yet another; far too little seen.

Ulex — Papilionaceae

Small/medium hardy to very hardy evergreen shrubs. Very familiar as native plants but too little grown in gardens. Almost leafless but with sharp spines and vivid yellow pea-like flowers with honey fragrance. Always best at the coast but thrives elsewhere in full sun on poor, dry, preferably acidic, soils; not for shallow, alkaline or rich soils. No routine pruning. Sow seed in cold-frame in autumn or spring or take semi-ripe cuttings in summer. ❀ *U. europaeus* (Gorse, Furze, Whin), chrome-yellow flowers, mid- to late spring, 1.5m/1m (5ft/3ft); *U. e.* 'Flore Pleno' (syn. 'Plenus'), compact hummock, semi-double yellow flowers, late spring, 1.5m/1m (5ft/3ft); *U. gallii* (Western Gorse), 'Mizen', prostrate habit, golden-yellow flowers, late summer to autumn, 30cm/30cm (1ft/1ft).

Ulmus *Elm* — Ulmaceae

Medium/large trees. Very hardy. Once an integral part of the British landscape but now hugely depleted due to Dutch Elm Disease. There are few areas where any elm can now be grown with much certainty that the disease won't appear. Most have good yellow autumn colour and small red flowers, usually hermaphrodite, in early spring, followed by green winged fruits. Thrives in any well-drained, fertile soil in sun. No routine pruning. Sow seed outdoors in autumn or spring, take semi-ripe cuttings in summer or remove rooted suckers in autumn (most hedgerow elm trees originated as suckers from a common rootstock). ❀ *U.* x *hollandica* 'Jacqueline Hillier' (syn. *U. elegantissima* 'Jacqueline Hillier'), medium shrub, dense suckering habit suitable for hedging, oval, small, double-toothed dark green leaves persist into winter, no flowers, 3.5m/2.5m (11ft/8ft); *U. minor* 'Dampieri Aurea' (syn. *U.* 'Wredei'), narrow conical tree, broad leaves suffused with golden-yellow, 10m/4m (33ft/13ft).

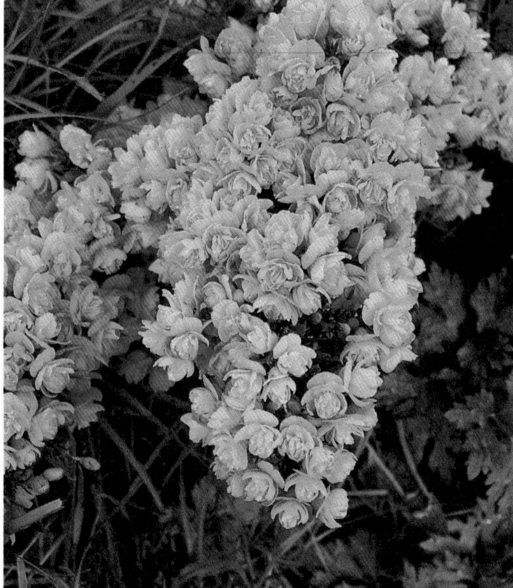

right *Ulex europaeus* 'Flore Pleno'. If the normal flowered native gorse is seen too infrequently in gardens, this wonderful double-flowered form is a positive rarity.

Uvularia *Bellwort* — Convallariaceae

Medium rhizomatous hardy ornamental. Infrequently seen woodland plants with graceful pendent flowers and an unusual colour for plants of this form. Leaves are borne on arching stems. Narrow, bell-shaped flowers with twisted petals. Requires a cool, shady site where the soil is moist but well-drained and enriched with leaf-mould. Sow ripe seed in a cold-frame or divide plants in autumn or early spring. ❀ *U. grandiflora*, clump-forming habit, ovate leaves of fresh bright green, bright yellow flowers hang down on slender stalks from late spring to early summer, 75cm/45cm (2½ft/1½ft); *U. g.* var. *pallida*, paler yellow flowers.

Vaccinium Ericaceae

Acidic soil fruits and small deciduous or evergreen shrubs and sub-shrubs. Barely hardy to hardy and suitable for acidic soils that don't dry out in summer; barely hardy forms need shelter but can be grown successfully in containers. No routine pruning. Sow seed in a cold-frame in autumn, take semi-ripe cuttings in mid- to late summer or layer.

Ornamental

V. delavayi, dwarf evergreen, barely hardy, shiny dark green leaves, tiny cream-white flowers, early summer, red fruits, 1m/75cm (3ft/2½ft); *V. floribundum* (syn. *V. mortinia*), low-spreading evergreen, barely hardy, dark green leaves red when young, pink flowers, early summer, red fruits, 1.5m/1.2m (5ft/4ft); *V. glaucoalbum*, spreading, dense evergreen, barely hardy, oval leaves of dark green with white undersides, white flowers late spring to early summer, black fruits with white bloom, 1.2m/1m (4ft/3ft); *V. nummularia*, dwarf evergreen, moderately hardy, thick, shiny, oval leaves, bronze when young, pink flowers, late spring to early summer, black fruits, 40cm/20cm (1½ft/8in); *V. vitisidaea* (Cowberry, Foxberry, Mountain Cranberry), dwarf evergreen, creeping by means of rhizomes, hardy, egg-shaped leaves of lustrous green, deep pink flowers, bright red fruits, 15cm/60cm (6in/2ft); *V.v.* Koralle Group, vigorous, invasive, abundant fruits.

Fruiting

V. corymbosum (Blueberry, Highbush Blueberry, American Blueberry, Swamp Blueberry), dense shrub, hardy, mid-green leaves with yellow to red autumn colour, white or pink flowers, edible sweet blue-black fruits, 1.5m/1.5m (5ft/5ft); *V. c.* 'Bluecrop', early to mid-season, good flavour, fairly heavy cropper, upright; *V. c.* 'Berkeley', mid-season, spreading; *V. c.* 'Earliblue', early, large fruit.

V. macrocarpon (Cranberry, American Cranberry), dwarf evergreen shrub and a very different and more vigorous plant than the native European cranberry, hardy, dark green leaves bronze in winter, pink flowers, edible red fruits, best in cool, moist soil in sun, 25cm (10in)/indefinite; *V. m.* 'CN' mat-like, spreading, large red fruit; *V. m.* 'Early Black'; *V. m.* 'Hamilton'.

V. myrtillus (Bilberry, Blaeberry, Whinberry, Whortleberry), vigorous, creeping shrub, hardy, glossy bright green leaves often red in autumn, pink flowers, blue-black fruits, invasive in fertile soils, 30cm (1ft)/indefinite.

above *Valeriana phu* 'Aurea'. One of rather a small group of herbaceous perennials that is grown for golden foliage rather than flower appeal.

Valeriana *Valerian* Valerianaceae

Large herbaceous hardy perennials (some rhizomatous) and medium shrubs (some evergreen). Thrive in any fairly fertile soil that is moist but well-drained, in full sun or partial shade and will also commonly establish in wall crevices. Useful, if undistinguished, border plants. Sow seed in a cold-frame in spring, take basal cuttings or divide plants in spring or autumn. ❀ *V. officinalis* (Common Valerian, Garden Heliotrope), clump-forming, short rhizomes, mid-green leaves, white or pink flowers, mid-summer, aromatic leaves attract cats, 1.2/1m (4ft/3ft); *V. phu* 'Aurea', open mound-shaped habit, rhizomatous perennial, divided leaves of golden-yellow in spring then age to mid-green in summer, flowers insignificant, best leaf colour in full sun, 1.2/1m (4ft/3ft).

Valerianella Valerianaceae

Small hardy annual grown as a leafy salad crop. Very hardy, will grow in most soil and positions. Silver-blue flowers in early spring. Sow in growing positions in spring and again in summer for a winter crop. ❀ *V. locusta* (Corn Salad, Lamb's Lettuce), small, neat rosettes of bright green leaves, use as a cut-and-come-again crop or cut the whole plant.

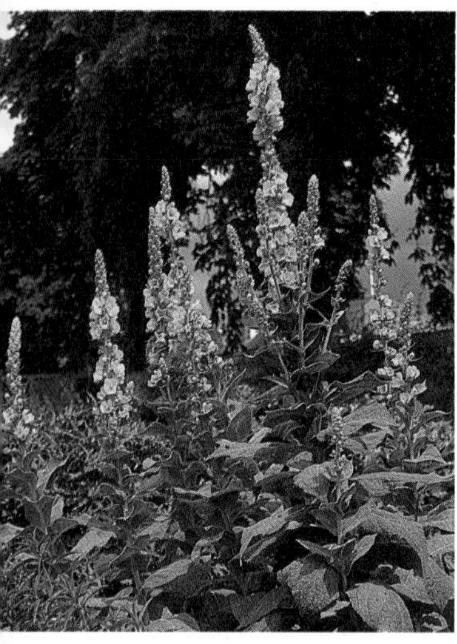

above *Verbascum thapsus.* I adore the mulleins, especially this native species; but if only they were longer lived.

Veratrum — Liliaceae

Large, very hardy rhizomatous ornamentals. Imposing yet easy plants for damp sites and with remarkably coloured flowers. All parts toxic if eaten. Requires a moist, fertile soil in sun or partial shade. Sow ripe seed in a cold-frame, divide mature plants in autumn or spring. ❀ *V. nigrum*, compact clump, dark green oval leaves, long narrow spike of black-purple flowers, late summer to early autumn, 1.2m/60cm (4ft/2ft).

Verbascum *Mullein* — Scrophulariaceae

Small/large biennials, annuals, perennials and sub-shrubs (some evergreen or semi-evergreen). Barely hardy to hardy. Very imposing and sometimes truly beautiful, although sadly short-lived, drought-tolerant plants for the back of the border. Basal rosette of leaves, some species with characteristically white woolly-felt-like foliage. Stout spires of flowers, early summer to autumn, usually yellow but white, pink, mauve and apricot colours too. Plant in full sun in a well-drained soil, very valuably tolerant of poor and/or alkaline soils. Sow seed in a cold-frame in spring or summer. Divide perennials in spring or take root cuttings in winter. ❀ *V. blattaria* (Moth Mullein), biennial, pale yellow flowers, unusually requires moist soil, 1.8m/30cm (5¾ft/1ft); *V. b. albiflorum*, white flowers; *V. bombyciferum* (syn. *V.* 'Broussa'), branching biennial or short-lived evergreen perennial, silver leaves and stems, yellow flowers, 1.8m/75cm (5¾ft/2½ft); *V. chaixii* (Nettle-Leaved Mullein), semi-evergreen perennial with white woolly leaves, yellow flowers, 1.2m/45cm (4ft/1½ft); *V. c.* 'Album', white flowers with mauve centres; *V.* x *phoeniceum* (Purple Mullein), 'Cotswold Queen', evergreen/semi-evergreen perennial, pale buff to amber flowers, 1.2m/30cm (4ft/1ft); *V.* x *p.* 'Gainsborough', silver-grey leaves, primrose-yellow flowers, 1.5m/30cm (5ft/1ft); *V.* x *p.* 'Pink Domino', rose-pink flowers with darker eye, 1.2m/30cm (4ft/1ft); *V. dumulosum*, evergreen sub-shrub, grey woolly leaves, yellow flowers, for rock garden, hardy if sheltered; *V.* 'Helen Johnson', buff to pink-brown flowers, 1.2m/30cm (4ft/1ft); *V.* 'Letitia', evergreen sub-shrub, blue-grey leaves, yellow flowers, for rock garden, 25cm/15cm (10in/6in); *V. nigrum* (Dark Mullein), semi-evergreen, dark yellow flowers, 90cm/60cm (3ft/2ft); *V. olympicum* (syn. *V. longifolium* var. *pannosum*), grey-white leaves, golden-yellow flowers, often dies after flowering, 2m/60cm (6½ft/2ft); *V. phoeniceum* (Purple Mullein), often grown as an annual, deep green leaves, pink, purple or white flowers, can self-seed, 1m/30cm (3ft/1ft); *V. thapsus* (Great Mullein, Aaron's Rod), biennial, white or grey leaves and woolly spires, yellow flowers, 2m/45cm (6½ft/1½ft).

Verbena *Vervain* — Verbenaceae

Small/medium annuals, perennials and sub-shrubs, some rhizomatous. Tender to hardy. Most importantly grown as half-hardy annuals or short-lived perennials for containers but some are valuable in borders. Most successful in full sun in a fertile soil. Sow seed in warmth in autumn or early spring, divide perennials in spring and take stem-tip cuttings in late summer. Unlike many tender perennials, they are not as successful when kept over winter as stock plants for taking cuttings in spring. ❀ *V.* 'Apple Blossom', raise as an annual, pale apple-blossom-pink, 25cm (10in); *V.* 'Blue Lagoon', raise from seed, blue flowers, 25cm (10in); *V. corymbosa*, spreading rhizomes, hardy perennial, blue/red-purple flowers, early to mid-summer, invasive in damp sites, 1.2m/1m (4ft/3ft); *V. hastata* (Blue Vervain), herbaceous hardy perennial, tiny blue to pink-purple flowers, mid-summer, 1.2m/60cm (4ft/2ft); *V.* 'Homestead Purple', herbaceous hardy perennial, purple flowers, long-flowering, 30cm/45cm (1ft/1½ft); *V.* 'Lawrence Johnston', spreading perennial, brilliant scarlet flowers, propagate by cuttings, 45cm/60cm (1½ft/2ft); *V. officinalis* (Common Vervain), hardy perennial, small mauve flowers from mid-summer to early autumn, 45cm/30cm (1½ft/1ft); *V.* 'Peaches and Cream', coral-pink ageing to cream-yellow; *V.* Romance Series, erect, bushy plants, various colours with white eye, 25cm (10in); *V. rigida* (syn. *V. venosa*) (Veined Vervain), tuberous perennial grown as annual, purple flowers, 60cm/30cm (2ft/1ft); *V.* 'Silver Anne', vigorous perennial, fragrant bright pink flowers that age to silver-white, 30cm/60cm (1ft/2ft); *V.* 'Sissinghurst' (syn. 'Saint Paul'), mat-like perennial, magenta-pink flowers, 20cm/1m (8in/3ft).

Veronica *Speedwell* — Scrophulariaceae

Small/medium annuals or perennial, some evergreen, some rhizomatous. Barely hardy to hardy. A distinctive and much loved group of plants with tiny flowers, often in characteristic spikes, suitable for summer borders and rock gardens, although the genus also includes some intractable if pretty weeds. Most thrive best in sunny, well-drained sites and are ideal plants for alkaline soils. Sow seed in cold-frame in autumn. Divide perennials in autumn or spring. ❀ *V. austriaca* 'Ionian Skies', semi-upright habit, evergreen, bright blue flowers, may need protection from winter wet, 20cm/60cm (8in/2ft); *V. a. teucrium* 'Crater Lake Blue', vivid sky-blue flowers; *V. a. t.* 'Royal Blue', deep blue flowers; *V. beccabunga* (Brooklime), usually evergreen, blue flowers with violet veins, unusual in a plant for wet soil or pool margin, take stem-tip cuttings or divide in summer, 60cm/1m (2ft/3ft); *V. chamaedrys* (Germander Speedwell), 'Miffy Blue', rhizomatous, bright green leaves, bright blue flowers, 30-50cm/50-80cm (1-1¾ft/1¾-2½ft); *V. cinerea*, prostrate, evergreen, grey leaves, purple-blue or pink flowers, can be invasive, 10cm/30cm (4in/1ft); *V. gentianoides*, mat-like, evergreen, glossy dark green leaves, pale blue flowers in short spikes, 30cm/40cm (1ft/1½ft); *V. longifolia*, bright blue flowers in tall, rather feeble spikes, 1m/30cm (3ft/1ft); *V. pectinata*, creeping evergreen, grey leaves, pale blue flowers, 10cm/30cm (4in/1ft); *V. p.* 'Rosea', rose-lilac flowers; *V. prostrata* (syn. *V. rupestris*), mat-like evergreen, dark green leaves, bright blue flowers in masses of short spikes, 10cm/45cm (4in/1½ft); *V. p.* 'Blue Sheen', bright blue flowers; *V. p.* 'Mrs Holt', pink flowers; *V. p.* 'Trehane', golden leaves, violet-blue flowers; *V.* 'Shirley Blue', dwarf, deep green leaves, bright blue flowers, 25cm/25cm (10in/10in); *V. spicata* (syn. *V. kellereri*), compact habit, hardy, mid-green leaves, blue flowers in tall, slender, strangely aromatic spikes, 30-60cm/45cm (1-2ft/1½ft); *V. s.* 'Alba', white flowers; *V. s.* 'Heidekind', silver-grey leaves, deep pink flowers; *V. s. incana* (syn. *V. incana*), hairy, silver-grey leaves, mid-blue flowers; *V. s.* 'Romiley Purple', bushy habit, dark blue flowers; *V. s.* 'Rotfuchs' ('Red Fox'), deep pink flowers; *V. wormskjoldii* (syn. *V. stelleri*), clump-forming, evergreen, violet-blue flowers.

above *Viburnum x burkwoodii* 'Park Farm Hybrid'. Perhaps the best flowering variety among a huge genus of really excellent garden shrubs.

left *Veronica spicata* 'Blaufuchs'. This simple flower grew in my own childhood garden and it's still one that I grow with great affection.

Viburnum Caprifoliaceae

Medium/large shrubs and small trees (some evergreen). Barely hardy to hardy and a quite invaluable if seldom highly distinguished group of shrubs offering, collectively, year-round interest of leaves, flowers and fruits. Most have white flowers, sometimes fragrant, and many of the deciduous species have good autumn colour. Cross-pollination needed for good crops of fruits. Viburnums thrive well in sun or partial shade, evergreens are shade tolerant. Almost all sites are suitable, even shallow soils over chalk, although large-leaved species should be sheltered from strong winds. No routine pruning unless grown as a hedge, when should be pruned twice each year. Sow seed in a cold-frame in autumn or take semi-ripe cuttings in summer. ❀ *V.* x *bodnantense*, large shrub, fragrant rose-tinted flowers, from autumn onwards, 3m/2m (10ft/6½ft); *V.* x *b.* 'Charles Lamont', similar to 'Dawn' but purer pink flowers; *V.* x *b.* 'Dawn', fragrant flowers, autumn to late winter; *V.* x *burkwoodii*, medium shrub, evergreen, dark green leaves with grey-brown felt-like undersides, pink buds, fragrant white flowers, late winter to late spring, 2.5m/1.8m (8ft/5¾ft); *V.* x *b.* 'Park Farm Hybrid', strong growing shrub with more spreading habit, fragrant flowers in late spring; *V.* x *carlcephalum*, large shrub, compact habit, often good autumn colour, pink buds, fragrant white flowers, late spring, 3m/1.5m (10ft/5ft); *V. carlesii*, medium shrub, downy dull green leaves with grey undersides, autumn colour, pink buds, sweet fragrant white flowers, late spring, black fruits, 2m/1m (6½ft/3ft); *V. c.* 'Aurora', red buds, fragrant pink flowers; *V. davidii*, small/medium shrub, low mound habit, evergreen, leathery, glossy dark green leaves, small, dull white flowers, early summer, bright blue fruits if several plants together,

1.5m/80cm (5ft/2½ft); *V. farreri*, medium/large shrub, leaves bronze when young, pink buds, fragrant white flowers, winter, sometimes red fruits, 2.5m/1m (8ft/3ft); *V.* x *hillieri* 'Winton', large shrub, semi-evergreen, leaves bronze-red in winter, cream-white flowers, early summer, red fruits ageing to black, 2m/80cm (6½ft/2½ft); *V.* x *juddii*, medium shrub, fragrant pink-tinted flowers, late spring, 1.8m/1.5m (5¾ft/5ft); *V. lantana* (Wayfaring Tree), large shrub, sometimes red autumn colour, cream-white flowers, late spring to early summer, red fruits ageing to black, 5m/4m (16ft/13ft); *V. opulus* (Guelder Rose), large shrub, spreading habit, maple-like leaves sometimes with good autumn colour, white flowers in early summer, red fruits from autumn through winter, likes boggy soils, 4.5m/2m (14¾ft/6½ft); *V. o.* 'Aureum', compact habit, bright yellow leaves that scorch in full sun; *V. o.* 'Compactum', small shrub, remains at 1.5m/1.5m (5ft/5ft); *V. o.* 'Nanum', dwarf shrub, often colours in autumn but seldom flowers; *V. o.* 'Roseum', cream-white flowers in globular heads; *V. o.* 'Xanthocarpum', clear golden-yellow fruits; *V. plicatum*, large shrub, wide-spreading with branches in layers creating a tiered effect, bright green oval leaves often with autumn tints, small cream-white flowers, late spring to early summer, red fruits ageing to black, 3m/1.8m (10ft/5¾ft); *V. p.* 'Lanarth', like 'Mariesii' but branches less horizontal; *V. p.* 'Mariesii', horizontal branching habit, good autumn colour, masses of large flowers; *V. p.* 'Pink Beauty', flowers age to pink, free-fruiting; *V.* 'Pragense', large shrub, spreading habit, evergreen, corrugated leaves of dark green with white felt-like undersides, pink buds, cream-white flowers, late spring, 2.5m/1.5m (8ft/5ft); *V. rhytidophyllum*, large shrub, fast-growing, evergreen, large corrugated leaves, glossy dark green above, grey beneath, small cream-white flowers in late spring, red fruits ageing to black, several plants needed for good crop of fruits, ideal for alkaline soils, 4m/1.5m (13ft/5ft); *V. sargentii* 'Onondaga', large shrub, vigorous, large, maple-like leaves, corky bark, young leaves maroon then red-purple in autumn, deep red buds, white flowers, bright red fruits, 4.5m/2m (14¾ft/6½ft); *V. tinus* (Laurustinus) large shrub, evergreen, glossy dark leaves, pink buds, white flowers, late autumn to early spring, metallic-blue fruits ageing to black, tolerates shade and coastal winds, 3.5m/2m (11ft/6½ft); *V. t.* 'Eve Price', dense compact habit, smaller leaves, carmine buds, pink-tinged flowers, the best form; *V. t.* 'Gwenllian', compact form with small leaves, deep pink buds, white flowers with pink flush; *V. t.* 'Purpureum', very dark green leaves, purple-tinged young leaves; *V. t.* 'Variegatum', cream-yellow variegated leaves, not for cold areas.

below *Viburnum tinus* 'Eve Price'. This is one of the real old shrub garden favourites and of its type, it is a variety that has never been surpassed.

Vicia — Papilionaceae

Hardy annual vegetable fruit, grown for pods. Among a group containing many familiar wild flowers and some weeds, the broad bean is of outstanding garden importance. It is the earliest bean to crop, arguably the easiest of the pea and bean family to grow and is one of the oldest cultivated plants known to man. Requires a deep, rich soil augmented with humus, moist but never waterlogged. Sow seed in autumn or in early spring, depending on variety. ❀ *V. faba* (Broad Bean). Among the main types, the Longpods are hardiest and have long pods. The Windsors have shorter, broader pods, mature later and are sometimes claimed to have a better flavour. Dwarf varieties are useful for growing under cloches but,

left *Vinca minor* 'Atropurpurea'. The vincas are almost unrivalled as ground cover in shade but the blue- and white-flowered forms are seen far more frequently than the mauves.

contrary to what is often said, they are not the best for small gardens, yielding less per area of ground. 'Aquadulce Claudia', longpod for autumn or early spring sowing, the hardiest type, 1.3m (4½ft); 'Bonny Lad', dwarf, 35cm (1¼ft); 'Express', longpod, early variety, 90cm (3ft); 'Hylon', longpod, late, very long pods; 'Imperial Green Longpod', longpod, large seeds and long pods, 90-135cm (3-4½ft); 'Jubilee Hysor', Windsor-type, late, large white beans; 'Red Epicure', red flowers, Windsor-type green pods with attractive red seeds, 90cm (3ft); 'The Sutton', longpod, for autumn or early spring sowing, dwarf, 30cm (1ft).

Vinca *Periwinkle* Apocynaceae

Small herbaceous hardy perennials and sub-shrubs, many evergreen. Fairly hardy to hardy. Invaluable ground cover in shady areas and tolerant of fairly dry conditions, although larger forms can be invasive. Flowers are produced in spring to early summer then on and off through the season. Cut back hard in spring to keep tidy and within bounds. Divide plants in autumn or spring, take semi-ripe cuttings in summer or remove rooted runners. ❀ *V. difformis*, evergreen, glossy dark green leaves, pale blue or white flowers, 30cm/60cm (1ft/2ft); *V. major*, evergreen, bright blue (dark violet) flowers, 35cm (1¼ft)/indefinite; *V. m.* 'Maculata' (syn. *V. m.* 'Aureomaculata'), dark yellow-green leaves with lighter margins, pale blue flowers; *V. m.* 'Variegata' (syn. *V. m.* 'Elegantissima'), light green leaves with pale yellow margin, rich lavender-blue flowers; *V. minor*, evergreen, glossy dark green leaves, blue-pink, purple or white flowers, 20cm/1m (8in/3ft); *V. m.* 'Argenteo-variegata' (syn. *V. m.* 'Variegata'), dull green leaves with pale yellow margins and mid-ribs, violet-blue flowers; *V. m.* 'Atropurpurea' (syn. *V. m.* 'Purpurea Rubra'), dark green leaves, dark purple flowers; *V. m.* 'Azurea Flore Pleno' (syn. *V. m.* 'Caerulea Plena'), dark green leaves, double dark blue (sky-blue) flowers; *V. m.* 'La Grave' (syns. *V. m.* 'Bowles Blue', 'Bowles Variety'), compact habit, dark green leaves, lavender-violet flowers.

Viola *Violet, Pansy* Violaceae

Small annuals, biennials and perennials (some evergreen, some rhizomatous). Half-hardy to very hardy. A very large, diverse and versatile group of remarkably similar looking plants; the characteristic 'face'-like appearance is instantly recognisable. The annuals are quite essential as bedding or container plants, while the perennials are underestimated for their use in shrubberies, at the front of borders and in rock gardens. Most have mid-green leaves either oval or heart-shaped, often evergreen. Thrive in any well-drained soil enriched with humus to keep it moist, in sun or partial shade, some of the perennials are more shade tolerant. Sow ripe seed in a cold-frame; sow in summer for winter-flowering forms. Divide perennials in spring or autumn or take stem-tip cuttings in spring or summer. The naming of this group is confusing and complex and I have chosen a system that makes sense to me.

Viola species and near-species (Perennial unless stated otherwise)

V. alba (syn. *V. obliqua* ssp. *alba*), white flowers with violet veins, late spring to early summer, 10cm/30cm (4in/1ft); *V. biflora*, small yellow flowers with purple-brown veins, mid- to late spring,

above *Viola labradorica*. Several of the species violas are fairly shade tolerant and this one is certainly an essential shade garden plant.

right *Viola* 'Baby Lucia'. This is the most delicately coloured of a small group of delightful summer flowered miniature pansies.

self-seeds, 5cm/30cm (2in/1ft); *V. canina* (Dog Violet, Heath Violet), rhizomatous, semi-evergreen, bright blue or violet flowers, spring and early summer, pretty but invasive; *V. c. alba*, white flowers; *V. cornuta* (Viola, Horned Violet), rhizomatous evergreen, white or lilac flowers, early to mid-summer, 15cm/30cm (6in/1ft); *V. c.* Alba Group, white flowers; *V. c.* 'Alba Minor', white flowers, dwarf; *V. c.* 'Minor', dwarf with lavender-blue flowers; (Cornuta Hybrids): 'Belmont Blue', pale sky-blue; 'Foxbrook Cream', cream-white; 'Victoria Cawthorne', purple-pink; *V. grisebachiana*, stemless, clump-forming, yellow or blue, 8cm/5cm (3¼in/2in); *V. hederacea* (syns. *Erpetion hederaceum, V. reniforme*) (Australian Violet, Trailing Violet), mat-like evergreen, white, cream or violet-blue flowers with twisted petals and white tips, summer to early autumn, not reliably hardy, 5cm/30cm (2in/1ft); *V. jooi*, stemless, clump-forming, red-purple flowers, mid- to late spring, 5cm/15cm (2in/6in); *V. labradorica* (syn. *V. adunca* var. *minor*) (Labrador Violet), semi-evergreen, dark green leaves, bronze-purple when young, pale purple flowers, spring and summer, a good shade plant, 8cm (3¼in)/indefinite; *V. odorata* (Sweet Violet, English Violet, Garden Violet), rhizomatous, semi-evergreen, fragrant blue or white flowers, spring and again early autumn, late winter and early spring, self-seeds freely, 8cm/15-30cm (3¼in/6in-1ft); *V. o.* 'Alba', fragrant white flowers; *V. riviniana* (Wood Violet, Dog Violet), semi-evergreen, blue-violet flowers, early spring to early autumn, can be invasive, 10cm/30cm (4in/1ft); *V. rupestris rosea* (Teesdale Violet), pink flowers, best in sunny, warm spot on well-drained soil, 10cm (4in); *V. septentrionalis* (Northern Blue Violet), pale to deep violet flowers, spring to early summer, 20cm/25cm (8in/10in); *V. sororia* (syn. *V. papilionacea*) (Woolly Blue Violet), rhizomatous, white flowers with violet-blue markings or deep violet-blue flowers, spring and summer, self-seeds, 10cm/20cm (4in/8in); *V. s.* 'Freckles', white flowers speckled with violet-blue; *V. tricolor* (Heartsease, Wild Pansy), annual or biennial, flowers are yellow or purple, both marked with white, flowers throughout the year, self-seeds freely but never a problem, 10cm/30cm (4in/1ft); (Tricolor Hybrids): 'Bowles Black', velvet, almost black flowers with small yellow eye, self-seeds, keep apart from other varieties or it will hybridize to produce purple flowers 10cm/20cm (4in/8in).

V. x *wittrockiana* (Pansy)

Winter-flowering types Ultima Series F1, medium-sized flowers in very broad range of colours, either plain or with faces; Universal Series F1, medium-sized flowers in a broad range of colours, including bicolours and faces.

Spring/summer-flowering types Varieties come and go rather quickly so I have given only a brief selection of the more durable; most are 15-20cm (6-8in). ❀ 'Allegro' F1 / F2, large flowers in broad colour range, with and without faces; 'Colour Festival' F2, large flowers in range of colours each with dark face; 'Floral Dance' F2 , range of bright colours, also for winter flowers; 'Imperial Series' F1 , large flowers in broad colour range including pastel shades, most with faces; Joker Series F2, medium bicoloured flowers in light blue, brown-gold, violet-gold and mixed colours, strong marked faces, winter hardy; 'Love Duet', pale cream with deep pink blotch; 'Majestic Series' F1,

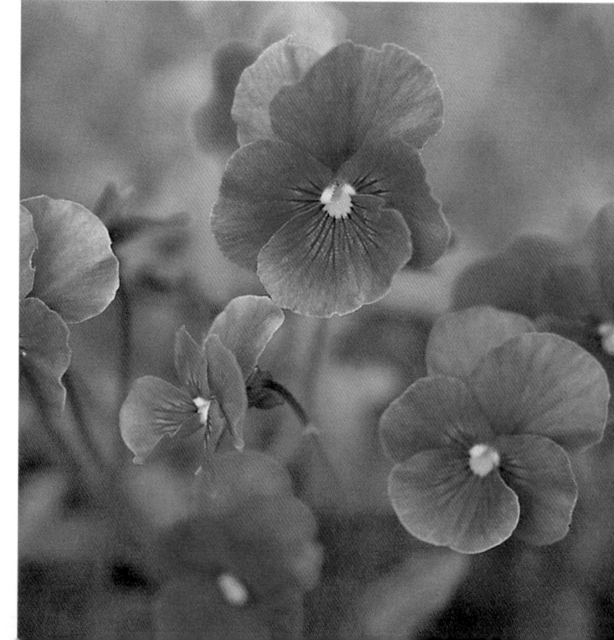

large flowers, vigorous plants; 'Padparadja' F2, intense orange flowers; Rococo Series, F2, ruffled blooms in red, pink, yellow, purple and blue.

Miniature Pansy types raised from seed; These are utterly charming plants, sometimes called Violas or *Viola tricolor* varieties. ❀ 'Baby Lucia', small clear blue flowers with yellow eye, spring and summer, 10cm (4in); 'Prince Henry', small dark purple flowers, spring to summer; 'Prince John', small bright yellow flowers, spring to summer.

Hybrid Violas

Rounded flowers with central blotch, often scented, 15cm/35cm (6in/1¼ft). ❀ 'Ardross Gem', pale pink to dark mauve with golden blotch; 'Chantreyland', large apricot-yellow flowers; 'Elizabeth', white flowers with mauve markings; 'Huntercombe Purple', purple flowers; 'Irish Molly', yellow-bronze flowers; Jackanapes', brown and yellow flowers; Maggie Mott', silver-mauve flowers with cream centre; 'Martin', velvet-purple with golden eye; 'Molly Sanderson', black flowers; 'Moonlight', fragrant cream-yellow flowers; 'Vita', small mauve flowers.

Hybrid Violets

Spurred flowers, usually sweetly scented, not very hardy, 30cm/30cm (1ft/1ft). ❀ 'Amiral Avellan' (syn. 'Admiral Avellan'), red with purple flush, fragrant; 'Coeur d'Alsace', fragrant salmon-pink flowers.

Hybrid Violettas

Sweet fragrance, flowers have central yellow blotch, 10cm/25cm (4in/10in). ❀ 'Buttercup', very fragrant, pale yellow flowers; 'Dawn', primrose yellow flowers; 'Little David', fragrant, cream-white flowers with frilled petals.

Double Violets

❀ 'Duchesse de Parme', fragrant, double mauve flowers in spring, needs cloche or frame protection over winter.

Vitis *Vine* Vitaceae

Large climbers, some self-clinging, and climbing fruit. Hardy or very hardy. Grown primarily for autumn colour, some have edible fruit. Insignificant flowers. Require a well-drained soil enriched with humus in full sun or partial shade. Clip ornamental varieties as necessary to limit to available space; for pruning of fruiting vines see companion volume. Sow seed in a cold-frame in autumn or spring, although named varieties of grapevines do not come true; take hardwood cuttings in late winter or root 'vine eye' cuttings in early spring. Layer in autumn.

Ornamental ❀ *V.* 'Brant', vigorous, lobed leaves turn red-purple in autumn, dark purple-black fruits, 9m (30ft); *V. coignetiae*, very large, rounded dark green leaves turn red in autumn, black-purple fruits, for best leaf colour grow in poor soil, 10-25m (33-80ft).

Fruiting Grapes can be grown for wine outdoors, or in mild areas for dessert use – although for reliable fruiting, greenhouse protection is strongly recommended (plant outside and train stem through the wall). Full sun and a moist but well-drained rich soil are essential. Hand pollinate indoor plants. Shade greenhouse in summer. Thin dessert grapes with pointed scissors if bunches are tightly packed. ❀ *V. vinifera* (Grapevine), lobed leaves, edible fruit, 9m (30ft); 'Chasselas', pale pink fruit, greenhouse type, early, moderate cropper; 'Léon Millot', black, outdoor type, mid-season, fairly heavy cropper but small bunches, fairly good resistance to disease; 'Madeleine Angevine', white, outdoor type, early, moderate cropper, 'Madeleine Sylvaner', white, outdoor type, early, moderate cropper; 'Müller-Thurgau', white, outdoor type, mid-season, moderate cropper, best as wine grape; 'Muscat of Alexandria', amber fruit, greenhouse type; 'Pirovano 14', black, outdoor type, early, heavy cropper; 'Schiava Grossa' (syn. 'Black Hamburgh'), black, greenhouse type, early to mid-season, heavy cropper; 'Seyal Blanc', white, outdoor type, heavy cropper, resistant to mildew; 'Siegerrebe', white, outdoor type, early heavy cropper.

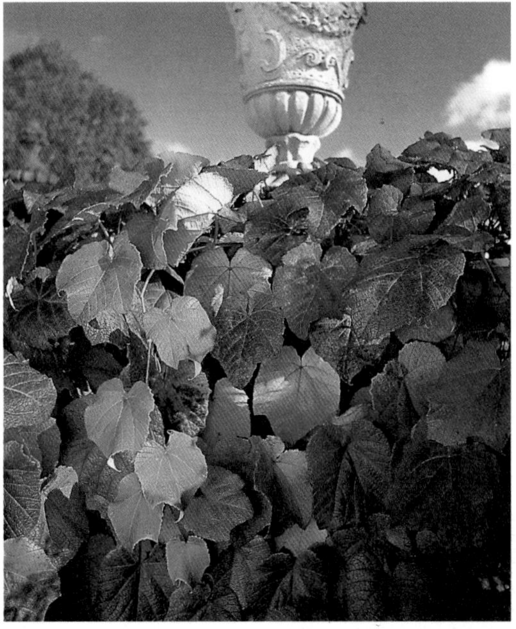

left *Vitis coignetiae*. The largest leaves of any vines and probably of any hardy climbing plants; so one to be placed with care.

above *Wisteria floribunda* 'Multijuga'. I can't think of any climbing plant with longer inflorescences; a truly spectacular variety.

Weigela Caprifoliaceae

Small/medium shrubs. Very hardy. Easy to grow flowering shrubs especially valuable for mixed borders; not really imposing enough as specimens. Clusters of funnel-shaped flowers, late spring to early summer. Succeed in any fertile soil that is well-drained but doesn't dry out in summer, most are suitable for sunny or partially shaded sites. Cut back old flowering shoots after flowering. Take semi-ripe cuttings in early summer or hardwood cuttings in autumn to winter. ❀ *W.* 'Briant Rubidor' (syns. 'Olympiade', 'Rubidor'), yellow or green leaves with yellow margin, carmine-red flowers, best in partial shade, 1.8m/1m (5¾ft/3ft); *W.* 'Bristol Ruby', vigorous, erect habit, dark green leaves, free-flowering, ruby-red flowers, 1.8m/1.5m (5¾ft/5ft); *W.* 'Eva Rathke', compact, slow-growing, dark green leaves, crimson flowers, 1.5m/1m (5ft/3ft); *W. florida* 'Foliis Purpureis', a slower growing dwarf form of the species, purple-flushed (bronze-green) leaves, pink flowers, 1m/1.5m (3ft/5ft); *W.* 'Florida Variegata', compact, grey-green leaves with white margin, 2m/2m (6½ft/6½ft); *W.* 'Looymansii Aurea', light golden leaves, pink flowers, best in partial shade, 1.5m/1.5m (5ft/5ft); *W. middendorffiana*, small shrub, bright green leaves, bell-shaped yellow flowers with orange markings, late spring, best in sheltered site in partial shade, 1.5m/1m (5ft/3ft); *W.* 'Newport Red', upright habit, large red flowers; *W.* 'Praecox Variegata', vigorous, leaves with cream-yellow margins that whiten with age, crimson buds, large fragrant pink flowers with yellow markings appear in late spring; *W.* 'Victoria', purple-flushed leaves, red flowers.

Wisteria Papilionaceae

Large, very hardy climbers. Beautiful flowering climbers, justifiably called the 'Queen' of climbing plants but they require considerable space and are unlikely to flower until about five years old. Pinnate leaves. Pea-like fragrant flowers borne on pendent racemes. Bean-like green seedpods form after hot summers. Plant in full sun or partial shade against a tall wall, pergola or old tree. The soil should be fertile and moist but well-drained. Once a framework has been established, hard prune previous season's sideshoots in winter and shorten leafy shoots to 20cm (8in) in late summer. Named forms do not come true from seed. Difficult to propagate but try basal cuttings from sideshoots in summer or layer low-growing lateral shoots in autumn or graft in winter. ❀ *W. floribunda* (Japanese Wisteria), stems twine clockwise, 'Alba' (syn. *W. multijuga* 'Alba'), fragrant white flowers tinted lilac, 4m (13ft); *W. f.* 'Multijuga' (syn. 'Macrobotrys'), purple and violet flowers, inflorescences 60cm (2ft) long; *W. f.* 'Rosea', pale rose-pink flowers tipped with purple; *W. f.* 'Snow Showers', pure white flowers; *W.* x *formosa* 'Isai', lilac-blue flowers, flowers as young plant; *W.* x *f.* 'Kokuryû (syn. 'Black Dragon'), double purple flowers; *W. sinensis* (Chinese Wisteria), stems twine anti-clockwise, violet-blue flowers open before leaves, 10-15m (33-50ft); *W. s* 'Alba', white flowers; *W. venusta* (Silky Wisteria), stems twine anti-clockwise, silky hairy leaves, lightly fragrant white flowers with yellow blotch, the largest in the genus, velvet seedpods, 9m (30ft).

Yucca Agavaceae

Small/medium evergreen shrubs. Tender to moderately hardy. Valuable for architectural shape and look especially effective in large containers – dramatic flower spikes a bonus – but inappropriate in old or 'cottage' gardens. Rosette of narrow, sword-shaped leaves. Tall racemes or panicles of bell-shaped flowers after four or more years. The hardier species can be grown in a hot, dry spot in full sun with a well-drained soil. Sow seed in warmth in spring or remove rooted suckers in spring. ❀ *Y. filamentosa*, moderately hardy, mid-green leaves with white threads, fragrant cream-white flowers in summer, even on young plants, 1m/1m (3ft/3ft); *Y. f.* 'Bright Edge', green leaves with a golden-yellow margin; *Y. f.* 'Variegata', leaves have cream-white margin; *Y. flaccida* 'Golden Sword', moderately hardy, mid-green to glaucous leaves with a central band of cream-yellow, free-flowering, 60cm/75cm (2ft/2½ft); *Y. f.* 'Ivory', large panicles of cream-white flowers with green markings; *Y. gloriosa*, tree-like with a stout stem, barely hardy, rigid leaves with spines, cream-white flowers with red tinge borne from mid-summer to early autumn, may not flower for five years, 1.5m/1m (5ft/3ft); *Y. g.* 'Variegata', leaves have cream-yellow stripes and margins; *Y. whipplei*, barely hardy, rigid, spiny leaves of grey-green, large fragrant flowers of green-white edged with purple, late spring to early summer, 1m/75cm (3ft/2½ft).

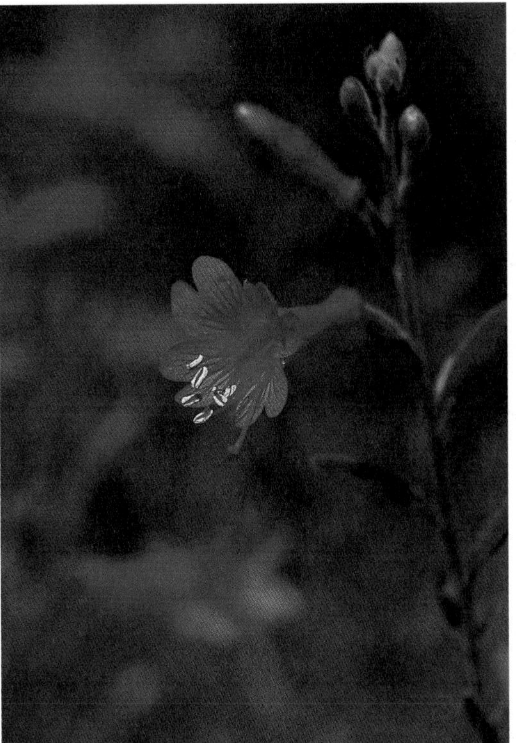

left *Zauschneria californica*. If you want bright colours in late summer and on into autumn, these Californian relatives of the Fuchsia will certainly provide it.

Zantedeschia

Arum Lily, Calla Lily Araceae

Medium rhizomatous ornamentals. Tender to barely/fairly hardy and grown for their dramatic flower spikes (spathes) and glossy leaves. Plant rhizomes in moist soil and mulch over winter, or plant in containers and take under protection. Also valuable pool margin plants in milder areas; plant in an aquatic planting basket in water to a depth of 15-30cm (6in-1ft). Sow ripe seed in warmth or divide plants in spring. ❀ *Z. aethiopica*, evergreen in mild areas, barely to fairly hardy, glossy bright green leaves, cream-white spathe, 90cm/50cm (3ft/1¾ft); *Z. a.* 'Crowborough', hardier than species; *Z. a.* 'Green Goddess', hardier than species, green spathe with white throat.

far left *Zantedeschia aethiopica* 'Green Goddess'. There are now many astonishingly coloured hybrid zantedeschias but they aren't hardy. This older and rather impressive variety nonetheless is an outdoor plant.

Zauschneria Onagraceae

Small/medium sub-shrubs or perennials, some evergreen, some rhizomatous. Barely hardy to moderately hardy and especially prized for their later, brightly F1 coloured flowers. Most are suitable for mixed borders. Lance-shaped leaves are downy and either green or grey-green. Clusters of funnel-shaped flowers from late summer to early autumn. A sunny position is essential, hardy if given a fertile, well-drained soil. In cold areas, choose a sheltered position at the foot of a warm wall. Sow seed in a cold-frame in spring or take

right *Zephyranthes candida*. A more romantic name than Flower of the West Wind would surely be hard to find.

basal cuttings in spring. ❀ Z. *californica* (syns. *Epilobium californicum, E. canum*) (California Fuchsia, Humming Bird Flower), rhizomatous, semi-evergreen to evergreen, moderately hardy, grey-green leaves, scarlet flowers, 45cm/45cm (1½ft/1½ft); Z. *c.* 'Dublin' (syns. 'Glasnevin', Z. ssp. *cana* 'Dublin'), longer flowers of bright orange-red, 30cm/30cm (1ft/1ft).

Zea — Poaceae

Vegetable fruit. Half-hardy. Needs a sunny, sheltered site and most likely to produce cobs in the south although modern varieties that mature early worth trying in other areas. Soil should be deep, organic and well-drained. Sow seed in pots in warmth in spring and plant in square blocks rather than rows to assist wind pollination. ❀ Z. *mays* (Sweet Corn), there are numerous varieties, generally from only one or two suppliers each and including 'Earliking' F1; 'Early Xtra Sweet' F1; 'Jubilee' F1; 'Kelvedon Glory' F1. From time to time, ornamental varieties with variously coloured seed cobs or variegated foliage are also offered.

Zenobia — Ericaceae

Medium semi-evergreen/deciduous hardy shrub. An unusual early summer-flowering plant for a moist, acidic soil in sun or partial shade. No routine pruning. Sow seed in cold-frame in late winter or take semi-ripe cuttings in summer. ❀ Z. *pulverulenta*, suckering habit, young shoots may be damaged by frosts, leaves have blue-white bloom when young, white bell-shaped flowers with anise fragrance, 182m/75cm (600ft/2½ft).

Zephyranthes — Amaryllidaceae

Small bulbous ornamentals. Half-hardy to barely hardy with delightful crocus-like flowers. Require a well-drained soil and sunny, warm position, ideally with cloche protection from winter rain. Sow ripe seed in warmth or separate offsets in spring. ❀ Z. *candida* (Zephyr Flower, Flower of the West Wind), evergreen, narrow rush-like leaves of dark green, pure white or pink-tinged flowers in late summer to autumn, 25cm/10cm (10in/4in).

Zinnia — Asteraceae

Annuals, perennials and sub-shrubs. Tender and grown as half-hardy annuals in mixed borders, containers, as edging and, very valuably, for cutting. Linear to oval or elliptic leaves, dahlia-like flowers in bright colours, including red, purple, yellow and orange, also white. Sow seed in warmth in mid-spring or in the flowering position in late spring. ❀ Z. *angustifolia* 'Starbright', low-growing, star-shaped single flowers, bright orange or white flowers, summer, suitable for ground cover and rock gardens, 25-35cm/30cm (10in-1¼ft/1ft); Z. *elegans*, bushy annual, hairy, oval to lance-shaped leaves, 60-75cm/30cm (2-2½ft/1ft), various single and double varieties in mixed colours are available, including 'Belvedere', dwarf, weather resistant, 30cm (1ft), and 'Whirligig', single flowers in red, yellow, purple, orange and white, with petals tinted with contrasting colour; Z. *haageana* 'Chippendale', light green, lance-shaped, hairy leaves, single red flowers tipped gold, 60cm/30cm (2ft/1ft); Z. *h.* 'Persian Carpet', semi-double, bicoloured maroon, purple, yellow, chocolate and cream flowers, better than most in poor weather conditions, 40cm/30cm (1½ft/1ft).

PLANT FAMILIES INTRODUCTION

A family is a group of related genera and is one of the basic divisions that botanists use for classification. Few popular gardening books dwell on plant families at any length but I have always found it both instructive and intriguing to learn which of my own plants are closely related. I have therefore listed here the salient features of the plant families that are represented in this book in the hope that you will also find a new dimension to your understanding of gardening.

The number of Families described here is of course only a part of the Plant Kingdom although including as it does, our most important garden plants, it is a surprisingly large fraction of the whole. I have included something like over 170 Families of flowering plants (plus some ferns and conifers). Depending on which botanical authority you believe, there are between 350 and 500 in total. So if you have in your garden a representative of every one of those I describe, you will have gained an idea of something of the breadth of the Plant Kingdom (although I have always believed that you should visit the Tropics to gain a real impression of what plants are capable).

There are many criteria by which genera are assessed by botanists in deciding whether to group them together in families and although I have listed the most important of these features, I have omitted some of the more technical matters such as details of flower structure. Nonetheless, I hope I have provided sufficient information to enable you to see that any one family represents a summation of characteristics. And although I have provided a comprehensive Glossary in my companion volume, *Stefan Buczacki's Gardening Dictionary*, I have additionally listed here in a List of Terms, those words used in the descriptions that may be unfamiliar and will help an appreciation of this part of the book.

BREAKDOWN OF EACH FAMILY ENTRY

With few exceptions, such as coniferous trees and ferns, I have listed for each family the following characteristics:

Monocotyledon or Dicotyledon (see List of Terms)

Global distribution: many families are restricted to the Tropics or Temperate regions; a few have a hemispheric restriction.

Leaf arrangement: the patterns by which the leaves are attached to the stem are generally in opposite pairs, alternately or whorled (see illustrations).

ALTERNATE OPPOSITE WHORLED

Leaf shape: although the details of leaf shape offer almost infinite variations, a basic division is into leaves that are Simple (an entity in itself, although one that may be variously shaped or indented), and leaves that are Compound (comprising several small parts or leaflets that are united to form a whole). (see illustrations).

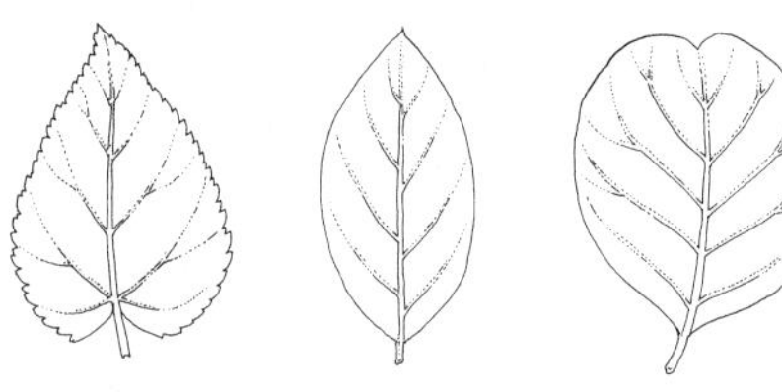

SOME SIMPLE LEAVES

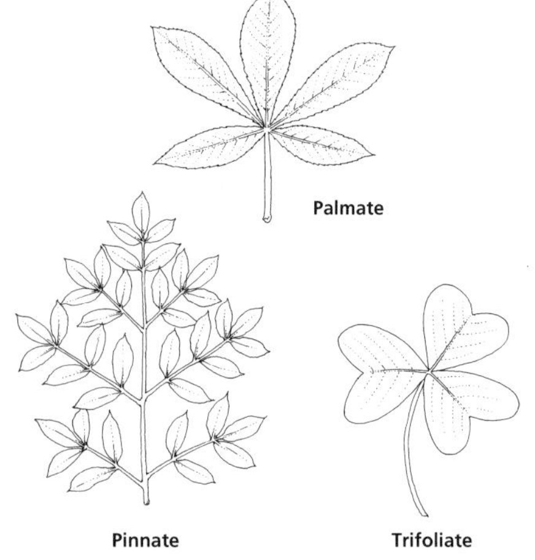

SOME COMPOUND LEAVES

Flower sex: flowers may be unisexual or bisexual; unisexual flowers sometimes, although not invariably, occurring on different plants.

Flower shape: although there is huge variety in flower shape, they may be divided into those that are Regular (capable of being divided into equal halves in two or more planes); and those that are Irregular (capable of being divided into equal halves in one plane only). (see illustrations).

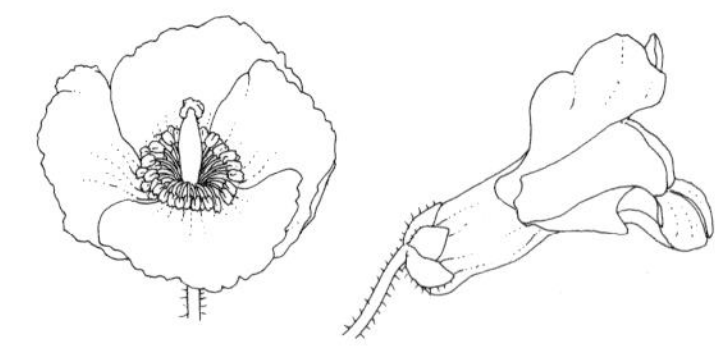

REGULAR FLOWER IRREGULAR FLOWER

Petal number: flowers may have a widely differing number of petals although the number, within a defined range, is generally consistent within families. I have not made a distinction between those flowers that have fused petals and those where they are separate and distinct.

Inflorescence type: flowers are arranged on a stem in either Solitary fashion or grouped together into inflorescences and these are of characteristic type. I have illustrated the major categories although it should be said that some inflorescences are so complex or obscure as almost to defy analysis. In a few instances such as the umbel of the Apiaceae or the head of the Asteraceae, the inflorescence type is highly characteristic. In other families, the range in form is considerable. (see illustrations – the numb ers denote the order of development of the individual flowers).

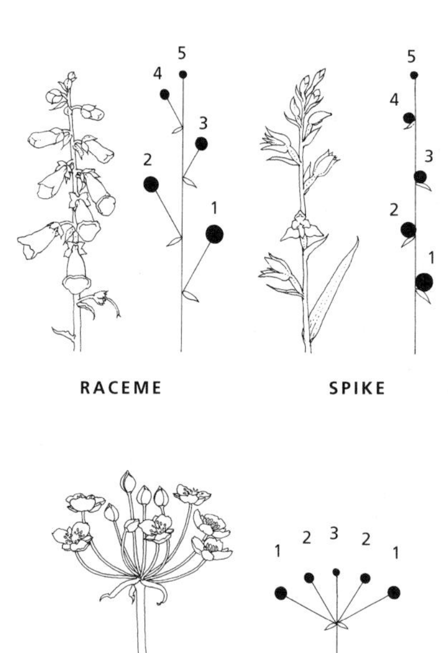

RACEME SPIKE

UMBEL

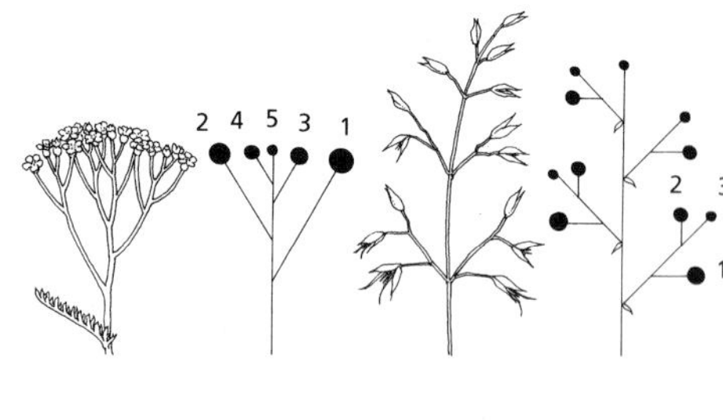

CORYMB PANICLE

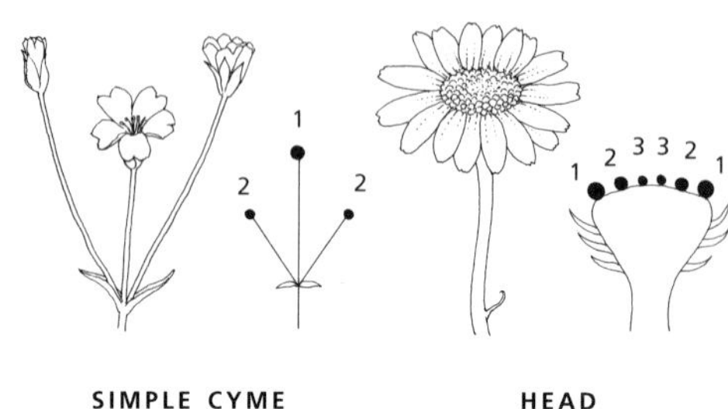

SIMPLE CYME HEAD

Fruit type: the type of fruit is sometimes a distinctive feature of particular families and it is seldom that any one family displays a very wide range in type.

Family size: I have indicated the approximate number of genera and species in each family. The range is vast and the book includes the extremes with so-called monotypic families (1 genus and 1 species) like the Davidiaceae at one end, and the Asteraceae (1,300 genera, 21,000 species) and the Orchidaceae (800 genera, 21,000 species) (respectively the largest groups of Dicotyledons and Monocotyledons) at the other. Family size is not necessarily a criterion of horticultural importance however. A remarkable family in this respect is the Rubiaceae with nearly 11,000 species, most fully hardy in temperate gardens, but only a handful having any ornamental merit or appeal.

Genera described: finally, I have listed for each family those genera that are described in this book.

Some plant families are remarkably uniform. The 22 genera and 800 species of the Primulaceae for example vary little. It is pretty easy to decide at sight if a plant belongs here; their leaf and especially their flower form is highly constant, and all have the same type of fruit. By contrast, the Rutaceae are extremely diverse, with little consistency among their 160 genera and 1,650 species. It is families such as this that are often split up by botanists on the basis of more detailed study. Perhaps the classic family in this regard is the huge Monocotyledonous group the Liliaceae which is constantly being sub-divided.

LIST OF TERMS

ACHENE – a dry fruit with one seed, formed from a single carpel and with no specially developed method of opening for seed liberation.

ANGIOSPERM – flowering plant. All flowering plants belong to the group Angiospermae which differs from the Gymnosperms (conifers and their relatives) by having the ovules borne within an enclosed ovary which, after fertilisation, becomes a fruit.

AXIL – the angle between the upper side of a leaf stalk or branch and the stem from which it emerges.

BERRY – a succulent, many-seed fruit such as a tomato or gooseberry. Many fruits popularly called berries are botanically something quite different, often a drupe.

BULB – a vegetative reproduction and storage organ comprising a very short stem (the basal plate) from which the roots arise, with a mass of swollen, overlapping immature leaves.

CALYX – collectively, the sepals of a flower.

CAPITULUM (see Head)

CAPSULE – a dry type of fruit formed from a compound ovary and which liberates its seeds by splitting longitudinally.

CARPEL – the female reproductive parts of a flowering plant, comprising an ovary and ovules, a stigma and a style.

CATKIN – type of inflorescence; a hanging spike.

CORM – a vegetative reproduction and storage organ comprising a swollen stem base with buds in the axils of the scale-like leaf remains of the previous season.

COROLLA – collectively, the petals of a flower.

CORYMB – type of inflorescence with individual flower stalks becoming shorter towards the top so that all flowers appear at the same level, as in candytuft.

COTYLEDON – also called a seed leaf; leaves that form part of the embryo of a plant within the seed. They are simpler than the later, true leaves and often contain nutrient for the emerging seedling. The two big divisions of flowering plants, the Monocotyledons and the Dicotyledons are characterised by one and two cotyledons respectively. Gymnosperms have varying numbers.

CYME – type of inflorescence in which, unlike a raceme, terminal flowers form and so the continued growth of the inflorescence depends on the production of new growing points, as in *Lamium*.

CYPSELA – small, dry one-seeded fruit similar to acheme.

DICOTYLEDON – one of the two main groups of flowering plants, characterised by having two cotyledons emerge from the germinating seed. Dicotyledons generally have relatively small, more or less rounded leaves by contrast with the long, typically grass-like leaves of Monocotyledons.

DRUPE – a type of fruit in which an outer skin and inner fleshy layer enclose a single hard seed.

FERN – non-flowering green plant, reproducing by means of spores but having fairly advanced conducting and other tissues. Many species are widely used in gardens for their ability to grow in damp moist places and for the attractiveness of their leaves or fronds.

FLORET – reduced form of flower, typical of the family Asteraceae where the mass of apparent petals in each 'flower' is in reality a collection of many individual florets. The petal-like outer ones are termed ray-florets, the tubular ones making up the central area, the disc florets.

FLOWERS – the reproductive structure of most important garden plants, except ferns. Flowers are evolved, modified leafy shoots and display an enormous variety of form, colour and/or scent, almost all adaptations to facilitate pollination by either wind or animals, often insects.

FOLLICLE – a dry fruit formed from a single carpel, containing more than one seed and splitting along a suture.

FRUIT – the ripened, fertilised ovary of plant, containing one or more seeds.

GENUS (pl. genera) – a classificatory group containing closely related species; similar genera are themselves grouped into a Family.

GYMNOSPERM – conifers and related plants in the group Gymnospermae. Most produce seeds exposed in cones and the group includes many very important garden trees.

HEAD – type of inflorescence; a disc like structure comprising many individual small flowers in a single head.

INFLORESCENCE – a flowering shoot, a collection of flowers together forming an entity.

LEAF – plant organ in which most photosynthesis takes place. In Dicotyledons, the leaf is typically more or less rounded and divided into a flattened blade and stalk. In Monocotyledons, it tends to be elongated and strap-like with parallel veins. Leaves may be modified to form hooks, tendrils and other structures for secondary roles.

LEGUME – type of fruit, also called a pod, characteristic of the family Papilionaceae, formed from a single carpel and splitting along the mid-rib to expose the seeds.

PALMATE – of leaves; shaped like the palm of a hand.

PANICLE – type of inflorescence, highly branched, strictly a raceme of cymes but also used to mean a raceme of racemes.

PETAL – one of the parts forming the corolla of a flower, often conspicuous and brightly coloured. Evolutionarily, a modified leaf.

PINNATE – of a leaf composed of more than three leaflets arranged in two rows along a common stalk, as in ash. Bipinnate and tripinnate leaves are those in which the leaflets are themselves pinnate.

POME – type of fruit in which the seeds are surrounded by a tough layer as in apple.

RACEME – type of unbranched inflorescence with the flowers arranged in sequence on a central stem and with no terminal flower.

SEPAL – one of the parts that forms the calyx of a flower, usually positioned outside the petals and green and leaf like although some important groups of plants (the Ranunculaceae for example) have brightly coloured sepals that take the place of petals in bestowing the colour to the flowers.

SPADIX – type of inflorescence; a club-like spike of unisexual flowers (males above, females below) enclosed in a large spathe. Characteristic of the Araceae.

SPATHE – large ear-like bract enclosing an inflorescence, usually a spadix as in members of the family Araceae.

SPECIES (note that the word has no singular) – abbreviated to sp., the cornerstone of the classification and naming of organisms but one whose definition is not widely understood. A species is a collection of individual organisms that are readily able to breed among themselves but not generally able to breed with organisms belong to other species.

SPIKE – type of inflorescence, a raceme with the flowers all stalkless.

STEM – part of a plant bearing leaves, buds and flowers, normally green and aerial but may be variously modified. Some stems (rhizomes) for example are subterranean, others much abbreviated (the basal plate of a bulb) or swollen (potato tubers) but all can be recognised and distinguished from roots or other organs by the presence of buds.

UMBEL – type of inflorescence with individual flower stalks all arising from the top of the main stem, typical of the family Apiaceae.

PLANT FAMILIES INCLUDED IN THIS BOOK

Acanthaceae Dicotyledons. Mainly tropical herbaceous plants, climbers, some shrubs, few trees, leaves usually opposite, simple, flowers bisexual, usually irregular or two-lobed, four or five petals, fruit usually a capsule. Over 300 genera and 4,000 species, around 40 cultivated as ornamentals. *Acanthus*, *Thunbergia*.

Aceraceae Dicotyledons. Mostly North temperate trees and shrubs, leaves opposite, simple or compound, often palmate, flowers unisexual, regular, in racemes, usually four to five greenish 'petals', fruits winged. Two genera, over 100 species, many cultivated as ornamentals. *Acer*, *Dipteronia*.

Actinidiaceae Dicotyledons. Tropical and sub-tropical trees, shrubs and climbers, leaves alternate, simple, flowers uni- or bisexual, regular, inflorescence various, usually five petals, fruit a berry or capsule. Three genera, over 350 species, a few cultivated for fruit or as ornamentals. *Actinidia*.

Adiantaceae Worldwide, herbaceous ferns, many very small. 56 genera, over 1,000 species. *Adiantum*.

Agavaceae Monocotyledons. Mainly tropical American, mainly in arid regions, short-stemmed herbaceous plants or sparsely branched trees, leaves alternate, usually in rosettes and often spiny and succulent, flowers usually bisexual, regular, solitary in racemes or panicles, usually with petals in whorls of three. 18 genera, nearly 600 species, many cultivated, mainly as ornamentals. *Agave*, *Cordyline*, *Phormium*, *Yucca*.

Aizoaceae Dicotyledons. Tropical and sub-tropical, mainly South African succulent herbaceous plants, leaves opposite, often basal, flowers bisexual, usually solitary, no petals but many petal-like parts, fruit a capsule. 120 genera, nearly 2,500 species, many cultivated as ornamentals. *Dorotheanus*, *Tetragonia*.

Alismataceae Monocotyledons. Worldwide, mainly North temperate, perennial aquatic and marsh plants, two types of alternate leaves, submerged and aerial, flowers unisexual or bisexual, regular, inflorescence usually a branched umbel, three petals, usually white, fruit a cluster of achenes. 13 genera, nearly 100 species, several cultivated as ornamentals. *Alisma*, *Sagittaria*.

Alliaceae Monocotyledons. Herbaceous bulbous plants, often strongly smelling, leaves narrow, often tubular, flowers bisexual, regular, inflorescence an umbel, usually six petal-like parts, fruit a capsule. Around 23 genera, 750 species, several cultivated as vegetables (onions) and ornamentals. Sometimes grouped with Liliaceae. *Agapanthus*, *Allium*, *Ipheion*, *Nectaroscordum*.

Aloeaceae Monocotyledons. African, sparsely branched succulent trees or herbaceous plants, flowers usually bisexual, regular, usually with petals in whorls of three. Seven genera, over 500 species, several cultivated, mainly as ornamentals. *Aloe*.

Alstroemeriaceae Monocotyledons. Central and South American herbaceous plants with rhizomes, leaves narrow, flowers bisexual, slightly irregular, in umbels, six petal-like parts, fruit a capsule. Two genera, nearly 20 species, few cultivated as ornamentals. *Alstroemeria*.

Amaranthaceae Dicotyledons. Tropical and warm temperate herbaceous plants, climbers, shrubs or rarely trees, leaves alternate, opposite or whorled, simple, flowers bisexual, regular, small, no petals, three or five papery parts, fruit a capsule, achene or berry. 60 genera, 900 species, few cultivated as food or ornamentals. *Amaranthus*, *Celosia*, *Gomphrena*, *Iresine*.

Amaryllidaceae Monocotyledons. Worldwide herbaceous plants with bulbs, corms or rhizomes, leaves mainly basal, flowers bisexual, solitary or in umbels, regular or irregular, six parts, fruit a capsule or berry. 70 genera, about 850 species, many cultivated as ornamentals. Sometimes grouped with Liliaceae. *Crinum, Cyrtanthus, Galanthus, Leucojum, Narcissus, Nerine, Sternbergia, Zephyranthes.*

Anacardiaceae Dicotyledons. Tropical, sub-tropical, Mediterranean and temperate north American trees, shrubs or climbers, leaves usually alternate, simple or compound, flowers usually unisexual, regular, usually five petals, fruit a one-seeded drupe. 73 genera, 850 species, few cultivated for food or as ornamentals. *Cotinus*, *Rhus*.

Anthericaceae see Liliaceae.

Apiaceae (formerly Umbelliferae) Dicotyledons. Worldwide, especially North temperate, herbaceous plants or rarely shrubs or trees, leaves alternate, often pinnately compound, flowers small, bisexual, regular or irregular, five petals, in characteristic umbels, fruit complex. Over 400 genera and over 3,000 species, many cultivated as important vegetables and kitchen herbs. *Aegopodium*, *Ammi*, *Anethum*, *Angelica*, *Anthriscus*, *Apium*, *Astrantia*, *Azorella*, *Chaerophyllum*, *Coriandrum*, *Daucus*, *Eryngium*, *Foeniculum*, *Hacquetia*, *Levisticum*, *Myrrhis*, *Pastinaca*, *Petroselinum*, *Pimpinella*.

Apocynaceae Dicotyledons. Worldwide, mainly tropical shrubs and trees with many climbers, leaves opposite, simple, often a milky sap, flowers bisexual, regular, five petals, solitary or in racemes or cymes, fruit various, seeds often with a feathery plume. Around 200 genera and nearly 2,000 species, a few important cultivated ornamentals. *Trachelospermum*, *Vinca*.

Aponogetonaceae Monocotyledons. Mainly Tropics of Old World, aquatic plants, leaves alternate with long stalks, flowers bisexual, regular in long spikes, flower parts one to three, fruit mainly a group of follicles. One genus, around 45 species, one or two cultivated as ornamentals. *Aponogeton*.

Aquifoliaceae Dicotyledons. Worldwide trees and shrubs, leaves alternate, simple, flowers usually unisexual, regular, in cymes or clusters, four to five petals, fruit a drupe. Two genera, around 400 species. Many cultivated as ornamentals. *Ilex*.

Araceae Monocotyledons. Mainly tropical herbaceous plants and woody climbers with milky, bitter sap, leaves stalked, often very broad, flowers minute, on a spadix enclosed in a spathe, four-six petals, fruit usually a berry. 115 genera, around 2,000 species, many cultivated as ornamentals, especially aquatics, also as food in the Tropics. *Acorus*, *Arisarum*, *Arum*, *Calla*, *Lysichiton*, *Orontium*, *Zantedeschia*.

Araliaceae Dicotyledons. Mainly tropical, herbaceous plants, shrubs and trees, often spiny, leaves alternate, flowers unisexual or bisexual, regular in umbels, usually five petals, fruit a berry or drupe. 15 genera, 1,400 species, many cultivated as ornamentals. *Aralia*, *x Fatshedera*, *Fatsia*, *Hedera*.

Araucariaceae Mainly tropical and southern temperate coniferous trees, leaves simple, leathery, needle-like to flattened, male cones cylindrical, catkin-like, female cones large, more or less spherical, terminal. Two genera, 32 species, very few cultivated as ornamentals. *Araucaria*.

Aristolochiaceae Dicotyledons. Mainly tropical, herbaceous plants and climbers, leaves alternate, usually compound, flowers bisexual, regular or irregular, inflorescence various, three flower parts, often strangely shaped and foul smelling, fruit a capsule. Seven genera, around 600 species. *Aristolochia*, *Arisarum*, *Asarabacca*.

Asclepiadaceae Dicotyledons. Mainly tropical, herbaceous plants, shrubs and climbers, usually with milky sap, leaves opposite, simple, flowers bisexual, regular, solitary or in racemes or cymes, five petals, fruit of one or two follicles. 350 genera, over 3,000 species, a few cultivated as ornamentals. *Asclepias*.

Asparagaceae Monocotyledons. Old World Tropics and temperate regions, herbaceous plants, shrubs and climbers, leaves reduced to scales or spines, flowers minute, bone on the cladodes, singly or in clusters, six flower parts, fruit a berry. Four genera, over 100 species. Sometimes grouped with Liliaceae. Few cultivated as food or ornamentals. *Asparagus*.

Asphodelaceae Monocotyledons. Worldwide, rhizomatous herbaceous plants, leaves narrow, flowers solitary, in racemes or panicles, six flower parts, fruit a capsule. Sometimes grouped with Liliaceae. *Asphodeline, Asphodelus, Eremurus, Kniphofia.*

Aspidiaceae see Aspleniaceae.

Aspleniaceae Including for convenience Aspidiaceae and Athyriaceae. Worldwide herbaceous ferns, including some climbers and epiphytes. Fronds simple to multi-pinnate, sub-divided on basis of arrangement of spore-bearing bodies. 78 genera, 2,700 species, several cultivated as ornamentals. *Asplenium*, *Cyrtomium*, *Dryopteris*, *Matteuccia*, *Onoclea*, *Polystichum*, *Athyrium*.

Asteraceae (formerly Compositae) Dicotyledons. Worldwide, herbaceous plants, shrubs or trees, sometimes with milky sap, leaves variable, flowers unisexual or bisexual, regular or irregular, in heads, petals three or five, fruit a form of achene, usually feathery. 1300 genera, over 21,000 species, the largest family of Dicotyledons. Many cultivated as ornamentals, vegetables and herbs. *Achillea, Ageratum, Anaphalis, Antennaria, Anthemis, Arctotis, Argyranthemum, Arnica, Artemisia, Aster, Bidens, Boltonia, Brachycome, Brachyglottis, Buphthalmum, Calendula, Callistephus, Carlina, Centaurea, Chamaemelum, Chrysanthemum, Chrysogonum, Cicerbita, Cichorium, Cirsium, Coreopsis, Cosmos, Cotula, Crepis, Dahlia, Dimorphotheca, Doronicum, Echinacea, Echinops, Erigeron, Eupatorium, Euryops, Felicia, Gaillardia, Gazania, Gerbera, Helianthus, Helichrysum, Helipterum, Hieracium, Inula, Lactuca, Leontopodium, Leucanthemopsis,*

Leucanthemum, Liatris, Ligularia, Matricaria, Olearia, Onopordum, Osteospermum, Ozothamnus, Petasites, Raoulia, Rudbeckia, Santolina, Sanvitalia, Scorzonera, Senecio, Silybum, Solidago, x Solidaster, Stokesia, Tagetes, Tanacetum, Tithonia, Zinnia.

Athyriaceae see Aspleniaceae.

Azollaceae Tropical and warm temperate floating water ferns. 1 genus, six species, few cultivated as ornamentals but invasive aquatic weeds in many countries. *Azolla.*

Balsaminaceae Dicotyledons. Mainly Old World, herbaceous plants, leaves alternate, simple, flowers bisexual, irregular, solitary or in clusters or racemes, five petals, fruit an explosive capsule. Two genera, 850 species, few cultivated as ornamentals. *Impatiens.*

Begoniaceae Dicotyledons. Mainly tropical herbaceous plants and shrubs, leaves alternate, simple or compound, flowers usually unisexual, regular or irregular, flowers parts usually four, fruit a capsule or berry. Two genera, 1000 species, several cultivated as ornamentals. *Begonia.*

Berberidaceae Dicotyledons. Mainly North temperate herbaceous plants and shrubs, leaves usually alternate, simple, flowers bisexual, regular, solitary or in racemes or cymes, fruit a capsule or berry. 15 genera, around 600 species. Many cultivated as ornamentals. *Berberis, Diphylleia, Epimedium, Mahonia, Nandina.*

Betulaceae Dicotyledons. North temperate trees and shrubs, leaves alternate, simple, flowers unisexual, petals absent, fruit a nut, often winged. Six genera, about 150 species. Many cultivated as ornamentals, often grouped with Corylaceae. *Alnus, Betula.*

Bignoniaceae Dicotyledons. Mainly tropical, usually woody climbers or trees, leaves usually opposite, usually compound, flowers unisexual, irregular, inflorescence a cyme, five petals, fruit usually a capsule. 112 genera, 725 species, several cultivated as ornamentals. *Campsis, Catalpa, Eccremocarpus, Incarvillea.*

Blechnaceae Worldwide terrestrial herbaceous and 'tree' ferns and climbers. 10 genera, 260 species, several cultivated as ornamentals but few in temperate gardens. *Blechnum.*

Boraginaceae Dicotyledons. Worldwide, herbaceous plants, shrubs and trees, leaves alternate, simple, flowers bisexual, usually regular, inflorescence often a characteristically coiled cyme, five petals, fruit a small nut or drupe. 156 genera, 2,500 species, many cultivated as ornamentals. *Anchusa, Brunnera, Cynoglossum, Echium, Heliotropium, Lithodora, Mertensia, Myosotis, Omphalodes, Pulmonaria,*

Symphytum.

Brassicaceae (formerly Cruciferae) Dicotyledons. Worldwide in cool regions, usually herbaceous plants, leaves simple or divided, alternate, flowers bisexual, regular, solitary or in spikes or racemes, four petals, fruit usually a capsule. Nearly 400 genera and 3,000 species, some cultivated as ornamentals, some very important vegetables. *Aethionema, Alyssum, Arabis, Armoracia, Aubrieta, Aurinia, Barbarea, Brassica, Cardamine, Crambe, Draba, Eruca, Erysimum, Hesperis, Iberis, Lepidium, Lobularia, Lunaria, Malcolmia, Matthiola, Raphanus, Sinapis, Thlaspi.*

Buddlejaceae Dicotyledons. Mainly East Asian Tropics, mostly trees and shrubs, leaves often toothed, usually opposite or whorled, simple, flowers bisexual, regular, inflorescences various, four petals, fruit a capsule, berry or drupe. One genus, about 100 species, several cultivated as ornamentals, sometimes included in the family Loganiaceae. *Buddleja.*

Butomaceae Monocotyledons. Tropics and temperate parts of Europe and Asia, aquatic plants, leaves basal or alternate, flowers bisexual, regular, solitary or in umbels, three petals, fruit a follicle or group of follicles. Four genera, 13 species, few cultivated as ornamentals. *Butomus.*

Buxaceae Dicotyledons. Mainly tropical, usually trees or shrubs, leaves simple, opposite or alternate, flowers usually unisexual, regular, often in heads or spikes, three to six flower parts, fruit usually a capsule. Five genera, 60 species, few cultivated as ornamentals and for wood and oil. *Buxus, Pachysandra, Sarcococca.*

Caesalpiniaceae Dicotyledons. Mainly tropical, herbaceous plants, shrubs and trees, leaves usually pinnately compound, usually spiral, flowers usually bisexual, irregular, usually in racemes, spikes or heads, four to five petals, fruit a legume. 160 genera, around 2,000 species, some cultivated as ornamentals. *Cercis, Gleditsia.*

Calycanthaceae Dicotyledons. China and North America, shrubs or trees with aromatic bark, leaves opposite, simple, flowers bisexual, regular, solitary, petals absent, fruit a group of achenes. Two genera, around 10 species, few cultivated as ornamentals. *Chimonanthus.*

Campanulaceae Dicotyledons. Worldwide, mainly herbaceous plants, often with milky sap, leaves, usually alternate, simple, flowers bisexual, regular or irregular, inflorescence various, usually five petals, fruit a fleshy capsule. 87 genera, nearly 2,000 species, several cultivated as ornamentals. *Adenophora, Campanula, Codonopsis, Cyananthus, Hypsela, Jasione, Laurentia, Lobelia, Platycodon, Pratia.*

Cannabaceae Dicotyledons. Temperate areas of Europe and Asia, herbaceous plants or climbers, leaves alternate or opposite, simple or divided, flowers unisexual in cymes, flower parts usually four or five, fruit an achene. Two genera, three species. Cultivated as ornamentals and for fibres and narcotic resin. *Humulus.*

Cannaceae Monocotyledons. Tropical America, rhizomatous herbaceous plants, leaves spiral, flowers bisexual, irregular, paired, three flower parts, fruit a capsule. One genus, around 50 species, few cultivated as ornamentals. *Canna.*

Capparaceae Dicotyledons. Tropical and warm temperate regions, herbaceous plants or shrubs, leaves alternate, simple or compound, flowers bisexual, irregular, solitary or in racemes, usually 4 petals, fruit a capsule, berry or nut. 45 genera, around 700 species, few cultivated as ornamentals and kitchen spices (caper). *Cleome.*

Caprifoliaceae Dicotyledons. Worldwide but mainly North temperate, mainly shrubs and climbers, leaves opposite, usually simple, flowers bisexual, regular or irregular, inflorescence often a cyme, usually five petals, fruit a berry. 16 genera, around 400 species, several cultivated as important ornamentals. *Abelia, Diervilla, Dipelta, Kolkwitzia, Leycesteria, Lonicera, Sambucus, Symphoricarpos, Viburnum, Weigela.*

Caryophyllaceae Dicotyledons. Mainly North temperate regions, mainly herbaceous plants, leaves usually opposite, simple, flowers usually bisexual, regular, solitary or in a cyme, petals usually four to five, fruit a capsule or nut. Around 90 genera and 2,000 species. Many cultivated as important ornamentals. *Agrostemma, Arenaria, Cerastium, Colobanthus, Dianthus, Gypsophila, Lychnis, Sagina, Saponaria, Silene.*

Celastraceae Dicotyledons. Worldwide, mainly tropical, shrubs and trees, some climbers, leaves opposite or alternate, simple, flowers unisexual or bisexual, regular in racemes or panicles, fruit various, usually a capsule, berry or drupe. 70 genera, around 1,300 species, a few cultivated as important ornamentals. *Celastrus, Euonymus.*

Cercidiphyllaceae Dicotyledons. Oriental trees, leaves opposite or alternate, simple, flowers unisexual, no petals, fruit of separate follicles. One genus, one species. Cultivated as an ornamental. *Cercidiphyllum.*

Chenopodiaceae Dicotyledons. Worldwide, herbaceous plants and shrubs, often succulent, leaves alternate or opposite, usually simple, flowers unisexual or bisexual, regular, usually in cymes, flowers parts three to five, fruit an achene or nut. About 100 genera, 1,400 species, few cultivated as important vegetables and very few as ornamentals. *Atriplex, Beta, Chenopodium, Spinacia.*

Cistaceae Dicotyledons. Mainly warm North temperate regions, herbaceous plants or shrubs, usually opposite, leaves simple, flowers bisexual, regular, solitary or in racemes, three to five petals, fruit a capsule. Seven genera, around 175 species. *Cistus,* x *Halimiocistus, Halimium, Helianthemum.*

Clethraceae Dicotyledons. Mainly tropical and subtropical, shrubs and trees, leaves alternate, simple, flowers bisexual, regular, fragrant, in racemes or panicles, five to six petals, fruit a capsule. One genus, around 65 species. Few cultivated as ornamentals. *Clethra.*

Clusiaceae (formerly Guttiferae) Dicotyledons. Worldwide, herbaceous plants and shrubs, often with resinous, often brightly coloured latex, leaves usually opposite, simple, flowers unisexual or bisexual, regular, in cymes, two to 10 petals, fruit a capsule or berry. 48 genera, over 1,000 species, few cultivated as ornamentals. *Hypericum.*

Cobaeaceae Dicotyledons. Tropical American climbers, leaves alternate or opposite, pinnately compound, flowers bisexual, usually regular, usually in cyme-like inflorescence, five petals, fruit a capsule. One genus, 10 species, few cultivated as ornamentals. *Cobaea.*

Colchicaceae. see Liliaceae.

Commelinaceae Monocotyledons. Tropics and warm temperate regions, herbaceous plants, leaves alternate or spiral, simple, flowers bisexual, usually regular, usually in panicles or coiled cymes, usually three petals, fruit a capsule. Around 35 genera, 600 species, a few cultivated as ornamentals. *Commelina, Tradescantia.*

Convallariaceae. see Liliaceae.

Convolvulaceae Dicotyledons. Worldwide, climbers or sub-shrubs, often with milky sap, leaves alternate, simple, flowers bisexual, regular, solitary or in clusters or cymes, four to five petals, fruit a fleshy capsule. 58 genera, around 1,700 species, few cultivated as ornamentals and food crops. *Convolulus, Ipomoea.*

Cornaceae Dicotyledons. Mainly temperate hrubs and trees, leaves usually opposite, simple, flowers unisexual or bisexual, regular, in corymbs or umbels, usually three to five petals, fruit a drupe or berry. 13 genera, over 100 species, few cultivated as ornamentals. *Aucuba, Cornus, Griselinia.*

Corylaceae Dicotyledons. North temperate regions, trees, leaves alternate, simple, flowers unisexual, in catkins, no petals, fruit a nut. Four genera, around 50 species, many cultivated as ornamentals, often grouped with Betulaceae. *Carpinus, Corylus.*

Crassulaceae Dicotyledons. More or less world-wide, herbaceous plants and shrubs, leaves alternate or opposite, simple, succulent, flowers bisexual, regular, inflorescence various but usually a cyme or flowers solitary, petals various, fruit a group of follicles. 30 genera, around 1,400 species, several cultivated as ornamentals. *Aeonium, Chiastophyllum, Rhodiola, Sedum, Sempervivum.*

Cucurbitaceae Dicotyledons. Worldwide but mainly tropical, mainly herbaceous plants or climbers with tendrils, leaves alternate, simple, flowers usually unisexual, regular, solitary or in cymes, usually five petals, fruit usually a fleshy berry. Around 130 genera, over 700 species, several important food plants and ornamentals. *Cucumis, Cucurbita.*

Cupressaceae Worldwide coniferous trees, leaves usually scale-like in opposite pairs, cones small, woody, leathery or berry-like. 17 genera, 113 species, many cultivated as very important ornamentals. *Chamaecyparis,* x *Cupressocyparis, Cupressus, Juniperus, Microbiota, Thuja, Thujopsis.*

Cyperaceae Monocotyledons. Worldwide, herbaceous plants, leaves spirally arranged, stems triangular in section, flowers unisexual or bisexual in axils of spirally arranged bracts in spikes, flower parts various, fruit a nut-like achene. 100 genera, around 4,000 species, very few cultivated as ornamentals. *Carex, Eriophorum.*

Davidiaceae Dicotyledons. Chinese tree, leaves simple, alternate, flowers bisexual surrounded by males flowers, no petal but each flower with two showy white bracts, fruit a drupe. One genus, one species, sometimes grouped with Nyssaceae, widely cultivated as an ornamental. *Davidia.*

Dicksoniaceae Tropical American and warm southern hemisphere 'tree' ferns. Two genera, 25 species, few cultivated as ornamentals but rare in temperate gardens. *Dicksonia.*

Dipsacaceae Dicotyledons. Old World, mainly Mediterranean, mainly herbaceous plants, leaves opposite, simple or dissected, flowers bisexual, irregular, usually in a head, four to five petals, fruit a form of achene. 10 genera, around 250 species. Several cultivated as ornamentals. *Dipsacus, Knautia, Scabiosa.*

Ebenaceae Dicotyledons. Mainly tropical, shrubs and trees, leaves alternate, simple, flowers usually unisexual, regular, solitary or in cymes, four petals, fruit a berry. Two genera, about 500 species, a few cultivated as ornamentals, a few important timber trees (ebony). *Diospyros.*

Elaeagnaceae Dicotyledons. Worldwide, shrubs and trees, leaves alternate or opposite, simple, flowers unisexual or bisexual, regular, solitary or in various inflorescences, petals absent, fruit an achene. Three genera, 45 species, several cultivated as ornamentals. *Elaeagnus, Hippophae.*

Elaeocarpaceae Dicotyledons. Tropical, shrubs and trees, leaves usually spirally arranged, simple, flowers unisexual or bisexual, regular, inflorescence various, usually four to five petals, fruit a capsule or drupe. 11 genera, 220 species, very few cultivated as ornamentals. *Crinodendron.*

Epacridaceae Dicotyledons. Mainly Australasia, shrubs and trees, leaves alternate, simple, flowers bisexual, regular, in various inflorescences, usually five petals, fruit a capsule or drupe. 31 genera, around 400 species, few cultivated as ornamentals. *Cyathodes.*

Ericaceae Dicotyledons. Worldwide, herbaceous plants, shrubs or trees, leaves alternate or opposite, simple, sometimes needle-like, flowers bisexual, regular or irregular, solitary or in racemes or clusters, usually five petals, fruit a capsule, berry or drupe. Over 100 genera, over 3,000 species, many very important cultivated as ornamentals, especially on acidic soils. *Andromeda, Arbutus, Arctostaphylos, Bruckenthalia, Calluna, Cassiope, Daboecia, Enkianthus, Erica, Gaultheria, Kalmia, Kalmiopsis, Leucothoe, Menziesia,* x *Phylliopsis, Phyllodoce, Pieris, Rhododendron, Vaccinium, Zenobia.*

Escalloniaceae Dicotyledons. Mainly Southern Hemisphere, shrubs and trees, leaves mainly alternate, simple, often lobed, flowers bisexual, regular, in racemes, four to six petals, fruit a capsule or berry. 15 genera, 70 species, several important cultivated as ornamentals. *Corokia, Escallonia, Itea.*

Eucryphiaceae Dicotyledons. Australia and South America, shrubs and trees, leaves opposite, simple or pinnate, flowers bisexual, regular, solitary, four petals, fruit a capsule. One genus, about 10 species, most cultivated as ornamentals. *Eucryphia.*

Euphorbiaceae Dicotyledons. Worldwide, herbaceous plants, succulents, shrubs and trees, often with milky sap, leaves usually alternate, simple or compound, flowers unisexual, regular, in various inflorescences, five inconspicuous petals, fruit capsule-like or a drupe. 326 genera, 7,750 species, some important cultivated ornamentals. *Euphorbia.*

Fagaceae Dicotyledons. More or less world-wide, shrubs and trees, leaves usually alternate, simple, flowers unisexual, inconspicuous, males in catkins, four to seven flower parts, fruit a nut. Eight genera, around 600 species, many important cultivated timber trees, some ornamentals. *Castanea, Chrysolepis, Fagus, Quercus.*

Flacourtiaceae Dicotyledons. Mainly tropical, shrubs, trees and woody climbers, leaves alternate, simple, flowers unisexual or bisexual, regular, in various inflorescences, no petals, fruit a capsule or berry. 90 genera, around 1,250 species, few cultivated as ornamentals. *Azara.*

Garryaceae Dicotyledons. North America shrubs and trees, leaves opposite, simple, flowers unisexual in catkin-like inflorescences, no petals, fruit a berry. One genus, about eight species, several cultivated as ornamentals. *Garrya.*

Gentianaceae Dicotyledons. Worldwide, mainly herbaceous plants, leaves mostly opposite, simple, flowers bisexual, solitary or in panicles or cymes, four to five petals, fruit a berry-like capsule. 80 genera, 700 species, some important cultivated as ornamentals. *Gentiana.*

Geraniaceae Dicotyledons. Worldwide, usually herbaceous plants, leaves alternate or opposite, simple or compound, flowers usually bisexual, regular or irregular, usually in cymes, three to five petals, fruit usually a capsule or berry. 14 genera, over 700 species, many important cultivated ornamentals. *Erodium, Geranium, Pelargonium.*

Gesneriaceae Dicotyledons. Mainly tropical, herbaceous plants and shrubs, leaves opposite, usually simple, flowers bisexual, usually irregular, in cymes or solitary, five petals, fruit a capsule or berry. 146 genera, 2,400 species, several cultivated as ornamentals, but mainly as house-plants. *Haberlea, Ramonda.*

Ginkgoaceae Chinese tree, fan-shaped leaves, uniquely distinct catkin-like reproductive structures. Totally unlike any other living plant family; the classical 'living fossil'. One genus, one species, now widely cultivated as an ornamental. *Ginkgo.*

Glaucidiaceae Dicotyledons. Japanese herbaceous plant, leaves spirally arranged, dissected, flowers bisexual, solitary, no petals, fruit a head of follicles, flattened and winged. One genus, one species, sometimes grouped in the Paeoniaceae, cultivated as an ornamental. *Glaucidium.*

Globulariaceae Dicotyledons. Mainly Mediterranean herbaceous plants and sub-shrubs, leaves alternate or basal, simple, flowers bisexual, irregular, in heads, four to five petals, fruit a nut. One genus, 22 species, many cultivated as ornamentals. *Globularia.*

Goodeniaceae Dicotyledons. Mainly Australasia, herbaceous plants and shrubs, leaves usually alternate, simple, flowers bisexual, irregular, solitary or in heads, racemes or cymes, five petals, fruit usually a capsule. 16 genera, 430 species, few cultivated as ornamentals. *Scaevola.*

Grossulariaceae Dicotyledons. Temperate Northern Hemisphere and South America, shrubs, often with spines, leaves alternate, simple or lobed, flowers unisexual or bisexual, regular, in racemes, four to five petals, fruit a berry. One genus, 150 species, many cultivated as ornamentals or for their edible fruits. *Ribes.*

Haloradigaceae Dicotyledons. Worldwide, aquatic herbaceous plants, leaves very variable, sometimes huge, spirally arranged or basal, simple, flowers unisexual or bisexual, regular, inflorescences varied, up to four petals, fruit a nut or drupe. 10 genera, around 160 species, few cultivated as ornamentals. *Gunnera.*

Hamamelidaceae Dicotyledons. Mainly Tropics and Sub-tropics, shrubs and trees, leaves usually alternate, simple or lobed, flowers unisexual or bisexual, regular or irregular, in spikes, clusters or pairs, usually four to five petals, fruit a woody capsule. 28 genera, 90 species, several cultivated as early flowering ornamentals. *Corylopsis, Disanthus, Fothergilla, Hamamelis, Liquidamber, Parrotia.*

Hemerocallidaceae see Liliaceae.

Hippocastanaceae Dicotyledons. Tropical and temperate shrubs and trees, leaves opposite, palmate, flowers usually bisexual, irregular, in racemes, four to five petals, fruit a large capsule. Two genera, around 15 species, some important ornamentals. Aesculus.

Hostaceae see Liliaceae.

Hyacinthaceae see Liliaceae.

Hydrangeaceae Dicotyledons. Worldwide, herbaceous plants, shrubs or rarely climbers, leaves usually opposite, simple, flowers mainly bisexual (sometimes with sterile outer flowers in inflorescence), regular, in cymes, four to seven petals, fruit a capsule or berry. 17 genera, 170 species, many cultivated as ornamentals. *Carpenteria, Deutzia, Hydrangea, Kirengeshoma, Philadelphus, Schizophragma.*

Hydrocharitaceae Monocotyledons. Mainly tropical and warm temperate aquatics, leaves alternate, variable, flowers usually emerging from the water, unisexual or bisexual, regular, usually in a bifid spathe between two bracts, three petals, fruit usually a capsule. 15 genera, around 100 species, few cultivated as ornamentals, some only in aquaria. *Stratiotes.*

Hydrophyllaceae Dicotyledons. Mainly American herbaceous plants, leaves various, flowers bisexual, regular, in cymes, five petals, fruit a capsule. 22 genera, around 275 species, few cultivated as ornamentals. *Nemophila.*

Hypoxidaceae Monocotyledons. Irregularly worldwide, herbaceous plants with rhizomes or corms, leaves usually basal or alternate, flowers bisexual, regular, solitary or in racemes or heads, fruit a capsule or berry. Five genera, around 150 species, often grouped with the Amaryllidaceae. *Rhodohypoxis.*

Illiciaceae Dicotyledons. Asia and North America, shrubs and trees, leaves alternate or whorled, simple, flowers bisexual, regular, solitary, fruit a group of follicles. One genus, around 40 species, several cultivated as aromatic ornamentals. *Illicium.*

Iridaceae Monocotyledons. Worldwide, especially South Africa, usually herbaceous plants forming rhizomes, corms or bulbs, leaves alternate, often folded sharply inwards or pleated, flowers bisexual, regular or irregular, solitary or in racemes or panicles, six flower parts, fruit a capsule. 70 genera, around 1,500 species, many important cultivated ornamentals. *Crocosmia, Crocus, Dierama, Diplarrhena, Freesia, Gladiolus, Hermodactylus, Iris, Ixia, Libertia, Schizostylis, Sisyrinchium, Sparaxis.*

Juglandaceae Dicotyledons. North Temperate, shrubs and trees, leaves usually opposite, pinnately compound, flowers unisexual, males flowers in catkins, four flower parts, fruit a complex nut. Seven genera, 40 species, several important timber trees, ornamentals and nut trees. *Juglans.*

Juncaceae Monocotyledons. Worldwide, herbaceous plants, often forming rhizomes, occasionally woody, leaves usually basal, spirally arranged, stems circular in section, flowers usually bisexual, regular, in various types of inflorescence, six flower parts, fruit a capsule. Nine genera, around 350 species, a few cultivated as ornamentals. *Juncus.*

Lamiaceae (formerly Labiatae) Dicotyledons. Worldwide, herbaceous plants and shrubs, leaves opposite, simple or compound, aromatic, flowers mainly bisexual, irregular, usually arranged in whorls called verticils, fruit composed of four small nuts. 224 genera, 5,600 species, many cultivated as aromatic herbs or ornamentals. *Agastache, Ajuga, Ballota, Calamintha, Clinopodium, Glechoma, Lamium, Lavandula, Melissa, Melittis, Mentha, Molucella, Monarda, Nepeta, Ocimum, Origanum, Perovskia, Phlomis, Physostegia, Prunella, Rosmarinus, Salvia, Satureja, Scutellaria, Solenostemon, Stachys, Teucrium, Thymus.*

Lardizabalaceae Dicotyledons. Irregularly worldwide, mainly woody climbers, leaves alternate, compound, flowers usually unisexual, regular, inflorescence raceme-like, six petals, fruit a berry. Eight genera, 21 species, few cultivated as ornamentals. *Akebia, Decaisnea.*

Lauraceae Dicotyledons. Mainly tropical shrubs and trees, leaves usually alternate, simple, flowers unisexual or bisexual, regular, in cymes or racemes, four to six flower parts, fruit a drupe-like berry. 50 genera, around 2,000 species, few cultivated as ornamentals, as flavouring or fruit (avocado pear). *Laurus.*

Liliaceae Monocotyledons. Worldwide, herbaceous plants with rhizomes, corms or bulbs, leaves various, flowers usually bisexual, regular, solitary or in racemes or panicles, fruit a berry or capsule. In the broadest sense, about 290 genera, over 4,500 species but the family is often much reduced in size as parts are dispersed among other families. In this book, I have given separate descriptions for some of these, but Colchicaceae, Convallariaceae, Anthericaceae, Hemerocallidaceae, Hostaceae and Hyacinthaceae are retained here. Many cultivated as ornamentals. *Bulbocodium, Camassia, Cardiocrinum, Chionodoxa, Clintonia, Colchicum, Convallaria, Disporum, Erythronium, Fritillaria, Galtonia, Hemerocallis, Hosta, Hyacinthoides, Hyacinthus, Lilium, Liriope, Muscari, Ornithogalum, Ophiopogon, Polygonatum, Puschkinia, Scilla, Smilacina, Tricyrtis, Tulipa, Uvularia, Veratrum.*

Limnanthaceae Dicotyledons. Temperate North America, herbaceous plants, leaves alternate or basal, divided, flowers bisexual, solitary, three to five petals, fruit complex. Two genera, six species, few cultivated as ornamentals. *Limnanthes.*

Loganiaceae Dicotyledons. Tropical shrubs and trees, some climbers, leaves opposite, simple, flowers bisexual, regular, solitary or in cymes, no petals, fruit a capsule, berry or drupe. 29 genera, around 800 species, few cultivated as ornamentals, the Buddlejaceae is sometimes included in the family. *Desfontainea.*

Lythraceae Dicotyledons. Worldwide, herbaceous plants, shrubs and trees, leaves usually opposite or whorled, simple, flowers bisexual, usually regular, solitary or in racemes, two to six petals, fruit a capsule. 26 genera, 580 species, several cultivated as ornamentals. *Cuphea, Lythrum.*

Magnoliaceae Dicotyledons. Mainly North Temperate and Sub-tropical trees and shrubs, leaves alternate, simple, flowers bisexual, regular, solitary, fruit a group of follicles. 12 genera, around 200 species, many cultivated as ornamentals. *Liriodendron, Magnolia.*

Malvaceae Dicotyledons. Worldwide, herbaceous plants, shrubs and trees, leaves alternate, simple or divided, flowers usually bisexual, regular, solitary or in cymes, five petals, fruit various. 121 genera, 1,550 species, several cultivated as ornamentals, some for fibres (cotton). *Abutilon, Alcea, Althaea, Hibiscus, Hoheria, Lavatera, Malope, Malva, Sidalcea, Sphaeralcea.*

Menyanthaceae Dicotyledons. Temperate aquatic and marsh plants, leaves simple or with three leaflets, alternate, flowers bisexual, regular, solitary or in various types of inflorescence, five petals, fruit usually a capsule. Five genera, 40 species, few cultivated as ornamentals. *Menyanthes, Nymphoides.*

Mimosaceae Dicotyledons. Mainly tropical and sub-tropical, usually shrubs and trees, leaves usually spirally arranged, usually bipinnate, flowers usually bisexual, regular, usually in racemes, spikes or heads, four to five petals, fruit a legume. 58 genera, 3,100 species, sometimes grouped within Papilionaceae, several cultivated as ornamentals. *Acacia, Albizia.*

Moraceae Dicotyledons. Mainly tropical and North temperate, shrubs, trees and climbers, often with milky sap, leaves alternate or opposite, simple or divided, flowers unisexual, in small complex inflorescences, no petals, fruit a drupe. 50 genera, around 1,500 species, several cultivated as ornamentals, fruit (fig, mulberry) and some important food crops (breadfruit). *Ficus, Morus.*

Morinaceae Dicotyledons. Temperate Eastern Europe and Asia, herbaceous plants, leaves opposite or whorled, simple or dissected, often spiny, flowers bisexual, irregular, in complex whorls, four to five petals, fruit a form of achene. Three genera, 13 species, few cultivated as ornamentals. *Morina.*

Myricaceae Dicotyledons. Northern Hemisphere, shrubs and trees, leaves alternate, simple or divided, flowers usually unisexual, usually in catkins, fruit a drupe. Three genera, around 30 species, few cultivated as aromatic ornamentals. *Myrica.*

Myrtaceae Dicotyledons. Mainly tropical America and Australia, shrubs and trees, leaves opposite, usually simple, flowers bisexual, regular, inflorescences various, fruit a capsule or berry. 121 genera, 3,850 species, several cultivated as ornamentals, some important timber trees. *Callistemon, Eucalyptus, Leptospermum, Myrtus.*

Nyctaginaceae Dicotyledons. Mainly tropical, shrubs, herbaceous plants and woody climbers, leaves usually opposite, simple, flowers usually bisexual, regular, inflorescence a cyme, usually five flower parts, fruit an achene. 30 genera, around 300 species, few cultivated as ornamentals. Mirabilis.

Nymphaeaceae Dicotyledons. Worldwide, aquatic herbaceous plants with rhizomes, leaves alternate, simple, flowers bisexual, regular, solitary, petals absent, four to six petal-like parts, fruit various. Six genera, 60 species, many cultivated as ornamentals (water-lilies). *Nuphar, Nymphaea.*

Oleaceae Dicotyledons. Mainly Europe and North America, shrubs and trees, some climbers, leaves usually opposite, simple or compound (pinnate), flowers usually bisexual, regular, inflorescence often a panicle, usually four petals, fruit various. 24 genera, over 900 species, many cultivated as ornamentals, few fruit (olive). *Chionanthus, Forsythia, Fraxinus, Jasminum, Ligustrum, Osmanthus, Syringa.*

Onagraceae Dicotyledons. Mainly temperate herbaceous plants, leaves opposite or alternate, simple, flowers bisexual, usually regular, solitary or in racemes, two to four petals, fruit a capsule, berry or nut. 24 genera, 650 species, some important ornamentals, some weeds. *Clarkia, Epilobium, Fuchsia, Gaura, Oenothera, Zauschneria.*

Orchidaceae Monocotyledons. Worldwide, herbaceous plants, many epiphytic, some saprophytes, leaves usually alternate, flowers usually bisexual, irregular, solitary or in racemes or panicles, three petal-like parts, fruit a capsule. 800 genera, over 22,000 species, the largest family of flowering plants, many cultivated as ornamentals, few suitable for outdoors in temperate gardens, one crop plant (vanilla). *Dactylorhiza, Pleione*.

Osmundaceae Worldwide herbaceous ferns, some large, often in wet places, fronds usually one to three-pinnate, Four genera, 18 species, some cultivated as ornamentals. *Osmunda*.

Oxalidaceae Dicotyledons. Worldwide, herbaceous plants, shrubs and trees, leaves alternate or basal, compound, often trifoliate, flowers bisexual, regular, five petals, inflorescence various, fruit a capsule, often discharging explosively. Eight genera, 875 species, many cultivated as ornamentals, some pernicious weeds. *Oxalis*.

Paeoniaceae Dicotyledons. North temperate herbaceous plants and semi-shrubs, leaves alternate, compound, flowers bisexual, regular, usually solitary, five to nine petals, fruit a large follicle. One genus, around 25 species, many cultivated as ornamentals. *Paeonia*.

Papaveraceae Dicotyledons. Mainly North temperate herbaceous plants, often with milky sap, leaves usually alternate or basal, simple, flowers bisexual, regular, solitary, usually four to six petals, fruit a capsule. 23 genera, 210 species, many cultivated as ornamentals, some important narcotics. *Argemone, Chelidonium, Corydalis, Dicentra, Eomecon, Eschscholzia, Glaucium, Macleaya, Meconopsis, Papaver, Romneya, Sanguinaria*.

Papilionaceae Dicotyledons. Worldwide herbaceous plants, shrubs and trees, leaves usually alternate or spirally arranged, variable, simple to compound trifoliate, flowers usually bisexual, irregular, inflorescence usually a raceme, four to five petals, fruit usually a legume. 450 genera, around 11,300 species, many cultivated as very important food crops and ornamentals, many important weeds. *Amicia, Anthyllis, Caragana, Clianthus, Coronilla, Cytisus, Galega, Genista, Hippocrepis, Indigofera, + Laburnocytisus, Laburnum, Lathyrus, Lotus, Lupinus, Phaseolus, Pisum, Robinia, Sophora, Spartium, Tetragonolobus, Trifolium, Ulex, Vicia, Wisteria*.

Passifloraceae Dicotyledons. Mainly tropical American shrubs, trees and climbers, leaves alternate, simple or compound, flowers usually bisexual, regular, solitary or in cymes, usually five petals, fruit a berry or capsule. 18 genera, 150 species, some cultivated as ornamentals, few fruit. *Passiflora*.

Philesiaceae Monocotyledons. Southern Hemisphere shrubs or climbers, alternate or spirally arranged leaves, flowers unisexual, regular, solitary, six petal-like parts, fruit a berry. 8 genera, around 12 species, few cultivated as ornamentals. *Lapageria*.

Pinaceae Irregularly worldwide coniferous trees, leaves needle-like, spirally arranged, female cones usually woody with spirally arranged scales, male cones small, not woody. Nine genera, 194 species, many cultivated as ornamentals and very important timber trees. *Abies, Cedrus, Larix, Picea, Pinus, Pseudotsuga, Tsuga*.

Pittosporaceae Dicotyledons. Warm temperate and tropical Old World shrubs and trees, some climbers, leaves alternate or opposite, simple, flowers bisexual, regular, usually solitary, five petals, fruit a capsule or berry. Nine genera, around 240 species, some cultivated as ornamentals. *Billardiera, Pittosporum*.

Plantaginaceae Dicotyledons. Worldwide herbaceous plants or semi-shrubs, leaves variously arranged, often basal, simple, flowers unisexual or bisexual, regular, inflorescence usually a spike, three to four petals, fruit a capsule or nut. three genera, 250 species, few cultivated as ornamentals, some weeds. *Plantago*.

Platanaceae Dicotyledons. North Temperate trees, leaves alternate, simple, flowers unisexual, regular, in hanging racemes, three to five petals, fruit a prickly ball of achenes. One genus, around eight species, several cultivated as ornamentals. *Platanus*.

Plumbaginaceae Dicotyledons. Worldwide, shrubs, climbers and herbaceous plants, leaves alternate or basal, flowers bisexual, regular, inflorescence a cyme or raceme, flowers often in spikelets, fruit usually an achene. Around 22 genera, over 400 species, few cultivated as ornamentals and several grown as 'everlasting' flowers. *Acantholimon, Armeria, Ceratostigma, Limonium, Plumbago, Psylliostachys*.

Poaceae (formerly Gramineae) Monocotyledons. Worldwide herbaceous plants and bamboos, leaves alternate, sheathing, flowers usually bisexual in many-flowered spikelets, petals absent and flowers parts varied and distinctly different from most other plant families, fruit also a uniquely distinct caryopsis. 660 genera, around 9,000 species, economically the most important family of flowering plants, many cultivated as ornamentals and many hugely important food crops (cereals). *Agrostis, Alopecurus, Anthoxanthum, Briza, Calamagrostis, Chusquea, Cortaderia, Deschampsia, Elymus, Fargesia, Festuca, Glyceria, Hakonechloa, Helictotrichon, x Hibanobambusa, Himalayacalamus, Holcus, Hordeum, Imperata, Indocalamus, Lagurus, Milium, Molinia, Pennisetum, Phalaris, Phyllostachys, Pleioblastus, Stipa, Zea*.

Polemoniaceae Dicotyledons. Mainly American herbaceous plants, few shrubs and climbers, leaves alternate or opposite, simple or pinnately or other compound, flowers bisexual, usually regular, usually in cyme-like inflorescence, 5 petals, fruit a capsule. 20 genera, 275 species, few cultivated as ornamentals. *Phlox, Polemonium*.

Polygalaceae Dicotyledons. Worldwide, mainly tropical herbaceous plants and shrubs, leaves usually alternate, simple, flowers bisexual, irregular, inflorescence a raceme, spike or panicle, usually three petals, fruit usually a capsule. 18 genera, 950 species, few cultivated as ornamentals. *Polygala*.

Polygonaceae Dicotyledons. Mainly North temperate herbaceous plants, shrubs and climbers, leaves alternate or basal, simple, flowers unisexual or bisexual, regular, in racemes or cymes, thee to six flowers parts, fruit a nut. Around 30 genera, 800 species, some cultivated as ornamentals, few significant weeds. *Eriogonum, Fallopia, Muehlenbeckia, Persicaria, Rheum, Rumex*.

Polypodiaceae. Worldwide herbaceous ferns, mainly epiphytes, often with relatively undivided fronds. 52 genera, 550 species, few cultivated ornamentals in temperate gardens, some houseplants. *Polypodium*.

Portulacaceae Dicotyledons. Mainly New World herbaceous plants and shrubs, often succulent, leaves opposite or alternate, simple, flowers bisexual, regular, often solitary or in heads or other types of inflorescence, three to 18 petals, fruit a capsule. 19 genera, around 500 species, few cultivated as ornamentals, few as edible salads. *Calandrinia, Lewisia, Portulaca*.

Potamogetonaceae Monocotyledons. Worldwide submerged or emerging aquatic plants of fresh or brackish water, leaves alternate or opposite, flowers bisexual, regular, in a spike, no petals, fruit a drupe or achene. Two genera, over 100 species, few cultivated as ornamentals, often in aquaria. *Potamogeton*.

Primulaceae Dicotyledons. Worldwide, mainly herbaceous plants, leaves variously arranged but often basal, usually simple, flowers bisexual, usually regular, inflorescence various but often in whorls, five to seven petals, fruit a capsule. 22 genera, around 800 species, many cultivated and important ornamentals. *Anagallis, Cortusa, Cyclamen, Dionysia, Dodecatheon, Hottonia, Lysimachia, Primula, Soldanella*.

Proteaceae Dicotyledons. Southern hemisphere shrubs and trees, leaves alternate, simple, flowers usually bisexual, regular or irregular, inflorescence various, no petals but four petal-like flower parts, fruit a follicle, nut or drupe. Around 75 genera, 1,300 species, some cultivated as ornamentals although notoriously tricky to grow. *Embothrium*.

Ranunculaceae Dicotyledons. Mainly temperate herbaceous plants, few shrubs, some climbers, leaves usually alternate, simple or compound, flowers bisexual, regular or irregular, petals variable, few to many, fruit usually an achene or follicle. 50 genera, around 2,000 species, many cultivated as very important ornamentals although many poisonous, some important weeds. *Aconitum, Actaea, Adonis, Anemone, Caltha, Cimicifuga, Clematis, Delphinium, Eranthis, Helleborus, Hepatica, Nigella, Pulsatilla, Ranunculus, Thalictrum, Trollius*.

Resedaceae Dicotyledons. North temperate herbaceous plants and shrubs, leaves alternate, simple, flowers unisexual or bisexual, irregular, inflorescence a spike or raceme, two to eight petals, fruit a capsule, follicle or berry. Six genera, 75 species, very few cultivated as ornamentals for their fragrance. *Reseda*.

Rhamnaceae Dicotyledons. Tropics and North temperate regions, shrubs and trees, leaves usually alternate, simple, flowers unisexual or bisexual, regular, inflorescence corymbs, cymes or clusters, four to five petals, fruit drupe-like or a capsule. 53 genera, 875 species, several cultivated as ornamentals. *Ceanothus, Colletia, Rhamnus*.

Rosaceae Dicotyledons. Worldwide, herbaceous plants, shrubs, trees or rarely climbers, leaves usually alternate, simple, flowers usually bisexual and regular, inflorescence various, usually four to six petals, fruit variable, achenes, follicles, collections of drupelets or pomes. 115 genera, 3,200 species, a hugely important family, many cultivated as ornamentals and important fruit. *Acaena, Alchemilla, Amelanchier, Aruncus, Chaenomeles, Cotoneaster, Crataegus, Cydonia, Dryas, Exochorda, Filipendula, Fragaria, Geum,*

Holodiscus, Kerria, Malus, Mespilus, Photinia, Physocarpus, Potentilla, Prunus, Pyracantha, Pyrus, Rosa, Rubus, Sanguisorba, Sorbaria, Sorbus, Spiraea, Stephanandra.

Rubiaceae Dicotyledons. Worldwide herbaceous plants, shrubs and trees, leaves opposite or often whorled, simple, flowers usually bisexual and regular, inflorescences various, four to five petals, fruit a capsule or berry. 631 genera, 10,700 species, remarkably few cultivated as ornamentals, many weeds. *Asperula, Coprosma, Galium, Phuopsis.*

Ruscaceae see Liliaceae.

Rutaceae Dicotyledons. Tropics and warm temperate regions, herbaceous plants, shrubs and trees, leaves alternate or opposite, simple or compound, flowers usually bisexual, usually regular, three to six petals, inflorescence various, fruit fleshy, often a capsule. 160 genera, 1,650 species, some cultivated as ornamentals, some very important fruit (*Citrus*). *Choisya, Dictamnus, Ruta, Skimmia.*

Salicaceae Dicotyledons. Worldwide shrubs and trees, leaves alternate, simple, flowers usually unisexual, in catkins, no petals, fruit a capsule, seeds woolly. Two genera, over 300 species, widely cultivated as ornamentals and as timber trees. *Populus, Salix.*

Sapindaceae Dicotyledons. Mainly tropical shrubs, trees and woody climbers, leaves usually alternate, compound, flowers unisexual, regular or irregular, inflorescence various, cymes, racemes, panicles, four to five petals, fruit various. 145 genera, 1,300 species, few cultivated as ornamentals, even fewer in temperate gardens. *Dodonaea, Koelreuteria.*

Saururaceae Dicotyledons. Irregularly distributed herbaceous plants, leaves alternate, simple, flowers bisexual, regular, inflorescence a spike, raceme or head, no petals, fruit a follicle or fleshy capsule. Five genera, seven species, few cultivated as ornamentals. *Houttuynia.*

Saxifragaceae Dicotyledons. Mainly North temperate herbaceous plants, leaves alternate or basal, usually simple, flowers bisexual, usually regular, usually four to five peals, inflorescence a raceme, fruit a capsule. 30 genera, 475 species, many cultivated as ornamentals. *Astilbe, Astilboides, Bergenia, Darmera, Heuchera, x Heucherella, Rodgersia, Saxifraga, Tellima, Tiarella, Tolmeia.*

Scrophulariaceae Dicotyledons. Worldwide herbaceous plants, shrubs and trees, leaves alternate or opposite, usually simple, flowers bisexual, irregular, inflorescence various, four to five petals, fruit usually a capsule, 220 genera, 4,500 species, many cultivated as ornamentals, some common although rarely significant weeds. *Antirrhinum, Asarina, Calceolaria, Chaenorrhinum, Chelone, Chionohebe, Collinsia, Cymbalaria, Diascia, Digitalis, Erinus, Hebe, Linaria, Mazus, Nemesia, Parahebe, Paulownia, Penstemon, Phygelius, Rhodochiton, Scrophularia, Verbascum, Veronica.*

Simaroubaceae Dicotyledons. Mainly tropical shrubs and trees, leaves alternate, simple or compound, flowers usually unisexual, regular, inflorescence various, up to eight petals, fruit various. 23 genera, around 170 species, few cultivated as ornamentals. *Ailanthus.*

Solanaceae Dicotyledons. Worldwide, herbaceous plants, shrubs and trees, many highly toxic, leaves alternate simple, flowers bisexual, regular or irregular, inflorescence often a cyme or flowers solitary, five petals, fruit a berry or capsule. 90 genera, 2,600 species, many cultivated as ornamentals or as food crops (potato, tomato). *Browallia, Brugmansia, Capsicum, Cestrum, Lycopersicon, Nicotiana, Nierembergia, Petunia, Physalis, Salpiglossis, Schizanthus, Solanum.*

Stachyuraceae Dicotyledons. Eastern Asian shrubs and herbaceous plants, leaves alternate, simple, flowers bisexual, regular, solitary or in clusters, 4 petals, fruit a berry. One genus, six species, few cultivated as ornamentals. *Stachyurus.*

Sterculiaceae Dicotyledons. Mainly tropical shrubs and trees, leaves alternate, simple or compound, flowers unisexual or bisexual, regular, solitary or in clusters, usually five petals, fruit various. 73 genera, 1,500 species, few cultivated as ornamentals. *Fremontodendron.*

Styracaceae Dicotyledons. Eastern Asian, Mediterranean and American shrubs and trees, leaves alternate, simple, flowers bisexual, regular, inflorescence a raceme, panicle or cluster, four to eight petals, fruit a drupe or capsule. 12 genera, 165 species, few cultivated as ornamentals. *Halesia, Styrax.*

Tamaricaceae Dicotyledons. Mainly Mediterranean and East Asian shrubs and trees, leaves usually alternate, scale-like, flowers bisexual, regular, usually in racemes or panicles, four to six petals, fruit a capsule. Five genera, 90 species, few cultivated as ornamentals. *Tamarix.*

Taxaceae Irregularly distributed worldwide trees, leaves needle-like, spirally arranged, small, soft, fruit-like reproductive structures. Six genera, 18 species, several cultivated as important ornamentals, some timber trees. *Taxus.*

Taxodiaceae Irregularly distributed temperate coniferous trees, leaves needle-like, spirally arranged. Cones woody, spherical. 10 genera, 13 species, several cultivated as important timber trees, few ornamentals but generally too large for gardens. *Cryptomeria, Metasequoia.*

Theaceae Dicotyledons. Warm temperate and tropical shrubs and trees, leaves alternate, simple, flowers bisexual, regular, inflorescence a raceme or panicle or flowers solitary, five to 14 petals, fruit a capsule or berry. 30 genera, 520 species, some cultivated as ornamentals and one important crop plant (tea). *Camellia, Stewartia.*

Thelypteridaceae Worldwide terrestrial ferns with simply pinnate fronds. 30 genera, 900 species, several cultivated as ornamentals but few in temperate gardens. *Phegopteris.*

Thymeleaceae Dicotyledons. Worldwide shrubs and trees, leaves alternate or opposite, simple, flowers usually bisexual, regular, inflorescence various, four petals, fruit a drupe, nut or capsule. 50 genera, 750 species, few cultivated as ornamentals. *Daphne.*

Tiliaceae Dicotyledons. Worldwide, mainly shrubs and trees, leaves alternate, simple, flowers bisexual, regular, inflorescence a cyme, four to five petals, fruit a capsule or drupe. Few cultivated as ornamentals. *Tilia.*

Trilliaceae Monocotyledons. North Temperate herbaceous, rhizome-forming plants, leaves opposite or commonly whorled at top of stem, flowers bisexual, regular, flowers solitary, flowers parts in groups of three, fruit a capsule. Four genera, 60 species, several cultivated as ornamentals. *Trillium.*

Tropaeolaceae Dicotyledons. Central and South American herbaceous plants, leaves alternate or opposite, simple, flowers bisexual, irregular, solitary in leaf axils, five petals, fruit complex. One genus, around 80 species, several cultivated as ornamentals. *Tropaeolum.*

Typhaceae Monocotyledons. Worldwide herbaceous marsh plants, leaves narrow, alternate, flowers minute in two unisexual spikes, one on top of the other, flowers parts scale-like, fruit dry. One genus, around 15 species, few grown as ornamentals. *Typha.*

Ulmaceae Dicotyledons. Northern hemisphere shrubs and trees, leaves alternate, simple, flowers unisexual or bisexual, irregular, solitary or clustered, four to nine flower parts, fruit usually a drupe. 16 genera, around 140 species, several cultivated as ornamentals and few used for timber. *Ulmus.*

Valerianaceae Dicotyledons. Mainly North temperate herbaceous plants, leaves opposite, simple, flowers bisexual, irregular, inflorescence a cyme, five petals, fruit a cypsela. 17 genera, around 400 species, several cultivated as ornamentals. *Centranthus, Valeriana, Valerianella.*

Verbenaceae Dicotyledons. Mainly tropical herbaceous plants, shrubs and trees, leaves opposite, simple or compound, flowers bisexual, irregular, inflorescence various, five petals, fruit usually a drupe or berry. 91 genera, 1,900 species, few cultivated as ornamentals. *Aloysia, Callicarpa, Caryopteris, Clerodendrum, Lantana, Verbena.*

Violaceae Dicotyledons. Worldwide herbaceous plants and shrubs, leaves alternate or basal, simple, flowers usually bisexual, regular or irregular, solitary or in clusters, five petals, fruit a capsule or berry. 20 genera, 1,000 species, few cultivated as important ornamentals. *Viola.*

Vitaceae Dicotyledons. Tropical and warm temperate woody climbers, leaves alternate, compound, flowers unisexual or bisexual, inflorescence a cyme, four to six petals, fruit a berry. 13 genera, around 800 species, several cultivated as ornamentals and some fruit (grapevine). *Ampelopsis, Parthenocissus, Vitis.*

Winteraceae Dicotyledons. Tropical and southern temperate shrubs and trees, leaves alternate, simple, flowers unisexual or bisexual, regular, in cymes or fascicles, two to many petals, fruit a follicle or berry. Six genera, 80 species, few cultivated as ornamentals. *Drimys.*

Zingiberaceae Monocotyledons. Tropical rhizome forming herbaceous plans, leaves in two ranks, flowers bisexual, irregular, inflorescence a raceme, cyme or head, three petals, fruit usually a capsule. 40 genera, 1,000 species, few cultivated as ornamentals but some important spice plants (ginger, turmeric). *Roscoea.*

ENGLISH/LATIN NAMES USED IN PLANT DICTIONARY

A

Aaron's Rod *Verbascum thapsus*
Absinthe *Artemisia absinthium*
African Daisy *Arctotis*
African Marigold *Tagetes erecta*
Alder *Alnus*
Alder Buckthorn *Rhamnus frangula*
Alecost *Tanacetum balsamita*
Alexandrian Laurel *Danae*
Allegheny Monkey Flower *Mimulus ringens*
Almond *Prunus dulcis*
Alpine Balsam *Erinus alpinus*
Alpine Catchfly *Lychnis alpina*
Alpine Pasque Flower *Pulsatilla alpina* ssp. *apiifolia*
Alpine Pink *Dianthus alpinus*
Alpine Poppy *Papaver alpinum*
Alpine Toadflax *Linaria alpina*
Alum Root *Heuchera*
Alyssum *Lobularia maritima*
Amaranth *Amaranthus*
American Blueberry *Vaccinium corymbosum*
American Cranberry *Vaccinium macrocarpon*
American Land Cress *Barbarea verna*
Angel's Trumpet *Brugmansia*
Angelica Tree *Aralia elata*
Anise *Pimpinella anisum*
Anise Basil *Ocimum basilicum* 'Horapha'
Aniseed *Pimpinella anisum*
Apple Mint *Mentha suaveolens*
Apricot *Prunus armeniaca*
Arrowhead *Sagittaria*
Arum Lily *Zantedeschia*
Asarabacca *Asarum*
Ash *Fraxinus*
Asparagus *Asparagus*
Asparagus Pea *Tetragonolobus purpureus*
Aspen *Populus tremula*
Aster *Aster/Callistephus*
Atlas Cedar *Cedrus libani* ssp. *atlantica*
Aubergine *Solanum melongena*
Aubretia *Aubrieta*
Auricula *Primula auricula*
Australian Violet *Viola hederacea*
Austrian Pine *Pinus nigra*
Autumn Crocus *Crocus sativus/Colchicum*
Autumn Snowflake *Leucojum autumnale*
Avens *Geum*

B

Baby's Breath *Gypsophila paniculata*
Balloon Flower *Platycodon*
Balsam *Impatiens*
Baneberry *Actaea*
Barley *Hordeum*
Basil *Ocimum*
Bastard Balm *Melittis*
Bachelor's Buttons *Ranunculus acris* 'Flore Pleno'
Bay *Laurus*
Bay Laurel *Laurus nobilis*
Bean *Phaseolus/Vicia*
Bear's Breeches *Acanthus*
Bearberry *Arctostaphylos*
Beauty Bush *Kolkwitzia*
Bedding Alyssum *Lobularia maritima*
Bedstraw *Galium*
Balm *Melissa*
Beech *Fagus*
Beech Fern *Phegopteris*
Beet *Beta*
Beetroot *Beta*
Bell Flower *Campanula*
Bell Heather *Erica cinerea*
Bells of Ireland *Molucella laevis*
Bellwort *Uvularia*
Bent Grass *Agrostis*
Bergamot *Monarda*
Bhutan Pine *Pinus wallichiana*
Bidi-Bidi *Acaena*
Bilberry *Vaccinium myrtillus*
Bindweed *Calystegia/Convolvulus*
Birch *Betula*
Bird Cherry *Prunus avium*
Bird's-Eye Primrose *Primula farinosa*
Birthwort *Aristolochia clematitis*
Bishop's Wort *Stachys officinalis*
Bittersweet *Celastrus*
Black Mulberry *Morus nigra*
Black Mustard *Brassica nigra*
Black Walnut *Juglans nigra*
Blackberry *Rubus fruticosus*
Blackcurrant *Ribes nigrum*
Blackthorn *Prunus spinosa*
Bladder Cherry *Physalis alkekengi*
Blaeberry *Vaccinium myrtillus*
Bleeding Heart *Dicentra*
Blessed Thistle *Silybum marianum*
Bloodflower *Asclepias curassavica*
Bloodleaf *Iresine*
Bloodroot *Sanguinaria*
Blue Gum *Eucalyptus globulus*
Blue Passion Flower *Passiflora caerulea*
Blue-Eyed Grass *Sisyrinchium angustifolium*
Blue-Eyed Mary *Omphalodes verna*
Bluebell *Hyacinthoides non-scripta*
Blueberry *Vaccinium corymbosum*
Bog Arum *Calla/Lysichiton*
Bog Bean *Menyanthes*
Bog Myrtle *Myrica gale*
Bog Rosemary *Andromeda*
Bonnet Bellflower *Codonopsis*
Bosnian Pine *Pinus heldreichii* var. *leucodermis*
Boston Ivy *Parthenocissus tricuspidata*
Bottle Brush *Callistemon*
Bowles' Golden Grass *Milium effusum* 'Aureum'
Bowles' Mint *Mentha* x *villosa f. alopecurioides*
Box *Buxus*
Box Elder *Acer negundo*
Bramble *Rubus fruticosus*
Bramble *Rubus ulmifolius* 'Bellidiflorus'
Brandy Bottle *Nuphar lutea*
Brass Buttons *Cotula*
Brewer's Spruce *Picea breweriana*
Broad Bean *Vicia faba*
Broad Buckler Fern *Dryopteris dilatata*
Broccoli *Brassica oleracea* Italica Group
Bronze Fennel *Foeniculum vulgare* 'Purpureum' f. 'Bronze'
Brooklime *Veronica beccabunga*
Broom *Genista*
Brown Mustard *Brassica juncea*
Brussels Sprouts *Brassica oleracea* Gemmifera Group
Buckthorn *Rhamnus*
Buffalo Currant *Ribes odoratum*
Bugbane *Cimicifuga*
Bugle *Ajuga*
Bulb onion *Allium cepa*
Bullace *Prunus insititia*
Burnet *Sanguisorba*
Burning Bush *Dictamnus*
Bush Basil *Ocimum basilicum* var. *minimum*
Bush Honeysuckle *Diervilla*
Bush Violet *Browallia*
Busy Lizzie *Impatiens walleriana*
Butcher's Broom *Ruscus*
Butterburr *Petasites*
Buttercup *Ranunculus*
Butterfly Flower *Schizanthus*
Butterfly Weed *Asclepias tuberosa*

C

Cabbage *Brassica oleracea* Capitata Group
Cabbage Tree *Cordyline*
Calabrese *Brassica oleracea* Italica Group
Calamint *Calamintha*
Calico Bush *Kalmia latifolia*
California Fuchsia *Zauschneria californica*
California Poppy *Eschscholzia*
Californian Lilac *Ceanothus*
Californian Tree Poppy *Romneya*
Calla Lily *Zantedeschia*
Camash *Camassia*
Camomile *Chamaemelum nobile*
Campion *Silene*
Canadian Poplar *Populus* x *canadensis*
Canary Creeper *Tropaeolum peregrinum*
Candytuft *Iberis*
Canna Lily *Canna*
Cape Figwort *Phygelius capensis*
Cape Gooseberry *Physalis peruviana*
Caraway Thyme *Thymus herba-barona*
Cardoon *Cynara cardunculus*
Carline Thistle *Carlina*
Carnation *Dianthus*
Carrot *Daucus*
Catchfly *Lychnis/Silene*
Catmint *Nepeta cataria*
Catnip *Nepeta cataria*
Caucasian Fir *Abies nordmanniana*
Caucasian Lime *Tilia x euchlora*
Caucasian Spruce *Picea orientalis*
Cauliflower *Brassica oleracea* Botrytis Group
Cedar *Cedrus*

Cedar of Lebanon *Cedrus libani* ssp. *libani*
Celeriac *Apium graveolens rapaceum*
Celery *Apium graveolens dulce*
Celery Mustard *Brassica rapa* Chinensis Group
Century Plant *Agave*
Chard *Beta*
Checker Mallow *Sidalcea*
Cheddar Pink *Dianthus gratianopolitanus*
Cherry Laurel *Prunus laurocerasus*
Cherry Pie *Heliotropium*
Cherry Plum *Prunus cerasifera*
Chervil *Anthriscus cerefolium*
Chickweed *Cerastium*
Chicory *Cichorium intybus*
Chilean Bell Flower *Lapageria*
China Aster *Callistephus*
Chinese Broccoli *Brassica oleracea* Alboglabra Group
Chinese Cabbage *Brassica rapa* Pekinensis Group
Chinese Chives *Allium tuberosum*
Chinese Gooseberry *Actinidia deliciosa*
Chinese Lantern *Physalis alekengi* var. *franchetii*
Chinese Leaves *Brassica rapa* Pekinensis Group
Chinese Necklace Poplar *Populus lasiocarpa*
Chinese Wisteria *Wisteria sinensis*
Chives *Allium schoenoprasum*
Chocolate Vine *Akebia*
Christmas Box *Sarcococca*
Christmas Rose *Helleborus niger*
Christmas Tree *Picea abies*
Cider Gum *Eucalyptus gunnii*
Cigar Flower *Cuphea ignea*
Cinnamon Basil *Ocimum basilicum* 'Cinnamon'
Cinquefoil *Potentilla*
Clarkia *Clarkia*
Climbing Snapdragon *Asarina*
Clock Vine *Thunbergia*
Clover *Trifolium*
Cobnut *Corylus avellana*
Cobweb Houseleek *Sempervivum arachnoideum*
Cockscomb *Celosia argentea* var. *cristata*
Cockspur Thorn *Crataegus crus-galli*
Coleus *Solenostemon scutellarioides*
Colorado Blue Spruce *Picea pungens*
Comfrey *Symphytum*
Common Candytuft *Iberis amara*
Common Comfrey *Symphytum officinale*
Common Holly *Ilex aquifolium*
Common Jasmine *Jasminum officinale*
Common Lilac *Syringa vulgaris*
Common Marjoram *Origanum vulgare*
Common Myrtle *Myrtus communis*
Common Pasque Flower *Pulsatilla vulgaris*
Common Polypody *Primula vulgare*
Common Rosemary *Rosmarinus officinalis*
Common Rush *Juncus effusus*
Common Sage *Salvia officinalis*
Common Thyme *Thymus vulgaris*
Common Valerian *Valeriana officinalis*
Common Vervain *Verbena officinalis*
Common Walnut *Juglans regia*
Common Yarrow *Achillea millefolium*
Common Yew *Taxus baccata*
Cone Flower *Echinacea Rudbeckia*
Coralberry *Symphoricarpos*
Coriander *Coriandrum sativum*
Corn Salad *Valerianella locusta*
Corn-cockle *Agrostemma*
Cornflower *Centaurea cyanus*
Cornish Heath *Erica vagans*
Corsican mint *Mentha requienii*
Costmary *Tanacetum balsamita*
Cotton Grass *Eriophorum*
Cotton Lavender *Santolina chamaecyparissus*
Cotton Thistle *Onopordum acanthium*
Courgette *Cucurbita pepo*
Cowberry *Vaccinium vitis-idaea*
Cowslip *Primula veris*
Coyote Willow *Salix exigua*
Cranberry *Vaccinium macrocarpon*
Cranesbill *Geranium*
Creeping Buttercup *Ranunculus repens*
Creeping Jenny *Lysimachia nummularia*
Creeping Soft Grass *Holcus mollis*
Creeping Willow *Salix repens*
Cress *Lepidium*
Cross-Leaved Heath *Erica tetralix*
Crowfoot *Ranunculus*
Crown Imperial *Fritillaria imperialis*
Crown Vetch *Coronilla*
Cuckoo Flower *Cardamine pratensis*
Cucumber *Cucurbita sativa*
Cudweed *Artemisia ludoviciana*
Cup and Saucer Vine *Cobaea scandens*
Cup Flower *Nierembergia*
Curled Parsley *Petroselinum crispum*
Curled Spearmint *Mentha spicata* 'Crispa'
Currant *Ribes*
Cypress *Cupressus*

D

Daffodil *Narcissus*
Daisy Bush *Olearia*
Dame's Violet *Hesperis*
Damson *Prunus insititia*
Dark Mullein *Verbascum nigrum*
Dawn Redwood *Metasequoia*
Day Lily *Hemerocallis*
Day-Flower *Commelina*
Dead-nettle *Lamium*
Deodar *Cedrus deodara*
Dill *Anethum*
Dittany *Dictamnus*
Dock *Rumex*
Dog Violet *Viola canina/Viola riviniana*
Dog's Tooth Violet *Erythronium*
Dogwood *Cornus*
Dorset Heath *Erica ciliaris*
Douglas Fir *Pseudotsuga menziesii*
Dove Tree *Davidia*
Dutch Crocus *Crocus vernus*
Dutchman's Pipe *Aristolochia macrophylla*
Dwarf Bean *Phaseolus vulgaris*
Dwarf Flowering Almond *Prunus glandulosa*
Dwarf Russian Almond *Prunus tenella*
Dwarf Siberian Pine *Pinus pumila*
Dwarf Snapdragon *Chaenorrhinum*
Dyers' Camomile *Anthemis tinctoria*

E

Eastern Hemlock *Tsuga canadensis*
Eau de Cologne Mint *Mentha x piperita f. citrata*
Edelweiss *Leontopodium*
Egg Plant *Solanum melongena*
Egyptian onion *Allium cepa* Proliferum Group
Elder *Sambucus*
Elephant's Ears *Bergenia*
Elm *Ulmus*
Endive *Cichorium endivia*
English Hawthorn *Crataegus laevigata/Crataegus monogyna*
English Oak *Quercus robur*
English Yew *Taxus baccata*
European Larch *Larix decidua*
Evening Primrose *Oenothera*
Everlasting *Antennaria*

F

Fairy Moss *Azolla*
False Acacia *Robinia pseudoacacia*
False Camomile *Boltonia*
False Cypress *Chamaecyparis*
False Heather *Cuphea hyssopifolia*
False Mallow *Sphaeralcea*
False Solomon's Seal *Smilacina*
False Spiraea *Sorbaria*
Fat Hen *Chenopodium bonus-henricus*
Feather Grass *Stipa*
Fennel *Foeniculum vulgare*
Fescue *Festuca*
Feverfew *Tanacetum parthenium*
Field Poppy *Papaver rhoeas*
Field Scabious *Knautia arvensis*
Fig *Ficus*
Figwort *Scrophularia*
Filbert *Corylus maxima*
Finocchio *Foeniculum vulgare* var. *dulce*
Fire Lily *Cyrtanthus*
Firethorn *Pyracantha*
Flame Creeper *Tropaeolum speciosum*
Flax Lily *Phormium*
Fleabane *Erigeron*

Floating Heart *Nymphoides*

Florence Fennel *Foeniculum vulgare* var. *dulce*

Flower of the West Wind *Zephyranthes candida*

Flowering Almond *Prunus triloba*

Flowering Currant *Ribes sanguineum*

Flowering Rush *Butomus*

Flowering Tobacco *Nicotiana alata*

Fly Honeysuckle *Lonicera caprifolium*

Foam Flower *Tiarella*

Forget-Me-Not *Myosotis*

Fountain Grass *Pennisetum alopecurioides*

Four o'clock Plant *Mirabilis jalapa*

Fox-Tail Barley *Hordeum jubatum*

Foxberry *Vaccinium vitis-idaea*

Foxglove *Digitalis*

Foxglove Tree *Paulownia tomentosa*

Foxtail Grass *Alopecurus*

Foxtail Lily *Eremurus*

French Bean *Phaseolus vulgaris*

French Lavender *Lavandula stoechas*

French Marigold *Tagetes patula*

French Sorrel *Rumex scutatus*

French Tarragon *Artemisia dracunculus*

Fringe Cups *Tellima*

Fritillary *Fritillaria*

Fuchsia Flowered Gooseberry *Ribes speciosum*

Furze *Ulex europaeus*

G

Garden Cress *Lepidium sativum*

Garden Heliotrope *Valeriana officinalis*

Garden Sorrel *Rumex acetosa/Rumex scutatus*

Gardeners' Garters *Phalaris arundinacea* var. *picta*

Garlic *Allium sativum*

Gean *Prunus avium*

Gentian *Gentiana*

Germander *Teucrium*

Germander Speedwell *Veronica chamaedrys*

Gherkin *Cucurbita sativa*

Giant Hyssop *Agastache*

Gland Bellflower *Adenophora*

Globe Daisy *Globularia*

Globe Flower *Trollius*

Globe Mallow *Sphaeralcea*

Globe Thistle *Echinops*

Glory Flower *Eccremocarpus*

Glory of the Snow *Chionodoxa*

Glory Pea *Clianthus puniceus*

Goat's Beard *Aruncus*

Goat's Rue *Galega*

Godetia *Clarkia*

Golden Chestnut *Chrysolepis*

Golden Club *Orontium*

Golden Elder *Sambucus nigra* 'Aurea'

Golden Knee *Chrysogonum*

Golden Rain Tree *Koelreuteria paniculata*

Golden Rod *Solidago*

Golden Shield Fern *Dryopteris affinis*

Golden Willow *Salix alba var. vitellina*

Good King Henry *Chenopodium bonus-henricus*

Gooseberry *Ribes uva-crispa* var. *reclinatum*

Gorse *Ulex europaeus*

Ginger Mint *Mentha x gracilis*

Granny's Bonnet *Aquilegia vulgaris*

Grape Hyacinth *Muscari*

Grapevine *Vitis vinifera*

Great Mullein *Verbascum thapsus*

Great White Cherry *Prunus* 'Taihaku'

Great Yellow Gentian *Gentiana lutea*

Greater Celandine *Chelidonium*

Greater Spearwort *Ranunculus lingua*

Greek Basil *Ocimum basilicum* var. *minimum*

Ground Elder *Aegopodium*

Ground Ivy *Glechoma hederacea*

Globe Artichoke *Cynara* Scolymus Group

Guelder Rose *Viburnum opulus*

Gum Tree *Eucalyptus*

H

Hair Grass *Deschampsia*

Hamburg Parsley *Petroselinum crispum* var. *tuberosum*

Hard Fern *Blechnum*

Hare's Tail Grass *Lagurus*

Harlequin Flower *Sparaxis tricolor*

Hart's Tongue Fern *Asplenium scolopendrium*

Hawk's Beard *Crepis*

Hawkweed *Hieracium*

Hawthorn *Crataegus*

Hazel *Corylus*

Hazelnut *Corylus avellana*

Heartsease *Viola tricolor*

Heath *Erica*

Heath Violet *Viola canina*

Heather *Calluna/Erica*

Hedge Bedstraw *Gallium mollugo*

Hedgehog Holly *Ilex aquifolium* 'Ferox'

Heliotrope *Heliotropium*

Hemlock *Tsuga*

Hemp Agrimony *Eupatorium cannabinum*

Herb Bennett *Geum urbanum*

Herb Fennel *Foeniculum vulgare*

Highbush Blueberry *Vaccinium corymbosum*

Highclere Holly *Ilex x altaclarensis*

Himalayan Honeysuckle *Leycesteria*

Hinoki Cypress *Chamaecyparis obtusa*

Holly *Ilex*

Holly Fern *Polystichum*

Hollyhock *Alcea*

Holm Oak *Quercus ilex*

Holy Thistle *Silybum marianum*

Honesty *Lunaria*

Honey Locust *Gleditsia triacanthos*

Honeysuckle *Lonicera*

Hoop Petticoat Daffodil *Narcissus bulbocodium*

Hop *Humulus*

Hornbeam *Carpinus*

Horned Poppy *Glaucium*

Horned Violet *Viola cornuta*

Horse Chestnut *Aesculus*

Horse Mint *Mentha longifolia*

Horseradish *Armoracia*

Hound's Tongue *Cynoglossum*

Houseleek *Sempervivum*

Humming Bird Flower *Zauschneria californica*

Hyacinth *Hyacinthus*

I

Ice Plant *Sedum spectabile*

Iceland Poppy *Papaver nudicaule*

Incense Rose *Rosa primula*

Indian Bean Tree *Catalpa*

Indian Paintbrush *Asclepias tuberosa*

Indian Root *Asclepias curassavica*

Irish Heath *Erica erigena*

Irish Yew *Taxus baccata* 'Fastigiata'

Italian Broccoli *Brassica oleracea* Italica Group

Italian Parsley *Petroselinum crispum* var. *neapolitanum*

Ivy *Hedera*

Ivy-leaved Toadflax *Cymbalaria muralis*

J

Jacob's Ladder *Polemonium*

Jacob's Rod *Asphodeline*

Japanese Blood Grass *Imperata cylindrica* 'Rubra'

Japanese Cedar *Cryptomeria*

Japanese Holly Fern *Cyrtonium falcatum*

Japanese Larch *Larix kaempferi*

Japanese Painted Fern *Athyrium niponicum* var. *pictum* 'Pictum'

Japanese Privet *Lonicera japonicum*

Japanese Quince *Chaenomeles*

Japanese Shield Fern *Dryopteris erythrosora*

Japanese White Pine *Pinus parviflora*

Japanese Wineberry *Rubus phoenicolasius*

Japanese Wisteria *Wisteria floribunda*

Jasmine *Jasminum*

Jerusalem Artichoke *Helianthus tuberosus*

Jerusalem Sage *Phlomis fruticosa*

Judas tree *Cercis*

June Berry *Amelanchier*

Juniper *Juniperus*

K

Kale *Brassica oleracea* Acephala Group

Katsura *Cercidiphyllum*

Kerosene Bush *Ozothamnus ledifolius*

Kidney Bean *Phaseolus vulgaris*

Kidney Vetch *Anthyllis vulneraria*

Kilmarnock Willow *Salix caprea* 'Kilmarnock'

Kingcup *Caltha*

Kingfisher Daisy *Felicia*
Kiwi fruit *Actinidia deliciosa*
Knapweed *Centaurea*
Knotweed *Persicaria*
Kohl-rabi *Brassica oleracea* Gongylodes Group
Korean Fir *Abies koreana*
Kowhai *Sophora tetraptera*
Kybean Gum *Eucalyptus parvifolia*

L

Labrador Violet *Viola labradorica*
Lacebark *Hoheria*
Lad's Love *Artemisia absinthium*
Lady fern *Athyrium filix-femina*
Lady's Bedstraw *Galium vernum*
Lady's Mantle *Alchemilla*
Lady's Smock *Cardamine pratensis*
Lamb's Ears *Stachys byzantina*
Lamb's Lettuce *Valerianella locusta*
Lamb's Tails *Stachys byzantina*
Lamb's Tongue *Stachys byzantina*
Lantern Tree *Crinodendron*
Larch *Larix*
Laurustinus *Viburnum tinus*
Lavender *Lavandula*
Lawson Cypress *Chamaecyparis lawsoniana*
Leadwort *Plumbago*
Leek *Allium porrum*
Lemon Balm *Melissa*
Lemon Basil *Ocimum basilicum* var. *citriodorum*
Lemon-scented Verbena *Aloysia triphylla*
Lemon Thyme *Thymus* x *citriodorus*
Lent Lily *Narcissus pseudonarcissus*
Lenten Rose *Helleborus orientalis*
Leopard Plant *Ligularia*
Lesser Celandine *Ranunculus ficaria*
Lesser Reedmace *Typha angustifolia*
Lettuce *Lactuca*
Lettuce-Leaf Basil *Ocimum basilicum* 'Napolitano'
Leyland Cypress *x Cupressocyparis leylandii*
Lilac *Syringa*
Lily *Lilium*
Lily of the Valley *Convallaria*
Lily Turf *Liriope/Ophiopogon*
Lime *Tilia*
Linden *Tilia*
Livingstone Daisy *Dorotheanus*
Lobster Claw *Clianthus puniceus*
Lodgepole Pine *Pinus contorta*
Lombardy Poplar *Populus nigra* var. *italica*
London Plane *Platanus* x *hispanica*
London Pride *Saxifraga* x *urbium*
Loosestrife *Lysimachia/Lythrum*
Lovage *Levisticum*
Love-in-a-Mist *Nigella damascena*
Love-lies-bleeding *Amaranthus caudatus*
Lungwort *Pulmonaria*
Lupin *Lupinus*

M

Madonna Lily *Lilium candidum*
Maiden Pink *Dianthus deltoides*
Maidenhair Fern *Adiantum*
Maidenhair Spleenwort *Asplenium trichomanes*
Maidenhair Tree *Ginkgo*
Male Fern *Dryopteris filix-mas*
Mallow *Malva*
Manipur Lily *Lilium mackliniae*
Maple *Acer*
Marguerite *Argyranthemum*
Marigold *Tagetes*
Marjoram *Origanum*
Marrow *Cucurbita pepo*
Marsh Mallow *Althaea officinalis*
Marsh Marigold *Caltha*
Martagon Lily *Lilium martagon*
Marvel of Peru *Mirabilis jalapa*
Masterwort *Astrantia*
May *Crataegus laevigata*
Mayweed *Matricaria*
Meadow Buttercup *Ranunculus acris*
Meadow Rue *Thalictrum*
Meadowsweet *Filipendula ulmaria*
Mediterranean Buckthorn *Rhamnus alaternus*
Medlar *Mespilus*
Melon *Cucumis melo*
Mexican Orange *Choisya*
Mexican Sunflower *Tithonia*
Mibuna *Brassica rapa*
Michaelmas Daisy *Aster*
Mignonette *Reseda*
Mile-a-Minute Vine *Fallopia baldschuanica*
Milfoil *Achillea*
Milkweed *Asclepias*
Milkwort *Polygala*
Mint *Mentha*
Miss Willmott's Ghost *Eryngium giganteum*
Mizuna *Brassica rapa*
Mock Orange *Philadelphus*
Moneywort *Lysimachia nummularia*
Monk's-hood *Aconitum*
Monkey Flower *Mimulus*
Monkey Puzzle Tree *Araucaria araucana*
Montbretia *Crocosmia*
Monterey Pine *Pinus radiata*
Montezuma Pine *Pinus montezumae*
Morning Glory *Ipomoea*
Moss Locust *Robinia hispida*
Moth Mullein *Verbascum blattaria*
Mountain Ash *Sorbus aucuparia*
Mountain Avens *Geum montanum/Dryas octopetala*
Mountain Cranberry *Vaccinium vitis-idaea*
Mountain Gum *Eucalyptus dalrympleana*
Mountain Heather *Phyllodoce*
Mountain Pine *Pinus mugo*
Mt. Etna Broom *Genista aetnensis*
Mugwort *Artemisia vulgaris*
Mulberry *Morus*
Mullein *Verbascum*
Musk Flower *Mimulus moschatus*
Mustard *Brassica*
Mustard Greens *Brassica juncea*
Myrobalan *Prunus cerasifera*
Myrtle *Myrtus*

N

Naked Ladies *Colchicum*
Nasturtium *Tropaeolum majus*
Navelwort *Omphalodes*
Nectarine *Prunus persica* var. *nectarina*
Needle Grass *Stipa*
Nettle-Leaved Mullein *Verbascum chaixii*
New Guinea Hybrid Busy Lizzies *Impatiens* New Guinea Group
New Zealand Burr *Acaena*
New Zealand Flax *Phormium tenax*
New Zealand Spinach *Tetragonia tetragonioides*
New Zealand Wind Grass *Stipa arundinacea*
Night Scented Stock *Matthiola longipetala*
Ninebark *Physocarpus*
Northern Blue Violet *Viola septentrionalis*
Norway Maple *Acer platanoides*
Norway Spruce *Picea abies*

O

Oak *Quercus*
Oatgrass *Helictotrichon*
Ocean Spray *Holodiscus discolor*
Old English Lavender *Lavandula angustifolia*
Old Man *Artemisia absinthium*
Onion *Allium*
Opium Poppy *Papaver somniferum*
Orache *Atriplex*
Orange Mint *Mentha* x *piperita f. citrata*
Oregano *Origanum vulgare*
Oregon Grape *Mahonia aquifolium*
Oriental Mustard *Brassica juncea*
Oriental Poppy *Papaver orientale*
Oriental Spruce *Picea orientalis*
Ornamental Quince *Chaenomeles*
Our Lady's Milk Thistle *Silybum marianum*
Oxlip *Primula elatior*

P

Paeony *Paeonia*
Pagoda Tree *Sophora japonica*
Painted Nettle *Solenostemon scutellarioides*
Pak-Choi *Brassica rapa* Chinensis Group
Pampas Grass *Cortaderia*
Pansy *Viola* x *wittrockiana*
Panther Lily *Lilium pardalinum*
Paper-Bark maple *Acer griseum*
Parrot's Beak *Lotus berthelotii*
Parsley *Petroselinum*
Parsnip *Pastinaca*
Pasque Flower *Pulsatilla*
Passion Flower *Passiflora*
Pea *Pisum*
Pea tree *Caragana*
Peach *Prunus persica*
Pear *Pyrus*
Pearlbush *Exochorda*
Pearlwort *Sagina*
Pearly Everlasting *Anaphalis*
Pedunculate Oak *Quercus robur*
Pennycress *Thlaspi*
Pennyroyal *Mentha pulegium*

Pepper *Capsicum*
Peppermint *Mentha x piperita*
Periwinkle *Vinca*
Persian Ironwood *Parrotia*
Peruvian Lily *Alstroemeria*
Pheasant Berry *Leycesteria*
Pheasant's Eye Narcissus *Narcissus poeticus* var. *recurvus*
Pheasant's Tail Grass *Stipa arundinacea*
Pickaback Plant *Tolmeia*
Pimpernel *Anagallis*
Pine *Pinus*
Pineapple Mint *Mentha spicata* 'Variegata'
Pink *Dianthus*
Plane Tree *Platanus*
Plantain *Plantago*
Plantain Lily *Hosta*
Plum *Prunus domestica*
Plume Poppy *Macleaya*
Plume Thistle *Cirsium*
Poached Egg Plant *Limnanthes douglasii*
Polypody *Polypodium*
Pondweed *Potamogeton*
Poor Man's Orchid *Schizanthus*
Poplar *Populus*
Poppy *Papaver*
Portuguese Heath *Erica lusitanica*
Pot Marigold *Calendula*
Potato *Solanum tuberosum*
Potato Vine *Solanum jasminoides*
Prairie Mallow *Sidalcea*
Prickly Poppy *Argemone*
Primrose *Primula vulgaris*
Prince of Wales' Feathers *Celosia spicata*
Privet *Ligustrum*
Pumpkin *Cucurbita pepo*
Purple Basil *Ocimum basilicum* var. *purpurascens*
Purple Loosestrife *Lythrum salicaria*
Purple Moor Grass *Molinia caerulea* ssp. *caerulea* 'Variegata'
Purple Mullein *Verbascum phoeniceum*
Purple Toadflax *Linaria purpurea*
Purslane *Portulaca*
Pyrethrum *Tanacetum coccineum*

Q

Quaking Grass *Briza*
Quamash *Camassia*
Quince *Cydonia*

R

Radish *Raphanus*
Ragged Robin *Lychnis flos-cuculi*
Rape *Brassica napus*
Raspberry *Rubus idaeus*
Red Basil *Ocimum basilicum* var. *purpurascens*
Red Cedar *Thuja*
Red Currant *Ribes rubrum*
Red Hot Poker *Kniphofia*
Red Oak *Quercus rubra*
Reed Canary Grass *Phalaris arundinacea* var. *picta*
Reed Grass *Calamagrostis*
Reedmace *Typha*
Rhubarb *Rheum*
Rock Cress *Arabis*
Rock Rose *Cistus/Helianthemum*
Roman Mugwort *Artemisia pontica*
Rose *Rosa*
Rose Acacia *Robinia hispida*
Rose Campion *Lychnis coronaria*
Rose of Sharon *Hypericum calycinum*
Rose Root *Rhodiola rosea*
Rosebay Willow-Herb *Epilobium angustifolium*
Rosemary *Rosmarinus*
Rowan *Sorbus aucuparia*
Royal Fern *Osmunda regalis*
Rue *Ruta*
Runner Bean *Phaseolus coccineus*
Rush *Juncus*
Russian Comfrey *Symphytum* x *uplandicum*
Russian Sage *Perovskia*
Russian Tarragon *Artemisia dracunculoides*
Russian Vine *Fallopia baldschuanica*

S

Sacred Bamboo *Nandina*
Sage *Salvia*
Salad Burnet *Sanguisorba minor*
Salad Rocket *Eruca*
Salt Bush *Atriplex*
Sandwort *Arenaria*
Savory *Satureja*
Savoy *Brassica oleracea* Capitata Group
Sawara Cypress *Chamaecyparis pisifera*
Saxifrage *Saxifraga*
Scabious *Knautia/Scabiosa*
Scarlet Oak *Quercus coccinea*
Scented Mayweed *Matricaria recutita*
Scorzonera *Scorzonera hispanica*
Scotch Thistle *Onopordum acanthium*
Scots Flame Flower *Tropaeolum speciosum*
Scots Pine *Pinus sylvestris*
Sea Buckthorn *Hippophae*
Sea Holly *Eryngium*
Sea Kale *Crambe maritima*
Sea Lavender *Limonium*
Sea Pink *Armeria*
Sedge *Carex*
Self Heal *Prunella*
Sensitive Fern *Onoclea sensiblis*
Sessile Oak *Quercus petraea*
Shallot *Allium cepa* Aggregatum Group
Sheep Laurel *Kalmia angustifolia f. rubra*
Sheep's Bit *Jasione*
Shellflower *Chelone*
Shirley Poppy *Papaver rhoeas* 'Shirley Singles'
Shrub Verbena *Lantana*
Shrubby Plumbago *Ceratostigma*
Shrubby Veronica *Hebe*
Silky Wisteria *Wisteria venusta*
Silver Fir *Abies*
Silver Willow *Salix alba* var. *sericea*
Skullcap *Scutellaria*
Skunk Cabbage *Lysichiton*
Slipper Flower *Calceolaria*
Sloe *Prunus spinosa*
Smoke Bush *Cotinus*
Snake's Head Fritillary *Fritillaria meleagris*
Snake's Head Iris *Hermodactylus*
Snapdragon *Antirrhinum*
Sneezewort *Achillea ptarmica*
Snow Gum *Eucalyptus pauciflora*
Snow Poppy *Eomecon*
Snowbell *Styrax*
Snowberry *Symphoricarpos*
Snowdrop *Galanthus*
Snowflake *Leucojum*
Snowy Mespilus *Amelanchier*
Soapwort *Saponaria officinalis*
Solomon's Seal *Polygonatum*
Sorrel *Rumex*
Sour Dock *Rumex acetosa*
Southernwood *Artemisia abrotanum*
Sow Thistle *Cicerbita*
Spanish Bluebell *Hyacinthoides hispanica*
Spanish Broom *Spartium junceum*
Spanish Gorse *Genista hispanica*
Spear Grass *Stipa*
Spearmint *Mentha spicata*
Speedwell *Veronica*
Spider Flower *Cleome*
Spider Lily *Tradescantia*
Spiderwort *Tradescantia*
Spinach *Spinacia*
Spleenwort *Asplenium*
Spotted Laurel *Aucuba*
Spring Gentian *Gentiana verna*
Spring Greens *Brassica oleracea* Capitata Group
Spring Onion *Allium cepa*
Spring Snowflake *Leucojum vernum*
Sprouting Broccoli *Brassica oleracea* Italica Group
Spruce *Picea*
Squash *Cucurbita pepo*
Squill *Scilla*
St. Bernard's Lily *Anthericum liliago*
St. Dabeoc's Heath *Daboecia*
St. John's Wort *Hypericum*
Stagshorn Sumac *Rhus typhina*
Star Jasmine *Trachelospermum*
Star Thistle *Centaurea*
Statice *Limonium*
Sticky Catchfly *Lychnis viscaria*
Stock *Matthiola*
Stokes' Aster *Stokesia*
Stone Cress *Aethionema*
Stonecrop *Sedum*
Stork's Bill *Erodium*
Strawberry *Fragaria*
Strawberry Tree *Arbutus*
Strawflower *Helichrysums bracteatum/Helipterum*
Striped Squill *Puschkinia*
Sulphur Flower *Erigonum umbellatum*
Sumac *Rhus*

Summer Hyacinth *Galtonia candicans*
Summer Savory *Satureja hortensis*
Summer Snowflake *Leucojum aestivum*
Sunflower *Helianthus annuus*
Sun Rose *Helianthemum*
Swamp Blueberry *Vaccinium corymbosum*
Swamp Foxtail Grass *Pennisetum alopecurioides*
Swamp Milkweed *Asclepias incarnata*
Swan River Daisy *Brachyscome*
Swede *Brassica napus* Napobrassica Group
Sweet Basil *Ocimum basilicum*
Sweet Bay *Laurus nobilis*
Sweet Box *Sarcococca*
Sweet Brier *Rosa eglanteria*
Sweet Cherry *Prunus avium*
Sweet Chestnut *Castanea*
Sweet Cicely *Myrrhis*
Sweet Coltsfoot *Petasites*
Sweet Corn *Zea mays*
Sweet Flag *Acorus*
Sweet Grass *Glyceria*
Sweet Marjoram *Origanum majorana*
Sweet Pepper Bush *Clethra alnifolia*
Sweet Rocket *Hesperis*
Sweet Woodruff *Galium odoratum*

T

Tamarisk *Tamarix*
Tansy *Tanacetum vulgare*
Tasmanian Snow Gum *Eucalyptus coccifera*
Tassel Bush *Garrya*
Tassel Hyacinth *Muscari comosum* 'Plumosum'
Tea Tree *Leptospermum*
Teesdale Violet *Viola rupestris rosea*
Thai Basil *Ocimum basilicum* 'Horapha'
Thorn *Crataegus*
Thrift *Armeria*
Thyme *Thymus*
Tickseed *Coreopsis*
Tiger Lily *Lilium lancifolium*
Toad Lily *Tricyrtis*
Toadflax *Linaria*
Tobacco Plant *Nicotiana*
Tomato *Lycopersicon esculentum*
Trailing Bellflower *Cyananthus*
Trailing Violet *Viola hederacea*
Transvaal Daisy *Gerbera*
Tree Cabbage *Brassica oleracea* Tronchuda Group
Tree Heath *Erica arborea*
Tree Mallow *Lavatera*
Tree of Heaven *Ailanthus*
Tree Onion *Allium cepa* Proliferum Group
Tree Paeony *Paeonia suffruticosa*
Trumpet Flower *Campsis*
Trumpet Gentian *Gentiana acaulis*
Tulip *Tulipa*
Tulip Tree *Liriodendron*
Turkish Hazel *Corylus colurna*
Turnip *Brassica rapa* Rapifera Group
Turnip Rooted Parsley *Petroselinum crispum* var. *tuberosum*
Twisted Hazel *Corylus avellana* 'Contorta'
Twisted Willow *Salix babylonica pekinensis* 'Tortuosa'

V

Valerian *Centranthus/Valeriana*
Variegated Land Cress *Barbarea vulgaris variegata*
Variegated Yellow Rocket *Barbarea vulgaris variegata*
Veined Vervain *Verbena rigida*
Vernal Grass *Anthoxanthum*
Vervain *Verbena*
Vine *Vitis*
Viola *Viola cornuta*
Violet *Viola*
Viper's Bugloss *Echium vulgare*
Virginia Creeper *Parthenocissus quinquefolia*
Virginian Cowslip *Mertensia pulmonarioides*
Virginian Stock *Malcolmia maritima*

W

Wake Robin *Trillium*
Walking-Stick Cabbage *Brassica oleracea* Tronchuda Group
Wall Germander *Teucrium chamaedrys*
Wallflower *Erysimum cheiri*
Walnut *Juglans*
Wand Flower *Dierama*
Water Arum *Calla*
Water Avens *Geum rivale*
Water Fern *Azolla*
Water Figwort *Scrophularia auriculata*
Water Fringe *Nymphoides peltata*
Water Hawthorn *Aponogeton distachyos*
Water Hyacinth *Eichornia*
Water Lily *Nymphaea*
Water Mint *Mentha aquatica*
Water Plantain *Alisma*
Water Soldier *Stratiotes aloides*
Water Violet *Hottonia palustris*
Wayfaring Tree *Viburnum lantana*
Welsh Onion *Allium fistulosum*
Welsh Polypody *Polypodium cambricum*
Western Gorse *Ulex gallii*
Western Hemlock *Tsuga heterophylla*
Western Mugwort *Artemisia ludoviciana*
Whin *Ulex europaeus*
Whinberry *Vaccinium myrtillus*
White Currant *Ribes rubrum*
White Cypress *Chamaecyparis thyoides*
White Fir *Abies concolor*
White Mugwort *Artemisia lactiflora*
White Mulberry *Morus alba*
White Mustard *Sinapis alba*
White Pine *Pinus strobus*
White Poplar *Populus alba*
White Spruce *Picea glauca*
White Water Lily *Nymphaea alba*
Whitebeam *Sorbus aria*
Whorlflower *Morina longifolia*
Whortleberry *Vaccinium myrtillus*
Widow's Tears *Commelina*
Wild Basil *Clinopodium vulgare*
Wild Buckwheat *Eriogonum*
Wild Carnation *Dianthus caryophyllus*
Wild Daffodil *Narcissus pseudonarcissus*
Wild Ginger *Asarum*
Wild Pansy *Viola tricolor*
Wild Pink *Dianthus plumarius*
Wild Rye *Elymus*
Wild Service Tree *Sorbus torminalis*
Wild Sweet William *Dianthus barbatus*
Wild Thyme *Thymus serpyllum*
Willow *Salix*
Willow Gentian *Gentiana asclepiadea*
Willow-Herb *Epilobium*
Willow-leaved Pear *Pyrus salicifolia*
Winter Aconite *Eranthis*
Winter Cherry *Physalis alkekengi*
Winter Flowering Cherry *Prunus* x *subhirtella* 'Autumnalis'
Winter Flowering Heather *Erica carnea*
Winter Flowering Iris *Iris unguicularis*
Winter Flowering Jasmine *Jasminum nudiflorum*
Winter Hazel *Corylopsis*
Winter Heath *Erica carnea*
Winter Heliotrope *Petasites fragrans*
Winter Savory *Satureja montana*
Winter's Bark Tree *Drimys winteri*
Wintersweet *Chimonanthus*
Witch Hazel *Hamamelis*
Wood Betony *Stachys officinalis*
Wood Lily *Trillium*
Wood Sage *Teucrium scorodonia*
Wood Sage *Teucrium*
Wood Violet *Viola riviniana*
Woodruff *Asperula*
Woolly Blue Violet *Viola sororia*
Woolly Willow *Salix lanata*
Worcesterberry *Ribes divaricatum*
Wormwood *Artemisia*

Y

Yarrow *Achillea*
Yellow Floating Heart *Nymphoides peltata*
Yellow Horned Poppy *Glaucium flavum*
Yellow Water Lily *Nuphar lutea*
Yew *Taxus*

Z

Zephyr Flower *Zephyranthes candida*

The publishers wish to thank the following organisations for their kind permission to reproduce the photographs in this book:

Acknowledgements in Source Order

Stefan Buczacki Plant Dictionary

Acton Beauchamp Roses 261

A-Z Botanical Collection 47, 52 Bottom Right/Andrew Brown 231 Bottom Right/Anthony Cooper 172 Top Right, 179 Bottom Right/Peter Etchells 57/Terence Exley 208 Bottom/Bob Gibbons 177/David Hughes 62 Top Left, 164 Bottom Right/J Malcolm Smith 251 Top/Neil Joy 68 Bottom Left/Geoff Kidd 10 Top Right, 77 Top Left, 104 Top Left, 224 Top Right/F Merlet 232 Top Left/Malcolm Richards 55/Dan Sams 11 Centre Left/Moira C Smith 19 Centre Right/Roger Standen 94 Top Left/Bjorn Svennson 200 Top Right/Adrian Thomas 21, 60, 124, 137, 284 Top Centre Left, 292 Bottom Right/Dr Vivienne Tyrey 197 Bottom Right/Malkolm Warrington 18 Bottom Right/Jo Whitworth 154/Andy Williams 118 Bottom

Right /Nick Wiseman 78 Bottom Left/A Young 14 Bottom Left

Pat Brindley 228 Top Left, 237 Bottom, 240 Top Right, 240 Centre Left, 293 Centre Right

Brogdale Horticultural Trust 196 Top Left

Professor Stefan Buczacki (B&B Photographs) 206 Top Left, 208 Top Left, 257 Top Right, 292 Centre Left, 300 Bottom Right

Eric Crichton 108 Top Centre, 112 Centre Right, 112 Bottom Left, 128, 132, 141 Bottom, 143 Bottom Right, 166 Bottom Centre, 166 Top Left, 169 Top Right, 185 Top Right, 188, 191 Bottom, 194 Bottom Right, 195, 202 Bottom Left, 202 Top Left, 216 Top Left, 217 Top Right, 232 Top Right, 239 Top Right, 260 Bottom Right, 263, 272 Top, 277, 295, 296

Garden Picture Library David Askham 65 Top Right, 83, 196 Bottom Right, 260 Top Left/Kim Blaxland 281 Top/Chris Burrows 175 Bottom Right/Rex Butcher 254 Bottom Left/Brain Carter 36, 38 Top Left, 54 Bottom Right, 68 Top Right, 90 Bottom Left, 101 Top Right, 115 Bottom Right, 125, 133 Bottom Left, 150 Bottom Right, 170 Bottom Left, 174 Top Left, 176, 192 Bottom Left, 215, 250, 286 Top, 287 Bottom Centre, 289 Top/Densey Clyne 31 Top Left, 243/Karin Craddock 41 Bottom Right/David England 251 Bottom Right, 278 Top/Robert Estall 262 Bottom/Ron Evans 231 Top Right/Christopher Fairweather 294 Bottom Left/John Glover 46 Bottom Right, 58 Top Left, 74 Top Right, 82 Bottom Right, 88 Bottom Right, 92 Top Left, 119, 123 Centre Left, 133 Top Right, 149 Centre Right, 156 Top Left, 193, 206 Bottom, 237 Top, 248 Centre Right, 249 Top Right, 252 Bottom Right, 298, 300 Top/Sunniva Harte 179 Top Left, 259, 279 Bottom/Neil Holmes 13 Bottom Right, 17 Bottom Right, 39, 40 Bottom Right, 147, 149 Top Left, 271 Top, 287 Top, 293 Top/Michael Howes 48 Top Centre Right, 93 Bottom Right/Jacqui Hurst 17 Top Centre/Lamontagne 145, 268 Bottom Right/Clive Nichols 116/Marie O'Hara 51 Top Left/Jerry Pavia 41 Top Left, 213 Top Left, 224 Bottom left, 264 Bottom /Philippe Bonduel 221 Top Left/Howard Rice 13 Left, 27 Bottom Left, 34 Top Right, 65 Bottom Centre Right, 76 Top Right, 90 Top Left, 115 Top Right, 127 Bottom Right, 135, 156 Bottom Right, 160, 168 Bottom, 246 Bottom Left, 262 Top Left, 267, 273 Top, 280 Bottom Right, 285, 290 Bottom Left/David Russell 172 Centre Left, 204 Top Left/J S Sira 12, 53 Top Right, 75, 102 Bottom Right, 171, 283/Friedrich Strauss 272 Bottom Right/Brigitte Thomas 153, 256/Juliette Wade 190 Top Left, 238, 265/Mel Watson 88 Top Left, 203 Bottom Right/Didier Willery 48 Bottom Left, 62 Bottom Right, 95, 97 Centre Right, 146 Bottom Left, 180 Bottom, 202 Centre Right, 244, 245 Bottom Right/Steven Wooster 50, 53 Bottom Right

John Glover 20 Top Left, 92 Bottom Right

Reed Consumer Books Ltd. Front Cover Top Right, 2, 16 Bottom Right, 25 Top Right, 28 Bottom Right, 43 Bottom Left, 51 Centre Right, 56 Top Right, 58 Bottom Right, 61 Top Right, 96 Top Right, 98 Bottom Left, 102 Top Left, 108 Centre Left, 111 Centre Right,114 Bottom Right, 123 Top Right, 129 Centre Right, 152 Top Left, 181 Top Left, 184 Bottom, 186, 201 Centre Right, 212 Bottom, 221 Centre Right, 253, 270 Centre Left, 284 Bottom Right, 297 Bottom Left, 304/Michael Boys 23, 46 Top Left, 54 Top Left, 113, 130, 159 Top Right, 203 Top Right/Jerry Harpur Spine, Front Cover Bottom Centre, 4, 15, 22, 24 Centre Right, 25 Bottom Left, 120 Bottom Right, 121, 122 Top Left, 134 Top Left, 134 Bottom Right, 164 Top Left, 178 Bottom Right, 181 Bottom Right, 189, 191 Top Left, 198 Bottom Right, 212 Top Left, 218, 220 Top Left, 252 Top Left, 275, 289 Bottom Right, 290 Top, 303 Top/Neil Holmes 73, 74 Bottom Left, 245 Centre Left/Andrew Lawson Endpapers, Front Cover Top Centre, 3, 7, 10 Left, 49, 59, 64, 65 Centre Left, 69, 70 Top Left 71 Bottom Left, 71 Top Right, 72 Bottom Right, 85 Top Left, 89 Centre Right, 91, 98 Top Right, 110 Top Left, 114 Top Left, 118 Top Left, 122 Bottom Right, 126, 136, 144, 152 Bottom Right, 158, 159 Bottom Left, 167, 194 Top Left, 213 Centre Right, 222 Top Left, 222 Bottom Right, 223, 225, 226 Top Left, 228 Bottom Right, 257 Bottom Left, 274 Bottom Right, 282 Top/Peter Myers Front Cover Top Left, 129 Bottom Left/Steven Wooster 157, 210, 258 Top, 258 Bottom Left

George Wright Front Cover Bottom Left, Front Cover Bottom Right, 1, 31 Bottom Right, 103, 107 Top Left, 117 Bottom Right, 161, 170 Top Right, 183 Top, 247, 254 Top Right, 255 Bottom Right, 266 Top Left, 281 Centre Right, 282 Bottom Left, 301

Harpur Garden Library 34 Bottom Left, Garden Owner Bob Flowerdew 42 Top Left, White Hart Royal Hotel, Glos. 43 Top Left, Coton Manor, Northants 63 Top Right, Grower Jim Marshall 101 Centre Left, Andrew Lawson 18 Top Left, 20 Bottom Right, 26 Top Right, 27 Top Right, 29, 30, 33, 37, 40 Centre Left, 66 Top Left, 86 Bottom Right, 94 Bottom Right, 100 Top Right, 105, 109 Top Right, 120 Top Left, 131, 140, 142, 150 Top Left, 151, 163, 169 Bottom Left,173, 180 Top Left, 182, 187 Bottom Right, 192 Top Right, 198 Top Left, 200 Bottom Left, 201 Centre Left, 205 Top Right, 205 Centre Right, 209, 211, 214, 230 Bottom Right, 233, 236, 239 Bottom, 242 Top Left, 255 Centre Left, 269 Top Right, 270 Top, 274 Top Left, 279 Top, 280 Top, 294 Top, 303 Bottom Left

S & O Mathews 35 Bottom Left, 100 Bottom Left

Clive Nichols Photography 5, 61 Bottom Right, 72 Top Left, 220 Bottom, 227, 229, 268 Top, 297 Top

Photos Horticultural 16 left, 56 Bottom Left, 80, 86 Top Left, 96 Centre Left, 111 Top Left, 138 Top Right, 139, 168 Top Left, 174 Bottom Right, 271 Bottom Right, 276 Top

Howard Rice/Potatoes courtesy of GM & AE Innes, Aberdeen 278 Bottom Centre Right

J S Sira 175 Top

Harry Smith Collection 11 Bottom Right, 14 Top Right, 19 Centre Left, 24 Top Left, 26 Centre Left, 28 Top Left, 35 Top Right, 38 Bottom Right, 42 Bottom Centre Right, 44 Top Left, 45, 52 Top Left, 63 Centre Left, 66 Bottom Right, 67, 76 Bottom Left, 77 Bottom Right, 78 Top Right, 79, 81 Bottom Right, 81 Top Right, 82 Top Left, 84, 85 Centre Right, 87, 89 Top Left, 93 Top Left, 97 Bottom Left, 99, 104 Bottom Right, 106 Bottom Left, 109 Bottom, 110 Bottom Right, 117 Top Left, 138 Bottom Left, 141 Top Right, 143 Top Right, 148, 155, 162 Top Left, 165, 178 Top Left, 183 Bottom Right, 184 Top Left, 185 Bottom Right, 190 Bottom Right, 199, 204 Centre Right, 205 Bottom Centre, 207, 217 Bottom Left, 219, 230 Top Left, 234 Top Right, 234 Bottom Left, 241, 242 Bottom, 246 Top Right, 248 Top Left, 249 Bottom Left, 264 Top, 266 Bottom Right, 273 Bottom Right, 276 Bottom Right, 286 Bottom Right, 302

Supplied courtesy of Suttons Seeds 44 Bottom Right, 127 Top Left, 235

Supplied courtesy of Thompson & Morgan 291

Jo Whitworth/Savill Gardens, Surrey 32, 107 Centre Right, RHS Wisley, Surrey 108 Centre Right, Loseley Park & Garden, Surrey 146 Top Right, Secretts Garden Centre, Surrey 162 Bottom Right, 187 Top Left, Iden Croft Herbs, Kent 197 Top Left, 269 Bottom, Hollington Herb Garden, Berks 288, 226 Bottom Left

Justyn Willsmore/RHS Wisley 299, Sir Harold Hillier Gardens & Arboretum, Hants 216 Top Centre Right